IRONY IN THE
MEDIEVAL ROMANCE

IRONY IN THE MEDIEVAL ROMANCE

D. H. GREEN

CAMBRIDGE UNIVERSITY PRESS

CAMBRIDGE

LONDON · NEW YORK · MELBOURNE

Published by the Syndics of the Cambridge University Press
The Pitt Building, Trumpington Street, Cambridge CB2 1RP
Bentley House, 200 Euston Road, London NW1 2DB
32 East 57th Street, New York, NY 10022, USA
296 Beaconsfield Parade, Middle Park, Melbourne 3206, Australia

First published 1979

Printed in Great Britain
at the University Press, Cambridge

Library of Congress Cataloguing in Publication Data

Green, Dennis Howard, 1922–
Irony in the medieval romance.

Bibliography p.
Includes indexes.
1. Romances–History and criticism.   2. Irony in literature, I. Title.
PN683.G7   809.1'9   78–14930
ISBN 0 521 22458 6

CONTENTS

PREFACE

I owe a debt of gratitude to two colleagues who, by inviting me to hold forth on a topic of my own choosing, assisted me, more perhaps than they realise, in putting my thoughts on medieval irony in order and on to paper. The first such stimulus came from Professor Hans Kuhn who invited me to direct the medieval section of the Fifth Graduate Workshop in German at the Australian National University, Canberra in May 1971, and who generously accepted the theme of this book as the topic for that session. The second stimulus, no less valuable than the first, came from Professor Fredi Chiappelli, Director of the Center for Medieval and Renaissance Studies at the University of California, Los Angeles, who likewise invited me to the Center in 1975. To both these colleagues, and also to those who participated at Canberra and at Los Angeles, I am immensely indebted for their encouragement to finish this work.

To other friends and colleagues I am glad to record my warm thanks for reading my manuscript and giving me the benefit of their advice: Hans Fromm, Peter Ganz, Peter Johnson and Marianne Wynn. Franz Bäuml and Michael Curschmann have helped by their constant readiness to share my concerns and discuss my problems with me.

My thanks are also due to the Council of Trinity College and to the Electors to the Tiarks Fund at Cambridge, both of whom gave financial support for the publication of this book.

Trinity College, Cambridge   D.H.G.
April, 1978

[vii]

ABBREVIATIONS

AfK	*Archiv für Kulturgeschichte*
AUMLA	*Journal of the Australasian Universities Modern Language Association*
BJRL	*Bulletin of the John Rylands Library*
CAIEF	*Cahiers de l'Association Internationale des Etudes Françaises*
CCM	*Cahiers de Civilisation Médiévale*
CL	*Comparative Literature*
CM	*Cornhill Magazine*
CN	*Cultura Neolatina*
CT	*Canterbury Tales*
DVjs	*Deutsche Vierteljahrsschrift für Literaturwissenschaft und Geistesgeschichte*
EG	*Etudes Germaniques*
ELH	*Journal of English Literary History*
EM	*English Miscellany*
ESt	*Englische Studien*
FMLS	*Forum for Modern Language Studies*
FR	*French Review*
FS	Festschrift
GLL	*German Life and Letters*
GR	*Germanic Review*
GRM	*Germanisch-romanische Monatsschrift*
ILRL	*Istituto Lombardo, Rendiconti, Classe di Lettere*
JEGP	*Journal of English and Germanic Philology*
LG	*Literaturgeschichte* (further details will be found in the Bibliography under the author's name)
LMS	*London Medieval Studies*

LR	*Lettres Romanes*
MA	*Moyen Age*
MÆ	*Medium Ævum*
MF	*Minnesangs Frühling*, ed. C. von Kraus (Leipzig, 1944)
MGH	*Monumenta Germaniae Historica*
MHG	Middle High German
MLN	*Modern Language Notes*
MLR	*Modern Language Review*
MPh	*Modern Philology*
MPL	J. P. Migne, *Patrologiae cursus completus. Series Latina*
MSD	K. Müllenhoff and W. Scherer, *Denkmäler deutscher Poesie und Prosa aus dem 8.–12. Jahrhundert*, 3rd ed. (Berlin, 1892)
MSt	*Mediaeval Studies*
NM	*Neuphilologische Mitteilungen*
NMS	*Nottingham Medieval Studies*
PBB	*Paul und Braunes Beiträge*. (T) stands for the Tübingen series
PhM	*Philological Museum*
PhQ	*Philological Quarterly*
PMLA	*Publications of the Modern Language Association of America*
RES	*Review of English Studies*
RF	*Romanische Forschungen*
RhM	*Rheinischer Merkur*
RJb	*Romanistisches Jahrbuch*
RPh	*Romance Philology*
RR	*Romanic Review*
SMV	*Studi Mediolatini e Volgari*
StFr	*Studi Francesi*
StPh	*Studies in Philology*
TLS	*Times Literary Supplement*
UTQ	*University of Toronto Quarterly*
WS	*Women's Studies*
WW	*Wirkendes Wort*
YFS	*Yale French Studies*
YWMLS	*Year's Work in Modern Language Studies*
ZAA	*Zeitschrift für Anglistik und Amerikanistik*

ZfdA	*Zeitschrift für deutsches Altertum*
ZfDk	*Zeitschrift für Deutschkunde*
ZfdPh	*Zeitschrift für deutsche Philologie*
ZfdW	*Zeitschrift für deutsche Wortforschung*
ZfrPh	*Zeitschrift für romanische Philologie*

I

INTRODUCTION

For a Germanist to devote a book to the presence of irony in the medieval romance stands in need of justification nowadays, for both the hunt for irony in medieval literature and the very preoccupation with it have called forth objections. There are some, like Batts,[1] who doubt the relevance of irony to medieval literature at all and protest against the anachronistic application of what is held to be a specifically modern mode to an earlier period (although in practice Batts himself uses the term which in theory he rejects).[2] Others fall back to another position and, like Kramer,[3] deny irony to a German author such as Hartmann, but concede it to his predecessor Chrétien, thereby tacitly admitting the equally important point that irony was therefore employed in the romance from its beginnings at the hands of Chrétien. Others again are suspicious of the fashionable standing of irony in literary studies and unwilling to be taken in by a passing mode (Wells approves of a scholar's approach because he sees in it a welcome 'antidote to the current fashion for realism and irony').[4] We may share this reluctance, but also recognise that a critical method need not be wrong just *because* it is currently practised. Elsewhere irony has deservedly fallen into disrepute when very real difficulties of interpretation can be swept aside with a reference to an underlying irony.[5] To this kind of criticism the answer must be to learn the lesson from irony as a questioning mode by

[1] See Batts, *Humanitas*, p. 39. See also below, p. 14.
[2] E.g. *ibid.*, already on p. 40 ('the real irony of this situation') or p. 48.
[3] Kramer, *Erzählerbemerkungen*, pp. 142ff., 152 and 180.
[4] Wells, *YWMLS* 34 (1972), 508.
[5] See Wehrli's criticism of P. W. Tax in his review in *ZfdPh* 82 (1963), 416, or the same point made repeatedly by Frappier in his criticism of F. X. Newman (ed.), *Meaning*, in *Amour*, pp. 61ff. (see especially pp. 64, 66 and 92).

not stopping short of such questions as: what precisely do we mean by irony? How can we recognise when it is being employed? What is its function in any given passage? By asking such questions we shall also avoid the disconcerting need to defend ourselves, like Cleanth Brooks,[1] against the charge of believing *all* poetry to be ironic or the equally embarrassing imputation that we actually prefer obscurity and ambiguity to clarity and simplicity.[2] Finally, although the argument about scholarly fashions can be inverted (Donoghue gives it as his 'impression that in recent years irony has lost some of its prestige'),[3] even this can be made into a virtue if we see the distance this implies as increasing the chance of objectivity by allowing us to stand back from current polemics.

Each of these recently voiced objections can therefore be answered in theory or in practice. This makes it even more significant that, in isolation and in scattered observations, the theme of irony has played a more and more prominent part in critical evaluations of the romance. In the field of French literature Ménard has written at length on humour in the courtly romance and has discussed irony repeatedly,[4] Haidu has analysed two of Chrétien's romances in the light of their comedy and irony,[5] whilst Frappier, although rightly critical of any facile appeal to irony as an answer to our problems of interpretation, has many fine observations on the irony employed by Chrétien as the founding father of the new genre.[6] In German literature it is Hartmann about whom opinions are still not settled (some deny him irony, whilst others, now in the majority, grant it him),[7] but the position is much clearer with his two leading colleagues.

---

[1] *College English* 9 (1947/48), 231ff.
[2] See the salutary argument of Booth, *Fiction*, pp. 367ff., on this point.
[3] In his review of Booth, *Irony*, in *TLS* (6 December 1974), p. 1358.
[4] Ménard, *Rire*.
[5] Haidu, *Distance*.
[6] As one example for many cf. Frappier, *Amour*, p. 65, fn. 11: 'Qu'il y ait une part d'ironie dans le *Chevalier de la Charrette*, je n'en disconviens pas. Mais le point délicat est de déterminer la tonalité exacte de cette ironie.' On the irony employed in *Flamenca* see Lewent, *ZfrPh* 53 (1933), 60ff.
[7] The first group of Hartmann scholars includes Kramer (see above, p. 1, fn. 3) but also Bumke, *Literaturbeziehungen*, p. 31 and Jackson, *Faith*, p. 58. In the second group I include Milnes, *GLL* 14 (1960/61), 241ff.; Sacker, *GR* 36 (1961), 5ff.; Cramer, *Euphorion* 60 (1966), 36f.; Ruh, *Epik*, pp. 115 and 132; Jackson in Owen (ed.), *Romance*, pp. 65ff., although this list could easily be lengthened.

Bumke's critical bibliography of work on Wolfram often uses the word irony[1] (even though the author apparently attaches little importance to this, since he does not include the word in his index), L. P. Johnson has written on dramatic irony in *Parzival*[2] and Nellmann's sketch of Wolfram's narrator is aware of the ironic implications of this theme.[3] To judge by externals, irony has been most readily acknowledged in the case of Gottfried, for Borovski and Kunzer have written monographs on his use of irony,[4] and Clausen's thesis on the narrator in *Tristan* gives a quarter of its space to the same subject.[5] In English studies Chaucerian irony is no recent discovery,[6] so that the appearance of a monograph on ambiguities, mainly of an ironic nature, in *Troilus and Criseyde*[7] is hardly surprising. Even in the case of *Sir Gawain and the Green Knight*, about which scholars seem to be reluctant to use the concept expressly, irony has certainly been discussed.[8] These are only random examples, but there would be little point in adding to them, since scholarship is not a matter of democratic head-counting. Instead, I use this point to make it clear that irony has played a considerable part in recent work on the romance, that it is time to move on from isolated observations to the general question of the function of irony in the romance as a genre and that, whether it be blessed or cursed with the feature of modishness, this is a problem which amply repays sustained and concentrated analysis.

If our focus is to be concentrated we cannot avoid facing one of the questions mentioned above and saying what exactly we mean by the irony to be found in medieval literature. In other words, we cannot, as happened in a survey of Thomas Mann's irony,[9] dispense with a working definition: this is a trick which can be played only once, and even then one may doubt whether

---

[1] Bumke, *Forschung*, pp. 72, 88, 96, 146, 298f., etc.
[2] Johnson, *Ironie*, pp. 133ff.
[3] Nellmann, *Erzähltechnik*, see index under 'Ironie'.
[4] Borovski, *Ironie*, and Kunzer, *Tristan*.
[5] Clausen, *Erzähler*, pp. 152ff.
[6] For an assessment of the present state of research on this question see Ramsey in Rowland (ed.), *Companion*, pp. 291ff.
[7] Gordon, *Sorrow*.
[8] E.g. by Clark, *MÆ* 40 (1971), 10ff.; Burrow, *Poetry*, pp. 41f.; Hunt, *FMLS* 12(1976), 1ff.
[9] Heller, *Mann*, pp. 235ff.

it was successful. I have attempted a definition of medieval irony elsewhere,[1] suggesting that there are eight component features which I shall enumerate here in theoretical terms so as to provide the basis of the argument in the following chapters, without adducing the illustrative material quoted in my earlier article.

The simplest definition, occupying a traditional place in classical rhetoric, is to regard irony as a statement in which the real meaning is the opposite of the apparent meaning. Accordingly, Donatus defines the rhetorical trope *ironia* as *tropus per contrarium quod conatur ostendens*,[2] Isidore of Seville sees it in a similar light: *Ironia est sententia per pronuntiationem contrarium habens intellectum*,[3] and both illustrate their definition by referring to derision through what appears to be praise, just as, to quote a vernacular example, Wolfram refers to the ugly Cundrie in *Parzival* as *diȝ gæbe trût* (314,6), where his context makes it clear that he means the opposite of what he says.[4] Yet this definition, however traditional, is unsatisfactory as a total statement, since it says both too much and too little. Too much, because not every example of irony goes as far as meaning the opposite of what is said. Too little, because this definition would be equally applicable to lying.

Alternative definitions of rhetorical irony take account of such doubts by avoiding any extreme statement involving the term *contrarium*, common to Donatus and Isidore, and by suggesting that the real meaning merely diverges from the apparent meaning. Pompeius therefore substitutes *aliud* for *contrarium* (*ironia est, quotienscumque re vera aliud loquimur et aliud significamus in verbis*)[5] and Isidore implicitly does the same when he classifies irony (in his sense of deriding through apparent praise) under rhetorical allegory, which he terms *alieniloquium*.[6] The advantage of this slight change of definition is that whilst the word *aliud* or *alienum* can embrace the term *contrarium*, it need not necessarily imply that the meaning is the direct opposite of the statement and can

---

[1] See Green, *Alieniloquium*, pp. 119ff.
[2] *Ars*, p. 401.
[3] *Etymologiae*, I 37, 23.
[4] The epithet *gæbe* can hardly be applied straightforwardly to one who *was gevar den unglîche/die man dâ heizet bêâ schent* (313, 2f.) and Cundrie's appearance disqualifies her from being anyone's *trût* (313,30: *niht nâch friundes minne ger*).
[5] *Commentum*, p. 310.
[6] *Etymologiae*, I 37, 22.

therefore cover other types of ironic obliqueness. Yet we pay a price for this gain since the definition, as it now stands, is applicable not merely to lying, but also to allegory (which is why Isidore can include irony under allegory). Before we can differentiate irony from these related phenomena, however, a number of further refinements of the definition are called for.

The first of these concerns the two levels on which an ironic statement can be understood, one on which the poet's real meaning is conveyed to, and understood by, the initiated and one on which his ostensible meaning is taken as the truth by the uninitiated. These different levels may be represented by different characters within the work, or they may be incorporated in different sections of the audience or in the same audience at different stages of their understanding of the work, or finally, by the distinction between poet and narrator. Because of the various ways in which these different levels of understanding may be built into the work it is unsatisfactory to confine this type of discrepancy, as does Fowler, to the audience alone when he talks of the double audience of an ironic utterance.[1] It is pressing the term 'audience' unjustifiably to say that a character in a work, making a statement which the audience recognises as unwittingly ironic, himself constitutes the uninitiated audience, and it is quite misleading to confuse the fallible or ignorant narrator with the audience. For these reasons we must exclude any specific reference to the audience alone, and suggest an element of withholding on the part of the poet, who may convey his real meaning to the initiated, but presents an apparent meaning to the uninitiated. But the withholding may affect a character, the audience or the narrator.

The next refinement consists in the suggestion that irony presupposes conscious intention (of a character in the work or of the poet) and cannot arise fortuitously. This might appear to be self-evident, but there are two features of medieval literature and the conditions in which it was created which could give rise to the appearance of irony where none was intended. The first

[1] Fowler, *Dictionary*, p. 295: 'Irony is a form of utterance that postulates a double audience, consisting of one party that hearing shall hear and shall not understand, and another party that, when more is meant than meets the ear, is aware both of that more and of the outsiders' incomprehension.'

of these is the semantic ambivalence of so much medieval vocabulary,[1] for such ambivalence, like ambiguity of any kind, is a potential weapon in the armoury of irony, but we can only term it
ironic when we are convinced that the ambivalence is not simply
a given fact of the language concerned, but has been consciously
exploited by the poet as part of his ironic intention. In short, we
need to be persuaded that the ambiguity is not accidental, but
has been purposely built into the episode by the poet. The same
is true of a second feature of medieval literature, its traditionalist
aspect or the way in which a work may be the result of a collective
enterprise over the generations, so that different historical layers,
representing different attitudes to the theme, will be incorporated
in a work and create the illusion of a multiplicity of perspectives
which need not be attributed to any one author as a conscious
ironic intention. We can best exclude the danger of seeing irony
where none was meant by asking after the degree of conscious
artistry with which the poet imposes his view of things on the
material handed down to him (where such independence is
lacking it will be dangerous to assume the presence of irony).
This means, however, that we must find a place for conscious
intention in any definition of medieval irony.[2]

As the next step, we have to describe the relationship between
the real meaning and the apparent meaning of the ironic statement as not merely divergent, but also as incongruous. This
addition is called for because it is the unsuspected dissimilarity
or contrast between one dimension and another which distinguishes irony from metaphor. The two figures are alike (and this
is why we must consider metaphor in defining irony) in that
both mean something different from what they actually say, but
whereas metaphor emphasises the links between the two meanings,[3] irony stresses what separates them.[4] Whereas the real

---

[1] Cf. Hoffmann, *Semasia* 1 (1974), 37ff.
[2] To insist on conscious intention on the part of an author, and on our need to
detect its presence, might seem to involve me in the intentional fallacy. I am less
worried about this after the rigorous and salutary words of Hirsch, *Validity*,
pp. 11ff.
[3] Cf. Quintilian, *Institutio* VIII 6, 8: *metaphora brevior est similitudo*.
[4] Lausberg, *Elemente*, §226, distinguishes in these terms between metaphor
('Krieger/Löwe': 'Verhältnis des Abbildes') and irony ('tapfer/feige': 'Verhältnis
des Gegensatzes').

meaning of the metaphor parallels its ostensible meaning (the two are congruous), in irony their relationship is one of dissimilarity and contrast, sometimes, but not always, going as far as opposition (the two are incongruous).

This aspect of metaphor happens also to be true of allegory, so that the reference to incongruity in our definition of irony serves to distinguish it from allegory as well as metaphor. The two figures of irony and allegory have long been regarded as close to one another,[1] so that the etymology of *allegoria* (to say something other than what is meant) is equally true of irony. Irony and allegory, like irony and metaphor, both say one thing and mean another. But whereas allegory establishes a correspondence between statement and meaning, irony insinuates a contrast. The correspondences with which allegory works may be partial, involving no more than a comparison,[2] or total, suggesting identification (cf. the frequent use of *id est* in exegesis), just as the contrasts of irony may likewise be partial (*aliud . . . aliud*) or total (*per contrarium*). Even where the correspondence may be no more than partial it is on this that allegory concentrates to the exclusion of those features where differences obtain,[3] whilst irony focuses on points of contrast and grants these a greater importance than any similarities. What is ignored by the allegorist can be seized upon by the ironist and adapted to very different ends.

At the first stage of our search for a definition (when looking at the provisional suggestion that the real meaning of an ironic statement is the opposite of the apparent meaning) I suggested, amongst the reasons for dissatisfaction with this common definition, that it made no distinction between irony and lying. To take account of this we must recognise that the divergence and incongruity lie between the 'real or intended' meaning and the 'apparent or pretended' meaning. By using such verbs as 'intend' and 'pretend' we draw attention once more to the purposeful activity

[1] Quintilian, *Institutio* VIII 6, 54–7, therefore classifies irony under allegory, whilst Pompeius, *Commentum*, p. 310, finds it necessary to clarify his definition of irony by showing how it differs from allegory.

[2] E.g. Gottfried's *Tristan* 16969: *der marmeline esterich/der ist der stæte gelich/an der grüene und an der veste.*

[3] Thus Honorius Augustodunensis, *Expositio in cantica canticorum*, MPL 172, 148, can maintain *Leo Christum significat propter fortitudinem, quia vicit diabolum,* but also *Leo significat diabolum . . . propter saevitiam.*

of the ironic poet: it is he who consciously decides that his pretence shall be seen through and arranges through his choice of signals that this shall be possible. In this he differs from the hypocrite whose plan of deception may be scotched, against his wishes, by someone recognising his fabrication for what it is.[1] A more decisive point is made, however, by the distinction between the two verbs 'intend' and 'pretend'. An element of pretence is unavoidably present, since the ironist means something other than what he says and the pretence must be at least superficially plausible if some are to take it, for however short a time, as the speaker's true meaning.[2] But irony differs from hypocrisy in that the element of pretence shared by both should be accompanied, in the case of irony alone, by the poet's intention to destroy this pretence and negate the illusion by allowing the truth to be visible at the same time. In consciously letting the truth shine through the appearance of what he says the ironist resembles the allegorist and differs from the hypocrite, but in working with an incongruity between the truth and what he says he resembles the hypocrite and differs from the allegorist. The ironist leaves work for the audience to do; they must make his truth their own by reacting against what he appears to mean, so that his purpose in saying something other than what he means is not to deceive with a lie, but to awaken to a truth.[3]

We may round off our definition by extending it beyond *ironia* as a rhetorical figure, which is all we have considered so far. As we use the word irony today, we apply it not merely to a figure of speech, but also to a situation or action incongruously different from our expectations, as if in mockery of what things had seemed to promise. In other words, we acknowledge the irony of situation alongside rhetorical irony. Where the latter presupposes an ironist who so uses words as to allow us to share his view of things, the former involves a situation or outcome of events which implies no more than an observer. Knox[4] has taught us that, apart from some odd exceptions, what we now call the

---

[1] Cf. Weinrich, *Linguistik*, p. 13.
[2] Without such pretence there would be no uninitiated as victims. Cf. Hass in Schaefer (ed.), *Ironie*, p. 59.
[3] Cf. Birney, *PMLA* 54 (1939), 638.
[4] Knox, *Word*.

irony of situation was not recognised as irony in English and hence designated by the term reserved for rhetorical irony until about the middle of the eighteenth century.[1] Even if this extension of the English word from rhetorical irony to the irony of situation took place only then, it is highly likely that some aspects of the irony of situation, although not designated by the term, were felt as such at an earlier date. Knox points in the direction where this can be illustrated, to the conception of a mythological or supernatural power as a cosmic mocker, behaving like an ironist in apparently saying one thing to man, but really meaning something quite different.[2]

Taking account of these separate points we arrive at a definition of irony which, for all its clumsiness, pays some regard to the complexity of the phenomenon:

Irony is a statement, or presentation of an action or situation, in which the real or intended meaning conveyed to the initiated intentionally diverges from, and is incongruous with, the apparent or pretended meaning presented to the uninitiated.

This is the definition with which I shall be working in the chapters that follow. As the steps of the argument have shown, this definition is meant to distinguish the concept irony from similar, but not identical modes of speech in medieval literature, it takes no account of various subcategories within irony (e.g. verbal irony and dramatic irony),[3] which will instead be described in the relevant chapters. If it be objected that such terms for subcategories of irony are specifically modern and not to be found in rhetorical tradition, classical or medieval, my answer must be that the same is true of most of our critical terminology and conceptual apparatus, employed by us to ask questions of literary texts which were for the most part not even realised as possible questions at the time when these texts were composed. Apart from the most narrowly rhetorical interpretations of a medieval text by a modern scholar, we approach such a text nowadays with

[1] The semantic history of the corresponding word has not been investigated, to my knowledge, for any other language, but I see no reason why the position should be markedly different from that in English.
[2] We shall return to this problem later, under the heading of dramatic irony, pp. 277ff.
[3] I have discussed these subcategories briefly in *Irony*, pp. 5off.

quite different presuppositions from those of its author, so that it is from our modern intellectual needs that I draw my justification in categorising irony in a manner largely unknown to earlier rhetoric. The position here is hardly different from Knox's demonstration of the development of the specifically modern concept of the irony of situation: here too what we understand by this now can be illustrated from medieval literature even though the word *ironia* was not applied to these examples in the Middle Ages.

If the author of a book on irony cannot be absolved from defining this term, he may be forgiven not going into equal detail with related terms like comedy, humour, satire and parody, because of the immense scope of terms which go beyond literature and touch upon philosophical and psychological questions,[1] and also because Gaier, for example, needed more than a hundred pages to produce a provisional definition of satire,[2] after devoting three times as many pages to interpreting the term's implications in a number of works. Accordingly, I shall attempt only to sketch how I see the general border between irony and these other terms, recognising that it often shades off into a very indeterminate zone.

Whereas all these concepts presuppose a discrepancy between appearance and reality, comedy presents this discrepancy neutrally and free of any valuation, satire attacks this state of affairs, whilst humour grants a value to what it laughs at and shows a sympathetic understanding of human imperfections.[3] If we wish to fit irony into this differentiation by Wiegand it will be to suggest that it shares a critical attitude with satire, but differs from this more aggressive and direct weapon by insinuating its point, hinting at what is not actually said.[4] Parody I regard in the following pages as a stylistic form of irony, an exaggerated imitation of a style or genre in order to imply criticism,[5] resting like irony on a discrepancy between ostensible meaning (a work

---

[1] Cf. Wehrli, *Literaturwissenschaft*, p. 87 and Fromm, *DVjs* 36 (1962), 322f.
[2] Gaier, *Satire*, pp. 329ff.
[3] See Wiegand on 'Komische Dichtung' in Kohlschmidt and Mohr (edd.), *Reallexikon*, I 869.
[4] See Allemann on 'Ironie', *ibid.*, I 756.
[5] Cf. Allemann, *ibid.*, p. 757 and Muecke, *Compass*, p. 78.

in the genre imitated) and real meaning (a criticism of what is imitated).

How this tentative distinction between the various terms may work in practice can be shown with reference to Wehrli's essay on Wolfram's humour.[1] He starts by analysing the purely comic aspects of the scene of the three drops of blood in the snow (e.g. the correlation of hero with hawk or the automatism of Parzival's reverie, reminiscent of Bergson's definition of the comic, 'du mécanique plaqué sur du vivant').[2] But humour, irony and parody are also present in this episode. Wehrli sees humour, for example, in Wolfram's equipment of his narrative with various dimensions (in this case the way in which the scene opens out into the larger themes of love and the Grail),[3] just as Mohr has likewise understood the relationship between Parzival and Gawan in the whole work in terms of humour.[4] We pass on to irony, however, once we realise that in his remarks on the unexpectedness of King Arthur in a snowy landscape instead of his conventional spring-time setting the poet is implicitly ironising the conservative expectations of his listeners, whom he further mocks by disguising the fact that, despite this implicit criticism, he later mischievously follows the very tradition which he here rejects.[5] Finally, the possibility of parody is introduced by Wolfram having as one of the targets of his irony his French source, for Chrétien's time-scheme had suffered from illogically introducing Arthur on every occasion at a Whitsun festival which came round again too swiftly to be credible.[6] Thanks largely to Wehrli it is possible to identify comedy, humour, irony and parody in this one episode and in that process to see how in practice irony may be distinguished from cognate concepts.

As regards the particular romances I discuss in this book, I have unashamedly tackled my theme from a Germanist's point

---

[1] Wehrli, *Humor*, pp. 104ff.
[2] *Ibid.*, p. 106 (cf. also pp. 107 and 111). Bergson's definition comes from Bergson, *Rire*, p. 50.
[3] Wehrli, *Humor*, pp. 109f. (see also p. 116).
[4] Cf. Mohr, *Euphorion* 52(1958), 15f.
[5] I am anticipating here, in a very compressed form, the argument which I develop below, pp. 40ff. Wehrli, *Humor*, p. 108, draws attention to yet another way in which the comedy of this scene opens out into irony.
[6] See below, pp. 40f.

of view, but because I wish to illustrate that irony is latent in the genre as such and is not just to be found in this or that work I have used a comparative approach in trespassing upon other literatures, whilst recognising that if this method had been used by a French or English specialist the emphasis might have fallen quite differently. I have selected my romances primarily with an eye to their aesthetic quality and historical importance, and for this I make no apologies. This means that I include Chrétien's works as a matter of course,[1] but also the *Tristan* romance (Béroul and Thomas) as well as the Provençal *Flamenca*, chosen in preference to the Arthurian *Jaufre* in the hope that it demonstrates that the irony of love is not confined to *Tristan*. This choice of French works dictated the selection of German ones: the romances of Hartmann and Wolfram as successors of Chrétien, and of Gottfried as a representative of the *Tristan* tradition in Germany.[2] As English examples I have taken the leading example of Chaucer's *Troilus and Criseyde* (showing by that choice that I regard it still essentially as belonging to the romance tradition)[3] and the anonymous *Sir Gawain and the Green Knight*. Because of the late flourishing of the vernacular romance in English literature these last two examples come about two centuries later than the other works, but I hope to have made a virtue out of this chrono- logical discrepancy if I have successfully shown that, no matter in what period or in what vernacular tradition, the medieval romance, as composed by poets of the first rank, was a genre eminently receptive to irony and that there are a number of recognisable reasons, aesthetic and sociological, why this should be so.

This should make it amply clear that my chief concern is with the romance genre, not with any particular representative, so that there is no sustained discussion of the function of irony in any one work, but at the most, at recurrent points, a discussion of

---

[1] Apart from *Guillaume d'Angleterre*, because of the uncertainty whether this work is really by Chrétien.

[2] With an occasional reference to Eilhart's *Tristrant*.

[3] Cf. still Young, *PMLA* 53 (1938), 40ff., Lenaghan, *Clerk*, pp. 31ff. and Jordan, *YFS* 51(1974), 223ff. When Muscatine, *Chaucer*, p. 132, denies the term 'romance' to Chaucer's work because of what he calls 'the romance's entertainment of a univalent idealism' he is strangely forgetful of the realistic elements which he has himself traced in the genre of the romance (pp. 41ff.).

isolated passages. This method was forced upon me by what I regard as the primary necessity to establish the presence of irony in this genre from the beginning, to an extent and with a sophistication not true of all narrative literature. Only after this has been demonstrated for the genre as such can one justifiably take the further step of organising the problem round a particular author or work, asking then such questions as how Chrétien's use of irony differs from that of his German successors or how these German poets differ amongst themselves. But these are questions which must be answered elsewhere.

2

THE POSSIBILITIES OF
IRONY IN COURTLY
LITERATURE

We may take as our starting-point an article by Batts[1] in which he expresses reservations about invoking irony in the interpretation of medieval literature. His doubts are two. On the one hand irony is for him so intangible that it is difficult or impossible to tell when it is actually meant, whilst on the other he questions the very justification of expecting to find ironic ambiguity in medieval literature.[2] The aim of this chapter is to suggest that it is both valid to expect irony in the courtly romance and possible to detect cases where it is employed.

Rhetorical considerations

The case for expecting to find irony can best be argued by reference to the rhetorical nature of so much medieval literature, for rhetoric attributed an established place to irony, whilst most of the poets with whom we are concerned are known to be rhetorically schooled and therefore theoretically aware of the possibilities of irony. Of the classical origins of the term and concept irony[3]

[1] Batts, *Humanitas*, pp. 37ff.
[2] *Ibid.*, p. 39: 'The quality of irony is its very intangibility; the nature of its expression is such as often to conceal the real meaning beneath an imperturbably urbane pronouncement of the contrary. Who then is to decide what is irony and what is not?' and 'It is true that one may expect levels of meaning in medieval works, written as they were for an audience for whom the three or fourfold method of exegesis was a commonplace, but it is misguided to suppose a type of sophistication which relies upon ambivalence of standpoint, between, say, author, narrator, and characters. Such an approach is possibly appropriate in an age where the relativity of truth can be a subject for discussion, but not for the Middle Ages, when there was only one truth.'
[3] See Ribbeck, *RhM* N.F. 31 (1876), 381ff.; Büchner, *Hermes* 76 (1941), 339ff.; Behler, *Ironie*, pp. 15ff.

it can be said that the rhetorical tradition, with its definition of irony as a derisive mode of speech which says one thing while meaning the opposite, was of decisive importance.[1] Cicero is aware of the role of Socrates as a prototype of irony and stresses the important social or urbane function of this mode of speech (*de Graecis autem dulcem et facetum festivique sermonis atqui in omni oratione [dis]simulatorem, quem* εἴρωνα *Graeci nominarunt, Socratem accepimus*),[2] but he also gives it a place in his *De oratore*.[3] This is also the case with the *Rhetorica ad Herennium*[4] (attributed to Cicero in the Middle Ages), Quintilian's discussion of tropes and figures in his *Institutio oratoria*,[5] or the grammatical treatise of Donatus.[6] The importance of these examples lies not so much in the authority of the rhetoricians concerned or even in their finding a systematic place for irony within classical teaching on rhetoric and grammar, as in the survival of knowledge of these authors in the Middle Ages. Their texts therefore represent one of the important channels through which knowledge of the classical concept irony was disseminated in the postclassical period. Donatus was thoroughly well-known to the Middle Ages,[7] yet if the other authors are extensively used only from a later date (Quintilian from the end of the eleventh century, Cicero and the *Rhetorica ad Herennium* from the twelfth),[8] this did not preclude their being utilised in the flowering of rhetoric which began again in the twelfth century and made them accessible to the rhetorically trained amongst the vernacular authors of the courtly period.[9]

This direct channel of textual transmission is only one of the ways in which knowledge of classical rhetoric and grammar, and

---

[1] Cf. Behler, *Ironie*, pp. 24f. On the frequency of this definition see Green, *Alieniloquium*, pp. 120ff., on its deficiency *ibid.*, pp. 123ff.

[2] *De officiis* I 30, 108.

[3] III 53,203: *alia dicentis ac significantis dissimulatio.*

[4] IV 34,46: (*Permutatio*) *ex contrario ducitur sic, ut si quis hominem prodigum et luxuriosum inludens parcum et diligentem appellet.*

[5] VIII 6,54–8 and IX 2,46–51.

[6] *Ars grammatica* III 6 (401,30–402,5).

[7] Paré, *Renaissance*, p. 152.

[8] On Quintilian see Mollard, *MA* 5 (1934), 81ff., 161ff. and 6 (1935), 1ff.; on Cicero Grosser, *Studies, passim*; on the *Rhetorica ad Herennium* Faral, *Arts*, pp. 99ff. and Grosser, *op. cit.* Much useful information is given by Hunt, *FMLS* 6 (1970), 1ff.

[9] Hunt, *art. cit.*

of the role they conceded to irony, could reach the twelfth century. Classical rhetoric and grammar could also be excerpted and incorporated in derivative compilations of the Middle Ages,[1] especially important because of the wish to harmonise the categories of the classical rhetoricians and grammarians with biblical exegesis[2] and because of the indirect survival of the classical schools of rhetoric in the form of the monastic schools of the Middle Ages.[3] We find such early medieval authorities as Isidore of Seville, Julian of Toledo and Bede[4] incorporating what they had acquired from classical authors in their own rhetorical works and finding a place for irony and its cognate tropes, but revealing by the often stereotyped order in which these tropes are discussed and by the identical illustrations of them which constantly recur that a recognisable rhetorical tradition has survived the collapse of the Roman Empire. Since the works of these early medieval authors (especially the *Etymologiae* of Isidore) themselves become traditional in the Middle Ages, they constitute a second channel through which knowledge of the rhetorical potentialities of irony was transmitted to the twelfth century.

A third channel, more intangible but none the less important, is represented by the oral instruction provided by the monastic schools of the Middle Ages, in whose curriculum the rhetorical and poetic traditions of antiquity still survived.[5] To this curriculum we largely owe the survival of our primary classical texts and also the secondary compilations of medieval scholars, but it would be wrong to see instruction in medieval schools as exclusively dependent on written works and as not largely taking place in the oral encounter between teacher and pupils in the classroom. If so, we have to reckon with a dissemination of rhetorical tradition which never, or only rarely, found its way onto parchment – of its nature and extent little can be said, but of its existence there can be no doubt. In the case of German literature a fortunate chance has preserved for us, in Notker's

---

[1] *Ibid.*, pp. 7f.
[2] Cf. MacQueen, *Allegory*, pp. 49f. on Bede's importance in this respect.
[3] Hunt, *art. cit.*, p. 6 and Reiber, *Studie*, pp. 23 and 30f.
[4] Isidore, *Etymologiae* I 37, 23–5 and II 21,41; Julian of Toledo, *De vitiis et figuris* 74f. (pp. 35f.) and 80–7 (pp. 36f.); Bede, *De schematibus et tropis* 615,35–616,3.
[5] See Reble, *Pädagogik*, p. 54 (quoted by Strauss, *Redegattungen*, p. 12, fn. 1).

De arte rhetorica,[1] a written example of what was once used in oral instruction, for the mixture of Latin and German, as in Notker's other works, captures something of the classroom atmosphere at St Gallen. At one stage Notker, without explicitly naming it, speaks of what his definition (*ubi aliud dicitur et aliud intellegitur*) shows to be *allegoria*,[2] the heading under which rhetoric traditionally included *ironia* and related modes of speech. Again without mentioning it by name, he then talks of irony, defining and illustrating it in so traditional a way that there is little difficulty in seeing that this is what he must have in mind (*Hęc aliena . sed propinqua sunt. Item per contrarium intelleguntur sententię . ut in conuetudine* (sic!) *latinorum interrogantibus . quesiuit nos aliquis respondetur . bona fortuna . i.* Hel unde salida . *et intellegitur nemo . quod durum esset . i .* unminnesam . zesprechenne . *Similiter teutonice postulantibus obsonia promittimus sic .* Alles liebes gnuoge . *et intellegitur per contrarium propter grauitatem uocis*).[3] The theory of irony can have been no stranger to Notker's pupils at St Gallen.

A fourth and last channel is provided by those rhetorical handbooks, still largely traditional, which were composed in the twelfth and thirteenth centuries. In the twelfth century Hugh of St Victor refers to irony in his *De grammatica*[4] and Matthew of Vendôme betrays his acquaintance with it when, under the trope *allegoria*, he says that seven types are to be distinguished,[5] for these seven types are traditional in rhetoric and are led by *ironia*. In the thirteenth century Buoncompagno da Signa gives a definition and several examples of irony in his *Rhetorica antiqua*,[6] whilst Geoffrey of Vinsauf refers to what must be seen as irony by

---

[1] Ed. Piper, *Schriften*, I 623ff.

[2] *Ibid.*, 674,4f. Cf. the definition given by Donatus, *Ars grammatica* III 6 (401,26): *Allegoria est tropus, quo aliud significatur quam dicitur.*

[3] *Ibid.*, 674,19–26. For Notker's definition cf. that given by Donatus for *ironia* (*op. cit.*, 401,30): *ironia est tropus per contrarium quod conatur ostendens.* Notker's example is also given by Donatus under *charientismos* (*op. cit.*, 402,9ff.), a subtype of *allegoria* and closely related to *ironia* (cf. Lausberg, *Handbuch* §1244, p. 730).

[4] 321,10–15. It is difficult to tell whether *Nonia* (321,10) is a scribal error or a modern misprint, but it is clear that *ironia* is what is meant, because the definition and illustration of *ironia*, and then of *antiphrasis* as *unius uerbi ironia*, agree closely with Donatus on *ironia*.

[5] *Ars versificatoria* 43 (p. 177): *Hujus tropi quamvis septem sint species, de minus ventilata, scilicet de aenigmate, prosequendum est.*

[6] The definition has been edited by Benton, *Clio*, p. 37.

the term *significatio per ambiguitatem*.[1] If some of these examples from the thirteenth century come later than the rise of the courtly romance, this is of little import given the manifestly traditional nature of medieval teaching on irony, the occurrence of so many references to it in the preceding centuries, and the non-datable, but long-lived presence of an oral, pedagogic tradition alongside written handbooks. Through any one of these channels knowledge of rhetorical irony could have reached courtly authors working in the vernacular and equipped them with the means of making use of irony in their own works.

The accessibility of rhetorical irony is relevant to our problem only if we can be sure that the vernacular authors concerned were rhetorically trained and made practical use of what they had been taught. Although much work still remains to be done, it is already clear that the courtly romance is, with one main apparent exception, the work of literate authors who had enjoyed a rhetorical training. For the French romance Hunt has discussed the rhetorical background to the Arthurian prologue in general terms, concentrating on Chrétien,[2] whilst Bertolucci has extended the inquiry to a rhetorical commentary on two complete works of Chrétien, *Erec* and *Cligès*.[3] The same scholar has also provided a similar commentary on Thomas's *Tristan*.[4] In the German field Hartmann and Gottfried are the obvious candidates for such treatment, not least because each composed a passage describing the formal education of the hero which there are grounds for supposing to be autobiographical in tone.[5] Gruenter has therefore established that Hartmann's rhetorical training probably contained elements of forensic oratory in particular.[6] Salmon has correlated Hartmann's narrative practice with the theoretical rules of medieval poetics,[7] and something very similar was undertaken by Sawicki for Gottfried's *Tristan*.[8] For England the field has been well ploughed in

---

[1] *Poetria nova* 1545: Ille vir egregius: *vox haec sonat* optimus. *Aut vir*/Pessimus *oblique nos respicit*; *hic sonat. Haec vox*/*Transvertit visum, vel peccat visus in istis*/*Ambiguis. Res est cooperta, et risus apertus.*
[2] *FMLS* 6 (1970), 1ff. and 8 (1972), 320ff.
[3] *SMV* 8 (1960), 9ff.   [4] *SMV* 6/7 (1959), 25ff.
[5] On Hartmann's passage see Schönbach, *Hartmann*, pp. 221ff., and on Gottfried's Sawicki, *Gottfried*, pp. 25ff.
[6] *DVjs* 26 (1952), 49ff.   [7] Salmon, *Works, passim.*
[8] *Op. cit.*

the case of Chaucer from the time of Manly[1] (although opinions differ as to the aesthetic benefits to be gained from a rhetorical schooling, no one seriously questions that Chaucer was so trained and reveals it in his poetry). Less has been done in the case of *Sir Gawain and the Green Knight*, but enough to demonstrate that here too practice is informed by theory and that the poet can achieve some of his most striking effects by working within (and occasionally against) the poetic and rhetorical norms of his day.[2]

In this brief survey I have confined myself for practical reasons to those vernacular poets who will mainly engage our attention, but have so far omitted Wolfram on the grounds that some would deny him literacy and therewith the most elementary presupposition for a rhetorical training. I am not convinced of Wolfram's illiteracy[3] and would even argue that he may well have been acquainted with the general prescriptions of medieval rhetoric, even if not formally trained. Much of what Pörksen has established for his technique in *Willehalm*[4] shows that, whether or not Wolfram had a rhetorical training like Gottfried, his style has many parallels with what medieval rhetoric demanded of the author.[5] We need not assume that Wolfram knew that he was using this or that rhetorical device (for rhetoric was descriptive as well as prescriptive), but the fact that his style can so often be related to it (and presupposes its conventions even when it goes against them) suggests a general acquaintance with rhetoric, which could well have come not so much from the schoolroom as from close observation of the poetic practice of his contemporaries.[6]

---

[1] See the survey of recent research by Payne, *Chaucer*, pp. 38ff.

[2] Cf. Pearsall, *MLR* 50 (1955), 129ff. and Silverstein, *MPh* 62 (1964/65), 189ff.

[3] See Green, *Oral*, pp. 163ff.

[4] Pörksen, *Erzähler*. Cf., for example, p. 109 ('Wolfram steht also in der Tradition der Rhetorik...Auch der Forderung Quintilians...entspricht Wolframs Vorgehen') and p. 221 ('Zu diesem Eindruck trägt vor allem die oft originelle Abweichung vom überlieferten Typus bei, das spannungsreiche Verhältnis zur Konvention').

[5] The converse argument conducted by Nellmann, *Erzähltechnik*, pp. 165ff., denies rhetorical influence on the narrator's interventions not merely in the case of Wolfram, but with regard to Middle High German literature at large. Even Nellmann does not contest the importance of rhetorical influence in other respects, however.

[6] Something like this has been suggested in the case of *Sir Gawain and the Green Knight* by Pearsall, *MLR* 50 (1955), 133f., and by Schirmer in the case of many authors of 'Mären' (see *Versnovelle*, pp. 124f.).

Rhetorical tradition, reaching courtly authors from classical antiquity along four different channels, therefore made accessible to them its theory and practice of irony, but can it be said that they made any use of this opportunity? In some measure this question can already be answered positively, for some of the rhetorical analyses of these authors have made explicit reference to irony or to a related mode of speech. On Thomas's *Tristan* Bertolucci has grouped a number of passages under *ironia* and rather more under the (potentially) ironic figure of *litotes*.[1] The same author also gives a number of examples of *litotes* for Chrétien's *Erec* and *Cligès*,[2] whilst Haidu has discussed at greater length numerous examples of irony in *Cligès* under various rhetorical headings.[3] Sawicki has done the same thing (on a very restricted scale) for Gottfried,[4] whilst Payne's survey of Chaucer's use of rhetoric includes one example of Chaucer ironising the rhetorical tradition itself[5] and concludes with the suggestion (of much wider import) that rhetoric, by raising questions about the correlation of language with truth, contributed towards Chaucer's complex ironic perspective.[6] These are pointers, but too few to answer the question raised above. Yet if we now consider the possibility that rhetorically trained authors did make use of irony we run into the other difficulty raised by Batts. How can we be certain whether any passage is to be read ironically or straightforwardly,[7] especially at our distance in time from the medieval texts?[8] The difficulty we face is twofold: how are we to recognise a passage as ironic (on what signals, inserted by the author, are

---

[1] *SMV* 6/7 (1959), 54, 38 and 41.   [2] *SMV* 8 (1960), 45 and 50.
[3] Haidu, *Distance*, pp. 25ff.   [4] *Op. cit.*, pp. 123f.
[5] *Op. cit.*, pp. 45f.   [6] *Ibid.*, p. 55.
[7] Wachinger has put his finger on a danger in modern interpretation of the *Nibelungenlied*, and of medieval literature at large (*Studien*, p. 140): 'Man ist versucht, die Schwächen des NL möglichst gering und die dichterische Qualität möglichst hoch einzuschätzen, und dabei will man vor allem die vorhandenen Widersprüche bagatellisieren, weginterpretieren *oder gar als bewußte Kunst ausdeuten*' (my italics). If Pope complained to Joseph Spence that the point of a couplet in one of his poems had been widely misunderstood because most readers were unable to read between the lines, this is hardly the danger we face today.
[8] Cf. the warning by Körner, *Nibelungenlied*, p. 109: 'Bekanntlich ist für eine nachgeborene Zeit nichts schwerer zu erkennen als die feine Linie, welche vormals zwischen Ernst und Scherz lief; leicht erscheint uns heute komisch, was ursprünglich pathetisch gemeint war, noch leichter übersehen wir zartere humoristische Färbung.'

we dependent?), and, since irony can obviously achieve more subtle effects with concealed signals,[1] how are we to reach agreement on these more sophisticated instances?

Signals to irony

Although some of the original signals available in the live situation of narrator and audience (gesture, change of tone, greater emphasis) are irretrievably lost to us and are only known as possibilities because the rhetorical handbooks refer to them,[2] none the less the range of signals built into the text and still accessible to us is a wide one and runs from the explicit to the merely implicit, from an example which I take to be certain to problematic cases where agreement has not yet been reached.[3] The unmistakable example is provided by *Waltharius*, which is not surprising since the Latin poet can make use of the technical rhetorical term *ironia* in giving his signal, whilst his vernacular colleagues have no similarly explicit term at their disposal.[4] The passage in question comes when Hildegund suspects Waltharius of teasing her with the idea of marriage whilst such a thought is far from his mind (235: *Virgo per hyroniam meditans hoc dicere sponsum*), so that this insight into her feelings shows her conceiving the discrepancy between Waltharius's statement and what she takes to be his meaning as amounting to a mockery of her. This example establishes beyond all doubt that irony was a mode of speech available to medieval poetry and that we are justified

---

Cf. Allemann, *Prinzip*, p. 20.

[2] Cf. Donatus, *Ars grammatica* III 6 (402,2: *Hanc nisi gravitas pronuntiationis adiuverit, confiteri videbitur quod negare contendit*), Diomedes, *Ars grammatica* II (462,16: *haec ab ironia differt, quod ironia pronuntiando et adfectu mutat significationem, antiphrasis vero diversitatem rei nominat*) and Bede, *De schematibus et tropis* (616,1: *Inter ironiam autem et antifrasin hoc distat, quod ironia pronuntiatione sola indicat quod intellegi vult, antifrasis vero non voce pronuntiantis significat contrarium, sed suis tantum verbis, quorum est origo contraria*). See also Isidore, *Etymologiae* I 37,23.

[3] I have discussed the various types of signal more fully elsewhere, *Recognising*, pp. 11ff.

[4] French *gaber* or *ramposner*, German *spotten* or *schimpfen* can admittedly be used to indicate ironic speech, but their range is wider so that there is no absolute certainty as with Latin *ironia*. The rich vocabulary of irony in Old French has been treated by Ménard, *Rire*, pp. 447ff., but nothing similar has been done for German terminology.

in looking for it elsewhere, even though its signals may not always be so clearcut.

If the medieval vernaculars lack a word as explicit as *ironia*, we come closest to the position in *Waltharius* whenever the narrator intervenes to show up the irony of an initial statement by its immediate reversal in a straightforward one. In *Cligès* Fénice, supposedly lying mortally ill, hoodwinks her husband by playing on the topos of love as a sickness which only the lover can heal.[1] She refuses to see the doctors summoned by her husband, saying that she places her trust in only one healer, one who disposes of her life and death (5635: ...*ele dit que ja n'i avra/Mire fors un qui li savra/Legieremant doner santé,/Quant lui vendra a volanté./Cil la fera morir ou vivre,/An celui se met a delivre/Et de santé, et de sa vie*). Lest we miss the point, the narrator now steps forward and distinguishes between what the husband and the court believe her to mean (5642: *De Deu cuident que ele die*) and what she actually has in mind (5643: *Mes molt a male entancion,/Qu'ele n'antant s'a Cligés non:/C'est ses Dex qui la puet garir/Et qui la puet feire morir*). With this intervention the irony is made retrospectively clear, even if not so clear as with a word as explicit as *ironia*.

We move one step away from such directness when the remark which produces the ironic incongruity is no longer made by the occasionally visible narrator, but instead by one of the figures in the story, as when Wolfram describes Gawan and Orgeluse riding away together on horseback after they have first met. She asks him to ride on before her, adding that otherwise she would fear to lose him (515,30: '*ez wære et schade, ob ich verlür/sus ahtbæren gesellen*'). One ironic aspect of this remark is clear from what has gone before, since the lovestruck Gawan has already revealed Orgeluse's fascination for him and his hope to wear down her resistance by sheer persistence (515,21 f.), so that there is hardly any danger that she might lose him by leaving him out of her sight. Yet the other irony of her words (she would esteem it a *schade*, if she were to lose so *ahtbære* a companion) is implied by her previous offhand dismissiveness and is made painfully clear by the frankness of what she now says (516,2: '*got müeze iuch vellen!*'). An initial hint of irony, in itself slight and

---

[1] On the ironic potentialities of this topos, see below, pp. 208ff.

intangible, is here reinforced by the directness of the subsequent remark.

The obviousness of a signal grows less, and more reliance is placed on the audience's powers of discrimination, when the information is no longer conveyed by an explicit commentary, but is given in a descriptive remark which could be taken on the level more of narrative than of interpretation. When, in *Yvain*, Calogrenant springs politely to his feet as Guinevere approaches this calls forth a reaction from Keu in the form of apparent praise (71: ...*Par De, Calogrenant!/Mout vos voi or preu et saillant,/ Et certes mout m'est bel, que vos/ Estes li plus cortois de nos*; 77: *S'est droiz que ma dame le cuit,/Que vos aiiez plus que nos tuit/De corteisie et de proesce*). Yet this praise is revealed as a pretence in two ways. First, within Keu's speech itself by a disclosure of his true attitude placed between these two passages (75: *Et bien sai, que vos le cuidiez,/Tant estes vos de san vuidiez*), so that Calogrenant's reputation for courtesy is spitefully equated with his stupid belief that this is so. Secondly, by the narrator's introduction to Keu's speech (69: *Et Kes, qui mout fu ranposneus,/Fel et poignanz et afiteus,/Li dist...*). These words are primarily descriptive, and yet they tell us how to read the words that follow. If he is malicious and sharptongued, then we know, even before he shows his hand in the middle of the speech, that his praise of another should not be taken at face value. That we are correct in this is confirmed by the Queen's reproachful reaction to Keu's words (90: *Enuieus estes et vilains/De ranposner voz conpaignons*; 134: *Costumiers est de dire mal*). Praise is revealed as spiteful criticism,[1] but the initial description of Keu warns us that this will be so.

If the descriptive remark as a signal to irony can sometimes be reduced to one word alone,[2] the poet goes further in the demands he makes on his listeners' attentiveness when the one-word signal has lost even its descriptive function and stands out much less obviously. We are now dealing with the suggestion of irony by means of an apparently superfluous word, whose true function is to call into doubt our certainty as to what is really happening.

---

[1] I have discussed the irony of criticism masquerading as praise elsewhere, *Damning*, pp. 117ff.
[2] As with Gottfried's *Tristan* 13723 (*betrogen*) or Wolfram's *Parzival* 651,7 (*zorn*).

This is the case in *Cligès*, when Chrétien describes Arthur's departure for Brittany and his decision, on the recommendation of his barons, to entrust his realm in his absence to Count Angrés of Windsor (423: *Par le consoil de toz ansanble/Fu comandee, ce me sanble,/Au conte Angrés de Guinesores,/Car il ne cuidoient ancores/ Qu'il eüst baron plus de foi/An tote la terre le roi*). If things are really as they seem, the word *ancores* is superfluous and its presence could then be explained only as a convenient rhyme. If we hesitate to accept such an explanation with a poet of Chrétien's skill, then *ancores* must have a rôle to play in hinting that there will come about a state of affairs when Angrés will no longer be regarded as the most trustworthy baron in Arthur's realm. Since this state of affairs soon arises, taking the form of the count's rebellion in Arthur's absence and seizure of London (1045ff.), I take it that *ancores* is not superfluous and that it alerts us to the dramatic irony of Arthur entrusting his kingdom to one so soon to betray him. Other one-word signals to dramatic irony can be provided by verbs such as French *cuider*, or German *wænen, dünken*,[1] but in all such cases, because the meaning of the verb can vary from 'to be under a delusion' to 'to hold a justified belief', we need confirmatory evidence that the context is itself ironic and that the verb must therefore suggest a discrepancy between fond beliefs and intractable reality. This is the case with the *Cligès* passage just quoted, for there could be no certainty that the use of *cuider* is necessarily ironic ('the barons foolishly thought that he was trustworthy') without the further support of *ancores* in the same context.

Under the next heading we lose the more obvious signal of a seemingly superfluous word, but emphasis is now provided by a demonstrative. Just as the use of a verb like *wænen* prompted us to make a comparison between what is believed and what is the case (and thereby to register a discrepancy), so can the occurrence of a demonstrative like 'this' suggest its counterpart 'that' and thereby insinuate a comparison and ultimately an incongruity. In Chrétien's *Perceval* Gauvain mockingly says to Keu that he will avoid the injuries which Perceval has just inflicted on the

---

[1] Similar examples are provided by the use of *gedenken* or of the auxiliaries *wolte* and *solte*. See my examples in *Recognising*, pp. 28ff.

latter in unhorsing him (4410: *Ja n'an avrai le braz maumis,/Et sanz chenole desloiier,/Que je n'aim mie tel loiier*). The function of *tel* is to draw our attention to *loiier*, to invite us to compare the idea of reward with the situation of Keu's humiliating defeat and injuries, to consider how far such an outcome may be regarded as a reward and to conclude that *loiier* is meant ironically, either as a gift with which Keu would gladly have dispensed or as a more fitting reward than he could realise for having attacked Perceval so rashly.

Hartmann similarly concludes his description of the turmoil at Castle Limors, when Erec awakens from the dead, kills the count and puts his followers to flight, by humorously bringing the narrator's self into the context (6641: *ich enkam ze solher brûtloufte nie*). As with Chrétien's *tel*, the task of *solh* is to make us pause at the substantive it qualifies, to inquire into its justification. Having been brought this far, we can now be left to ask the obvious questions – at what wedding festivities are ghosts, killings and skirmishes the order of the day? Can there really be any talk of a *brûtlouft* when force has been used against the bride and when, as Erec's appearance makes amply clear, Enite is not even a widow and therefore free to marry again? That even the definite article could be used as a demonstrative signal is shown by Wolfram's reference to Gramoflanz and Itonje brought together in Guinevere's company (725,3: *ouch saz der künec Gramoflanz/zuo der, diu ir liehten glanz/mit weinen hete begozzen./daz hete sie sîn genozzen*). That *geniezen* is intended ironically is clear, since it is a strange advantage which a woman gains from her lover if her beauty is covered by tears, but so far this irony is only implicit, without any pointer. If we imagine a stress falling on *daz*, then this word could almost be replaced by *sus* and would invite us to consider how far this situation fell short of what is normally understood by *geniezen*. With this example we reach a point where it is not the presence of a particular word, but the emphasis that falls on it which suggests the possibility of irony. In other words, we catch a glimpse here of the medieval narrative situation, where irony could be pointed out by the reciter's tone of voice.

From this point we shall be concerned with various types of non-verbal signal, the first of which is provided by the contrast between the ironic statement and the context in which it is made. After Chrétien's Perceval encounters the Grail-king fishing and is told how to reach the castle where he is to spend the night, we are shown how he gratefully catches sight of the castle at the end of his journey (3058: *Li vaslez cele part avale/Et dit que bien avoiié l'a/Cil qui l'avoit anvoiié la./Si se loe del pescheor...*). The statement that the fisher king has well directed him onto the right path (*bien avoiier*) is borne out by the context (Perceval has just glimpsed the castle and now praises his informant for his accurate instructions), so that there are no grounds for suspecting irony here. Yet almost the same remark is made by Perceval a little earlier in a very different situation, since on leaving the fisher king he rides up to a mountain-top from which he sees not the nearby castle, but bare, uninviting terrain (3037ff.). He now accuses himself of stupidity in following such faulty advice (3040f.) and curses the man who led him astray, but in words which almost literally anticipate those with which he soon afterwards thanks the king, once he does catch sight of the castle (3042: *Deus li doint hui male vergoingne/Celui qui m'a anvoiié,/Si m'a il or bien avoiié/Que il me dist que je verroie/Meison quant ça amont seroie!*). If in the later passage the phrase *bien avoiier* was fully justified, the same cannot be said of the earlier occasion, where it is contradicted by the bare landscape, by Perceval's self-accusation and by his curse. The discrepancy between statement and context is here so glaring that it can only be irony when Pereceval says that he has been well guided at the moment when he is convinced that he has been put on the wrong track. Yet our perception of this irony cannot be due to any exclusively verbal signal, since the two lines uttered by Perceval in this ironic passage are identical with what he says in the non-ironic passage. What alerts us here is not what is actually said, but the incongruity between what is said and the context. No verbal signal may be used, but even without this we can be sure of the poet's ironic intention.

Irony can also be signalled by the tacit parallelism between two episodes. When Gottfried's Tristan gains the upper hand over Morolt so that his opponent sinks to the ground he taunts him (7065: *'wie do, wie do?' sprach Tristan/'so dir got Morolt, sag an,/ist dir dirre mære iht kunt?/mich dunket, du sist sere wunt;/ich wæne, din dinc übele ste'*). That this jeering remark is ironic is suggested by the presence of *mich dunket* and *ich wæne*, not in the sense that Tristan's victorious elation is about to be undermined by events, but in the sense that these phrases suggest pedantic caution, whereas the situation admits of no doubt about the extremity which Morolt now faces. But the irony comes earlier and is more defiant, since Tristan's opening words (*wie do, wie do*) are more than a cry of triumph, they take up the words with which Morolt, after wounding Tristan with the poisoned sword, had jeered at him (6931: *'wie do?' sprach Morolt 'wiltu jehen?/hier an mahtu wol selbe sehen,/daz nieman unreht vüeren sol:/din unreht schinet hier an wol'*). Tristan's repetition of his opponent's taunt is hardly fortuitous, for the link between the two jeers is strengthened by what follows in each case. Just as Morolt then reveals the nature of the poisoned wound and the fact that only his sister can heal it,[1] so does Tristan say that, however things may stand with himself, Morolt clearly needs medical treatment.[2] Similarly, Tristan's words about justice triumphant[3] take up Morolt's earlier claim and give it the lie. By casting back Morolt's taunt in his face Tristan is rubbing it in that the wheel has turned full circle and that his opponent's earlier confidence was misplaced. Yet none of this irony is actually indicated by Tristan's words *wie do, wie do*, it emerges only from their echo of Morolt's words.

Finally, a signal can also be given by the presence of different levels of irony within a given passage. In *Troilus and Criseyde* the narrator ensures by explicit commentary that we grasp the irony of the opening situation in which Troilus, mocking others ensnared by love, is about to become a victim himself (I 211: *O blynde world, O blynde entencioun!/How often falleth al the effect contraire/Of surquidrie, and foule presumpcioun;/For kaught is proud, and kaught is debonaire./This Troilus is clomben on the staire,/And litel weneth that he moot descenden;/But al day faileth thing that fooles wenden*). What is not immediately so clear is the wider implication of this commentary. In its present context it applies to what is just about to happen, to Troilus's fall from the proud rejection of love to the humility imposed upon him by love. But in the wider

---

[1] *Tristan* 6935ff.   [2] 7070ff.   [3] 7075ff.

context provided by a knowledge of the whole work these lines later acquire greater significance, for they also ironically fore-shadow his fate as a lover, his fall from the pride of an unquestion-ing lover to the bitter knowledge won by his loss of Criseyde.[1] These different levels of irony are temporal (the contrast between the present situation and future events), but the difference can be brought about by other means, such as the contrast between the knowledge of a figure in the work and what the audience knows of the situation.[2] In *Flamenca*, for example, the count of Aussuna, engaged in conversation with Flamenca, yields his place to Guillem as the latter joins them (7516: *Em pes levet, e quais per juec/El dis*: '*Sener, en dreg d'amor/Vos farai ara gran honor,/Quar ma cosina-us laissarai/E josta leis vos asseirai,/E pregar l'ai, si-l plas, de vos*'). On one level this is an example of ironic social banter, for the count doesn't mean what he says (*e quais per juec*), presumably because he realises that a knight like Guillem will not need another's good offices in establishing contact with a courtly lady. On another level, however, the lovers and the audience realise what the count does not know, namely that the long-standing affair between Guillem and Flamenca renders any kind of introduction and word on his behalf superfluous.[3] What the count intended as the polite irony of social intercourse is itself ironised by the situation of which he has no full knowledge.

Failures in recognition

This abbreviated survey has shown us various types of signal (to which more could be added), helping both us and the medieval audience to recognise the poet's intention, but they range from the rare explicitness of *Waltharius* to cases (especially within the bracket of non-verbal signals) where discussion and disagreement are certainly possible.[4] Because so many of these signals avoid

---

[1] Cf. Martin, *Fools*, p. 43.
[2] This amounts of course to dramatic irony, which I discuss below, pp. 250ff.
[3] Cf. Lewent, *ZfrPh* 53 (1933), 60.
[4] These less explicit signals concern above all cases where there is a discrepancy between statement and context (often to be construed in the widest sense), parallelism between often widely separated passages, or the presence of several layers of irony.

any heavy explicitness and can thereby achieve very subtle effects, it is possible both that some medieval listeners may not have noticed the signal and that some modern readers may disagree as to whether irony is being indicated. That some medieval listeners failed to see a signal we need not doubt, quite apart from the way in which Wolfram divides his audience into its more and its less perceptive members.[1] Not to be seen for what it is, after all, is a risk run by all indirect modes such as irony and even satire.[2] If this risk is greater in the case of readers coming centuries later, it was also greater for a medieval German audience than for a French one, if we accept Ruh's point that German courts were less sophisticated, more in need of a helpful narrator's commentary (and therefore more in danger of floundering whenever he was less than explicit).[3]

Courtly authors can sometimes draw a parallel between their own use of irony and that employed by characters in their work,[4] but in the latter case they are sometimes ready to illustrate that the irony was not always perceived. This is true in Chrétien's *Lancelot* of Guinevere's heartless teasing of Lancelot once he has freed her from captivity (4205: *et sel cuidai ge feire a gas,/mes ensi nel cuida il pas*), or more tellingly, in *Perceval*, of the inexperienced young hero's inability to see through Keu's mocking recommendation to help himself to the Red Knight's equipment (4120: *Cil qui ne sot le gap antandre/Cuida que il voir li deïst*).[5] Failures of understanding within the poet's narrative world are likely to have had their counterparts in the real world of his audience.[6]

---

[1] *Parzival* 1,16 and 2,5. Cf. Haas, *Tumpheit*, pp. 31ff. and Nellmann, *Erzähltechnik*, p. 5.

[2] Cf. Worcester, *Satire*, pp. 42f.

[3] Cf. Ruh, *Epik*, p. 108, who also makes the important point that the German narrator's commentary need not always be meant for the whole of his audience, so that this division of his audience comes close to the position acknowledged by Wolfram with his listeners (see above, fn. 1).

[4] See below, pp. 48ff.   [5] Green, *Recognising*, p. 15.

[6] Cf. the example discussed by Owen, *FMLS* 2 (1966), 192ff., especially pp. 195f. (whether or not we agree with Owen's suggestion that the author was Chrétien). Another example is possibly provided by the ivory comb with a parallel depiction of two scenes from *Cligès* and *Tristan* (referred to by Gnaedinger, *Musik*, p. 9, fn. 12), for here two literary themes are seen as parallels which for Chrétien stood rather in parodic opposition (see Fourrier, *Courant*, pp. 124ff.). The difficulty, however, is to tell whether the parody has not been seen or has been deliberately rejected.

Even without such a reference built into the work this was almost certainly the case with the careful chronology of *Parzival* where, as Weigand[1] has shown us, Wolfram's mockery of Chrétien for always conventionally introducing Arthur in a springtime Whitsun setting does not prevent him, behind a suitable smoke-screen, from doing precisely the same thing himself when describing the reunion of Parzival with Gawan and Arthur at Joflanze.[2] If the picture of a modern scholar sitting at his desk in the 1930s to calculate a medieval poet's time-references is not a surprising one, I find it impossible to conceive a member of Wolfram's contemporary audience similarly checking these references on the fingers of his hand over a number of recitals. In other words, the poet's hoodwinking of his audience must have been a private joke, but one in which, as with the ironist's misleading of others, it was theoretically possible for any audience to join at any time.

In view of the objections raised by Batts, however, it is more important to consider the failure of modern readers to acknowledge cases of irony in these works than to engage in speculation as to whether medieval listeners also failed. That the difficulties facing us are very real and that Batts's point is an important one (even though my conclusion differs from his) I hope to show by considering some cases where critical opinion has differed sharply over the question of irony. These cases may concern points of detail, they may affect central features of the work, or they may touch upon general problems of medieval literature.

Under points of detail I single out first the use of the word *clûse* in the *Kaiserchronik* to refer to the tower in which Crescentia successfully imprisoned the wicked Dieterich during her husband's absence (11 722: *Duo rûmten si die clûse/unt giengen von dem hûse*). Burdach briefly considered the possibility of reading the word ironically (the prison in which chastity is enforced upon Dieterich is presented as if it were a religious retreat in which he voluntarily embraces it) only to reject it as improbable, without giving any reasons.[3] He may be correct, but there are pointers in the opposite

---

[1] Weigand, *Parzival*, pp. 56 and 61f. The article reprinted here was originally published in German in *PMLA* 53 (1938), 917ff.
[2] See also below, pp. 40f.
[3] *ZfdPh* 60 (1935), 314f.

direction, for others have detected traces of a mischievous humour in this scene and discovered irony in the passage introduced
by these lines.[1]

Another contested detail comes at the close of Gottfried's
survey of the love-poets of his day (4816: *si unde ir cumpanie/
die müezen so gesingen,/daz si ze vröuden bringen/ir truren unde ir
senedez clagen:/und daz geschehe bi minen tagen!*). Some see in this the
indirect expression of a wish that these lyric poets may put an
end to their complaints about unreciprocated love, whilst others
reject this reading and take the lines straightforwardly (in Mohr's
words: 'Möchten sie im Liede ihr Leid zur Freude für die
Aufnehmenden verwandeln, jetzt, in meiner Zeit, in der Kunst
in diesem Sinne möglich geworden ist').[2] Another detail of
Gottfried's work, the landscape setting to the May festival held
by Marke, has been interpreted as ironic by Batts,[3] who suggests
that the tentative phrasing used in some of the descriptive phrases
(55off.: *sulen sin, ervröuwen sol, bringen solte*) is meant to be aimed
parodically at those poets who cultivate this kind of idealised,
but unrealistic landscape description. Kunzer[4] has instead pointed
out that this wording appears to be conventional, recurring not
merely in Gottfried's own description of the love-grotto landscape (where parody of this kind can hardly be present), but also
in Hartmann's works, i.e. precisely in those romances at which
Gottfried, if his intention had been polemical, must be assumed
to have aimed his ironic barb.

---

[1] Mischievous humour has been proposed for this scene by Teubert, *Crescentia-
Studien*, p. 28, Helff, *Studien*, p. 25, and Hamm, *Legenden*, pp. 37f. (but rejected by
Baasch, *Crescentialegende*, p. 91), whilst irony has been suggested by Shaw, *Darstellung*, pp. 157, 164 (especially fn. 68) and 292f. (especially fn. 47) for a number of
distinct reasons.

[2] The ironic reading of these lines has received support from Nickel, *Studien*,
p. 63; Ranke, *Allegorie*, p. 36; Nauen, *Bedeutung*, p. 88; Fromm, *DVjs* 41 (1967),
342f.; Gnaedinger, *Musik*, p. 48 and Wapnewski, *Lyrik*, pp. 214f. The direct
reading is proposed by Bindschedler, *Gottfried*, pp. 22f. and Mohr, *Minnesang*,
p. 228, although I find the reasons advanced by Mohr less than convincing. He
cannot find support by reference to Gottfried's valuation of his own artistry in
the prologue, since this parallel presupposes that Gottfried regards the art of the
love-poets as highly as he does his own, whereas this is precisely the point which
has to be established. Nor is the reference to Walther's poem on the death of
Reinmar any more convincing, since the lines quoted from Walther themselves
contain an ironic point (Georgi, *Preisgedicht*, p. 158, and Green, *Damning*, pp. 129f.).

[3] Batts, *Neophilologus* 46 (1962), 227.

[4] Kunzer, *Tristan*, p. 91, fn. 8.

An example of quite another kind is Hartmann's Laudine, or rather the poet's defence of her against the charge of fickleness and wish to dissociate himself from Chrétien's more cynical motivation (*Iwein* 1863ff.). Whereas this passage was once generally read (and still is by some) straightforwardly as an idealising gloss by an ethically more serious German adaptator (or one didactically concerned to inculcate courtly standards among his more provincial German listeners),[1] it is symptomatic of the rôle which irony is coming to play in the interpretation of medieval literature that these lines are now more commonly read ironically.[2] By using an indirect mode instead of the plainer method of sarcasm, Hartmann's ultimate effect would therefore be comparable with Chrétien's: both authors distance themselves from their narrative action.

Disagreement over an ironic interpretation can also affect more central features of a work. In the case of the *Millstätter Exodus* de Boor[3] has suggested that the disparity between theme and style (e.g. the full exploitation of military pathos in order to deny its relevance to the situation) is meant ironically as a conscious deflation of the secular heroic style. I have rejected this view elsewhere,[4] mainly on the grounds that what appears in this case to be a discrepancy to us need not have appeared in this light to the twelfth century[5] and that there is no reason to assume irony here which, if it were present in such passages, would colour our interpretation of the whole work and the purpose for which it was written. Something similar is true of Kalogreant's definition of *âventiure* at the beginning of Hartmann's *Iwein*, only this time it is de Boor who, by viewing this as a programmatic statement of the chivalric code, takes it seriously[6] and as intended positively both by Kalogreant and by Hartmann. Others however have seen

---

[1] Cf. Ehrismann, *LG* II 2, 1, pp. 176f.; Kramer, *Erzählerbemerkungen*, p. 145.

[2] E.g. Ohly, *Struktur*, p. 108; Ruh, *Epik*, p. 108; Jackson, *Observations*, p. 71; Peiffer, *Funktion*, pp. 59ff.; Nölle, *Formen*, pp. 22f.

[3] Cf. de Boor, *LG* I 151.

[4] Green, *Exodus*, pp. 305ff.

[5] In other words, I regard this as a case where Körner's warning (quoted above, p. 20, fn. 8) has to be taken very much to heart.

[6] Cf. de Boor, *LG* II 65. There is hardly any need to point out the irony of my disagreeing with de Boor both when he proposes an ironic reading (of the *Millstätter Exodus*) and when he fails to observe irony (as with Kalogreant). It is similarly ironic that, having criticised the generalisations of Batts about the

in it an example of the poet ironically distancing himself from this definition.[1] Wolfram's presumed illiteracy (*Parzival* 115,27: *ine kan decheinen buochstap*) is another such example of scholarly dissension. Is this a straightforward statement of fact which we must take into account in assessing his style and mode of composition,[2] or do we have to read it less directly, as a topos with its own literary, but not necessarily autobiographical implications, or as a humorously ironic statement which was meant to be seen through?[3] These readings have not lacked their advocates, but on our interpretation of this single verse depends our view of Wolfram's style and of the position he occupies in the transition from oral to written composition which largely coincides with the rise of the continental romance. How pointed the contrast between opposing views on the question of irony can become may best be illustrated by a head-on difference of opinion in the case of Chaucer's *Troilus and Criseyde*. For C. S. Lewis 'the "ironic" Pandarus is not to be found in the pages of Chaucer', whilst Robertson is equally convinced that 'the character of Pandarus is a masterpiece of medieval irony'.[4]

On wider problems of medieval literature I shall confine myself to one example. German scholarship has largely dwelt upon the didactic aspects of Hartmann's work and the idealising style in which he presents his view of courtly life, stressing that he has thereby either missed or rejected Chrétien's more realistic and ironic tone.[5] For one period of scholarship this was a sign of his 'German seriousness' and ethical preoccupations, but lately it has been seen as a failure on his part to appreciate the more sophisticated art of his French source. More recently, however,

---

inadmissibility of entertaining medieval irony, I should then not find it possible to accept his own ironic interpretation of the landscape description of Gottfried's May festival. But at least these disagreements may illustrate how much work still needs to be done in the field of medieval irony.

[1] E.g. Ohly, *Struktur*, pp. 101f.; Sacker, *GR* 36 (1961), 7f.; Batts, *Humanitas*, p. 40; Cramer, *Iwein*, pp. 181f. (note to v. 526); Nayhauss-Cormons-Holub, *Bedeutung*, pp. 147f.; Désilles-Busch, *Don*, pp. 117f.; Kaiser, *Textauslegung*, pp. 110ff.

[2] Cf. Horacek, *Buochstap*, pp. 129ff., and Grundmann, *AfK* 49 (1967), 391ff.

[3] See Ohly, *ZfdA* 91 (1961/2), 1ff.; Eggers, *Litteraturam*, pp. 162ff.; Willson, *NMS* 14 (1970), 27ff.; Green, *Oral*, pp. 163ff.

[4] Lewis, *Allegory*, p. 191 and Robertson, *Preface*, p. 479.

[5] Cf. Bumke, *Literaturbeziehungen*, p. 31; Jackson, *Faith*, p. 58; Kramer, *Erzähler-bemerkungen*, p. 152.

important reservations have been suggested. Even Hartmann's idealising style can be devoted to critical as well as laudatory ends,[1] and he can find justification for this in rhetorical prescriptions. His narrator's commentary is not always so naïvely in harmony with the narrative as the rival view would have it.[2] Finally, a comparison of Hartmann's versions with Chrétien's, concentrating on those points where the German has failed to exploit an irony present in his source, fails to consider those cases where he introduces an irony absent from Chrétien's text.[3] The scope of the question, however, extends far beyond Hartmann's works alone, for it has been argued that not just he, but 'many German authors failed to perceive the ironical overtones in French literature and reacted to a system of values which they believed to be there',[4] in other words that the abandonment or weakening of irony might well be true of most German adaptations of French romances. How we interpret such a passage as Hartmann's defence of Laudine could therefore ultimately open out to the question how we regard the relationship between French and German courtly literature.

The point of this rapid survey has not been to settle the issues raised, but simply to suggest that on various levels (points of detail, central features of a work, wider problems of literary history) the question of irony is relevant, and not just peripherally, that to consider the presence of irony involves difficulties worthy of discussion and that there is something to be gained from treating these problems explicitly and systematically. This is preferable to the isolated attention which has so far been given to the problem and certainly better than either rejecting the possibility out of hand because of a reluctance to consider it more closely for medieval literature[5] or conversely, accepting it without more ado because it provides an easy explanation of

---

[1] Green, *Damning*, pp. 121ff. and *Praise, passim.*

[2] Peiffer, *Funktion*, pp. 27ff.

[3] As is the case with the hospitality extended to Erec by Coralus, cf. Green, *Damning*, pp. 148f. An equally telling example is provided by Hartmann's omission of Chrétien's ironic praise of Enide (2413ff., soon afterwards undermined by 2559ff.). Hartmann rejects this passage not because he is averse to irony at large, but because he wishes here to direct it against Erec exclusively (cf. 2924ff.). Cf. Green, *Praise*, p. 804.

[4] Jackson, *Faith*, p. 55.   [5] E.g. Reinhold, *Tendenzen*, p. 82.

a discrepancy for which it would otherwise be difficult to account.[1]
I mention both these possibilities because I am far from accepting
irony in every instance where it has been proposed (to confine
myself to the examples listed above, I have my doubts about
de Boor's interpretation of the *Millstätter Exodus* or Batts on
Gottfried's springtime festival scene) and because, even where
I incline towards the view that irony is present, I need not agree
with the way in which this irony is then interpreted (Chaucer's
Pandarus I regard as an ironic figure, but not because I accept the
Robertsonian doctrine that what appears as *fin'amors* in medieval
literature is mere parody and therefore automatically ironic).
I concede that there is such a thing as a false hunt for irony[2] and
that there is a danger of subjectively turning medieval literature
into an image of our own modern concerns.[3] Yet I also think that,
by taking this into account and paying due regard to signals
built into the text, it is possible to isolate from the examples
where differences of opinion are still possible a number of cases
where the presence of irony is much more likely, and it is to some
of these that I now turn.

Detection of irony

Irony can be detected with reasonable certainty when it is presented in the form of a pattern so clear-cut that it would be difficult
to attribute the patterning to chance. An example of such a
pattern[4] forcing us to draw the obvious conclusion is provided
by Chaucer in his *Troilus and Criseyde* at the point where he
underlines the ironic result of the Trojans' eagerness to ransom
Antenor. Any listener familiar with the matter of Troy would
remember him as responsible, together with Aeneas, for treacher-
ously negotiating with the Greeks, for delivering the Palladium

---

[1] Cf. the words of balanced criticism in a review article by Frappier, *Amour*, pp. 64 and 66.
[2] Cf. Jackson in a review of Mowatt's translation of the *Nibelungenlied*, MLR 59 (1964), 671f.
[3] As pointed out by Brewer in a review, *MLR* 68 (1973), 634. If Brewer sees the image as that of 'a modern North American liberal Freudian agnostic' I should wish to add irony to this mental equipment. That it is in danger of becoming one of our modern heresies has been argued polemically by Booth, *Reason*, pp. 327ff.
[4] Cf. Durling, *Figure*, pp. 57f.

to them and for thereby opening the way to the downfall of Troy. Chaucer takes care that we should appreciate the irony of the Trojans seeking to obtain the freedom of the man who will later betray them by generalising expressly on men unwittingly bringing about their own harm (IV 197: *O Juvenal, lord! soth is thy sentence,/That litel wyten folk what is to yerne,/That they ne fynde in hire desir offence*). He then leads from this *sententia* to the particular illustration (IV 201: *and, lo, here ensaumple as yerne./This folk desiren now deliveraunce/Of Antenor, that broughte hem to meschaunce*). So far the irony is quite obvious (especially to one who knew his romance of Troy), but this is only part of the pattern. In his next stanza the poet specifies Antenor's future offence (IV 204: *For he was after traitour to the town/Of Troye: allas, they quytte hym out to rathe!*), but then connects the theme of Antenor with another theme which has recently been voiced (IV 195f.). He reminds us that the Trojans were able to ransom Antenor from the Greeks only at the cost of handing over Criseyde in exchange (IV 207: *Criseyde, which that nevere did hem scathe,/Shal now no lenger in hire blisse bathe;/But Antenor, he shal come hom to towne,/And she shal out*; *thus seyde here and howne*).

The two themes are depicted as complementary, but the force of the generalising *sententia* which introduces Antenor in these stanzas is that it prompts us to ask whether there might not be a comparable irony about Criseyde's situation. What these lines expressly mention is Antenor's future betrayal (*he was after traitour*) and Criseyde's past loyalty (*which that nevere did hem scathe*), but what they omit to mention is Antenor's past loyalty (which clearly lies behind the Trojans' eagerness to secure his release) and Criseyde's future betrayal. Three points in this four-point pattern are known to the listeners, but it is the recognisability of the pattern which prompts us to look behind the praise of Criseyde's past loyalty and discern the outlines of her future betrayal – not of Troy, but of Troilus, so that Chaucer sees the same kind of human failing lying behind the fall of a city and a lover's personal loss.[1] That the poet can rely on the listener completing the obvious

---

[1] That Chaucer achieves some of his more intangible, but powerful effects by this parallel between the fate of the city and the fortunes of the lover has been suggested by Curry, *Chaucer*, pp. 250f.

pattern for himself is also clear from the placing of these stanzas very near the opening of Book IV, close to the proem in which mention had been made of Criseyde's imminent betrayal of her lover (IV 15: *For how Criseyde Troilus forsook, Or at the leeste how that she was unkynde,/Moot hennesforth ben matere of my book*). This warning may alert the listener, but it is still the balanced patterning of the later stanzas which forces upon him the conclusion that the laudatory mention of Criseyde's past loyalty may be true, but is irrelevant to the situation which has now arisen.

Ironic patterning of another kind occurs in Wolfram's references to the relationship between Parzival and Lähelin, this time of a complexity (rather than obviousness) which suggests a conscious intention at work. I have discussed this elsewhere from the point of view of knightly homicide and Johnson has treated it in the context of dramatic irony,[1] so that a lengthy demonstration is here superfluous. Dramatic irony is present in the encounter between Parzival and Trevrizent, where the hermit talks about the knight who came to the Grail-castle without asking the redeeming question and fails to realise that Parzival is that knight. Led astray by the Grail-horse on which Parzival had come to him and by his knowledge that Lähelin had penetrated Grail-territory where, by killing the knight Lybbeals, he had likewise obtained possession of a Grail-horse, Trevrizent asks Parzival point-blank whether he is Lähelin (474,1: *Hêrre, sît irz Lähelîn?*). We know the facts of which the hermit is still ignorant and can appreciate the threefold dramatic irony of the encounter so far (Trevrizent's ignorance of Parzival's presence at Munsalvæsche, his misunderstanding about the Grail-horse, his confusion of Parzival with the arch-enemy of his dynasty), but the irony of the scene is now taken a stage further. Parzival denies that he is Lähelin (475,4: *hêrre, in binz Lähelîn*) but, by adding that he once slew a knight and robbed the corpse (as Lähelin had done against Lybbeals), reveals that he is little better than a Lähelin, so that his denial in 475,4, whilst factually true, is shown in the same breath to be ethically untrue. Moreover, Parzival's mention of the knight he has himself killed and stripped takes us back to his encounter with Ither, to the scene where he had himself compared

[1] Cf. Green, *Homicide*, pp. 49ff. and Johnson, *Ironie*, p. 143 and *MLR* 63 (1968), 615.

his opponent with Lähelin (154,25: *du maht wol wesen Lähelîn*) at the moment when, about to kill and rob his adversary, he is to prove himself another Lähelin. The ironic equations between Parzival and Lähelin are many and variegated, they are present not for the sake of ironic density as an end in itself, but rather to suggest to the listener that what he knows to be factually untrue may yet have a symbolic bearing on Parzival's position – but in a sense which temporarily escapes both him and Trevrizent.

The probability of irony is also much greater when there is not just one pointer, but a number of distinct levels of evidence to suggest it. One such example, Hartmann's praise of Erec after his victory at his wedding tournament,[1] is apposite here, for the hero is described in such superlative terms that some have seen it as an example of straightforward praise[2] (2811: *Êrec der tugenthafte man/wart ze vollem lobe gesaget./den prîs hete er dâ bejaget,/ und den sô volleclîchen/daz man begunde gelîchen/sîn wîsheit Salomône,/ sîn schœne Absolône,/an sterke Samsônes genôz./sîn milte dûhte si sô grôz,/diu gemâzete in niemen ander/wan dem milten Alexander*). I suggest instead that the evidence for irony is present in various forms. One consideration concerns the placing of this passage. Coming at the close of the first part of the work (before the crisis at Karnant) this 'crowning success' is shown by the events that follow to be only superficial and provisional, for if Erec's success had in fact been as complete as this eulogy suggests, then his *verligen* would have been impossible and there would have been no subsequent narrative. This suggests that this climax of the first part is a false climax and that any praise of Erec at this point is ironic praise, not so much untrue as irrelevantly true.

Another suggestion is provided by the comparison of Erec with Absalom, for this figure was seen conventionally both positively (as the prototype of masculine beauty) and negatively (as a murderer and rebel),[3] as a Janus figure who could be employed, as by Hartmann in *Der arme Heinrich*,[4] to suggest negative features behind positive ones or to indicate that certain

---

[1] I have discussed this passage at greater length in *Praise*, pp. 798ff.
[2] E.g. Pörksen, *Erzähler*, p. 158; Fechter, *PBB* (T) 83 (1961/62), 303; Cormeau, *Hartmann*, p. 8.
[3] Cf. Fechter, *art. cit.*, pp. 302ff.
[4] V. 84ff.

virtues may be irrelevant if not backed up by other qualities.[1] The use of this figure warns us that Erec's positive features may have their ambiguous implications too, that they protect him against a fall as little as Absalom's beauty shielded him. Yet Hartmann compares Erec with other figures besides Absalom, so that to be convinced of the presence of irony we need to be shown a common feature, shared by these figures in Hartmann's passage *and* by Erec as well, which exposes them all to Hartmann's criticism, even at the moment when he is apparently praising these four for their separate virtues and Erec for possessing all these attributes together. We find this clue in the relationship of these men to women, as conventionally seen in medieval literature. Despite his wisdom, Solomon fell victim to his concubines and was guilty of idolatry.[2] Absalom's beauty fitted him to be a victim of love's omnipotence and he belongs to the frequently invoked 'slaves of love'.[3] Samson, as the victim of Delilah, obviously has a place here, the more so since he can serve as a warning to warriors and is therefore relevant to Erec's neglect of his chivalry.[4] Finally, Alexander's dalliance with Candace means that his position can be compared with Samson's or Absalom's.[5] These figures, despite their separate virtues, were therefore all enslaved by woman, but within barely 100 lines of this eulogy the same will be shown to be true of Erec in his *verligen* at Karnant.[6] The force of Hartmann's comparison goes much further than we at first suspect, it covers a negative feature common to Erec and these positive exemplars – behind this praise, behind the comparison with such worthy figures there lurks Erec's failure, soon to be revealed to us. Hartmann implicitly qualifies this eulogy of Erec's achievement in order to prepare us for his fall from grace,

[1] Cf. Fechter, *art. cit.*, p. 304: 'Absalom und andere Idealtypen beweisen, dass hervorragende Eigenschaften nicht genügen oder nichts nützen, wenn andere sittliche, intellektuelle, materielle Qualitäten fehlen.' Fechter then makes an important concession to my argument ('Das kann ernst oder ironisch gesagt sein'), but does not apply this possibility to the passage from *Erec*.

[2] I Kings 11,1ff.

[3] Cf. Fechter, *art. cit.*, p. 305 and Maurer, *DVjs* 27 (1953), 194.

[4] See Maurer, *art. cit.*, pp. 195f. and Ogle, *RR* 9 (1918), 13f.

[5] Cf. Frauenlob 141,2ff. and Oswald von Wolkenstein, No. 3, II 17: *küng Alexander, mächtig, hön,/von frauen viel, und Absolon, der schön.* On another love affair of Alexander cf. Ross, *Alexander*, especially pp. 12ff.

[6] V. 2924ff.

and Endres has shown, with regard to two of the qualities for which he is praised (*wîsheit* and *milte*), how the poet uses two methods for this purpose.[1] He prompts us to ask what exploits actually qualify Erec for such praise (thereby insinuating the further question whether this praise is justified) and he contrasts this praise at the close of the first part with the crowning eulogy at the end of the whole work (if the latter outshines the former, then again we are led to ask how apposite the early superlatives may be at this provisional stage in Erec's career).[2] The irony of this passage does not constitute a recognisable pattern (like the ransom of Antenor with Chaucer or the relationship between Parzival and Lähelin with Wolfram), but is instead made visible by the different kinds of evidence which allow us to suspect its presence.

An example of the same type is provided by Wolfram's humorous outburst about king Arthur and the setting in which he is normally depicted in Arthurian literature (281,16: *Artûs der meienbære man,/swaz man ie von dem gesprach,/z'einen pfinxten daz geschach,/odr in des meien bluomenzît./waz man im süezes luftes gît!*).[3] If we claim this passage as eminently ironic, this is because four distinct lines of argument converge to make this probable. In the first place, the poet is here parodying the Arthurian topos of the spring-festival, the conventional expectation that a court as ideal as Arthur's could not fail to come together against the unchanging backcloth of an ideal landscape, in turn demanding the ideal season.[4] Wolfram achieves his effect (which amounts to a deflation of the conventional picture of Arthur and his court comparable

---

[1] Endres, *Studien*, pp. 33ff. and 112f.

[2] I have argued (*Praise*, pp. 795ff.) that Hartmann's technique of praising a character on the brink of disaster (thereby ensuring a dramatic effect, but also imbuing the praise with irony) is certainly not isolated. He also employs it in his legends (*Der arme Heinrich* 29ff. and *Gregorius* 296ff.), where Pörksen is prepared to acknowledge it (*Erzähler*, p. 161), but also in *Iwein* 2426ff. (so that I cannot accept Pörksen's suggestion that the technique is confined to the legends alone). Cf. also Wolfram's *Parzival* 311,9ff. On this passage see also Haug, *DVjs* 45 (1971), 696ff.

[3] On the humorous aspects of this passage see Madsen, *Gestaltung*, pp. 74ff.

[4] On Whitsun as the conventional time for a court festival, above all in Arthurian literature but not confined to it, cf. Caliebe, *Horant*, pp. 19 and 72 (especially fn. 3). See also Hilka's edition of *Perceval*, pp. 667, fn. to v. 2785. Professor D. J. A. Ross reminds me that some French *pastourelles* are set in midwinter as a reaction to the conventional springtime opening.

with the critical distance from the Round Table which he else-where adopts)[1] by confronting this stylised view of Arthur with a touch of reality, commonly glossed over in other romances (281,21: *diz mære ist hie vaste undersniten,/ez parriert sich mit snêwes siten*). Conscious of the falsification of reality which the conventional Arthurian ideal already implies, Wolfram gives a jolt to habitual expectations by bringing in weather of quite a different type and far from ideal[2] – his awkward reminder of what reality is like casts an ironic light on the narrator's commentary (*waz man im süezes luftes gît!*), suggesting how little this idealising view accords with reality.

Yet if the idealised picture of Arthur is one of the targets of Wolfram's irony, we need not be surprised if he also mocks the poet responsible for first propagating this picture, Chrétien, concentrating on the lack of realism or consistency in the French poet's time-scheme in his *Perceval*. Weigand has pointed out Chrétien's inconsistency in having Arthur celebrate Whitsun at Orcanie (8888) despite the fact that (on a shortened time-scale operating with days and not permitting us to assume the passage of years) the French poet had earlier shown Arthur likewise celebrating Whitsun (2785).[3] In part this is because Chrétien is more concerned with an idealising presentation of Arthur to which an improbably recurrent Whitsun-setting is fully adequate, but in part Chrétien was unable to master some of the chrono-logical problems with which his narrative confronted him, especi-ally when he had to synchronise the two strands dealing with Perceval and Gauvain.[4] Chrétien's difficulties in this respect, but also Wolfram's mastery of this problem, have been well brought out by Weigand. Since this presupposes that, in order to correct him, Wolfram must have perceived Chrétien's inconsistencies and been dissatisfied with them, we can take his apparently

---

[1] See below, pp. 319ff.

[2] This does not mean that I do not accept the possibility (as Deinert, *Ritter*, pp. 18ff., has convincingly shown) that the snow landscape may not also have another rôle to play, but merely that I see Wolfram as skilfully making use of the motif to serve more than one end.

[3] Weigand, *Parzival*, pp. 21ff.

[4] *Ibid.*, pp. 29ff., 33, 36f., 39, 41. On Chrétien's use of chronology see also de Riquer, *FR* 4 (1957), 119ff.; Goosse, *LR* 12 (1958), 305; Frappier, *MA* 64 (1958), 78ff. and 84ff.

generalising remark about Arthur's eternally springtime setting
as containing a very personal barb, a criticism of his source for
mishandling the time-scheme. The common factor to these two
points by Wolfram (his mockery of the idealised picture of Arthur
and of the inconsistent chronology to which this leads Chrétien)
is his wish for at least an elementary form of narrative realism,
the recognition that Arthur's court must sometimes have been
exposed to harsh climate and that there is only one Whitsun in
any year.

Wolfram's irony goes further in this passage, since it also
involves self-irony and irony at his listeners' expense. For all his
criticism of the Whitsun convention Wolfram had himself introduced Arthur in this conventional manner when narrating
Clamide's journey to the Round Table after his defeat by Parzival
(216,13: *mit sölher massenîe lac/durch hôchkezît den pfinxtac/Artûs
mit maneger frouwen*). Wolfram thereby pays his tribute to the
convention, but since he does it only once this does not involve
him in Chrétien's unrealistic contradiction, and his listeners can
accept this early conventional reference without realising that an
attack will later be launched against such unquestioning acceptance. Wolfram's dig at Chrétien's muddled chronology also
amounts to the sly admission that he had once misled his listeners
into thinking that his work was no different.

It is only at a later stage that Wolfram ironises his listeners
even more effectively. As we saw earlier,[1] it is not true simply to
say that the German poet pays his tribute to this convention
only once. He does so in fact twice (over a timespan of years, so
that he can now avoid Chrétien's chronological improbability),
but conceals the second occasion from the casual listener. When
Arthur and his Round Table are depicted for the last time in the
work (as Parzival and Gawan join them at Joflanze) we are
given enough scattered information to tell that this must have
taken place seven weeks after Parzival's arrival at Trevrizent's
cell. Since the earlier scene fell on a Good Friday, the last appearance of Arthur must coincide with Whitsun, as Weigand has
painstakingly calculated. Wolfram nowhere says this pointedly,
but he gives his audience enough material for them to reach this

[1] See p. 30.

conclusion independently, although it is dubious whether anyone before Weigand, let alone any medieval listeners, ever hit upon the idea of collating the poet's time-references. In ironising Chrétien Wolfram is therefore also ironising his own audience, unaware that he is having his fun with them by doing exactly the same as what he criticises in the case of his source. It is this multiplicity of targets (the conventional Arthurian ideal, Chrétien's chronology, Wolfram's introduction of Arthur in Book VI, and his unsuspecting audience), constituting so many distinct levels of evidence, which makes the presence of irony overwhelmingly probable in this short passage.

In addition to patterning and the various levels of evidence as indications of irony, there are passages with different levels of irony which, taken together, strengthen the assumption that irony is present and intended.[1] I shall confine myself to two examples, from Gottfried and Wolfram. The former, describing the fears and temporary loss of mastery of the situation by the young Tristan when he has been set ashore by the Norwegian merchants after his abduction, says of him: *Nu wie gewarp do Tristan?/Tristan der ellende? ja,/ da saz er unde weinde alda* (2482ff.). These words by the narrator are spoken from Tristan's point of view and in this sense they are perfectly correct: Tristan has been abducted from his family and set ashore in a foreign land where he knows nobody, he is indeed *der ellende*. But by taking Tristan's part the narrator is able to remind us that he (and, through him, we too) knows more than Tristan. We have known from the beginning that Rual and Floræte are not Tristan's parents and that his mother comes from Cornwall, and we have just been told that it is in Cornwall that the Norwegians have set him ashore (2466ff.). This superior knowledge passed on to us by the narrator means that we must look askance at him when he calls Tristan *der ellende*, since we know that in terms of blood kinship he is more at home here than in Parmenie.[2] Lest the dramatic irony of this superior knowledge escape us, the narrator's subsequent

---

[1] Cf. also the examples, treated above (pp. 27f.) in the context of signals to irony, from *Troilus and Criseyde* and *Flamenca*.

[2] Cf. the narrator's reference to Marke at this stage of the action (3382: *der unverwande vater sin*).

commentary makes it quite explicit (3379: *Nu Tristan derst ze huse komen/unwizzend, alse ir habet vernomen,/und wande doch ellende sin*).

This is the one level of irony in this passage, brought about by the irony of events in leading Tristan to this particular situation, but it is in turn transcended by irony on another level. In the factual sense it may be ironic to call Tristan *der ellende* at this point, since the facts known to us conflict with his partial view of events. But he may none the less be called *der ellende* in another (symbolic) sense, since he is shown before long to be a stranger to the values of the courtly world he finds at Tintagel and this quality of distance from courtly values later comes to be even more true of his position as the lover of Marke's wife. In this respect Tristan is *der ellende*, his qualities are *vremede*,[1] he is the antithesis of the courtly world and its social values, but this sense of *ellende* is no longer the same as the purely factual and geographical one employed in the initial dramatic irony. The irony of this passage therefore works on two levels and in two directions. At first we are encouraged to react against the apparently mistaken view that Tristan is in strange surroundings in Cornwall, but then, with a change of function in the operative word, we are driven to recognise that the initial statement is after all correct, if on quite a new level.

Irony on at least two levels is constructed by Wolfram in the scene of Parzival's first encounter with Sigune.[2] Again, the first level is made up of dramatic irony. The young boy, touched by Sigune's grief, reacts generously by wishing to avenge the wrong done to her (141,27: *swenne ich daz mac gerechen,/daz wil ich gerne zechen*), but Sigune, conscious of the mortal danger awaiting him if he were to encounter Orilus, the cause of her sorrow, deliberately puts him on the wrong path so as to guard him from this risk (141,30: *sie wîste in unrehte nâch:/sie vorhte daz er den lîp verlür*).[3] This insight into her motives, granted us by the narrator, gives us the superior knowledge necessary to appreciate the irony of the eager would-be knight following the wrong path in the belief that it is the right one. Sigune sends him on this path

---

[1] On this aspect of Tristan see Hahn, *Raum*, pp. 88ff.
[2] Cf. Harms, *Homo*, p. 227.
[3] See Gibbs, *MLR* 63 (1968), 872.

because she thinks that this will be the safe one for him, keeping him from any chance of meeting Orilus. But in another sense (no longer of physical danger, but of mortal peril to his soul) the path pointed out to Parzival by Signe is indeed dangerous, since it leads him to the situation just outside Nantes where he falls disastrously from grace in killing Ither and in beginning his chivalric career with the sin of homicide.[1] As with the *Tristan* passage, a first level of dramatic irony has built upon it a second level on which irony is made effective by now taking a concept from the first level in an unexpected sense. But with Wolfram we may even go a step further if we argue, with Harms, that Parzival's killing of a relative in the person of Ither is ultimately the means by which he attains to a recognition of his own sinfulness (that he is himself little better than Lähelin or the Orilus from whom Signe strove to keep him), to a reconciliation with God without which he could never have come to be Grail-king. Judged on this last level, Signe would indeed have guaranteed his safety, but not in the physical sense which she had in mind in first setting him on the wrong path. As with Gottfried's passage, the irony operates on different levels and moves in two directions: physical danger is avoided on the first level of dramatic irony, but this is next revealed as bought at the cost of exposing Parzival's soul to danger, whilst finally the to-and-fro of this movement comes to rest with the salvation of his soul at the close of the romance. It is a complex ironic structure covering most of the hero's career and well fitted to showing up the unpredictable vicissitudes through which he has to pass, as well as the benign providence ultimately ensuring the positive conclusion.

Ironic characters

There is a final class of evidence suggesting that we are justified in looking for irony in courtly literature and that it is a mode of speech well known to courtly authors. This evidence is provided by the many instances in the literary depiction of verbal encounters where one figure assumes that another has employed irony in addressing him. In such cases the assumption or presence of

---

[1] See Mohr, *Schuld*, pp. 196ff., and Green, *Homicide*, pp. 44ff.

irony within the poet's fictional world implies a poet acquainted with irony and making use of it in the verbal construction of this world.

The most obvious example we have already encountered in *Waltharius*, where Hildegund's accusation that the hero is mocking her hopes *per hyroniam* (it makes no difference that her reproach should be unfounded) is proof that this author was acquainted with irony and made use of it on at least this occasion. Elsewhere, although we may lack such explicitness, ironic characters are certainly not lacking. In Chrétien's *Lancelot*, as in *Waltharius*, Arthur raises the possibility of irony in what Keu has just said (96: '*Est ce a certes ou a gas?*'), only to be told, again as in the Latin epic, that his words are to be taken straightforwardly (97: *Et Kex respont: 'Bias sire rois,/Je n'ai or mestier de gabois,/einz praing congié trestot a certes*). Gottfried makes use of sardonic irony in the combat between Tristan and the giant Urgan when the latter, having killed his opponent's steed (16 026f. and 16 038), jeers at Tristan whom he thinks he has at his mercy (16 028: *der ungehiure rise erschrei/und rief Tristanden lachend an:/'so gehelfe iu got, her Tristan!/engahet niht ze ritene/geruochet min ze bitene,/ob ich iuch müge ervlehen,/daz ir mich min lantlehen/mit genaden und mit eren/vürbaz lazet keren!'*). The irony here is suggested by Urgan's laughter (16 029), which in turn rests on the discrepancy between what he says and what the situation demands. The conventional phrase *so gehelfe iu got* acquires a new force if used when Tristan has apparently been deserted by God, the request not to ride away quickly (16 031) derives its point from Tristan's loss of his horse, whilst the request to be good enough to wait for him can only be meant jeeringly when the giant is convinced that his unmounted opponent has no choice, so that the use of excessive politeness (*geruochet* and *ob ich iuch müge ervlehen*) only drives home the full discrepancy between words and situation.

Because of the part conceded to trickery and deceit the *Tristan* story grants ample opportunity for the exercise of irony, particularly dramatic irony.[1] The scene of the ambiguous oath is a telling example with Béroul and Gottfried, both of whom make

[1] See below, p. 254.

it clear that they conceive Isold's formulation not as a lie, but as ironically meaning one thing to some and something quite different to others.[1] With Béroul the situation at the ford has been cunningly contrived by the lovers so that Yseut should be carried across on his back by Tristan disguised as a leper, thus permitting the queen to formulate her oath accordingly (4205: *Q'entre mes cuises n'entra home,/fors le ladre qui fist soi some,/Qui me porta outre les guez,/Et li rois Marc mes esposez;/Ces deus ost de mon soirement*). From these words alone it would appear that the queen's intention was simply to deceive all those present, but irony comes into the question when we take into account the problem of her audience. She addresses her words not simply to her husband and his court, but also to God and St Hilary, as is made clear by the words introducing her oath (4199: *Or escoutez que je ci jure,/De quoi le roi ci aseüre:/Si m'aït Dex et saint Ylaire,/Ces reliques, cest saintuaire,/Totes celes qui ci ne sont/Et tuit icil de par le mont,/Q'entre mes cuises n'entra home...*). The two audiences which I regard as necessary for an ironic statement are here provided by God and St Hilary on the one hand and the court on the other, so that the queen addresses both simultaneously, has to convince each of the truth as they see it[2] and can only achieve this by means of ironic ambiguity. If the detail about Yseut also addressing her oath to her metaphysical allies had not been included, ironic ambiguity would still be present, but on a different level, for the two audiences would now be provided by the characters in the narrative scene (apart from Yseut) on the one hand and the narrator and his listeners on the other, for they are privy to facts concealed from the internal audience. Since Yseut is shown addressing two groups of listeners simultaneously and conveying a different meaning to each, it is she who is the ironist in this scene (and behind her, of course, Béroul), but if the appeal to God and St Hilary had been missing, then only Béroul could be called the ironist. In either case, the scene implies an author aware of the potentialities of irony and capable of exploiting them.

---

[1] See Green, *Alieniloquium*, pp. 151ff.

[2] Cf. Frappier, *CCM* 6 (1963), 446: 'Il faut le reconnaître: on se condamne à ne plus rien comprendre au récit de Béroul et à la version commune en général du moment qu'on admet la possibilité d'un langage hypocrite envers le ciel de la part des amants et de ceux qui ont épousé leur défense.'

The same is true of Gottfried's corresponding scene, and for the same reason. With him the lovers have arranged a similar 'accident' on the way to Isold's trial by ordeal, so that she too can formulate her oath ambiguously (15706: *vernemet, wie ich iu sweren wil:/daz mines libes nie kein man/deheine künde nie gewan/noch mir ze keinen ziten/weder zarme noch ze siten/ane iuch nie lebende man gelac/wan der, vür den ich niene mac/gebieten eit noch lougen,/den ir mit iuwern ougen/mir sahet an dem arme,/der wallære der arme*). As with Béroul, the German Isold is shown to be an ironist (as well as Gottfried himself) by the way in which she too addresses her oath not just to the assembled audience, but also to the invisible audience of God and the saints (15717: *so gehelfe mir min trehtin/ und al die heilegen, die der sin,/ze sælden und ze heile/an disem urteile!*).[1]

These last examples have shown us that behind an ironic fictional character there necessarily stands an ironic author and

---

[1] On a similar example from Eilhart's *Tristrant* see Green, *Alieniloquium* pp. 153ff. *Flamenca* has an example in small compass in the verbal encounter between Archimbaut and Alis, who says (1544: *Alis respon, et arodilla/Si dons, pueis dis: 'Sener, e vos,/Gens bainas plus soven que nos/E lai estatz plus longamen'*). This is not the case, whether in the literal meaning of taking a bath or in the concealed sense of what we know goes on in the bath-house, and Alis knows perfectly well that this is not so (1548: *Poissas ne ri, car sap que men,/Quar unquas, pueis que mollier pres,/ No-s bainet ne-il venc neis em pes,/Ni-s resonet ungla ne pel*). Yet as she makes her mocking remark to Archimbaut Alis also glances at her mistress (1544: *et arodilla/ Si dons*) to make sure that this member of her audience shall be aware of her irony. The same point is made more obviously (it is part of the burlesque treatment of the jealous husband that he can be mocked so openly) when Archimbaut inquires after his wife's health (4583: *E dis: 'Qu'en faitz? ses mellurada?/Ben garretz quant seres disnada'./'Sener, so respon Margarida,/Ben agra obs mieilz [fos] garida';/E fa-il de la lenga bossi./Cascuna en som poin s'en ri*). We know what is implied by the ironic use of the topos of healing love's sickness (see below, pp. 208ff.), but by her drastic mockery Margarida makes it obvious to her companions, if not to her bemused victim.

The association of an ironic character with an ironic poet becomes even closer in the case of Chaucer's Wife of Bath. Winny has shown (*Wife*, pp. 9ff) that she is depicted as enjoying and fully in control of her own ironies (p. 9: 'Where her behaviour involves ironies, the Wife is herself their most appreciative critic'; p. 10: 'The Wife is entirely aware of the contradictions of her attitude, and shares the joke of her quick-witted duplicity with the pilgrims'; p. 11: 'So far from being unconscious victim of irony, the Wife is its master and exponent'). But she is also comparable with the poet in this respect (p. 11: 'Like Chaucer himself, she possesses the power of critical perception which gives a narrative its cutting edge') and even in some measure is his spokesman (p. 15: 'Through the Wife, Chaucer seems to be declaring his hostility to the moral outlook which could impugn the whole function of woman within marriage, and by implication the creative process in which the poet himself is involved'; p. 16: 'The poet who gives her this assurance and vitality is an invisible partner in her triumph').

that although sometimes the irony may not be attributable to a character in the work it can still be the mode of speech adopted by the author. We have reached the point in our argument where at last we catch a glimpse of the ironic poet as a reality of courtly literature. Other examples of this association of ironic author with ironic figure are not far to seek. If Keii is the one figure of Arthur's court from whom one can almost always expect ironic mockery,[1] if, like Chaucer's Pandarus, he represents a negative element amidst the courtly idealisms,[2] he has also been compared with the court-fool, enjoying like the poet the privilege of holding out a mirror to the court and telling it awkward truths.[3] Without this meaning that the views expressed by Keii are shared by the poet, the poet's use of this figure to show up certain failings of the court brings the two very close together and suggests that the step from Keii's mockery to the poet's irony is not always a great one.

Quite a different example is provided by Gottfried's depiction of Tristan's skilful control of Marke's responses by using the rhetorical devices of the inability and modesty topos to achieve his purposes by insinuation when he is to be equipped for knighthood.[4] Since these are the devices also employed by the poet (especially in the prologue and the literary digression)[5] there is at least a parallel between Tristan's ironic manipulation of the king and Gottfried's of his audience. Wolf has also drawn attention to the parallel (taking the form of a literary borrowing) between Wace's self-ironical search for the marvels of Broceliande in the *Roman de Rou* and Chrétien's utilisation of this in a similar tone in Calogrenant's account of his adventure at the well.[6] We move into quite another sphere when Wolfram, at the close of *Parzival*, allows us to perceive that the irony of events (brought

[1] It is not by chance that so many of my examples in *Recognising* should concern this figure, whether in French or German literature. On this aspect of Keii cf. also Milnes, *GLL* 14 (1960/61), 243ff. Haupt, *Truchsess*, misses a golden opportunity by largely ignoring this aspect of the character to whom his monograph is devoted, even though he treats of 'Formen der Komik' in one of his chapters (pp. 121ff.).

[2] On this aspect of Pandarus see Lewis, *Allegory*, p. 191.

[3] Cf. Eroms, *Vreude*, p. 142.

[4] See Kunzer, *Tristan*, p. 73.

[5] On Gottfried's employment of these rhetorical devices in the prologue and literary digression see Clausen, *Erzähler*, pp. 21ff. and 170f.

[6] Wolf, *Sprachkunst* 2 (1971), 16ff.

about, as Parzival rebelliously thinks, by a mocking God),[1] is identical with the irony of the poet ultimately in control of these events in his fictional world (827,17: ...*Parzivâls, den ich hân brâht/dar sîn doch sælde het erdâht*).

Final clarity is reached when the narrator or poet (there is little point in attempting a distinction when irony admitted by the former must also be conceded to the latter) reveals himself more explicitly as an ironist. Hartmann's narrator in *Erec* is forced to admit as much by his naïve interlocutor, slowly coming to see that the narrator has been ironic at his expense (7512: '*dû redest sam ez sî dîn spot'./wê, nein ez, durch got./'jâ stât dir spotlîch der munt'.*[2]*/ich lache gerne zaller stunt*). Wolfram also wryly confesses to his irrepressible tendency to mock, even on serious occasions (*Parzival* 487,11: *wes spotte ich der getriuwen diet?/mîn alt unfuoge mir daz riet*).[3] These are only glimpses, but they confirm what we have elsewhere been led to suspect, that the poet who skilfully exploits the irony of his own fictional creatures cannot be denied having an interest in irony himself.

We may meet the objections raised by Batts which formed our starting-point by claiming that irony was made available to courtly authors by a rhetorical tradition going back to classical antiquity, that with varying degrees of probability irony can be shown to have been made use of by them, and that, again with a range extending from the explicit to the merely possible, these poets operate with a variety of signals to make their irony recognisable. These conclusions justify us in considering, in successive chapters, the two major themes which attracted ironic exploitation in the romance (chivalry and love) and also various problems of narrative technique in which irony is of undeniable importance.

---

[1] See Green, *Alieniloquium*, p. 158. See also pp. 282f. for further discussion of the same problem.

[2] We have here an indication of one of the non-verbal gestures or signals to irony which the medieval narrator could make use of during recital.

[3] On this confession see Schröder, *Akzente* 6 (1955), 568ff. (whose conclusions go much further than the text warrants) and Madsen, *Gestaltung*, pp. 66ff.

3

IRONY AND CHIVALRY

The courtly romance is the literary attempt, undertaken by a class which had gained cultural dominance, to justify its position within medieval society. It does this largely by idealising the desirability and feasibility of the concerns of knighthood,[1] amongst which we are hardly surprised to find the profession of arms. Courtly literature therefore legitimises knighthood by optimistically granting it in art a success which did not always come its way in life and by largely glossing over the difficulties encountered and objections raised. We find this self-idealisation present from the beginnings of the new genre, in Hartmann's *Erec*,[2] where numerous stylised devices are employed to make this flattering depiction of chivalry aesthetically acceptable. Is it likely, in view of this tendency, that authors so concerned to idealise knighthood would also have been ready to admit critical doubts and to relativise the kind of picture which we find in this first Arthurian romance? Is it conceivable that, alongside their manifest wish to legitimise chivalry, these authors may also have applied irony to this theme?

Realistic details

This objection may be met in part by the reminder that the medieval romance is a complex phenomenon, that it finds room for realistic details within an idealising framework,[3] and that its

---

[1] See Auerbach, *Mimesis*, p. 131 and Köhler, *Ideal*, p. 32. Cf. also Borst, *Saeculum* 10 (1959), 228 and Ehrismann, *LG* II 2, 139.

[2] What is true of the German poet is also largely true of his French source, Chrétien, but I take Hartmann's romance as an example here because in this chapter I draw my material largely from German literature.

[3] See Köhler, *Ideal*; Fourrier, *Courant*, and Knoll, *Studien*.

critical self-awareness does not stop short of a scrutiny of what it
holds dearest.[1] Accordingly, it is not difficult to collect examples
where poets make use of the potentialities of irony even in a
chivalric context.[2] In view of his well-known reservations about
knighthood, Gottfried does not surprise us by the ironic implications of Marke's chivalric recommendations to the freshly
knighted Tristan (a listener acquainted with the theme would
catch the force of 5029: *wis diemüete und wis unbetrogen* and of
5034: *ere unde minne elliu wip!*).[3] Moreover, Marke, equipping his
nephew for combat, unwittingly gives him two pieces of gear
which symbolically anticipate the triangular relationship in which
both are later involved with Isold.[4] An ironic light is cast again
on the king's chivalric advice by the narrator's commentary on the
brutally effective, but unchivalric way in which Tristan gains
vengeance on Morgan (5623: *sus hæter sich verrihtet/und al sin dinc
beslihtet*).[5]

1 Cf. Désilles-Busch, *Don*, p. 204 (with regard to the motif of one knight sparing
another in combat): 'Hier kann man, wie auch an anderen Zentralproblemen der
Zeit...die Bewußtseinsstufe der Gesellschaft an dem Grad der Selbstkritik
ablesen.'
2 Generally in this chapter I discuss examples from Gottfried first, since his remoteness from knighthood is most obvious and easy to register, then Wolfram's
Parzival, where the presence of a Grail-sphere does much to relativise the self-
sufficiency of an Arthurian ideal of chivalry, then Hartmann's *Iwein*, because of the
greater reservations shown here by the poet in comparison with *Erec*, which I
place last for treatment.
3 The virtue of humility may not be central to Tristan's career, but his gift of
deceitfulness certainly is. The innocuous recommendation to love and honour
all women derives its sting from the fact that in contemporary love-poetry worship
of womankind was meant to cloak, and yet reveal, love for *one* woman in particular,
so that dramatic irony lies in Marke unwittingly recommending his nephew to
love a woman who, as the listeners would know, is to be none other than Isold.
On the irony of Marke's chivalric advice at large see Fromm, *DVjs* 41 (1967),
347f. and Haug, *Aventiure*, p. 109. It acquires a particular literary and parodic
point from Gottfried's deviation from his source at this point by borrowing details
from Hartmann's *Gregorius* (Tax, *Wort*, p. 32). The target of Gottfried's irony is
therefore Hartmann's chivalric ideal as much as Marke.
4 Thus the dart on Tristan's helmet foretells his love (6594ff.) from which Marke
will be the first to suffer, and the boar depicted on his shield (6614ff.) is later
explained symbolically in Marjodo's dream (13511ff.). On the boar see Beck,
Ebersignum, pp. 134ff., Hatto, *AUMLA* 25 (1966), 36 and Speckenbach, *Eber*,
pp. 471ff.
5 On the ironic parallel and contrast between these lines, summing up the way in
which Tristan had procured justice for himself, and Marke's conventionally idealising recommendation (5147: *daz du dich da verrihtest/und din dinc da beslihtest/nach
vrumen und nach eren*) see Tax, *Wort*, p. 37 and Combridge, *Recht*, p. 43. The latter
rightly points out that in the narrator's commentary the emphasis falls on the word

We find similar examples with Wolfram, for whom knighthood meant so much more than for Gottfried. The young Parzival's belief that he can perform exploits with his *gabylôt* is ironised at the very moment when his knightly blood causes him to react in a chivalric manner to what he has just learned. When his mother tells him of Lähelin's killing of Turkentals (128,11: '*diz rich ich muoter; ruocht es got,/in verwundet noch mîn gabylôt*'), the irony here is that he kills not his enemy Lähelin, but his kinsman Ither with this very weapon. In instinctively reacting to Sigune's bereavement with a knightly gesture (139,9: *dô greif der knappe mære/zuo sîme kochære*), he is not pulled up in his tracks, as Wolfram's listeners would have been, by the incongruity of what he finds (139,11: *vil scharphiu gabylôt er vant*). But it is not only the young simpleton's ambitions that can be so ironised. Wolfram also directs his laughter at Gawan himself in his climactic adventure at Schastel Marveile, rubbing it in just how great is the gap between a knightly exploit on horseback and Gawan's ludicrous clinging to the revolving bed (567,19: *Sus reit er manegen poynder grôz*).[1]

Nor are examples lacking even in the case of Hartmann. Iwein's chivalry is not exactly magnified when he owes his escape from the situation at Ascalon's castle not to any exploit of his own (for this had merely put him in this humiliating position), but to the assistance given by Lunete, whose *unhövescheit* (1189) Hartmann takes care to mention.[2] The poet also keeps his distance from the many tournaments attended by Iwein in his year's absence from Laudine – in striking contrast to *Erec* he does not describe them at all, but disposes of this year in no more than 22 lines,[3] a refusal to be involved which is reminiscent of Gottfried's attitude to the tournament which followed Tristan's knighting ceremony.[4]

---

sus, 5623 (see Green, *Recognising*, pp. 31ff. on the use of this and other demonstratives as a signal to irony) and that, although Tristan's exploit has served his material interest (*nach vrumen*), doubt must attach to the words *nach eren*.

[1] On the ironic implications of this line and its connections with both Tristan and Parzival see Green, *Aventiure*, pp. 149ff. Once again *sus* is used as a pointer to irony.

[2] The irony lies in a knight being dependent here on a woman, and one at that who is described as uncourtly. See Ohly, *Struktur*, p. 106.

[3] 3037–58. Cf. Ohly, *op. cit.*, p. 110.

[4] Hartmann does not describe these tournaments, because he rejects Iwein's excessive concern with knighthood and consequent neglect of love, whilst Gottfried has no interest in tournaments or knighthood as such. Hartmann believes that

These reservations about chivalry become even stronger when Iwein's period of madness in the wood is described (3257: *der ie ein rehter adamas/rîterlîcher tugende was,/der lief nû harte balde/ein tôre in dem walde*), for this level of degradation has been reached not by the neglect of chivalric pursuits (as with Erec), but by Iwein's wholehearted preoccupation with tournaments which enhanced his knightly renown.[1] Even in *Erec*, where Hartmann first puts forward his chivalric ideal, such doubts can be hinted at, as in the detail that it is Erec's armour (meant to symbolise his false conception of chivalry at this stage) which blinds him to dangers and to calls on his chivalry.[2]

Such examples could be multiplied, but to do so would still not remove the objection that they may be random examples only, too scattered to suggest that irony can be directed against aspects of the chivalric ideal on a broad front. To be assured of this we must look at the question in a wider context, asking whether realistic details in the romance amount to a questioning of the idealisation undertaken by Chrétien and Hartmann, how far this questioning concerns various knightly combats or the concept 'adventure' itself and to what extent the theme of trial by combat is also affected.

Criticism of knighthood is no rarity before the romance, but when we turn to knightly authors we find not so much an outright condemnation as a number of shrewdly realistic comments which bear on the idealisation of chivalry found in Hartmann's *Erec* and, by implying reservations, could suggest a reluctance to accept this simplistic solution and therewith a tacit agreement with some of the clerical objections to knightly practice. Again, we are not surprised to find Gottfried's attitude to chivalric

knighthood and love should be harmonised, whilst Gottfried has no wish to jeopardise the absolute claims of love by associating it with any other value.

Many of the points in Hartmann's romances which I discuss in these pages are also to be found in Chrétien's. I discuss them in this context, because I am primarily concerned with German material at this stage and not because I wish to maintain the German poet's originality in introducing such irony.

[1] Ohly, *op. cit.*, p. 113. On the renown which Iwein's success in tournaments brings him cf. vv. 3048f. – there is consequently an ironic discrepancy between this knightly *prîs* and the human degradation to which Iwein is brought, which casts a dubious light on the value of such renown. On the dubious value of courtly renown see also pp. 291ff. and Green, *Damning*, pp. 145ff.

[2] Cf. Ohly, *op. cit.*, p. 72.

idealisation so remote as to amount to a refusal to be taken in by its pretensions. He therefore deflates the comforting belief of the conventional romance that victory in combat goes to the just cause by realistically stressing instead the fortuitous to-and-fro of warfare (366: *wan zurliuge und ze ritterschaft/hœret verlust unde gewin:/hie mite so gant urliuge hin;/verliesen unde gewinnen/daz treit die criege hinnen*).[1] He also shrewdly sees knightly combat as an affair of strength pitted against strength, leading to the destruction of political order (6419: *man hat uns doch hie vor gezalt,/gewalt hœre wider gewalt/und craft wider crefte./sit man mit ritterschefte/lant unde reht sol swachen,/herren ze schalken machen/und daz ein billich wesen sol...*).[2]

Gottfried is not the only one to show us this reverse side, for Wolfram can similarly shatter illusions. His Gahmuret, far from showing disinterested altruism, insists on hard and fast reward for his services (17,11: *er bôt sîn dienest umbe guot,/als noch vil dicke ein rîter tuot,/oder daz s'im sageten umbe waz/er solte doln der vînde haz*) and does not naïvely believe that the arrival of one knight will make much difference to the fortunes of a besieged city (24,25: *ich pin niht wan einec man:/swer iu tuot od hât getân,/dâ biut ich gegen mînen schilt:/die vînde wênec des bevilt*).[3] Elsewhere, the narrator undermines conventional idealism by describing an occasion when the formalities of a tournament quickly degenerated into an angry rough-and-tumble (78,5ff.).[4] Hartmann, too, is capable of such insights. In *Iwein* Lunete frankly exposes to her mistress how much reliance she may place on the knights in her retinue (2163: *irn habet niender selhen helt/ern lâze iuch nemen swen ir welt,/ê er iu den brunnen bewar*). Even his first romance, in its picture of Coralus impoverished and rejected by society, concedes the contemporary fact of knightly violence and injustice, whilst

---

[1] Cf. Weber, *Tristan*, II 84 and Stein, *DVjs* 51 (1977), 338ff.

[2] The force of Tristan's criticism of knighthood is heightened by the rebuke in v. 6425. Although Tristan utters these words with reference to the situation existing between Cornwall and Ireland, which is the particular reason why rights are to be ignored and noblemen enslaved, he generalises his remark by his opening words (6419–21) into a criticism of *ritterschaft* at large.

[3] On these two passages see Green, *Auszug*, pp. 65 and 84.

[4] Cf. also Green, *Homicide*, pp. 34f. In *Willehalm* 428,3ff. Wolfram also breaks with the literary conventions of his day in reminding us of the military contributions of *arme rîter* alongside the deeds of kings on whom so much attention fell.

the detail added to the description of Iders's previous success in
the sparrowhawk contest as proof of his lady's supreme beauty
(210: *nû sagete man daz mære/daz dâ manec wîp schœner wære/dan des
ritters vriundîn./dô was sîn vrümekeit dar an schîn:/er was alsô vorhtsam/
daz er in mit gewalte nam./in getorste dâ nieman bestân:/strîtes wart er
gar erlân*) is another admission that violence may defeat justice in
the contemporary knightly world.

Yet we have to be careful how we interpret such realistic
touches in an otherwise idealised narrative, for they may well be
examples of an authenticating realism, meant to strengthen the
ideal and render it circumstantially more credible,[1] rather than to
question it. Thus, in the examples just quoted Gahmuret's
insistence on a concrete reward gives way to the courtly desire to
serve a lady (29,21ff.) and to the stylised motives of the Arthurian
knight, *strît und minne* (35,25). The unlikelihood of one man making
any difference is contradicted by the reaction of the besieged
pagans to his timely arrival (21,2: '*frouwe, unser nôt/ist mit fröuden
zergangen./den wir hie haben enphangen,/daz ist ein rîter sô getân,/daz wir
ze vlêhen immer hân/unsern goten, die in uns brâhten*') and by the course
that events now take.[2] In the case of both Coralus and Iders,
Erec arrives on the scene like a fairytale hero just in time to put
things right, emphatically so in the case of Iders, since we are
told that if he had gained the victory on this third occasion the
prize would have remained his for good (204ff.).[3] These realistic
touches are therefore subordinate to the idealising tendency, they
strengthen it rather than cast doubt on it, but this does not mean
that the same is true of all such touches. I turn now to the far
from negligible array of examples where a similar display of
realism is meant to contrast with the conventional chivalric ideal
and to cast an ironic light on its make-believe nature.

Gottfried's Tristan

Gottfried again causes us no surprise by his depiction of knighthood in action. A poet who converts a highlight of chivalric
literature, a knighting ceremony, into a literary digression, who

---

[1] Cf. the words of Stevens, *Romance*, p. 169, on realistic details in the romance.
[2] Green, *Auszug*, p. 84.   [3] Cf. Rosskopf, *Traum*, pp. 167f.

complains that such descriptions have been overdone by others (4618: *mit rede also zetriben*) and who, in refusing to treat the tournament that followed, contemptuously refers those interested to the squires present,[1] stands in no close relationship to the values of chivalry. Because he sees through the literary idealisation of these values Gottfried, more than any contemporary, depicts knighthood baldly and harshly, stripped of its glittering trappings, as collective warfare and not as stylised adventures,[2] as an affair of battles involving bloodshed, destruction and rapine.[3] The first such war to be presented, Riwalin's campaign against Morgan, lacks the glossy attractions of the conventional Arthurian encounter: initiated for no more defensible reason than the youthful Riwalin's *übermuot* (299),[4] it involves the ransoming of cities threatened with destruction (351f.), a material aspect of contemporary warfare which recurs elsewhere in Gottfried's descriptions of warfare (e.g. Cornwall and Ireland). Violence and ruthlessness are features of contemporary warfare to which Gottfried is ready to grant space. What they drive out is the idealisation of chivalry, since such unredeemed brutality is not worthy, in his eyes, of serving as a vessel for the higher values which Hartmann had seen in Erec's knightly calling. Victory in combat, far from being a pointer to a knight's ethical position or the justice of his cause, is an affair of strength or cunning, which explains why warfare, divorced from the immutabilities of the moral order, is revealed as the to-and-fro of chance, changing strength and shifting allegiance (366ff.).

Gottfried does retain some tenuous links with the chivalric world of the romance, but these features are present more so that he may parody than emulate them. This is true of his employment of a term like *ritterschaft*. The disillusioned view of warfare just mentioned (366: *wan zurliuge und ze ritterschaft...*), seeing it

---

[1] 5056ff. This episode has been placed in a wider setting by Stein, *DVjs* 51 (1977), 300ff.

[2] Apart from the judicial combat between Tristan and Morolt and the hero's two encounters with mythological creatures (the dragon and the giant Urgan) all the encounters depicted in Gottfried's work are massed battles.

[3] On these characteristics of knightly warfare as described in *Tristan* see Mersmann, *Besitzwechsel*, pp. 175f.

[4] On the ironic way in which this *übermuot* is presented under the guise of praise see Green, *Damning*, pp. 152ff.

as a fortuitous to-and-fro involving gain and loss,[1] conceals an ironic barb directed against the pretensions of chivalry in the deflating use of terms from the sphere of trade, that vulgarly practical sphere from which knighthood kept a superior distance.[2] Tristan's words to Morgan (6419ff.) further lessen the ideal claims of *ritterschaft* by equating it with the brutalities of *gewalt* and *craft*, by questioning its justification (6425: *und daʒ ein billich wesen sol*) and by identifying chivalry with the irresponsible arrogance of the young Riwalin.[3] On one occasion when Tristan is shown not serving Isold with a knightly exploit, but hoping to gain for her the magic dog Petitcreiu by engaging in combat with the giant Urgan (16166: . . . *daʒ Tristan dar gerüeret kam/und leite an dise ritterschaft/alle sine maht und sine craft*), this is subsequently questioned by Isold's rejection of the gift.[4] She shows herself truer to the poet's view of love in refusing any offer of consolation for her lover's absence than does Tristan in thinking that she can be served in this way.

Chivalry is revealed as a stopgap when Tristan turns to knightly exploits after his banishment in order to forget the pains of separation (18438: *nu gedahter, solte im disiu not/iemer uf der erden/so tragebære werden,/daʒ er ir möhte genesen,/daʒ müese an ritterschefte wesen*). But Gottfried is not content with this demotion of chivalry to the rank of the second-best: he further ironises it by making clear his disapproval of Tristan for following the faulty advice of Ovid in seeking relief for the pains of love[5] and, in a contemptuous dismissal reminiscent of his refusal to depict the knighting tournament, by turning his back on Tristan's knightly deeds.[6] The irony is even more pointed when the term *ritterschaft* is not applied to behaviour of which the poet disapproves, but to

---

[1] Cf. 367 and 369.

[2] As is illustrated in *Parzival*, Book VII, when Gawan is more than once insulted by being deliberately taken for a merchant instead of a knight (e.g. 353,25ff.). On Wolfram's ironic exploitation of such passages see below, p. 211, fn. 2.

[3] Cf. Tristan's words (6420: *gewalt hære wider gewalt/und craft wider crefte*) with the narrator's judgment on Riwalin (272: *übel mit übele gelten,/craft erzeigen wider craft*). Cf. also Heinzel, *Schriften*, p. 23 and Snow, *Euphorion* 62 (1968), 369.

[4] Cf. Jackson, *Anatomy*, p. 155.

[5] On Gottfried's disagreement with Ovid, and on his ironisation of Tristan by having him act in accordance with Ovid's precepts, see Meissburger, *Tristan*, 7ff.

[6] 18455ff. See also below, pp. 73f.

a context in which no knightly exploit is even involved, as with Tristan's leap to Isold's bed (15186: *Tristan der minnen blinde tete/ den poinder und die ritterschaft*). Here the irony lies in the discrepancy between the conventional understanding of these technical terms and the use to which Gottfried puts them, together with the implication that this is how he conceives Tristan's daring exploits.[1]

If a term like *ritterschaft* can be so parodied, we are not surprised to find Gottfried ironising in different ways some of the combats in which Tristan is engaged. This is true of his first combat, the encounter with Morgan, since it is depicted as a clear case of murder. The poet may not expressly criticise Tristan, but the facts speak for themselves. The hero's choice of words is deliberately insulting from the beginning, whilst Morgan receives him with courtesy[2] (the reversal of the situation where the courteous Erec addresses the provocative giants is a pointer to Gottfried's deflation of his hero's chivalry). What is depicted is the brutally aggressive killing of an unarmed opponent, without any formal declaration or warning.[3] The deed stands out as an example of daring and deception, but it is certainly not a model of courtesy or chivalry, for such impractical models are ignored by the hero in his undeviating concern to find the most effective means of realising his purpose. The ugliness of the deed is brought out by the physical details of the description[4] (5451ff., which comes revealingly from a poet elsewhere concerned to avoid *rede, diu niht des hoves sî*, 7954). It is not in part redeemed, like Parzival's equally murderous initial exploit, by youthful ignorance, since this is the deed of one trained in courtly conduct and freshly advised by Marke to be *höfsch* (5045) and *wolgezogen* (5030) and whose chivalry had been recommended to God's care (5042ff.). If God's automatic approval of such ruthlessness is called into doubt, it cannot even be claimed that, however dubious his methods, at least Tristan's claims on Morgan are just ones. Here too Gottfried suggests that, even though Tristan acts as if justice were on his side, this is not the case,[5] that his primary motive is vengeance at all costs (so that his behaviour closely resembles that

---

[1] See below, p. 77.
[2] Cf. Haug, *Aventiure*, p. 109.
[3] Jackson, *Anatomy*, p. 148.
[4] Haug, *op. cit.*, p. 109.
[5] The legal ambiguity of Tristan's position has been well brought out by Combridge, *Recht*, pp. 27f.

of his restless father).[1] His success he owes to ruthlessness and deception, not to the justice of his case,[2] which explains why the eminently courteous Rual had stood aloof from the undertaking at the beginning.[3]

Different methods are employed in the encounter with Morolt. We are allowed to entertain the view that, although Morolt's claim may be legally justified, moral justice is on Tristan's side, defending Cornwall against the imposition of human tribute, but that Tristan is himself unchivalrous in behaviour, coldblooded in his tactics and merciless in the moment of victory.[4] God and justice may be invoked to support the hero in this combat, but Gottfried's irony lies in his having these two allegorical powers lend their support to a far from morally praiseworthy protagonist. His tactics may not be as despicable as Morolt's reliance on a poisoned sword, but his exploitation of every opportunity and taunting of his defeated opponent have more in common with the reality of medieval combats than with the chivalric magnanimity displayed in courtly literature. The outcome is also realistically different from the ethical optimism of literary convention. Morolt is not mercifully spared (like Iders or Mabonagrin), but is squalidly killed off, whilst Tristan's wound is not healed and forgotten with miraculous ease (like Erec's in the care of Guivreiz's sisters), but festers disgustingly for some time. Even Tristan's argument before the combat, when he appears to come closest to the ideal view of a knight defending a just cause, is not without its calculated ambiguity.[5] Tristan has cunningly prepared his tactics: he does not rest his case on God or justice (rather does he subordinate them to his own ends), nor does he rely on chivalric magnanimity, but instead he calculatingly weighs every advantage and seizes every opportunity. Even where his cause is morally just, this does not have a direct bearing on his own behaviour.

By various methods Gottfried so narrowly circumscribes the knightly field of action by realistic details that no room is left

---

[1] Cf. Combridge, *op. cit.*, p. 28 and Bindschedler, *Gottfried*, p. 19, fn. 1.
[2] Combridge, *op. cit.*, p. 43.
[3] 5555: *iedoch geriet er die geschiht/umb Morganes schaden niht.*
[4] Jackson, *Anatomy*, pp. 151f.; Kunzer, *Tristan*, pp. 61 and 68.
[5] This has been convincingly discussed by Haug, *Aventiure*, pp. 110f.

for the idealised view of combat sketched in Hartmann's *Erec*. Tristan's encounter with Morgan in the wider context of a collective clash of arms sets the tone for what follows, and the only single encounters which are attributed to the hero in the course of the narrative (Morolt, dragon, Urgan) are equally unedifying. All other military combats are massed encounters, far removed from Hartmann's idealised adventure by that fact and by the gruesome realism with which they are presented. Even a leading concept such as *ritterschaft* is not exempt from parody. None of this may surprise us in an author for whom chivalry is at best a distraction from the serious business of love, but what does deserve comment is that his literary antipode, Wolfram, can also make use of realistic details in order to ironise the chivalric ideal formulated by Hartmann. Their purposes may be quite different (Gottfried wishes to break down the union between chivalry and love[1] established by Chrétien and Hartmann because he sees it as qualifying the overriding claims of love, whilst for Wolfram Hartmann's ideal solution is deficient because of its element of make-believe), but both agree in relativising the chivalric ideal by inserting discordant realistic touches.

Wolfram's Parzival

Wolfram's *Parzival* differs from the general distinction between massed encounters in the epic and solitary adventures in the Arthurian romance[2] by granting considerable space to both in the same work. These pitched battles are commonly the occasion for the hero to be at the centre of activity, so that our attention is focussed primarily on him (we have seen this in Gahmuret's arrival at the besieged city of Zazamanc, where he is greeted almost as a secular redeemer, and something similar is true of the

---

1 Cf. Jackson, *op. cit.*, p. 155: 'It is hard to escape the conclusion that Gottfried rejects the connection between success in combat and success in love.'

2 Each part of this distinction needs to be slightly qualified, for the epic does depict the occasional single combat within a pitched battle and the romance sometimes describes massed combat. But Désilles-Busch, *Don*, pp. 153ff., has amply demonstrated that the single combat in the epic is by no means the same thing as the solitary adventure in the romance, whilst the massed combat in the romance frequently occur as the type of realistic detail in a mainly idealised narrative which we are discussing.

analogous stage in his son's career, when Parzival brings relief to Pelrapeire). It is none the less significant that Wolfram chooses to draw our attention to the protagonist in the more true-to-life situation of a massed encounter rather than in the fictional stylisation of a solitary adventure. Realism is also present to the extent that these pitched battles result in slaughter,[1] since the conventional device of *sicherheit*, frequently used in the solitary adventure as a means of avoiding the awkward fact of knightly homicide,[2] cannot be universally employed in the countless skirmishes which make up a collective battle scene. By introducing such scenes into a genre normally concerned with single encounters (here Wolfram differs significantly from Hartmann) the later author confronts us with the truth that knighthood involves the killing of other knights and that no amount of idealising glosses should allow us to forget this unpalatable fact.[3]

If this background of collective warfare and massed killing is common to Wolfram and Gottfried, making it difficult for either to share Hartmann's ethical optimism, we may ask whether Wolfram makes use of realistic details elsewhere in order to stress the make-believe nature of knightly encounters demanded by the genre. Since in his day the Arthurian romance meant above all Hartmann's work, Wolfram voices his realistic awareness of what knighthood involves in the form of a parody of Hartmann's skirting of the problem, he takes details of *Erec* a step further in order to underline the untenability of Hartmann's wishful thinking.

Wolfram's parody of his predecessor's chivalric ideal (implying not that it was wrong as a goal but that it took insufficient account of reality)[4] may be shown in the sketch of the fate of Gurnemanz's knightly sons, inserted when the old man can no longer contain his grief on learning that Parzival has decided to ride further

---

[1] Gahmuret's arrival at the besieged city of Zazamanc occurs under the auspices of Isenhart's death (16,4ff.; cf. also 27,21ff.), whilst the number of dead and wounded is also hinted at (54,7–10; cf. also 19,27ff.). Parzival's arrival at Pelrapeire shows us even more emphatically the reality of death on the battlefield (182,8ff.; 205,9ff.; 208,15ff.; 215,30f.).

[2] See Green, *Homicide*, pp. 21f. and Désilles-Busch, *Don*, pp. 66ff.

[3] Green, *op. cit.*, pp. 35ff.

[4] In other words, Wolfram's attachment to chivalry (even though he is more realistically aware of what it involves than Hartmann) keeps him from the extremism of Gottfried's wholesale rejection of the knightly ideal.

afield.[1] In each case Wolfram suggests a link between a character in his work and one in *Erec*, but he also implies, as is commonly the case with his allusions to Hartmann, that the other author had stopped short of facing certain awkward facts about knighthood.[2] These facts concern death, for Gurnemanz's sons have all been killed in the pursuit of chivalry, but by introducing a literary link with his predecessor's romance Wolfram suggests that the chivalric ideal proposed in *Erec* is unacceptable because it takes no account of this aspect of knighthood.

Gurnemanz tells Parzival that his eldest son, Schenteflurs, met his end in defending Condwiramurs against Clamide and his seneschal Kingrun (177,27ff.), but of this Clamide it is later said that he is *der künec von Brandigân* (210,5). This 'king of Brandigan' (the office, not the particular holder) must have been well known to Wolfram's listeners, since it occurs in *Erec*, applied to Ivreins (9645), as the title of the lord of the castle in whose vicinity Erec's final combat with Mabonagrin is fought out. It follows from this that Clamide and Ivreins must be holders of the same office at different times, and it has been suggested that Wolfram's king of Brandigan must have come after Hartmann's.[3] This has a bearing on Wolfram's attitude to the solution proposed by Hartmann at the conclusion of *Erec*, as we see if we correlate Hartmann's account with Wolfram's development of it.

For Hartmann Brandigan was where *des hoves vreude* was to be found (8002ff.), a fact to which the lie is given so long as Mabonagrin's bloodshed and violence bring grief over the king-

---

[1] The fate of Gurnemanz and his sons has been well discussed by Rosskopf, *Traum*, pp. 181ff., even though his discussion forms part of a wider thesis which I find quite unacceptable (cf. *MLR* 70 (1975), 220ff.).

[2] Rosskopf, *op. cit.*, p. 181, rightly stresses that Chrétien offers nothing comparable in his depiction of Gornemant.

[3] See Rosskopf, *op. cit.*, pp. 183f. There is another passage in *Parzival* where it is even more clearly implied that the events narrated in this work are to be dated later than those dealt with in *Erec*, namely the boastful claim made by Orilus that he defeated Erec (his brother-in-law) in a joust at Karnant (134,14f.). This encounter cannot have taken place before Erec's wedding tournament, for Hartmann expressly tells us that this was his hero's first tournament (2252f.); it cannot have occurred during the wedding tournament, since Erec himself is the universally acknowledged victor on this occasion. The reference in Wolfram's work must therefore be to the period *after* the conclusion of Hartmann's narrative, to the period when, as we are told in the epilogue (10122ff.), Erec no longer neglected chivalry.

dom, for Erec's victory restores the earlier order of things (9753: *hie begunde sich êrste mêren/diu vreude ûf Brandigân*). This is an optimistic solution fully in accord with Hartmann's ideal conception of chivalry, but it can hardly have satisfied his successor's more realistic view. For him Clamide, a later king of Brandigan, is the cause of needless bloodshed in his attacks on Pelrapeire for the selfish reason of imposing his will upon Condwiramurs, his kingdom is again a source of grief and death in all of which Mabonagrin is once more as fully involved as he had been in the reign of Ivreins before his defeat at the hands of Erec.[1] Yet if the kingdom of Brandigan is again a hotbed of knightly violence, the suggestion behind Wolfram's development of Hartmann's theme is that the solution brought about by Erec's victory was no lasting one, that Mabonagrin has once again lapsed into his old murderous ways and that *des hoves vreude* is again a tragic misnomer. If Erec's solution was of short duration, this is because Hartmann's optimistic terms of reference took no account of the reality of knightly violence, because no credence could be given to Mabonagrin's suspiciously quick conversion.

This interpretation is borne out by what we are told of the other two sons of Gurnemanz, for in their case, too, Wolfram turns a situation found in *Erec* parodically upside down. The second son, Lascoyt, was killed by Iders (178,11: *mîn ander sun hiez cons Lascoyt./den sluoc mir Îdêrs fil Noyt/umb einen sparwære*), once again an allusion to the first Arthurian romance in German, since Erec's first adventure took place at the tournament of Tulmein, where he defeated *Îdêrs fil Niut* (465) in the contest for the sparrowhawk. What Wolfram's transfer of a situation in his predecessor's work to the different context of his own means is that a tournament which, as a stylised chivalric pastime, is no place for knightly homicide in Hartmann's narrative world[2] has been converted into a scene of death. Hartmann had hinted at this possibility (but more for reasons of aesthetic tension than of realism) in having his Iders threaten Erec with death (708ff.), but the point of this is blunted when Erec gains the upper hand and

---

[1] I have discussed the murderous activities of Clamide, Iders and Mabonagrin in *Homicide*, pp. 51ff.

[2] In other words, Hartmann's tournament lacks the realistic element of uncontrolled violence and possible death conceded by Wolfram in *Parzival* 78,5ff.

refuses to kill the other knight.[1] Whether Iders, victorious in his last two encounters, had dispatched his earlier opponents as he threatened to in Erec's case we are nowhere told by Hartmann, but Wolfram, by seizing on this possibility and illustrating it in the case of an old knight grieving for the loss of all his sons in combat, has not just hinted at death in theory, he has confronted us with its tragic results. In Hartmann's well-regulated chivalric universe such things are not discussed, whilst Wolfram, by highlighting them, shows that his colleague's narrative world is too well regulated to be credible.

Where the encounter between Lascoyt and Iders stands in the relative time-scales of *Erec* and *Parzival* we cannot tell, as we could approximately in the case of Ivreins and Clamide, but if Lascoyt was one of Iders's victims before Erec's arrival at Tulmein, Wolfram's concern is to confront us with a reality of knighthood which his predecessor had glossed over. If, more probably, Lascoyt encountered Iders *after* the events narrated by Hartmann, this can only mean that Wolfram shows us Iders lapsing into his old ways after Erec has passed out of his ken, just as he had implied the same with Mabonagrin in his collusion with Clamide. Whichever chronology we accept, Wolfram is parodying the artificial optimism with which alone Hartmann was able to construct his narrative *ad majorem militis gloriam*.

Mabonagrin, who has so far come across Gurnemanz's horizon only as the henchman of Clamide in the killing of Schenteflurs, now steps to the fore in his own right. Parzival is told that his host's third son, Gurzgri, met his end at Schoydelakurt at the hands of the bloodthirsty Mabonagrin (178,20: *gein Brandigân der houbetstat/kom er nâch Schoydelakurt geriten./da wart sîn sterben niht vermiten:/dâ sluog in Mabonagrîn*). As with his allusion to Iders, Wolfram's reference to Mabonagrin's murderous activity stresses the difference between Hartmann's world and his own. In the

---

[1] Despite Iders's earlier threat to kill him in combat (708ff.) Erec shows him mercy when his opponent asks him for it (1009f.), even though Hartmann's terms of reference in this romance might have justified Erec in killing a murderous opponent. The reason why Erec shows mercy at this stage is probably the markedly fairytale atmosphere of this first part of the work, together with the need to finish this part with a happy ending comparable with that achieved with Mabonagrin's defeat and conversion.

carefully contrived optimism of the earlier romance Mabonagrin had been introduced at a time when he was just about to be defeated and when *des hoves vreude* was about to be restored, whilst Wolfram's reference to Mabonagrin lacks this comforting background by showing us Erec's opponent as the victor, offering no mercy to Gurzgri and thereby continuing his reign of terror. Whereas the outcome of the Schoydelakurt episode with Hartmann had been the happy demonstration that justice will triumph over all odds in a knightly encounter, Wolfram has changed his focus to bring out a different lesson, the possibility that superior strength can win the day in support of an unjust cause and that things may not be organised for the best in the best of all possible chivalric worlds. If the grief-stricken words of Gurnemanz have rightly been taken as a lament for the suffering which knighthood brings in its train, this should not blind us to Wolfram's more particular purpose in this episode. By building in pointers to Hartmann's first romance and by suggesting the unreality of its presuppositions he is making use of parody to indicate the deficiencies of Hartmann's ideal of chivalry.

Hartmann

The tendency of our argument has been to suggest that both Gottfried and Wolfram were dissatisfied, for very different reasons, with the chivalric ideal established for German literature in *Erec* (whether Gottfried had this particular work in mind must remain open to doubt, but with Wolfram this seems to be the case). What is decisive for the emergence of an ironic view of chivalry in the German romance is the fact that similar reservations, although nothing like so emphatic, have even been detected in Hartmann's *Iwein* and are also to be faintly discerned in his *Erec*, not as a head-on confrontation with his major thesis of the chivalric ideal, but rather as worrying discrepancies in a minor key which his thesis fails to take into account (and it is precisely on features such as these that Wolfram was able to build).

The critical point in *Iwein* has long been recognised as the encounter of Kalogreant (and then Iwein) with Ascalon. Several factors suggest that an apparently straightforward chivalric

adventure introduced by a theoretical definition of adventure
need not command the poet's total allegiance. The fact that this
adventure is first described by Kalogreant some years after he
sought it out[1] (and is then presented to us as Iwein's experience)
is not without effect on our reception, since Kalogreant narrates
with superior hindsight and is in a position to exercise self-
irony by mocking his earlier hopes. We are shown a knight of
the Round Table terrified out of his wits by the tempest he
causes,[2] then anxious to make his peace with Ascalon *wan er was
merre danne ich* (733), aware that 'his greatest success' in the
encounter is that his lance broke in two (741f.), and left lying by
his opponent (747) without so much as a glance (750f.). Deprived
of his horse and forced to return on foot, Kalogreant has to take
off his heavy armour[3] and thereby symbolically reveals himself as
lacking in chivalry. Such ignominy is prepared for by the victim's
wry admission of how he first approached the magic well. The
surprising conjunction of *âventiure* with *unmanheit* (631:...*sît ich
nâch âventiure reit,/ez wære ein unmanheit/obe ich dô daz verbære*)
reveals the unexpected picture of an Arthurian knight having to
prompt himself into undertaking an exploit, but within two lines
this prompting is exposed, by the superior knowledge acquired
from ten years' meditation on his disgrace, as the advice of *mîn
unwîser muot* (635). What we are given here is the unusual depiction
of an encounter from the point of view of the loser, of one who can
afford after this lapse of time to look down upon his earlier folly.
This undermining of an adventure from the loser's angle is confirmed from Ascalon's point of view, for we learn enough of his
attitude to see that the encounter also rests on a very shaky legal
and ethical basis.[4] Since Kalogreant lacks any practical purpose
in this exploit, the damage he causes is heightened by being so
needless. Ascalon is right in accusing him of being *triuwelôs* (712)
and of *hôchvart* (715), for he has laid waste his lands by an unprovoked attack without a formal declaration of feud, an offence

---

[1] Cf. v. 260.
[2] 666ff. That this is meant to be seen as characteristic of Kalogreant is suggested
by his similar reaction when he first catches sight of the wild man's beasts (412ff.).
[3] 773ff.
[4] Cf. Ohly, *Struktur*, p. 102, Wiegand, *Studien*, p. 277 and Désilles-Busch, *Don*,
pp. 172f.

which amounts to *âne schulde...grôzen schaden* (728) from the innocent victim's point of view.[1] From both angles, from that of the ignominious loser and that of the outraged victim, this adventure is exposed as a very dubious undertaking.

Kalogreant's account serves another function in its bearing on his listeners. After being told of the legal position, no knight at Arthur's court stands up for the cause of justice or speaks on behalf of Ascalon, the victim of devastation. Instead, their solidarity is with one of their own kind, their concern is to seek vengeance for Kalogreant and they are not deterred by the thought that they might be repeating the injustice already perpetrated. To this extent Iwein, as one of the listeners, is no different from the other members of the Round Table (his thirst for vengeance is even heightened by his kinship with Kalogreant),[2] but his motives separate him from his fellows when we are told first of his need to gain the adventure for himself by beating Gawein to the well[3] and subsequently of his fear of Keii's mockery if he should fail.[4] But Iwein, in now setting out, is in a different position from Kalogreant ten years ago, since he is aware, as his predecessor could not grasp so clearly, that he is committing an injustice on one who has caused him no harm.[5] It is his need for *êre* at all costs which blinds him to such considerations, as is revealed by the way in which all he retains of Kalogreant's account are the external pointers to the scene of the adventure, nothing of his colleague's implied criticism.[6]

It is in the light of this scene that we have to judge Iwein's encounter with Ascalon. The narrator makes great play of not wanting to describe the combat in detail[7] (his reluctance on this score shows as much distance from the theme as does Gottfried

---

[1] See Cramer's edition of *Iwein*, pp. 185f. (note on v. 712).
[2] 803ff.   [3] 911ff.
[4] 1062ff.   [5] Cf. Désilles-Busch, *Don*, p. 173.
[6] See Schweikle, *Iwein*, p. 13.
[7] 1029ff. The narrator's words could also be taken as implying his refusal to repeat what he had already adequately described in the case of Kalogreant, but if this had been his only reason, it would have been perfectly possible to abbreviate the second scene without any explicit explanation (especially when the reason advanced is so transparently lame). Even if we accept Cramer's suggestion (*Iwein*, p. 189, note to v. 1029) that Hartmann is here mocking Chrétien's verbosity in his description of the combat, this still implies that Hartmann wished to distance himself from such a knightly scene.

in the case of Tristan's knighting tournament). But he advances
so transparent a reason for this (he confuses the levels of fiction
and reality by saying that no one else was present who could have
informed him)[1] that we are led to suspect an ulterior motive.
Moreover, the absence of any eyewitness serves another purpose,
allowing the narrator to plead his ignorance (which I take as a
cover for his distaste) on the further ground that, since one of the
combatants was killed and since Iwein was *ein sô hövesch man* (1040)
that he could not possibly have bragged about his exploit, the
narrator could not be expected to know anything of the course of
the encounter. This apparent praise of Iwein's good breeding is
undermined by several considerations. In *Erec*, and elsewhere in
Iwein, Hartmann illustrates in narrative practice his belief that
for one knight to kill another is an offence against ideal courtesy,[2]
so that the exception in this case must be explained by more
telling reasons than the demands of plot. A little later, when we
are shown Iwein's anxiety to capture his opponent, alive or dead,
in order to escape Keii's ridicule,[3] it is quite clear that Iwein *is*
prepared to boast with the tacit trophy of a corpse (if not in
words) and that this is indeed his driving motive. How shortlived this impression of Iwein's good breeding is meant to be is
suggested by the detail that Iwein, after dealing his opponent
a mortal blow, pursued the dying Ascalon *âne zuht* (1056).[4] If this
detail were not meant to convey some further criticism of the
hero's conduct, it is difficult to see what point is served by the
circumstantial parallel (and contrast) presented later (once Iwein
has begun to practise a chivalry of compassionate service of
others) by the scene in which Iwein pursues Aliers to the gate of
his castle, but this time spares his defeated foe.[5] This parallel
prompts us to ask why, if it is right for him to show mercy to one

[1] 1032ff.
[2] Cf. Green, *Homicide*, pp. 19ff.   [3] 1062ff.
[4] This phrase has been discussed in detail by Salmon, *MLR* 69 (1974), 556ff., who
suggests a non-pejorative reading. Although Salmon is undoubtedly right in his
reservations about the way in which Wapnewski (*Hartmann*, pp. 69f.) places the
whole weight of his interpretation on these two words, none the less his own
reading can only appeal to a passage from the *Livländische Reimchronik* for parallel
support, whilst it is methodologically unsound to restrict an interpretation to
these words alone, without taking the wider context into account at all.
[5] 3766ff. Cf. Ohly, *Struktur*, p. 114, Oh, *Aufbau*, p. 120, and Kern, *ZfdPh* 92 (1973),
341f.

who has proved himself to be in the wrong, it should not be meant as a blemish on his chivalry when he deals ruthlessly with one who has done him no harm and is instead the innocent victim of unprovoked aggression. It is by discreet means such as these that Hartmann invites us to question the use to which knighthood is put in this episode, to ask whether an adventure conducted in this manner, even if it fulfils the terms of Kalogreant's definition of *âventiure* to the wild man,[1] is meant to command our unthinking assent.[2]

By comparison with this episode in *Iwein* the hints of a questioning of chivalry in *Erec* are scattered and faint, and can be regarded as significant only in the light of what later emerges in *Iwein* and then with Wolfram and Gottfried. Amongst these hints we find remarks made in each of Erec's encounters with his most chivalric opponent, Guivreiz. On the first occasion Guivreiz is depicted as a knight who loses no opportunity to seek chivalry (4304ff.) and who, seeing that Erec is a knight, presupposes the same attitude with him (4336ff.) and therefore challenges him to single combat. Yet in reply to this Erec shows a remarkable reluctance to engage in what he regards as an uncalled-for combat (4359: *ir sult...|...mich mit gemache lân,|wan ich enhabe iu niht getân.|ich hân verre geriten|und hân solh arbeit erliten|daz aller mînes herzen rât| unwilleclîchen stât).*[3] The second reason advanced here is purely external, but the first (*wan ich enhabe iu niht getân*) registers a certain discontent with adventure for the sake of adventure, a doubt as to whether this is justification enough, and can be compared with the self-characterisation of the wild man in *Iwein*, meant to contrast critically with Kalogreant's meaningless quest for combat (484: '*swer mir niene tuot,|der sol ouch mich ze vriunde hân*'). This passing flicker of doubt is not integrated into the rest of the work since it harmonises neither with the undoubted praise which is

---

[1] Hartmann's questioning of the type of chivalry illustrated in this scene would become more insistent if we were to accept even Kalogreant's definition as ironic. On this, see below, pp. 79ff.

[2] Batts has made a further important point in observing that in *Iwein* the knightly code is rarely acknowledged beyond Arthur's circle and that even here it seems to be ineffectual (*Humanitas*, pp. 49f.). This is confirmed by the similar position with the concept adventure, which is likewise not acknowledged by all (see below, pp. 81f.).

[3] Cf. Désilles-Busch, *Don*, pp. 122f.

elsewhere lavished on the chivalric Guivreiz nor with the manner in which Erec's own adventures are presented. Yet it can be linked with a passage in the second encounter between Erec and Guivreiz, where it is Erec who deliberately seeks combat, meets his only defeat in the work and regrets the folly of his adventurousness and regards his defeat as a form of expiation (7010: *swelh man tœrlîche tuot,| wirts im gelônet, daz ist guot.|sît daz ich tumber man|ie von tumpheit muot gewan|sô grôzer unmâze|daz ich vremder strâze|eine wolde walten|unde vor behalten|sô manegem guoten knehte,|dô tâtet ir mir rehte.|mîn buoze wart ze kleine,|dô ich alters eine|iuwer aller êre wolde hân:|ich solde baz ze buoze stân*). Erec accepts this defeat as a merited punishment (to that extent the harmony of Hartmann's chivalric world is retained intact); he accuses himself of arrogance in needlessly challenging Guivreiz and his party, rather than prudently stepping aside and thereby better protecting himself and Enite.[1] Yet the range of Erec's self-criticism may extend further than this last encounter[2] (in fighting Iders he had been concerned with a self-centred pursuit of *êre* and vengeance); he may be looking back on a period in his life when his knighthood consisted in a simple search for combat and condemning his desire to confront all comers as *unmâze*. Even so, the decisive point is that in these two encounters with Guivreiz it is the knight who deliberately seeks an encounter without due cause (first Guivreiz, then Erec) who, like Kalogreant, meets with defeat, and it is the function of these two utterances by Erec to alert us to the general import of this faint questioning of adventure as an end in itself.

This is not all, for Erec's confession to Guivreiz qualifies the value of only some of his past exploits (in his first encounter with Guivreiz he had tried to avoid combat, and his rescue of Cadoc from the giants and of Enite from Oringles could hardly be criticised as self-centred). At a later point, however, Hartmann manages to relativise all of Erec's adventures. This wholesale ironisation in retrospect comes when Erec learns at Arthur's court of the death of his father and of the necessity for him to

---

[1] Cf. Harms, *Kampf*, p. 124.
[2] As is suggested by Ehrismann, *LG* II 2, 169; Schwietering, *LG*, p. 155; Harms, *Kampf*, p. 126.

return home and rule his country (9971: *nû was des sînem lande nôt/daz er sich abe tæte/ solher unstæte/und daz er heim vüere:/daz wære gevüere/sînen landen und sîner diet*). By using such a word as *unstæte* (which I take in a sense like 'gadding about') the narrator implicitly criticises all Erec's adventures on his journey as unimportant by comparison with the tasks which now await him. At this point reality breaks into what has hitherto been the realm of fiction – a political, regal reality, indicating that Erec has duties which exceed that of fulfilling his own chivalric nature and can even call him away from Arthur's court. Without expressly saying so, Hartmann subordinates knight-errantry to this political reality;[1] he has Erec abandon his youthful *unstæte* for the business of life, for which he has now been prepared. This comes near to a tacit revocation of knightly exploits, a palinode at the close of the work faintly comparable to the switch by Andreas Capellanus from love to misogyny or by the narrator at the close of *Troilus and Criseyde* from love to Christian charity. These other poets (like Hartmann, although more explicitly) abandon fiction for reality (here I take misogyny as the sexual reality of the medieval celibate clergy and Christian charity as its dogmatic reality) and thereby qualify the ultimate truth of their fiction.

Adventure

These last considerations have touched upon another problem, the concept adventure, to which we must now address ourselves as another sphere in which the knightly exploit can be subjected to scrutiny. Once again it is Gottfried's reservations that are most obvious, although these are by no means absent from Wolfram and from Hartmann, at least in his *Iwein*.

Gottfried makes his position clear by composing a romance in

---

[1] The position at the close of this romance can be compared with an episode from Joinville's *Histoire de Saint Louis*. Urged to join the crusade by Louis, Joinville refuses, saying that the destruction of his people by others during his absence on an earlier occasion had taught him that he could best serve God's will by remaining in France to help protect his people and that a ruler could therefore imitate Christ more effectively by remaining at home as a protection than by exposing them to danger by his absence on a crusade. See Joinville's *Histoire* cxliv (pp. 261f.). What Joinville specifically calls the *aventure* of the expedition provides a parallel between his view of the crusade and Hartmann's view of Erec's past adventures.

which the chivalric quest for adventure plays no part.[1] There is hence no call for the term *âventiure* to perform the chivalric function which it has with Hartmann and Wolfram (on the rare occasions when Gottfried still so uses it, a negative usage is generally visible). Instead, he shifts the balance of the word towards the sense of chance or fortune, as in the phrase *von aventiure*[2] (a usage which is also to be found in the Arthurian romance, but still in conjunction with knightly concerns from which Gottfried has largely separated it). But where Arthurian literature employs *âventiure* in the foreground sense of chance in order to imply ultimately a providential control of events in favour of the knightly hero, Gottfried can reveal his doubts about *aventiure* as an agent for such overall harmony behind the chaos of fortuitous happenings.[3]

If this overall control is called into question in *Tristan*, it is not surprising that the individual knightly encounters which in *Erec* had demonstrated this guidance should now be exposed to the possibility of irony. This is true of the rare occasions when Gottfried depicts Tristan in the context of a conventional knightly adventure, for he takes care to indicate his distance from the straightforward use of the concept. Conventional adventures occur at one stage in Tristan's life, in the period of his banishment when, to alleviate the pains of separation, he plunges into knightly activity in order to induce oblivion (18 455: *gelückes unde linge/an manlichem dinge/und aventiure erwarber vil*). Yet the similarity of this chivalric period in the hero's life to the conventional quest of the Arthurian knight is only superficial, because behind it Gottfried's attitude is very different from that of Hartmann. For the earlier author such adventures were meaningful pointers to his hero's ethical progress, whilst Gottfried sees them only as *fabelen* (18 463), to be distinguished from the truth (18 465f.) and therefore fit only to be thrown to the wind (18 464).[4] He accord-

---

[1] On the divorce of Gottfried's romance from the values of chivalry see Jackson, *Anatomy*, pp. 142ff. On his attitude to the concept adventure see Haug, *Aventiure*, pp. 88ff.

[2] Haug, *op. cit.*, p. 92, fn. 10 and Stein, *DVjs* 51 (1977), 344f. (On the implications of this for dramatic irony in Gottfried's work see below, p. 282). Haug's arguments have been criticised by W. Schröder, *ZfdA* 104 (1975), 323ff.

[3] Cf. the two passages discussed by Hahn, *Raum*, pp. 101f.

[4] See Green, *Oral*, pp. 261f.

ingly turns his back on such exploits (18 458: *der ich aller niht gewehenen wil*), just as he had refused to have anything to do with the knighting tournament, and links them with Ovidian advice to the lover (to seek forgetfulness in activity, especially as a soldier) about whose falsity he leaves us in no doubt.[1]

Tristan is so rarely depicted in terms of chivalry that the chances of mocking the convention in his case are severely limited. If Gottfried is to be really effective in his ridicule he will be better served by a figure who sees himself in such conventional terms and whose discomfiture will involve the principle for which he stands. We find such a figure in the Irish steward, for the episode devoted to his claims is characterised by the threefold use of knightly adventure in parodic terms. He is introduced by the statement that when other knights set out for their exploits (8954: *durch gelücke und durch manheit*)[2] the steward always joined them, but for no other reason than that people should talk about him in terms of knightly adventure (8957: *durch niht, wan daz man jæhe,/daz man ouch in da sæhe,/da man nach aventiure rite,/und anders was ouch niht dermite*). How skin-deep this concern for chivalry is the narrator then tells us by the ironic use of a laudatory, chivalric adverb (8961: *wan ern gesach den trachen nie,/ern kerte belderichen ie*). When the steward comes across the dragon, already safely killed by Tristan, his words (9157: *hiest aventiure vunden*) are a parody of the true knight's elation at finding what he has sought (as with Hartmann's *Erec* 8527ff.), for no adventure can be carried out by proxy[3] or against a dead adversary. In describing the steward's ludicrous attack on the corpse in deliberately conventional terms (charge on horseback, swordfight on

---

[1] See above, p. 58, fn. 5. For these reasons I do not think that the positive reading of *aventiure* in *Tristan* 18457, suggested by Schröder, *ZfdA* 104 (1975), 326, in opposition to Haug, goes far enough.

[2] This double formula sums up two of the essential ingredients of chivalric adventure, as depicted in the romance. Significantly, the element of apparent chance or *gelücke* (behind which stands a providential control of events) is irrelevant in Tristan's case in view of his careful planning and self-reliance, whilst the element of knightly valour or *manheit* is signally lacking in the steward's exploits. For opposite reasons neither of these rivals incorporates the conventional idea of adventure.

[3] Or rather, if it is so carried out (as in the case of Sifrid on behalf of Gunther at Isenstein in the *Nibelungenlied*) this is not without its own humour and irony. On this see Mayer, *Humor*, pp. 26ff.

foot) with a fair sprinkling of French loanwords and references to the steward serving his lady Isold with such deeds,[1] Gottfried is heightening the parody of the situation whose irony works in two ways: as a deflation of this grotesque figure, but also as a suggestion of the hollowness of conventional chivalry. So taken up with the chivalric ideal is the steward that he can conceive of no other reason for tackling the dragon, so that when he boastingly reports his victory and prudently adds that another knight has probably met his end in fighting the dragon he can only picture this knight as a counterpart to himself (9234: *ein aventiurære,/der ouch nach aventiure reit*). It is revealing that the terminology of conventional chivalry and love-service is employed not in the actual combat in which Tristan dispatches the dragon, but only in the sham pretence put up by the steward.

Wolfram's reservations about conventional chivalry may lack Gottfried's radicalism, but they are disturbing for all that. He employs the concept *âventiure* in several of its positive functions (it is a guarantee of God's support of chivalric endeavour,[2] an active demonstration of compassion and the wish to relieve distress,[3] and the means by which the knight may rise above the level of mere necessity).[4] But in addition, Wolfram shows a greater realism than Hartmann by suggesting that *âventiure*, the hub of knightly activity, also involves the real danger of homicide, that the knight who sets out to right wrongs is also the knight whose actions involve him in bloodshed,[5] an offence which is heightened to the extent that *âventiure*, freely undertaken, lacks the excuse of necessity and must be regarded as an irresponsible playing with human life.[6] This dichotomy within Wolfram's conception of *âventiure* makes his view of knighthood much more complex than Hartmann's, it rests on a paradox rather than on the simplicities of wishful thinking and explains how his dissatisfaction with Hartmann's oversimplified ideal could issue in parody (as with his elaboration of the history of Gurnemanz's sons) or, within the terms of his own narrative, in irony.

---

[1] Cf. 9165f. as well as 8950ff. and 9093ff. On the irony of these last two passages see Green, *Recognising*, p. 30.
[2] Cf. Green, *Aventiure*, pp. 105f.   [3] See Mohr, *Hilfe*, pp. 173ff.
[4] I have argued this in the case of Gahmuret's exploits, *Auszug*, pp. 62ff.
[5] Green, *Homicide*, pp. 34ff.   [6] Ibid., pp. 13f. and 18f.

The makings of such irony are provided by the parallel figures of Parzival and Gawan. Both are knights and set out in search of knightly exploits, but Wolfram is much readier to depict Gawan engaged in adventure than Parzival, for whom he has higher things in store. This contrast, lying beneath the parallel between the two, is brought out by the way in which *âventiure* in the sense of knightly exploit is used 16 times of Gawan, but only 6 times of Parzival,[1] a discrepancy which is all the more remarkable in a work whose author sees Parzival as *dirre âventiure hêrre* (140,13). Parzival is an Arthurian knight like Gawan, so that it is fitting that an eminently Arthurian term like *âventiure* should be applied to him as well as to Gawan. But Parzival is much more than this, he is the only Arthurian knight to pass beyond this kind of chivalry and enter the realm of the Grail where *âventiure* need not have the same function as in Arthur's world. Moreover, twelve of the cases where *âventiure* is applied to Gawan's chivalry refer to his crowning exploit at Schastel Marveile,[2] whereas none of the six examples with Parzival concerns his climactic adventure, the analogue to Gawan's, at Munsalvæsche. Whilst Gawan's adventures, even his crowning one, all remain within the world of *âventiure*, Parzival's major experience takes him beyond this sphere. This conjunction of two parallel, but contrasting careers means that the world of adventure which sufficed for Erec[3] no longer suffices to explain the career of Parzival – to the extent that this career embraces other things the previously self-sufficient world of adventure is relativised.

Wolfram enriches this point by suggesting that the conventional adventure is no longer sufficient and has to give way to a new view of the knightly exploit, to which Parzival alone is granted access. If the poet illustrates this transition to a new world of adventure in the scene at the Grail-castle to which the hero alone

---

[1] Green, *Aventiure*, pp. 145f. The occasions for Gawan are as follows: 318,20; 399,1; 540,12; 553,12; 557,11; 557,27; 559,20; 563,27; 564,9; 566,30; 587,12; 605,27; 617,19; 619,30; 620,17; 659,9. For Parzival they are: 223,23; 333,16; 333,26; 435,11; 446,5; 679,12.

[2] Of the examples for Gawan given in the preceding footnote only 399,1; 540,12; 553,12 and 557,11 do not refer directly to the adventure of Schastel Marveile.

[3] Apart from the narrator's relativising remark at the end of his adventures, 9971ff.

is called, his aesthetic tact is such that he cannot plant his hints too obviously in this critical scene, but instead he builds his allusions into its analogue, the scene of Gawan's adventure at Schastel Marveile. Doubts as to how genuinely chivalric Gawan's adventure is to be are raised when the knight, arriving at Schastel Marveile for his supreme testing, is disconcerted on being told to dismount and leave his horse at the gateway.[1] These are strengthened when we learn that his adventure is to take place on a magical bed, of all places – this is where he has to prove his valour, not on horseback (567,19: *Sus reit er manegen poynder grôz*). How suspect this is in the case of a crowning exploit is suggested in the case of another romance hero of Wolfram's time whose 'adventures' take place in bed, for Gottfried can ironically use the same word *poynder* of Tristan's leap to Isold's bed (15 186ff.).[2] Gottfried uses chivalric terminology to describe an amorous exploit, stressing thereby the gulf between his hero and the deeds of a knightly hero, whilst Gawan's exploit, although not an erotic one, is just as little chivalric as Tristan's.[3] Wolfram's purpose is clearly burlesque, to take down this ideal Arthurian knight a peg or two by placing him in a humiliating position where his chivalry is of no avail,[4] but behind this deflation he has a serious purpose, to invite us to ask whether Parzival in his analogous adventure may not also be placed in a situation where chivalric valour is irrelevant.

A hint of Gawan's later predicament is dropped when Parzival comes to the court of Gurnemanz (163,22ff.: invited to dismount, he refuses to do so because he naïvely equates knighthood with the simple fact of being on horseback) and then to the Grail-

---

[1] Cf. 561,5f., 561,12f. and 564,9ff. I have discussed these passages elsewhere *Aventiure*, pp. 148f.

[2] See above, p. 59.

[3] Gawan's chivalry is also deflated somewhat by Wolfram emphasising that he is the passive victim of events at Schastel Marveile. The poet accordingly uses the phrase *die âventiure erlîden* five times in this episode (557,26f.; 605,27; 617,19; 620,17; 659,9), and nowhere else in the work. See Green, *Aventiure*, pp. 149f.

[4] In other words, Wolfram has deliberately placed Gawan in the same sort of situation where his chivalry is of no use to him as the author of the *Alexanderlied* had done in confronting his hero with the queen of the Amazons, for in this position there is no honourable place for knightly warfare (see Green, *Alexanderlied*, p. 260). The criticism of Alexander's knighthood first voiced by a clerical author has here been taken up as a reservation felt by a knightly poet himself.

castle, for although he is now more amenable in dismounting and discarding armour and weapons (and is therefore symbolically stripped of all his knightly appurtenances) he soon regrets this when imagining a provocation which he cannot punish[1]. Even though he reacts in a knightly manner, Parzival has been led to a situation where no conventional knightly adventure awaits him, but rather a simple question of compassion. He cannot see this, because he is blinkered by knightly concepts, as is confirmed on the day after his failure to ask the question when he still persists in the belief that knightly assistance in battle is what Amfortas requires of him.[2] He fails to grasp that something other than knighthood is called for, that his testing is no military one (the only kind of trial he can conceive for a knight), but an ethical one of compassion. Behind this lies the poet's dissatisfaction with the ethical optimism of the romance, the assumption that every case of suffering can be relieved by knightly intervention with weapons. This knightly reaction may at times be justified, but it can provide no complete answer to human suffering – Parzival has to learn that compassion (rather than its particular expression in the form of knightly intervention) is more important and is called for at the Grail-castle. By thus carefully circumscribing the field in which adventure may be effective Wolfram has shown the limitations of Hartmann's chivalric ideal, the need to realise that adventure provides only a limited answer to the suffering which the knight felt himself called upon to relieve.

In subordinating the knightly test of adventure to a higher form of moral trial Wolfram comes close to the author of *Sir Gawain and the Green Knight*, for the position of the English hero resembles Parzival's. He is prepared for a knightly test of bravery (at an appointed time and place), but this blinds him to the actual moral test to which he is earlier subjected in Bertilak's castle. The English romance, like the German, may depict the undeniable merits of chivalric adventure, but it also cuts its pretensions down to size by defining its limitations and depicting the field of action to which it is irrelevant. It is perhaps because of this

---

[1] 227,23f.; 229,1f.; 229,8ff. On this episode see Weigand, *Parzival*, pp. 75ff., but also Bumke, *Wolfram*, pp. 291ff. and Schröder, *ZfdA* 100 (1971), 112.

[2] 246,11f. and 248,19ff.

unimportance of the knightly exploit in the English romance that
the dangers which Gawain meets on his journey from Logres to
the Wirral, the encounters which await the knight errant of the
Arthurian world, are listed with such breathless rapidity that no
time is left to recount them (720: *Sumwhyle wyth wormeʒ he werreʒ,
and with wolues als,/Sumwhyle wyth wodwos, þat woned in þe knarreʒ,/
Boþe wyth bulleʒ and bereʒ, and boreʒ oþerquyle,/And etayneʒ, þat hym
anelede of þe heʒe felle).*[1] The excess of alliteration in these lines has
been called comic[2] (deliberately, in view of its skilful handling
elsewhere), which is probably another way of deflating the type
of adventure which Gawain, like Parzival, expects and beyond
which his real testing is to take him. What this testing of Gawain
and Parzival suggests is the fact that in these two romances the
hero may still be a knight, whilst his crowning adventure is no
longer specifically knightly, but rather an ethical trial which, if
we ignore the details of setting and description, could befall any
man. Nor are these authors the only ones to retain a knightly
hero whilst abandoning the key role of the chivalric adventure.
This is what Gottfried does in leading his hero through the adventures of the world of love, whilst of Chrétien's *Yvain* it has been
asked, with regard to the hero's liberation of the 300 captive
women in the cloth-factory of the *chastel de Pesme Avanture*,
whether we can really believe that Chrétien naïvely thought that
such wrongs, reflecting Flemish conditions in the latter half of
the twelfth century, could be happily righted by no more than
a blow with the sword.[3] If we hesitate to ascribe such simplicity
to so sophisticated an author, then we must recognise that here
too there is an implied limit set to what the hero can accomplish
by knightly means. Here too we have been brought to the limits
of the world of chivalric adventure.

   This mention of *Yvain* must now take us to Hartmann's *Iwein*,
to consider the way in which he too qualifies the idealised view

---

[1] Where the author of the *Alexanderlied* (V 686ff.) can list the places his hero passed
  through with a rapidity which in his case amounts to an epic hyperbole (cf.
  Bertau, *Literatur*, I 244f.) which is not meant to be questioned, the later poet uses
  precisely the same stylistic feature to suggest his distance. On the ironic use of
  hyperbole see below, pp. 194ff.

[2] Cf. Barron in his edition of *Sir Gawain and the Green Knight*, pp. 11f. and also the
  same author in *Romance*, p. 13.

[3] See Bertau, *Literatur*, I 569.

of adventure he had put forward in *Erec*. In his encounter with the wild man Kalogreant mentions that he is seeking adventure (525), which prompts the creature from the non-courtly world to ask what that is (527). The situation resembles that of Herzeloyde when Parzival asks her what she means by God after she has mentioned the word (119,17ff.). Just as Herzeloyde is forced to speak down to the mental level of her son in telling him about God, so is Kalogreant compelled to give the barest definition[1] (530: *ich heize ein riter und hân den sin/daz ich suochende rîte/einen man der mit mir strîte,/der gewâfent sî als ich./daz prîset in, und sleht er mich:/gesige aber ich im an,/sô hât man mich vür einen man,/und wirde werder danne ich sî*). The situation in which Kalogreant defines his activities tells us much about how we are to view them, for he cannot fall back on the idealising conventions of the romance (which mean nothing to the wild man), but has to use the baldest terms. Stripped of its pretence, adventure is revealed as a primitive code of behaviour. Whoever defines it in this way reveals that he acknowledges military activity as self-sufficient and that he is content to build his reputation upon a simple equation of knightly strength with value, even if the demonstration of knightly strength means the killing of a knightly opponent.[2] When Iwein and the Round Table set out, after Kalogreant has finished his account, to seek the adventure for themselves (and to gain vengeance on behalf of one of their kind from an innocent victim already once affronted) they reveal that they accept Kalogreant's definition.

Moreover, the definition is self-contained in two senses. It sees adventure as confined socially to two adversaries of knightly rank and makes no mention of any motives for single combat, of any values (ethical or legal) which it may serve.[3] It is this absolute self-sufficiency and consequent divorce from values which places

---

[1] Ohly, *Struktur*, pp. 101f. Wiegand, *Studien*, p. 275, criticises this observation by Ohly ('Denn es geht nicht an, von einem im *Iwein* nicht belegten *Aventiure*-Begriff als "Wertbegriff" aus den hier episch verwirklichten zu beurteilen'), but ignores the fact that Hartmann presupposes knowledge of *Erec* in his later romance (2792ff.) and can therefore equally presuppose acquaintance with the ideal of compassionate chivalry to which Erec ultimately attained.

[2] I follow here Lachmann's reading of 534 (*ersleht er mich*), based on the MSS Abcz. Cf. also Désilles-Busch, *Don*, pp. 117f.

[3] Oh, *Aufbau*, p. 89.

Kalogreant's definition on a lower level than the second series of chivalric exploits performed by Erec to assist those in need and which makes of the Arthurian knights who accept it swash-buckling ruffians who conceal their crudity under a courtly veneer. How true this is Hartmann implies by depicting the Round Table's readiness to seek this adventure even though they know from Kalogreant's account that it involves injustice against someone outside their circle or by the way in which Gawein unthinkingly offers his knightly services to the elder daughter of the Graf vom Schwarzen Dorn without stopping to inquire into the merits of the case (it is precisely she who is in the wrong).[1] This self-sufficient exclusiveness of Arthurian adventure is the reason why the wild man is ignorant of it and needs an explanation. His social rank as peasant cuts him off from the world of adventure, but also his peaceful walk of life. That Hartmann attached greater importance to the second consideration emerges from the fact that the wild man is not the only one to be ignorant of adventure. Kalogreant has previously come across the knightly lord of the castle who expresses his amazement that his guest should be seeking adventure, since no other guest of his has done this (373: *des wundert in vil sêre,/und jach daz im nie mêre/ dehein der gast wære komen/von dem er hæte vernomen/daz er âventiure suochte*). This is not the case in Chrétien's version,[2] so that Hart-mann, by making this lord of the castle share the wild man's distance from adventure, has changed the point of this episode. It is no longer the ignorant wild man who stands isolated, but rather Kalogreant with his oversimplified and self-sufficient definition of *âventiure*.[3]

The deficiencies of this definition are confirmed by further indications. The contrast between Kalogreant and the wild man offers a number of shocks to conventional expectations. To the arrogantly condescending question of the knight (487: *waz crêatiure bistû?*) there comes a reply suggesting what they have in

[1] 5635ff.   [2] *Yvain* 256ff.
[3] Cf. Schweikle, *Iwein*, pp. 8f. This reinforces the point made by Batts (see above, p. 70, fn. 2) about the exclusiveness of the Arthurian concept of adventure: it is of course remote from the non-chivalric wild man, but also from the knightly lord of the castle who entertains Kalogreant, and it is accepted more with anger than as a knightly challenge by Ascalon.

common (488: *ein man*), to which is added a slight rebuke (*als dû gesihest nû*). The statement of the wild man's attitude to life (484: *swer mir niene tuot,/der sol ouch mich ze vriunde hân*) implies a superiority to the needless damage caused by the knight's violence. The quiet adequacy of the wild man, exercising control over his beasts, is a foil to the calamitous failure which awaits Kalogreant at the end of his chosen path. These doubts about Kalogreant and the knighthood for which he stands are reflected in other episodes. When Lunete gets Laudine to accept her argument that Iwein must be the better man because he defeated Ascalon in combat (1955ff.) she is using the same argument as in Kalogreant's definition of adventure, the equation of strength with value. To the extent that we are expected to see through Lunete's argument as sophistry this casts a dubious light on Kalogreant's view of the knight's task.[1] Kalogreant's inadequate conception may find expression in the self-irony with which he humorously presents his own discomfiture from the vantage-point afforded by the lapse of ten years, but in Iwein's case this same inadequacy is revealed more tragically in the killing of an innocent man. That this more tragic aspect of a falsely conceived chivalry was uppermost in Hartmann's mind is suggested by its recurrence in the episode of the captive maidens in the *Pesme Aventiure*, for their fate is the direct result of the folly of their young lord who rode out in quest of adventure and was compelled to hand them over as hostages. Like Kalogreant, this knight meets with failure in his adventure, but, as with Iwein's encounter with Ascalon, the cost has to be borne by someone else.

The deficiency of Kalogreant's definition is finally brought out by its inferiority not simply to the compassionate chivalry which Erec had come to exercise on his quest, but also to the understanding of his own obligations to which Iwein himself later attains. When asked to champion the cause of the younger sister he expresses his readiness in general terms which far surpass Kalogreant's level (6002: *swem mîns dienstes nôt geschiht/und swer guoter des gert,/dern wirt es niemer entwert*), showing by his insistence on the condition *swer guoter* that, unlike Gawein in the same episode, he now subordinates his chivalry to ethical principles. By

[1] Green, *Damning*, pp. 166f.

this means Hartmann is enabled to rescue a chivalric ideal endangered by the self-sufficiency of Kalogreant's view, but the chivalry to which Iwein attains, because it brings active help to those in need, is also superior to the passive harmlessness displayed by the wild man.[1] However much the poet may relativise the faulty view held by Arthurian knights, it is to the knight Iwein that the honour eventually falls of practising a chivalry not merely superior to theirs, but of greater value to society than the passivity of the wild man.[2] Hartmann employs irony not to destroy the basis of all chivalry, but rather to safeguard a refined version of its potentialities.[3]

Trial by combat

If it can be occasionally suggested that knightly adventure need not always serve the cause of justice, that sometimes an innocent or worthy knight may be killed in single combat, and that, even if there may be a providential control of events, this may not always be exercised through the specific means of chivalric encounters, these isolated reservations amount, when taken together, to doubting whether divine judgments are reliably to be assessed by the outcome of a clash of arms. The ironic scrutiny of the medieval trial by combat is the final problem I wish to consider in this chapter.[4]

The belief in God's readiness to intervene in the affairs of this world and to proclaim justice by directing the course of events is much older than the courtly romance, although courtly authors are prepared to adapt it to their own ends, amongst them the welcome demonstration that chivalric combat can be used to

---

[1] Cf. Kern, *ZfdPh* 92 (1973), 345f.

[2] This means that between the *Alexanderlied* (where the gymnosophist in his questioning of Alexander plays a role similar to that of the wild man in his encounter with Kalogreant) and *Erec* a means had been found of justifying knighthood in positive terms not earlier available. This essential acquisition of the Arthurian romance remains unaffected by Hartmann's employment of irony in *Iwein*.

[3] Unlike the position with the depiction of encounters (see above pp. 68ff.) or with regard to Arthur and the Round Table (see below, pp. 315ff.) where there are traces of irony, however faint, there seem to be no questionings of the *âventiure* ideal in Hartmann's *Erec*.

[4] The authority on this subject is now Nottarp, *Gottesurteilstudien*. Useful material, especially from the literary point of view, has been assembled by Meiners, *Schelm*, pp. 105ff. Cf. also Désilles-Busch, *Don*, pp. 128ff. and Bloch, *Literature*, especially pp. 18ff. and 46ff.

determine the truth and settle a legal issue, and that God is willing to offer support to chivalry in such cases. This is the kind of motif which lends itself with little difficulty to Hartmann's idealisation of knighthood, especially in view of the time-honoured antiquity of this belief, fed by biblical accounts of miracles and legendary reports on divine intervention especially in support of martyrs,[1] and strengthened by the fact that trial by combat, itself of Germanic antiquity,[2] had been early adapted to Christian ends and was employed in the legal practice of the Middle Ages.[3] Unlike the chivalric adventure or the miraculous way in which Erec can avoid killing a fellow knight in the course of his career, this motif has the advantage that it is no artificial literary invention, but instead one substantiated by legal practice and biblical authority. Trial by combat, which is what concerns us, is one variant of the general phenomenon of trial by ordeal. What the two have in common is the fact that in either case the result of the test (whether of arms or not) is decisive for the judgment of those taking part,[4] so that an event which takes place in the here and now is felt to reflect divine judgment of the situation. Where trial by combat is not possible (as in the case of women), legal provision can be made for the appointment of someone to champion their cause,[5] a detail which is reflected in Hartmann's depiction of the combat between Iwein and Gawein.

Legal practice and belief are reflected in contemporary literature on this point whenever the outcome of a judicial combat is taken as a reliable sign of guilt or innocence, especially when reference is made to what in human eyes would seem to be the initially disadvantageous position of the successful contestant, for divine intervention can be readily assumed in such an event.[6] This is illustrated in the *Rolandslied* in the case of the judicial combat, as a means of establishing Genelun's guilt, between Tirrich and Binabel (fighting on behalf of his kinsman Genelun). The odds seem to be uneven, favouring Binabel's size and strength (8873ff.) and inducing pessimism in Tirrich's supporters (8879ff.). But

---

[1] Meiners, *op. cit.*, p. 105.   [2] Nottarp, *op. cit.*, pp. 50ff.
[3] Nottarp, *op. cit.*, pp. 213ff. and Meiners, *op. cit.*, p. 109, fn. 7.
[4] Meiners, *op. cit.*, p. 107.
[5] See Désilles-Busch, *Don*, p. 130 and Nottarp, *Gottesurteilstudien*, pp. 294ff.
[6] Meiners, *Schelm*, p. 109.

this is no merely physical combat, for Tirrich proclaims that God presides over it and is concerned to bring out the truth about Genelun's position (8834: *Dâ scol got sîn wârhait/hiute hie erzaigen,/ daz er mit lugen unt mit mainaiden/di untriuwe hât begangen*), making use of the human combat to manifest a divine judgment (8840: *Ich wil durh got huite gerne vechte/unt wil mit mîme swerte/di wârhait erherte/in des hailigin Cristes namen*). In the light of these facts Tirrich appeals to the Old Testament example of David and Goliath as proof that God's intervention in support of the just cause can strengthen the hand of a weaker man (8847ff.), maintaining that what was possible in biblical days is still to be expected (8851: *Got hât înoch di selben gewonhait*).

Such unquestioning faith in the automatic nature of God's assistance in judicial combat is especially welcome to romance authors, anxious to provide a metaphysical support for knightly concerns. We find Hartmann utilising the same apparatus in Erec's encounter with the two giants, i.e. not in what can strictly be called a judicial combat (for no legal case is involved), but rather in an ethical combat between cruelty and compassion. The author appeals to the same biblical precedent as the poet of the *Rolandslied* (5561: *wan daz der mit im was/der Dâvîde gap die kraft/ daz er wart sigehaft/an dem risen Gôliâ:/der half ouch im des siges dâ/daz er in mit gewalte/volle gevalte/und im daz houbet abe sluoc*). This is called for not just because Erec is engaged in combat with giants at this point, but also because this is the first occasion for the narrator expressly to tell us that God is assisting the knight Erec.[1] The confidence in this divine ordering of events which the *Rolandslied* and *Erec* presuppose is also shared by fictional characters, for example by Iwein as he comes to the rescue of the unjustly accused Lunete (5167: *ouch hete mîn her Îwein/grôzen trôst zuo den zwein,/daz got und ir unschulde/den gewalt niene dulde/daz im iht missegienge*) and then when he sees that he has to face three adversaries (5273: *waz von diu, sint iuwer drî?/wænet ir daz ich eine sî?/got gestuont der wârheit ie:/mit ten beiden bin ich hie./ich weiz wol, sî gestânt mir:/sus bin ich selbe dritte als ir*).

Such unshaken belief should not blind us to the fact that there is evidence of another medieval attitude to the belief in God's

---

[1] I have assembled the material on which this argument rests in *Pathway*, pp. 172f.

intervention.[1] The number of fabulous stories recounting examples
eventually grew so large that the obvious reaction did not fail to
present itself in the form of parodies of such miracles,[2] which
could be directed against not merely the later excesses of this
genre, but also the earlier, simpler examples. What is exposed to
irony is the genre as such and the belief on which it rests. A frequent form of parody depicts the ultimate victor, objectively not
in the right, manipulating the formalities of judicial combat so
that the external requirements are duly met,[3] often by means of
an ambiguously formulated oath. God yields to such formal
correctness and the successful outcome of the combat reflects
this. Along quite another line objections could be raised out of
a pragmatic conviction that experience did not bear out the
reliability of this procedure,[4] or as criticism by the Church of
the Germanic practice which it at first had little choice but to
accept, modifying it as best it could and eventually abolishing it
in 1215.[5] However unshaken the examples from the *Rolandslied*
and *Iwein* appear to be, they are composed at a time when the days
of the belief on which they rest were already numbered.

Perhaps for this reason another episode in *Iwein*, the combat
between Gawein and the hero which takes on judicial form because
it is the means of settling the legal dispute between the two sisters,
suggests incipient doubts about the efficacy of this practice.
These doubts do not concern the fact that Gawein abuses the
practice by doing combat for the wrong cause, for criticism here
is directed against the abuse, not the practice as such. Instead, the
practice is reduced to an absurdity by the way in which the combat is not allowed to proceed to its conclusion (which should
have involved Gawein's defeat), by Arthur's intervention to

---

[1] This more critical attitude was amply strengthened by the abuse of the practice.
On this see Nottarp, *Gottesurteilstudien*, p. 215 and Meiners, *Schelm*, p. 106. On
other aspects of the gradual move away from trial by combat see Bloch, *Literature*,
pp. 119ff. and 189ff.

[2] Meiners, *Schelm*, pp. 106f., fn. 4.

[3] Meiners, *Schelm*, p. 110, with a reference to Konrad von Würzburg, *Engelhard*
3671–4992.

[4] Désilles-Busch, *Don*, p. 135, fn. 132, quotes a doubt expressed by the Langobardic
ruler Liutprand: *Quia incerti sumus de iudicio Dei, et multos audivimus per pugnam sine
iustitia causam suam perdere* (*MGH Leges* IV 156, 16f.). On the changing (and often
critical) attitudes towards the practice see Nottarp, *Gottesurteilstudien*, pp. 317ff.

[5] Nottarp, *Gottesurteilstudien*, pp. 346ff.

settle the legal dispute (if he can do so now, why did he not do it beforehand?) and by the way in which even Arthur's settlement is not strictly speaking a legal one (for the party in the wrong receives no punishment), but is brought about by a verbal trick so transparent that, if the elder sister had only had her wits about her, his solution would have been easily frustrated.[1] No word is said about God's rôle in such a scene, but it is clear that, even though Arthur carries things off by a hair's breadth, more reliance is placed on the fairness of his intervention than on God's.

A similar indecisiveness is to be found in Chrétien's *Lancelot*,[2] in the scene where the hero fights in a judicial combat in order to defend his mistress Guinevere against the charge of adultery levelled at her by Meleagant who has been misled by ambiguous signs to assume a relationship between the queen and Keu. The irony of this situation lies in Meleagant's correct suspicion that the queen is adulterous, but unfounded belief that Keu is the culprit, rather than Lancelot. If Meleagant had been shrewd enough to accuse the queen of adultery in general terms, without the mistaken reference to Keu (4965ff.), Lancelot would have been in no position to formulate his technically truthful oath, denying that Guinevere had ever slept with Keu (4971ff.). We are shown enough in this scene to realise that human stupidity and alertness can together make a mockery of a legal procedure which depends entirely on empty verbal formalities. After such an introduction the combat between Meleagant and Lancelot then sheds its character of trial by combat and becomes an ordinary duel (when Meleagant's father stops the fighting there is no further talk of Guinevere's guilt or innocence).[3] Like Hartmann, Chrétien blurs the issue and avoids an outright criticism of trial by combat, but it is none the less possible to glimpse something of his dissatisfaction.

In this respect Gottfried is much more radical. In the scene of Isold's trial with the red-hot iron he makes no secret of his failure to believe that God intervenes as soon as He is called upon to

---

[1] On this episode see Milnes, *GLL* 14 (1960/61), 247f., Batts, *Humanitas*, p. 49 and Désilles-Busch, *Don*, pp. 135ff.

[2] Cf. Désilles-Busch, *Don*, pp. 139f.   [3] 5010ff.

make justice manifest. He does this, first, on the same level as Chrétien in *Lancelot* by having Isold formulate an ambiguous oath, like Lancelot's, which has the double purpose of hoodwinking Marke and his court and at the same time binding God to this correct observance of formalities.[1] When she emerges unscathed from the ordeal (15 731f.) we are witnesses of this clever manipulation of a farcical procedure which has nothing to do with the establishment of the legal truth. But whereas Chrétien had allowed Lancelot's combat with Meleagant to shed its character of trial by combat and shade over into a straightforward single combat, Gottfried avoids this easy way out. He has Isold's oath (15 706–20) precede her grasping of the iron (15 731) by only a few lines, so that there is no time, as with Chrétien, for the metaphysical dimension of this trial to fade from view; we are not allowed to forget that God is involved in this mockery of justice. Having involved Him so explicitly, Gottfried can now voice his scorn in terms which go beyond this particular occasion (15 733: *da wart wol goffenbæret/und al der werlt bewæret,/daʒ der vil tugenthafte Crist/wintschaffen alse ein ermel ist*), confirming that what is criticised in this episode is not merely Isold's behaviour, but also the hollowness of a legal institution which can be so twisted into being a travesty of justice.[2]

If Gottfried can express his scorn for the legal convention in a case like this, where no trial by combat is involved, he is unlikely to be more hesitant when chivalry itself is involved, as in Tristan's combat with Morolt. Tristan converts a single combat into one concerned with the justice of the case for his own shrewdly calculated purposes,[3] to force God to intervene on his behalf (6781: *got muoʒ binamen mit mir gesigen/oder mit mir sigelos beligen*), a stratagem by which (quite apart from the justice of the case) Tristan manipulates God as effectively as does Isold in the trial-scene. If trial by combat can be criticised as a subordination of God to all too human purposes, Gottfried can hope to reduce it to absurdity by mocking this aspect of the convention. He does this not just in this manipulation of God by Tristan, but also in the way in which he himself, as narrator, humanises God's

---

[1] On the irony of this ambiguous oath see Green, *Alieniloquium*, pp. 152f.
[2] See Combridge, *Recht*, pp. 110f.   [3] Cf. Haug, *Aventiure*, pp. 110f.

activity in this scene. In order to equalise matters between Tristan and Morolt (with the strength of four men) he allegorises the resources on which Tristan can call, including the two abstract powers of *got* and *reht* (6883). But to account for the narrative tension of a combat where things seem to go initially against the hero, the narrator must show these two powers as slow to come to their champion's help (6978ff.), rather as if they were two capricious Olympian gods.[1] Even when they do come (6996ff.) the ironic point is that God is now no more than one ally amongst four[2] and Tristan eventually wins not so much because he has God on his side as because he can field four fighters against his adversary's *vier manne ritterschaft*. The issue is settled not on any metaphysical level, but on a numerical plane where strength has to be balanced against strength.[3]

In conclusion, let us return to our opening question and ask again how likely it is that courtly authors may have praised chivalry and at the same time subjected it to irony. Is it conceivable that the central ideal of chivalry should have been the object of such criticism? In the case of Gottfried the answer is simple, for chivalry is no ideal in his eyes, he is therefore free to criticise it, and his ironisation of chivalry is meant as a defence of his ideal love.[4] Wolfram, in turn, can ironise the Arthurian ideal or, more particularly, he can parody Hartmann's *Erec*, not because he rejects his predecessor's wish to find a literary justification of knighthood, but rather because of dissatisfaction with the artificial terms in which Hartmann had sought to achieve this. By criticising the Arthurian ideal he hopes to ensure permanence for the Grail ideal instead. Hartmann, at least in *Iwein*, can afford to ironise an irresponsible quest for adventure for its own sake because the position he ultimately wishes to defend is the ideal

---

[1] This apposite comparison has been made by Kunzer, *Tristan*, p. 64.

[2] Cf. Weber, *Tristan*, I 126f.

[3] Weber, *ibid.*, pp. 117f., makes the valid point about the narrator's commentary 7224–30 (in which Morolt's defeat is ascribed to God's intervention to punish his arrogance) that the narrator is here, as elsewhere, speaking more on behalf of the young Tristan than himself: 'Man wird sich...hüten müssen, darin ein gültiges Eigenbekenntnis des Dichters zur göttlichen Vorsehung und Gerechtigkeit zu erblicken. Eher wäre gerechtfertigt, aus der betonten, der Redeweise des jugendlichen Siegers nachgebildeten Sprechart eine leise Ironie über ein so primitives Aufrechnen herauszuhören.'

[4] See below, pp. 116ff.

of a compassionate chivalry in the service of others.[1] He can reject the self-sufficiency of Kalogreant's knighthood only because this ultimate ideal is more positive and more explicitly chivalric than the wild man's passive quietism. Elsewhere, one can argue that the poet's irony leaves what is for him the nucleus of the ideal intact and unchallenged, whilst mocking those very imperfect figures who see it only according to their own lights.[2] It would be going too far to conclude from parodies of trial by combat that every poet concerned denied the miraculous power of God or the biblical authority of David's fight with Goliath, for the target lies elsewhere: human credulity and readiness to claim divine support for one's own cause.[3] Even where the hero is led to a climactic adventure which is not specifically chivalric in form, it is still a knightly hero on whom this literary honour is conferred. It is not so much the chivalric ideal which attracts criticism as particular literary aspects or variations of it which are regarded as inessential or unable to do justice to the difficult task of devising an aesthetic justification of medieval chivalry.

[1] Wolf, *Sprachkunst* 2 (1971), 15, fn. 42, speaks similarly of 'der ironischen Auseinandersetzung des Erzählers mit dem vereinseitigten aventiure-Begriff Kalogreants, aus der dann im Iwein-Teil auch Ethisches herausentwickelt wird'.

[2] Cf. Mowatt, *Irony*, p. 53: 'The irony is directed not at the ideals themselves, but at people who do not know how to use them.'

[3] Cf. Meiners, *Schelm*, p. 112: 'Nicht gegen den Glauben an die Macht Gottes oder die Autorität der Bibel richtet sich der Spott: gegen die Gedankenlosigkeit, die das Heilige und Wunderbare zum Alltäglichen gemacht, die religiöse Spannung zerstört, das Nachdenken über die irdische Wirklichkeit erstickt hat, wird hier zu Felde gezogen.'

4

IRONY AND LOVE

In turning to the second secular concern of courtly literature we may start by asking the same question as in the case of chivalry. Have we any right to expect an ironic view, with its reservations and even criticism, of a value which, as countless medieval poets remind us, was regarded as the inspiration of all virtues? The theory that love was *omnium bonorum radix et causa principalis* can therefore be proposed by Andreas Capellanus,[1] whilst individual poets concentrate on its effects on men, as with the view of Bernart de Ventadorn that it is love and its service which make a man excellent (*Per re non es om tan prezans/com per amor e per domnei*),[2] an opinion voiced by poets as different as P. de Capdeuil (*Qu'amors es caps de trastotz bes,/E per amor es hom guays e cortes,/ Francs e gentils, humils et orgulhos*),[3] Reinmar (*MF* 157,31: *Und wiste ich niht daz si mich mac/vor al der welte wert gemachen, obe si wil,/ ich gediende ir niemer mêre tac*) and Gottfried (187: *liebe ist ein also sælic dinc,/ein also sæleclich gerinc,/daz nieman ane ir lere/noch tugende hat noch ere*). These are categorical statements apparently excluding any suggestion of doubt or hesitancy. To argue an undercutting of an ideal of love praised in such superlatives suggests the wilful malice of a Keii, the desire to see shortcomings where others have registered only virtues. What then is the evidence that there is not simply a place for Keii in the romance[4], but also for his kind of attitude when assessing the literary treatment of love, that the praise of love as an ennobling force is not the whole

---

[1] *De amore* I 6 C (ed. Trojel, p. 69).
[2] Ed. Lazar, 11, 25f.   [3] Quoted by Jeanroy, *Poésie* II 99.
[4] In the sense suggested by Lewis, *Allegory*, p. 172: 'Above all it protects itself against the laughter of the vulgar – that is, of all of us in certain moods – by allowing laughter and cynicism their place *inside* the poem.'

story and that it needs to be qualified by an awareness of its failings?

If I start with a reminder that love has always been exposed to humour because of the discrepancy between emotional pretensions and physical needs, this is not because I wish to invoke a psychological generalisation to suggest that medieval authors must have mockingly made fun of love. Instead, my purpose is to underline the historical point made by Curtius that classical literary theory saw love as belonging to the realm of comedy[1] and that the continuity of this theory is suggested by the role of the *comoedia* in Medieval Latin literature[2] or by the way in which Walter of Châtillon includes *Veneris copula* amongst *ridicula*.[3] If there are tangible literary historical, rather than vaguely psychological grounds for suspecting that even in courtly literature love may have been the object of banter as well as admiration, we should pay closer attention to numerous passages where the possible attitude of good-humoured or scornful mockery of lovers and their ways can actually be built into the narrative.

All the world may love a lover, but it is still quick to laugh at his more ludicrous antics. In *Ille et Galeron* lovers may resort to secrecy as much because of their vulnerability to ridicule as for any other reason (3928: *Amors gabent et les amans;/Cil est plus gabes c'Alemans/Qui cortois est et velt amer*). It is part of the irony of the situation in which Chaucer's Troilus finds himself after falling in love with Criseyde, that just before this he is depicted as mocking at those who suffer the pangs of unrequited love (I 194: *He wolde smyle, and holden it folye,/And seye hym thus, 'god woot, she slepeth softe/For love of the, whan thow tornest ful ofte'*). This banter he is at first compelled to keep up when, after being struck by love's dart, he comes out of the temple and puts on as good a front as he may (I 328: *And ay of loves servantes every while,/Hym self to wrye, at hem he gan to smyle;/And seyde, 'lord, so ye lyve al in lest,/Ye loveres! for the konnyngeste of yow,/That serveth most ententiflich*

---

[1] Curtius, *Literatur*, p. 431, quotes Servius on Book IV of Virgil's *Aeneid*: *nam paene comicus stilus est: nec mirum ubi de amore tractatur*. See also Curtius, *ibid.*, p. 390, fn. 3.

[2] On this see Cloetta, *Beiträge*, vol. 1; Cohen, *Comédie*; and Beyer, *Schwank* pp. 18ff.

[3] Ed. Raby, *Oxford*, Nr. 195, 20f. and 24f. On the poem see Moleta, *Arcadia* 5 (1970), 226ff.

and best,/Hym tit as often harm therof as prow;/Your hire is quyt ayeyn, ye, god woot how,/Nought wel for wel, but scorn for good servyse;/In feith, youre ordre is ruled in good wise'). The irony of this situation concerns Troilus rather than the lovers whom he mocks when he is about to join their ranks, but by his behaviour he illustrates the possibility that a lover's ways did not always call forth sympathy and understanding.[1] If this instance of mockery belongs to the prehistory of Troilus's career as a lover, the same certainly cannot be said of Reinmar, whose difficult relationship with a not always sympathetic audience underlies much of his love-poetry. This conviction of not being appreciated as a poet who sings of love speaks out of his complaint at the ridicule to which this can expose him (*MF* 197,9: *Ungefüeger schimpf bestêt mich alle tage*). Even if this is directed at Walther's polemics there are grounds for thinking that his rival may have made himself the spokesman of those at the Viennese court who could not take Reinmar's pose at its face value.[2] One can therefore argue that the poems of the German lyricist who most unquestioningly incorporates the values of love also provide the evidence that there were some amongst his listeners who were not so uncritical.

Realistic details

Reinmar's reference to the reality of a court audience sometimes resistant to his pose reminds us that, in the case of the chivalric ideal, realistic details incorporated into the romance could imply a reluctance to accept an all too simple idealisation of knighthood. Comparable realistic details with a bearing on the theme of love are not far to seek, especially with regard to two central features: the idealised nature of women and of the love-experience itself.

What needs to be stressed on the first score is the undercurrent of antifeminism, of an attitude quite different from conventional

---

[1] The irony of Troilus's situation, so soon to be a victim like those whom he mocks, does not affect the grounds on which he bases his mockery. What he primarily sees in love-service, like Hartmann von Aue in *MF* 218,5ff., is the laughable disparity between service and reward (I 333 and 335: *Nought wel for wel, but scorn for good servyse*). The scorn displayed for such a one-sided relationship allows Troilus to finish with the ironic observation (I 336: *In feith, youre ordre is ruled in good wise*).

[2] Cf. von Kraus, *Reimar* III 9 and de Boor, *LG* II 288f.

idealisation.[1] In his *Erec* Chrétien has Galoain utter a generalisation curtly dismissing flattery of women,[2] whilst *Yvain* contains similar uncomplimentary insights voiced not merely by a character, but by the narrator, as when he accuses women of wilfulness (1640: *Mes une folor a an soi,|Que les autres fames i ont,|Et a bien pres totes le font,|Que de lor folies s'escusent|Et ce, qu'eles vuelent, refusent*) and inconstancy (1749: *Ez vos ja la dame changiee|De celi, qu'ele ot leidangiee*).[3] The author of *Flamenca* allows himself a more malicious comment in his praise of the heroine's beauty by adding that if other women were agreed that she was beautiful there must have been something to it (558ff.), whilst Andreas Capellanus, attempting to turn his friend Gualterius from erotic pursuits, paints a picture of the false charms of women with such a detailed list of their faults that Nykrog, in discussing the more blatant antifeminism of the fabliau, has been able to take Andreas as a Virgilian guide on his descent into the *Inferno* of the feminine soul.[4]

Such insights, ranging from the shrewd to the cynical, are not confined to France. Hartmann's *Erec*, in criticising his wife's disobedience in breaking the silence enjoined upon her, connects his chastisement of her with what he has often heard of women in general (3242: *daz ich von wîben hân vernomen,|daz ist wâr, des bin ich komen|vol an ein ende hie:|swaz man in unz her noch ie|alsô tiure verbôt,| dar nâch wart in alsô nôt|daz sis muosten bekorn*), thereby lapsing into a generalised antifeminism like that of the narrator in *Yvain*. In his *Iwein* Hartmann's narrator agrees with Chrétien's in generalising the object of his criticism (1866: *doch tete sî sam diu wîp tuont:|sî widerredent durch ir muot|daz sî doch ofte dunket guot.|daz sî sô dicke brechent|diu dinc diu sî versprechent,|dâ schiltet sî vil maneger mite*).[5] He likewise generalises beyond the point at issue when

[1] This point was suggested in passing by Nickel, *Studien*, pp. 29f. See also Miller, *WS* 2 (1974), 335ff., Ferrante, *Woman*, and Kahn Blumstein, *Misogyny, passim*.

[2] V. 3350ff.

[3] The dramatic insistence of *Ez vos* in this example effectively suggests the narrator's exasperation with the ways of women.

Galoain's views in *Erec* and the narrator's views in *Yvain* are not necessarily the poet's, but the expression of such views is enough to suggest their currency in courtly circles at the time.

[4] *De amore* III (Trojel, pp. 340f.) and Nykrog, *Fabliaux*, pp. 195ff.

[5] It makes no difference that Hartmann's narrator should refuse to see in this a reason to think ill of women (1872ff.) or that the whole passage could be meant

mentioning the dejected silence of the women prisoners (6293: *ouch nam er war daz lützel hie/überiger rede ergie,/der doch gerne vil geschiht/ dâ man vil wîbe ensament siht*).[1] Even Gottfried, whose devotion to love is subject to less qualifications than that of other poets and who can imply that Isold lived up to this ideal better than his hero, is not free of caustic comments on the nature of woman, as with Isold's tears before Marke (13 900: *wan daz si kunnen weinen/ ane meine und ane muot,/als ofte so si dunket guot./Isot diu weinde starke*), her excuse for seeming to be fond of Tristan (13 987: *man sprichet von den vrouwen daz,/si tragen ir manne vriunden haz*)[2] or her account to Marke after the encounter in the orchard (14 958: *triure und üppeclichiu clage/deist min und aller vrouwen site;/hie reine wir diu herze mite/und liutern diu ougen./wir nemen uns dicke tougen/ein michel leit von nihte/und lazenz ouch inrihte*).

As with most of these cases, when the hero of *Sir Gawain and the Green Knight* learns the truth about his testing at Bertilak's castle he is not content with criticising his hostess, the one woman responsible for his failure, but launches into a conventional tirade against the wiles of women, citing fellow victims from the Old Testament.[3] Whatever may be said for or against the appositeness of such a commonplace at this point, it demonstrates that even the secular romance with its idealising concerns could find a place for a tradition of antifeminism which has its antecedents in classical antiquity,[4] was reinforced by clerical criticism throughout the Middle Ages[5] and was introduced into the romance by the

---

ironically (see Green, *Damning*, pp. 16off). What counts is that this is a generally held view of women which the narrator can count on being immediately recognised as such.

[1] Cf. also the way in which the elder sister seeks to excuse herself by sheltering behind feminine weakness at large, 7674ff.

[2] Again, it matters little that Isold's statement should be palpably untrue when applied to Tristan as Marke's friend. What counts is that she should be able to appeal to a generally held belief, uncomplimentary to women, in order to extricate herself from a difficult position.

[3] V. 2414ff. See Burrow, *Reading*, pp. 146ff.

[4] Cf. Jackson, *Anatomy*, p. 8, on Virgil's attitude to Dido's sensual hold over Aeneas and the sympathy which this attitude would arouse among medieval antifeminists. See also Bullough, *Viator* 4 (1973), 485ff., especially p. 486, and Hansen, *Frauengestalten*, pp. 148ff. Frappier, *Amour*, p. 18, observes that medieval antifeminism is particularly apparent in romances dealing with a classical theme. On the critical attitude shown towards love in these romances see Ferrante, *Conflict*, pp. 137ff.

[5] On this tradition in English literature and its general background see Utley, *Rib*, *passim*. See also Ferrante, *Woman*, pp. 17ff.

fact that many of the earliest romance authors, in Northern France at least, were clerics who could not completely deny their background.[1] When these works depict a knight adopting a similar tone, it may be psychologically convincing that he does so under the impact of anger (Hartmann's Erec or in *Sir Gawain*) or annoyance (Chrétien's Galoain), but the revelation of such uncourtly sentiments at a moment of crisis suggests that even in literature the adulation of woman was a fragile affair. As for the position in contemporary reality, what we know of the hardheadedness of feudal marriage practice[2] suggests that the dismissive attitude of a Galoain may have been shared by most men.

As to a realistic assessment of love itself, even in the *Tristan* tradition, even in the courtly strand in which adulterous love is presented as a positive value, Thomas is prepared to take stock of what is actually involved. Two informative examples have been discussed by Le Gentil.[3] He shows how Thomas's casuistical analysis (1084ff.) of which of the four persons involved after Tristan's marriage suffered most amounts to a critical exposure of the courtly *ménage à trois*. The courtly pattern is also unflatteringly reduced to sensual needs in the reproaches which the poet has Brengvein level at Ysolt in the course of their quarrel (1265ff.).

Much more discreetly Chaucer can ironise the religious hyperboles of courtly love literature in the scene when Troilus, at last in Criseyde's bed, addresses a prayer of thanks to the divinities of love (III 1254: ...'O Love, O Charite,/Thi moder ek, Citherea the swete,/After thi self next heried be she,/Venus mene I, the wel-willy planete'). The irony lies in the terms he uses, the confusion of a pagan love with Christian charity.[4] In the next two stanzas (III 1261ff.), as so often in the literary tradition to which Troilus is depicted as still belonging, the imagery of Christian worship is applied to a situation of secular love, but the poet's parodic intention becomes clear once we realise that the first of these stanzas is taken direct from Dante's *Paradiso*,[5] where it constitutes a prayer for the granting of the beatific vision. It must have been

---

[1] See Nykrog, *Fabliaux*, p. 239 (quoting Schürr), Tiemann, *RF* 72 (1960), 422 and Frappier, *Amour*, p. 18.

[2] See Schlösser, *Andreas*, pp. 286ff. and Wiegand, *Studien*, pp. 10ff.

[3] In *RPh* 7 (1953/54), 120ff.   [4] Gordon, *Sorrow*, p. 36.

[5] *Paradiso* 33, 13ff. (see Root in his edition of *Troilus*, pp. 484f., note to III 1262–7).

a well-read and alert member of the audience who could grasp the similarity and yet the difference between the situations in which Troilus and Dante the pilgrim find themselves (each is about to be granted a very different kind of bliss)[1] but, as we saw with Wolfram's time-references to Arthur's Whitsun festivals,[2] this is not of itself a valid argument against an ironic intention. Moreover, the target of this irony may not be Troilus himself[3] (who cannot be blamed for his ignorance of the Christian divine law against which he offends), but rather the medieval convention of describing human love in terms taken from religious imagery, for here no such plea of ignorance can be entertained. In this passage Chaucer both belongs to this tradition of medieval literature (for it assists him in producing some of his most intensely lyrical passages) and, by virtue of an ethical intention, stands critically aloof from it.

As with the theme of chivalry, the incorporation of such realistic details in a genre whose overall tendency is idealisation has the makings of irony (especially if we also take into account the comic potential of the theme of love) and in this last example from Chaucer I have followed Gordon in explicitly using the word irony. But to talk of irony in medieval love literature nowadays means running the risk of being taken for a Robertsonian, so that it is incumbent on me to state clearly where the literary possibility with which I am concerned differs from the work of D. W. Robertson. The American scholar maintains that wherever the message of medieval poetry, even of a secular nature, is not immediately reconcilable with the Christian doctrine of charity, the intent of that poetry must be allegorical (and therefore ultimately reconcilable),[4] so that works which apparently advocate the doctrine of *fin' amors* are in reality ironic in intention.[5] Despite the common ground of irony I believe that this argument goes much too far. It leaves in obscurity the question whether the

---

[1] See Wenzel, *PMLA* 79 (1964), 547. [2] See above, pp. 41f.

[3] Gordon, *op. cit.*, p. 39. [4] See Robertson, *Criticism*, p. 14.

[5] Robertson, *Preface*, p. 205 (where the word 'satiric' is twice employed) and *Concept*, p. 3 (where the same situation is described as 'ironic and humorous'). I must make it clear at this point that my disagreement with Robertson does not result from his transposition of the argument from allegory to irony, for this is perfectly justified in terms of the rhetorical closeness of these two tropes (see Green, *Alieniloquium*, pp. 144ff.).

Christian antithesis between *caritas* and *cupiditas* is the pervading theme of medieval secular literature and, if not, what exceptions there might be.[1] Any possible exceptions are not discussed and the impression is given that the argument is universally applicable. A lack of differentiation on yet another score has disturbed Frappier.[2] He objects that 'courtly love' is used quite simply as a blanket term for what are in fact different forms of love which must be kept apart within medieval literature and distinguished from any postmedieval derivatives such as romantic love. When Robertson labels them all indiscriminately as the same human weakness of idolatrous passion he is applying an ethical yard-stick[3] and ignoring the multiplicity of literary forms.

Difficulties also arise over the criteria by which Robertson would distinguish between a straightforward literary depiction of ordered sexual love and an ironic portrayal of its opposite. These are discussed very much in passing[4] and, for the rest, recourse is had to the argument that when the values behind such a medieval trope as allegory perished or were no longer understood in the modern age the trope itself perished, so that we are left with what appears to be no more than a literal statement.[5] This is a dangerously circular form of argument (a general assumption about medieval allegory is invoked as a demonstration that it must be present in this or that case, from which Robertson presumably was first led to his general assumption, even though no other pointers are present). The postmedieval reader has to 'take the underlying ironic meaning as it were on trust, solely on the grounds that it would have been clear to a medieval audience'.[6] Also ignored is the fact that medieval authors

---

[1] In his review article of Robertson's *Preface* (*ELH* 30 (1963), 190) Kaske has made a similar, and important, point: 'To the extent that illicit sexual love is thought to have flourished in the Middle Ages (and when has it not?), it becomes difficult to believe that we will find so unvarying a judgement of it in literature written by medieval men; to the extent that we suppose such love did not particularly flourish, it becomes difficult to believe (even in the light of its important allegorical significance) that it could have remained the object of so tireless and intense a disapproval.'

[2] Frappier, *Amour*, p. 64.

[3] Which is what makes one question the accuracy of his statement about his intentions in *Concept*, p. 14 ('Perhaps I should pause briefly to emphasize the fact that I am not trying to make Chaucer a Puritan').

[4] *Preface*, p. 233ff. See Kaske, *ELH* 30 (1963), 189.

[5] *Preface*, p. 288.   [6] See Gordon, *Sorrow*, p. 8.

were concerned to build into their narrative various types of signal to irony ranging from the merest hint to the quite explicit,[1] so that it seems doubtful whether the clues to Robertson's tropes of allegory and irony are always as external as he suggests.

Finally, if the love literature of the Middle Ages is to be read uniformly as an ironic condemnation what are we to make of the existence of works which parody the love theme (such as *Aucassin et Nicolette*)?[2] If Robertson is correct, this would confront us with parodies of something already parodic and with the impossibility of telling whether we are dealing with no more than a literary double bluff or are facing an unending vista of further complexities. If, as Robertson holds, there was no such thing as 'courtly love' in the Middle Ages,[3] how are we to interpret such parodies of something which never existed, such attacks without a target?[4] We overcome these difficulties if we avoid the two major errors in Robertson's line of argument. We must learn to differentiate between various views of love in the Middle Ages (so that irony now takes the form of a parodic criticism of one view in favour of another) and abandon the claim that irony is universally applicable to the literary depiction of love (so that irony would now be detectable only in a number of separate allusions, no longer as a continuous level of meaning divergent from the literal statement, a truth which has long since been acknowledged in the case of the allegorical trope[5] which Robertson rightly sees as allied with irony). It is with these more modest suggestions of an irony of love that this chapter will be concerned.

In the light of this we may return to the theoretical objection to the possibility of criticising love in courtly literature with which this chapter began. If the lover's lady really is unfailingly perfect

---

[1] As I have tried to show in my article, *Recognising*.

[2] I cite only one example here, but the problem extends very much further when we take into account the parody of courtly love to be found in the fabliau (cf. Nykrog, *op. cit.*, pp. 72ff.) and the *Schwank* (see Schirmer, *Versnovelle*, pp. 237ff.).

[3] *Concept*, p. 1. It hardly needs to be added that Robertson's denial that there was any such thing as courtly love in the Middle Ages is very different from Frappier's criticism of the ambiguity of the term *amour courtois* in modern criticism (*Amour*, pp. 1ff.).

[4] Cf. Frappier, *ibid.*, p. 64.

[5] E.g. Hatto, *Aventiure*, p. 100. Similarly, despite his rejection of Robertson's theory of an overall irony, Frappier is perfectly ready to consider the possibility of irony at many points in medieval works (*Amour*, pp. 65, fn. 11, 81, 83, 92).

it is difficult to account for Chaucer's use of irony in describing Criseyde's reluctance to embark on an affair with Troilus,[1] for when Pandarus has stage-managed the setting for love's consummation Criseyde's reactions are presented to us as arising from very mixed motives (III 918: *This accident so pitous was to here,/And ek so lik a sooth at prime face,/And Troilus hire knyght to hir so deere,/His prive comyng, and the siker place,/That though that she dede hym as thanne a grace,/Considered alle thynges as they stoode,/ Ne wonder is, syn she dide al for goode*). What is implied here is that Criseyde may not have been completely taken in by this contrived accident, which appears to her not as the truth, but *like* the truth, moreover only in appearances (*at prime face*). The tangible considerations of her lover's *prive comyng* and *the siker place* in which they find themselves now play a part in her decision. All these considerations are meant to qualify the force of the last clause, *syn she dide al for goode*. In this tug-of-war between the conventional highflown sentiments of *fin' amors* and the heroine's shrewd assessment of her position and acceptance of what Pandarus may be up to the ethical fiction of the love doctrine still has a part to play, but no longer an unqualified one. Whatever the qualities which love may teach its devotees, they certainly need not exclude self-interest and a shrewd sense of caution.

This is expressed more directly when a reference to love's instruction is connected with one of the stratagems to which lovers, especially those in the courtly triangle, have recourse. Flamenca thus hits upon a means of replying to Guillem's whispered complaint without being observed by her jealous husband (4335: *Res non es Amors non ensein:/Flamenca fes un cortes gein*). This point is made with greater force, because the affront to conventional morality is more shocking, when Gottfried's narrator comments on the lovers' decision to ask Brangæne to take Isold's place on the wedding-night (12447: *alsus so leret minne/durnehtec-liche sinne/ze valsche sin vervlizzen,/die doch niht solten wizzen,/waz ze sus getaner trüge/und ze valscheit gezüge*). These words cast an ironic light on the claim made in the prologue that no one may have *tugende* or *ere* without love's instruction[2] and give further force to

---

[1] Discussed by Gordon, *op. cit.*, p. 104.
[2] See Combridge, *Recht*, p. 103, fn. 145, and Peiffer, *Funktion*, pp. 171ff.

Tristan's abrupt dismissal of the still inexperienced Isold's belief that love for her would have taught even the Irish steward courtly virtues (11632: *Tristan sprach*: '*disiu mære/sint mir ein aventiure./daz wider der natiure/kein herze tugentliche tuo,/da gehœret michel arbeit zuo*:/*ez hat diu werlt vür eine lüge,/daz iemer unart garten müge*'). Tristan makes a denial here in the case of the steward which the narrative confirms on the occasion of the lovers' first deception, namely that the conventional view of a direct relationship between the experience of love and a growth in moral stature is at the best very dubious.[1] This is also suggested in the case of Tristan and Isold by the passage in Chrétien's *Cligès* where Fénice rejects for herself Isold's shameful position between two men (3112: *Amors en li trop vilena*).[2] Instead of enhancing her courtly virtues the experience of love is seen here as having degraded Isold, a recognition of love's negative potential which is also found in a more subdued key in Hartmann's *Erec*, exemplified in the persons of Erec himself, Galoein and Mabonagrin. Of the amoral nature of love in the scene of Yvain's wooing of Laudine it has been said that 'the God of Love...can adopt very devious tactics and can show himself shameless, cynical, and unmindful of any but his votaries'.[3] This is a far cry from the conventional idealisation of love as the fount of all virtues, but both facets of love (its enhancing alongside its amoral or degrading effects) are to be found in courtly literature which in examples such as these can achieve humorous and ironic effects precisely by exploiting these discrepancies.

Even in the medieval genre which devoted its energies most exclusively to the cultivation of an ideal of love, the lyric, irony is no stranger. This possibility can be accounted for if we regard paradox as the statement or presentation of a discrepancy and irony as its purposeful exploitation,[4] for the introspective analyses of the love-lyric abound in musings on the paradoxical nature of

---

[1] Schirmer, *Versnovelle*, p. 181, points to the significant divorce between the love-plot and the lovers' acquisition of courtly virtues – since they demonstrate these virtues to perfection before the love-plot starts, the ethical function of love, as conventionally seen, is rendered superfluous.

[2] Cf. Pollmann, *Liebe*, p. 304.   [3] See Whitehead, *Wooing*, p. 333.

[4] On F. Schlegel's view of irony as 'die Form des Paradoxen', see Bahr, *Ironie*, p. 174.

love. In so far as the lady is depicted in the love-lyric as perfect she partakes of the impersonality and immobility of perfection, but there are many lyrics where this is a source of disquiet for the poet, raising awkward questions as to whether perfection may not mean inhumanity or whether immobility may not be a cloak for indifference. On the one hand the love-lyric finds it necessary to indulge in such idealisation (for it holds out the best hope of likewise idealising courtly life and its aspirations), whilst on the other hand it is the poet in his role of lover who suffers from, and occasionally rebels against, the consequences of such insistence on the lady's perfection. Reinmar was perceptive enough to see the force of this paradox and to grasp that it constituted the nucleus of his love-poetry (165,37: *Zwei dinc hân ich mir für geleit,/ diu strîtent mit gedanken in dem herzen mîn:/ob ich ir hôhen werdekeit/ mit mînem willen wolte lâzen minre sîn,/ode ob ich daz welle daz si græzer sî/und si vil sælic wîp stê mîn und aller manne vrî./diu tuont mir beidiu wê*). For the poet to place all his hopes in one human being (whom he idealises in order to justify these hopes), for him to convert life into one long act of homage and service of a woman on whom he has projected the image of his own strivings is a rash excess which invites failure, since it is based on a distortion of life to which no human being can for long conform.

It is such rashness which Chaucer portrays in *Troilus and Criseyde* (his depiction of the lover's fervour, coloured with the religious imagery conventional in the love-lyric, raises doubts as to the absolute validity of the object of his devotion), but the problem as such is latent in medieval love-poetry itself. But other paradoxes also abound. As Kuhn has stressed,[1] this lyric tradition is informed by a tension between the lover's hope for bliss and the suffering to which he is inevitably exposed, between its ethical pretensions and the adultery, actual or potential, on which it rests, between its social context and the antisocial nature of a love which must seek secrecy. Even the attitude which convention forces the lover to adopt is paradoxical, for only the truly courtly can be a true lover, yet *fin' amors*, by leading him into extravagance of feeling and behaviour, renders him incapable of observing

[1] Kuhn, *Dichtung*, p. 10.

moderation, one of the cardinal virtues of courtliness.[1] It is at such points that irony can be applied, at those cracks in the façade where the discrepancy between what is and what should be becomes visible. If the paradoxes of *fin' amors* do not of themselves constitute irony, they at least provide the material with which the ironist may work.[2] And we find him at work in the love-lyric of both France and Germany, above all at those moments when we can observe the poet in the act of seeing through the convention and momentarily standing back from it with critical detachment.[3]

The difference of genres

If a poet can understandably stand back from convention most easily when criticising a rival, this suggests that one way out of the Robertsonian dilemma might be, as Frappier has proposed, to pay full regard to the variety of the views of love in medieval literature and to see the irony of love as largely arising from the clash between them, and the use of irony as a weapon in that encounter.[4] This is the point to bear in mind when considering

---

[1] Sutherland, *Meditation*, p. 165.

[2] This has been brought out by Siekhaus in an article (*DVjs* 45 (1971), 237ff.) devoted to the technique of *revocatio* in *Minnesang* which he regards as an expression of the paradoxes that inform this poetry. In his survey he twice recognises that this type of exploitation of a paradox can issue in irony, once when discussing an image used by Rudolf von Fenis (p. 247) and once when dealing with a poem by Bernger von Horheim (p. 251) which forms the starting-point of the article.

[3] This happens most readily when the love convention is seen in a wider context, such as the crusades, as in Hartmann's poem *MF* 218,5ff. or Hausen's *MF* 47,9ff. (on the final stanza see Kienast, *Scheltliet*, above all pp. 37ff.). It also happens whenever one poet parodies a rival, as with Walther 111,22ff. with regard to Reinmar (cf. von Kraus, *Reimar* III 6ff. and *Walther*, pp. 396ff., Kralik, *Walther*, and Wapnewski, *Euphorion* 60 (1966), 1ff.) or, in turn, with Wolfram's parody of Walther's poem in his lyric 5,16ff. (on this see Scholte, *PBB* 69 (1947), 414f., Wapnewski, *GRM* 39 (1958), 321ff., Scholz, *Walther*, pp. 145ff. and Wapnewski, *Lyrik*, pp. 174ff.).

[4] I stress this clash between rival views as productive of parody not because I think it the only source of the ironisation of love in medieval literature, but rather because this needs to be stressed in answer to Robertson's failure to differentiate between these rival conceptions of love. Another equally important source of irony, in regard to love as much as to chivalry, lies in the juxtaposition of realistic features alongside high-flown idealism. Walther can do this in his feud with Reinmar by means of the awkward reminder that unwearying devotion and length of service on the part of the lover necessarily involve the unthinkable idea of an aging mistress (73,17f.). Geltar shows as little belief in the love-poet's pose of prolonged suffering as does Wolfram (*Parzival* 587,7ff.) by mentioning a realistic consideration which this artificial pose conveniently ignores (Kraus, *Liederdichter*

the position in the narrative genre of the romance. In the first place, the difference of genre between the lyric and the romance heightens the possibility of irony in the latter. One reason for this is that the transposition of the theme of love from the lyric to the narrative genre means a transfer from an introspective, self-contained poetic realm (where attention and energy are largely restricted to the problem of love, artificially isolated) to a different type of fictional universe where the lover is also a man of action concerned with the world around him and where the literary theme is knightly action as well as lover's sentiment.[1] By this change of genre the theme of love is no longer regarded hermetically, but has to justify itself against competing claims, so that the narrative world of the romance opens up the same kind of wider horizon invoked by Chaucer in his relativisation of Troilus's headstrong fervour. Significantly, where this generalisation about the hermetic nature of medieval love-poetry may not be regarded as valid (as with the type of lyric where the rival claims of love and the crusade are treated or in a *genre objectif* such as the *pastourelle*), the same kind of relativisation can be detected as I am suggesting for the romance. With Hausen or Hartmann, the result of bringing in the theme of the crusade is to unmask the falsity of the belief in the self-contained exclusiveness of love,[2] whilst the *pastourelle*, by confronting the courtly class with the reality of the non-courtly world, similarly lends itself to a parody of the courtly ideal.[3]

The move from the lyric to the narrative is also a geographical move from Provence to Northern France. This means that (apart from the *Tristan* and *Lancelot* themes) love loses something of its fixation on the adulterous (or at least extramarital) affair, it now leads normally to marriage and conforms to the norms of society, of knighthood and of the Church.[4] It is Chrétien's achieve-

I 78: *ir sît ze veiz bî klagender nôt:/wær ieman ernst der sich alsô nâch minnen senet,/ der læg inner jâres friste tôt).*

On the more general possibilities of irony and parody in German love-poetry see also Moret, *Débuts*, pp. 231ff.

[1] On this see Ferrante, *Conflict*, pp. 135ff.   [2] Cf. p 103, fn. 3.

[3] On this aspect of the pastourelle see Jackson, *PhQ* 31 (1952), 156ff., Köhler, *Trobadorlyrik*, pp. 193ff. (dealing with Marcabru, but with wider implications) and Wapnewski, *Euphorion* 51 (1957), 147ff.

[4] Cf. Lazar, *Amour*, p. 14 and Frappier, *Amour*, pp. 13f.

ment to have brought about this reconciliation of love with the other norms of his day and to have fused them all into a unified ideal, but the result was that love lost its unique and absolute claims and that the need to find a place for it in a wider social setting meant another form of possible clash between the fiction of *fin' amors* and the needs of reality. Yet if it was Chrétien's wish to harmonise love with social needs and thereby to qualify its absolute claims which lies behind the rejection of this unified ideal by the *Tristan* versions of Thomas and Gottfried, this does not mean that with these *Tristan* versions we simply revert to the position maintained in the lyric. Here again the difference between the two genres asserts itself and confronts the love of the *Tristan* story with another type of reality. By this I mean that at the point where the social problems of love really begin, where it cannot avoid the realities of the world in which it has its being and where the dormant conflict between love and honour comes out into the open, the love-lyric is normally silent and (apart from the exceptional case of the *genre objectif*) refrains from penetrating beyond its own charmed circle. But this is not the case with *Tristan*, if only because the narrative genre is more committed to filling in the background with convincing details. Where the lyric can merely hint at (or keep silent about) the awkward presence of a husband, the narrative has to take him into account.[1] Whilst the lyric is concerned with the theme of love, the *Tristan* story deals with the conflict between love and society, a shift of emphasis partly resulting from the change in genre, but producing a vantage-point from which the values of the lovers may potentially be regarded from outside and with a measure of distance. The same is true of a last feature of the narrative genre which applies not merely to *Tristan*, but to any romance which treats the theme of love. Whereas the lyric presents the experience of love from the partial point of view of one of the partners (it is therefore a genre of the first person – again the exception of the *genre objectif* confirms my case), the action of a narrative genre is presented in the third person from the overall point of view of a narrator who can take account of the actions and sentiments of both partners (and of a wider sector of reality than is accessible to them).[2] To take

[1] Cf. Kolb, *Euphorion* 56 (1962), 243.   [2] Pollmann, *Liebe*, p. 259.

into account both the lover *and* his beloved brings with it the possibility of ironising the ignorance of one of them;[1] it amounts to another widening of the dimensions of the esoteric world of the love-lyric.

Reasons of genre therefore prevent us from considering, like Robertson, the love-lyric and the romance as presenting one unified doctrine of love. But there is another reason why we should avoid this trap. If the polemics and parodies which are to be found in the love-lyric suggest that even this genre is not undifferentiated, but consists of individual poets whose views are often widely at variance,[2] the same is equally true of the broader question of the depiction of love in medieval literature at large. Here we owe much to Frappier's campaign of enlightenment against the misleading ambiguities of the term *amour courtois*, which he sees as dangerous because of the blanket way in which it has been employed, without regard for some very different literary stances.[3] Frappier's suggestions have been worked out in detail by Lazar,[4] and together they advise us compellingly to differentiate first between the kinds of love depicted in the Provençal lyric and in the romances of Northern France, but then also to distinguish, within the literary context of the North, between the love presented in the Arthurian romance and that described in the *Tristan* tradition. They propose different terms to take account of these three basic types (*fin' amors, amour conjugal* and *amour-passion* respectively) and they are fully alert to the possible need for further refinements, e.g. with regard to such works as *Cligès* and *Lancelot*.[5] If we follow their lead we shall avoid the ambiguities of a misleading, because too general, term like *amour courtois*, we shall escape from the dilemmas of

---

[1] See below, pp. 136, fn. 2, 173f., 180ff. and 253.

[2] This point has been well made by Gilson, *Théologie*, p. 193.

[3] Frappier, *Amour*, pp. 1ff.   [4] Lazar, *Amour, passim*.

[5] A further differentiation to which both Frappier and Lazar pay too little attention is the view of love presented in various romances with a classical theme, for this cannot simply be identified with any of the three basic types which they otherwise put forward. On this particular view see Wolff, *Schriften*, pp. 143ff. and Jones, *Theme, passim*. If I have paid no further attention myself to this fourth type in what follows, this is because the classical romance plays a very minor rôle in the literary polemics on the theme of love in courtly literature, which in turn is probably because this type of romance assisted the rise of the secular romance at large, but rapidly became out of date with the introduction of the *matière de Bretagne*.

Robertson's line of argument and we shall see that the kaleidoscope of differing views in medieval literature provided even more scope in the romance than in the lyric for clashes of opinion between different schools of thought and for the use of parody and irony in the conduct of their arguments.

The romance and the love lyric

The first clash of opinion concerns the reaction of the romance to the conception of love cultivated in Provence, for if there are signs that the doctrines of the south influenced the north[1] it is equally undeniable that the romance of Northern France was not uncritical of Provençal theory. Telling evidence of this is the polemical encounter with Provençal doctrine, involving the use of parody, to be found already in Chrétien's *Erec*. A sign of the reservations with which Provençal ideas are greeted in the different social and literary climate of the north is Chrétien's attempt to reconcile love with the institution of marriage and with the practice of chivalry (both possibilities are ignored by Provence, whilst the first is denied outright in the *De amore* of Andreas Capellanus).[2] In *Erec* Chrétien illustrates a narrative fusion of love with marriage by depicting his hero, stylised in the courtly manner, finding fulfilment in marriage. Accordingly, he stresses in somewhat theoretical terms that the couple are both lovers *and* man and wife, as at the time of their marriage (2438: *A sa fame aloit donoiier.|De li fist s'amie et sa drue*), and the theoretical formulation of this and other statements suggests that Chrétien is putting forward his view against the tenet of the incompatibility of love with marriage.[3] A comparably programmatic statement is made by the narrator in *Cligès* (6753: *De s'amie a feite sa fame,|Mes il l'apele amie et dame*). The polemical force of this is revealed by the express negative formulation added (6755: *Ne por ce ne pert ele mie|Que il ne l'aint come s'amie,|Et ele lui tot autressi*), for this remark

---

[1] Pollmann, *Liebe*, p. 281.

[2] *De amore* I 6 F (ed. Trojel, p. 153): *Dicimus enim et stabilito tenore firmamus, amorem non posse suas inter duos iugales extendere vires.*

[3] Cf. also Enide's answer to the question asked by Oringle (4688: *S'ele estoit sa fame ou s'amie.|L'un et l'autre', fet ele, 'sire!'*). It is important that this point is taken over intact by Hartmann (6172: '*was er iuwer âmîs oder iuwer man?'|'beide, herre'*).

is directed against the view that love and marriage are irreconcilable, just as the further observation (6759: *Et chascun jor lor amors crut*) is aimed at the theory advanced in *De amore* that if a pair of lovers marry their love will suffer a decline.[1]

Yet Chrétien also brings the theme of love and knighthood up for discussion at the time of Erec's marriage and consequent idleness.[2] At the peak of the wedding festivities the poet eulogises Enide's courtly virtues (2417ff.) and says that so perfect are her qualities that whoever was able to serve her was made more worthy by that privilege (2428: *Qui li pooit feire servise,/Plus s'an tenoit chiers et prisoit*). This is a generalising remark in the Provençal spirit, but what effect does this paragon of courtly virtues have on the man who serves her? According to the Provençal doctrine that service of a lady enhances a man's virtues Erec should now be conducted to courtly perfection, but instead the opposite happens (2434: *Mes tant l'ama Erec d'amors/Que d'armes mes ne li chaloit,/Ne a tornoiemant n'aloit*). In other words, Erec falls in the courtly hierarchy of values (in which chivalry has its place for Chrétien) because he devotes himself exclusively to the value which is supposedly the source of all virtues.[3] By giving himself over to what Provence sees as an absolute good Erec offends against chivalry, another key-value in Chrétien's system. The poet stresses here the gulf between the fiction of *fin' amors* and reality as seen in Northern France, he shows his awareness that love cannot be practised in isolation, but has to be reconciled with social obligations, that it cannot therefore be an absolute value, but is at the most a relative one. Chrétien poses this problem in the scene of Erec's *recreantise*, but his polemical intention is clear if we compare his description of Erec's fall with what Andreas Capellanus imputes to a lover, here representative of *fin' amors*, courting his lady. This lover uses the following argument: *Nam ab amoris aula semotae sibi tantummodo vivunt ex earum vita nemine sentiente profectum; prodesse autem nulli volentes pro moritus* [*sic*! read

---

[1] *De amore* II 4 (ed. Trojel, p. 249): *Sed et superveniens foederatio nuptiarum violenter fugat amorem*. Cf. Schumacher, *Auffassung*, p. 75.

[2] Pollmann, *Liebe*, pp. 286ff. Pollmann appears to consider the possibility of parody here (p. 287), but then to take it back (p. 289), an uncertainty which seems unjustified in the light of the remarks made by Zaddy, *Chrétien*, pp. 44ff.

[3] Pollmann, *op. cit.*, pp. 272f.

mortuis] *saeculo reputantur, et earum fama nullatenus est digna relatu sed momento prorsus silentii subhumanda. Quae vero amoris student vacare solatiis, suae videntur probitatis incremento studere et aliorum profectui deservire.*[1] Again, Chrétien illustrates this attitude (put forward as a positive recommendation in the *De amore*) in narrative action, and its disastrous consequences. Instead of withdrawing from Love's court, Erec keeps away from his own court at Karnant and behaves as Andreas's lover recommends, but the result for him is not enhancement of his reputation, but its destruction, not a life of service to others, but one of social futility.[2]

Amongst examples of a parody of the lyric poets' love-ideal in the German romance[3] I propose to discuss a scene in Gottfried's *Tristan*. This has the advantage of illustrating that parody need not arise from the wish to accommodate love with marriage and chivalry (two values quite foreign to Gottfried) and that the clash between Gottfried's views and those of the 'Minnesänger' was sharp enough to generate a parodic attitude as critical as Chrétien's. The difference between Gottfried and the 'Minnesänger' can be seen with regard to the (originally) feudal ideal of *triuwe*, for the theme of the lover serving his lady in the hope of *lôn* or *genâde* is absent from his account of the loves of Riwalin and Tristan. Moreover, Gottfried does not conceive *triuwe* as a horizontal bond between two equal partners in love, but rather as a bond bringing

---

De amore I 6 G (ed. Trojel, pp. 157f.). These words are admittedly spoken by a man of the higher nobility (*nobilior*) to a woman of the same class, so that the argument is applied to the social disgrace that would befall a woman who withdrew from the court of Love. There is no reason to assume that it would not be equally applicable to a man, and therefore to one in Erec's position.

[2] It has been shown by Hrubý, *DVjs* 38 (1964), 337ff. and by Kramer, *Erzählerbemerkungen*, pp. 158ff. that the literary polemics conducted by Chrétien in this work against the Provençal doctrine meant little to Hartmann in the different literary situation in Germany, so that the parody present in the French romance has been removed from the German version. This does not mean, however, (as Kramer believes) that irony is not present in Hartmann's *Erec* at all, but rather that it has changed its target and that we must look for it elsewhere. One obvious example in the German work which is not present in the French source is Erec's reception by Coralus (cf. Green, *Damning*, pp. 148f.).

On Chrétien's parody of the Provençal conception of love in *Lancelot* see Pollmann, *Liebe*, pp. 284ff. and Bogdanow, *MLR* 67 (1972), 50ff.

[3] For reasons of space I leave aside the complex question of Wolfram's attitude to contemporary love-poetry and the possibility of his using parody to express his opinion. On two telling examples of this see Scholz, *Walther*, pp. 42ff. and 69ff.

about the complete union of the lovers (1358ff.). With this conception of *triuwe* Gottfried reacts against the dominant conception of love in *Minnesangs Frühling*. Hausen, Morungen, Reinmar employ feudal terms of a relationship which in effect is more onesided than the feudal bond, for whereas the feudal lord is in duty bound to reward a loyal vassal, the lady of the love-lyric more commonly remains indifferent to the lover (*MF* 134,15: *an sô hôhe stat dâ sîn dienest gar versmât*). In the context of unrequited love *triuwe* becomes very much a onesided virtue, standing for the lover's readiness to serve even without reward (*MF* 159, 10ff.).[1]

If Gottfried differs here from *Minnesang* (despite a measure of common ground), it is not surprising that he should polemicise against it in the form of parody. He does this by altering one character, the Irish steward, in the direction of the ideal of *Minnesang*, so that the defeat of this figure amounts to a deflation of the ideal he incorporates. Gottfried introduces the steward in terms of his relationship with Isold (8948: *der einer von den vieren/ truhsæze was der künigin;/der was ouch unde wolte sin/der jungen küniginne amis,/wider ir willen alle wis*). *Amis* is a term of *fin' amors*, but this relationship is devalued by Gottfried in his realistic conversion of the inequality of the *fin' amors* relationship into a downright refusal by Isold to have anything to do with the steward (8952). The poet here defends the right of a woman to choose her own lover (rather than simply be put on a pedestal and worshipped by him). This deflation is confirmed by v. 8950, where we do not have a simple repetition, because the task of *wolte sin* is to undermine *was*, to show the reality behind the pretension, the fact that this relationship is not reciprocal and therefore not love.[2]

---

[1] Gottfried's reaction to the essential onesidedness of *minne* does not stand alone. Hartmann, before finally abandoning this *minne* for divine love, threatens to seek reciprocal love among women of humble rank (*MF* 216,29ff.) and Walther carries out the threat in his lyrics of *niedere Minne*. In narrative literature, Hartmann and Wolfram develop the theme of reciprocal love, like Chrétien, by praising married love, whilst it is left to Gottfried to take the more difficult course of praising a love which is both reciprocal and extramarital.

[2] Cf. also the use of the same auxiliary verb in 9093ff. (*Der truhsæze, alse ich han gesaget,/der der sæligen maget/vriunt unde ritter wolte sin*). On the ironic use of this and other auxiliaries see Green, *Recognising*, pp. 28ff.

In the steward's verbal encounter with Isold's mother he is further exposed to ridicule (9906: *du weist der vrouwen art ʒe wol;| du bist dar in ʒe verre komen:|eʒ hat dir der manne art benomen*; 9914: *du minnest, daʒ dich haʒʒet;|du wilst, daʒ dich niht enwil:|diʒ ist doch unser vrouwen spil;|waʒ nimest du dich hie mit an?|so dir got, du bist ein man,|laʒ uns unser vrouwen art*). With these lines the poet scores two bull's eyes. He first reveals the weak point of *Minnesang*, its fundamental effeminacy and over-refinement, also repugnant to Wolfram (*Parzival* 115,13ff.). If Wolfram rejects for himself the role of a poet serving his lady with song, he makes it clear what poet he has in mind, for eight lines earlier (115,5ff.) he refers to Reinmar's praise of his lady at the expense of all others (*MF* 159,5ff. and 9), the poem parodied by Walther (111,23ff.) and criticised by Gottfried (8294ff.).[1] But Gottfried makes it clear that when he criticises the effeminacy of *Minnesang* he too is thinking of Reinmar, for the Irish queen's words to the steward (9914: *du minnest, daʒ dich haʒʒet*) allude to the typical pose of Reinmar (*MF* 166,31: *sît si mich haʒʒet, diech von herzen minne*).[2] Hartmann, too, had expressed dissatisfaction with Reinmar's kind of stance, namely in the crusading poem in which he abjures *minne* in favour of a divine love of which he can boast (*MF* 218,25: *daʒ ich dâ wil, seht daʒ wil alse gerne haben mich*) and Gottfried makes the same point as Hartmann through Isold's mother (9921: *habe dine mannes sinne|und minne, daʒ dich minne*). Reinmar therefore stands in the cross-fire of several poets dissatisfied with *Minnesang* (Wolfram, Walther, Hartmann). To these we must add Gottfried and see in his parody of Reinmar a criticism of the ideal of *minne* for which Reinmar stood in the eyes of so many of his contemporaries.

Arthurian and Tristan *romances*

Yet Chrétien and those who follow him in Germany had more to do than make clear the difference between their position and

---

[1] Scholz, *Walther*, pp. 76ff.

[2] Cf. Nickel, *Studien*, pp. 31f. The second parallel adduced by Nickel (*Tristan* 9915: *du wilt, daʒ dich niht enwil* and Reinmar, *MF* 199,14: *liebes des enhân ich niht,|wan ein liep daʒ mîn niht wil*) is weaker, both because of the uncertain authorship of the love-poem and because Gottfried's verbal echo is more distant. But it can still be argued that Gottfried is parodying in general terms an attitude characteristic of the love-poet at large and of Reinmar in particular.

that of the love-lyric. They faced a danger nearer home in the shape of the *Tristan* story, unsettling to the harmony established by Chrétien by its advocacy of the absolute claims of love and by the realistic view, beneath the courtly trappings with Thomas and Gottfried, it takes of human love and its consequences for society, presenting it as a force strong enough to bring the lover into conflict with society.[1] Here too the clash of views between the Arthurian and the *Tristan* romances can involve mutual criticism and the use of parody, both when Chrétien states his distance from the implications of the *Tristan* story and when Gottfried implies his rejection of a central facet of the Arthurian romance's reconciliation of love and chivalry.

To understand the literary reaction to the *Tristan* story we must realise that although the courtly society of Thomas's day which accepted the Provençal ideas about extramarital love in Northern France (Eleanor of Poitou, Marie of Champagne) was unlikely to take offence at the depiction of illicit love as such, it was however likely to reject the antisocial implications of his work, since these cut the ground from beneath courtly society itself. Nor do we have to look far to imagine the form which this literary rejection, on behalf of courtly society, of Thomas's romance took, because *the* literary exponent of these ideals at this time was Chrétien himself. If there are grounds for thinking that Thomas may have taken Chrétien's *Erec* into account (in rejecting the social implications of Chrétien's Arthurian ideal),[2] here we have to look at the converse side of this literary relationship, at Chrétien's rejection of Thomas's view. Chrétien was acquainted with the *Tristan* story throughout his career, although it is doubtful whether we can talk of his 'obession' by this theme[3] or whether we can interpret references to the story already in his *Erec* as critical, rather than simply as examples of a rhetorical figure ('fairer than Isold', like 'fairer than Helen') where the emphasis falls more on the supreme qualities of the person praised than on any deficiencies in the model surpassed.[4]

It is only in *Cligès* that the tone of Chrétien's allusions to the

---

[1] Cf. Ferrante, *Conflict*, pp. 11f.   [2] Cf. Mölk, *GRM* 12 (1962), 96ff.

[3] Cf. Fourrier, *Courant*, p. 123. Chrétien refers to having composed a work on this subject (*Cligès* 5), but this may have been no more than a *conte* or *lai*.

[4] See Baehr, *Sprachkunst* 2 (1971), 45ff.

Tristan story becomes markedly sharper, betraying at times a definite enmity in their linguistic formulation. Fénice sees it as degrading for her love for Cligès to be compared with that of Tristan and Isold and is ashamed even to mention their names (3105ff.), she refuses to flee with her lover from her husband because this would resemble the position of the other lovers (5250ff.), she rejects violently for herself the situation which Isold accepted, shared between a husband and a lover (3113f.) and she sees the love of Tristan and Isold as devoid of all courtly values (3112: *Amors an li trop vilena*). Between the opinions voiced in *Cligès* (not merely by Fénice, who is no more than a figure in the work, but also by the poet in his detailed organisation of the narrative structure as a sustained parody of *Tristan*)[1] and Chrétien's earlier, essentially receptive and neutral attitude to the *Tristan* story there is no continuity, but instead a clean break. Most attempts to explain the sharpness of polemical accent in *Cligès* presuppose a change of attitude on the part of Chrétien which must have been radical enough to imply a revocation of his own previous work (so that Fénice's words, 3108: *Don tantes folies dit l'an,|Que honte m'est a raconter*, would apply equally to his own poem *Del roi Marc et d'Iseut la blonde*). Rather than presuppose a change in Chrétien the poet about which we have no other evidence it is safer to assume a change in the literary treatment of the *Tristan* story (about which we do know something).[2] We know from his *Erec* that at this early stage Chrétien was acutely conscious of the danger to the courtly ideal represented by a false conception of love, and we know that Thomas's treatment of the *Tristan* story stressed the antisocial nature of love as part of his positive ideal. It is very probable, therefore, that it was this new *Tristan* version by Thomas which alerted Chrétien to the danger to his courtly ideal, so that what must have attracted Gottfried to Thomas's version[3] is precisely what repelled Chrétien. This means that the *Tristan* story was known to Chrétien at the start of his career in the form of the *version commune* (treating an illicit love, but still clearly subordinating it to social values), but

[1] On this see van Hamel, *Romania* 33 (1904), 465ff., Fourrier, *Courant*, pp. 124ff. and Lazar, *Amour*, pp. 226f.

[2] I follow here the convincing argument of Baehr, *art. cit.*, pp. 54f.

[3] Cf. Jackson, *Anatomy*, pp. 36f.

a decade later the position was drastically changed with the appearance of Thomas's work. His incorporation of the courtly ideal into the *Tristan* story now alerts Chrétien to their fundamental contradiction. As the literary guardian of courtly values, he would be alive, more than most, to any danger to his newly established synthesis.

Chrétien's answer is given in his *Cligès*, above all in the polemical passages voiced by Fénice and the parodic plot with its details taken over from *Tristan* for the purposes of caricature, both of which make of *Cligès* what has been termed an *Anti-Tristan*.[1] By imitating details of Thomas's story in this new plot and by developing them *ad absurdum* Chrétien rejects Thomas's presuppositions, but it is significant that Chrétien's plot-machinery creaks somewhat and illustrates his difficulties in refuting his rival.[2] Even Chrétien can only avoid the dilemma of Tristan and Isold by contriving the convenient death of Fénice's unloved husband. Moreover, in order to maintain his polemical truth against Thomas (only the man to whom the woman gives her heart may possess her body) Chrétien is forced to motivate on two occasions by the supernatural means of a magic potion. Once, to induce a sleep which gives the appearance of Fénice's death and, earlier, the grotesque potion which puts the husband to sleep, but tricks him into believing that he made love to his wife (only thus can she be preserved for her lover and thereby avoid Isold's promiscuity). It is difficult to know how to assess this faltering motivation. Perhaps these unreal, improbable elements betray Chrétien's suspicion that the ideal of love, reconciled with marriage and society, was just as much a fairytale as the motifs to which he has recourse here, whilst the *Tristan* story might after all be truer to contemporary reality. In any case, *Cligès* illustrates the force of the impact made by Thomas's version, forcing Chrétien to meet the challenge by a sustained parody in which he hopes to ironise aspects of his rival's position, but in which (by an irony which he certainly did not intend!) he may have been led to reconsider whether the optimism of the solution proposed in *Erec* was justified.

[1] Cf. Hofer (in agreement with Foerster), *Chrétien*, p. 113.
[2] See Lazar, *Amour*, pp. 227ff. and Baehr, *art. cit.*, pp. 55f.

The use of parody in the encounter between the Arthurian and the *Tristan* romances is not confined to a criticism of the courtly version of *Tristan*, as we see when we consider the position with Gottfried. Despite some common ground shared by Gottfried and his Arthurian rivals (both are opposed to the love-ideal of the lyric) the differences between these two types of romance invite Gottfried in his turn to make use of parody, especially with regard to the social dimension in which the Arthurian romance illustrates its ideal of love. If Gottfried attempts to excise this dimension, this does not mean that it is absent from his work altogether (as we have seen, this is theoretically conceivable only in the lyric, not the narrative genre). Instead, he depicts this social dimension either as divorced from the ideal of love (thus, none of Tristan's knightly exploits is performed in the service of Isold)[1] or as opposed to it (in the institution of marriage or in Marke's court).[2]

In one other respect does Gottfried abandon a social aspect of love common to the love-lyric and to the Arthurian romance. Both make use of the feudal imagery of service (in the Arthurian romance of Chrétien or Hartmann this act of subordination still underlies the reciprocity of the man and wife relationship, for the woman serves the husband as her lord, whilst the man serves his wife as his mistress). Even this reciprocal subordination goes too far for Gottfried, who is not content with *triuwe* as a bond between equals, but sees it as a complete union, to the necessary exclusion of concepts like service and reward.

Gottfried formulates his ideas on this in the *rede von minnen* (12 183ff.), especially in connection with the complaint that love is nowadays for sale (12 300: *Minne, aller herzen künigin,/diu vrie, diu eine/diust umbe kouf gemeine!*). What he has in mind, as we shall see in connection with the Irish steward, is the contemporary conception of love in the mercenary terms of a reward for services

---

[1] This is true even of his combat with the giant Urgan if we take into account that the gift of the dog Petitcreiu (which was Tristan's purpose in seeking this adventure) is rejected by Isold as irrelevant to her position. The one exploit by Tristan which comes close to being a chivalric adventure is undermined by Isold's refusal to play her allotted part. See also above, pp. 58f.

[2] On this aspect of Gottfried's work see especially Jackson, *Anatomy*, pp. 142ff.

rendered, subjecting love to calculations of possible gain, as in the lyric's recurrent metaphors of *dienst*, *gnâde* and *lôn*. For Gottfried love must be freely bestowed, beyond all thought of merit or not, because it is for him an absolute and therefore comparable with the Christian concept of grace (*gratia*), given to man irrespective of his deserts (*gratis*). If we recall the argument imputed to the Countess of Champagne by Andreas Capellanus[1] that lovers give each other everything freely (*gratis*) under no compulsion of necessity, whilst married people are in duty bound to give in to each other's desires, it is probable that Gottfried's depiction of love as above all mercenary considerations was also aimed at contemporary feudal marriage-practice. In short, Gottfried's rejection of feudal service within love separates him from both the love-lyric and the Arthurian romance; he shows considerable insight in discovering what they have in common beneath all their surface polemics. On this common ground he differs from them both.

Gottfried's rejection of the service–reward motif in the context of love amounts to a rejection of the feature by which the Arthurian romance harmonised the twin ideals of love and chivalry: knightly exploits as service rendered to the lady, her love as the knight's reward. This fusion of two secular ideals had been Chrétien's accomplishment in initiating the genre of the Arthurian romance, yet it is this recent gain which Gottfried now undoes by separating chivalry from love.[2] From the point of view of Chrétien and his German successors this provocative move must have seemed irresponsible, jeopardising the balance between two ideals so recently achieved, but Gottfried must have acted thus because of the absolute value he attaches to love, seeing it as superior to all mercenary considerations. How far his refusal to accept the doctrine of service and reward in love went may be gauged by his construction of the episode of the dragon combat and the Irish steward's claims as a parody of it. We have already considered the episode in the context of Gottfried's attitude to the love-lyric, so that if it crops up again in connection with his

---

[1] *De amore* I 6 F (ed. Trojel, p. 153): *Nam amantes sibi invicem gratis omnia largiuntur nullius necessitatis ratione cogente. Iugales vero mutuis tenentur ex debito voluntatibus obedire et in nullo se ipso sibi invicem denegare.*

[2] Stein, *DVjs* 51 (1977), 300ff.

attitude to the Arthurian romance as well, this is because he has perceptively seen what these two genres have in common (love as a reward for service) and in his parody aims to kill two birds with one stone.

The scene of the wooing of Isold implies a strong criticism of the medieval practice (in the romance) of granting the woman as a prize to the victorious knight, for it depicts a situation in which Isold narrowly escapes being handed over to a cowardly, deceitful and murderous knight only at the cost of being married off to a king she has never seen and certainly never loves.[1] Love may have no part in these arrangements, yet this is the normal way in which a couple is brought together in the Arthurian romance. The victorious knight may gain the lady as his prize, but what has this to do with love? Or with her feelings? Yet the steward is really on a lower level than Marke, for he cannot even excuse himself by the sensual attractions which later draw Marke to Isold. Instead, the steward does not desire Isold as a person, but as a possible means of inheriting the Irish throne, and therefore as a thing. She is his by right of conquest, a woman exchanged for a dragon's head and reduced to the level of goods and chattels, which is the aspect of the knight serving a woman in the Arthurian romance that Gottfried is attacking here. He criticises not just the steward, but the whole system. He makes his point by showing up the steward's claims as false, but also by frequent explicit references to the heart of the matter, the fact that a woman should be exchanged for a thing and that, without her feelings being consulted, she should be made into a reward for services rendered.[2]

It is natural that it should be the steward who first mentions the mercenary aspect of Isold as a mere reward (9803: *swelh ritter disen serpant/slüege mit sin eines hant,/ir gæbet ime ʒe solde/iuwer tohter Isolde*),[3] but this is then taken up scornfully by others. First by the mother (9821: *der also rilichen solt,/als min tohter ist, Isolt,/ungedienet haben wil/entriuwen des ist alʒe vil*; 9838: *swer aber so hohes lones gert,/*

---

[1] Jackson, *Anatomy*, p. 79.

[2] Cf. Mersmann, *Besitʒwechsel*, pp. 190ff.

[3] That it should be the Irish king who has proclaimed his daughter as a reward for the dragon-slayer shows that Gottfried is attacking not merely the steward, but also the system to which the king, too, conforms.

da er sin niht verdienet hat,/entriuwen, deist ein missetat; 9851: *sin wirt aber gewunnen niht/mit also cleiner geschiht*), but then by Isold herself (9853: '*nein zware*', sprach diu junge Isot/' durch also mæzliche not/enwil ich niemer veile sin'). The repetition of this theme in so small a compass is significant. Between them these passages stress (1) the great reward (*rilichen solt, so hohes lones*); (2) the negligible service rendered (*also cleiner geschiht, also mæzliche not*); and (3) the discrepancy between these two as a suggestion that the reward has not been truly merited (*ungedienet, niht verdienet*). In fact we know that this reward has not been merited by the steward (since we know that his claims are false), but the two Isolds make their point *before* the falsity of his claims has been demonstrated. What is suggested is that no possible service could merit this reward, not just because of Isold's unique beauty, but because any woman, as a person, is unique and not to be treated as a thing, as a material reward (9855: *enwil ich niemer veile sin*). Any exploits on the field of combat are a negligible service, undeserving because a woman's heart can only be won emotionally, not by such externals. To act otherwise (as in the Arthurian romance) is to apply legalistic, not emotional standards and thereby to degrade woman to the level of an object.

That this interpretation is generally valid (and not just in this particular case) is borne out by the use of similar terminology when Isold later laments being handed over to an unknown husband (11590: *ine weiz, wie ich verkoufet bin*), when Marke by his insensitivity on the wedding-night betrays that one woman is like another to him and that all are 'things' in his eyes (12607: ...*daz ie so schœne messinc/vür guldiniu teidinc/ze bettegelte würde gegeben*), and above all in the Gandin episode when Tristan angrily reproaches Marke with having given Isold away in exchange for a performance on the harp, i.e. with having treated her as much as a reward or thing as the Irish steward in claiming her (13443ff.). Ultimately, Marke therefore turns out to be as bad as the steward. Both, whether actively (the steward) or passively (Marke), regard woman as an object of barter. This is the position in the Arthurian romance (cf. Erec and Enite in the tournament at Tulmein)[1] and it is this approach to love which Gottfried rejects as an insult to

---

[1] On this see Wiegand, *Studien*, pp. 90ff.

woman (making of her a thing) and to love (converting it into the mercenary transaction which he lamented in the *rede von minnen*).[1]

The romance and the fabliau

We have seen that parody in connection with the theme of love can arise from the variety of different attitudes within the range of courtly literature: from differences within the love-lyric, from differences of genre operating between the lyric and the romance, as well as from different conceptions of love separating the romance from love-poetry and the Arthurian romance from the *Tristan* romance. To these we have to add a final distinction: the presence of widely differing genres within the repertoire of courtly literature. By this I mean the recent discovery that the fabliau and the *Schwank* are in their origins courtly narrative genres and as such must take their place alongside the courtly romance.

For Bédier[2] the place of the fabliau within medieval literature was obvious. By contrast with the courtly genre of the romance it was essentially a bourgeois genre, and it was this sociological origin which for him explained the realism of the fabliau and what he saw as its occasional satire on the knightly class. Bédier was also aware that some fabliaux bear all the marks of having been meant for courtly consumption,[3] but he treats these cases as

---

[1] Another example of Gottfried's parody of the love-ideal of the Arthurian romance has been discussed by Schindele, *Tristan*, pp. 80f. It concerns the description of the lovers' seclusion in the love-grotto, more particularly the comment that in this ideal setting they had no need of the company of Arthur's court (16859ff.) and that they were happy in their seclusion (16847: *ouch muote si daz cleine,/daz s in der wüeste als eine/und ane liute solten sin*). The comparison with Arthur suggests a comparison with Hartmann's Arthurian world, but even apart from this the allusion to the Schoydelakurt episode in *Erec* is clear, above all in the contrast between *Tristan* 16847ff. and *Erec* 9438 (*wan bî den liuten ist sô guot*). An antisocial form of love which Hartmann had rejected is here affirmed by Gottfried as a positive ideal, who makes his position clear by converting his predecessor's reference to *liute* into its antithesis. Chrétien's target in his corresponding scene had been the esoteric nature of the love depicted in the Provençal lyric (Zaddy, *Chrétien*, pp. 44ff.). Hartmann takes over his general outline for this scene because it fits in with the social nature of his love-ideal, without intending any parody of the contemporary love-lyric (see above, p. 109, fn. 2). Finally Gottfried parodies Hartmann's position because of the essentially antisocial nature of love as *he* conceives it. This does not mean that Gottfried's *Tristan* now simply reverts to the position of the Provençal love-lyric, but that both happen to agree on a particular point foreign to the Arthurian romance.

[2] Bédier, *Fabliaux*.   [3] Bédier, *Fabliaux*, pp. 376ff.

exceptions by arguing a confusion in courtly taste involving a confusion of genres.[1] What he dismissed as marginal has recently come to be accepted as a central feature of this genre. For the fabliau it is Nykrog and for the *Schwank* Fischer and Schirmer who have maintained that this genre belonged in origin to courtly literature[2] and that if it later formed part of the literary diet of the bourgeoisie it shares this widening of social appeal with other courtly genres such as the romance and the love-lyric. This is not the occasion for discussing the variety of arguments deployed by these scholars,[3] but if we accept their conclusions this will drastically affect our view of the range of courtly taste. If not merely the romance, but also the fabliau was addressed to a courtly audience, we can no longer argue with Bédier in terms of an antithesis between courtly idealism and bourgeois realism,[4] but must acknowledge that a courtly audience could appreciate both styles. Once we reach this point, we cannot stop short of the question whether these two aspects of courtly taste remained

[1] *Ibid.*, pp. 382ff.

[2] See Nykrog, *Fabliaux* (together with the important review article by Tiemann, *RF* 72 (1960), 406ff.), Fischer, *Studien*, and Schirmer, *Versnovelle*.

[3] The arguments advanced on behalf of the courtly origins of this genre cover a wide range of possibilities, including such variegated points as the presence of a markedly literary and rhetorical style (Nykrog, pp. 36ff., Schirmer, pp. 1ff.), of a courtly or even aristocratic public (Bédier, pp. 376ff., Nykrog, pp. 20ff., Fischer, pp. 244f.), the signs of a cultivated class of poets, whether professional or amateur (Fischer, pp. 208ff. and 219), but also the occurrence of details within the genre which could only have been appreciated by an audience sufficiently well acquainted with courtly literature at large, such as literary allusions (Fischer, pp. 228ff.), the theme of love-casuistry (Nykrog, pp. 94ff., Schirmer, pp. 247ff., 265ff.) and the parody of courtly literature (Nykrog, pp. 72ff., Schirmer, pp. 237ff.). The question of dating (Nykrog, p. 4, still maintained that there is no occurrence of the word *fabliau* before 1200) has now been resolved in favour of an earlier occurrence (Tiemann, pp. 409f. and 420), so that there is no objection to regarding the genesis of the fabliau as contemporary with the rise of other genres in what is acknowledged as courtly literature, a possibility which is strengthened by the still earlier existence of the so-called Latin fabliau (cf. Faral, *Romania* 50 (1924), 321ff., Beyer, *Schwank*, pp. 18ff., 51ff. and 64ff., and Dronke, *RF* 85 (1973), 275ff.).

I attach particular importance to Tiemann's expansion of Nykrog's narrower conception of courtly authorship so as to include clerics active at courts – both because this parallels what is known of French courtly literature in other respects (cf. Frappier, *Chrétien*, pp. 16ff.; see also below, pp. 359ff.) and because a similar case has been convincingly made out for the *Schwank* by Schirmer, pp. 299ff.

[4] If Nykrog has cast radical doubt on the epithet 'bourgeois' in this term, Fischer (*Studien*, pp. 128ff.) has also pointed out how necessary it is to qualify our understanding of the word 'realism' as applied to this genre (see also Nykrog, *Fabliaux*, p. 229).

separate in the watertight compartments of distinct genres or whether they might not be found together in the same genre. If, following Nykrog and his colleagues, it is to the second possibility that we give our assent, this means that what the fabliau has to tell us about courtly literature confirms, from quite a different angle, our suspicion that courtly poets were not simply preoccupied with a romantic idealisation of love, but were also aware of elements of make-believe in that ideal and were particularly quick to spot them when they occurred in the work of a rival poet.

What I am suggesting is that the juxtaposition of the fabliau alongside the romance cannot be free of implications for the romance, that the presuppositions of the one genre serve as a commentary on the assumptions of the other.[1] The poet can discreetly invite us to make a comparison, and here we detect his suggestion that there are important links betwteen the two genres and that it is part of courtly taste to realise this fact and its implications. An example is provided by the conjunction of two very different types of narrative from the first day of the *Canterbury Tales*, the *Knight's Tale* alongside the *Miller's Tale*, the romance next to the fabliau.[2] No sooner has the Knight concluded his romantic tale of the love of two knights for Emelye than the drunken Miller brushes the Host aside, insisting that he is to tell *his* tale now. By such dramatic means Chaucer has juxtaposed a love romance and an obscene fabliau, but by introducing a structural parallel between the two narratives[3] he highlights their differences. Like the Knight's tale, the Miller's is one of the rivalry of two lovers for a young woman, but whereas the courtly tale depicts love as idealised ardour, the characters in the fabliau are concerned with the immediate gratification of desire. How polemically the Miller's account of love is conceived is revealed by its link with the preceding tale. The Knight has just con-

---

[1] This is of course the tenor of Muscatine's stimulating book, *Chaucer*, whose value is only slightly reduced by its appearance in the same year as Nykrog's work and therefore its operation with Bédier's thesis that the fabliau is essentially a bourgeois genre.

[2] On the conjunction of these two tales on the first day see Frost, *RES* 25 (1949), 302ff., Stokoe, *UTQ* 21 (1951/52), 120ff., and Ruggiers, *Art*, pp. 54ff.

[3] Cf. Frost, *art. cit.*, p. 303.

cluded with a few words about his young couple on the conventional note of 'they lived happily ever after' (3101: *For now is Palamon in alle wele,/Lyvynge in blisse, in richesse, and in heele,/and Emelye hym loveth so tendrely,/And he hire serveth al so gentilly,/That nevere was ther no word hem bitwene/Of jalousie or any other teene*), but with a snort of disbelief the Miller rejects this sketch of married life and proceeds to show us the other side of the picture (3124: *By armes, and by blood and bones,/I kan a noble tale for the nones,/With which I wol now quite the Knyghtes tale*). The emphasis on *quite* is unmistakable (especially in contrast to the Host's use of the same verb a few lines earlier)[1] and tells us that the Miller is not simply keeping to the bargain of telling a tale, but is more specifically providing an answer to the Knight's view of things.[2] His fabliau is an external means, complementing the internal ironies of the *Knight's Tale*,[3] of placing that romance, and the ideal fiction of love it expresses, at a distance from the audience. By that I do not wish to suggest that the poet adopts the crudity of the Miller's position as his own, but nor can the poet be equated with the Knight. Instead, each tale and each teller makes a comment on the other, and if we smile at the Knight's touching ingenuousness, while warming to the nobility of his mind, it is one of the functions of the fabliau to reinforce this slight sense of distance from the Knight's world of values, which we can admire without living in it so wholeheartedly.

Even more telling are the cases where fabliau features are built into a romance, where they can serve the disruptive purpose of commenting on its values. It has been observed, for example, that in the crucial bedroom scenes of the third fitt the English romance *Sir Gawain* is moving through, or disturbingly close to, fabliau country.[4] When Gawain hears the lady of the castle steal into his bedroom, we are invited to react to the situation in a manner characteristic of the fabliau and to ask the obvious question as to the whereabouts of her husband. Such doubts are laid to rest when the lady assures Gawain that they will not be disturbed (1231: *My lorde and his ledeȝ ar on lenþe faren,/Oþer*

---

[1] 3118f.

[2] Cf. Stokoe, *UTQ* 21 (1951/52), 121f. and Ruggiers, *op. cit.*, p. 56.

[3] See Frost, *art. cit.*, p. 304 and Thurston, *Ambivalence, passim*.

[4] Burrow, *Reading*, p. 75.

burne₃ in her bedde, and my burde₃ als,/þe dor drawen and dit with a derf haspe). This stock situation of the fabliau (the inconvenient appearance of the husband) is discounted from the beginning, but for the poet to go out of his way to deny the possibility is rather like Gottfried protesting his ignorance as to whether Riwalin began his unprovoked campaign against Morgan out of *übermuot* or not (342f.): it immediately alerts us to the possibility which is supposedly being denied. In *Sir Gawain* this is made clear in the same passage, for if the fabliau contingency of the returning husband is excluded we can hardly be out of a fabliau situation when the wife feels it necessary to reassure Gawain on the absence of her husband and on the fact that she has safely bolted the bedroom door behind her.[1] Quite apart from other fabliau elements at this stage of the work,[2] this detail is enough to highlight the common ground between this romance situation and a stock motif of the fabliau. For a member of the audience whose view of love in the romance was one of highflown sentiment this reminder of how close the romance lay to the fabliau must have been unsettling.

Tristan *and the fabliau*

An example like this is open to the objection of being so isolated as to be unrepresentative, but there are other cases where fabliau elements play a central part in the romance. As an example I take the continental stage in the genesis of the *Tristan* story when, as Schoepperle has shown,[3] many elements from French courtly literature were added to the plot (e.g. Tristan's exploits undertaken for Isold's sake, the playing down of marriage in the figure of the second Isold), including a number of fabliau motifs. One reason for the adoption of such motifs is the essentially

---

[1] *Ibid.*, p. 76.

[2] Burrow, *op. cit.*, pp. 77f., observes that the only known parallel to the exchange of winnings motif occurs in the *Miles Gloriosus*, one of the so-called Latin fabliaux of the twelfth century, and that the idea of the exchange of winnings involves seeing the wife's favours as a commodity which can be won. This is a motif which recurs in the fabliau in the crude sense of a mercantile transaction (cf. Schirmer, *Versnovelle*, pp. 205f.), whereas the courtly romance or lyric will disguise it either in idealising terms (as in the idea of a knight gaining his lady's favours by chivalric exploits, attacked by Gottfried) or by rendering it innocuous (as in Reinmar's threat to steal a kiss from his lady, parodied by Walther).

[3] Schoepperle, *Tristan* I 112ff.

episodic nature of this continuation of the *Tristan* story.[1] The focus in this part of the story is on a sequence of scenes in which the lovers either are together at court and have to outwit the husband and his henchmen or are separated by the jealous husband and manage to come together briefly. The poets who worked on this part of the story would therefore be driven to derive assistance from a genre like the fabliau which provided readymade numerous episodes on the theme of outwitting a jealous husband. Yet if the fabliau sketches sexual love as an antithesis to the idealism of *fin' amors* (as a burlesque revelation of what lies behind such courtly pretensions), it also stands closest to the *Tristan* story in courtly literature, for here too we find love depicted (although not exclusively) as an elementary passion. When the fabliau operates with the comic figure of the suspicious, but outwitted husband, this has its counterpart in Marke, even though he is enriched (especially by Gottfried) with non-comic, tragic attributes. Similarly, in the fabliau's depiction of a cunning and amoral wife, using any means to achieve her ends, we recognise the outlines of Isold's character, and this can even extend to the fabliau picture of the wife's sexual insatiability, as with Gottfried's comment, however discreetly phrased, on Isold at the start of the garden scene (18 126ff.) and on her compulsion to seek immediate relief (18 139ff.). With her, as with Marke, this is no mere fabliau encounter (even though it has points in common), as is revealed by the heights reached in the departure-scene after the lovers have been discovered. As for Tristan, he shares with the fabliau lover the qualities of cunning and rashness in successfully emerging from every hazardous meeting with Isold, but although he constantly outwits the husband (as in the fabliau) this is not the thematic point of these scenes in *Tristan*, but rather the lovers' readiness to risk all for love.[2]

The three leading characters in the Tristan story therefore have essential similarities with three stock figures in the fabliau, but in addition there are many parallels in the themes and situa-

---

[1] On this see Fuchs, *Tristanroman* and Stein, *DVjs* 51 (1977), 344.

[2] In similar terms (and by no means confining himself to the *Tristan* story) Dronke, *RF* 85 (1973), 292ff., has stressed that the recurrence of identical motifs in the romance and the fabliau highlights the very different poetic ends to which this material is put.

tions described. The theme of the husband sharing his wife with another man[1] is common in the fabliau, where the situation can arise unwittingly (as in *Der Wirt*,[2] cf. the relationship between Marke and Tristan) or as a result of a rash promise given by the shortsighted husband (as in *Rittertreue*,[3] cf. Marke and Gandin). The triangular relationship constitutes the pattern of *Tristan* and of many fabliaux which base most of their comic complications on this relationship.[4] Similar complications exist in *Tristan*, not however to arouse mirth (although that may be an incidental part of our reaction to Marke's credulity), but to establish tension in the opposition between the lovers and society. In most such triangular relationships in the fabliau the central and dominating figure is the woman, never short of an idea for hoodwinking the husband or devising a way out of a dangerous situation. With Gottfried, too, Isold's wits are sharpened by the needs of her situation as a married mistress, as Gottfried makes clear in his commentary on her idea to substitute Brangæne on the wedding night (12 447ff.). But whereas the fabliau depicts the triangular relationship by focussing on the wife and husband, so that the lover is only the occasion for the conflict between these two, in *Tristan* the focus is changed to the lover and his mistress, whilst the husband is no more than an obstacle between them. The result of this change is to elevate love above the claims of marriage, whilst the fabliau is basically interested only in the comic tensions within marriage, so that the *Tristan* story makes use of fabliau themes for a new purpose, subordinating them to its depiction of the love between Tristan and Isold. *Huote* or surveillance is another theme shared by the fabliau and *Tristan*.[5] The fabliau treats it humorously (as in the poet's advice to the husband in *Der Wirt*)[6] as a means of emphasising the wife's cunning and the strength of her sexual needs, but whereas Gottfried is just as critical of *huote* (cf. 17871ff.) he deploys his argument as part of his stress on the voluntary nature of love, where nothing can be gained by compulsion (17917ff.), a truth to which even Marke ascends when he banishes the lovers from

---

[1] Cf. Schirmer, *Versnovelle*, pp. 210ff.
[2] Ed. Niewöhner, *Gesamtabenteuer*, pp. 125ff.
[3] Ed. Pfannmüller, *Novellen* II 5ff.   [4] Schirmer, *op. cit.*, pp. 208ff.
[5] *Ibid.*, pp. 204f.   [6] 249: *doch sol ir man/ir hüeten baz, ob er ez kan.*

the court (16566ff.). Once more, Gottfried subordinates criticism of *huote* (which he shares with the fabliau) to the depiction of a positive ideal of higher love.[1]

These two contributions from French courtly literature to the development of the *Tristan* story (aspects of love poetry from the second half of the twelfth century, together with elements from the fabliau, a genre developing in the vernacular in the same period) complement one another in *Tristan* as much as in the repertoire of courtly literature.[2] First, thematically: the fabliau elements in *Tristan* reverse the coin of idealised love, point out its human shortcomings by reminding us that even Tristan and Isold have a number of features in common with the most vulgar adulterers of the fabliau world. The presence of ideal elements alongside fabliau motifs results in a more complex picture of love than could be presented by either of these literary traditions in isolation. Secondly, in a structural sense: whereas the elements incorporated into *Tristan* from French love-poetry of the day idealise the relationship between the lovers (Tristan's exploits for the sake of Isold, Kaherdin and Camille, or Kaherdin and Gargeolain), the fabliau elements place the lovers more in the context of society, they no longer treat of Tristan and Isold in isolation, but in their relationship to Marke and his followers. Whilst the relationship between the lovers may be an ideal one, fully positive when taken by itself, it comes to be seen very differently in a wider social context, as a betrayal and an offence in the eyes of others, a conclusion which agrees with Nykrog's analysis, based on quite different presuppositions, of the fabliau *Un chivalier et sa dame et un clerk*.[3]

---

[1] Newstead (*RPh* 9 (1955/56), 269ff. and *Growth*, pp. 130f.) has shown that two episodes in the *Tristan* story have close fabliau parallels: the ambiguous oath by which Isold escapes punishment (for a parallel in German *Schwank* literature, *Der Pfaffe und die Ehebrecherin*, ed. Niewöhner, *Gesamtabenteuer*, pp. 47f., see Schirmer, *Versnovelle*, pp. 305f.) and the lovers' meeting beneath the tree. The Oriental provenance which Newstead has established for this fabliau material is no argument against its possible influence on the *Tristan* story, since Arabic tales of this type were already known in the West by the early twelfth century, as in the *Disciplina clericalis* (cf. Tiemann, *RF* 72 (1960), 417ff.). Thomas himself betrays some knowledge of this work (cf. the edition of Wind, pp. 12 and 63, fn. to v. 760, and also Jonin, *Personnages*, p. 380).

[2] Nykrog, *Fabliaux*, pp. 235ff.

[3] *Ibid.*, pp. 68f., especially p. 69: 'Le triangle courtois a ainsi deux visages, l'un pénible, l'autre sublime, et du point de vue littéraire il y a entre eux une différ-

What is true of *Tristan* could be illustrated from other courtly works which share motifs with the fabliau. The outwitted husband is no stranger to courtly literature, where the scorn in which he is held may not be tempered (as with Gottfried) by a realisation of the tragedy of his situation (cf. the burlesque treatment of marital infidelity in the *Mantel* of Heinrich von dem Türlin or in his *Crône*).[1] How this situation can be treated humorously even by a poet who thinks as highly of marriage as Wolfram is shown by his presentation of the episode in which Clinschor, as a punishment for an adulterous adventure, is treated as drastically as Abélard, for after the account of his fate Gawan's reaction is described (657,10: *des wart aldâ gelachet/von Gâwâne sêre*).[2] This episode makes it clear how a model of courtesy may react in a fabliau manner to this kind of situation; it suggests that the situation could be regarded in two distinct ways both of which are part of courtly literature. Even the dawnsong, that genre of courtly literature which acted as a safety-valve for the idealising demands imposed by the love convention, can also occur in the fabliau, where it can be discreetly misapplied for parodic purposes.[3] Chaucer follows the fabliau in this when, in *Troilus and Criseyde*, he concludes the lyrical intensity of the night of love in Book III with a deflating change of tone, for Troilus takes his leave in terms which recall, but tacitly question, this courtly situation, and we are told (III 1534: *Retorned to his real paleys soone,/He softe into his bed gan for to slynke,/To slepe longe, as he was wont to doone*).[4] These lines measure the ideal against the restrictions of reality: whereas the dawnsong concludes on a note of lover's ardour undiminished, here we are afforded an anticlimactic glimpse of a world in which the flesh has its limitations. Yet this parody of the dawnsong is no prerogative of the fabliau. We find it in the courtly lyric, with Steinmar who confronts the fictional situation with reality by asking whether any lover would be ready

ence de *style*: le conte romantique place la femme et l'amant au premier plan, en repoussant le mari à l'arrière-plan comme une menace vague; le conte comique insiste sur les relations entre le mari et la femme, l'amant étant souvent réduit à l'état d'ombre ou de 'ressort' pur.'

[1] *Der Mantel* 569ff., *Diu Crône* 918ff. and 2299off.
[2] Cf. Schirmer, *Versnovelle*, p. 209.
[3] *Ibid.*, pp. 212ff.
[4] Cf. Kaske, *Aube*, pp. 167ff. (especially p. 175).

to trust his fate to a watchman who had betrayed his lord by letting him in,[1] and already with Wolfram who devotes a dawn-song to the theme of married love (5,34ff.)[2] and reminds us of the potentially corruptive situation of a knight demeaning himself to rely on such an accomplice.[3]

The reality against which the courtly ideal is measured in such examples not merely reminds us of human weaknesses which endanger that ideal, it also affords an opportunity for the type of obscenity which we readily associate with the fabliau, but are less happy to detect in the romance.[4] Yet even the fabliau gener-ally prefers the type of circumlocution which we find in the romance to the outright obscenity,[5] whilst on the other hand Wolfram can be very direct, as in his descriptions of the wedding-night of Parzival and Condwiramurs, of what Gahmuret would have done if it had been he, rather than his inexperienced son, who met the charming Jeschute, and of the erotic play between Gawan and Antikonie.[6] Even this directness has not protected Wolfram from some of his modern interpreters. What he says of Gawan on his wedding-night seems clear enough (643,28: *er vant die rehten hirzwurz/ . . ./Diu wurz was bî dem blanken brûn*), but this has not prevented one scholar from seeing the passage as a symbolic reference to Christ and the Virgin,[7] whereas Wolfram's purposes I take to be much more human and certainly less virginal.

In returning in conclusion to the theoretical objection which was our starting-point (have we any right to expect an ironic questioning of the ennobling force of love in courtly literature?) we find ourselves facing the question as to where, in any assess-ment of parody, the greater weight of the irony is to fall: on the characters and situations of the parodic work or on the characters

---

[1] Ed. Bartsch, *Minnesänger*, p. 176 (XIX 5, 1ff.).

[2] Borck, *Untersuchungen*, p. 55 (quoted by Wapnewski, *Wächterfigur*, p. 81).

[3] Wapnewski, *Wächterfigur*, pp. 87, 88, 89, and *Lyrik*, pp. 245 ff. This view has now been called into question by Johnson, *Sîne klâwen*, pp. 314ff.

[4] On obscenity in the fabliau see Nykrog, *Fabliaux*, pp. 208ff., in the *Schwank* Schirmer, *Versnovelle*, pp. 216ff., and in medieval literature at large Stempel, *Obszönität*, pp. 187ff.

[5] Nykrog, *op. cit.*, p. 209 and Schirmer, *op. cit.*, p. 217.

[6] *Parzival* 193, 12f.; 139,15ff.; 407,1ff. (cf. Schirmer, *op. cit.*, p. 218).

[7] See Knight Bostock, *MLR* 52 (1957), 235ff. Against this interpretation see Eis, *Priamel*, pp. 181ff. and Bumke, *Wolfram*, pp. 310f. (with a reference to Krogmann, *ZfdPh* 67 (1942), 7ff.).

and situations of the work parodied? In many cases there can be little doubt but that most of the ironic weight falls on the persons and events of the foreground story, on the grotesque attempts of peasants and priests in fabliaux or of peasants in Neidhart's poetry[1] to ape courtly ways. Their attempt to live up to courtly gallantry beyond their emotional grasp and social standing involves them in such ludicrous folly that they stand out as the objects of the poet's scorn. It is the non-courtly world which is here ironised, whilst the courtly world and its values remain unaffected. Yet the obviousness of this particular target should not blind us to the possibility that the poet may alternatively direct his irony at the courtly world itself. That courtly literature was capable of self-irony is clear from the differentiated views on love and the parodies of rival conceptions which it embraces. When Chrétien parodies Provençal doctrine or Gottfried attacks the view of love put forward in the Arthurian romance, each is criticising a rival whose views are part of courtly literature. The parody remains within the courtly world as an internal debate, however rancorous it may sometimes become.

A similar possibility exists with regard to the contrast between the romance and the fabliau, for the deflationary criticism implicit in the latter genre may also be directed at courtly society and not simply at those outsiders whose attempts to enter the charmed circle make them ridiculous. Nykrog, who places greater weight on the criticism of the non-courtly world,[2] sees the irony in the discrepancy between an ideal and those who cannot live up to it, but theoretically this is just as much applicable to members of courtly society who fall short of their own ideal as to those who do not belong to this society. In this connection I attach great importance to Gaier's analysis of Neidhart's satirical and ironic devices, in which he argues that the poet's criticism, whilst also directed at the peasants' foolish aping of a courtliness beyond their grasp, is fundamentally aimed at a courtly society endangered not so much by attacks from without as by its own internal corruption.[3] Bédier was one of the first to see that in the fabliaux

---

[1] On this see Günther, *Minneparodie* and Gaier, *Satire*, pp. 7ff.
[2] Nykrog, *op. cit.*, pp. 95 and 104.
[3] Gaier, *op. cit.*, pp. 65ff., 86ff. and 91.

powerful barons are not immune to the marital misfortunes of
lesser mortals and that, by being placed in such belittling situations, these members of the courtly world are themselves made
foolish.[1] Since this type of criticism only concerns the individuals
who fail to live up to courtly standards it still leaves the courtly
ideal unaffected,[2] just as the various parodies of this or that type
of love we have considered do not amount to a rejection of all
secular love as such (this is where we differed from Robertson),
but merely to a repudiation of a rival view in favour of the poet's
own. The result is that the frontiers of the courtly ideal may be
more narrowly defined, not that its secular ground is abandoned
altogether.

The implications of irony grow more critical, however, when
it is applied to the inadequacies of courtly life itself, although
even here we must be careful not to see the criticism as more
radical than it really is. When Chaucer parodies the romantic
emotionalism of Troilus at his moment of bliss or when he has
him look down from heaven on the petty doings of this world[3]
he is not so much debasing the lover's concerns as putting them
in their place, reminding us of the existence of a higher love and
of realistic considerations which the romantic ignores. When
Hartmann praises the divine love which draws him overseas on
a crusade he turns his back on the courtly pretensions of the
minnesinger, but avoids any absolute rejection of their concerns[4]
and leaves it open whether his attitude may not be dictated by the
pressing, but restricted needs of this particular crusade and

---

1 Bédier, *Fabliaux*, p. 327, fn. 2.
2 This possibility of ironic self-criticism within courtly literature itself makes me
doubtful of Jackson's suggestion (*PhQ* 31 (1952), 159) that because the pastourelle
commonly depicts the knight in an unfavourable light this genre cannot have been
cultivated in courtly circles. When he argues that it was probably written by or
under the influence of clerics, this still does not exclude the likelihood of the
pastourelle as a courtly genre, because of the literary function of clerics at so many
French courts (see above, p. 96, fn. 1 and p. 120, fn. 3).
3 See Everett, *Essays*, pp. 134ff., Bethurum, *PMLA* 74 (1959), 516ff. and Donaldson,
Speaking, pp. 84ff.
4 Cf. *MF* 218,3: *Sich rüemet* manger (not 'everyone'), 218,15: ...*dazs* ir eteslîchen
bæte (not 'all of them'), 218,21: ofte *misselingen* and 218,26: *verliesen* under wîlen
wânes vil (not 'always'). It is difficult to imagine all these passages as understatements, so that the poet's question (218,14: *wâ sint diu werc?*) is directed only to
those *minnesinger* from whom he has heard nothing but words, not to those who
(like Hausen) have matched words with deeds by going on a crusade.

whether, on its conclusion, he might not be accessible to secular *minne* again. Beyond these cases there remains a hard core of examples where the courtly ideal is not simply put in its place, but shown up as deficient or misleading, as when Andreas Capellanus finally rejects the love whose rules he has himself codified, revealing this love as a game whose artificial character does not escape him.[1] How characteristic of courtly literature this last category is could only be ascertained by a complete survey which this chapter cannot claim to be, but I suspect that its incidence is fairly restricted and that irony, when used of love in medieval literature, is like the ironisation of chivalry in that it refines and differentiates what it is applied to, instead of rejecting it out of hand.

[1] Nykrog, *op. cit.*, p. 205.

5

IRONY AND NARRATIVE
TECHNIQUE

In the last two chapters we have been concerned with two major
themes of the romance, but now we must consider the way in
which the narrative is organised to bring out any ironic implications of these themes. Of the countless possibilities which this
opens up[1] I shall concentrate on one central problem: the aesthetic
organisation of time.[2] This has the advantage that it has been
treated by Günther Müller and his school[3] and that it lies close
to a problem which recurs in medieval rhetoric and poetics: the
distinction between *ordo naturalis* (events are presented in the
chronological sequence of their happening) and *ordo artificialis*
(having begun in the middle or at the end, the poet narrates
subsequently what came before).[4]

Although most theoreticians distinguish between these two
orders, Bernard of Utrecht concedes the possibility of combining
them in the same work.[5] There is also evidence to suggest
that the natural order was associated with the veracity of
religious writings and the artificial order with the fictional nature
of works of art.[6] Benson has shown that even a conventional

---

[1] A stylistics of irony, whether as a whole or broken down according to genres,
periods or authors, is an urgent desideratum. The only work like this known to
me is de Novais Paiva, *Contribuição*, who draws most of her examples from the
works of Eça de Queirós.

[2] See Lämmert, *Bauformen*, who opens his inquiry with a section devoted to 'der
sukzessive Aufbau des Erzählwerks'.

[3] See Müller, *Bedeutung*; *Erzählzeit*; *DVjs* 24 (1950), 1ff. Müller's method has been
applied to medieval German literature by Luxenburger, *Zeitgestaltung*, and Schorn,
Zeit. See also Grisebach, *Zeitbegriff*, and Thomsen, *Darstellung*.
See especially Faral, *Arts*, pp. 55ff. and Brinkmann, *Wesen*, pp. 44f.
Faral, *op. cit.*, p. 57: [ordo] *utrum sit scilicet artificiosus vel naturalis vel commixtus sit.*

[6] Cf. the tantalisingly brief comment by Ohly, *ZfdA* 91 (1961), 13 and the expansion
of this idea by Strunk, *Kunst*, pp. 154ff.

romance,[1] following the adventures of its hero in their temporal sequence, cannot avoid the artificial order whenever an antagonist is introduced. From the point of view of the hero (and of the audience accompanying him) this opponent is generally a stranger, entering the story from outside and *in medias res*, whose motives and prehistory have to be recapitulated at a later stage. In practice, all the romances we shall discuss contain examples of the artificial order.

This may explain why all of Chrétien's works (with the exception of *Cligès*, which follows a genealogical pattern in devoting an earlier part to the hero's parents) begin according to the artificial order, plunging into the midst of events and subsequently giving what account of the prehistory may be necessary.[2] So strong is Chrétien's need for this artificial order that he employs it even in *Perceval* (a romance whose theme of the hero's slow progress might have suggested a straightforward biographical pattern) by giving an account of the prehistory only subsequently in the words of Perceval's mother (407ff.).[3] The fact that Wolfram alters this and, by adopting a genealogical pattern for his first two books, gives the events of the prehistory in the natural order rejected by Chrétien,[4] like the presence of a prehistory in *Tristan* devoted to an earlier generation, cannot be used as an argument that these other romances abandon the artificial order altogether, for there are many other instances where they make use of it. Instead, their deviation from Chrétien implies that they are ready to make use of both orders and that, particularly in the case of Wolfram, their poetic purpose may only partially agree with Chrétien's.

With the artificial order we may expect to find passages where the narrative switches from one time-sequence to another. I

---

[1] Benson, *Art*, pp. 170f. Benson is talking of *Sir Gawain and the Green Knight*, which is far from being a conventional romance, but what he describes is true of any romance in which the hero encounters an adventure.

[2] Kellermann, *Aufbaustil*, p. 43, who rightly stresses (fn. 1) the need to determine whether Chrétien is here dependent on Virgil. Ziltener, *Chrétien*, pp. 15ff., discusses this possibility, but is too ready to solve the problem in terms of a direct imitation. On the shortcomings of Ziltener's work see Frappier, *RPh* 13 (1959), 50ff.

[3] We shall see below (pp. 149f.) that Chrétien's overriding concern in *Perceval* was quite different.

[4] See especially Bertau, *Literatur*, pp. 778ff.

propose to consider them under three temporal headings: the present (we switch from one strand of action to a simultaneous one), the future (an anticipation of things to come) and the past (events of the past are shown up in a new light because of what has since come about). My argument will be that whilst such passages are not always necessarily ironic, they are potentially so and that medieval poets frequently made use of such chronological switches in order to suggest an ironic reading without having to point it out in so many words.

Interlace technique

To suggest that medieval narrative can switch repeatedly from the narrative present to a simultaneous point in another strand in the plot is another way of describing the technique of interlace, first pointed out in its labyrinthine complexity by Lot in the prose *Lancelot* and then by Frappier and Vinaver.[1] They rightly see that the technique was brought to perfection only in the thirteenth century (although not without its precedents in the twelfth) and that its mode of operation was suggestive rather than explicit ('It consisted less in explaining the action in so many words than in forging significant and tangible links between originally independent episodes; it aimed at establishing, or at least suggesting, relationships between hitherto unrelated themes').[2] What this technique means is that one strand of the narrative can be abandoned at one point in favour of another, which can then be forsaken for another. The result is a narrative complexity which earlier scholarship saw as a bewildering maze, but which we now recognise as a coherent pattern from which no one detail could be removed without disturbing the rest.[3] How apposite this technique was to the needs of later romance-writers has been stressed by Lewis.[4] When the various narrative strands are concerned with this or that knightly quest (as we should expect from an Arthurian romance) the fact that the adventure which we are following is liable at any moment to be superseded by another

---

[1] See Lot, *Étude*, pp. 17ff.; Frappier, *Étude*, pp. 347ff; Vinaver, *Form, passim* and *Rise*, pp. 68ff.

[2] Vinaver, *Rise*, p. 68.   [3] Lot, *op. cit.*, p. 28; Vinaver, *Rise*, pp. 71f.

[4] In *Major British Writers* (ed. Harrison) I 98. Quoted by Vinaver, *Rise*, p. 76.

persuades us that in this vast forest (that symbol of uncertain fate in which these adventures generally are set)[1] this perpetual dovetailing of adventure into adventure goes on into seeming infinity, that life really is, as these romance-writers sought to show, one long chivalric adventure.

Interlace on this scale and of this complexity is absent from the romance before the thirteenth century, but the early romance none the less has examples of its simpler employment whenever the narrative follows two separate strands for a time, as in the more obvious cases of Chrétien's *Lancelot* (Lancelot and Gauvain) and *Perceval* (Perceval and Gauvain). Something similar, yet not strictly interlace, is also to be found in *Yvain*. Here the adventures which dovetail into one another[2] differ in being held together by the one hero who performs them, whereas elsewhere the switch to another narrative strand means a switch to another knight.[3] Whether this technique in the courtly romance owes anything to the similar intermeshing of adventures in the Hellenistic love-romance still remains to be established, despite the growing probability that the Hellenistic romance influenced the medieval genre.[4] Yet the fact that interlace in the earlier romance is much less complex is irrelevant to our problem if it can be shown that Chrétien and others were ready to use it for an ironic purpose.

This function of interlace, effecting unexpected or disconcerting conjunctions, can certainly be found in the romance. In Thomas's *Tristan* the words with which he introduces a new strand devoted to Ysolt after the lovers' separation (701: *Ysolt en sa chambre suspire/Pur Tristran qu'ele tant desire;/Ne puet en sun cuer el penser/Fors ço sul que Tristran amer*) derive their ironic force from

---

[1] On this see Stauffer, *Wald*.

[2] On the dovetailing of adventures in this work see Frappier, *Yvain*, pp. 63ff., who also points out that this technique first makes its tentative appearance with Chrétien in the relationship between the white stag and sparrowhawk adventures in his *Erec*.

[3] This has been well observed by Ruberg, *Raum*, p. 133, fn. 11.

[4] See Kellermann, *Aufbaustil*, pp. 67f. On the Hellenistic romance at large see Perry, *Romances*, on its possible connection with the medieval romance Ruh, *Epik*, pp. 54f., and with the *Tristan* story in particular Schwander, *Fortleben*. To look for possible antecedents here (i.e., in another narrative genre, whose influence on the medieval romance is most likely) certainly seems more promising than to suggest the possible influence of Ovid's *Metamorphoses* (cf. Vinaver, *Rise*, p. 76).

the contrast with what they replace, since the preceding strand has dealt with Tristan's unworthy doubts about her love for him and his consequent marriage with the second Ysolt.[1] In *Cligès* Chrétien depicts the infatuation of Alexander for Soredamors, giving him a long lover's complaint and making it clear that he has no idea whether his feelings are reciprocated. This ignorance of the lover is then ironised by the words with which the narrator switches to a description of Soredamors's anguish (865: *Granz est la conplainte Alixandre,/Mes cele ne rest mie mandre/Que la dameisele demainne*), an irony of the mutual ignorance of lovers which is also exploited by Gottfried in the case of Riwalin and Blanscheflur.[2] The fortunes of war can bring about confusion as great as those of love, as when Chrétien switches from one scene to another with the comment (2113: *Li Greu defors grant dolor mainnent,/Et cil dedanz formant se painnent/Comant il lor facent savoir/Don grant joie porront avoir*), thereby stressing the futility of the Greeks' lamentations with which the preceding strand had been abandoned.

A telling example occurs in Chrétien's *Lancelot* when the poet switches to the strand dealing with Meleagant, demanding whether Lancelot has been seen (6734: *Puis li requiert de Lancelot,/li mauvés traïtres provez/se puis fu veüz ne trovez*). There is irony present in this situation, since we know, as Gauvain does not, that Meleagant has made a captive of Lancelot and therefore has no need to ask this question (which is why the poet adds, 6737: *ausi con s'il n'en seüst rien*). But there is also an irony in the connection between this opening of a new strand and the close of the preceding one, for at the end of this we have been informed that Lancelot has made good his escape. Although he cannot know it, Meleagant has every reason to ask after his foe's whereabouts (which is why Chrétien now adds further, 6738: *nel feisoit il, nel sot pas bien,/mes il le cuidoit bien savoir*). The dramatic irony of Meleagant, cheated by events just when he thinks himself their

---

[1] 133ff.

[2] In his debate with himself Riwalin wonders whether his feelings for Blanscheflur are returned by her (877ff.), but when the narrative switches to consider what is going on in her mind we are immediately alerted to the futility of his doubts and fears (957: *Ouch vergie sin senelich geschiht/die seneden Blanschefliure niht:/diu was ouch mit dem selben schaden/durch in als er durch si beladen*).

master, is strengthened by the placing of this passage at the point of interlace between two separate strands.[1]

For the German romance I must content myself with examples from Wolfram and Gottfried. At the end of Book VIII in *Parzival* we are shown Gawan, having sworn to search for the Grail, setting out on that quest (432,29: *nâch dem grâle im sicherheit gebôt:/er reit al ein gein wunders nôt*). Accordingly, when we next revert to the Gawan strand, we are given a brief recapitulation of his adventures since setting out (504, 1ff.) and are reminded that both Vergulaht and he were in search of the Grail (503, 21ff.). Both these passages are placed at points of interlace (where we abandon and then come back to the Gawan plot). Between them they establish continuity in his adventures over the period when he has been lost to view, but their ironic force again lies in their placing, for they mark out the period of time in which the narrative reverts to Parzival (Book IX) and shows *him* in the Grail-territory to which Gawan vainly seeks access. These passages ultimately stress the futility of Gawan's attempts to reach a sphere which is reserved for Parzival alone.

As a revealing example from Gottfried's work I take the apparently unemphatic passage with which he tell us of the lovers' early morning walk in the surroundings of the love-grotto (17347: *Des selben morgens was Tristan/und sin gespil geslichen dan/ bihanden gevangen/und kamen hin gegangen/vil vruo und in dem touve/ uf die gebluoten ouwe*...). These lines are an example at once of interlace (they take us back to the lovers after we have been following the strand of Marke's hunt and of his huntsman following tracks which lead him to the surroundings of the grotto) and also of the artificial order (in factual time the lovers' walk had come before the huntsman's arrival on the scene, so that the tracks he has followed merge into the footprints left by them in the dew).[2] By reversing the natural order (and signalling it by his interlace comment *Des selben morgens*) Gottfried has given ironic force to his lyrical description of the lovers in their paradise-like surroundings. We now know (as they do not, and as we should not have known if the poet had followed the natural order) that this idyll

---

[1] On the general implications of this technique in *Lancelot* see Kelly, *Sens*, pp. 157ff.
[2] On this detail see Rathofer, *ZfdA* 95 (1966), 27ff.

is threatened and that the world of the court is beginning to move in on the lovers once again.[1]

Two examples may suffice for the English romance. In *Troilus and Criseyde* the narrative forks after Criseyde has departed from Troy and there is a consequent contrast between Troilus's hopes for her return and what we are shown of her in the Greek camp. In describing the crucial scene with Diomede as taking place on the tenth day (V 842), whereas Boccaccio had timed it on the fourth, Chaucer has heightened the ironic tension between the two strands of the action by synchronising the seduction with the eager waiting of Troilus, convinced that Criseyde will return on this day.[2] In the light of what we have learnt from the Diomede scene we can judge the futility of Troilus's hopes when the narrative returns to him (V 1100: *This Troilus, as I byfore have told,/ Thus driveth forth, as well as he hath myght./But often was his herte hoot and cold,/And namely that ilke nynthe nyght,/Which on the morwe she hadde hym bihight/To come ayeyn*). We also know how to judge Troilus's optimism when he convinces himself that he sees Criseyde approaching in the distance (V 1156ff.) and are in fact independent of the brutal contrast of Pandarus's realism[3] in assessing the truth of the situation.

Sir Gawain and the Green Knight can be said to be constructed according to an interlace design, for its Chinese-box structure (the adventure of the Green Knight's challenge ultimately gives way to Gawain's testing at the castle) is nothing other than large-scale interlace, since the first adventure occupies the first and fourth parts of the poem, whilst the temptation episode falls in the second and third parts. But this effect is carried further still, for the temptation episode is itself built according to an interlace pattern: the temptation is divided into three scenes (three bedroom encounters on subsequent mornings), inserted into the simultaneous scenes of the lord's hunting on these three days. Each day therefore starts with the lord's departure for the hunt and ends with his return, but inserted into this each day is a scene in which the narrator brings us back to the castle and shows us

---

[1] What results from Gottfried's employment of the artificial order and of interlace at this point has been well discussed by Gruenter, *Bauformen*, pp. 40ff.
[2] See the note on V 842 on p. 545 of Root's edition.
[3] Cf. Muscatine, *Chaucer*, pp. 146f.

what is happening in Gawain's bedroom in the meanwhile, pin-pointing his change-over on each occasion (moving from the hunt to the castle and then back again) with an interlace formula.[1] This is interlace technique of a high degree of artistry, but so far the two strands seem thematically too remote from one another (hunting and an attempted seduction) for their relationship to be ironic. We approach this possibility, however, once we recall the common medieval use of hunting as a metaphor for love[2] and realise, following Savage,[3] that the lady is as intent on her prey in the bedroom as the lord on his in the woodland, that the type of animal hunted each day parallels Gawain's reaction to the lady's approaches each day[4] and that Gawain is as much ensnared by his own guile on the third day as the fox is in the forest.[5] It is ironic that Gawain, like the fox, is brought low by his resorting to the trickery which was to save him. It is even more ironic that we are asked to judge the behaviour of a model of courtesy in the light of a beast of vermin, a creature of duplicity. It is this irony which the poet expresses not by any explicit remark, but by the tacit interweaving of these two strands by interlace.[6]

Narrator's anticipations

From a time-switch in the present (from one strand of action to a simultaneous one) we pass to a switch from the present to the future, to those anticipations of future events which disrupt the even chronological flow of narrative by bringing in another dimension. As a means of organising the time-scheme such anticipations, affording a view of the future from the limited perspective of the present, occur in most narratives, but in the

[1] These chronological switches are 1178f. and 1319f. for the first day, 1468–70 and 1560f. for the second, 1729–32 and 1893f. for the third.

[2] See Spearing, *Gawain-poet*, pp. 215f., Thiébaux, *Stag*, pp. 89ff. and also below, pp. 210f.   [3] *JEGP* 27 (1928), 1ff.

[4] This is the persuasive point of Savage's article. Spearing is not convinced (*op. cit.*, pp. 216f.), but still concedes the importance of the parallel between the two strands (a hunt to the death is going on both in the castle and in the forest), registers a close convergence of the two hunts on the third day in particular, and draws attention to the significant use of the perfect tense in v. 1895.

[5] Savage, *art. cit.*, pp. 5f.

[6] The irony which can occur in medieval interlace does not go as far as the irony in Flaubert's famous scene at the Comices Agricoles in *Madame Bovary* (on this see Turnell, *Novel*, pp. 270ff.) but it stands in the same tradition of stylistic irony.

particular form of the 'epische Vorausdeutung' they have come in for much discussion, especially with regard to the *Nibelungenlied*.[1] We need not confine ourselves to this type of formula, for any anticipation of future events represents a momentary abandonment of a continuous temporal narrative just as much as the use of interlace technique to switch from one strand to another.[2] Taking anticipation of the future in this wider sense, we may ask whether it is employed in the romance as a way of ironising the ignorance of actors in the narrative present by giving information to the audience which is withheld from them. If this can be answered positively, this technique would contribute as much to the establishment of dramatic irony as the interlace technique. Both afford the audience a wider view of things than is available to the restricted vision of actors in the story, whether by a glimpse of the future or by a revelation of what is happening elsewhere at the same time.

To state the problem this way suggests one restriction in assessing the ironic implications of this technique. Although in a genre such as the legend a prophecy may convey an objectively valid view of the future,[3] in a secular narrative such as the romance we have to distinguish between the narrator's (theoretical)[4] omniscience and the actors' ignorance of the future.[5] Irony can only be entertained as a possibility when the future is anticipated in a remark by the narrator from his unique vantage-point, not in an utterance made within the story itself, whose protagonists can at the best express hopes for the future and, if they claim knowledge of the future, commonly invite an ironic reversal as a punishment for their hubris. In this sense of a distinction

---

[1] On this technique at large see Gerz, *Rolle*; Burger, *Vorausdeutung*, pp. 125ff.; Reiffenstein, *Erzählervorausdeutung*, pp. 551ff. (see also Lämmert, *Bauformen*, pp. 139ff.). On its use in the *Nibelungenlied* see in particular Bonjour, *EG* 7 (1952), 241ff.; Beyschlag, *PBB* 76 (1954), 38ff.; Wachinger, *Studien*.

[2] Reiffenstein's reproach to Burger (*Erzählervorausdeutung*, p. 554, fn. 6) for unhelpfully extending the scope of the 'epische Vorausdeutung' need not affect us, for we are concerned with any type of anticipation of future events in the narrative. In this the 'epische Vorausdeutung' plays an important, but not unique rôle.

[3] Burger, *art. cit.*, p. 126.

[4] The use of a word like 'theoretical' is necessary because the narrator can for tactical reasons from time to time disclaim knowledge of events.

[5] This vital distinction (of greater importance than Lämmert's between 'zukunftsgewisse' and 'zukunftsungewisse' anticipations) is made by Wachinger, *op. cit.*, pp. 5f.

between what the narrator knows (and allows us to know with him) and what the actors fondly think they know irony has indeed been established in the use of this formula in the *Nibelungenlied*. Burger, discussing the difference between this epic and the heroic lay, speaks of a 'fast ironisch zu nennende Distanz des Erzählers von der dargestellten Welt'[1] and Wachinger refers more than once to the irony resulting from the difference in perspective between the actors and the narrator.[2] Can the same be said of anticipatory remarks in the courtly romance?

The irony of arrogant brutality assuming that it is in control of the situation is exploited in Hartmann's *Erec*, but he can bring this home to us by means of a narrator's observation of what the future really has in store. When Erec approaches the second band of robber-knights, we are shown how, anticipating an easy victory, they divide up the spoils beforehand (3329ff.), but then we are told by the narrator how premature this was (3347: *ouch vluren si ir liezen*). This is a remark by an omniscient narrator, aware of the future, as the robbers are not and Erec even less so, for he is not aware of what they are planning (3348: *Êrecke was diu rede unkunt*) or even of their existence, since he has to be warned of this by Enite (3379ff.). The narrator allows us to share his vantage-point, but if we look down from it on the ignorance of the actors it is at the arrogance of the robbers that this irony is directed.[3] The same is true of the plans of Count Oringles to to marry Enite by force, for the narrator interposes three remarks in quick succession which put this intention in its proper perspective (6351: *got hete den gewalt und er den wân*; 6355: *er gedâhte, des lîhte niht geschach,/mit ir vil guote naht hân*; 6357: *ichn ruochte, trüge in sîn wân*). The first of these remarks implies that the narrator has an insight into God's plans for the future,[4] so that

---

[1] *Art. cit.*, p. 139. Burger gives us no idea of what his reservations, lurking in the word 'fast', may be.　　　　[2] *Op. cit.*, pp. 24ff.

[3] The irony of this passage is enhanced by the way in which one of the robbers goes so far as to claim justice for himself in dividing up the spoils (3331: *man sol si im nemen, daz ist reht*; 3336: *dô sprâchen si alle gelîche,/si würde im billîche*). Where justice in fact lies is made quite clear by the narrator's assessment (3343: *daz was doch ungenædeclich,/wan ez diente von rehte/Êrecke dem guoten knehte*), by his anticipation of the future and by the course which events now take.

[4] Here again we encounter an ironic contrast between the narrator's view of things and what an actor thinks to be the truth. The suggestion that God has a hand in

the use of irony at this offender's expense delineates an ethical world-order in which God is in full control. Having made this clear with this first anticipation of the future, the narrator can now afford to play with the situation by using understatement where our knowledge renders it inapposite. In v. 6355 *lîhte* falls laughably short of what we now grasp of God's plans, whilst in v. 6357 the use of a conditional clause and hypothetical subjunctive is again not called for after the certainty of v. 6351.[1]

How careful we must be in distinguishing narrator's prophecies from those of actors within the story is brought out when Erec arrives at Brandigan, for the narrator warns us of what is to come (8059: *ze vreise sînem lîbe*) and then inserts fully fourteen prophecies by the inhabitants of what they see as Erec's approaching death.[2] Such emphasis apparently gives weight to the dangers of this climactic adventure, but is ultimately undermined by Erec's victory giving the lie to all these prophecies. Only the narrator (who, we now see, warned us only of mortal danger, not of certain death) emerges with credit as reliable. Erec's disdain for such old wives' superstition, conveyed to us by the narrator (8123: *deheines swachen gelouben er phlac./er enwolde der wîbe liezen/ engelten noch geniezen./swaz im getroumen mahte,/dar ûf enhete er dehein ahte./ern was dehein wetersorgære*), expresses, I suspect, something of Hartmann's reservations about the use of dreams and prophecies in the heroic epic as if they were valid anticipations of the future.[3]

---

things at this stage (6351) takes up the point made when Count Oringles was first introduced, namely that God had sent him to prevent Enite from committing suicide (6117: *den got dar gesande*; 6123: *den hâte got dar zuo erkorn/daz er si solde bewarn*), but contrasts ironically with Oringles's conviction that God has sent him to Enite so that he may marry her, even against her will (6251: *mich wæne in sæliger zît/ze iu got her gesendet hât*). The narrator makes it clear that God certainly stands behind events, but also that He is operating in a way quite different from what Oringles imagines. In short: *got hete den gewalt und er den wân*.

[1] A similar anticipation that events will give the lie to hopes is made by Kalogreant (*Iwein* 690: *jâ wând ich vreude ân ungemach/unangestlîchen iemer hân:/seht, dô trouc mich mîn wân*). This example only appears to be voiced by an actor within the story (and therefore not necessarily as a reliable forecast), since in reality Kalogreant is here both the protagonist and the narrator of events which, lying now in the distant past, he can survey as a whole from his present vantage-point.

[2] Details are given by Endres, *Studien*, pp. 52f.

[3] Again we have to distinguish between prophetic dreams which, occurring in a religious epic like the *Rolandslied*, are felt to be objectively true (on this aspect of the *Chanson de Roland* see Steinmeyer, *Untersuchungen*) and the portents which are

Wolfram uses anticipatory formulas to show up the futility of human wishes. Herzeloyde's plan to keep Parzival from chivalry (117,22ff.) is not merely ironised as futile at the moment she announces it (117,29: *Der site fuor angestlîche vart*), we are even allowed to see its irrelevance beforehand, first during her pregnancy (109,10: *wan diu truoc in ir lîbe/der aller ritter bluome wirt*) and then after her son's birth, where the plan to keep him from chivalry (112,19f.) clashes with what the narrator tells us of his chivalric future (112,28: *er wart mit swerten sît ein smit*). The power of God or of an ethical world-order may not be in the background here, as with Hartmann; instead it is the force of *art*, the chivalric inclinations passed on from Gahmuret to his son, which proves superior to human planning. It can also be the uncontrollable fortunes of war that scotch all plans, as when we are told in advance that the very man to urge an attack is to fall in that combat (205,9: *den rât gap Galogandres,/der herzoge von Gippones:/ der brâht die burgære in nôt,/er holt' och an ir letze den tôt*) or it can be the organisation of the work around Parzival's slow progress to maturity which allows the narrator to foretell a time when his hero will regret what he has just done (161,7: *sît dô er sich baz versan,/ungern het erz dô getân*).[1] Elsewhere, as we have seen with the interlace formula concerning Gawan's forthcoming adventures at the end of Book VIII (432,30: *er reit al ein gein wunders nôt*), the irony lies in the false impression we are allowed to gain. Since this remark follows a line dealing with Gawan's quest for the Grail, we are tempted to read the forecast as referring to Grail adventures like those encountered by Parzival. This is not the case, as we learn later, yet the narrator's forecast remains a truthful one, but only if we separate it from its apparent connection with the Grail-world.

If anticipations of the future in Gottfried's *Tristan*, like those in the *Nibelungenlied*, are more commonly concerned with the

to be found in a secular work like the *Nibelungenlied* (on these see Wachinger, *op. cit.*, pp. 32ff.).

[1] The narrator's comment thus casts an ironic light on Iwanet's congratulations to Parzival for having killed Ither (156,12: *dô sageter Parzivâle danc/prîses des erwarp sîn hant/an dem von Kukûmerlant*). I see no necessary indication of irony in this earlier passage, but we have to regard it differently when we are told how Parzival will later view this episode.

negative turn which events are about to take, this lies mainly with the theme of the lovers having constantly to outwit the attempts of society to keep them apart, a conflict between love and society which is insoluble and must always call into question any momentary union of the lovers.[1] This is not to say that Gottfried cannot use this technique like Hartmann to suggest the punishment of hubris. He indicates this twice in his sketch of Riwalin's youthful heedlessness (262: *wan daz er ze verre wolte/ in sines herzen luften sweben/und niwan nach sinem willen leben;/daz ime ouch sit ze leide ergie*; 308: *do wander, des doch niene geschach,/daz er iemer also solte leben/und in der lebenden süeze sweben*), ironising these high spirits from superior knowledge of their short duration and the suffering they will bring. Elsewhere, in place of the tragic destiny in control in the *Nibelungenlied* or the ethical workings of providence with Hartmann, we find the suggestion that love is in charge of things, leading them to an outcome different from what is vainly hoped. This is implied by the detail that Marke himself equips Tristan with the helmet of which the narrator says (6594: *dar uffe stuont diu strale,/der minnen wisaginne,/diu sit her mit der minne/an ime vil wol bewæret wart*), by the reference to Isold as she departs from Ireland (therefore before the scene of the love-potion) as *sin unverwande amie* (11488) or by the narrator's warning when the chambermaid picks up the potion in mistake for wine (11672: *nein, ezn was niht mit wine,/doch ez ime gelich wære...*). Repeated warnings of this kind add up to an impression that, however different, the lovers' destiny is as ineluctable as that which drives towards catastrophe in the *Nibelungenlied*. This is why an episode or new state of affairs can often commence with a narrator's forecast opening up to the listeners a deeper prospect than is visible to the actors, as with the start of the

---

[1] Cf. Clausen, *Erzähler*, p. 47. On the relationship between anticipations of coming catastrophes (as in the *Nibelungenlied*) and those which suggest a providential control of events (as with Hartmann) see Burger, *art. cit.*, pp. 141ff. and Reiffenstein, *art. cit.*, pp. 565f. Both argue that the technique was taken over from heroic into clerical literature (with a corresponding change from 'Unheilsvorausdeutungen' to 'Heilsvorausdeutungen', from heroic tragedy to providential control) and then adopted from clerical literature by courtly authors as part of their secular and basically optimistic view of things. Seen in this light, Gottfried's work again emerges as more tragic in its implications than the conventional romance.

Marjodo episode (13485: *der minnære Tristan/der stal sich tougen-liche dan/an sine strichweide/ze manegem herzeleide/im selben unde der künigin*).[1]

Concealment by the narrator

This situation is changed when we come to the third type of time-switch (showing up past events in a new light from the vantage-point of the present), for this is used not merely to reveal how ignorant or mistaken a character may have been in the past, but also to suggest that this partial vision was shared by the audience. Whereas the narrator's forecasts took the audience into his confidence, so that their shared knowledge ironised the ignorance of actors in the present, this gradual revelation of the truth about past events places actors and listeners on the same level; both are ironised for their ignorance in the past. Since both techniques can be employed in the same work, the listeners, unlike the actors, experience the events of the story discontinuously on two levels, at times as bewildered and perplexed as the actors and at times granted by the narrator a superior view of things. What the implications of this shifting view-point of the audience can be we shall consider later.

One way for the narrator to control the information he feeds to his audience is for him to abandon his omniscient stance and, with a welcome gain in dramatic tension, move closer to the audience by himself expressing doubts, fears, uncertainty as to how things may turn out, or closer to the restricted vision of the actors in wishing a successful outcome to events which he claims are as open and uncertain for himself as for those involved. Hartmann's narrator wishes Erec well on a number of occasions (e.g. 6698: *nû müeze got gesenden/disen ellenden,/Êrecke und Ênîten,/ ros dâ si ûfe rîten*),[2] but by doing this he is involved in the pretence that, like protagonist and listener, he has no means of foretelling the narrative future. Which is an effective way not merely of heightening tension, but also of keeping his listeners in ignorance, forcing them into a position close to that of Erec.

---

[1] Cf. also 15043ff. and 18119ff.
[2] Examples are to be found in Roetteken, *Kunst*, pp. 198f. and Herchenbach, *Präsens*, p. 41.

The same method is also used by Chrétien in Yvain's entertainment at the castle of Pesme Avanture (5424: *Or doint Des, que trop ne li cost/Ceste losange et cist servise!*), a remark which at once opens the vague prospect of dangers and successfully closes off all possibility of enlightenment at this stage.

In Parzival's encounter with his halfbrother Feirefiz Wolfram's narrator[1] likewise disregards the fact that his narrative is supposed to deal with events that have unrolled in the past and can therefore be surveyed by him in their totality. Instead he puts himself (and thereby his listeners) into the fictional present and into a state of uncertainty as to what the future may hold. In this sense he can utter his wishes (738,18: *gelücke scheidez âne tôt!* and 742,14: *got ner dâ Gahmuretes kint!*). In the second case we can detect, behind the façade of ignorance, the skilled dispositions of an author who knows what is afoot, since his wish on behalf of Gahmuret's son ironically covers not merely Parzival himself, but also his halfbrother.[2] By pretending not to know, the narrator restricts his field of vision to that of a spectator, giving what purports to be an eyewitness account of events unfolding in the present and whose result he cannot yet know. He thereby similarly restricts the perspective in which the audience can view these events.

Wolfram is especially skilled in developing other devices to explain his pretended ignorance. At the start of Book IX, when the narrative returns to Parzival who has been lost to view for some time while foreground events were devoted to Gawan, he uses the personification *frou Âventiure* to provide his listeners with information on Parzival, to bring them up to date just before he comes on to the stage again.[3] So far, the function of this personification seems to be to purvey information, rather than withhold it, but there are two qualifications to this apparently informative function. In the first place, if the listeners need to be brought up to date by *frou Âventiure*, this means that over the last few books, by the device of switching the narrative almost exclusively to Gawan, they have indeed been deprived of information. Of greater

---

[1] Cf. Nellmann, *Erzähltechnik*, pp. 152ff.
[2] See Green, *Alieniloquium*, p. 127.
[3] Cf. Ohly, *Cor*, pp. 470ff.; Green, *Irony*, p. 55; Nellmann, *Erzähltechnik*, pp. 98f.

importance is the fact that the narrator pretends to be in the same position. His importunate requests for enlightenment (433,8: *wie vert der gehiure?*; 433,15: *wie vert er nuo?*; 433,16: *den selben mæren grîfet ʒuo...*; 433,23: *nu prüevet uns*; 433,24: *hât er Munsalvæsche sît gesehen...*; 433,27: *gebt uns trôst*; 433,29: *lât hœren uns diu mære*; 434,2: *nu erliuhtet mir die fuore sîn*; 434,4: *wie hât Gahmurets sun gevarn...*; 434,8: *habt er sich an die wîte...*; 434,10: *sagt mir*) serve two ends. They create tension and heighten the listeners' expectancy, but they also confirm the fiction of the narrator's ignorance and justify its deployment on other occasions. This pretence of ignorance is the method the narrator employs to keep his listeners in the partial ignorance necessary for them to equate themselves with Parzival. In the thirty lines of dialogue between the narrator and the personification the former sees himself in the first person singular, in his unique capacity as narrator, only towards the end of the dialogue (434,2 and 10) as he prepares to address himself to the task of narration once more. Before this he makes use of the first person plural (433,22, 27 and 29), seeing himself at one with the listeners, because both narrator and listeners are ignorant and in need of enlightenment (or rather, this is what the narrator insinuates). The technique is similar to Wolfram's use of phrases like *unser ritter* (16,19) of Gahmuret and *unser tœrscher knabe* (138,9) of his son.[1] The use of the plural possessive establishes a bond of sympathy between the audience and the hero, but also a link between the audience and the narrator by means of which the latter can suggest that their ignorance is also his. Whereas it is of course he who is rhetorically wishing this ignorance upon them.[2]

The ignorance in which the narrator leaves his listeners on occasions is destined to be progressively lifted as the story proceeds. Like Parzival, they may be described as *træclîche wîs* (4,18), even though at points provided by the narrator's forecasts their enlightenment may be in advance of Parzival's. At one stage

---

[1] Nellmann, *op. cit.*, pp. 48ff.

[2] The double bond which Wolfram forges in this way for rhetorical purposes (including the ironisation of hero and audience alike) is quite different from the frequency with which Chaucer refers to his hero as 'this Troilus' (see Coghill, *Troilus*, pp. xxivf.), thereby ironising him alone, referring to him as if he were an exhibition piece.

the narrator even talks of releasing information in controlled instalments, in the so-called 'Bogengleichnis' which may also be a defence of the artificial order which this procedure involves (241,1: *Wer der selbe wære,/des freischet her nâch mære./dar zuo der wirt, sîn burc, sîn lant,/diu werdent iu von mir genant,/her nâch sô des wirdet zît,/bescheidenlîchen, âne strît/unde ân allez für zogen*).[1] Although Hartmann's narrator uses a similar delaying tactic in *Erec* when addressing his audience (7828: *des enist noh niht zît./wie gebitelôs ir sît!/wer solde sîn mære vür sagen?*),[2] only to give the information immediately afterwards, there is no need to assume that Wolfram is likewise teasing only in the short term. It may be, as Nellmann suggests,[3] that the names in question are soon afterwards divulged to Parzival (and to the audience) in his encounter with Sigune (250,22ff.), but it is imposing a literalist straitjacket on Wolfram's imagination to insist that *nennen* can only mean 'to give the name' and not also 'to explain, to give a full account',[4] and that the

[1] On the rhetorical function of the 'Bogengleichnis' see Curschmann, *DVjs* 45 (1971), 638ff.; Groos, *MLN* 87 (1972), 391ff.; Nellmann, *Erzähltechnik*, pp. 89ff.; Spitz, *Bogengleichnis*, pp. 247ff. To the suggestion made by Groos (that the 'Bogengleichnis' is to be connected with the artificial order) Curschmann keeps an open mind (p. 640), whilst Nellmann (p. 93, fn. 77) rejects it without giving any argument.

[2] Nellmann (*op. cit.*, p. 90, fn. 68) refers to similar passages from Chrétien.

[3] *Op. cit.*, p. 90.

[4] Thus Benecke–Müller–Zarncke (*Wörterbuch* II 1, 306) list for *name*, in addition to the meaning 'Name', two further semantic spheres. The first of these is 'Stand, Begriff, Würde, Wesen, Beschaffenheit' and the second 'Person' in the sense of 'eine bestimmte Stellung einnehmend, eine bestimmte Eigenschaft tragend'. Under the first heading the examples given show that *name* can combine the meaning 'name, title' with 'honours, privileges, rank' (*Erec* 5468, *Iwein* 3188, *Tristan* 4409) and that it can at times imply 'rank, station' (*Tristan* 1655) or 'reputation, honour' (*Tristan* 1619). Likewise, Wolfram can use the word to mean 'name, title' and also 'honours, privileges, rank' (*Parzival* 134,2), but also in the general sense 'concept' (*Parzival* 173,3). Under the second heading the examples include *Iwein* 163 and Walther von der Vogelweide 19,9. To these we can add Wolfram's use of the word to indicate 'rank, qualities' (*Parzival* 123,9) or 'qualities' alone (*Parzival* 233,19).
For the verb *nennen* itself Benecke–Müller–Zarncke (II 1, 311) give, in addition to 'nenne, gebe einen Namen', the more extended meaning 'ernenne zu etwas, erkläre für etwas' (cf. *Erec* 2580). A similar usage occurs in *Parzival* 21,29 and 740,27. Elsewhere, Wolfram uses the verb to mean 'to talk about' (545,19), 'to explain, to describe' (414,21) and 'to tell all about' (369,13). These examples, especially the last, suggest that Wolfram's use of *nennen* in 241,4 need not be confined to the meaning 'to give the name', suggested by Nellmann, but can also extend to Trevrizent later telling us all about, explaining and describing what lies behind the events at Munsalvæsche.

narrator's remark cannot also extend to his words in Book IX,[1] introducing the scene in which we learn from Trevrizent so much more about Munsalvæsche than from Sigune. These words take up the theme of the earlier passage (453,1: *swer mich dervon ê frâgte/unt darumbe mit mir bâgte,/ob ichs im niht sagete,/umprîs der dran bejagete./mich hat ez helen Kyôt,/wand im diu âventiure gebôt/daz es immer man gedæhte,/ê ez diu âventiure bræhte/mit worten an der mære gruoz,/daz man dervon doch sprechen muoz*). Even in the later passage, where we stand on the brink of Trevrizent's revelations about the Grail, the narrator, as in the dialogue with *frou Âventiure*, still presents himself as dependent on instructions from someone else (here his 'source', Kyot) and refers to *diu âventiure* not as a personification, but as an independent authority. At the moment when he is about to supply information the narrator creates the impression that he may not be in full control of its supply. As with the *frou Âventiure* dialogue, informativeness may give way to lack of information. Or in terms of the audience: the superior knowledge conveyed to them by the narrator's forecasts may alternate with situations where his (pretended) ignorance puts them again on a par with Parzival.

Such a technique of gradually widening horizons, of a piece-meal revelation which in retrospect shows earlier misconceptions in a very ironic light is admirably fitted to the Parzival story, but precisely because Wolfram combines it with the complementary one of sometimes giving his listeners information still withheld from the hero it can be more easily grasped in Chrétien's version. The French romance is organised more thoroughly than its German counterpart on an inductive principle in that the hero (and the listeners who accompany him) is led from the unknown to the known.[2] This does justice to the theme of an inexperienced youth to whom the world presents a series of discoveries to be made. By narrating the story from Perceval's restricted point of view Chrétien has forced a similar restriction on his audience, so that their enlightenment very largely keeps pace with his. But this technique bears on more than just the character of the hero

[1] Nellmann (*op. cit.*, p. 89, especially fn. 67) has to admit that this is how others have generally read the passage.

[2] See Kellermann, *Aufbaustil*, pp. 42f.; Frappier, *Chrétien*, p. 174; Bertau, *Literatur*, pp. 605ff. and 777f.

(whose extreme naïveté could be peculiar to him alone). The limited viewpoint with which it works allows the poet to present the Grail-kingdom (which we experience from Perceval's blinkered point of view) as a convincingly mysterious realm and to organise his narrative around the central motif of the quest, conceived as a movement from ignorance to enlightenment. To the extent that the artificial order starts in the middle of things and initially narrates much which is not immediately understood and only later made clear, it serves the same purpose as Chrétien's focus on Perceval's point of view.

In taking over this subject-matter Wolfram was largely bound to a similar technique, despite his complication of the work's structure by introducing occasional vantage-points from which his listeners could see further ahead than Parzival.[1] Like Chrétien, but with many changes of detail, he works with the principle of progressive enlightenment of both hero and audience, even though the pace at which each advances may not be the same. This can be illustrated in his plotting of Parzival's miraculous guidance to the Grail-castle, a narrative problem which, like Chrétien in his presentation of the mysteries of the Grail-kingdom, he solved by making use of a subjective focus which gradually widens to allow us to glimpse progressively more implications.[2]

Wolfram's Parzival

The truth with Parzival, we eventually learn, is that he sets out on his travels as the unwitting beneficiary of providential assistance, but then forfeits this by his failure at Munsalvæsche. Our initial uncertainty about the scenes in question means that we fail to grasp at the time that they illustrate the hero's providential guidance, so that our subsequent enlightenment parallels that of Parzival as he learns the truth from Trevrizent. Wolfram's

---

[1] In other words, I disagree with Bertau who sees Wolfram's technique too much in terms of an absolute contrast with Chrétien's (op. cit., pp. 788ff.). I see him as partly adopting his predecessor's method, but also making use of another narrative principle. On the presence of these two complementary features in Wolfram's technique see below, pp. 164ff.

[2] The argument of the following pages abbreviates what I have said elsewhere in Weg, pp. 11ff. and, in a very much wider context, in Pathway, pp. 174ff.

method is to give us information about the knight's travels, but
in such a way that we can be expected not to grasp its significance
at the time. By rhetorical means he therefore puts us in the same
position as his hero, who witnesses events without seeing their
meaning. His methods in implying, without stating, that Parzival
is preternaturally guided at the start of his journey have been
analysed in detail.[1] They comprise suggestions that Parzival's
singleminded effort, the haste and speed of his travel, constantly
take him along the correct path,[2] as well as the use of gradation
to strengthen the impression that he heads without the slightest
deviation for the next event that awaits his coming.[3] But such
passages are ambiguous so that on a first hearing the audience is
likely to take them only in their innocuous sense. The haste with
which Parzival travels could be simply a mark of the eagerness
with which a young boy sets out in search of Arthur and chivalry.
The same is true of the gradations with which his speed is suggested, but even when extraordinary feats are implied in covering
immense distances there is still no reason why we have to see in
this the miraculous intervention of providence. Parzival may
cover a great distance on leaving Graharz (161,17: *gewâpent reitz*
der tumbe man/den tac sô verre, ez hete lân/ein blôz wîser, solt erz hân
geriten/zwêne tage, ez wære vermiten), but this may be the inexperienced enthusiasm of one just introduced to knighthood, riding
his horse to death, where another would have more prudently
spared it. Condwiramurs may wonder at the speed with which he
journeyed from Graharz to Brobarz (189,22ff.) and his speed may
be even more remarkable on his way to Munsalvæsche (224,22ff.),
but with an author given to hyperbole[4] we should hesitate to
read anything more into such remarks.

Even when the narrator refers to these journeys with apparent
explicitness he still remains fundamentally ambiguous. We are
told that Parzival does not lose his way in the wild country
between Graharz and Brobarz (180,15: *Doch reit er wênec irre*) or

---

[1] The features of Wolfram's technique have been established by Wynn, *Speculum* 36
(1961), 393ff. My approach differs from hers in that I am concerned to show that
Wolfram first suggests Parzival's miraculous guidance by remarks which are
deliberately ambiguous and that he allows us only later to grasp their full implications.   [2] Wynn, *art. cit.*, pp. 399f.
[3] *Ibid.*, pp. 400f.   [4] E.g. *Willehalm*, 62,11ff.

even on his ride to the Grail-castle from Lake Brumbane (226,10: *Parzivâl der huop sich dan,/er begunde wackerlîchen draben/den rehten pfat unz an den graben*), even though the risk is great enough here for Amfortas to have to warn him (226,6ff.). But there is still no reason to assume anything but a happy chance, the good fortune that accompanies the hero of a fairytale.[1]

Finally, conscious ambiguity seems to lurk behind Parzival's ride to Munsalvæsche (224,19: *mit gewalt den zoum daz ros/truog über ronen und durchez mos:/wandes wîste niemens hant*). If the knight's horse is directed by no one's hand, this could imply that Parzival allows it to take its own path (because he is riding at random and does not know the way) or that there is nobody to show him the way[2] (so wild and deserted is the region). Yet behind these two obvious readings lies another which we are not meant to perceive so readily – and here for the first time we touch upon other possibilities, ambiguously present in all these references, but clarified only later. If no one's hand (or better in this context: no man's hand)[3] guides Parzival's horse and if none the less it takes him through wild country straight to the Grail-castle, it is possible to see in this phrasing a suggestion that it is the hand of God that guides the hero on this critical stage of his journey,[4] the God for whom one of the poet's circumlocutions is *diu hœhste hant*[5] and who later answers a plea of Parzival by guiding his horse to Trevrizent's cell (452,9ff.). Such explicitness is missing from this

---

[1] In other words, Parzival's good fortune in finding the way on these occasions could be a sign of the *sælekeit* or *geschiht* which Hartmann is perfectly ready to invoke in the case of Erec when he makes good his escape from Limors (6713: *alse doch sîn sælekeit/volleclîche dar an schein*) and when he encounters Guivreiz again (6868: *alsô vuoctez diu geschiht*). But Hartmann in each case can only realise his purpose when we discern the hand of God behind what appears to be no more than chance or good fortune, so that God has to be explicitly mentioned for the point to be made (6726: *ez vuocte et gotes wille* and 7070: *nû hete in an der genâde sant/ûz kumbers ünden gesant/got und sîn vrümekeit*). It is similarly impossible to be sure with Parzival whether he has actually received divine guidance. The poet may hint at the possibility, but refuses to pin himself down.

[2] See Walshe, *LMS* 1 (1939), 343.

[3] I base this reading on the fact that the genitive of the pronoun can be *niemens* or *niemannes* and that the word can sometimes be divided into two (*nie + man*), cf. *Iwein* 573, 1175, 3646. I agree with the remark in Benecke–Müller–Zarncke, *Wörterbuch* II 1, 42, that such divided forms are (syntactically) not the same as *nieman*, but their semantic force is the same, and it is this which Wolfram exploits.

[4] Wynn, *Speculum* 36 (1961), 401.

[5] Cf. Adolf, *Neophilologus* 19 (1934), 260ff.

earlier passage because the fact of Parzival's guidance is to be revealed only retrospectively, after it is already forfeit. As the knight approaches Munsalvæsche we cannot know that God's hand is at work. Even though no one's hand may guide his horse, we know nothing yet of the significance of Lake Brumbane or of the castle to which he finds his way[1] and therefore have no grounds for seeing miraculous guidance in his arrival there, by contrast with his being led to Trevrizent's cell. Equally, we know nothing at this stage of God's readiness to guide a knight who places his trust in Him by abandoning his reins.[2]

But how does the poet make it subsequently clear that Parzival was in fact guided miraculously to a predestined goal? The turning-point is his failure at the Grail-castle, for when he departs on the following morning, eager to catch up with the Grail-knights and offer his military assistance, he loses their track and for the first time fails to keep to the right path (249,5: *do begunde krenken sich ir spor:/sich schieden die dâ riten vor./ir slâ wart smal, diu ê was breit:/er verlôs si gar: daz was im leit*).[3] If this remark stood alone, it could be regarded as purely fortuitous (like the earlier passages indicating that Parzival had found the way, apparently by chance). Instead it is prefaced by the narrator's first explicit statement about the hero's journeying (249,1: *Der valscheite widersaz/kêrt' ûf der huofslege kraz./sîn scheiden dan daz riuwet mich./alrêst nû âventiurt ez sich*). The auspices for Parzival finding the right way seemed to be good, in fact better than before, for he had horse-

---

[1] Our ignorance is heightened by Wolfram's withholding of place names from us at this stage. We know that Parzival comes to a lake in the vicinity of a castle, but the lake is simply termed a *sê* (225,2) and its name *Brumbâne* is given for the first time only very much later (261,27), when Parzival encounters Jeschute and Orilus. Similarly, although Parzival has now penetrated into Grail-territory and soon comes to the Grail-castle itself, the names *Terre de Salvæsche* (251,4) and *Munsalvæsche* (251,2) are first mentioned to him, and to us, by Sigune, once he has left the Grail behind him. Initially, therefore, we realise as little of the meaning of this realm as does Parzival himself.

[2] In the later episode, where God guides Parzival's horse to Trevrizent, we are told both that the rider slackened his reins (452,10: *den zügel gein den ôren für/er dem orse legete*) and that he issued a challenge to God to guide his steed (452,5: *mac gotes kunst die helfe hân,/diu wîse mir diz kastelân/dez wægest umb die reise mîn!/sô tuot sîn güete helfe schîn./nu genc nâch der gotes kür!*). In the earlier episode we are told only that Parzival dropped his reins (224,19: *mit gewalt den zoum daz ros/truog über ronen und durchez mos*). It looks as if Wolfram took care to omit any express reference to divine guidance from this earlier scene.

[3] Wynn, *Speculum* 36 (1961), 402.

tracks to follow, whereas earlier he had struggled through track-less terrain (180,6f.) or followed unknown paths (226,6). Despite this, it is only now that he loses his way, a novelty which is stressed by the narrator's use of *alrêst*. Now for the first time he rides at random, subject to the vagaries of chance[1] and liable to lose his way. This is borne out by the subsequent narrative. Parzival has so far forfeited the miraculous guidance which he unconsciously enjoyed earlier that he spends years trying to find Munsalvæsche again. The journey once accomplished with miraculous speed and directness now gives way to blind groping, extended over years and apparently leading nowhere.

In this scene when Parzival departs from Munsalvæsche Wolfram brings it home to us that his hero had previously benefited from miraculous guidance. By letting us see this only now, at the moment when he loses it, the poet lets us feel the magnitude of Parzival's loss, but he also lets us realise belatedly that the narrator's earlier remarks were ambiguous and that, like Parzival, we failed to grasp the facts of his situation. We can now appreciate that Parzival's haste was not just the mark of an eager, youthful knight (although it may have been that as well) or simply an example of hyperbole (although this is an undeniable aspect of Wolfram's style), but primarily an indication of miraculous guidance, allowing him to avoid every sidetrack and overcome every obstacle. Even the remark that no man's hand guided Parzival's horse begins to reveal the possibility of a concealed allusion to divine guidance.

When Parzival leaves the Grail-castle we know for certain only that the guidance now lost must have been miraculous, not necessarily divine. For this further certainty we have to wait several years, until his approach to Trevrizent's hermitage. The

---

[1] I take the verb *sich âventiurn* to imply the element of chance (cf. Green, *Âventiure*, p. 103), a meaning which is also present in other cases where Wolfram employs the noun *âventiure*, for example with regard to Feirefiz's random journey to Europe in search of his father (748,24: ...*dar inne diu reise mîn/nâch âventiure wart getan*). In this pagan's view, however, his journey has not been ultimately fortuitous, since it is crowned with the unexpected success of meeting, not his father, but his half-brother, a success for which he thanks the pagan divinities that guided him (748,14ff.). But Feirefiz is not the hero of his work and Wolfram can therefore allow us in his case to catch sight of the providential framework immediately, whereas with Parzival we have to struggle, like him, to recognise the fact of guidance at all.

pilgrim-knight has just recommended Parzival to seek out the hermit's cell nearby, pointing out that he has only to follow his track (448,21). But for Parzival, whose thoughts have been turned towards God again by this encounter and by learning that it is Good Friday, this offer of a track is not enough, it is as ambiguous as the narrator's initial remarks about his journeying[1] and need not imply that God is intervening in his life again. He therefore rides away, considering the possibility that God might help him and in this mood he deliberately turns back from the track pointed out to him (451,23: *er kêrt sich wider, dannen er dâ reit*). In doing this he issues a challenge to God (452,5: *mac gotes kunst die helfe hân,/ diu wîse mir diz kastelân/dez wægest umb die reise mîn!*), loosens his reins, abandons the horse to God. And the horse now takes him to nowhere else but the hermit's cell (452,13: *gein Fontâne la salvâtsche ez gienc*). Whereas the departure from Munsalvæsche made it clear that Parzival's former guidance had been miraculous, this scene where it is restored shows the divine nature of such guidance. The audience learns the truth retrospectively and in controlled instalments, so that they partly share their ignorance with Parzival.[2]

But Wolfram's artistry is even more subtle. Not content with arranging for us to learn of Parzival's initial divine guidance retrospectively and in two instalments, he suggests that even during Parzival's period of estrangement from God and rides at random God is still in control of events, however indirectly. On this different level of God's intervention Wolfram illustrates how the wrong path taken by Parzival (and this is the period when we

---

[1] One might even argue that Parzival, like Hartmann in his description of Erec's good fortune (see above, p. 152. fn. 1), is not content with an ambiguity and can only be satisfied by an unmistakable indication. Just as Hartmann has to add the word *got* explicitly, so must Parzival be convinced by an obviously providential intervention. This suggests that Wolfram's references to Parzival's early journeying (see especially the argument of Wynn, *Speculum* 36 (1961), 393ff.) are left deliberately obscure and are not in themselves enough to imply that his travels are divinely guided. Final certainty is provided only retrospectively—we are in as much need of proof as Parzival himself.

[2] The emphasis needs to fall on the word 'partly' here, for although our growth to certainty largely parallels Parzival's, Wolfram has not failed to exploit the ironic possibilities of a discrepancy between our knowledge of the situation and his. We therefore learn, as he does not, that miraculous guidance was withdrawn after he left Munsalvæsche (249,4) and we are also informed that God was in control as Parzival began to approach the hermit's cell (435,12). See below, pp. 16of.

expect him to take the wrong path) turns out to be the right path for him, however circuitously it may take him to his goal.[1] On such occasions he alerts his audience to the fact that the path taken is the wrong one – his explicitness, given in the episode itself and not retrospectively, differs from his technique with Parzival's preternatural guidance. The reason for this difference is clear. By telling his listeners early the poet may hope to disarm and lull them into a sense of false security, into the belief that, since this is the wrong path, no predetermined adventure can await the knight. Since the mistake is presented as a human error, we cannot yet be in a miraculous realm where the hero is guided unerringly to the adventure meant for him alone.

When he leaves Munsalvæsche after his failure Parzival is under the impression that Amfortas is in need of his knightly assistance.[2] On noticing the hoofmarks outside the castle he assumes that the Grail-knights have ridden out in the military service of their lord and sets out in pursuit of them, meaning to render his host the same service. However, the tracks soon fade away and Parzival loses his way (249,5ff.). Important though this point may be (it shows that guidance has been withdrawn from the hero as a result of his behaviour at the Grail-castle, even though the listener may still have no idea why this should merit such a punishment),[3] it conceals another detail of Wolfram's artistry. Parzival may have set out hoping to assist Amfortas and may have lost his way, but on quite another level (which the listener cannot be expected to understand immediately) he does find his way. At the moment when we learn that he has lost the Grail-knights' tracks we are also told that, guided by the voice of a woman lamenting, he comes across Signe (249,11f.). This meeting is a disastrous one for Parzival, since Signe

---

[1] This problem, both in connection with the period of Parzival's rides at random and elsewhere in the work, has been briefly discussed by Gibbs, *MLR* 63 (1968), 872ff.

[2] Cf. 246,1ff. and 248,19ff.

[3] This passage provides the audience with information not available to Parzival and at the same time, by alerting them to further aspects of the situation which they cannot understand, brings them closer to Parzival's position of incomprehension. On the double movement of this and similar passages (reminiscent of what the narrator says in the Prologue of the type of listener he has in mind, 2,5: *ouch erkande ich nie so wîsen man,|ern möhte gerne künde hân,|welher stiure disiu mære gernt| und waz sie guoter lêre wernt*), see below, pp. 164ff.

curses him when she learns of his omission at Munsalvæsche and it is from her that he learns something of the enormity of his error. But in learning of the opportunity which he has squandered Parzival is also learning something positive about the mysteries of the Grail, something about his own kinship with that world. It is not by chance that in his first meeting with Sigune, in the Arthurian setting of Bertane, Parzival learns from her details about chivalry, whereas the second encounter, in Terre de Salvæsche, is concerned with the mysteries of the Grail-castle.[1] Although he may be cursed at this second meeting, he is now being judged on a higher level than earlier and the accusation has an essential part to play in the journey which brings him to Munsalvæsche again. It is the first station on his way to realising that the help he is to bring Amfortas is not the military assistance which he imagines to be required.[2] If Parzival loses track of the Grail-knights this is because he is not yet ready to give Amfortas the only kind of help that can miraculously save him. In losing their track, however, he finds the way to Sigune who, by her accusation, teaches him vital truths about himself and the Grail. In losing the track which he intended to follow (but which was the wrong one for him, for it could have led him nowhere in his wish to serve his host) he finds a path which, however irrelevant it may seem to his wishes of the moment, leads him, by a roundabout way necessitated by his own folly, to the goal of his wishes. We may not realise this at the time, since we cannot yet grasp the paradox that the path *away* from the Grail and its knights is the only path which will lead him back to it. Equally we are meant to miss the point that, although Parzival seems to have lost his path at this stage, his journeying is still under preternatural guidance, even if more indirectly than before.

A similar impression (the faint outlines of guidance behind the appearance of losing his way) is conveyed by Parzival's next meeting with Sigune, just before his arrival at Trevrizent's hermitage.[3] Sigune's earlier anger has now evaporated and she is touched by the constancy of his endeavour to find his way back

---

[1] This point has been well made by Wynn, *MLR* 56 (1961), 41f.
[2] See Mohr's valuable demonstration of this in *Hilfe*, especially pp. 187 and 190.
[3] 435,15ff.

to the Grail. In an attempt to help him she tells him that, since her food is brought to her by Cundrie from Munsalvæsche (438,29ff.) and since this messenger has only recently left her, there is every hope that Parzival might be able to follow her track and come to the Grail-castle again (442,9: *si sprach: nu helfe dir des hant,/dem aller kumber ist bekant;/ob dir sô wol gelinge,/ daz dich ein slâ bringe,/aldâ du Munsalvæsche sihst,/dâ du mir dîner freuden gihst./Cundrîe la surziere reit/vil niulîch hinnen*). This is a repetition of the earlier situation when Parzival departed from Munsalvæsche, for there too he had set out following clear, fresh tracks (248,17f.). There too he had hoped to catch up with the Grail-knights ahead of him, just as Sigune now tells him that he has every chance of overtaking Cundrie (442,21: *ich rât daz du ir rîtes nâch:/ir ist lîhte vor dir niht sô gâch,/dune mügest si schiere hân erriten*). But as on the earlier occasion Parzival soon loses these tracks, however hopeful things had seemed on his setting out (442,24: *dane wart niht langer dô gebiten,/urloup nam der helt aldâ:/dô kêrter ûf die niwen slâ./Cundrîen mûl die reise gienc,/daz ungeverte im undervienc/eine slâ dier het erkorn./sus wart aber der grâl verlorn*).[1] In contrast to his journeys through wild country before he came to the Grail-castle, the desolate, trackless landscape now really does represent an obstacle, it is the cause of his losing his way, a fact which the narrator sums up resignedly (443,5: *nu lât in rîten: war sol er?*).

If this scene, in which Parzival leaves Sigune hoping to catch up with Cundrie, resembles the earlier scene when, hoping to catch up with the Grail-knights, he came to Sigune, we may press the parallel further. Is it not possible that, although he loses track of Cundrie, he finds another path which, however roundabout, is the only path for him – just as his earlier path to Sigune was the necessary one at that stage? Just after we are told that Parzival has lost track of Cundrie his encounter with a Grail-knight is described (443,6f.). This brings it home to us that Parzival is actually in Grail-territory and can only narrowly have missed being led to Munsalvæsche, but after this joust Parzival rides on at random (445,27: *do reit er, ern wiste war*). Even though an

---

[1] The use of the word *aber* in *sus wart aber der grâl verlorn* is a clear indication that we are meant to see these two episodes in connection with each other.

unspecified period of time comes between this encounter and the next (446,3ff.) it is in fact only a few lines later (seconds later in narrative time) that Parzival meets the pilgrim-knight who is the means whereby he comes to Trevrizent's cell. In terms of the narrative there is an unbroken continuity in these encounters with Sigune, the Grail-knight, the pilgrim-knight and Trevrizent. We are led to the conclusion that if Parzival had not lost his way after leaving Sigune he may never have come across Trevrizent, but since it is Trevrizent who absolves him from sin (502,25f.) and reconciles him with God (741,26f.), the ironic truth is that only by losing the way which Sigune had pointed out does Parzival find his way back to God.[1]

This again provides a parallel with the scene in which Parzival came across Sigune after leaving the Grail-castle. In this earlier scene the reason for his losing track of the Grail-knights and consequent inability to give Amfortas the military assistance he thought was required was that help of his kind was out of place. Parzival had to learn, at great cost to himself and to the suffering Amfortas, what kind of assistance was called for in the context of the Grail. Similarly, although Sigune reveals her sympathy for the hero by putting him on Cundrie's tracks she does not realise the extent of his estrangement from God. Only after this has been healed by Trevrizent can there be any possibility of Parzival being worthy of the Grail, so that his path to Munsalvæsche leads not in Cundrie's tracks, as Sigune thinks, but indirectly via Trevrizent's cell. In both cases Parzival appears to lose his way because he is not yet ready for any direct approach to his goal. The path along which he wanders when we (and he) think that he has hopelessly lost his way is the only path which will bring him in his present condition to the destination he seeks.

This method reveals a narrator who deliberately leads his audience astray (just as God appears to be doing the same with Parzival) by allowing them to think that Parzival is lost. In reality, the episodes in which these misleading suggestions are

---

[1] This is paralleled by the irony of the situation in which the pilgrim-knight's daughters, out of Christian compassion with Parzival, attempt to persuade their father to invite Parzival to accompany them (448,27ff.). If their attempt at charity had been successful Parzival would never have met Trevrizent, so that all that followed from this encounter would have been irrevocably lost.

made are scenes which illustrate the knight's providential guidance, even if this now takes place on a level which the audience does not expect. The same effect can be achieved when the author exploits not the ambiguity of situation, but the ambiguity of language, as with *Parzival* 224,21 (*wandez wîste niemens hant*), where we learn only retrospectively that, if Parzival's steed was guided by no human hand, this must be because of divine control of his travels.

Revealing and concealing

In the last few pages I have devoted so much space to Wolfram's romance because the *Parzival* story lends itself particularly well to a technique which stresses the hero's incomprehension of the situations in which he finds himself and which brings this home to the audience by ensuring that, like him, they initially fail to grasp what is at stake. Although the narrator's technique of forcing a restricted vision on his audience by expressing fear or uncertainty is already used by Hartmann, there is little doubt but that Wolfram derived his more far-reaching technique, together with his story, from Chrétien.[1] But whereas Chrétien had used the technique of piecemeal revelation almost exclusively,[2] keeping his audience at much the same level of enlightenment as Perceval himself, Wolfram adopts this method, but combines it with the technique of giving his listeners occasional wider views than are available to Parzival, above all by his anticipatory remarks. By this twofold method Wolfram's audience is brought sometimes closer to Parzival (by virtue of their shared blindness to the implications of events), but sometimes closer to the narrator (whenever both have superior knowledge). Although in general terms Wolfram allows his listeners to flounder almost as much as Parzival over the question of miraculous guidance on his travels, he supplies them with information denied him: first when this guidance is withdrawn from him after leaving Munsalvæsche (249,4: *alrêst nu âventiurt ez sich*) and then when it is about to be

[1] Here again I differ from Bertau in not seeing Wolfram's technique as so radically the opposite of Chrétien's as he suggests (*Literatur*, p. 777).

[2] Chrétien can occasionally abandon this technique, as when (possibly by oversight) he allows Perceval to understand more of the situation by hearing than was possible without also seeing (v. 100f.). On this detail see Mergell, *Parzival*, p. 20, and Bertau, *Literatur*, p. 775.

restored to him as he begins to approach Trevrizent's cell (435,12: *sîn wolte got dô ruochen*). Parzival can have no idea of these two points revealed to the audience, nor can he suspect, as they may, that the withdrawal of guidance may have something to do with his omission at the Grail-castle. It is by the creation of a shifting perspective which now appeals to the listeners' superiority and now undermines their certainty by reminding them of what they do not know, that Wolfram can relativise the convictions of his audience, inducing in them a frame of mind receptive to the questioning of conventional values which is one of the functions of his irony.

However well he may use these techniques in combination, Wolfram is not alone in using both in the same work. Here we may return to the fact that, in addition to the natural and artificial orders, there was a theoretical possibility of the *ordo commixtus* (both orders in the one work).[1] This combination of two narrative orders is closer to Wolfram's combination of two narrative techniques (the one withholding and the other conveying information) than might appear at a first glance. Of crucial importance is Benson's argument that the two narrative orders demand two distinct narrative points of view: an omniscient one in the natural order, but an unavoidably partial or restricted view in the artificial order.[2] To begin, with the natural order, at the beginning and to narrate all events in the sequence in which they took place means that there is no opportunity for a surprise effect by suddenly reverting to the past in order to show it anew in the light of the present. But to begin, with the artificial order, *in medias res* means that some events will have to be recapitulated later and that until then the listeners' view of things is incomplete. If most romances are in fact examples of the *ordo commixtus*, how far can it be said that their combination of two different time-sequences (and therewith of two different narrative points of view) is utilised for ironic purposes?

Certainly there is the possibility of irony whenever the poet operates with a double perspective. The irony of this lies in the contrast between the extent of the audience's knowledge (thanks to the forecast given by the narrator) and the extent of its ignor-

---

[1] See above, p. 132, fn. 5, on Bernard of Utrecht.   [2] Benson, *Art*, pp. 170f.

ance (resulting from its misapplication of this information). Two examples from Hartmann's *Erec* have been mentioned by Endres.[1] One concerns the congratulations and good wishes for the future showered upon Erec and Enite at the time of their marriage (2200: *die sprâchen alle/mit gelîchem schalle/wol den hôchzîten:/Êrecke und vrouwen Ênîten/wunschten si aller sælekeit./diu was in doch nû bereit/lange unde manec jâr./ir wunsch wart volleclîche wâr,/wan zwei gelieber wurden nie/unz ez der tôt undervie*). If we had only the first five lines of this quotation it would be nothing more than a wish for the future voiced by actors and therefore not necessarily of any objective validity. The following five lines change the position, however, by the confirmation that these wishes were amply fulfilled, given by the omniscient narrator. This narrator's forecast is in its turn confirmed by subsequent events, for this prophecy of future fairytale happiness for the couple is taken up again at the close of the work. Their *sælekeit* is expanded at some length in vv. 10115ff., as is the reference to their eventual death (2209) in vv. 10125ff. Yet what this forecast leaves out of account is the whole span of the narrative with its events bringing anything but immediate *sælekeit*, rather an estrangement between man and wife, suffering, despair and the danger of death. If Hartmann is operating with two time-spans here whilst allowing his listeners to think that there is only one, he thereby ironises the conventional fairytale association of the marriage of a couple with immediate *sælekeit*.[2]

Two time-spans, one immediate and the other long-term, are also evident in the lengthy passage (6471ff.) in which Count Oringles attempts to convince the apparently recently widowed Enite that her social conditions have changed for the better,[3] for now she has the opportunity to marry one of such high standing as himself. His argument operates with the contrast between negative and positive, between past and present, between the condition in which he has found her and the wealth he can confer on her. What he cannot realise is that all his positive terms (which he sees as his immediate gift to her in the present) are also

---

[1] Endres, *Studien*, pp. 54f. and 68f.
[2] I have discussed another example of Hartmann's ironisation of the happy ending of the fairytale in *Erec* (*Praise*, pp. 798ff.).
[3] See Green, *Alieniloquium*, pp. 125f.

applicable to the near future, when Enite will be restored to happiness and social esteem at the side of her husband, so that the count's flattering prophecy, although voiced by a character within the narrative, ironically turns out to be true, but hardly in the sense in which he meant it.

Double time-perspectives of this kind are particularly common in *Sir Gawain and the Green Knight*, where the structure of the plot (the temptation theme set within the beheading theme) creates the conditions for their occurrence. When Gawain has agreed to stay with Sir Bertilak at his castle (an agreement followed by the fatal exchange-of-winnings arrangement) and his host replies exultantly (1089: '*ʒe han demed to do þe dede þat I bidde;/Wyl ʒe halde þis hes here at þys oneʒ?*'),[1] his words acquire a double relevance, which only becomes clear once we have been enlightened on the identity of the host with the Green Knight. We come to wonder retrospectively whether Gawain's promise is to his affable host or to the more threatening figure of the Green Knight, whether the promise is to be redeemed in the bantering context of the exchange of winnings or at the cost of Gawain's head. A threatening dimension is also visible (but not necessarily seen) when the host, on the brink of Gawain's departure, says to him (1969: '*In god fayþe*', *quoþ þe godmon*, '*wyth a goud wylle/Al þat euer I yow hyʒt halde schal I redé*'). On the face of it this is the polite offer of a generous host, but once we come to suspect the identity of Sir Bertilak with the Green Knight, the promise takes on a distinctly grimmer look. In both cases the irony lies in the presence of two possible time-schemes (an immediate one, sociable and apparently innocuous, and a long-term one whose implications are more threatening) and in the consequent contrast between what the audience may think it has been told and what lurks behind such statements.

The same effect is produced whenever the conjunction of two different perspectives is brought about by intertwining in the same episode the two points of view, one in which the audience is in complicity with the narrator and therefore knows more than the actor and the other in which the listeners' ignorance brings them close to the actor. We find an example of this in the scene

---

[1] Would it be going too far to suggest that the words *at þys oneʒ* might imply that the promise will be kept rather sooner than Gawain imagines?

in which Hartmann's Enite is lamenting the apparent death of her husband and contemplating suicide. We should recall the uncompromising way in which this scene starts. Erec is so wounded and exhausted from his combat with the giants that he is called *der halptôte man* (5730), but then his last reserves of strength ebb away and he collapses (5737: *einen solhen val er nam/daz er lac vür tôt*). For Enite this is the sign that Erec is dead. Even for the listeners the phrasing is highly uncertain (is he in fact dead or does he merely seem to be?), but the long lament which Enite now begins sweeps them over to her point of view. When in the course of this lament she refers to herself as *mir vil gotes armen* (6032) she is likely to command the listeners' sympathies. But this close agreement between Enite and the audience (neither has any real knowledge of what is afoot) gives way to a very different position later when she attempts to commit suicide (6062ff.), for the audience is now given a commentary by the narrator which allows them to survey the situation as Enite cannot (6069: *wan daz irz got verbôt/und ir leben gevriste/mit genædeclîchem liste/dar an daz si begunde/dem swerte dâ ze stunde/vluochen dô siz gesach*). This is only the first of God's interventions at this point (a little later we are told that Enite's repeated suicide attempt was frustrated by the arrival of Oringles, sent there by God, vv. 6115ff.). The function of these narrator's comments is to place the listeners in a privileged position which shows them more of the situation than when they see it, with however much dramatic tension, from the restricted viewpoint of the actor.

A conjunction of restricted viewpoint alongside superior vantage-point is of particular interest in Wolfram's *Parzival*. His 'Bogengleichnis' (241,1ff.), a passage which forces temporary ignorance on the audience in connection with the mysteries of the Grail and for which eventual enlightenment is completely given four books later, is surrounded by a cluster of narrator's forecasts. With a greater density and frequency than before these tell us something about the implications which escape Parzival (242,18: *ez wirt grôz schade in beiden kunt*; 245,4: *ir boten künftegiu leit/sanden im in slâfe dar*; 249,4: *alrêst nu âventiurt ez sich*; 249,9: *mære vriesch dô der junge man,/dâ von er herzenôt gewan*).[1] This cluster

---

[1] Cf. Nellmann, *Erzähltechnik*, pp. 89f.

tells us what Parzival cannot know, that things are going disastrously wrong and he is acting mistakenly. On the one hand we are therefore given information which he sorely needs himself, whilst on the other hand the 'Bogengleichnis' keeps us in the same state of ignorance as Parzival. This means that Wolfram can rescue for his own work the advantages of dramatic tension and openness to mystery which characterised Chrétien's work, but can also exploit to the full the possibilities of dramatic irony in allowing his listeners the occasional superiority to his hero.

That there is no necessary conflict between these changing viewpoints[1] (they rather work together to relativise the audience's convictions and make them receptive to Wolfram's questioning) can be shown by the way in which even this cluster of forecasts gives only partial information and leaves many questions unanswered. When the narrator shrieks his grief at the parting of Parzival from Amfortas and forecasts suffering for them both (242,18), this gives the audience more knowledge than Parzival, but only at the cost of prompting them to ask why this should be so, a question which is answered for them only by Trevrizent.[2] Similarly, although it is made quite clear to us that the hero's nightmare presages his future suffering (245,4f.), we have no comprehension why all this should follow from the failure to ask a question and again have to wait until Book IX for enlightenment.[3] When we are told that Parzival's rides at random now begin for the first time (249,4), this conveys essential information to us about his past journeying which is withheld from him, but still conceals the fact that miraculous guidance will still operate in his favour, but indirectly, until it is mentioned again expressly as Parzival draws near to Trevrizent. The forecast that Parzival will be told grievous news by Sigune (249,9f.) informs us slightly in advance of him, but if Parzival at the end of his encounter with Sigune, although willing to make amends, is still at a loss to see what he has done wrong,[4] this is equally true of the audience.

---

[1] Nellmann, *op. cit.*, p. 89, apparently suggests this and then seeks to remedy the position by arguing that the deferment of information announced by 241,1ff. lasts only a bare 300 lines.

[2] 483,19ff.

[3] 484,13ff.

[4] 255,23: *ich wandel, hân ich iht getân.*

Both they and Parzival have to wait to be informed by Trevrizent.[1] Every one of these forecasts, in the act of giving the listeners more information than is available to the hero, also withholds some essential fact from them which is released to both parties only in Book IX. These passages (whose function of informing the listeners is obvious) operate in a less obvious manner with a tension of information withheld which, like the 'Bogengleichnis' with which they seem to contrast, stretches from Book V to Book IX.

Nor is this the only example of the tension of information withheld stretching from Book V to Book IX. The same is true of the relationship between what Parzival experiences on his visit to the Grail-castle, how he interprets what he sees, and what Trevrizent later tells him of the significance of things there. This relationship between the two Books has been brought out by Deinert in connection with the rôle played by astronomy in Wolfram's work.[2] He too makes the point that what is first presented in Book V from Parzival's uncomprehending viewpoint is later depicted in its coherence by Trevrizent who, acquainted with both the Grail-world and astronomy, is able to give an objective survey to complement and correct Parzival's subjective experience. The audience learns with Parzival that the conjunction of circumstances on the day when Parzival came to Munsalvæsche was favourable as on no other day to prompting the question which had to be asked *ungewarnet*,[3] that disparate details such as the bloody spear and the summer snowfall really belong together[4] and add up to a miraculous concatenation of events by Providence with the purpose of tacitly guiding Parzival to ask the redeeming question. What to Parzival at the time were separate, meaningless details are revealed by Trevrizent as part of the providential plan of bringing Parzival to Munsalvæsche to ask the question of Amfortas.

If the nature of Parzival's journeying is only revealed retrospectively (first that it was miraculously guided, then that it was divinely assisted), the same is true of events once he has been

---

[1] 484,13ff. The three questions thus raised earlier in the audience's mind and answered subsequently by Trevrizent are all discussed by him in the passage 472,21ff. as well.

[2] Deinert, *Ritter*, pp. 12ff.   [3] *Ibid.*, pp. 14f.   [4] *Ibid.*, pp. 18 and 22f.

brought to his providential goal, for the subjective perspective of Book V is widened, corrected and ironised by the objective view supplied by Trevrizent.[1] But if Parzival's experience of events in Book V is mistaken, this is not necessarily always the case with the listeners who accompany him and witness events primarily from his point of view, for in the Grail-castle episode the narrator makes a number of revelations to the audience which allows them to see a little more than the hero. They are told, for example, that Amfortas lies at death's door (230,20), whereas Parzival is not told this and even if he may suspect it from what he sees, this is nowhere indicated. They are told the name of the Grail, the fact that it was the *wunsch von pardîs* and *erden wunsches überwal* and that it demanded chastity of its guardians (235,20ff.). Again they alone are warned that it is *der sælden fruht, der werlde süeze* and that it is almost as valuable as heaven itself (238,21ff.) and they are alerted to the gravity of Parzival's omission in not asking the question (240,3ff.). All of these narrator's comments, like his forecasts at this point, both give information and, by stimulating curiosity, show that they also withhold it, but together they plot a line which shows the listeners being given more guidance as to what is at stake than Parzival himself. By means of this they are able to judge him as well as sympathise with him.

To analyse this double technique (giving and withholding information, drawing his listeners now further from Parzival, now closer to him) in the overall relationship between these two Books is impossible here, but it can be illustrated in the smaller compass of Parzival's second encounter with Jeschute. This scene has been analysed (especially by contrast with Chrétien) in regard to dramatic irony,[2] but not with an eye to the way in which Wolfram releases information to his listeners and which is here the basis of his dramatic irony. Jeschute immediately recognises Parzival when she sees him again because of his extreme beauty which has obviously made an impression on her (258,1: *Dô Parzivâl gruoz gein ir sprach,/an in si erkenneclîchen sach,/*

---

[1] Tax (*Trevrizent*, pp. 119ff.) has analysed a similar technique in Wolfram's depiction of the encounter between Parzival and Trevrizent and likewise stresses its ironic implications.

[2] Cf. Salmon, *PBB*(T) 82 (1960), 107ff.

er was der schœnste über elliu lant;/dâ von s'in schiere het erkant).[1]
When she goes on to say that the wretched condition to which
she is now reduced (this has already been described to us, when
Parzival first catches sight of her, both in terms of her horse and
her own person, 256,14ff.) is the result of Parzival's meddle-
someness (258,5ff.), the audience is meant to recall two facts
from an earlier scene which will tell them whom Parzival here
confronts.[2] From Jeschute's husband they have already learned
that she is the sister of Erec (134,6) and that Orilus, angry at
what he takes to be his wife's infidelity, imposes upon her a
punishment similar to that which her brother inflicted on his
wife, Enite (136,23ff.). When the audience, coming across
Jeschute again and seeing her as Parzival sees her, is told of her
tattered clothing and of the wretched state of her horse, they can
immediately surmise that this must be Jeschute, but this possibility is denied to Parzival. The two remarks about her brother
Erec and the punishment which Orilus will inflict upon her were
addressed to her alone by her husband (Parzival has passed out of
this earlier scene and knows nothing of this), and when Parzival
sees her again she has been presumably rendered as unrecognisable by suffering and neglect as Sigune when Parzival meets her
for the second time.[3] Confident that he is correct, Parzival therefore denies Jeschute's claim that he is responsible for her condition (258,17: *jane wart von mîme lîbe/iu noch decheinem wîbe/laster
nie gemêret/(sô het ich mich gunêret),/sît ich den schilt von êrst gewan/
und rîters fuore mich versan*). This remark is quite truthful, but its
irony lies in its unconscious irrelevance, since the boy Parzival
was not yet a knight when he first met Jeschute. Parzival has
clearly not recognised whom he has before him, and this is
paralleled by the anonymous manner in which the narrator refers
to her, as it were from Parzival's point of view, simply as a
frouwe (256,15, 24, 29; 257,5).

---

[1] Jeschute had earlier rashly admitted to the impression which Parzival's beauty
had made on her (133,17f.), a confession which can only have confirmed her
husband's suspicions.

[2] The point about Wolfram's technique in this encounter is that he does not immediately mention Jeschute's name. He puts us initially in the same position as
Parzival, but gives us the means to rise superior to him.

[3] 249,21f. and 252,27ff.

This is the position up to the moment when they speak to each other. Jeschute recognises Parzival, it has been made possible for the audience to recognise her, but Parzival fails to do so. As the encounter proceeds, no development in insight is possible in Jeschute's case, since she grasps the facts from the beginning. As regards the audience there is some room for a growth in certainty, since the narrator's implicit style could have left the obtuse members unenlightened. This possibility is removed, first when the narrator refers to the husband by name (260,25: *der herzoge Orilus*), then eventually to Jeschute herself (262,25). The position with Parzival is not so clearcut. The narrator goes on using Parzival's point of view,[1] referring to her anonymously (*frouwe*: 258,24, 30; 259,27; 260,7; *blôziu frouwe*: 260,19; 261,22; *diu frouwe mit ir blôzem vel*: 268,19), but by the end of the episode, even though no formal recognition scene has been given, we are meant to see that Parzival has at last recognised the facts of the situation, for he phrases his oath to Orilus accordingly (269,20: ...*ob missetân/disiu frouwe habe, dô diz geschach/daz ich ir fürspan von ir brach./och fuort ich mêr goldes dan./ich was ein tôre und niht ein man,/ gewahsen niht pî witzen*). With Parzival we are therefore shown his initial ignorance of the facts (his rejection of Jeschute's reproach, and the use by the narrator, adopting Parzival's standpoint, of anonymous terms for Jeschute) and his final acknowledgement of the situation. Where Parzival's actual recognition came between these two points we are not told. It would be tempting to see the first stirrings of doubt in one phrase used by the narrator (260,3: *diu blôze herzogîn*) since from her mere appearance Parzival has no means of telling whether Jeschute is a duchess, unless he is beginning to recognise her. Against this there speaks the fact that we have no means of telling whether the narrator might not be speaking here in his own voice.[2] Apart from this, we can say

---

[1] Parzival employs the word *frouwe* as a term of polite address to Jeschute (258,15; 259,5, 15) and he also uses it of her when addressing Orilus (265,21; 266,9), but he nowhere uses the phrase *frou Jeschûte*, used by the narrator once he reveals her name (262,5; 263,24; 264,22; 268,8,12).

[2] Furthermore, although in their first encounter Jeschute's rank as a *herzogîn* had been revealed to the audience (129,27ff.), no mention of this had been made to Parzival. It might still be possible to rescue the suggestion that the narrator's reference to *diu blôze herzogîn* indicates the beginnings of Parzival's doubt if we were to read it not in any subjective terms of Parzival's psychology, but as an

that in this encounter we are shown things largely from Parzival's point of view, but are also given hints which place us in a position of advantage over him.[1]

In this one episode, as in the large-scale relationship between Books V and IX, the poet arranges that we share Parzival's doubts and bewilderment and therefore feel sympathy with him, and yet occasionally stand aloof and appreciate the irony of his situation, judging him from the broader perspective provided by another viewpoint. The creation of more than one viewpoint, the ability to see more of the total situation from one viewpoint than from the other, the shifting perspective which this provides, all this invites us to be more than passive recipients of a story,[2] it encourages us to scrutinise Parzival's experience from various angles and to adopt as our own the critical and questioning mode which is characteristic of the romance[3] and which it is one of the tasks of irony to propagate.

objective statement by the narrator meant purely as an external indication of where Parzival now stands. This would be confirmed by the important observation made by Harms that Wolfram's narrator indicates the failure of two combatants to recognise each other by himself referring to them anonymously during their period of misunderstanding, reverting to the use of their names only as they come to recognise each other. See Harms, *Kampf*, pp. 156f. on the use of this technique in Parzival's combat with Gawan and p. 164 on the anonymity of Feirefiz when he encounters Parzival. Hartmann makes use of the same device in depicting the combat between Iwein and Gawein (Harms, pp. 129f.).

I hope that this point, concerned with Parzival and Jeschute, may go some way to meet Mohr's doubts about the relationship between Parzival and Orilus in the same scene (*Euphorion* 52 (1958), 12). My point is that the narrator describes events here largely, but *not* completely, from Parzival's point of view. It is this slight discrepancy that allows us to see more than he can.

[1] Benson, *Art*, pp. 185ff., gives an informative discussion of the narrator's alternating points of view in *Sir Gawain* and of the alternation between an overall view and a restricted standpoint which this technique forces upon his audience.

[2] Chrétien's Calogrenant makes a similar point in the introduction to his account of his adventure (150: *Cuer et oroilles me randez!/Car parole oïe est perdue,/S'ele n'est de cuer antandue*). On the function of Calogrenant's 'prologue' as a substitute for Chrétien's see Gallais, *CCM* 7 (1964), 491. Hartmann has retained the point made by Calogrenant (*Iwein* 251ff.), but has made nothing of Chrétien's game with the prologue.

[3] See Vinaver, *BJRL* 46 (1963/64), 484ff., especially pp. 488 and 497.

6

VERBAL IRONY

At this point we must turn from themes and narrative technique to the various categories of irony we encounter in the romance. We shall concentrate on five categories[1] in the five chapters that follow, proceeding from the most small-scale type of irony to those with much wider implications. But to start with a category which I call verbal irony demands a word of explanation since all literary irony may be said to be verbal, whether it operates with the contrast between the real and apparent meanings of a statement or with the discrepancy between an utterance and its context, whilst the irony of situation[2] presupposes an artist who exploits it verbally. Even the use of gesture or intonation as a pointer to irony in the context of a public recital is still a signal to a verbal expression of irony. Instead, I use the term verbal irony in the more restricted sense of irony conveyed by the choice of one particular word (a restriction which comes close to the rhetorical definition of the figure antiphrasis as *unius verbi ironia*)[3] and propose to consider small-scale cases of irony under such headings as verbal ambiguity, oxymoron, litotes, inversion and divergence. I call such cases small-scale because their range is generally so restricted that the discrepancy between statement and context is immediately apparent; irony is present as a minute verbal phenomenon involving the shortest time-lag between hearing and understanding whereas the examples which will engage us in the following chapters operate with a much larger time-scale. This is not to say that verbal irony cannot be adapted

[1] I have discussed the main features of these five categories in *Irony*, pp. 50ff.
[2] On the irony of situation and its verbal presentation by the poet see Green, *Alieniloquium*, pp. 156ff., and below, pp. 250ff.
[3] Cf. Donatus, *Ars grammatica* III 6 (402,3).

to wider purposes and used as a recurrent stratagem by which the author may control his overall effects, but even here the individual examples which constitute this larger strategy are still small-scale cases whose irony is generally immediately apparent.

Verbal ambiguity

If I start with the possibility of irony provided by verbal ambiguity,[1] this is because Trier has taught us to recognise the wide range of meanings present in so many medieval terms[2] (what he says of medieval German is also applicable to other languages). Such semantic ambivalence does not constitute irony of itself[3] but it provides an author with ample opportunities to exploit it. We have no need to agree with Robertson's thesis about the ironic depiction of love in medieval literature in order to accept the force of his observation: 'The fact that the word love (*amor*) could be used for either Charity or cupidity opened enormous possibilities for literary wordplay.'[4] In the case of the vocabulary of love the situation is rendered more complex (and the possibilities of ironic wordplay are increased) by the presence of two-way literary traffic: love-poetry of the courtly period acquired much of its vocabulary and imagery from religious poetry,[5] whilst religious poetry in its turn could adapt secular poetry to its own ends.[6] Such reciprocal borrowings mean that many leading terms occupy an indeterminate position between secular and religious, an ambiguity which can only have increased the possibilities of irony for an author disposed to make use of it.

Yet it is not just to the semantic fluidity of medieval speech that we have to look in order to explain the prevalence of verbal ambiguity and its ironic exploitation. We also have to take into account the social dimension of courtly literature, such factors

---

[1] Booth, *Irony*, p. 48, has helpfully quoted from Smith, *Closure*, p. 254: 'Both irony and ambiguity are "pluralistic" ways of speaking, evasions of committed speech.'
[2] Trier, *Wortschatz, passim*. See also Hoffmann, *Semasia* 1 (1974), 37ff.
[3] I have discussed this point in another context, *Alieniloquium*, pp. 132f.
[4] Robertson, *Speculum* 26 (1951), 28.
[5] One aspect of this question has been discussed by Kesting, *Maria-Frouwe*, especially pp. 89ff.
[6] Cf. Weise, *Gotik*, pp. 131ff. The problem has been treated in the particular case of Seuse by Bizet, *Suso*.

as the demands of courtly etiquette in social converse. By this I mean the need to avoid such antisocial faults as boasting (encouraging thereby the use of understatement), coarseness of speech (best avoided by verbal ambiguity) and direct criticism of others (easily shunned by saying the opposite of what is meant, of criticising under the pretence of praising),[1] but also the more positive value attached to the art of courtly conversation (*talkyng noble*), especially the *luf-talkyng* or *dalyaunce* between the sexes in which words can mean everything or nothing.[2] Language and social convention thus combined to encourage a mode of indirect and uncommitted speech which could make ample use of irony – language by its semantic ambivalence and convention by the need to oil the wheels of social intercourse, the one providing the means and the other the incentive for using an indirect mode of speech.[3]

How consciously this verbal ambiguity could be used in a social context can be illustrated from the point of view both of the practitioner and of the recipient. We are shown both sides of the game of courtly double speech in an episode in *Flamenca* depicting one stage in the slow and far from certain declaration of feelings between lover and lady. Because of the unfavourable circumstances in which their encounters take place (at intervals at church, barely one or two syllables can be whispered by one party on each occasion) each has ample opportunity to think out in advance what short word or phrase will best entice the other into a further confession without exposing his or her own position too obviously. On one such occasion Flamenca, by now alert to what Guillem has in mind, takes advice with her female companions and is recommended to couch her next reply in such ambiguous terms that Guillem will be encouraged to advance a step further without any certainty as to her true feelings (5024: *Respondet li un mot doptos/Qui-l fassa bon entendement/E-l don*

---

[1] On this practice see Green, *Damning*.

[2] Cf. the stimulating words of Stevens, *Music*, pp. 159ff., on this aspect of courtly life, even though what he has to say is confined to England.

[3] I do not wish to imply by these words on courtly conversation that I regard the situation at German courts around 1200 as comparable in refinement and sophistication with what obtained in twelfth-century France or fourteenth-century England. My point is simply that at any court, to whatever varying extent, the needs of social intercourse encourage an essentially indirect mode of speech.

amor ab espavent). Following this advice, Flamenca chooses her ambiguous word accordingly (5029: *Car cest motz es aissi cubertz/ que ja per lui non sera certz/Qu'ieu l'ami ni desesperatz*). Such foresight pays dividends, for on hearing her reply the lover is overcome by a mixture of doubt and hope, as had been planned for him (5049: *Pero qui ben i vol entendre/Ben sembla que mais deja penre/ Vaus hoc que vaus non tal doptansa./Ben atrobet mot de balansa*). That Guillem is as skilled in this verbal game as Flamenca is indicated by the way in which he immediately grasps the ambiguity which he was meant to see, by his recognition that *un motz doptos* (5024) is characterised by its ambiguity or *doptansa* (5051), that what she intended as a *motz...cubertz* (5029) is for him equally a *motz de balansa*. How close Flamenca's use of ironic ambiguity (revealing the truth in instalments and without committing herself, rather like Wolfram in hinting at Parzival's preternatural guidance)[1] comes to the poet's exploitation of verbal ambivalence is suggested by Guillem's admiration of her verbal adroitness, for he twice uses a technical term for composing poetry (*atrobar*, 5052 and 5055) to describe her dexterity. Flamenca's skill with words reflects the poet's, and we have to weigh his words as carefully for their implications as Guillem does hers.[2]

With Chrétien Lunete can also display her skill in using ambiguous phrasing for ulterior purposes, as when she takes Yvain from his place of concealment and introduces him to the widow of the knight he has just killed. Although she has just successfully arranged things with Laudine, she cannot refrain from teasingly warning Yvain of the imprisonment that awaits him (1938: *Et parole par coverture/De la prison, ou il iert mis*), but the hint conveyed to us (not to Yvain) by the phrase *par coverture* warns us that this can hardly be meant literally. What is at stake is then made clear by the narrator's commentary that follows (1940: *Que sanz prison n'est nus amis./Ele a droit, se prison le claimme;/ Que bien est an prison, qui aimme*). Lunete's words *par coverture*, like Flamenca's *motz cubertz*, operate with two levels of meaning, in this case with the discrepancy between a literal understanding

---

[1] See above, pp. 150ff.
[2] An English counterpart to the Provençal *motz de balansa* would be Chaucer's description (*Troilus* V 897ff.) of *ambages* as *double wordes slye* and as *a word with two visages*.

of what she says and the metaphor of the prisoner of love[1] which she has in mind.

At one point in *Cligès* we witness the thought processes of the victim (as with Guillem in *Flamenca*) and follow her attempts to reach certainty. Fénice ponders over the meaning of Cligès's parting words to her (he takes his leave of one 'to whom he altogether belongs')[2] and is conscious of two possible meanings. She hopes that the positive one is what he had in mind (4328: *Aprés, por boene boche feire,/Met sor sa leingue un po d'espece:/Que ele por trestote Grece,/An celui san qu'ele le prist,/Ne voldroit que cil qui le dist/L'eüst ja pansé par faintié*). But she recognises that there is no certainty that her reading is correct (4359: *Mes ele n'an est pas certainne,/Por ce i met et cure et painne/A encerchier et a aprandre/A quoi ele s'an porra prandre;/En plusors menieres l'espont*), above all in view of the everyday meaning of his words as a polite commonplace (4388: *Mes ce me resmaie de bot/Que c'est une parole usee,/Si repuis bien estre amusee;/Car tiex i a qui par losange/Dïent nes a la gent estrange/ 'Je suis vostres, et quanque j'ai',/Si sont plus jeingleor que jai./Don ne me sai auquel tenir,/Car ce porroit tost avenir/Qu'il le dist por moi losangier*). In this monologue of Fénice we catch a glimpse of the ambiguities of courtly speech, meaning either everything or nothing and allowing Cligès to make a discreet confession without apparently committing himself.

In German literature it is Gottfried who is especially fond of illustrating this kind of position. We come across it first when Riwalin, to whom Blanscheflur has just made an observation as ambiguous as Cligès's to Fénice,[3] considers her remark in closer detail and interprets it eventually as signifying love for him (794: *er trahte maneger slahte,/waz Blanschefliure swære/und dirre mære wære./ir gruoz, ir rede betrahter gar,/ir suft, ir segen, al ir gebar/ daz marcter al besunder/und begunde iedoch hier under/ir siuften unde ir süezen segen/uf den wec der minne wegen*). Tristan himself is depicted in a situation similar to that of his father, mentally analysing the possible implications of an ambivalent word just used by Isold (11989: *do si lameir so dicke sprach,/er bedahte unde besach/anclichen*

---

[1] On this topos see Maurer, *DVjs* 27 (1953), 182ff.
[2] *Cligès* 4282f. See below, p. 181.
[3] *Tristan* 754ff. See below, pp. 181f. A similar example occurs in Isold's groping after the significance of the name Tantris, 10100ff.

unde cleine/des selben wortes meine./sus begunder sich versinnen,/lameir daʒ wære minnen,/lameir bitter, la meir mer:/der meine der duht in ein her). In these passages Gottfried concentrates on the recipient's task of interpretation, on his mental struggle to seize upon the truth behind conflicting possibilities. In projecting this task into the narrative action he is illustrating, like the author of *Flamenca* in the case of Guillem, the similar task confronting the listeners who are to understand the poet's own words, bringing it home to them what is involved in comprehending a literary work, to use Hartmann's words, with the heart as well as the ears.[1]

Muecke has referred to another type of ambiguity, the eighteenth-century practice of pretending to praise by saying, for example, that a book is written with equal learning and spirit or affords the reader as much improvement as entertainment.[2] The irony of such examples, which rests on a comparison whose linguistic formulation ('equal', 'as much as') invites us to take it positively rather than negatively, is not unknown to the medieval romance. In Chrétien's *Perceval* the command by Orguelleuse for Gauvain to ride ahead on his decrepit nag (7209: *Mes aleʒ et si vos teisieʒ,/Qu'or estes vos si aeisieʒ/Con je vos voloie veoir)*[3] is revealed as ironic by the discrepancy between his shameful situation and the use of a word implying that he is comfortable (*aeisieʒ*). When she says that he is now as much at ease as she wished to see him (*si...con*), the listener's reaction is to take this positively, since she after all employs a positive term *aeisieʒ*. Logically, however, there is no reason why the comparison should not be meant at the other end of the scale ('as ill at ease as she wished to see him') and it is towards this less obvious reading of the comparison

---

[1] *Iwein* 249ff. Cf. Chrétien's *Yvain* 149ff.

We move from verbal ambiguity used by a character to the same possibility exploited by the poet (and also from a sophisticated awareness of what is at stake to naïve inexperience) when we come to the ambiguities of Obilot's words in connection with Gawan. On these see Mohr's 'Nachtrag 1965', pp. 281ff., to his essay *Obie*, as reprinted in Rupp, *Wolfram*, pp. 261ff., and also Zimmermann, *Kommentar*, p. 208.

[2] Muecke, *Compass*, pp. 71f.

[3] I have discussed this passage in a wider context in *Recognising*, p. 39. In what follows I several times make reference to this essay, but this is not as repetitive as it might seem, for here I am concerned with various types of verbal irony, whereas the aim of the essay was to distinguish the signals to irony which were available to the medieval poet.

that the contrast between utterance and context drives us.[1] In a passage where Hartmann's Iwein replies to Keii's spiteful criticism a similarly ambiguous comparison is made when Iwein says that his opponent knows how to make his reproaches tactfully (862: *ouch kan erz mir wol undersagen/mit selher vuoge als er ie pflac*). The function of *selher* is twofold here, for it acts in itself as a pointer to irony,[2] but also suggests a comparison ('with as much courtly tact as he has always shown') which further underlines the irony, for we have already been shown that it is Keii's inveterate practice to show anything but self-control in his backbiting.[3]

Comparisons of degree lend themselves particularly well to this technique. When it is a question of suggesting how restricted the open fields in the midst of woodland are Wolfram can employ the word *breit* (398,20: *etslîchz sô breit daz ein gezelt/vil kûme druffe stüende*), allowing the more common positive meaning of the adjective to obscure temporarily the fact that, as a neutral term of measurement, it can also be used in a negative context. Orgeluse's words to Gawan, ordering him to ride in front of her for fear that she might lose so esteemed a companion (515,30: *'ez wære et schade, ob ich verlür/sus ahtbæren gesellen'*), are meant ironically,[4] but this purpose is again served by the strictly neutral formulation, for the words 'a companion as esteemed as yourself' can clearly be read in two ways.[5] In other cases Wolfram can employ the typifying comparison with the norm, so common in the idealising style of the romance, for an ironic purpose.[6] In talking in the Prologue of women with false hearts he says (3,12): *ist dâ daz herze conterfeit,/die lobe ich als ich solde/daz safer ime golde.*

---

[1] A more obvious example of the same method occurs in *Perceval* 8668f. (*Mes tu sez autant de la lune/Con tu fez del chastel, ce cuit*).

[2] On the employment of demonstratives as pointers to irony see Green, *Recognising*, pp. 30ff.

[3] Cf. *Iwein* 137ff. and 810ff.

[4] This is made clear by the words with which she immediately follows this remark (516,2: *'got müeze iuch vellen!'*). Cf. Green, *Recognising*, p. 18.

[5] Again the presence of irony is signalled by a demonstrative (*sus*) in 516,1 and by the implied comparison.

[6] Although such comparisons with the norm have been seen, in the case of Hartmann, as characteristic of his idealising style and therefore as an indication that his style is not ironic (cf. especially Kramer, *Erzählerbemerkungen*), there are also cases, which cannot simply be ignored, where the comparison with the norm can be utilised for ironic purposes. On these see Green, *Damning*, pp. 121ff.

The formulation is a positive one, but the point of the comparison is to show that the one deserves as *little* praise as the other.[1]

This still gives no account of the ironic exploitation of the semantic ambiguity of so many medieval terms, a subject too vast to be treated in anything but a highly selective manner. An isolated example of this technique is provided by the word with which Hartmann's Kalogreant describes the splendour of the magic well in its natural setting (603: *und vant dâ grôȥ êre*). This sense of *êre* (the splendour[2] of the scene which he found there) for the moment conceals the other sense of *êre* ('victory in combat')[3] which Kalogreant did not find on this occasion. Gottfried can play on the double meaning of the word *spil* ('entertainment, pastime' or 'loveplay') in the erotically highly-charged episode of the love-grotto.[4] He also adds to his derision of the Irish steward's claims to the hand of Isold by having him unwittingly reveal himself in his account of the dangers he has undergone (9219: *und waȥ er angeste hie mite/und kumberlicher næte erlite*). He means *angest* in the objective sense of 'danger', whereas we know from the description of his cowardice in dealing with a safely dead dragon that this word is more true in the subjective meaning of 'fear, fright'.[5] In the 'Schwertleite' digression (where the narrator subjects much contemporary literary practice to criticism under the pretence of praising it as superior to his own lack of skill) the mask of humility is worn so that we shall see through it (4924: *so cleine als ich gesinnet bin*). The word *cleine*,

---

[1] Cf. Wolfram's employment of a similar comparison with a negative purpose, to stress how little wit the young Parzival had in riding all day along a shallow stream without thinking to ford it (129,12: *den tag er gar derneben reit,/als eȥ sînen witzen tohte*).

[2] Maurer, *Leid*, pp. 274ff., discusses the semantic scope of *êre* in Hartmann's work. His treatment of *Iwein* (pp. 276f.) is selective, but he includes the meaning 'Pracht' in his survey of the word in *Erec* (p. 275). In his edition Cramer translates *êre* in v. 603 by 'Herrlichkeit'.

[3] Cf. Maurer, *op. cit.*, p. 274 ('Erfolg, Glück' in *Erec*) and p. 276 ('Sieg' in *Iwein*).

[4] Cf. Gruenter, *Euphorion* 55 (1961), 391f.

[5] Gottfried uses *angest* in the objective sense in v. 1259 to indicate the danger and suffering in which Riwalin lies because of his wound, but elsewhere the subjective sense is recognisable (e.g. 9310: *nu la din angesten sin*; cf. 9346f.). The same ambiguity also occurs when the steward unwittingly condemns himself in using the adverb (9809: ...*durch daȥ ich minnete daȥ wip/und wagete den lip/dicke engeslicher danne ie man*). What this claim amounts to has already been shown us earlier (8953ff.), above all by the ironic use of *belderichen* in v. 8962 (on this see below, p. 185).

apparently there to imply how little intelligence the narrator possesses, also retains in Gottfried's usage its earlier meaning of 'skilled, perceptive'[1] and can therefore suggest precisely the opposite of what seems to be said.[2] When two lines later we are told of the literary attempts of Gottfried's contemporaries (4926: *dar an sich also manic man/versuochet und verpirset hat*) the obvious meaning of *sich versuochen* ('to try one's hand') gives way, by its association with the more clearly negative *sich verpirsen*, to a far from complimentary nuance ('to go astray by seeking in the wrong direction').[3] Wolfram's acquaintance with the same technique, especially useful in flirtatious badinage, is borne out by the first encounter of Gawan with Orgeluse. To the courtly gesture with which he places himself gallantly at her disposal (530,6: *mîn vart von hinnen wirt getân/al nâch iuwerm râte*) she responds with words (530,8: *sie sprach 'der kumt iu spâte'*) which transfer *rât* from his apparent meaning ('at your command') to an erotic meaning ('the lady's favours'). She thereby hints that she has seen what intentions really lie behind such courteous behaviour.[4]

These examples of ambiguity concern only isolated points, but there are occasions where these recur so frequently that the whole passage takes on an ironic colouring. The first morning's bedroom encounter between Sir Gawain and the lady of the castle

---

[1] Cf. *Tristan* 11 436: *mit also cleinen sinnen.*

[2] I owe this point to Hahn, *ZfdA* 96 (1967), 220.

[3] Gottfried elsewhere exploits the possible ambiguity of reflexive verbs with the *ver-* prefix. In describing the dramatic irony of the Irish queen devoting all her medical skill to curing Tristan, one whom she would sooner have killed if she had been aware of his identity, he plays on the two meanings of *sich versinnen*, denoting both 'sich auf etwas besinnen' and 'sich irren' (7920: *und swes si sich versinnete,/daz ime ze senfte und ze vromen/und ze heile möhte komen,/da was si spate und vruo/betrehtic unde gescheffec zuo*). 'Whatever she could devise' here carries the nuance of making a drastic mistake. The same possibility exists in another passage where confident expectations are dashed. When Marke at the trial-scene cuts short the preliminaries and orders Isold to grasp the red-hot iron (15 725: *es dunket mich genuoc hier an,/alse ich michs versinnen kan./nu nemet daz isen uf die hant*), the meaning of this verb vacillates between the innocuous usage he has in mind ('as far as I can see') and a more ironic implication ('as capable as I am of making a mistake'). That Isold escapes unscathed is a confirmation that Marke has again fallen victim to the appearance of things.

[4] On this interpretation of the two functions of *rât* see Mohr, *Hilfe*, p. 178. On the ironic force of the passage in which Wolfram operates with both these meanings see Green, *Recognising*, pp. 48ff.

is a protracted and skilful example of this. The comic force of this courtly badinage (which is also an ironic force, for each knows that the other knows what is afoot) rests on the repeated manner in which innocuous terms from chivalry and social intercourse acquire sexual innuendoes and suggest intercourse of another kind when they are employed *à deux* in the setting of a bedroom.[1] The whole scene is informed by the irony of the double entendre, Gawain's repeated attempts to ignore the lady's erotic innuendoes and to fasten on the safer surface meaning of her remarks are countered by her successful endeavours to transfer the weight of their dialogue back to the field where she can hope to achieve her ends, and each contestant does justice to what the courtly art of *dalyaunce* expected from its participants. It is in the light of this constantly shifting linguistic pattern that we have to interpret the apparently blatant offer of the lady to Gawain (1237: *'ʒe ar welcum to my cors,/Yowre awen won to wale./ Me behoueʒ of fyne force/Your seruaunt be, and schale').*[2] At least appearances are preserved by the outward possibility that *my cors* need have no more than pronominal force[3] and could even involve wordplay on *cors* ('body') and *cor(t)s* ('courts'), just as *won* could likewise imply both 'delight' and 'dwelling'.[4] We may have little doubt but that the sexual implication is predominant, but as with the less blatant examples from other romances the point is that two linguistic levels are present in these words, so that an erotic attack can be launched on the one and, if necessary, a retreat into innocuous sociability made on the other.

Verbal ambiguity plays a decisive role in two characteristic scenes of the romance. The first is the stage in the narrative where one of the lovers tentatively confesses to the other, but in such veiled terms that a retreat is always possible without too much embarrassment. We have seen how different poets can employ the scene where the recipient unravels the truth of the ambiguous confession as an image for the manner in which the

---

1 These constant shifts in the linguistic formulation of this scene have been well analysed by Mills, *JEGP* 67 (1968), 612ff.
2 On these lines see Burrow, *Reading*, pp. 8off. and Clark, *MÆ* 40 (1971), 16ff.
3 Comparable therefore to *mon cors* in Old French and *mîn lîp* in Middle High German as circumlocutions for the first person singular pronoun.
4 Mills, *art. cit.*, p. 616.

ideal listener is to interpret the comparable ambiguities of the poet's statements, but now is the occasion to look at the kind of two-edged remark used in such concealed confessions. Flamenca's companions advise her to employ *un motz doptos*, she agrees with them in deciding on what she likewise calls a *motz cubertz*, and the recipient likewise concedes that her answer is an enigmatic one (*motz de balansa*). What Flamenca actually says, contracted to two syllables because of the difficulties under which they meet, is simply *qu'en puesc* (5028). We must see in this deliberate ambiguity a choice between two meanings, either the coldly uninviting 'What can I do about it?' (implying that she is not concerned in Guillem's fate) or the promising 'Tell me what I should do about it' (with its hint that she would gladly do it).[1] It is this open choice which leaves Guillem in as much doubt as before, seeing in these two syllables a source of hope, but also of alarm (5043: *'Cest motz aitan m'aporta/Que daus una part mi conorta/E daus l'autra part si m'esglaia'*), a failure to promise either clear gain or obvious loss (5047: *En* qu'en puesc? *non ai dan ni pron*), an avoidance of a straightforward yes or no (5048: *Ab* qu'en puesc? *non dis hoc ni non*). And this is precisely why these two syllables were chosen with such care.

Cligès takes equal care over the words with which he takes his leave of Fénice (4282: *Mes droiz est qu'a vos congé praigne/Com a celi cui ge sui toz*). Although we are not shown in his case, as with Flamenca, the ambiguous purpose behind his choice of words, we see the uncertainty they create in Fénice as she ponders over their import. Like Guillem, she can interpret them positively as a declaration of love (4382: *Ne ne deüst an nule guise/Cligés dire qu'il fust toz miens,/S'Amors ne l'a en ses liens*), but also negatively, implying in her case not the cold rebuttal which Guillem saw as his alternative reading, but the meaningless gesture of a polite term of social intercourse used of all and sundry. Gottfried's Riwalin is placed in a similar quandary by Blanscheflur's unexpected complaint to him (754: *si sprach: 'an einem vriunde min,/dem besten den ich ie gewan,/da habet ir mich beswæret an'*), for he takes *vriunt* in the obvious sense of a kinsman of hers whom he may have injured in the tournament (761: *und wande, daz er eteswen/ ir*

---

[1] Cf. Lewent, *ZfrPh* 53 (1933), 14.

mage, disen oder den,/unwizzend an der ritterschaft/gemachet hæte schadehaft). The audience is told straightaway by the narrator that this is a false reading of her words (767: *nein, der vriunt, des si gewuoc,/daz was ir herze, in dem si truoc/von sinen schulden ungemach,/ daz was der vriunt, von dem si sprach./iedoch enwester niht hie mite*), but Riwalin comes upon the truth only later, after closely considering her words and gestures. The words used by Isold on the voyage to Cornwall are more consciously literary[1] (11 986: *'lameir' sprach si 'daz ist min not,/lameir daz swæret mir den muot,/lameir ist, daz mir leide tuot'*) and the three stages of her remark point to the three meanings which Tristan discovers in the word *lameir*. It is ironically fitting that one so skilled in words as Tristan should at first fasten on the two meanings which could be, but are not involved here, but he is at least helped, as Guillem is not, by Isold's readiness to say that she meant *lameir* neither as *mer* nor as *sur* (12 004). Tristan is left with no alternative but to confront the sole remaining possibility (12 011: *do er des wortes zende kam,/ minne dar inne vernam*).

The other romance situation in which verbal ambiguity is crucially important occurs in works devoted to the triangle situation between husband, wife and lover, where at one stage in the narrative an oath has to be sworn to establish the innocence of one of the culprits. The *Tristan* story is an obvious case, with two corresponding examples from Béroul as well as Gottfried. Béroul's fragment opens with an incomplete scene (Marc spies on the lovers from a tree, but, unknown to him, they are aware of his presence and save themselves by acting out a charade) in which Yseult has to persuade her husband that his suspicions are unfounded. To make her statement the more convincing she brings God into the picture (22: *Mais Dex plevis ma loiauté,/ Qui sor mon cors mete flaele*). This now creates the ironic situation that, facing two audiences (God and her husband), she has to phrase her statement in such a way that each shall understand it in his own way, but that it shall still be acceptable to God as the formal truth. In this position she falls back on a conscious ambiguity (24: *S'onques fors cil qui m'ot pucele/Out m'amistié encor nul jor!*), which satisfies Marc, unaware of the substitution on his wedding-night,

---

[1] Cf. the parallels given by Hertz, *Tristan*, pp. 532f.

and which as a concealed reference to Tristan as her first lover offers no offence to the truth. The irony of this situation lies in the presence of two audiences[1] (God's omniscience is shared by the listeners, informed of facts which escape the outwitted husband) and in the way in which Marc is fobbed off by the formal truth of words whose deeper import is not grasped by him.

In his corresponding scene Gottfried works in essentially the same way. Here too Isold brings God into the situation (14755: *des si got min urkünde/und enmüeze ouch miner sünde/niemer anders komen abe*) and satisfies both her audiences by an ambiguous reference to her continuing to feel affection only for the man who first loved her (1476off.).[2] How ambiguity can achieve effects in small compass is brought out by a remark of Isold's to Tristan just before her oath (14752: *nu weiz ez aber got selbe wol,/wie min herze bin ziu ste*). This is indeed true (God does know the facts about their adultery), but Marke, whose doubts are about to be allayed by the oath, cannot realise that the truth about Isold's affection known to God is not identical with the truth of which the king now convinces himself.

The other occasion in both these *Tristan* versions (the trial-scene) is more dangerous for the lovers, since the threat of punishment is more tangible and legal formalities restrict their freedom to bend circumstances to their needs. None the less in each work Isold is able to break out of this dangerous constriction by carefully contriving an episode before the trial to which she can refer in formulating her oath and which provides her with the ambiguity she needs in this scene, too.[3]

---

[1] On the two audiences of irony see Green, *Alieniloquium*, pp. 129 and 150ff.

[2] *Ibid.*, p. 153.

[3] I have discussed these two passages in greater detail in *Alieniloquium*, pp. 151ff.

Although we cannot interpret it completely because of a gap in the MS at this point, enough remains for us to see that the oath with which Flamenca convinces her husband of her innocence (so that he relaxes his surveillance) is as ambiguous as any used in the *Tristan* story. She hoodwinks him by flattering his conviction of how efficient this surveillance has been (6685: *Mas certas bon plag vos faría:/Ma fe sobre sanz juraría,/Vezent mas donçellas, ades,/Qu'en aissi tostems mi gardes/Co vos m'aves saïns garada*). From these lines we can tell that two audiences are involved (on the one hand, Flamenca's companions and the saints by whom she swears, on the other hand Archimbaut himself). But if we paraphrase her words ('I shall henceforth impose as effective a guard upon myself as you have up to now') it is clear that we are dealing here with the type of ironic comparison considered above, pp. 176f. This is independent of the further irony that Archimbaut should be

The oxymoron

From ambiguity we pass to the figure of the oxymoron, which combines two contradictory concepts in narrow compass so as to make a unity of them. Since this figure belongs to the indirect mode of speech in meaning something other than what it literally says, it can be seen as a category or relative of irony.[1] For Freytag, to whom we owe a detailed study of this figure in the work of several medieval German poets, this connection with irony is a tenuous one,[2] because she (correctly) regards the two contradictory concepts of the oxymoron as *together* constituting the truth, whereas she sees irony as necessarily implying an antithesis between what is said and what is meant.[3] This is true only if we make the error of interpreting the relationship between the two meanings of an ironic statement as directly antithetical. This may be so with many (including the most obvious) examples, but not all, since irony can also arise from nothing more than a discrepancy or divergence between the two meanings,[4] both of which can be true, but in different ways. In such cases (if not in those where a flat contradiction is involved) both meanings of the ironic statement are true, as with the oxymoron both together

persuaded to relax his guard at the moment when his wife has begun an affair with Guillem.

The position is slightly different in Chrétien's *Lancelot*, when Lancelot defends Guinevere's reputation by swearing her innocence. Again, two audiences are involved within the narrative, since Lancelot swears by relics (4950f., 4961) and appeals to God (4954). But the difference arises in that Meleagant, convinced that Guinevere has spent the night with Keu (whereas we know that it was with Lancelot), stupidly specifies this in his formal accusation (4967ff.) instead of leaving it open. This enables Lancelot to swear with propriety that the Queen did not lie with Keu (4971 : *Et je t'an lief come parjur,|fet Lanceloz, et si rejur|qu'il n'i jut ne ne la santi*) and to seek divine vengeance on the calumniator (4974f.). When Lancelot pleads that God may make a *voire demostrance*(4976) he does not mean that God should expose the whole affair (including his own involvement and the Queen's actual guilt, unsuspected in this form by Meleagant), but rather that God should simply demonstrate the truth about the only formal accusation which has been made and denied. Lancelot sails very close to the wind here, but can do so because his opponent has played into his hands.

On the ambiguous oath in the *Roman de Renart* see Jauss, *Untersuchungen*, pp. 262f.
[1] Wackernagel, *Poetik*, p. 533 and Arbusow, *Colores*, p. 88. Both quoted by Freytag, *Oxymoron*, p. 11, fn. 14.
[2] Freytag, *Oxymoron*, p. 11.
[3] *Ibid.*
[4] On this distinction between direct contradiction and divergence, vital for any definition of irony, see Green, *Alieniloquium*, pp. 120ff.

constitute the truth, but show different aspects of it. To this extent at least there is an overlap between the oxymoron and irony which justifies us in looking at this figure.

In considering the possibility of an ironic employment of the oxymoron we have to discount those cases where the oxymoron is only apparent, where one of the concepts is used ironically so that after the reconstruction of its intended meaning the contradiction is resolved and the oxymoron destroyed. This is the case when Wolfram uses a euphemistic term as part of an apparent oxymoron, as when Meljahkanz is criticised (343,25: *er tregt der unfuoge kranz*) or the stiffness of Cundrie's hair is presented (313,20: *linde als eins swînes rückehâr*).[1] In both cases irony is clearly present: in *kranz* because the wreath of honour is normally used only of positive qualities, and in *linde* because this is a degree of comparison whose strictly neutral force we read positively only at our peril. Irony is present, but it is not the ironic use of an oxymoron, for the irony actually abolishes the oxymoron. The same is true of Gottfried's qualification of the Irish steward's turning to flight as 'brave' (8961: *wan ern gesach den trachen nie,/ern kerte belderichen ie*). We classify this conjunction of opposites as an oxymoron only as long as we fail to see the ironic force of *belderichen*.[2] In Tristan's claim to have had little trouble in cutting out the dragon's tongue (11261: *mit lihter arbeit*), the adjective is revealed as an ironic understatement of self-deprecation by its contrast with what the narrator himself says of this task (9058: *den giel er im uf brach,/mit micheler arbeit*).[3] If we accept the irony of these passages (whose force certainly resides, as Freytag wrongly claims of all irony, in the direct antithesis between statement and meaning), we cannot regard the apparent contradiction as really suggesting an oxymoron.

After making such allowances we still encounter cases where an oxymoron can be employed ironically. This can occur when a character's insufficient knowledge is at issue, by contrast with the information which the narrator places at his listeners' disposal. Gottfried's narrator comments on the irony that the kidnapped young Tristan should have been set ashore by the

[1] Cf. Freytag, *op. cit.*, p. 64.
[2] Freytag, *op. cit.*, pp. 150 (especially fn. 31) and 157.   [3] *Ibid.*, p. 185.

7-2

Norwegian merchants nowhere else but in Cornwall, his true home (3379: *Nu Tristan derst ȝe hu ˛komen/unwizȝend, alse ir habet vernomen,/und wande doch ellende sin*). Freytag calls this an example of 'Gedankenoxymoron' because the contradiction between *ȝe huse komen* and *ellende sin* exceeds the narrow limits of the verbal figure,[1] but the contradiction is a loose one in another sense as well. On the face of it, the antithesis between Tristan's belief that he is in a strange country and the fact that he is now in his homeland appears to be absolute, but this is toned down by the new dimension to the word *ellende* which is revealed at the Cornish court, the realisation that Tristan is inwardly estranged from courtly society altogether.[2] In this sense the irony of this passage, like the oxymoron, points to the truth that even though Tristan has come home to Tintagel he is inwardly estranged from the values of the court. Whereas the oxymoron operates on the literal, geographical level, the irony of this passage is effective in a metaphorical dimension.

An oxymoron can also be employed ironically when what is at stake is the discrepancy between appearances and reality, where again the audience may be given the means to judge the situation correctly earlier than the figure in the work. This is so when, in his encounter with Trevrizent, Párzival expresses his disillusionment with God (447,25: *ich diende einem der heizet got,/ê daȝ sô lasterlîchen spot/sîn gunst über mich erhancte*).[3] Since Parzival means the word *gunst* ironically to suggest its opposite (in his state of rebellion he cannot regard it as a sign of God's favour that he has suffered such disgrace), he can only mean the contradiction between *spot* and *gunst* as apparent and the oxymoron as unreal. But the further irony of this passage resides in the fact, unsuspected by the victim, that the oxymoron *is* a real one, since it is ultimately revealed as a proof of God's favourable disposition towards him that the disgrace that befell Parzival and the sufferings that arose from it are part of God's design to bring him to Munsalvæsche as Grail-king. We have in this passage a case where Parzival's bitter irony (*gunst*) it itself ironised by being ultimately shown to be true, but

---

[1] *Ibid.*, pp. 22 and 143.
[2] This deep estrangement has been brought out by Hahn, *Raum*, pp. 88ff.
[3] Freytag, *op. cit.*, p. 59, fn. 49.

in a way which Parzival cannot suspect because, despite the apparent superior knowledge inherent in his use of irony, he is still the prisoner of appearances and blind to the reality of God's controlling plan.[1]

Heroic irony

Verbal irony is restricted in its scope, as these examples have demonstrated, because the discrepancy between statement and meaning is immediately obvious. It is perhaps this frequent lack of long-range implications that explains why irony of this type is particularly common before the rise of the romance, in epic poetry where grim warrior humour often makes use of what might be called heroic irony[2] in its battle descriptions.[3] Irony of this type is still common in the single combats of the romance, so that we may see in heroic irony one possibility of a continuous ironic tradition in which the romance follows its predecessors in the epic. Such antecedents include the *Battle of Maldon* in England, where battle between the English and the Vikings is seen ironically as a (potential) reconciliation by means of the sword (60: *us sceal ord and ecg ær geseman,/grim guðplega, ær we gofol syllon*) and where weapons are regarded as the fitting tribute to render to the invaders (46: *Hi willað eow to gafole garas syllan,/ættrynne ord and ealde swurd,/þa heregeatu þe eow hilde ne deah*). In Germany the *Ludwigslied* likewise refers to the hero pouring out a bitter wine for his Viking opponents (53: *Her skancta cehanton sînan fîanton/ Bitteres lîdes*). In addition to this, heroic literature can invoke what has been called 'Standesironie'[4] by describing combat in terms taken from another walk of life. This is particularly effective when the person in question is not exclusively a warrior, so that trans-

---

[1] The two layers of this last example, where an ironic statement is itself ironised, are comparable to what I have shown to be a similar structure in a passage from Hartmann's *Erec* (*Recognising*, pp. 51f.).

[2] Cf. Schücking, *Ironie*, pp. 72ff. and also (without the term actually being used) in *Heldenstolz*, p. 9.

[3] By this I do not suggest that heroic irony can never be used with long-range functions in literature before the romance, for there are such examples in *Beowulf* or *Waltharius*. But there is still a marked difference between the preponderance of heroic irony in the epic and its relative infrequency in the romance, which is characterised as a genre by the further types of irony (long-range in their implications) which we shall be considering in the following chapters.

[4] Cf. Wolf, *Stil*, pp. 97ff.

fers can be made from his other profession, as in the *Nibelungenlied* with Volker's rôle as *spilman* (2002,1: *Sîne leiche lûtent übele, sîne zûge die sint rôt:/jâ vellent sîne dœne vil manigen helt tôt*). But such irony need not be confined to cases where the warrior gives battle with the tools of his trade as his weapon. We find other spheres being exploited for their imagery, above all because of the contrast they present: the practice of 'Minnetrinken' because of the powerful discrepancy between fighting and *minne* in the sense of love,[1] or the sphere of commerce because, whereas the warrior intends to give as good as he gets or even better, the merchant is out to keep all he receives and give nothing in exchange.[2]

Examples of heroic irony are frequent in the courtly romance where they also serve another useful purpose. The recurrent depiction of combat in terms of what it is not (e.g. love or friendship)[3] suggests, far more insistently than in heroic literature, that these knightly encounters were not after all a matter of life and death. In other words, such 'Standesironie' drastically tones down the issue, it places a stylistic barrier between the audience and the harsh reality of what takes place, it allows the author to maintain his façade of courtly refinement. Apart from this consideration of courtly taste, heroic irony is welcome for its own sake because the contrast offered by the intrusion of a completely different concept into a combat scene can shock the listener into a realisation of what is *not* presented by the poet. He can now leave it to the listener's imagination to fill in the crude and violent details which he hesitates to provide himself.

The non-military spheres from which this ironic imagery is drawn are generally no different from those utilised in heroic

---

[1] *Ibid.*, p. 100 and Wiercinski, *Minne*, pp. 32ff.
[2] Wolf, *op. cit.*, pp. 101f. Cf. also the edition of *Iwein* by Benecke and Lachmann, p. 347, note on v. 7200.
[3] The most effective use of terms from the sphere of love to describe a knightly combat is made by Hartmann in his description of Erec's encounter with Mabonagrin (cf. Kuhn, *Dichtung*, p. 144: 'Es ist mehr als eine Metapher, wenn der Kampf zwischen ihm und Mabonagrin als ein *minnen* dargestellt wird (9106ff.): er ist ein allegorischer Kampf, ein Kampf um die rechte Minneform'). On the introduction of *minne* (this time more in the sense of friendship) into an account of a combat cf. Hartmann's *Iwein* 701ff. In each case an originally ironic technique is also made to serve a non-ironic purpose, but the harshness of knightly combat is toned down by being ironically described in terms of what it so clearly is not. On the metaphor at large see Peil, *Gebärde*, pp. 152f.

literature. Battle can be referred to as enjoying sport, as in the condition which the giants insist on before they fight Yvain (5544: *Seus vos venez o nos deduire!*) or as a service rendered to one's foes in the description of the siege of Windsor in *Cligès*, when Alexander switches his attention from one opponent to another (1749: *Quant a celui ot trives prise,/A un autre offre son servise,/Ou pas ne le pert ne ne gaste:/Si cruelmant le fiert an haste/Que l'ame de son cors li oste,/et li ostex remest sanz oste*). Wolfram uses the verb *ermanen* in a sense close to 'teaching someone a thing or two', as when the Grail-knight challenges Parzival to combat (443,14: *ir wert schiere drumbe ermant/dâ von sich iwer gemüete sent*), or *gelônen* in the sense of paying someone back in a wholly negative sense, as in Gawan's struggle with Lischoys (542,9: *er dâhte 'ergrîfe ich dich zuo mir,/ich sols vil gar gelônen dir'*). The concept 'tribute' can take on ironic overtones as in the *Battle of Maldon* when Parzival fights with Gramoflanz (706,13: *sus enpfienc der künec Gramoflanz/sûren zins für sînen kranz*).[1] Gottfried uses the same image at the close of Tristan's combat with Morolt when the victor addresses his foe's companions (7115: *enpfahet jenez zinsreht,/daz ir dort uf dem werde seht,/und bringet iuwerm herren heim/und saget im, daz min œheim/der künic Marke und siniu lant/diu senden ime den prisant*). Here the irony is greatly enhanced by the fact that Morolt had actually come to Cornwall in search of the tribute which Ireland regarded as its due.

Litotes

One of the most noticeable effects of heroic irony brings it close to litotes or understatement: by avoiding direct reference to the facts of combat and bloodshed, it tones down their crudity and softens their impact. Psychologically, for those involved heroic irony may be a form of self-defence, but in literature it appears, like understatement, in situations that call for a strong emotional reaction, leaving it to the audience to supply what remains unsaid and thereby conveying more forcefully what is meant by saying

[1] Once more, a demonstrative (*sus*) acts as a pointer to irony. This is reinforced three lines later by the word *ouch* when an ironic understatement is used to describe the difficulties Parzival undergoes in this combat (706,15: *sîner vriwendinne künne/leit ouch bî im swache wünne*). The irony of Parzival's position is therefore 'also' applicable to Gramoflanz.

less than what is meant.[1] Understatement is therefore a rhetorical means of causing the listener to react forcefully against the obvious deficiency of a statement and thereby to do the poet's work for him in that the listener is driven to embrace an opinion emphatically which is identical with that which the poet has all along held.[2] Formally, there are two types of understatement. One amounts to a denial of the contrary, as in *vir non indoctus* (which is not the same thing as *vir doctus*, since the introduction of the crying irrelevance of *indoctus* compels the listener to react emphatically against the indirect suggestion). The other makes use of a minimum where circumstances call for a maximum (e.g. *lützel vröude* meaning 'keine Freude').[3]

Understatement was as welcome to courtly poets as to those working in the heroic tradition, since it could be readily used like heroic irony in the context of knightly encounters, but could also be employed in a much wider field. This wider usefulness is the result of two aspects of courtly literature: its idealising presentation of courtly values and its stress on what is socially fitting, on courtly decorum. Excessive praise invites an ultimate reaction of disbelief, but this can be guarded against whenever a poet, working within an idealising tradition, deliberately falls short of what is expected by making use of understatement. He thereby invites his listeners to react against this and to supply what he has been too tactful to give directly. Social decorum finds understatement useful above all at the negative end of the spectrum, to tone down the offence to courtly sensibilities by an open depiction of knightly violence or to cast a discreet veil over quarrelling, boastfulness, derision at court. The more under-

---

[1] Cf. Johnson, *Beauty*, pp. 290f., on the effects of litotes.

[2] On understatement in medieval German the decisive work is Hübner, *Ironie*. For Old English cf. Bracher, *PMLA* 52 (1937), 915ff., and for Old Norse Hollander, *PMLA* 53 (1938), 1ff.

Hübner has suggested that the disappearance of the simple negative *ni* contributed to the popularity of the second type of understatement in German. This is unlikely to be its sole explanation. Old Norse uses both types of understatement alongside an abundance of negatives, and Old French and Provençal make similar use of the second type (*po, petit, pauc*). The development of this type is hardly a replacement for a grammatical negative no longer in use, so that it can be regarded as a genuine form of irony.

[3] Hübner refers to these two types as the 'classical' and 'Germanic' forms of litotes respectively. I regard it as more important to distinguish between them than to employ this particular nomenclature.

statement is incorporated into the courtly mode of speech as a recurrent feature, the easier it is to maintain the appearance of decorum and cohesion at court.[1]

Understatement as a denial of the contrary is particularly common when the poet wishes to depict extreme beauty of any kind. He avoids the charge of exaggeration by indirectly inviting his audience to do his work for him, although he frequently leaves nothing to chance by adding a direct statement of what he really means. Chrétien describes the splendour of Laudine in regal attire as she greets King Arthur on his arrival at her court (2359–63), but then sums up her facial expression by a denial of what would have been completely out of place, given her pleasure at Arthur's visit (2364: *Ne n'ot mie la chiere iriee*). That there was indeed no cloud upon her face is then stated in positive terms (2365: *Ainz l'ot si gaie et si riant*), but the effect of this can only be increased by the listener's preliminary rejection of the inappositeness of the preceding line. The same technique is used in physical descriptions in *Flamenca*, of the beautiful blond hair of the countess of Nevers (denial of the contrary, 846: *E non ac ges los cabels pers*, followed by a direct statement of the positive, 847: *Ans son plus blon que non es aurs*) or of the strong hips of Guillem, as part of his idealising description on being first introduced (denial, 1614: *De las ancas non fon ges rancs*, followed by a positive, 1615: *Ans las ac grossas e cairadas*).

An extreme impression of any kind can paradoxically be conveyed by this type of understatement. Yvain's courtly reputation, when Lunete first mentions his name to her mistress, is well brought out by the indirect formulation of Laudine's reaction (1816: *Par foi! cist n'est mie vilains*), followed by a direct statement (1817: *Ainz est mout frans, je le sai bien*) whose force is strangely weaker, despite her asseveration *je le sai bien*. We are given a far more telling view of Orguelleuse's backbiting aggressiveness when this is expressed indirectly in *Perceval* (6878: *Qui n'estoit lante ne coarde/De dire a un chevalier honte*), just as Wolfram describes the vigour and energy of a combat by saying that this was no time for resting (211,27: *sin mohten vîrens niht gepflegen*, followed

---

[1] This social aspect of litotes (as of other features of courtly speech) has been stressed by Bayer, *Untersuchungen*, pp. 161f. and 181f.

by a direct observation, 211,28: *in was ʒe werke aldâ gegeben*) or stresses the splendour of the lights preceding the Grail by negative means (236,1: *Vorem grâle kômen lieht/(diu wârn von armer koste niht*)). Heavy irony or sarcasm can be used when it is a case of insulting someone while pretending to uphold courtly convention. This stance is taken up by Arthur towards the elder sister in Chrétien's *Yvain* (6408: *Je ne dirai pas toʒ voʒ buens*, followed by a positive, v. 6409) or by the impatient knights, held up by the importunate questioning of the stupid young Perceval (236: *'Ne set mie totes les lois'*), to name only these examples.

The second type of understatement (using a minimum where the situation calls for a maximum) occurs less widely in French (where *po* and *petit* are used in place of a superlative)[1] than in German, which disposes of a greater range of litotic expressions. *Tiure*, meaning 'rare' but standing for 'completely missing', is used in the description of what was lacking in Erec's reception by the impoverished Coralus (380: *diu wâren bî dem viure/des âbendes vil tiure*).[2] The fact that Iders had never before clashed with so doughty an opponent as Erec is conveyed by the word *selten* (773: *vil selten geschach im daʒ*). The excessive compliments heaped upon Iwein's chivalric prowess by Gawein are expressed by two understatements, 'a little' and 'sufficiently' (7638: *daʒ er im der êren bôt/ein lützel mêre danne gnuoc*). The rarity of meat and fish available to the three hundred captives in *Iwein* is underlined by *under wîlen*, meaning 'generally, for the most part' rather than 'occasionally' (6215: *eʒ wâren bî ir viure/under wîlen tiure/daʒ vleisch ʒuo den vischen*).[3] Wolfram uses *vil wênic* to mean 'nothing' when describing the starvation of a besieged city (184,18: *in trouf vil wênic in die koln*), but also *kleine* in the sense 'not at all'

---

[1] Examples are *Yvain* 3222ff. and 5579ff., where the narrator's further comments show that *po* and *petit* are used as understatements for 'not at all'. For Provençal *pauc* similarly used cf. *Flamenca* 4788ff.

[2] That *tiure* here means 'not available' and not 'rare' is made clear by the description that follows (382ff.). This kind of check is necessary if we are to be convinced that words like *tiure* are in fact being used litotically, rather than as straightforward statements.

[3] To take *under wîlen* in this sense means that in this case we have to read *tiure* literally, signifying 'rare'. Cf. Cramer's translation in his edition, 'im allgemeinen ...eine Rarität'.

(521,12: *mîn dienst iu doch vil kleine frumt*), *kranc* as 'none' (527,15:
...*der schuldec man,/dem ich nu kranker êren gan*),¹ *etslîch* ('some')
to suggest 'many' (771,28: *etslîches prîs geneiget*)² and the phrase
niht gar ('not completely') for 'not at all' (539,30: *daz enwart niht
gar geleistet dô*).³

Two further categories can be added. The first includes passages where an emphatic positive is rendered more acceptable by
the addition of 'somewhat', as in the bullying of Enide by
Oringle (4782: *Et li cuens auques l'angressoit/Par proiiere et par
menacier*).⁴ To the other category belong those numerous cases
where a word conveying moderation suggests 'moderately little',
and then, by understatement, 'nothing at all'. Chrétien's Erec
shows courtly restraint in this way as his encounter with Yder
reaches its verbal climax (857: *Que tot par mesure vos dot*). Hartmann's
narrator uses a corresponding construction very appositely when
saying that he cannot talk of gluttony at table at Erec's wedding-
feast, since, although much was generously offered, the guests
ate with courtly moderation (2129: *dâ was sô manec ritter guot/
daz ich iu zeiner mâze/wil sagen von ir vrâze:/wan si ahten mêre/ûf
ander êre/danne daz si vræzen vil*). Trevrizent dismisses the death
of Amfortas's pagan opponent with cursory irony (480,1: *den
heiden het er dort erslagen:/den sul ouch wir ze mâze klagen*). Gottfried
employs *mazlich* as a litotic adverb, once in a phrase where another

---

¹ In each case the context of these three examples suggests that we must regard
them as meaning much more than they appear to say. It goes against the length
and detail of the description of the starved inhabitants of Pelrapeire to imagine
that the narrator undermined this by using *vil wênic* literally rather than as a forceful understatement. It is quite improbable that Orgeluse used *kleine* straightforwardly and did not want to stress, at this first meeting, the magnitude of the
gulf between her and Gawan. And it is highly unlikely that, in using *kranker
êren*, Gawan meant that Urians was to *some* extent honourable after all.

² That *etslîch* in the context of Parzival's knightly exploits means very much more
than it says is implied by other remarks made in the same context (771,27: *vil
rîterschefte*; 773,4: *sô manege hôhe werdekeit*; cf. 772,26–8).

³ That *niht gar* must be an understatement for 'not at all' (i.e. Lischoys would have
nothing to do with Gawan's suggestion that he could safeguard his life by granting
him his *sicherheit*) is made clear by the following narrative detail that Gawan spared
his life even though no *sicherheit* was given (540,1: *Ûf liez er doch den wîgant/âne
gesicherte hant*).

⁴ Comfort, *Romances*, p. 62, translates this phrase: 'And the Count urged her mildly
by prayer and threat', apparently taking *auques* to qualify *par proiiere*. But it also
qualifies *par menacier* (so that we are led to ask how far threats, described as violent,
can be mild) and is used in conjunction with the emphatic verb *angresser*. These
considerations suggest that *auques* is being used as a litotes.

attribute reveals its function clearly enough (9079: *smal unde mazliche groz*), but elsewhere alone (19487: *und iuwer sinne senent sich,/ich wæne mæzlich umbe mich*). The irony of what Tristan here attributes to Isold (which we know to be unjustified because of what the narrator has shown us of her position in Cornwall) casts its own light on *mæzlich* and how we are to read it.

Litotes grows more complex when we find these two types combined in a double-layered understatement. Where the first type said that a man was not unwise and the second type substituted for 'not' a word like 'hardly', this compound type says that he was hardly unwise. This is not a case of one understatement cancelling out the other, but rather of conferring on it even greater emphasis (because of the greater shock effect) than a direct positive statement could convey. Wolfram's description of Galoes's generosity towards Gahmuret uses this procedure (10,6: *den künec wênec des verdrôz,/er enfultes im vier soumschrîn*), for *wênec* stands for 'not at all' and the reconstructed *niht verdriezen* is itself an understatement implying that he wasted no time or actually took pleasure in showing such magnanimity.[1] Gawan's account to Orgeluse of the rape committed by Urians magnifies the disgrace the perpetrator brought upon himself by means of a double litotes (526,6: *ouch bezalter dâ vil kleinen ruom/gein ir unwerlîchen hant*). *Vil kleine* implies 'none', whilst the very mention of *ruom* in so dishonourable a context drives us to read the phrase as meaning that he stood in disgrace as a result of this action. The intensity of universal lamentation can be suggested indirectly, as when Gawan insists on the perilous adventure of Schastel Marveile (562,9: *al die dâ wâren klageten:/wênc sie des verdageten*). Again we react against what is actually said in the direction which the author has mapped out for us: against *verdagen*, since this is the last thing we expect of lamentation, and against *wênc*, because its apparently qualifying force is contradicted by the emphasis of the preceding line.

Hyperbole

Understatement can therefore be classified as ironic because it does not completely say what is meant by falling short of what can be reconstructed as the poet's intention. The converse figure,

[1] Cf. 9,29f.

hyperbole or overstatement, also fails to say exactly what it means, this time because it says more than is meant. In neither case is the discrepancy necessarily ironic. Just as litotes can sometimes be used for reasons of genuine modesty or hesitancy, so can hyperbole be employed, above all in heroic literature, out of a conviction that this is the only adequate way to do justice to the magnitude of events (Bertau says of this attitude: 'Das Fieber der Hyperbel bestimmt die epische Temperatur: das Klima des Außerordentlichen').[1] But it is not difficult to imagine cases where overstatement, because of this discrepancy between what is said and what is meant (or what is meant to be regarded as credible), can be employed ironically. My reference to credibility shows us one way in which this is possible. When the excesses of heroic enthusiasm are scrutinised with critical detachment, either because familiarity has bred a measure of dissatisfaction or because the rise of the romance as a new genre provided a vantage-point from which the heroic epic could be looked at from a distance unthinkable while it was still the unquestioned narrative genre, doubts will soon fasten upon exaggerated feats and impossible numbers, the more so since the romance, as a questioning mode, raises questions which are foreign to the world of the epic. In addition, overstatement is a feature of parodic writing,[2] since to write an exact imitation of the original would defeat the parodist's end and to criticise it by understatement would run the risk of the parody not being recognised as such. Finally, hyperbole can also characterise ironic writing by serving as a pointer to the presence of irony: by ludicrous exaggeration (provided that we know that we are not to expect this from the author in question) we can be alerted to the need to pay critical attention, as with the impossibly highflown praise of marriage at the start of Chaucer's *Merchant's Tale*.[3]

---

[1] Bertau, *Literatur*, pp. 244f. For examples of heroic hyperbole in the *Rolandslied* which are not meant to be questioned, but are intended as an ideal worthy of sincere admiration see Wolf, *Stil*, pp. 8f.

[2] Muecke, *Compass*, p. 81.

[3] We are admittedly prepared to read this praise ironically since we already know from the Merchant's Prologue that he is unhappily married (1218: *I have a wyf, the worste that may be*), and his reaction, born of bitter experience, to the unreality of the *Clerk's Tale* with its idealised picture of the wife Grisilde prepares us for some self-identification in his story (cf. Hussey's edition of the *Merchant's Tale*,

When all such possibilities have been suggested, it remains the case that overstatement is less frequently exploited ironically in the romance than its counterpart, understatement. The reason for this lies in the fact that the romance is still in essence an idealising narrative type which, for all its realistic deflations and ironic qualifications, still proposes at its heart a model for courtly civilisation. If doubts are voiced about the ideal or its feasibility, these will tend to be concerned with awkward details well this side of the ideal, realistic observations will deflate it and ironic qualifications undercut it. Or in rhetorical terms: since an overstatement of an already elevated ideal leaves much less room for manoeuvre, the discrepancy which irony postulates will more easily be found by understatement. For this reason we can treat the ironic potential of hyperbole in the romance much more briefly – it forms part of the total picture of verbal irony, but not an important part.

An example of this ironic procedure occurs at the close of the first German Arthurian romance.[1] True to its predominantly idealising vein, Hartmann draws the action to a close by praising his hero, returned to his kingdom, in superlatives that seem to admit no doubt. By his exploits he has achieved the highest possible praise amongst his contemporaries (10037: *dô hâte er sæleclîche/in manegem lande daz bejaget,/als uns diu wârheit von im saget,/daz niemens lop enstuont sô hô/under den die et lebeten dô/von manlîcher getât*). His achievements confer upon him almost miraculous status (10043: *an sînem lobe daz stât/daz er genant wære/Êrec der wunderære*)[2] and accordingly his presence is felt far and wide (10046: *ez was et sô umbe in gewant/daz wîten über elliu lant/was sîn wesen und sîn schîn*). These are superlatives indeed, but what follows is something strangely out of tune with this. The narrator

---

p. 78, note to v. 12). Even without this previous knowledge we are allowed to see through the praise of the married state with which the Merchant begins his tale (1267ff.), precisely because it is so excessive that the tension cannot hold and once or twice his true attitude shows through (e.g. 1317f. or 1391f.). On the many ironies of this passage see Hussey's edition, pp. 11ff. and 16f.

[1] Cf. Ruberg, *Bildkoordinationen*, p. 500.

[2] Erec's title *wunderære* refers above all to *wunder* in the secular sense of a heroic exploit, but is also meant to reveal a miraculous dimension which is part of what Wehrli has shown to be the close association between the two genres of the romance and the saint's legend (*Formen*, pp. 155ff.).

now incorporates a question, implying a critical objection, from an imagined member of his audience (10049: *sprechet ir: wie mohte daʒ sîn?*) which he answers by explaining the earlier suggestion of his hero's omnipresence in purely rational terms (10050: *waʒ von diu, schein der lîp nû dâ,/sô was sîn lop anderswâ./ alsô was sîn diu werlt vol:/man sprach et niemen dô sô wol*). With this last line we revert to the earlier superlative praise of the hero, but now we regard it in a different light, since we know that it is not meant as the miracle which it seemed to be, but merely as a metaphor. By inserting an imaginary critical question which brings his eulogy down to earth and which he answers in the same rationalising vein the narrator has delicately ironised the hyperbolical topos 'all the world sings his praise' and shown up the limitations of the convention.[1] By this procedure something of the best of both worlds has been achieved. The closing line of the passage leaves no room for doubt about Erec's elevated status, but by incorporating the critical point the narrator can also assure his listeners that he is no unthinking victim of traditional practice and flatter them into believing that his perspicacity is really theirs.

Wolfram's style includes similar examples.[2] He uses the conventional equation of beauty with light, but exaggerates it by attributing an impossible force to it and at the same time, by incorporating a realistic detail, invites incredulity and mocks the claims of hyperbole. How he goes to work can be seen with Herzeloyde and Orgeluse. Both are described as so beautiful as to be resplendent (84,13: *vrou Herzeloyde gap den schîn*; 638,16: *diu herzoginne wær sô lieht*). This metaphorical brilliance is then raised to a superlative level which at the same time, by the comparison of this metaphorical light with a source of physical light,

[1] By concluding on this light note of doubt the poet is doing something similar to what we saw in the case of Erec's adventures (see above, pp. 71f.). Hartmann is still hesitant to ironise the conventional happy ending in *Erec* (by contrast with the more open conclusion of *Iwein*). The happy ending is maintained at the conclusion of the romance (10 115ff.) and is potentially criticised only at the conclusion of the first part of the narrative with the couple's *verligen* (see Green, *Praise*, pp. 798f.), at a position in the work where the subsequent narrative corrects this first hint of doubt and leads us eventually to the conventional type of conclusion. On the position with *Iwein* see Green, *Damning*, pp. 162ff. and *Recognising*, pp. 44ff.

[2] Pointed out by Wolff, *Schriften*, pp. 268f.

is placed in a real context, the illumination of a castle hall. With Herzeloyde we are told that even if the candles had gone out she would have shed light enough (84,14: *wærn erloschen gar die kerzen sîn,/dâ wær doch lieht von ir genuoc*). When the same point is later made of Orgeluse (638,17: *wære der kerzen keiniu brâht,/dâ wær doch ninder bî ir naht:/ir blic wol selbe kunde tagen*), it acquires added point from the detail that the candle-illumination of the palace has just been mentioned (638,9ff.). By such hyperboles, especially by obviously going one step too far to be taken seriously, Wolfram can convey an impression of extreme beauty and yet protect himself against the accusation of mere unthinking exaggeration. This procedure can be compared with Hartmann's. Both poets begin with superlative praise in metaphorical terms, both introduce the awkward fact of reality (Hartmann by his feigned critical question, Wolfram by the other term in his comparison), and both finish with praise on a new level, with the poet laughing at the form his praise has taken and inviting his listeners to share this deflation of hyperbole with him.

There remain two more types of verbal irony for consideration. In one what is said is the opposite of what is meant and in the other what is said is unexpectedly different or divergent from what is meant, without being its direct antithesis. We find this distinction made in various rhetorical handbooks (some refer to the relationship between the two meanings of an ironic statement as *contrarium*, others describe it in terms of *aliud* or *alienum*).[1] The distinction is an important one when it comes to defining irony as practised in medieval literature, for whereas the terms *aliud* and *alienum* are broad enough also to include ironic statements where the intended meaning is the opposite of the pretended one, the converse is by no means equally true, since *contrarium* is too restricted to find room for those cases where the meanings are merely divergent. However important this point is in establishing a working definition, it need not force us in discussing the use of irony to lump together two aspects which for the sake of clarity are best treated separately. I propose therefore to consider first examples of verbal irony where the true meaning is the opposite of the apparent (the irony of inversion), and then cases where

---

[1] On this distinction see Green, *Alieniloquium*, pp. 120ff., especially p. 124.

the realisation of what is at issue opens up an unexpectedly different, but not antithetical dimension (the irony of divergence).

The irony of inversion

The irony of inversion is very effective when it is used involuntarily by a figure in a work, unaware of the fact, realised by the audience, that his assessment is directly opposed to the actual state of affairs, so that dramatic irony enters at this point to give added force. What I have in mind can be illustrated from a scene in Chrétien's *Erec* where an evil character voices an opinion which men of good will know to be the opposite of the case. When Count Galoain attempts to win Enide over to his treacherous plan to kill Erec, his unsuspecting guest, the words he uses to persuade her are an ironic commentary on himself (3410: *Tenez, ma foi je vos fianz,/Dame! Leaumant come cuens,/Que je ferai trestoz voz buens*). The fact that a count is bound to standards of loyalty rebounds against himself, for the loyalty he promises to Enide is inseparable from the disloyalty he proposes to practise against Erec, whilst to act entirely in accord with Enide's interests (*trestoz voz buens*) would demand an immediate abandonment of his plot.

The situation here is close to what we find in *Sir Gawain*, where twice an act of dishonest concealment is claimed as an act of loyalty.[1] Once when Gawain accepts the green girdle on the lady's terms and avoids declaring these 'winnings' to his host (1862: *And bisoȝt hym, for hir sake, disceuer hit neuer,/Bot to lelly layne fro hir lorde; þe leude hym acordeȝ/þat neuer wyȝe schulde hit wyt, iwysse, bot þay twayne for noȝte*). Then later, when Gawain's guide suggests that, if he abandons his quest, he need not fear to be betrayed by him (2124: *þat I schal lelly yow layne, and lance neuer tale/ þat euer ȝe fondet to fle for freke þat I wyst*).[2] In each case, as with Chrétien's Galoain or Steinmar's criticism of the role of the watchman in the dawnsong situation,[3] the supposed loyalty to one person is revealed as disloyalty to another.

[1] Cf. Clark, *MÆ* 40 (1971), 14.
[2] There is the further irony that Gawain sees through the temptation and rejects the offer on the second occasion, but not on the first, so that his earlier failure renders the later victory valueless.   [3] See above, pp. 127f.

In turning from the irony of inversion in which the unwitting speaker is the victim to cases where such irony is consciously used by the speaker we are hardly surprised to find the narrator to the forefront, saying the opposite of what he means and confident that his listeners will grasp his meaning. Hartmann's narrator, in describing Erec's *verligen* at Karnant, shows us at some length how his followers criticise his behaviour amongst themselves and, convinced of the decline in their lord, withdraw in disgust from his court (2966ff.). At the same time the narrator makes it clear that he shares their critical attitude (2974: *mit rehte*). This makes it the more telling that the narrator sums up this disaster which has overtaken Erec with the words (2983) *den lop hete er erworben*, whose irony lies in the application of a positive term (*lop*) to a situation which those involved and the narrator are agreed in seeing as destructive of Erec's reputation. If we can imagine even a slight metrical stress falling on the word *den*, thus bringing out its demonstrative force, this would act as a signal to irony,[1] inviting us to compare the word *lop* with the negative description which has just gone before and to register the fact of an absolute contradiction between them. This apparent praise must therefore be read as its opposite.[2]

The narrator can also be sure that this technique will not misfire and his words be wrongly taken at their face value when, a little later, he gives the speech of the leading robber-knight to his companions as he catches sight of his intended victim. The robber proclaims his intention to kill Erec (3212) and to take Enide for himself (3213). He also unashamedly describes the encounter as the naked robbery (3206: *an disem roube*) which it clearly is, in the narrator's eyes as well, since he first introduces this ruffianly group as *drîe roubære* (3116). When his companions agree with the ringleader that he has the first claim to Enide, the narrator's choice of word for this (3215: *dô gewerten si in der êre*) ironically underlines the fact that to be the first in such unprovoked aggression is instead a signal dishonour.

Wolfram's *Parzival* is particularly rich in such examples. In the

---

[1] For other cases where the definite article, stressed so as to serve as a demonstrative, acts as a pointer to irony, see Green, *Recognising*, p. 34.
[2] Green, *Damning*, pp. 150ff.

description of the tournament at Kanvoleis the narrator refers to the knights taking part who are unseated and fall on the grass (75,17: *daz velt etswâ geblüemet was,/dâ stuont al kurz grüene gras:/ dâ vielen ûf die werden man,/den êre en teil was getân*). Whatever term may be used to describe the lot that befalls them, 'honour' can hardly be justified in their case, especially if we bear in mind that *êre* can also imply 'victory in combat', which is the opposite of what these unseated knights achieve.[1] The humorous scene at the castle of Gurnemanz in which Parzival is served by courtly maidens as he takes his bath also contains its narrator's ironic point. We are told that the hero is not put out by this feminine company and scorns to hide himself in a bathwrap (167,21: *man bôt ein badelachen dar:/des nam er vil kleine war*), which attracts a comment from the narrator (167,23: *sus kunder sich bî frouwen schemen*), ironically praising him for a quality which he has just shown him not to possess or to have ignored on this occasion.[2] The procedure here is the same as with Erec's loss of reputation at Karnant. First the narrative facts are presented which allow us to judge the situation adequately (Erec's decline, Parzival's total lack of embarrassment) and then we are given the narrator's contradictory commentary (Erec's supposed *lop*, Parzival's ability to *sich schemen*), but with a demonstrative pointer (*den, sus*) which invites us to measure the distance between narrative and commentary and recognise the presence of irony of inversion.

The siege of Pelrapeire calls forth a number of similar observations. The siege and the starvation of the inhabitants have been caused by Condwiramurs rejecting the hand of Clamide, who then attacks her city in the hope of forcing things his way. The narrator comments on the suffering of the city-dwellers (184,19: *des twanc sie ein werder man,/der stolze künec von Brandigân:/sie arnden Clâmîdês bete*), using the verb *arnen* ironically, meaning not so

---

[1] The irony of the *êre* that awaited Kalogreant at the magic well lay in the contrast between the two meanings 'splendour' and 'victory', only one of which was present here (see above, p. 178). Now the contrast is between *êre* in the sense of 'honour' or 'victory' and the facts of the situation described.

[2] The irony of this praise is signalled by the demonstrative *sus* (167,23) and reinforced by the litotes *vil kleine* (167,22) as well as by the sly humour of the commentary 167,27ff. where, as Marti indicates in the footnote in her edition (p. 195), the phrase *wîpheit vert mit triuwen* (167,29) is a parody of words earlier meant seriously (116,13: *wîpheit, dîn ordenlîcher site,/dem vert und fuor ie triuwe mite*).

much 'reap the benefits of' as 'suffer in consequence'.[1] When the narrator jokingly brings his own person into the picture, comparing the starvation of Pelrapeire with his own impoverished circumstances, he ironically refers to his poverty as if it were comfort (185,6: *alze dicke daz geschiht/mir Wolfram von Eschenbach,/ daz ich dulte alsolch gemach*). Once again it is the function of a demonstrative (*alsolch*) to bring about a comparison between what has just been described (184,29ff.) and the present commentary.[2] Shortly afterwards we are taken back to the theme of starvation at Pelrapeire, only to be surprisingly told that the citizens flourished well on their food (190, 27: *dô was der burgære nar/ gedigen an dise spîse gar*). When the next line explains what the results of this feeding are (190,29: *ir was vor hunger maneger tôt*) we realise that *nar* and *spîse* stand for an almost total lack of sustenance and that *gedîhen*, so far from meaning 'to flourish', is meant to sum up the inhabitants' wretched state already described in detail (184,7ff.).

Although the narrator in Gottfried's *Tristan* is much more reticent about such inversions in his comments, they are not absent from his work. We may mention his observation on the fact that when Riwalin attacks Morgan's territory his enemy's towns have to surrender and offer ransom whether they like it or not (353: *reht alse liep als ez in was*), for the use of *liep* is the direct opposite of what is required by the situation.[3] If the irony of this phrase affords us a glimpse of the mocking contempt in which the young Riwalin holds his enemy, a similar derision, expressed by the narrator adopting the standpoint of one with whom he sympathises, is conveyed by the comment on yet another successful hoodwinking of Marke by Isold (14010: *Marke der zwivelære/ der was da wider ze wege komen*). As we have been enabled to judge in the scene which this sums up, if there is any track on to which the deceived husband has been led it is more likely to be the garden path than the direct road to truth. These words express the

---

[1] Cf. the similarly ironic use of *geniezen* in 725,6 (Green, *Recognising*, p. 34).
[2] Green, *Recognising*, p. 32.
[3] As in the examples discussed above (pp. 176f.) the irony of this remark lies in the ambiguity of the phrasing. The use of the positive term *liep* invites us to read these words positively, whereas the comparative phrasing *alse liep als* could logically just as much imply the negative meaning intended.

opposite of the truth, but do so by the narrator adopting Isold's position, for from the point of view of her interests the husband has been led in the right direction when he has been misled. Not derision, but superiority can be brought out by this technique when the narrator addresses his audience directly. In the description of the Morolt combat he confidently maintains that, in contrast to what his source says and his own listeners no doubt expect this is no single encounter, but a fight between two groups of four. The narrator successfully concludes his demonstration by saying (6890: *uz den gebilde ich schiere/zwo ganze rotte oder ahte man,/ als übel als ich doch bilden kan*). This poetic triumph is meant to suggest that *übel* stands for its opposite,[1] that here too the apparent modesty that informed the scene of Tristan's knighting is to be taken as a proof of poetic skill and of the narrator's awareness of that skill.

With the narrator of the romance making such use of the irony of inversion it is not surprising to find him so arranging things that characters in his narrative likewise exploit this opportunity. Bearing in mind how Gottfried's narrator used the device to reveal an attitude bordering on mockery, or superiority, we may ask what type of character commonly shows such features and whether we might not expect to find this kind of irony used by him. An obvious candidate is Keii, and indeed the irony of inversion is frequently employed by him. The scene at the start of Chrétien's *Yvain* where Calogrenant, seeing the approach of Guinevere, courteously jumps to his feet is a case in point, since Keu now addresses him in words which are seemingly complimentary (71: '*Par De, Calogrenant!/Mout vos voi or preu et saillant,/ Et certes mout m'est bel, que vos/Estes li plus cortois de nos/...|S'est droiz que ma dame le cuit,/Que vos aiiez plus que nos tuit/De corteisie et de proesce*). There can be little doubt that we have to read these words as meaning the opposite of what they say (Keu is not pleased, but disgruntled).[2] The narrator introduces this speech with a thumbnail sketch warning us how to react (69: *Et Kes, qui mout fu ranposneus,/Fel et poignanz et afiteus,/Li dist...*), halfway through

---

[1] Again, the irony of these lines is brought about by the ambiguity of the comparative phrase *als übel als*.

[2] On this passage see Green, *Recognising*, p. 19.

Keu temporarily drops his mask and speaks with more open criticism (75: *Et bien sai, que vos le cuidiez,/Tant estes vos de san vuidiez*), and Guinevere's reaction to Keus's words shows us that she has seen through the pretence of politeness (90: *Enuieus estes et vilains/De ranposner voz conpaignons*). And if this is not sufficient guidance, we find Hartmann depicting this opening scene in just the same way, revealing an apparent compliment as a sarcastic form of criticism (*Iwein* 113ff.).[1]

A similar occasion, suggesting that we are right to expect such heavy irony as characteristic of this figure, occurs in *Perceval* when the young hero first arrives at Arthur's court, naïvely asks to be given the Red Knight's equipment and is told by Keu that he has every right to these arms (1003: *'Amis, vos avez droit:/Alez li tolir or androit/Les armes, car eles sont voz./Ne feïstes mie que soz/Quant vos por ce venistes ci'*).[2] That we are correct in reading these words as the irony of inversion is again made clear by the descriptive *inquit* formula used by the narrator, telling us something of Keu's mood and of how we may judge him (1001: *Li seneschaus, qui fu bleciez,/De ce qu'il ot s'est correciez/Et dit...*) and by the critical reaction of one of the bystanders, this time King Arthur, who takes Keu to task (1008: *'Keus', fet li rois, 'por Deu merci!/Trop dites volantiers enui'*, and 1017: *Vilenie est d'autrui gaber*).[3]

If an important member of the Round Table is so sharp-tongued, it would be an impossible idealisation of human nature if the others were not to reply with like coin, thereby showing that irony is a convenient safety-valve for the tensions and antagonisms present within courtly society. The irony of inversion can in its turn be directed against Keii himself. In *Perceval* Gauvain, about to set out to bring back Perceval to the Round Table after Keu's disastrous failure, is goaded by Keu's sarcasm to hit back at his tormentor with the same verbal weapon. He refers jeeringly to Keu's wounds received at Perceval's hands (4408: *Je l'an amanrai, par ma foi,/Se j'onques puis, biaus douz amis,/Ja n'an avrai le braz*

---

[1] *Ibid.*, pp. 26f.   [2] Green, *Recognising*, p. 20.

[3] The irony of Keu's words is also revealed in Arthur's recapitulation of this episode. He quotes Keu's words to Perceval (4417–9), passes his own commentary on the mood in which they were spoken (4114–6) and stresses that Perceval failed to understand the sense in which they were uttered (4120: *Cil qui ne sot le gap antandre/Cuida que il voir li deïst*).

maumis,/Et sanz chenole desloiier,/Que je n'aim mie tel loiier). When the sparks fly as they do here, one may wonder whether the polite address *biaus douz amis* still just maintains the fiction of courtesy, but with the word *loiier* (again underlined by the pointer *tel*) there can be no doubt that the idea of reward is meant in the sense of punishment.[1] Hartmann's Iwein can also hit back, when Keii mocks him for his decision to repeat Kalogreant's adventure, by using his adversary's own weapon of pretended politeness in 'gratefully' accepting Keii's reprimands (862: *ouch kan erz mir wol undersagen/mit selher vuoge als er ie pflac,/die niemen wol gezürnen mac./ mîn her Keiî der ist sô wîs/und hât selch êre und selhen prîs/daz man in gerne hœren sol).* The irony of this passage rests on the ambiguity of *mit selher vuoge als er ie pflac,* on the fact that Iwein then reveals his true opinion in equating his adversary with a yapping dog and in refusing to act on that level himself (875ff.) and on the narrator's comment on this verbal exchange (879: *Hie was mit rede schimpfes vil).* Once again we find a formula of polite address (865: *mîn her Keiî)* being used, perhaps as an ironic screen, at a moment of personal antagonism.[2]

---

[1] *Ibid.,* p. 31.

[2] Other characters from whom one might expect malicious irony of inversion include Chrétien's equivalent of Wolfram's Orgeluse in her more spiteful moments. Her derision of Gauvain, forced to make do with a broken-down nag, represents a good example. Exactly how she means her apparently positive statement (7178: *'Ha! certes, or va bien la chose!')* to be understood is made clear by the narrator's following *inquit* formula (7179: *Fet la pucele ranposneuse).* Moreover, the force of her complimenting Gauvain on his knightly appearance (7186: *Ore estes vos bien a hernois!/Or seez vos sor buen destrier,/Or sanblez vos bien chevalier/Qui pucele doie conduire!)* is clear from its contrast with the actual description of the wretched beast (7161ff. On the significant first line of her 'compliment' see Green, *Recognising,* pp. 36f.). The ironic ambiguity of her concluding remark (7210: *Qu'or estes vos si aeisiez/Con je vos voloie veoir)* has already been discussed (p. 176).

The female companions of Chrétien's counterpart to Wolfram's Obie prove themselves to be as waspish as their mistress, as witness the remark made by one of them to a page to whom she addresses (at the moment when she accuses him of folly, 5121) an ironic compliment (5125: *Si vos feites buen escuiier).* When she recommends this page to take what he wants from the passive Gauvain who has so far kept aloof from the fighting (5134ff.) she switches her fire to Gauvain (5132: *Et veez le plus deboneire/Chevalier qui onques fust nez!).* Her bitter scorn tells us on both occasions that she means the opposite of what she literally says.

Of quite a different nature is Trevrizent's irony of inversion in his conversation with Parzival (488,22: *wir sulen bêde samet zuo/herzenlîcher klage grîfen/und die fröude lâzen slîfen,/sît dîn kunst sich sælden sus verzêch).* In the last line the hermit uses two inversions. By his reference to Parzival's 'skill' (*kunst)* he means rather his bungling stupidity in losing his chance at Munsalvæsche, and by his choice of *verzîhen*

These two examples raise a final possibility of the irony of inversion which cuts across the distinction we have been following (used by the narrator or by a figure in the narrative). In either case we find that at a moment of animosity or derision a term of polite address (*biaus douz amis, mîn her Keiî*) can be used so incongruously as to suggest irony, a lashing scorn behind a façade of politeness. It is certainly also irony, as well as politeness, which makes the Green Knight welcome Gawain on his own ground with the words *Now, sir swete* (2237), knowing as he does that this is the prelude to chopping off Gawain's head.

However, some of the romances written around 1200 allow us to say more accurately when their courtesy is meant ironically. The position can be reconstructed best for Old French and in particular Chrétien thanks to Foulet's work on polite forms of address.[1] Although he is primarily concerned with the differences between terms like *dan, sire* and *messire*, this is irrelevant to our problem and I shall simply discuss the cases where any of these terms is used with an ironic afterthought. *Dan* is used in *Ypomédon*, above all to convey a pejorative nuance (combinations like *dan fol* and *dan asoté* are revealing).[2] A reflection of this is to be found in Chrétien's *Perceval* (he uses *dan* altogether very infrequently)[3] where the counterpart of Wolfram's Obilot witnesses Gauvain's defeat of Meliant from a tower (5529: *Qui de la tor ot bien veü/ D'une fenestre ou ele fu/Dan Meliant de Liz cheoir,/Si dist: 'Suer, or poëz veoir/Dan Meliant de Liz gisant,/Que vos aliiez si prisant'*). The narrator's use of *dan* in v. 5531 is dictated by the younger sister's use of it two lines later, where there can be little doubt about her mocking intentions towards her sister, pointing out the victory

he means, not that Parzival renounced this opportunity, but rather that Providence rejected him when he failed to rise to the occasion. The use of such irony is particularly effective here, since Trevrizent has just this moment been told that it was Parzival who came to the Grail-castle and neglected to ask the question. The hermit cannot avoid revealing something of his shock and grief, yet to express his reaction too directly would go against his concern to win Parzival back to a trust in God. In such circumstances the indirect mode of ironic speech is admirably suitable.

[1] Foulet, *Romania* 71 (1950), 1ff.
[2] *Ibid.*, p. 7.
[3] Haidu, *Distance*, p. 123, fn. 29, has concluded from Foulet's analysis: 'The fact that Chrétien did not use *dan* until the *Perceval*, where it is still used without ironic intent as well..., suggests that it was acceptable in certain circumstances, but old-fashioned and therefore subject to ironic use.'

of the knight previously jeered at and the humiliating defeat of one earlier praised (5534). When in the same episode one of the ladies in the castle mocks at the folly of a young page for missing a unique opportunity, she addresses him with the same dubious politeness (5120: *Danz escuiiers, se Deus m'aït,/Mout estes or fos estapez*).[1] Even more telling is Chrétien's use of *messire*, as analysed by Foulet. Until *Yvain* this title is confined to the illustrious Gauvain himself, but in this work we find it shared between Gauvain and the hero (which could be accepted without further comment), but also, surprisingly, with Keu.[2] The explanation of this inclusion of Keu, as Foulet has seen, is that the seneschal is often ironised by being mockingly honoured with this title.[3]

Mockery of this kind (deflation by means of a false honorific) has been proposed for *Parzival*, but not yet analysed in the detail shown by Foulet. Johnson[4] has built on the observation made by Blamires[5] that, although Wolfram refers frequently to Gawan as (*mîn*) *hêr Gâwân*, he rarely uses the same title of his hero. He points out that the few cases where Parzival is so described are ironic in function. Three of these cases occur clustered together in the scene where Cundrie appears at Arthur's court (315,9,26; 316,25). In itself this is enough to imply the possibility of irony because this is the scene in which Cundrie launches her bitter attack against Parzival for his failure at Munsalvæsche, the force of which is greatly enhanced by the uneasy presence of apparently polite addresses to her victim. Particularly revealing is the apparent oxymoron in 316,25: *gunêrter lîp, hêr Parzivâl!* That such politeness is indeed ironic can be confirmed by two further points: by the fact that Cundrie, when she appears to announce the crowning

---

[1] This adds to the irony of the remark which we have already considered (see p. 205, fn. 2).

[2] Neumann, *Wolfram*, pp. 368f., reminds us that in his *Iwein* Hartmann too can make use of similar ironic politeness towards Keii (2508ff.) and also Iwein (1127ff.).

[3] In the midst of the quarrel between Keu and Calogrenant, where the former is shown to be in the wrong, he is twice scornfully addressed with cold politeness (113,133). The same is true of Keu's later quarrel with Yvain (613,633) and when it is recalled by Yvain later (895). When Keu bursts out once more against the absent Yvain, the polite formula suggests testy impatience, first on the part of the narrator (2207, 2228), then on the part of Gauvain (2209) – although the narrator's usage in v. 2207 may be dictated by Gauvain's two lines later (like the use of *dan* in *Perceval* 5531 and 5533).

[4] *MLR* 64 (1969), 69f.

[5] Blamires, *Characterization*, p. 366.

honour of Grail-kingship that has now befallen Parzival, avoids the dubious honorific and addresses him simply as *Parzivâl* or as *Gahmuretes suon*,[1] and by the occurrence of the same ironic address *hêr Parzivâl* when the hero encounters Sigune for the third time.[2] The ironic use of this polite address is not confined to Parzival. When the narrator brings his hero for the first time to Arthur's court and fears the reception the inexperienced youth will be given at this sophisticated centre he brings Hartmann, as the originator of the Arthurian ideal in German literature, into his account (143,21: *mîn hêr Hartman von Ouwe,/frou Ginovêr iuwer frouwe/und iuwer hêrre der künec Artûs,/den kumt ein mîn gast ze hûs./bitet hüeten sîn vor spotte*). This looks like a polite acknowledgement of Hartmann's literary authority in Arthurian matters, but this is revealed as a dubious subservience (hinting rather at a polemical relationship between the two poets) when the narrator issues threats to these figures from Hartmann's world and thereby stresses his independence of one whose title *mîn hêr Hartman* does not protect him from such attacks.

The irony of divergence

The concluding type of verbal irony embraces those cases where the relationship between statement and meaning is not directly contradictory, as with the irony of inversion, but instead divergent, opening up an unexpected dimension which adds to our understanding of the original statement. Irony of divergence frequently operates with a distinction between a literal and metaphorical reading, where the metaphor can be taken from any number of different spheres of which only two can be mentioned here. The topos of the sickness of love and the image of the lover as one who has the means to ease the suffering he has caused lend themselves to this kind of exploitation. We have seen something of the potentiality of this topos in *Cligès*, in the scene in which Fénice refuses to see any doctor recommended by her

---

[1] 782,5 and 781,3. Cf. Johnson, *art. cit.*, p. 69.
[2] 440,29, where the irony is increased by the sardonic question that follows (440,30f.). Johnson, *art. cit.*, p. 70, is in error in saying that Sigune, in addition to going over to *du* in the same scene, *also* reverts to the simple *Parzival*. The text does not bear this out.

husband and places her trust in a doctor who has power over life and death, whom the Emperor takes to be God, but in whom we have to see her lover.[1] Without any express commentary of this kind Gottfried briefly alludes to the same theme by having Blanscheflur, when she has determined to visit the apparently mortally wounded Riwalin, disguise herself as a doctor (1277: *ouch jach diu meisterinne,/si bræhte ein arzætinne,/und erwarp, daz man si zuo zim liez*).

What Gottfried tactfully leaves implicit is developed expressly in the episodic poem *Tristan als Mönch*, which concludes with a scene comparable to that in *Cligès*. The listeners are alerted to the fact that Isold is physically healthy (2546: *do sprach die frouwe wol gesunt*) and here too it is the anxious husband who invites his own deception by worrying about a possible cure for his wife (2543: '*liebe frouwe, wuste ich doch/ob artzenye icht horte do zuo,/das man siu gewinnen duo*').[2] Isold exploits Marke's vulnerable anxiety by getting him to send for the monk Wit whom she describes as a trained doctor from Salerno, but who is none other than Tristan in disguise. Just as we are told that Isold is really in good health, so do we learn that Tristan in fact has no medical knowledge (2568: *...umb artzeliche liste,/von den er cleine wiste*). This is then ironically denied in the metaphorical sense of the lover's healing power when Isold, later asked how she feels, attributes her improved state to the attentions of her doctor (2634: *siu sprach: 'noch ungenoden wol,/des man yemer dancken sol/disem vil guoten man,/der myn so wol gepflegen kan*'). The narrator sums up, drawing the ironic conclusion (2652: *owe, wellichen artzat/sime wibe Marcke erwelt hat!/und wuste er wer er wære,/wie gerne er sin enbære!*) and comparing Marke's position with that of Ysengrin in *Reinhart Fuchs* (2656ff.).

Another work which turns the topos to good use is *Flamenca*. The husband's optimistic suggestion that Flamenca will feel better after she has eaten (4583f.) is rebutted by a remark which allows Archimbaut to feel that his wife's position is more critical, for she will need a better remedy than that (4585: '*Sener, so respon*

---

[1] See above, p. 22.
[2] These two points have their counterparts in *Cligès* 5627f. and 5631. Both strengthen the irony of the situation.

Margarida,/Ben agra obs mieilz fos garida'). That there is more to this than meets the husband's eye is made clear by the feminine reaction to this sally (4587: *E fa-il de la lenga bossi./Cascuna en som poin s'en ri*). Precisely what kind of cure is meant is revealed in a repetition of this scene. Archimbaut asks his wife what is wrong with her (5670), to which she replies that she desperately needs a doctor for a heart-complaint (5671: *'Sener, al cor ai una gota/Que m'auci e m'afolla tota,/E cug que d'aquesta morrai/Si conseill de mege non ai'*). Archimbaut again makes light of this (5675ff.), which prompts Flamenca to ask for leave to visit the bath-house again (5678: *'Bel sener cars, autra vegada/D'aquesta gota me senti,/Mas quan mi bainhei ne gari'*). This makes good sense in terms of the metaphor which she has in mind, but which eludes her husband, since it is in this bath-house that she has contrived to meet her lover in the past. The final touch is given when Archimbaut gives her leave to go there 'if that will give her pleasure' (5689: *'Domna, ieu vueill ben que-us baines,/E d'aisso no-us estalbies/Que non annes, se-us plas, als bainz'*).

Another metaphor well adapted to ironic usage is the topos of hunting as an image of love. We have seen it skilfully exploited on the grand scale in the third section of *Sir Gawain*, where the action alternates between the erotic temptation in Gawain's bedroom and the hunting in the nearby woodland and where the hunt is meant to pass comment on the state to which Gawain is reduced in the bedroom.[1] But it is with Gottfried that this topos is made to yield most in the way of irony. He can use it as a simple metaphor in describing Tristan moving stealthily, like a huntsman, towards his assignation (13485: *der minnære Tristan/ der stal sich tougenliche dan/an sine strichweide*). He can also exploit its ironic potential when he applies it to the lover's relationship to the rest of society, underlining the different manner in which each is meant to understand it.[2] The crucial passage occurs when Tristan makes an excuse for not joining Marke's hunting party, pleading illness but in reality anticipating a favourable opportunity to rejoin Isold briefly (14372: *sin weidegeselle/Tristan beleip*

---

[1] See above, pp. 138f. A comparable example from Wolfram's *Parzival* has been discussed by Schnell, *PBB* (T) 96 (1974), 246ff., especially pp. 256ff.

[2] Cf. Clausen, *Erzähler*, p. 80 and Green, *Alieniloquium*, pp. 139f.

da heime/und enbot dem œheime,/daʒ er siech wœre./der sieche weidenœre/ wolt ouch an sine weide). Here the two metaphors we are considering come together. Tristan is a huntsman in the literal sense known to all (he is Marke's master of the hunt), but also in the erotic sense suspected by Marke (this is why he is called Marke's *weidegeselle* even at the moment when he does not take part in Marke's hunt and it accounts for the presence of *ouch* in v. 14377). But he is also ill, not in the humdrum sense which he dangles before Marke, but in the metaphorical sense of the topos. This sickness is meant to explain his inability to hunt on the literal level, but also his absolute necessity to hunt metaphorically. If we accept the force of this deeply ironic passage it casts a new light on what can now be seen as the irony of Marke appointing Tristan to be his chief huntsman (3370ff.), thereby unwittingly preparing his own fate as surely as when he equips Tristan for combat, placing on his head the helmet with the symbolic arrow of love (6587ff.). It also casts a new light on the young Tristan's fabrication to the two pilgrims when he catches sight of the Cornish hunting-party, claiming that this is the group from which he has earlier been separated (2695ff.). As elsewhere,[1] his fabrication unwittingly anticipates the future, but in an ironically different way. To the pilgrims Tristan claims that he actually belongs to Cornwall and that he has lost his way while hunting, but the future shows us that it is in the course of hunting (in the metaphorical sense) that he irrevocably separates himself from courtly society and ends up where he started in Cornwall, on the outside.[2]

---

[1] Cf. Wolf, *Technik*, pp. 398ff. and Grosse, *WW* 20 (1970), 289ff.

[2] Another metaphor which lends itself to ironic treatment is the image of the knight as a merchant (see above, p. 188 and Grosse, *art. cit.*, p. 295). When Obie, reacting angrily to Obilot's claim that Gawan is to be her knight, scornfully mocks him (above all because of the rich equipment he carries with him and his passive aloofness from the combat so far) for being a merchant rather than a knight (353,26: *dort sitzt ein webselœre:/des market muoʒ hie werden guot./sîne soumschrîn sint sô behuot,/dîns ritters, tœrschiu swester mîn*), her irony consists in insultingly behaving as if she really believed the noble Gawan to be a vulgar merchant. Her words *dîns ritters*, far from being a last-minute concession, mean 'the man whom *you* are foolish enough to take to be a knight'. Yet if we take the comparison as a metaphor and not as the factual truth (which is also what we have to do with the imagery of healing or hunting), the irony ultimately works against the mocker, for knightly combat can often be depicted in terms of a commercial transaction and the knights themselves as merchants (e.g. Hartmann's *Erec* 862ff. and *Iwein*

Verbal irony, as we have considered it in this chapter, is essentially *unius verbi ironia*, although not necessarily confined, as this rhetorical definition would have it, to antiphrasis alone. Its effects are short-term, for even where the procedure is used more extensively by repetition (as with the hunting and temptation scenes in *Sir Gawain*) on each occasion the impact is an immediate one, at least to the listener alert to the poet's nuances and signals. This will no longer be so in the following chapters in which we shall be preoccupied with types of irony whose effects are long-term and built more into the structure of the work than into the phrasing of a particular passage. Just as modern interpretations of medieval works see in them many more effects than can be directly attributed to the rules of rhetoric, so do these following types of irony go beyond the prescriptions for *ironia* in the rhetorical handbooks. The difference in each case is a measure of the poet's originality, of the creative use to which he put recommendations which others were content merely to follow as rules without thus extending their limits. But since these other types of irony generally achieve their effects by the verbal means we have been considering the verbal irony of this chapter constitutes the basis of what follows.

7189ff.). In this sense, but only in this sense, Gawan is indeed just as much a *wehselære* as Hartmann claims him and Iwein to be (7189: *sî wâren zwêne mære/ karge wehselære*). What Obie intended as an insult turns out to be the truth, but in a metaphorical sense which she did not have in mind. This is why Obilot, when Gawan's defeated opponent offers her his *sicherheit*, cannot refrain from a last jeering reference to her sister's misuse of the term merchant (396,5: '*hêr künec, nu habt ir missetân,/sol mîn ritter sîn ein koufman,/des mich mîn swester vil an streit,/ daz ir im gâbet sicherheit*').

7

IRONY OF THE NARRATOR

The theme of the narrator opens up a far-ranging problem of medieval literary history: are we justified in talking of the aesthetic function of the narrator and if so, when? By irony of the narrator I mean *either* the irony of remarks made by the narrator standing back from the story and commenting on it *or* the irony which can arise from a discrepancy between narrator and poet. In this latter sense our problem belongs to a wider one of all narrative literature. Since the essence of this literature lies in the relationship between the poet,[1] his story and his audience, and since this relationship implies the possibility of three points of view (of the poet, his characters, his audience), the potential[2] disparity between these has the makings of irony.[3] Our task will be to consider what rôle the narrator plays in this and how far this rôle is characteristic of the romance.

Oral and written composition

My argument rests on the belief that the romance brings something new into medieval vernacular literature, that it represents the transition from oral composition to written secular literature

[1] The three points of this relationship become four once we make a distinction between poet and narrator.

[2] Scholes and Kellogg, *Narrative*, p. 240, go too far when they claim that 'the narrative situation is thus *ineluctably* ironical' (my italics), but are nearer the truth when they say later that in this kind of situation 'irony must be either actually or potentially present'.

[3] Here we reach a point in our argument which is diametrically opposed to the argument by Batts (see above, p. 14, fn. 2) that it is misguided to assume an ambivalence of standpoint between author, narrator and characters in a medieval work of literature. Significantly, Batts does not face the challenge presented by recent work on the narrator in medieval literature.

and that this brings about a number of potential disparities that lend themselves to ironic exploitation of a new kind. This novelty of the romance can be demonstrated by contrasting it with what we know of the features of oral composition in so far as they are believed to apply to the medieval epic.[1]

Oral poetry is traditionalist as regards its mode of composition and the values it incorporates. An oral poet differs from a writer in making no conscious attempt to break with traditional phrases: he cannot do this because the rapidity of improvising recital forces him to fall back on standing formulas, the use of which gives him time to think ahead.[2] But the same is true in a much more fundamental sense. It is not merely formulaic tradition which leads a poet to tell his story in the accustomed way, oral poetry is characteristic of a type of society which follows time-honoured ways and feels at home in them, since 'an unlettered people will usually have a more homogeneous outlook than people whose tastes have been diversified by books',[3] they will take more for granted because of their shared beliefs. This implies that the traditionalist outlook of the oral poet is shared in essentials by his listeners, they are as much part of the tradition as he is. If the accustomed formula is indispensable to the extemporising poet, it is also appreciated by his audience. They too, like the reciter, can relax slightly on hearing a familiar phrase; the conservatism of primitive taste is comforted by the recurrence of the time-honoured.[4] The audience for oral poetry is a collective unity not just in the obvious sense that they are all present at the same performance, but also in the sense that they react to it in much the same way 'because their own lives conform to customary rules of which they are largely unconscious and therefore uncritical'.[5] This unity of beliefs, shared by poet and listeners alike, implies

---

[1] In what follows I have largely based myself on the following works: Lord, *Singer* (who has a concluding chapter on the medieval epic); Bowra, *Poetry*; Rychner, *Chanson*. See also especially Curschmann, *Speculum* 42 (1967), 36ff.; Bäuml and Ward, *DVjs* 41 (1967), 351ff.; Bäuml, *Übergang*, pp. 1ff.; Bäuml and Bruno, *DVjs* 46 (1972), 479ff.; Bäuml and Spielmann, *FMLS* 10 (1974), 248ff., as well as the more general works of Duggan, *Oral* and Finnegan, *Oral*.

[2] Cf. Lord, *Singer*, pp. 4f. and Bowra, *Poetry*, pp. 225f.

[3] Bowra, *Poetry*, p. 476.

[4] See Lord, *Singer*, p. 97 and especially Bowra, *Poetry*, p. 231.

[5] Bowra, *Poetry*, p. 476.

that oral poetry is led by its mode of composition and by the type of culture in which it flourishes to discount originality as a conscious aesthetic virtue. This does not mean that novel effects cannot arise (the application of a common stock of formulas to any particular theme creates a pull towards the new),[1] but rather that they are not consciously sought after.[2]

Another feature of oral poetry is the impossibility of distinguishing between the acts of composition and recital, for both are synonymous.[3] With written literature there is a gap between the moment of composition and the occasion for reciting or reading, a gap which confers an advantage on the literate poet over his audience denied to his improvising oral colleague for whom composition and recital are two aspects of the same process. If each oral performance is therefore unique and if the oral poem does not exist (except in the memory) apart from its performance, there is no such thing as an 'original' or a 'variant' and equally no 'author',[4] but instead a multiplicity of poet-reciters, since each recital is a separate act. Because of this the oral poem is generally anonymous – not in the Romantic sense of a 'dichtender Volksgeist', but because the oral poet cannot conceive himself apart from tradition.[5]

Two other features of oral poetry deserve mention. The presence of narrative inconsistencies[6] has often been commented on (Homer's nods) and arises from the pull between the stock of formulas and the requirements of the poem recited. Where the poet fails to resolve this tension an inconsistency results, which shows us that he is so bound up with the act of improvising recital that he has no chance to stand back from the urgency of composition to iron out contradictions. Oral recital is therefore essentially episodic, concentrating on what is immediate and

---

[1] The obvious example of this is the adaptation of the stock of formulas inherited from Germanic heroic poetry to the needs of Christian literature in Old English and Old Saxon alliterative verse. Scholes and Kellogg, *Narrative*, pp. 24f., quote the particular example of *eorla drēam* generating *engla drēam* to meet these new needs.

[2] Scholes and Kellogg, *Narrative*, p. 24.

[3] Lord, *Singer*, p. 13.

[4] Lord, *Singer*, pp. 101f.

[5] On the anonymity of heroic literature see Höfler, *DVjs* 29 (1955), 167ff.

[6] See Lord, *Singer*, pp. 94f. and Bowra, *Poetry*, pp. 299ff.

unconcerned with logical connections between one episode and another. What is true of the oral poet (he is so involved in his task that he has no time to bear in mind what has already been narrated or is still to come) is also applicable to his listeners. They too are swept along by his story, they have no chance to compare the narrative present with the past and are likely to be as uncritical in this respect as the poet. Unlike the readers of a written text, these listeners have no time to ask awkward questions since, like the poet in front of them, they are preoccupied with the events narrated at any one point of time.[1] A similar unwillingness to question the implications of the narrative emerges from the fact that its audience generally regards oral poetry as a record of historical fact, taking the place of written history in a society with no literate tradition.[2] Since it is the means of preserving the religious, historical and ethical values of its culture and of creating its sense of identity, its function goes far beyond the purely aesthetic. To call it into question in any way would amount almost to a loss of cultural identity. What the oral poet offers is a record of events which his listeners accept as much as himself. There is as little call for them to doubt the truth of his narrative as there is for him to present anything other than what he regards as historical truth.[3]

A coherent narrative tradition like oral poetry, resting on shared beliefs common to poet, listeners and narrative, offers few disparities out of which irony might evolve. Of the five categories of irony we are considering[4] only verbal and dramatic irony are feasible in oral poetry. Verbal irony we can accept as a possible feature of oral poetry. Its effect can be immediate enough for the oral poet and his listeners to cope with in the pressure of improvised recital,[5] and heroic irony and understatement occur

[1] Bowra, *Poetry*, p. 300.
[2] Bowra, *Poetry*, pp. 508ff.; Scholes and Kellogg, *Narrative*, pp. 28f. See also Bäuml and Spielmann, *FMLS* 10 (1974), 250, on the 'encyclopaedic function' of oral tradition in a preliterate society.
[3] Cf. Hennig, *DVjs* 39 (1965), 489ff. See also Rossmann, *Wahrheit*, from whose argument it is clear that the possibility of doubting the truth of one's own poem is utilised in German literature of the twelfth century for the first time in the *Alexanderlied*, significantly a precursor of the romance (Green, *Alexanderlied*, pp. 246ff.).
[4] In Chapters 6 to 10.   [5] See above, p. 171.

long before the rise of the romance.[1] With dramatic irony, the type of situation presented in many plots (the deception of one character by another, pride coming before a fall)[2] equips the audience with the means to appreciate it, whilst the preference for traditional stories, already known to the listeners in outline, heightens their perception of the implications of a situation in the light of what is still to come.[3]

Although the scope of these types of irony is restricted and their impact direct rather than subtle, they can be expected in oral poetry, whereas this cannot be said of the remaining types. It is difficult to conceive irony of the narrator (the exploitation of a disparity in knowledge between poet, characters and listeners or between poet and narrator) in a tradition resting on a unity of views shared by poet, characters and listeners and ignorant of any distinction between poet and narrator. This also renders fruitless any search for the irony of values, for in the homogeneous outlook of a preliterate society the listeners share the poet's values and are just as unlikely to call these into question. Finally, what may be termed structural irony (arising from a discrepancy between characters or scenes juxtaposed so as to suggest a contrast) is likewise improbable in oral tradition. If the poet and his listeners are so involved in the immediate episode that they fail to recall its connection with other episodes and hence to register any inconsistencies between them, it is improbable that structural irony, demanding a critical awareness of such connections, will be intended in orally composed works.

If the introduction of literacy and written composition opens up a range of possibilities undreamt of by oral poets what is it about written culture which makes it potentially more receptive to irony? A recent article has pointed to the greater distance which opens up between poet, written text and audience.[4] Because the act of composition is distinct for the literate poet from that of recital, he can stand back from it, revise it and take issue with it. In so far as his subject is a traditional one, he therefore takes issue

---

[1] See above, pp. 187ff.
[2] Examples would be the plot to kill Sifrid in the *Nibelungenlied* or the overweening self-confidence of Guntharius in *Waltharius*.
[3] On this aspect of dramatic irony see below, p. 255.
[4] Bäuml and Spielmann, *FMLS* 10 (1974), 248ff.

with that tradition which he no longer embodies, as the oral poet does. A similar distance opens up between the written text and the audience. In the recital situation, because the interventions of a narrator commenting on his work separate the audience from the work, and in reading, because the reader resembles the literate poet in being able to distance himself from the narrative and subject parts of it to a critical comparison, independently of any recital. This increase of distance amounts to a growing differentiation between literate poet, text and audience which had been inhibited in oral poetry by a shared recital situation which was also the act of composition. Since differentiation is fundamental to irony (the ability to distinguish between two meanings in an ironic statement) we are as much justified to expect irony from the growing differentiation brought about by written composition as from the differentiation between various types of love depicted in courtly literature.[1]

In what follows I propose to consider two kinds of differentiation to be found in the literate genre of the romance (between poet and narrator, between composition and recital) before reviewing some of the situations in which the narrator commonly employs irony, amongst which I include examples of a third kind of differentiation (within the audience of the romance). My argument is that the three-point relationship between poet, story and audience (or four-point, once we include the distinction between poet and narrator) is more heterogeneous with written literature than with oral poetry. It is because of the disparities in understanding to which this can lead that the irony of the narrator plays so important a part in the romance.

Poet and narrator

Our first distinction, between poet and narrator, has been conceded in modern literature mainly because of dissatisfaction with the autobiographical fallacy and its assumption that what the narrator says of himself must be true of the poet.[2] But it has not

---

[1] See above, pp. 103ff.
[2] Cf. Wellek and Warren, *Theory*, pp. 67ff., especially p. 72. On the general relation between poet and narrator in modern literature see Booth, *Fiction*.

been so readily admitted in medieval literature,[1] for the same reason now operating in reverse (to admit that the narrator might not be identical with the poet is to risk depriving ourselves of one of the few sources of information available to us on the medieval poet). This loss is partly made good by Nellmann's observation on Wolfram.[2] Whilst not everything said by the narrator about himself is true of Wolfram the poet, it would be going too far to claim that nothing is applicable to him, so that there still remains an overlap between the two (of an admittedly uncertain extent) which does not rob us of all information about the poet. For the critic who hankers after the biographical approach it is this overlap which is important (the extent of the common ground shared by poet and narrator). For us the crucial point is that these two are not identical, that a distinction has to be made even for medieval literature. That this discrepancy has ironic implications in medieval literature has been brought out by Scholes and Kellogg.[3] They make the point that writing and the distancing it permits enable the literate poet to add a potential irony to his story, but that this irony comes from the introduction, not of a narrator, but of a poet. What is new is not the narrator of the romance (he continues in a literary form, written into the text, the function of the reciter in oral tradition), but rather the presence of a poet behind him, controlling him at a distance. It is the presence of these two figures and the disparity between them that make for increased irony in the romance.

The distinction between these two figures, more readily conceded in the lyric than in narrative literature,[4] can be argued for the romance on several grounds.[5] The first concerns the biographical approach, the unjustifiable equation of art with life and the neglect of literary conventions, especially important in

---

[1] The application of this method to medieval literature has been rejected by Batts, *Humanitas*, p. 39; Schröder, *PBB* (T) 90 (1968), 325 (in reviewing von Ertzdorff, *Spiel*, pp. 135ff.); Bronson, *Art*, p. 37. Kramer, a pupil of Schröder, makes the same point in *Erzählerbemerkungen*, pp. 9f., but restricts it to his justified criticism of Mecke, *Zwischenrede*.

[2] Nellmann, *Erzähltechnik*, p. 13.

[3] Scholes and Kellogg, *Narrative*, pp. 52f.

[4] Cf. for example the comments on the different rôles in Walther's poetry by McFarland, *Lichtenstein*, p. 194. See also Röhrig, *Dichter*, and Jackson, *Mosaic* 8, 4 (1975), 147ff.

[5] In what follows I am largely indebted to Sayce, *Prolog*, pp. 63ff.

the Middle Ages, which this entails. How far Hartmann's repentance for having composed secular works and his conversion to a religious theme in the prologue to *Gregorius* may be interpreted autobiographically has been rendered problematic by Schwietering's collection of similar literary confessions of guilt, establishing a clear convention.[1] Schwietering's parallels do not prove that Hartmann's remarks, while belonging to this convention, may not also be autobiographically true, but they warn us of the dangers of an easy assumption. As with Nellmann on Wolfram, the narrator's remark may apply to the poet as well, but need not, so that in the absence of confirmatory evidence we should avoid overhasty conclusions. Because of the conventional nature of so much medieval literature it is difficult to tell whether a personal confession is lurking behind a traditional formula.[2] We may suspect it, but can rarely prove it, and for want of proof must continue to distinguish the narrator from the poet in such cases.

A similar conclusion is forced upon us by certain recurrent themes in medieval literature. In the dream-vision, for example, the poet projects himself into his own narrative by making of himself a fictional figure which, because of the literary tradition to which it belongs, cannot be equated with the real poet, although they may have certain features in common. How far this fictional disguise can go is shown by *The Book of the Duchess*. The dreamer is not Chaucer himself, but a *persona* of the poet, presented as naïve for the artistic reason that this allows him to ask a number of naïve questions and experience the forest as enchanted, so that it is enchanted for the audience as well.[3] The poet operates with this *persona* in the same way as Chrétien with the clearly fictitious figure of Perceval:[4] by illustrating his childlike nature and incomprehension he invites us to share his experience of the mysteriousness of life. In another theme treated by Chaucer, that of pilgrimage, the poet can be included as a figure in his own work, but again we should be careful how we interpret the figure of Chaucer the pilgrim.[5] He may be presented as easily taken in

---

[1] Schwietering, *Demutsformel*, now accessible in *Schriften*, pp. 140ff.
[2] Cf. Sayce, *Prolog*, p. 69.
[3] Cf. Spearing, *Criticism*, p. 14.   [4] See above, pp. 149f.
[5] On this see the important observations of Donaldson, *Speaking*, pp. 1ff.

by appearances (which has prompted the observation that a naïve Collector of Customs would be a paradoxical monster),[1] but the rhetorical purpose of this naïveté, as with the figure of understatement, is to prompt the audience to react against it and adopt what has been the poet's critical attitude all along. When Chaucer the pilgrim-narrator whitewashes the Prioress[2] and agrees with the Monk[3] we are being led towards the poet's true opinion which we accept as our own.

How these themes of the dream-vision and the pilgrimage could be combined is exemplified by Dante, but here too the distinction between poet and narrator must be upheld.[4] Dante the narrator may share features with Dante the poet (how could the poet afford to depict his own personality with less conviction and authenticating details than are bestowed on others?). But this pilgrim figure is also equipped with an allegorical dimension which places him on a different plane from the human individual Dante and which alone justifies his report on the Other World. On this level Dante the pilgrim, unlike the poet, can be presented as symbolic of mankind, as is made clear in the opening lines of the poem with their juxtaposition of singular and plural pronouns (*Nel mezzo del cammin di* nostra *vita/*Mi *ritrovai...*).

The contrast between pronouns also underlies another class of evidence discussed for Hartmann's *Gregorius* by Linke and Sayce.[5] They point out that the prologue and epilogue refer to Hartmann as the poet responsible for this work in the third person (171: *Der dise rede berihte,/in tiusche getihte,/daz was von Ouwe Hartman*), whereas elsewhere the first person pronoun is used to denote the narrator. Here at least the differentiation between poet and narrator in written composition finds clear linguistic expression, but it is not confined to this isolated example. In Germany most cases where the poet is mentioned by name in the prologue or epilogue use the third person,[6] whilst the position in France

---

[1] Cf. Kittredge, *Chaucer*, p. 45.   [2] Cf. Mann, *Chaucer*, pp. 128ff.
[3] *CT*, General Prologue 183.
[4] See Spitzer, *Traditio* 4 (1946), 416f.
[5] Linke, *Strukturen*, p. 35 and Sayce, *Prolog*, p. 71. See however Goebel, *ZfdPh* 94 (1975), 15ff.
[6] Sayce, *Prolog*, pp. 70f., with references to Ehrismann, *ZfdW* 5 (1903/4), 142f. and Iwand, *Schlüsse*, p. 138, fn. 70.

seems to correspond to what we find in *Gregorius* in that a distinction is generally made between the poet in the third person and the narrator in the first.[1] With so many examples to assist us it is easier to explain the literary reality behind this linguistic phenomenon. It betrays the awareness of these poets that their work was destined for public recital (which need not preclude the possibility of its being occasionally read)[2] and that they need not always be the reciter once their work had gained a wider popularity. They must have had this in mind in composing on parchment their prologues and epilogues as well as their narrator's interventions. Conscious that, for their audience, the narrator tends to be equated with the visible reciter in front of them, they write into their text narrator's interventions in the first person, whilst reserving for themselves as poets the third person. Whenever the poem was recited by someone other than the poet this distinction was literally justified since it reflects the reality that poet and reciter are different people. Even when the poet recited his own work the distinction is legitimate in that it points to the poet's two different activities (composing his text in advance, in written form, and reciting it), activities which are now, thanks to the intervention of writing, carried out at different times and under different conditions, no longer simultaneously.

Composition and recital

With this we have already moved over to our second distinction, between the acts of composition and recital, which Lord held to be a major criterion of written as against oral composition.[3] To argue that the romance has already made this move from oral to written is not to suggest that it can simply be equated with written literature in the modern sense. Unlike the modern novel the medieval romance was composed with a listening audience in mind (only some of whom might have the occasion to read it themselves). If it retains stylistic features which we might regard as oral (appeals to the listeners to keep quite, to pay attention)[4]

---

[1] Cf. Delbouille, *Chansons*, pp. 328ff. and Tyssens, *Jongleur*, pp. 688f.
[2] See below, p. 258, fn. 1. Cf. also Green, *Oral*, pp. 180ff.
[3] Lord, *Singer*, pp. 13ff.
[4] Cf. Gallais, *CCM* 7 (1964), 489ff. for the French evidence.

this is because the romance was written with this recital situation in view. The place of the romance within the development of narrative literature from oral poetry to the modern novel, meant for private reading, lies between these two; it shares public recital with oral poetry and written composition with modern literature. This last feature is the novelty of the romance over against oral poetry: the separation of composition in written form from oral recital.

Whilst the oral poet had his listeners visibly in front of him for the indivisible act of composition and recital, the writer is removed from this situation for the act of composition. He works for himself, protected from the urgency of improvised composition, able to revise his text and view it as a whole, and forced to put himself imaginatively, while he composes in writing, into the position of a reciter facing his audience. The introduction of writing leads to a distinction between poet and narrator, but also to a separation of composition from recital. This twofold differentiation tells us why the literate poet may have felt it necessary to write into his text a first-person rôle for his eventual reciter, for by it he may hope to safeguard himself against the tendency of professional reciters to introduce their own alterations into a work entrusted to them. When a writer does this he goes beyond merely imagining himself in the position of a reciter, for what was at first only a potential disparity between poet and reciter has now taken permanent form in the written text. Such poets have become aware of their new opportunities and responsibilities in composing written literature.[1]

This argument rests on the assumption that the romance is a transitional form, belonging neither to oral nor to print culture, but instead to manuscript culture,[2] that it presupposes recital before an assembled audience from a text previously composed in written form. I have discussed the outlines of this problem elsewhere[3] and shall confine myself here to two examples suggestive of this. With Hartmann's *Erec* we have little difficulty in seeing that it is no orally composed epic, but has crossed the frontier

[1] In this paragraph I have largely followed the observations made by a pupil of mine, Howard, *Relationship*, pp. 100ff.
[2] I have borrowed these useful terms from Brewer, *Troilus*, p. 196.
[3] Cf. Green, *Oral*, pp. 164ff.

into written literature. The poet refers to his source not as oral hearsay, but as a written text (8698: *ob uns daz buoch niht liuget*), composed by one author whom he names (4629[12]: *alse uns Crestiens saget*) and designates by the clerical, learned title *meister* (7299). Hartmann therefore had access to written literature in composing his work in a manner not true of oral transmission (that he could in fact read he tells us elsewhere).[1] But we cannot conceive him as a modern author, composing his work for an unseen reading public. Instead, he composed for a particular court before which to recite his written text – this is suggested by his references to a circle of listeners, present at the recital, whom he can fictionalise as interrupting him to ask questions and being put in their place for doing this.[2] We have to imagine Hartmann neither as an oral poet, extemporising from a stock of formulas, nor as a writing poet in the modern sense, but as a transitional type of poet, composing a written text which he has before him as he recites it to his audience, surrounding him. This is confirmed by one expression when Enite's horse is described (7303: *alzan genzlîchen wîz/sô disiu schilthalben was/von der ich iu nû dâ las,/alse swarz was disiu hie/dâ diu wîze abe gie*). The use of the verb *lesen* does not mean that this detail has been read in a source,[3] but rather that it has just been recited ('vorlesen') to the audience (*iu*). This verb implies that the reciter stands before his audience with his text in his hand. Rhetorically *Erec* is a work composed in writing and potentially open to the advantages which only written composition confers.

With Chaucer there are also indications that he composed his romance with the prospect of recital in mind.[4] The poem opens with a statement of the narrator's intention (I 1: *The double sorwe of Troilus to tellen/...My purpose is*). This is so general that it could be used of a writer addressing his readers, were it not that the narrator specifies the setting (I 5: *or that I parte fro ye*) and requests his listeners to pay attention (I 52: *Now herkneth with*

---

[1] *Der arme Heinrich* 1ff. and *Iwein* 21ff.
[2] Cf. Pörksen, *Erzähler*, pp. 94ff. and Nellmann, *Erzähltechnik*, pp. 43ff.
[3] This usage is certainly possible elsewhere, cf. *Erec* 9019.
[4] Cf. Brewer, *Troilus*, p. 196. See also the frontispiece of the Corpus Christi College, Cambridge, MS 61, fol. 1vo, showing Chaucer reciting *Troilus and Criseyde* at court. Reproduced in Loomis, *Mirror*, No. 68.

a good entencioun). He can address his audience directly (I 450: *This, trowe I, knoweth al this compaignye*), see them before him (II 30: *in this place*) and realise that they can interrupt him (V 1032: *And shortly, lest that ye my tale breke*). This rôle given to the narrator must have been very persuasive when the poet was the reciter and acted this part, but hardly less effective whenever someone else recited his poem. The possibility implicit in the use of distinct pronouns by French and German poets to distinguish themselves from reciters is voiced explicitly by the English poet when he addresses his own work in the epilogue (V 1797: *And red wherso thow be, or elles songe,/That thow be understonde, god I biseche*). This indicates that his work can circulate independently of Chaucer the poet – how it can do this is suggested by the word *red* and by the phrase with which he begins his address to his work (V 1786: *Go, litel book*). The verb *reden*, like German *lesen*, denotes the private act of reading (silently or aloud, but to oneself)[1] or a public reading in the sense of recital,[2] but in either case it presupposes a fixed written text. Lastly, Chaucer is also aware of a special partnership between himself and the individual reader whom he can even address as a solitary reader (V 270: *Thow, redere, maist thi self ful wel devyne/That swich a wo my wit kan nat defyne./On ydel for to write it sholde I swynke,/Whan that my wit is wery it to thynke*).[3] This is the nearest we come to the modern reception of literature, but with Chaucer it represents only one end of a spectrum that extends all the way from the physical presence of an audience assembled round a reciter which the romance shares with oral tradition. The breadth of Chaucer's spectrum suggests that, like Hartmann and others, he conceived his work as destined for public recital, composed it in writing with this end in view, but realised that it could circulate independently and even be read in solitude.

Two points follow from this transitional nature of the romance. The first is that many conventional phrases used by the narrator

---

[1] Cf. Chaytor, *Script*, pp. 13ff.
[2] See below, p. 258, fn. 1.
[3] For a German example cf. the manner in which the *Tristan* of Heinrich von Freiberg switches from the plural when assembled listeners are being addressed (2057: *und hæret*) to the singular in the case of the private reader (2644: *leser dises buoches, vornim*).

presuppose, and originate in, the situation of public recital. The poet has therefore written into his text the figure of the reciter, allotting him a rôle which would allow the poet some control over a possibly irresponsible reciter. Even if the poet were to recite his own work, this could still yield ironic effects because of the discrepancy between the poet, as known to his audience, and the rôle in which he has cast himself.[1] The written romance incorporates a dramatic imitation of the reciter's performance, but in so far as he is presented dealing with each situation as it arises[2] and apparently improvising, this projected reciter is conceived more in terms of an oral poet. The new method of reciting from a written text retains this amount of contact with oral composition (made possible since both are addressed to an assembled group of listeners); the new method imitates the old, but on the level of conscious artistry, prepared in advance and with a planned control impossible in oral improvisation.

The reciter, in his guise as narrator, is not the only figure which the literate poet incorporates in his text. He can also allot a place to the fictitious member of his audience, interrupting with a question or an objection which has to be dealt with before the reciter can continue. Here we glimpse what must have been a frequent occurrence in the medieval recital situation, but, as with the aesthetic transformation of the reciter into the narrator, this bugbear of the poet reciting in the baronial hall has been projected into the work and made subject to the poet's control. Given this figure's origins and the professional antipathy which the medieval poet must have felt for him, the poet uses his fictitious interruptor as a means of asserting his own superiority. In Hartmann's *Erec* the narrator answers questions raised by the interlocutor or anticipated by the narrator, but in either case the narrator's authority is enhanced by his skill in dealing with them, whilst in the more sustained description of Enite's horse this authority is increased by the obtuse stupidity which the interruptor displays.[3]

---

[1] Cf. Brewer, *Troilus*, p. 199.
[2] See above, p. 224, fn. 2.
[3] On the function of the narrator in this description scene cf. Jackson, *Observations*, p. 66; Pörksen, *Erzähler*, pp. 38, 44, 48f. and 186; Kramer, *Erzählerbemerkungen*, pp. 63 and 137.

This technique recurs, but is taken in a new direction, in Gottfried's *Tristan* when during the combat between the hero and Morolt the narrator anticipates a possible objection from a listener (6978: *nu sprichet daz vil lihte ein man,/ich selbe spriche ez ouch dar zuo:/'got unde reht, wa sint si nuo,/Tristandes stritgesellen?'*).

One point of this interruption is to stress the narrator's authority by virtue of his skill in dealing with this question, but this time, by contrast with the humiliation of Hartmann's interruptor in the scene devoted to Enite's horse, there is a greater sympathy between narrator and questioner (the narrator after all agrees with the force of the objection).[1] Gottfried's narrator is not concerned with making a fool out of the interruptor, he is instead pedagogically accustoming his listeners to this kind of critical questioning; he encourages this response by showing its justification in the act of providing his explanation. Elsewhere he insinuates the possibility that this attentive listener may even confirm the truth of a poetic detail by comparing it with the written source,[2] thereby persuading this ideal listener to stand back from the recital situation (as the poet had in consciously planning this in advance) in a way unthinkable in oral composition. This pedagogic concern with encouraging the right response from his more promising listeners brings Gottfried close to what Nellmann has shown with Wolfram's *Parzival*, where the narrator flatters his real listeners by making them aware of ideal listeners built into the work whom they strive to emulate.[3]

Deviations from the norm

In considering examples of irony of the narrator we shall be mainly concerned with the German and English romance. Examples in French are fewer and French scholarship has devoted much less attention to the figure of the narrator than English

---

[1] We have already seen (cf. above, pp. 88f.) why the poet draws attention to this point by arranging for the fictional listener to interrupt with this kind of critical question. It is his indirect way of playing down the importance of *got* and *reht*, Tristan's metaphysical allies, and of thereby mocking the convention of the trial by combat.

[2] *Tristan* 2018ff. See below, p. 258.

Nellmann, *Erzähltechnik*, pp. 1 and 5ff., especially p. 8.

and German scholarship. Unlike his German successors, Chrétien rarely interposes his narrator between audience and story, he presents his story more immediately and allows his audience to feel that they witness events taking place in the present.[1] Why a greater distance should open up between the German audience and events reported to them more indirectly, as if they belonged to the past,[2] through the mediation of the narrator still needs to be worked out. The reasons almost certainly include the need felt by the German poet to train his audience in a courtly sophistication which could not be so readily assumed as in France (hence his employment of a narrator to comment and explain)[3] and also the difference between a German adaptation and a French source[4] (the German can survey the story from the beginning as a whole, he can correct anomalies and find time for reflection). If the German (and English) narrator is more obtrusive, we should not interpret that as a sign of literary individuality in any modern sense. The narrator is a fictional creation of the poet, only partially identifiable with him, so that we cannot draw a sketch of the poet on the strength of his composite picture of the narrator.[5] Even where the narrator deviates from the traditional, laughs at it or criticises it, he nowhere abandons this conventional norm, but still presupposes it.[6] Indeed, he must if he is to rely on his audience observing his deviation and noticing the presence of irony.

In *Sir Gawain*, which is alliterative and formulaic, but none the less literate, very subtle points can be made by tacit infringements of the convention. Borroff demonstrates that the poet uses elevated synonyms for 'man, warrior' regularly in the alliterating position of the long line, with one exception concerning the

[1] On this aspect of Chrétien's narrative art see Kellermann, *Aufbaustil*, p. 39, and Drube, *Hartmann*, pp. 59ff. Cf. however Dembowski, *YFS* 51 (1974), 102ff.

[2] Drube, *op. cit.*, p. 59, points to the contrast between Chrétien's preference for the historical present and Hartmann's almost complete avoidance of it. Cf. Herchenbach, *Präsens*, pp. 102ff.   [3] Cf. Ruh, *Epik*, p. 108.

[4] See Fourquet's selected edition, *Erec. Iwein*, pp. 27ff. (he speaks of a 'fatalité du genre'). The same point has been made repeatedly by one of Fourquet's pupils, Huby, *Adaptation*, probably one of the most useful observations in an otherwise unconvincing book (cf. Green, *MLR* 65 (1970), 666ff.).

[5] How unacceptable this approach has now become can be seen from the quotation from H. Schneider given by Nellmann, *Erzähltechnik*, p. 12.

[6] This is the conclusion of the argument by Pörksen, *Erzähler*, p. 222.

word *freke* (241: *þerfore to answare watȝ arȝe mony aþel freke*).[1] Because the rule is followed (and we expect it to be followed) in all the other cases a special effect is achieved when it is ignored on this one occasion. This stylistic offence coincides with an offence against the rules in the narrative action, inasmuch as the event described involves an embarrassing discrepancy between the Arthurian knights' reputation for courage and their behaviour in this scene, their reluctance to answer the challenge. At the moment when this discrepancy is made evident the narrator uses an idealising term of them; his diction pays ironic lip-service to a quality conventionally shown, but absent in this case.

This example illustrates the use of only one (disparate) word; the hint is so slight that it demands a sensitive response, but elsewhere the deviation from what is expected concerns a larger narrative unit and is more conspicuous in its questioning of convention. Hartmann's scene describing Erec's reception by the impoverished Coralus twice, in quick succession, builds up the ideal appearances of a conventional display of courtly wealth, but allows this to collapse with the realistic reminder that none of this was possible in view of the host's poverty.[2] Here we can see the advantage enjoyed by the adaptor of an earlier version, for the target of this ironic deflation is Chrétien himself whose version had made use of the trappings of a courtly reception, even though circumstances spoke against it.[3] In addition, Hartmann's own audience, in so far as they too had expected the usual description,[4] must be involved in this criticism, the ultimate pur-

---

[1] Borroff, *Study*, p. 65.

[2] *Erec* 368ff. I have discussed this episode elsewhere, *Alieniloquium*, pp. 121f. and *Damning*, pp. 148f. That it is the narrator who is involved is brought out by two generalising remarks going far beyond the particular situation, 371 and 387ff. (*swes*).

[3] Cf. Chrétien's *Erec* 479ff. Chrétien describes a scene of genteel poverty, thus avoiding the absolute destitution which Hartmann presents. The French host may not have many servants, but at least he has one (485ff.), whereas the German text has none and Enite has to act as such herself (350f.). The *coutes porpointes et tapiz* (479, cf. Hartmann 385) may not be traditionally described as of rich material, but they are not accompanied by Hartmann's *strô* (382). The French *vavassors* can at least serve meat (488ff.) to his guest, whilst Hartmann's description of food sums up only what was *not* available (386ff.). By presenting the host's poverty in more radical terms Hartmann has created for himself the means of ironising his source.

[4] On this topos of courtly literature see Dürrenmatt, *Nibelungenlied*, pp. 106ff. That the listener's expectations are deliberately disappointed in this passage is made

pose of which is to train them to measure convention against circumstances, to inquire critically how far one is apposite to the other.

Literary conventions are also called into question when Gottfried traditionally starts his work with an emphatic eulogy of the hero of his 'Vorgeschichte', but then undermines this by inserting an apparently laudatory, but ultimately catastrophic detail about Riwalin's youthfulness, or when Wolfram's narrator comments, near the close of the Arthurian action in *Parzival*, on Arthur's generosity (730,11: *Artûs was frouwen milte:/sölher gâbe in niht bevilte*). In both works the target of the narrator's irony is a literary convention, but also those listeners who may have expected conformity to it at this point.

In *Tristan* it is the opening of the story, a point where the hero is conventionally eulogised.[1] The narrator gives every appearance of doing the same, but only later does it become clear that the first detail in this praise, Riwalin's youth, is the cause of his *übermuot*, which in turn leads to his death at the hands of Morgan. In that his narrator's praise turns out to be a two-edged compliment Gottfried agrees with other contemporary poets realistically aware of the deficiencies of this type of laudatory opening.[2] In *Parzival* the narrator's commentary concerns Arthur's generosity in giving away women in marriage(*frouwen milte*), since his remark refers to the three marriages which the king has just successfully arranged (729, 27ff.: Itonje and Gramoflanz, Cundrie and Lischoys, Sangive and Florant),[3] as a fitting flourish at what is almost the conclusion of the Arthurian action. One is reminded, by the insistence on fully three marriages, of the grand finale to an operetta in which the happy couples whose marriage has been arranged make their last appearance and of the way in which

---

clear by the discrepancy between Erec having to make do with his host's good intentions alone (393ff.) and the more conventional hospitality enjoyed by Kalogreant in *Iwein* (367f.). Cf. also Wolfram's *Willehalm* 265, 10ff.

[1] *Tristan* 245ff. See also Green, *Damning*, pp. 152ff.

[2] On the rhetorical distinction between the *initium a persona* and the *initium a re*, on the preference of German narrative works for the former and on the ways in which Gottfried and some of his contemporaries express disagreement with this conventional *laudatio* of the hero at the start of a work see Brackert, *Rudolf*, pp. 226ff.

[3] *Milte* is therefore justified by the repeated use of *geben* (729, 27 and 730, 3), *gâbe* (730, 10) and *bieten* (730, 7) in this context.

a romance, like a fairytale, can often conclude on this kind of note. By his linguistic trick, equating the king's giving in marriage with generosity in gifts, the narrator is making fun of this literary convention,[1] the more so since the note of fairytale happiness in the Arthurian world serves as a foil to Parzival's position. Reminded by such marital rejoicing of his own loneliness, he turns his thoughts to Condwiramurs (732, 1ff.) and departs, leaving the rejoicers to their own devices (733, 17ff.). His eventual happiness later includes marriage when he rejoins his wife, but the marital satisfaction of this couple is more firmly based than the easily won happiness of the Arthurian couples, for whom a conventional topos is an adequate expression.

The last examples have shown us a narrator standing at a distance from a literary convention which can sometimes embrace an element of praise, at first idealised but then undermined. One usage which combines convention with idealisation occurs so frequently in the German romance that it has been considered as an argument against the presence of irony in these works.[2] I refer to the comparison of a detail with the norm of how things always are (e.g. of Enite's modesty, *Erec* 1321: *einer megede gelîch*) or with the ideal of how things ought to be (e.g. of Erec, 2567: *als einem ritter gezam*).[3] In either case, the individual event is seen in terms of what recurrently happens on such an occasion, whilst in the latter case it is judged in the light of a courtly and knightly ideal of timeless validity. Such normative or idealising comparisons are frequent in the German romance and contribute towards its depiction of a positive secular ideal. Alongside them, however, we must set cases which, although less frequent, help to qualify that ideal and confer credibility on what might otherwise seem too obviously idealised. This same technique can be used to convey criticism rather than praise whenever the norm or ideal is negative, as in Enite's self-recriminations when she thinks she is

---

[1] Hartmann can ironise the same convention of concluding the narrative with a happy marriage, as when he qualifies the couple's marriage in *Iwein* (2426ff.) at the close of the first part of the plot and also their marital happiness at the conclusion of the whole work (8139ff.) by the use of suspiciously many conditional clauses and the telltale insertion of *wænlich*. On this see Green, *Damning*, pp. 162ff.

[2] Cf. Ehrismann, *LG* II 2, p. 164 and Brinkmann, *Wesen*, pp. 152 and 180.

[3] A complete list of examples with Hartmann is given by Pörksen, *Erzähler*, p. 126, fn. 3. I have discussed this general problem in *Damning*, pp. 118ff.

the cause of Erec's death (5943: *als von rehte tuot ein wîp/von sô grôzer missetât*; 5965: *ich tete als die tôren tuont*) or whenever we are shown a detail falling short of the norm or offending against the ideal, as with Keii's ignominious defeat (4733: *ungelîch einem guoten knehte*) or Galoein's treachery (3678: *daz was doch wider dem rehte*). Such contrary examples contribute towards a less thoroughly idealised climate in which criticism and even irony may flourish.

We find the ironic mode in *Erec* when, after the hero commands Enite to manage singlehanded the horses of his defeated opponents, the narrator describes her inability to cope by means of the stylistic feature which so often expresses a conformity between what is expected and what is achieved (3288: *der pherde si dô phlac/dar nâch als ein vrouwe mac:/baz si enkunde*). If the context had been one more suited to a woman's abilities, the generalising comparison *dar nâch als ein vrouwe mac*[1] could have had positive import, but in this situation it emphasises just how little a woman could cope with this task (*baz si enkunde*).

Since French examples are relatively infrequent we may conclude this section on the ironic use of the comparison with the norm with a passage from *Cligès* where the narrator makes himself visible to the same effect. The scene is the deception of Alis on the night of his wedding to Fénice. Like any deception this has the makings of dramatic irony,[2] for Alis has been given a potion which ensures that he leaves his bride untouched, whilst himself remaining unaware of this. After describing the taking of the potion, the narrator sums up what this means (3287: *Or est l'empereres gabez*), so that this information precedes our hearing about the ritual blessing of the marriage-bed by the clergy (3288: *Molt ot evesques et abez/Au lit seignier et beneïr./Quant ore fu d'aler gesir,/L'empereres, si com il dut,/La nuit avoec sa fame jut*). On a first hearing the phrase *si com il dut* sounds like a conventional one resembling those in the German romance which imply conformity between ideal and reality, between general practice

---

[1] This generalising comparison is another example of the type of ironic ambiguity (discussed above, pp. 176f.) which invites us to read it positively, whereas a negative interpretation is equally possible. Another example is *Parzival* 3, 13 (*die lobe ich als ich solde*), where no praise is called for.

[2] On the contribution of the theme of deception to dramatic irony see below, p. 253.

and a particular situation,[1] meaning in this case that Alis, as was
his obligation or as was expected of him, lay beside his wife that
night. But the conventional use of this formula would suggest that
the husband lay with his wife and made love to her, an implication which is excluded because of the potion, so that the phrase
must not be read in its conventional, but in a particular sense,[2]
meaning that he lay beside her, as he had to (because of the force
of the potion), without touching her. That Chrétien's narrator
was conscious of this exploitation of a standing phrase and wished
his listeners to see that conventional expectations are not adequate
to this situation is clear from the narrator's commentary, drawing
attention to the inappositeness of the usual reading of this phrase
(3293: *Si com il dut? Ai ge manti,/Qu'il ne la beisa ne santi;/Mes an
un lit jurent ansanble*). We are invited to look at a standing phrase
with fresh eyes, to recognise that here is a situation to which it
cannot be applied in the customary sense and to acknowledge that
the discrepancy amounts to irony.[3]

The narrator's pretence

The examples so far considered, whether the narrator deviates
from a convention or exploits a comparison with the norm or
ideal for ironic purposes, have shown us a narrator pedagogically
superior to his listeners, leading them to share his reservations
about the unthinking use of a conventional motif. But it has also
been a characteristic of the pedagogic strategy of the ironist since
Socrates[4] to pretend to know less than he does and to entice his
unwary listeners into an acceptance of his truth by turning their
conviction of superiority into an acknowledgement of inferiority.
With this we approach another category of the irony of the narrator in which he works with a pretence of ignorance, naïveté,
inexperience or modesty to achieve his ends.

---

[1] For the French romance cf. *Erec* 6886 and *Yvain* 4683f.

[2] This passage illustrates the general observation made by Bäuml and Spielmann,
FMLS 10 (1974), 254: 'The literate perceiver can isolate the word from the
depicted action and confront the word with the action it describes: if the description does not fit the action, irony is the result.'

[3] I have discussed other examples of the same procedure in *Damning*.

[4] On this Socratic irony see Sedgewick, *Irony*, pp. 19ff.; Behler, *Ironie*, pp. 16ff.;
Muecke, *Compass*, pp. 87ff.; Booth, *Irony*, pp. 269ff.

The use of ignorance for ironic purposes is a feature of Hartmann's narrator in *Iwein*. In *Iwein* the recurrent use of this technique[1] invites the listeners to consider for themselves what the narrator claims not to understand, an invitation which is a concealed form of emphasis. When the narrator says that he cannot describe the single combat between Iwein and Ascalon because there was no eyewitness who could have reported it to him (1029ff.), we are meant to be pulled up by the discrepancy between this and other situations where the absence of a witness is no impediment to poetic omniscience. We may now suspect that other reasons lurk behind this excuse: an implied criticism of the length at which Chrétien describes this combat[2] and a wish to convert this excuse into a criticism of Iwein (he is *hövesch* enough not to boast with words, but is willing to kill his opponent in order to boast with his corpse as a trophy).[3] Similarly, the narrator says that he cannot tell us how Iwein and Laudine exchanged hearts on parting from one another (2995ff.) and is reprimanded by *vrou Minne* for his obtuseness, but by means of this interlude the narrator distances himself in two ways (incomprehension, 3011f., and inexperience, 3015) from a topos which he tacitly questions by not accepting responsibility for it and instead passing it on to *vrou Minne*.[4] The narrator's commentary, apparently laudatory, first on the married state of Iwein and Laudine at the wedding ceremony (2426ff.), then on their future happiness at the end of the work (8139ff.), is meant to be questioned more closely, not merely because of the weighted pile-up of conditions to be met, but also because in each the final affirmation is weakened by being turned into mere surmise (2433 and 8148: *wænlich*).[5]

This last example points to a variant of the same procedure, the use of *wænen* to suggest not a discrepancy between belief and reality, but a pedantic and fussy uncertainty, which acquires ironic force when the point at issue is so trivial as not to justify

---

[1] See Jackson, *Observations*, pp. 7of.
[2] See Cramer's edition, p. 189, fn. to v. 1029.
[3] See above, p. 69.   [4] Cf. Green, *Irony*, p. 54.
[5] Jackson, *Observations*, p. 71, makes the point that even when the narrator comes out into the open in *Iwein* with a firm *ich weiz* (1875), this is only to make the unreliable assertion that he knows that women always change their minds out of *güete*.

such attention or so obvious that no doubts are called for.[1] In its rhetorical effect this employment of *wænen* can be compared with litotes. By a formulation which falls ridiculously short of what the situation deserves the narrator invites his listeners to react against the shortcomings of his judgment and to adopt the position into which he wants to manoeuvre them. I have discussed one example elsewhere in a wider context. When Wolfram's narrator describes Orgeluse's derisive words to Gawan (530, 3: *sie sprach hin z'im, ich wæne durch haz*), the audience already has every reason to see that this is the case and can safely be left to convert the narrator's hypothesis into their own conviction.[2] This verb can also be applied by the narrator, unnecessarily pedantic on points which all the world takes for granted, to the two spheres of knighthood and love where he can rest assured that his listeners' experience will provide their own corrective. In the description of a tournament the juxtaposition of riderless horses and knights on foot allows only one conclusion, so obvious that we do not need a hypothesis from the narrator, as at Bearosche (379,28: *manc vole âne sînen meister lief,/des hêrre dort ze fuoze stuont:/ich wæne dem was gevelle kunt*). We react against the naïveté of a narrator who can entertain another possibility, unaware that the boot is on the other foot, since we are thereby moving in the direction already mapped out for us.

This procedure is even more acceptable to the narrator in describing an erotic situation. By disclaiming knowledge of what actually took place he can avoid the charge of obscenity, knowing full well that his listeners' imagination will more than do his work for him. This is the case in *Parzival* with Gawan and Antikonie (407, 2: *er greif ir undern mantel dar:/ich wæne, er ruort irz hüffelîn*), where we do not need to be acquainted with Gawan's reputation as a ladies' man[3] to feel that we can dispense with *ich wæne*.

---

[1] On this use of *wænen* by the narrator of *Parzival* see Nellmann, *Erzähltechnik*, pp. 73f. and 139.

[2] Cf. Green, *Recognising*, pp. 48f. Nellmann, *Erzähltechnik*, pp. 139f., also makes the point that the irony of *ich wæne* in this line is further ironised by the fact that, although the listeners react against this pedantic uncertainty by being convinced of Orgeluse's hatred, they are in fact wrong, for the narrator has already warned them (516, 3ff.) against judging her motives too hastily (cf. also 614, 6f.).

[3] On Gawan's literary reputation see Nitze, *MPh* 50 (1952/3), 219ff.; Frappier, *RPh* 11 (1957/8), 332ff.; Owen, *FMLS* 4 (1968), 125f. See also Whiting, *MS* 9

The formula *ine weiʒ* is traditionally employed as a straight-forward statement of a narrator's refusal to be tempted down irrelevant sidetracks and his wish to remain master of his poetic household.[1] Like other statements of ignorance or uncertainty this formula can be employed ironically (which now makes of it something more individual than a formula) whenever this refusal is used not to excuse a narrator's inability to say more, but to prompt his listeners to do for themselves what he claims he cannot do for them. We find this in Riwalin's attack on Morgan when the narrator confesses ignorance as to what prompted him (342: *weder eʒ do not ald übermuot/geschüefe, des enweiʒ ich niht*). What looks like a charitable refusal to criticise Riwalin (he may have been provoked,[2] it need not be a case of arrogance) serves the opposite purpose if we recall that the word *übermuot* is used only three times in the work, on each occasion applied to Riwalin, and that the other examples come before this passage.[3] We already know that Riwalin is tarred with *übermuot*, whereas we know nothing of any provocation. By putting forward this explanation (although he seemingly refuses to be committed to it) the narrator alerts us to this possibility and leaves it to us to judge Riwalin's behaviour for ourselves.

Elsewhere in *Tristan* this formula can be used, like *wænen*, to glide over a delicate point in the love story. The narrator feigns diplomatic ignorance when Marke discovers the lovers asleep in the orchard (18212: *Tristan und diu künigin/die sliefen harte suoʒe,/ ine weiʒ nach waʒ unmuoʒe*), an ignorance which has already been denied by the sultry eroticism of this scene. The same device is used earlier when Marke discovers the lovers asleep in the grotto. Here the narrator comments on Isold's flushed appearance, con-fessing his inability to understand this point from his source (17561: *ine weiʒ von welher arbeit/diʒ mære spellet unde seit,/von ders erhitʒet solte sin*).[4] This time, not content with this apparently

---

(1947), 189ff. Unfortunately this aspect is very weakly brought out by Homberger, *Gawein*, where one might have expected to see it better emphasised.

[1] On the conventional use of this formula see Hatto, *Ignorance*, pp. 98ff. and von Lieres und Wilkau, *Sprachformeln*, pp. 121ff. and 179ff. See also Mayer, *Topoi*, pp. 231ff.

[2] Cf. Hollandt, *Hauptgestalten*, p. 19, fn. 7.

[3] 268, 299, 342. Cf. Hollandt, *op. cit.*, p. 19 and fn. 8, and Mersmann, *Besitzwechsel*, p. 175, fn. 1.   [4] Cf. Hatto, *Ignorance*, pp. 98f.

obtuse avoidance of the sexual explanation, the narrator goes further in his ignorance by putting forward an innocuous explanation (17570: *ja ich erkenne mich nu wol,/waz dirre arbeite was:/Isot was, alse ich iezuo las,/des morgens in dem touwe/geslichen zuo der ouwe/und was da von enbrunnen*). No *edelez herze* amongst the listeners would have accepted this rationalisation, and the narrator would have known this, so that his ignorance is the means of leading them to their certainty. In both cases the appearance of ignorance, presented as if it were courtly discretion, conceals a deeper irony at Marke's expense, so that we are here invited into a tacit collusion against the husband.[1]

From pretended ignorance it is a short step to another type of rhetorical irony, a claim for modesty by which the narrator flatters his listeners and controls their responses by seeming to be their inferior. To use a phrase like *ich wæne* implies a lack of complete certainty which points towards ignorance, and is also a form of modesty which, as its rhetorical purpose shows, is not meant as such. Equally, to say *ine weiz* can suggest ignorance, but also the modesty belonging to such ignorance, as shown by one of the modesty formulas used by Gottfried's narrator in trying to prepare Tristan in his knightly gear (4826: *ine weiz, wie in bereite*).

This scene of Tristan's knighting is one of the most cunningly contrived passages in the work,[2] so that the claim for modesty must be looked at twice when such self-conscious artistry is displayed, the more so since this passage accomplishes what the narrator claims he cannot achieve. How little store we are to set by such modesty and how we should see it instead as a cloak for achieving calculated effects, including a criticism of those to whom the narrator pretends he is inferior, may be seen from the

---

[1] Wolfram's narrator uses this formula ironically when he twice denies all knowledge of the time when Parzival drew near to Trevrizent's cell (435, 5; 446, 3ff.), but soon afterwards has the latter reckon out on a psalter the exact length of time of the knight's wanderings (460, 22ff.). The use of this formula on this occasion is part of the narrative technique by which Wolfram ensures that the audience shall (some of the time) experience things from Parzival's point of view (see above, pp. 146ff.).

[2] On this scene cf. above all Fromm, *DVjs* 41 (1967), 333ff.; Schulze, *PBB* (T) 88 (1966/67), 285ff.; Hahn, *ZfdA* 96 (1967), 218ff.; Clausen, *Erzähler*, pp. 21f. and 171f.; Stein, *DVjs* 51 (1977), 300ff.

words with which, having prepared Tristan's companions, he 'modestly' questions whether he can do justice to their leader (4591: *wie gevahe ich nu min sprechen an,/daz ich den werden houbetman/ Tristanden so bereite/ze siner swertleite,/daz man ez gerne verneme/und an dem mære wol gezeme?/ine weiz, waz ich da von gesage,/daz iu geliche und iu behage/und schone an disem mære ste*). This looks modest enough: the opening rhetorical question seems to imply that the narrator does not know how to prove equal to his task, which in turn is apparently confirmed by the *ine weiz* formula. But the narrator then defines his position within the three-point relationship between the narrator, his story and his listeners, saying that his difficulty is in trying to please his audience and do justice to the demands of his story. Again, this looks conventional, but this point is underlined by being made a second time (4595-6 and 4598-9) and by the emphasis on pleasing the audience in the second passage (in place of the simple *gerne*, 4595, we are told: *iu geliche und iu behage*, 4598). The narrator's real difficulty therefore lies with his audience, he cannot do justice to his story and at the same time give them what they want, which implies that their preferences conflict with the narrator's obligation to his story. When he describes what the courtly literature of his day has accomplished in the way of such description (4600ff.) and emphasises his inability to compete (4612ff.), he inserts a concluding criticism of these descriptions (4616: *ja ritterlichiu zierheit/diu ist so manege wis beschriben/und ist mit rede also zetriben*) which shows that his inability to compete amounts to a refusal to do so.[1] The literary convention established by these rivals is what the narrator's listeners want to hear from him, his inability to perform his artistic task *and* please them amounts to a criticism of their taste and of the literary convention to which they are attached. Both these criticisms (of the audience and of the colleagues) lurk behind a confession of modesty, which is thereby revealed as its opposite.

A pretence of humility can be harnessed to further ends in *Troilus and Criseyde*.[2] In an early remark of this kind (I 15: *For I, that god of loves servauntes serve,/Ne dar to love, for myn unliklynesse,/*

[1] Cf. Fromm, *DVjs* 41 (1967), 342 and 348.
[2] See Durling, *Figure*, pp. 44ff.

Preyen for speed, al sholde I therfor sterve,|So fer am I from help in derknesse) the narrator implies that his poetic office is like the Pope's as *servus servorum Dei* (how modest is it for a poet to see himself as a Pope amongst clerics?). At the same time he uses the religious humility of this title to maintain distance from the theme of love. He is himself no servant of Love (for he dare not love), but only the servant of these servants. Another reference to the narrator's clerical status comes in the Proemium to Book III where, in his appeal to Venus for poetic assistance, he refers to himself as the 'clerk' of her servants (III 40: *At reverence of hem that serven the,|Whos clerk I am, so techeth me devyse|Som joye of that is felt in thi servyse*). Here *clerk* has two meanings, both pointing in the same direction (a cleric or a writer). As a writer, the narrator knows of love only at second hand, from books, not from personal experience, whilst as a cleric he has no part in the secular love celebrated in the poem. Such shrinking from experience by his narrator is Chaucer's way of casting doubt on the love described in his poem and current at court. Just as Parzival's upbringing remote from the Arthurian world makes it easier for him to transcend Arthurian values and gain entry into the realm of the Grail, so does the inexperience in love shown by Chaucer's narrator qualify him to lead his listeners to call into question the absolute value of secular love. But this manipulation takes place under the guise of a narrator modestly disclaiming his ability to do justice to his theme.

Sometimes Chaucer's narrator remarks that the lovers' emotions surpass his ability to describe them. Professing the impossibility of doing justice to the delights of their lovemaking, he leaves this task to the willing imagination of those who know about such things (III 1310: *Of hire delit or joies oon the leeste|Were impossible to my wit to seye;|But juggeth, ye that han ben at the feste|Of swiche gladnesse, if that hem liste pleye!*). This invitation shows up the narrator as an envious outsider, as hinted at by the contrast between *ye* (1312) and *I* (III 1319: *O blisful nyght, of hem so longe isought,|How blithe unto hem bothe two thow weere!|Why ne hadde I swich oon with my soule ybought,|Ye, or the leeste joie that was there?*). Even this seeming inferiority has to be read ironically, because the story soon demonstrates (and the listeners have already been alerted to this outcome) that the lovers' joy is only shortlived and that it will not be worth sacrificing one's soul for it, let alone for the *least* of their joys. Again, the narrator's inexperience in love conceals his qualifications for teaching the truth.[1]

At times the narrator creates the impression of being so lacking in insight that in denying certain doubts he manages to suggest them to his audience. This can be done so carefully that we can assume the presence of the poet behind the narrator, leading the audience to entertain these doubts. This is particularly so with *Troilus and Criseyde*, so that once more I draw my examples from this work. Just as Gottfried's narrator insinuated the idea of Riwalin's arrogance in maintaining ignorance,[2] so does Chaucer's implant the suggestion that Criseyde came to love Troilus rather too suddenly in meeting this objection from a member of his audience. He protests that Troilus had to serve her first (II 678: *For which, by proces and by good servyse,/He gat hire love, and in no sodeyn wyse*), a defence which is true if *gat hire love* refers to the consummation of Book III, but not if we read it in terms of her growing preoccupation with him.[3] In any case, it is the poet who decides at this stage to mobilise his fictitious listener and have him bring forward this objection (II 666: *Now myghte som envious jangle thus:/'This was a sodeyn love; how myghte it be/That she so lightly loved Troilus/Right for the firste syghte, ye parde?'*). We must credit the poet with some intention in inserting this doubt at this point, but if it is to allow Criseyde's reputation to emerge more firmly established, this purpose is not well served by a defence weakened by ambiguity.[4]

To perceive the intentions of the poet working behind and through the narrator we have to pay attention, as Donaldson has taught us,[5] to his use of language. When the coming change in

---

[1] On this general feature of Chaucer's narrator with regard to the theme of love see Bethurum, *PMLA* 74 (1959), 511ff. Nellmann, *Erzähltechnik*, pp. 14ff., has some important words on the way in which the narrator of *Parzival* presents himself in deliberately humble, even ridiculous terms, pp. 14f. Chaucer's narrator develops his rôle above all (but not only) with the theme of love in mind, whereas the range of poses adopted by Wolfram's has no such clear focus. Both agree, however, in adopting a position of self-ridicule.

[2] *Tristan* 342f.

[3] Cf. Gordon, *Sorrow*, pp. 81f.

[4] See also Donaldson, *Speaking*, pp. 65f.

[5] *Ibid.*, pp. 65ff.

Troilus's position is announced at the start of Book IV (15: *For how Criseyde Troilus forsook,/Or at the leeste how that she was unkynde,/ Moot hennesforth ben matere of my book*) we must realise that the euphemism of v. 16 could only be effective if it stood in place of an emphatic statement. Coming *after* v. 15 and not replacing it, it constitutes an unconvincing anticlimax, so that the failure to play down v. 15 finishes by granting it more importance.[1] One word can be enough to attract the notice of an audience forewarned of Criseyde's betrayal of her lover, as when her reaction to the news of her exchange for Antenor is revealed to us (IV 673: *As she that hadde hire herte and al hire mynde/On Troilus iset so wonder faste,/That al this world ne myghte hire love unbynde,/Ne Troilus out of hire herte caste*). This sounds persuasive until we look into the function of the opening word *as*.[2] The sentence begins as if a simile were to follow ('Like a woman that…'), but what ensues is a direct description of Criseyde, subjected to the slight distancing achieved by the frustrated simile (to say that 'She acted as one who had set her heart on him' is not so unambiguous as 'She had set her heart on him'). This is a minuscule point, but the audience still has fresh in its mind the warning about Criseyde given in the Proemium to Book IV and will be alert to anything that justifies their distrust.[3]

The narrator's truthfulness

The passage where Chaucer's narrator appeals to *myn auctour* to suggest a doubt about Criseyde[4] may serve as a bridge to a last group of examples illustrating the irony of the narrator, his source-references and claims for truthfulness. Of the irony of *myn auctour* in this passage there can be no doubt, because the episode in which it occurs has no counterpart in Chaucer's source, a fact which would have been known, or accessible, to those among Chaucer's audience who knew their Boccaccio.

---

[1] *Ibid.*, pp. 69f. [2] *Ibid.*, pp. 70ff.
[3] Donaldson has interpreted (p. 78) another example of the ironic use of a frustrated simile (IV 953ff.) and the doubts raised by the narrator's assurance *treweliche* (IV 1415 and elsewhere). He tellingly compares this with 'the *surely* that scholars sometimes employ to support statements which they suspect their readers will feel to be most unsure' (pp. 73f.). [4] III 575ff.

This type of narrator's irony presupposes the practice of attesting the truth of a story (Nellmann has shown this to be particularly the case in the vernacular as opposed to classical or medieval Latin),[1] but also the awareness by vernacular poets and some of their audience that fictional truth is not the same as factual truth, that poetry is concerned with verisimilitude and consistency rather than historical truth. Nellmann explains the vernacular practice of claiming to speak the truth as a concession to the underdeveloped sense of fictional truth shown by the poet's knightly public,[2] adding that the doubts raised by some of Wolfram's more hair-raising source-references would only have been entertained as doubts by the more educated amongst his listeners for whom such claims to be speaking the factual truth in fiction were superfluous.[3] The irony of these remarks implies some listeners, probably the majority, who took these claims at their face value and others whose understanding of the needs of fiction enabled them to share his joke at the others' expense. With these references to the source or claims to be telling the truth we come to the third kind of differentiation within the romance as written literature, between the more sophisticated and the less perceptive within the audience, as hinted at in Gottfried's *Tristan* by the distinction between *ir aller werlt* and the *edele herzen*[4] or in *Parzival* by the division of the audience into *tumbe liute* and the *wîse(r) man*.[5]

Chrétien's position with regard to source-references is different from that of his German adaptors, as is revealed by his attack on other professional storytellers at the beginning of his *Erec* (19ff.). Informing this attack is not merely a repugnance for their spoiling any theme they touch, but above all the need felt by a literate poet to keep a safe distance between himself and their oral fabrications, the more so since his own work, although a literate and rhetorical composition, is based on such an oral tale (13: *un conte d'aventure*). If these oral tales are exposed to the charge of being irresponsible inventions because they lack the authority of

---

[1] Nellmann, *Erzähltechnik*, pp. 50f.
[2] *Ibid.*, p. 51.   [3] *Ibid.*, p. 57.
[4] *Tristan* 50 and 47. See Speckenbach, *Studien*, pp. 52f.
[5] *Parzival* 1, 16 and 2, 5 (a collective singular and therefore comparable with the plural in 1, 16). On these two terms see Haas, *Tumpheit*, pp. 31ff.

a written tradition, the same charge can be levelled against Chrétien who seeks to draw attention away from his own vulnerable position by distancing himself from his rivals in distinguishing between their irresponsibility and the respectable written status (23: *estoire*) of his own composition.[1]

Chrétien's followers in Germany are in a different position. They have no need to distract attention from their source's unreliability, they go back to written sources (Chrétien's own works) and can appeal to a literate authority. If these German poets are released from the ambiguity of Chrétien's position we might expect to find them dispensing with ambiguous source-references, avoiding irony in attesting the truth of their narratives, but this is not the case because they do not always follow their written French sources in every detail. The liberty which Chrétien had tacitly claimed for himself (to base his *conjointure* on oral material lacking written authority) is also exercised by his German adaptors in not always following him to the letter even when they base their claim for truth on the written authority of his text.

If these poets deviate from Chrétien for their own aesthetic purposes and still claim to follow their sources faithfully, this suggests that they have to reckon with some of their listeners expecting a faithful rendering of an authoritative source and judging the truth of a romance by its conformity to the written tradition it continues. For these listeners the convention of the source-reference still had a part to play as a defence of secular literature. But from the German poet's frequent alterations to his source we may conclude that he did not expect these listeners to recognise his alterations (they were therefore unacquainted with his source or not concerned to gain access to it) or to doubt his claim to be following an authoritative source. They are therefore characterised as unsophisticated and uncritical, but if the irony of the narrator's source-references has any point it must be meant for other members of his audience from whom a critical response could be expected, who do not naïvely equate

---

[1] On the problem facing Chrétien in this prologue see Köhler, *Trobadorlyrik*, pp. 13f. Criticism of colleagues for their clumsy handling of the story is not unknown to the French epic (cf. Mölk, *Literarästhetik*, pp. 1ff.), but Chrétien adapts this convention to the distinction between oral tradition and written composition.

the truth of a story with the truth of history and who can occasionally consult a French original.[1] These listeners are sceptical of
a narrative convention such as the source-reference and are open
to the irony of a narrator using this convention when he offends
against its spirit. To establish this irony we have to be convinced
that the poet alters his source, and that these alterations coincide
with the narrator's claim not to be doing this.

Narrator's irony of this kind is particularly characteristic of
Wolfram, Gottfried and Chaucer, if not always explicit. Without
going into the question of Kyot Lofmark has demonstrated the
unreliability of the narrator's claims in *Parzival* to be recounting
events found in his source.[2] He shows how in most cases the
claim to take specific information from his source is apparently
false,[3] how the narrator deceives his listeners even when claiming
to be faithfully following his source,[4] and how he makes use
of a source-reference when he seems pointedly to go his own
way.[5] Whether or not we follow Lofmark as far as his quasi-
biographical conclusion,[6] the majority of these source-references,
especially those confirming details of no significance, are clearly
not intended to be taken seriously. The narrator shares with some
of his listeners a humorous disrespect for the strict rule of source
authority.[7] If this resembles Chrétien's attitude it is more significant in Wolfram's case because, unlike the French poet, he
has no reason to make fun of this rule – other than the need to
imply his superiority to it and to educate his listeners towards
a similar attitude.

By contrast, the narrator of *Tristan* really seems to remain true
to his source. He says in the prologue that he follows the nar-

[1] On this possibility see below, pp. 257f.   [2] MLR 67 (1972), 820ff.
[3] Ibid., p. 825.   [4] Ibid.
[5] Ibid., p. 826.
[6] Ibid., pp. 831ff.
[7] Ibid., p. 826. To Lofmark's findings could be added the position with regard to
Wolfram's use of *âventiure* to mean 'source' in *Parzival*. I have shown elsewhere
(*Aventiure*, pp. 110ff.) that only two of the 32 cases where *âventiure* is used to mean
'source' have a counterpart in Chrétien's version to which they can refer. For the
rest, *âventiure* can refer to a source in episodes which are not included in Chrétien's
incomplete version or to a Kyot whose account we cannot check, or, even more
intangibly, to Kyot's own source. Finally, the narrator in *Parzival* can claim that
a detail comes from his French source, but in all these cases Chrétien has nothing
comparable.

rative of Thomas because this version comes closest to the truth (149: *sin sprachen in der rihte niht,/als Thomas von Britanje giht*; 161...*daz ich in siner rihte/rihte dise tihte*).[1] This is confirmed by the way in which he takes over the main outlines of Thomas's story as well as by the accuracy of most of his specific source-references. In short, Gottfried's narrator differs from Wolfram's in practising no deception on his audience over the relationship between his version and the Anglo-Norman one. Whenever he says that he follows Thomas, this is the truth. But this is still only part of the truth, for there are also occasions where the German version differs from the source.

The narrator can explicitly state that what he says diverges from the source and all other versions, so that he stands fully alone, as in his commentary on the combat between Tristan and Morolt (6866: *Nu hœre ich al die werlde jehen/und stat ouch an dem mœre,/daz diz ein einwic wœre,/und ist ir aller jehe dar an,/hien wœren niuwan zwene man./ich prüevez aber an dirre zit,/daz ez ein offener strit/von zwein ganzen rotten was;/swie ich doch daz nie gelas/an Tristandes mœre,/ich machez doch warbœre*).[2] He can also refer critically to those versions which have got a particular detail wrong, for example the suggestion that Marke was given the dregs of the love-potion on his wedding-night (12651: *ouch sagent genuoge mœre,/daz ez des trankes wœre,/von dem Tristan unde Isot/gevielen in ir herzenot./nein des trankes was nime:/Brangœne warf in in den se*). The point of this commentary is that Thomas's version had had Marke drink of the potion.[3] The line *ouch sagent genuoge mœre* therefore conceals a reference to Gottfried's source in particular, even if it is not singled out for mention as with the last example in v. 6867. Gottfried's narrator can also tacitly correct what is an inconsistency in his source without saying what he is doing or voicing any criticism, as in the detail that Marke was not accompanied by the dwarf when he came across the lovers asleep in the orchard.[4]

Each of these three types of commentary amounts to a dis-

---

[1] Cf. Schröder, *ZfdA* 104 (1975), 307ff.
[2] On the novelty of this allegorical dimension of the combat in the German version see Piquet, *Originalité*, pp. 156f.
[3] See Bédier's edition, I 157 and 167f. and Piquet, *op cit.*, pp. 229 and 238.
[4] Cf. Gottfried's *Tristan* 18192ff. with Thomas's version, vv. 4ff. See also Piquet, *op. cit.*, pp. 45f. and Wapnewski, *Abschied*, pp. 349 and 355.

satisfaction with Thomas's motivation, criticising him by means of the criterion of *raisun* which he had invoked in defence of his own work.[1] Although he is nowhere mentioned by name (as in the prologue) he is present as a target: explicitly in the first instance (*daz mære*, Thomas's version, is singled out from *al diu werlt*), implicitly in the second (*genuoge* includes Thomas, points to him above all), and tacitly in the third. When Gottfried's narrator claims in the prologue to follow the Anglo-Norman text because this incorporates the truth of the story, this pays no regard to this kind of remotivation.[2] The discrepancy between the two versions amounts to a questioning, in which those listeners acquainted with Thomas are invited to take part, of the simple acceptance of a source as authoritative.

In *Troilus and Criseyde* reference is made to Lollius as a source,[3] a name usefully suggestive of respectable, even classical authority for a medieval romance. What this involves can be seen in the narrator's introduction of the song in which Troilus, falling in love, expresses his feelings (I 393: *And of his song nat only the sentence,/As writ myn auctour called Lollius,/But pleinly, save oure tonges difference,/I dar wel seyn, in al, that Troilus/Seyde in his song, loo, every word right thus/As I shall seyn*). It may be true that Chaucer has taken a passage in one of Horace's *Epistles* to imply that Lollius was a literary authority on the Trojan war,[4] yet he cannot be absolved from knowing that the authority which he was mainly following was not a classical poet but Boccaccio[5] and that in this context Troilus's song comes not even from Boccaccio's *Filostrato*, but from one of Petrarch's sonnets.[6] Reference to this classical source (lost to posterity, so that the narrator's claim

---

[1] Cf. Thomas's *Tristan* 2134ff. and Ranke, *Tristan*, pp. 130f. and 133ff.

[2] In other words, a courtly poet who appeals to the criterion of reason when criticising others runs the risk of embarrassment when the same criticism can be levelled against his source, the guarantee of the truth of his own version. Where this is the case, the acknowledgement of this criterion will tend to undermine the authority of source-references. The way is now open for the poet (and those of his audience who accept the validity of his criterion) to appreciate the irony of what are now meaningless source-references.

[3] On these references to Lollius see Root's edition, pp. xxxviff.

[4] *Ibid.*, pp. xxxviiif.

[5] On Chaucer's relationship with Boccaccio in this work see Root's edition, pp. xxviiiff.

[6] See Root's edition, pp. 418f., notes on I 393–9 and 400–20. The poem by Petrarch, Sonnet 88, is given in the second note.

cannot be disproved)[1] is a means for the poet to distance himself from his story. It confirms his pretence that he is not qualified to give an original treatment of the story because he is a stranger to love, dependent on the superior experience of others, as when he submits his account to the listeners' more informed judgment (III 1408: *For myne wordes, heere and every part,/I speke hem alle under correccioun/Of you that felyng han in loves art,/And putte hem hool in youre discrecioun,/Tencresce or maken diminucioun/Of my langage*). Where a reference to a non-existent source is immediately ironic, submissiveness to the authority of listeners with greater experience is shown as ironic flattery at the end of the poem when the narrator gives way to the poet expressing his own authoritative concern that his text should not in any way be bowdlerised (V 1795: *So prey I god that non myswrite the*).[2]

This example is revealing in one other respect. If the narrator admits that his knowledgeable listeners are at liberty to influence his record in accordance with their understanding of love he is tacitly conceding that the emotional truth, as they see it, is a sufficient criterion when dealing with a work of fiction and that the factual truth which the source supposedly purveys can be ignored. To this flattery of the listeners there correspond examples from the German romance where the narrator politely pretends to give way to what his audience may decide about the narrative. In *Parzival*[3] the tournament at Kanvoleis is described in such terms (59, 26: *ine sagez iu niht nâch wâne:/gebiet ir, sô ist ez wâr*), like the combat between Parzival and Orilus (263, 30: *ruochet irs, sie tâten strîtes schîn*) or a meal at Schastel Marveile (639, 2: *welt ir, sie habent genuoc dâ gâz*). If events can be politely subordinated to the wishes of the audience, little case can be made out for a narrative line predetermined by what the source has laid down, so that subjection to a source is gently ridiculed by the listeners being invited into collusion with the narrator.

---

[1] The same happy advantage, in *Parzival*, is enjoyed by Kyot's informant, Flegetanis, who read the secrets of the Grail in the heavens (454, 17ff.), a convenience for anyone who bases his poetic account on him which even those who believe in the existence of a Kyot would not deny.

[2] On this authority of the poet, instead of the inferiority of the narrator, coming to the fore at the end of the poem see Durling, *Figure*, p. 63.

[3] Examples have been collected by Nellmann, *Erzähltechnik*, pp. 40f.

Although the listeners are given the appearance of control they are of course puppets of the narrator, their existence and suggestions are his fictions, so that it is not surprising to see the narrator exercising a humorously arbitrary control over events in his narrative, for which he rather than any source is directly responsible. In *Parzival* the narrator compliments himself on his politeness in landing the old king Utepandragun gently on flowers when unhorsing him at a tournament (74, 5ff.),[1] in *Tristan* he accuses himself, like a flustered master of ceremonies, of having impolitely forgotten to mention the lady Floræte earlier (5227ff.)[2] and can revert with a jolt, after a digression, to a character in the work as if he had been left dangling in the meanwhile, awaiting the puppetmaster (4824: *ie noch ist Tristan umbereit/ʒe siner swertleite*).[3]

The authority of the source is here squeezed out from two sides (in reality, only by the poet). What takes its place is the apparently arbitrary, but aesthetically regulated decision of what is best, offered to the listeners by the narrator who leaves them no real choice. With the narrator pushing himself forward obtrusively it is only to be expected that his interventions should undermine the naïve idea of factual truth based on conformity to a source. In *Erec* the narrator pushes his listeners drastically away from factual truth (and in the direction of fictional truth) when making a joking confession about a hyperbole (9209: *Got lône im derʒ geloube,/wan ich niht drumbe geswern enmac*). In describing the dress of Mabonagrin's mistress he draws a line between imagination and reality (8946: *welh ir roc wære?/des vrâget ir kamerære:/ich gesach in weiʒ got nie,/wan ich niht dicke vür si gie*).[4] In *Parzival* the authority of the source is undermined by being linked with a non-existent oath brazenly imputed to his listeners by the narrator (238, 8: *man sagte mir, diʒ sag ouch ich/úf iuwer ieslîches eit*), so that

---

[1] Cf. Wolff, *Schriften*, p. 272.
[2] On this and other examples see Clausen, *Erzähler*, pp. 56ff.
[3] Clausen, *op. cit.*, p. 57.
[4] The offhand manner in which Hartmann's narrator dismisses this question and refers his questioner to the *kamerære* (8947) is reminiscent of the contemptuous gesture of Gottfried's narrator in refusing to say anything about the tournament at Tristan's knighting ceremony (5059). With Gottfried this is because of his repugnance for the theme of knighthood, with Hartmann it hints at his impatience with a literalist understanding of poetic truth.

they are liars just as much as he (238, 11: (*sol ich des iemen triegen,/ sô müezet ir mit mir liegen*)).[1] The switch from *man* (standing for the source) in 238, 8 to *ich* three lines later, from *sagen* to *triegen*, is an indication that the authority for the poem is not the source, but the narrator (behind whom stands the poet) and that what it presents is not a factual truth taken over from the source, but an aesthetic truth for which the adaptor is responsible. The narrator's game with his audience is part of his way of educating them to realise this novel state of affairs.

As in other chapters, completeness has been out of the question and I have concentrated instead on suggesting some of the ways in which the change from oral to written composition in medieval secular literature, contemporary with the emergence of the romance, gives scope to the irony of the narrator. This comes about because the various kinds of differentiation characteristic of written composition lend themselves to the differentiation which is a feature of irony. If the irony of the narrator, unlike verbal irony, is not treated in the rhetorical handbooks, this is no different from their neglect of the aesthetic function of the narrator himself.[2] In neither case does the silence of the theoreticians justify us in ignoring what medieval poets achieved in practice in developing their artistry beyond the limits of what was laid down for them.

---

[1] Cf. Wolff, *Schriften*, pp. 272f. Other examples are given by Nellmann, *Erzähltechnik*, pp. 67f.

[2] Cf. Nellmann, *Erzähltechnik*, pp. 165ff.

8

DRAMATIC IRONY

The type of irony we now have to consider depends for its effects on the superior knowledge of the listeners, aware of a truth withheld from a character. This category contrasts with the irony of the narrator, at least with those cases where the narrator manipulates the responses of his audience and, by pretending ignorance or by a teasing uninformativeness, denies his listeners facts of the narrative.[1] The one type keeps the audience in ignorant suspense, as much at a loss as the character himself, whilst the other places them on a vantage-point not shared by the actor. Between them, these two types create a disturbingly shifting perspective, now flattering our sense of superiority and now undermining our certainty by bringing it home to us how much we do not know.[2]

If we regard dramatic irony in its own right, we have to ask how the listener is put in his position of superiority. The answer to this depends on how we understand dramatic irony. Three factors are called for.[3] In the first place, there must be a tension within the narrative, one character must be at loggerheads with another (be he man, God or any other abstract power) or at variance with circumstances. Secondly, in this situation governed by tension at least one of the characters must be ignorant of his circumstances, the situation as he sees it differs from the situation as it really is, there is a discrepancy between appearances and

---

[1] See above, pp. 233ff.
[2] I have made this same point in *Irony*, p. 57.
[3] I rely here on Sedgewick, *Irony*, pp. 48f., but have adapted his wording because he is concerned with the dramatic genre. Other important works on the subject are Thirlwall, *PhM* 2 (1833), 483ff.; Sidgwick, *CM* 22 (1907), 497ff.; Thompson, *Mock*. On tragic irony see Behler, *Ironie*, pp. 134ff.

reality. Thirdly, the audience must be aware of the real situation and of the character's failure to assess it correctly. The discrepancy between appearances and reality must not merely exist, it must also be seen to exist by the audience. Taken together, these factors mean that dramatic irony is the sense of discrepancy felt by an audience in face of a character acting in ignorance of his situation.[1] The audience know the facts, he does not; his view of his situation differs from the facts made visible to the audience; the promise held out to him by things is at variance with the outcome of events, he is beguiled by their appearance.

We need not go here into the association of this type of irony, as its name suggests, with the drama or the coinage of this name in connection with Greek drama in particular.[2] Although this type is especially at home in the setting of the theatre, it is also to be found outside it, in narrative literature. Despite the adjective 'dramatic' English critical usage is ready to apply the term 'dramatic irony' to the narrative genre as well, whilst in German practice the term itself seems to be missing, apart from attempts by English scholars to introduce it.[3] True to my origins, I follow this precedent in the present chapter.

Occasions for dramatic irony

Dramatic irony may be central to the drama (indeed, it represents one of the few means available to the dramatist for imposing his own point of view on a course of events in which he plays no evident part like the narrator in narrative literature).[4] But can it be said that its occurrence in narrative literature, specifically in the romance, is at all frequent? Even if we confine ourselves to points raised previously in our argument it is possible to answer this question positively. On the formal side, three features encourage the exploitation of dramatic irony in the romance: interlace technique, anticipations of the future, and *ordo artificialis*. Dramatic irony is present in the first whenever the events nar-

[1] Sedgewick, *op. cit.*, p. 49.
[2] On this see especially the works listed on p. 250, fn. 3.
[3] Cf. Salmon, *PBB* (T) 82 (1960), 95ff.; Green, *Irony*, pp. 56ff.; Johnson, *Ironie*, pp. 133ff.
[4] Johnson, *Ironie*, p. 135.

rated in the one strand of action show up the ignorance of the actors in the other strand (as in the contrast between the grief felt by Thomas's Ysolt for her absent lover and his unworthy doubts about her, culminating in his marriage, in the narrative strand just abandoned).[1] Dramatic irony is involved in a narrator's forecast of the future when he shares with us knowledge of a reversal denied to a character (as when the narrator lets us see, when Herzeloyde's plans to protect her son from knighthood are first voiced, that they will come to nothing).[2] It is also brought out by the *ordo artificialis* when the disturbance of the natural chronology gives us knowledge with which to judge a scene (as with Gottfried's reversal of the lovers' early morning walk in the surroundings of the grotto and the arrival of Marke's huntsman on the scene, allowing us to perceive the threat to their idyllic existence).[3] In each case the audience is given knowledge withheld from a character, but in each case a different narrative technique has been employed to produce dramatic irony. To the extent that these three features are commonly used in the romance we may expect them to be possibly harnessed to this purpose.

The romance is also predisposed towards dramatic irony by some of its themes. The themes of adventure and the quest mean that it is concerned with encounters,[4] but it only needs one party to be ignorant of the other's identity, and the audience to be made aware of this, for dramatic irony to be possible. The frequency of such encounters and the need to ring the changes on this type of episode account for the cases where one knight meets, but fails to recognise another.[5] The stratagems of war (where the narrator describes to his listeners the plans of one side, concealed from the other) and the frequent case of a knight preserving his anonymity whilst seeking adventure provide further examples.

On the non-military side we have seen dramatic irony in the

---

[1] See above, pp. 135f.   [2] See above, p. 143.   [3] See above, p. 137.
[4] Cf. Bindschedler, *DVjs* 31 (1957), 100: 'Alle Artus-Dichtungen sind Dichtungen der Begegnung.'
[5] Professor Ross has suggested to me that failure to recognise an opponent would be a normal feature from the adoption of the closed helm in the second half of the twelfth century. For a particular type of this failure in recognition see Mölk, *RJb* 15 (1964), 107ff.

mutual ignorance of each other's feelings often depicted in lovers trembling on the brink of confession[1] (when this is expressed by a switch from one lover's unjustified doubts to what is revealed of the other's emotional response we find the technique of interlace combining with mutual ignorance to provide an episode governed by dramatic irony). To this we must add the frequent deceits employed by lovers, whether more innocuously to guard their privacy from prying eyes (Gottfried's Riwalin and Blanscheflur) or because their illicit love makes it a matter of life or death for the lovers to hoodwink society (*Cligès*, *Tristan* or *Flamenca*). When the poet, to enlist our sympathies on behalf of his lovers, makes us privy to their subterfuges he is giving us the means to appreciate the dramatic irony of the deception of an unwanted husband and his henchmen. Since the theme of illicit love governs almost the whole narrative in such cases dramatic irony is coterminous with most of the plot, no longer with one episode in which two lovers hesitate to confess their feelings to one another.

Such thematic possibilities already account for so much of the largely conventional plot of the romance that one is justified in going one step further and asking how far the principle of dramatic irony informs the whole œuvre of a poet or any romance. Under the first heading Kellermann maintained the pervasiveness of dramatic irony in all of Chrétien's works,[2] which in the case of the founding father of this genre has implications for the romance at large. He stresses that Chrétien frequently juxtaposes appearances and reality in the course of the narrative, imbuing the action with a double meaning and the possibility of mistakes, surprises and deceptions,[3] a technique which may owe something to the surprise turns of the plot, based on separations and recognitions, of the Hellenistic romance.[4] From this possibility there

---

[1] See above, pp. 173f. and 180f.
[2] Kellermann, *Aufbaustil*, pp. 72ff.
[3] *Ibid.*, p. 72.
[4] Kellermann suggests this (*ibid.*, p. 79), and also the possible influence of Ovid's *Metamorphoses* (pp. 80f.). The influence of one type of romance on another seems much more probable than so specific a model as Ovid (even though the early Chrétien tried his hand at some Ovidian themes), since there are already grounds for thinking that the Hellenistic romance exercised some influence on its medieval successor (see above p. 135, fn. 4).

follow examples in all of Chrétien's works, amongst which Kellermann adduces the formally correct oath which allows Lancelot to imply Guinevere's innocence,[1] the two occasions when Yvain confronts his wife without being recognised by her or his combat with Gauvain,[2] and Chrétien's crowning example of the failure to recognise someone, the encounter between Gauvain and Guiromelant in *Perceval*.[3] This dramatic irony established for Chrétien means that this feature is also established for the romances of Hartmann and Wolfram.

The one important type of romance not led in the path of dramatic irony by Chrétien's genius is the *Tristan* story.[4] But the plot of this story, especially as it developed on the continent, provided opportunities for dramatic irony, above all in the many deceptions perpetrated by the lovers against Marke, but also in the disguises adopted by Tristan (as a leper, a pilgrim, a court-fool, even a monk). In this the continental Continuation makes use of episodes which have close parallels in the fabliau,[5] but a recurrent feature of the fabliau is the dramatic irony of the hoodwinked husband, especially in the heightened form of a dupe trapped in a snare of his own devising.[6] Because of this development the *Tristan* plot is pervaded with dramatic irony. Almost any treatment, by its choice of subject-matter, could hardly avoid taking over thematic examples of this type of irony, as is revealed by even Eilhart, hardly a poet sophisticated enough to be given to irony, treating at length the dramatic irony latent in the encounter between Marke and Tristan in his disguise of court-fool.[7]

---

[1] See above, p. 183, fn. 3.
[2] Kellermann, *op. cit.*, p. 74.
[3] *Ibid.*, pp. 76ff.
[4] The closest Chrétien comes to the *Tristan* theme is in his *Cligès*, of whose plot ambiguities Kellermann has said: 'Alle Verwendungen des Doppelsinns im Cliges aufzuführen, hieße den ganzen Roman nacherzählen' (*ibid.*, p. 73). Even here it would be difficult to determine how far Chrétien's use of dramatic irony in this work results from his parodic intentions or the *Tristan* plot itself.
[5] See above, pp. 123f.
[6] In her survey of Chaucer's dramatic irony Dempster (*Irony*, pp. 27ff.) suggestively sees fabliau material as one of the contributory factors in his elaboration of this type of irony.
[7] I have analysed the irony of Eilhart's scene of Tristrant disguised as a fool at Marke's court in *Alieniloquium*, pp. 153ff.

Traditional and novel themes

If there are occasions when we might expect dramatic irony in the romance, we now have to ask in what kinds of situation the poet found himself with regard to his audience. How far could he rely on them to supply the superior knowledge necessary for dramatic irony and how far did he provide them with this knowledge for his own rhetorical purposes? We can answer this by taking two details into account. Is the subject-matter of the work a traditional or novel one? Is the audience listening to its recital for the first time or on a subsequent occasion? On the variations between these possibilities the poet's ability to use dramatic irony largely depended.

Where the subject-matter is traditional the outlines of the story are known to the audience even when they are listening to a novel version of an old theme, so that the poet can rely on this knowledge when dealing with a situation of dramatic irony. This was already true of Greek drama, for the Attic spectator came to tragedy not to hear a new story, but to attend the working-out of an old one;[1] he carried with him to the theatre a previous knowledge of the plot which Sophocles could take for granted in building dramatic irony into *Oedipus Rex*. What is true of Greek drama is also largely true of medieval narrative, for most clerical and heroic literature dealt with conventional themes known to an audience of conservative taste. The author of the *Millstätter Exodus* could rely on knowledge of his biblical theme for his subject to carry its own dramatic irony when he described the splendid knightly equipment of the Egyptian warriors in pursuit of the Hebrews (3039ff.) at a point when, as his listeners knew from the Bible, all this was to be set at nought in the Red Sea.[2]

Heroic literature can exploit dramatic irony to the full because it largely consists of themes handed down through the centuries and well known in their plots long before they found their way onto parchment. In the *Nibelungenlied*, however, we do not have to remain content with a general consideration, since the emphasis on friendship and the juxtaposition of Kriemhild and Brünhild in the thirteenth *Aventiure* can only be appreciated by an audience

---

[1] Sedgewick, *Irony*, pp. 5of.   [2] Green, *Exodus*, pp. 97f.

aware of the imminence of their quarrel.[1] As with the *Millstätter Exodus*, the audience for the *Nibelungenlied* must have been acquainted with the outlines of the plot; their knowledge (which does not rely on the narrator's anticipations of the future) is the condition for a use of dramatic irony which can at times dispense with direct hints.

To suggest that dramatic irony could most readily be perceived with a traditional theme seems to weaken the case for this type of irony in the romance, one of the most radical innovations in medieval literature. This case can be partly redeemed if we consider the ways in which the new genre rapidly established its own conventions. This is true even of Chrétien's works, for Kellermann has shown that his romances together constitute a 'poetische Gesamtatmosphäre'. One work so far presupposes the others that an audience hitherto acquainted with only one of his romances knows in any other that *li rois* is Arthur, *la reïne* refers to Guenevere and *li seneschaus* can only signify Keu.[2] To be acquainted with one work is to know what outlines to expect in another and how these standard characters will behave (Keu, for example, must soon have established his rôle of malicious braggart whose boasting leads to his discomfiture).[3]

Once his audience came to expect stock characters and situations the poet could rely on their expectancy to produce his effects for him. If Keu boasts, we can savour the irony of his boasting to the extent that we know that he will be put in his place by an ignominious defeat.[4] If in his encounters the hero is threatened with death by an opponent (Erec by Mabonagrain),[5] we can assume from the convention that the hero overcomes all dangers[6] that the tables will be turned against the opponent and appreciate the dramatic irony of the biter bit. Even if the hero's opponents

---

[1] Wachinger, *Studien*, p. 24, especially fn. 1.
[2] Kellermann, *Aufbaustil*, pp. 7f.
[3] Cf. Haupt, *Truchsess*.
[4] In each of his four Arthurian romances Chrétien has Keu's arrogance followed soon afterwards by his ignominious defeat. Cf. *Erec* 3985ff. and 4045ff., *Lancelot* 82ff. and 257ff., *Yvain* 2178ff. and 2240ff., *Perceval* 4274ff. and 4298ff.
[5] Cf. the verbal threat of 5906ff. with the tacit warning of the empty stake, 5796ff.
[6] This is not to say that a poet cannot achieve a surprise effect by occasionally going against this convention, as is the case with Erec's second encounter with Guivret or with Gawain in *Sir Gawain*. But this effect can only be achieved because the convention already exists.

are giants (when Erec rescues Cadoc), the same convention combines with the biblical precedent of David and Goliath to assure us that the giant's confidence is ironically misplaced. (This assurance is independent of the remark by Hartmann's narrator that the God who helped David also came to Erec's assistance on this occasion.)[1] At times the knowledge necessary for the appreciation of dramatic irony comes to the audience not from the conventions of the genre, but from another work which the poet can assume is known to his listeners. Wolfram can presuppose with his *Titurel* audience a previous knowledge of his *Parzival* and of the story of Schionatulander and Sigune, and therewith the ability to appreciate the tragic background to their love not suspected by them.

Apart from such cases, where the conventional nature of the romance provides the knowledge indispensable for dramatic irony, this genre represents something new, the importation of the *matière de Bretagne* into the repertoire of continental literature and a freedom of scope which time-honoured themes from heroic and classical antiquity could not offer. This novelty is what Wolfram means when he says of his task in *Parzival* (4, 9: *ein mære ich iu wil niuwen*). As the first German poet to treat this theme he is giving the story a new linguistic form which it had never had before, but also reciting a novel theme to a German audience. The poet can no longer assume that his listeners possess the necessary knowledge; he must now contrive means of feeding them information.

Even in these circumstances, where the German adaptor is responsible for his version of a French romance, one can still imagine two possibilities of previous knowledge, although on a more restricted scale than with a traditional subject-matter. We can assume that the poet's patron may have known the outline of the plot and that he did not commission a German version without some idea of what the French original had to offer. With the patron (and perhaps with a small circle close to him) the poet

---

[1] 5561ff. That this explicit mention of God is not essential to the dramatic irony of this scene is clear from Chrétien's version in which no such remark is made. Apart from an exchange of words between the giants and Erec, meant to illustrate the giants' arrogant confidence (4430ff.), Chrétien can rely upon the traditional motif of the combat with giants to make its own point.

may have been able to assume a general knowledge adequate to the obvious examples of dramatic irony. But knowledge of the French original need not stop there. One of the tasks of the patron was to procure a copy of the French romance on which the German poet could work to commission, so that this manuscript would have been available at a German court (presumably not to the poet alone) while the work of adaptation was proceeding. Gottfried has this in mind when, with regard to the appositeness of his hero's name, he appeals to his source (2018: *diz mære, der daz ie gelas,/der erkennet sich wol, daz der nam/dem lebene was gehellesam*). If *mære* connotes Gottfried's source[1] and if he appeals to his audience's knowledge to confirm what he says, then the use of *gelesen* implies that some among Gottfried's listeners (however few) had read the French original and that he could rely on these to grasp some examples of his dramatic irony.

Although the romance treats of novel themes within the medieval repertoire, there is no certainty that the literary versions that have come down to us are the earliest versions that circulated. Already in his *Erec* Chrétien refers to a *conte d'avanture* (13) on which his story is based and which has been mangled by some of his colleagues, Thomas knows of other versions of the *Tristan*

---

[1] As in 1946 (*als wir daz mære hæren sagen*), for example. Cf. Schröder, *ZfdA* 104 (1975), 323, although I see no objection to reading 2018, as in 320 (Schröder, *ibid.*), as referring to the source. *Lesen* can be used in Middle High German to indicate the act of reading out loud, i.e. reciting to a group, as well as the private act of reading to oneself (see Crosby, *Speculum* 13 (1938), 416, fn. 3, Chaytor, *Script*, p. 15, Schröder, *art. cit.*, pp. 309ff. and Green, *Oral*, p. 188). I cannot imagine any way in which Gottfried may have implied the former meaning in 2018, since it is quite unlikely that a reciter of Gottfried's source (presumably a Frenchman) could be a member of the audience for Gottfried's German version. On the possibility of the private act of reading in the Middle Ages cf. Wolfram's *Parzival* 337, 3; Konrad von Würzburg, *Der Welt Lohn* 52ff. For the possibility in Norman England cf. Gaimar, *Lestorie des Engles* 6496: *Dame Custance en ad lescrit,/ En sa chambre souent le lit*. Another suggestion that the source is available for consultation in written form is provided by the narrator's comment on the arrival of the Irish marshal (8737: *und als daz mære hie vor gibt, / der da vor an daz mære siht*). *Mære* I take to refer to the source again, whilst the verb *siht* implies that it exists in a written form. Lofmark, *MLR* 67 (1972), 831, fn. 1, also interprets *Parzival* 734, 1ff. as implying knowledge of Chrétien's version on the part of some members of Wolfram's audience. In more general terms (with reference to a written source) Mohr considers the possibility of the more cultivated members of Wolfram's audience knowing the general outline of his story from Chrétien's version (*Obie*, p. 14), whilst Zimmermann, *Kommentar*, pp. 263ff. and 283, argues persuasively that Wolfram was acquainted with Chrétien's *Lancelot*. Such knowledge is hardly likely to have been confined to the poet.

story[1] and has reservations about them, Hartmann's *Erec* may have been preceded by a Rhenish version[2] and Gottfried's *Tristan* is preceded by Eilhart's version, which Gottfried may have known himself.[3] If these poets know these other versions it is quite unlikely that their listeners knew nothing of them. Here too we encounter the possibility of previous knowledge and hence the ability to recognise some examples of dramatic irony.

First and subsequent recitals

These are exceptional cases, however, for we should not exaggerate the number of those at German courts who could read a French manuscript and had the opportunity to do so. For the most part, the German poet faced listeners to whom his story was a novelty and who could bring no previous knowledge with them to a recital. In considering how a poet who wished to exploit the irony latent in his subject-matter faced up to this situation we must distinguish occasions when a work was recited before an audience for the first time from subsequent occasions (that we are justified in assuming more than one recital before the same audience is suggested by the small number of narrative works in circulation and by the economics of literary patronage).[4] Those who heard a work recited more than once were in a better position to appreciate points that must have escaped them on the first occasion, when they were unacquainted with the outline of the plot and not always able to appreciate the discrepancy between what is said or done at any point and what the future holds in store. At a first recital these listeners (if they are given no hints by the narrator) will be in a position comparable with that of a character, ignorant of the future and not necessarily capable of judging the present correctly. Unlike a fictional character they enjoy the artistic privilege of being able to witness the same events unrolled before them on subsequent occasions. On these

---

[1] *Tristan* 2107ff. Cf. Fourrier, *Courant*, pp. 27ff.
[2] Tilvis, *NM* 60 (1959), 29ff. and 129ff.
[3] Cf. Lichtenstein's edition of Eilhart, pp. cxcvff. and Bédier's edition of Thomas, II 81ff.
[4] Cf. Gallais, *CCM* 7 (1964), 488f. For Wolfram's *Parzival* cf. Hirschberg, *Untersuchungen*, p. 52, fn. 18.

occasions they will savour the point of Gottfried's Marke equipping Tristan with a shield emblazoned with a boar, for now they
will recall the symbolism of Marjodo's dream, a detail that still
lay in the unknown future when first they came to Tristan's
combat with Morolt.[1]

Examples like this, whose dramatic irony would be unsuspected at a first recital, are not uncommon in the romance. Unless
we make the unlikely assumption that in every case the poet
enjoyed the private pleasure of making a point which he withheld from his audience,[2] we may see in them an indication that
the poet reckoned with more than one recital, with an effect
which would be all the stronger for the delayed impact. Keeping
this distinction between a first and subsequent recital in mind,
we can appreciate the concealed force of the following cases, in
each of which dramatic irony would be revealed only on the
later occasion.

When Chrétien's Erec is welcomed by his people after gaining
the hand of Enide (2398: *Onques nus rois an son reaume/Ne fu plus
lieemant veüz/N'a greignor joie receüz*) or when the narrator praises
Erec's virtues in superlative terms (2263ff.) an audience hearing
this for the first time cannot know that this is about to be disproved by his behaviour at Carnant, whilst at a second recital
their knowledge of what follows will throw a different light on
both passages. The same is true of *Yvain* when Laudine rejoices
that Arthur and his court are about to visit her (2320f.), for
neither she nor a 'first-night audience' can realise at this stage
that Gauvain will use this occasion to entice the newly married
hero away from his wife. When Perceval takes his leave of his

---

[1] *Tristan* 6614 and 13 511ff. Cf. Beck, *Ebersignum*, pp. 134ff. and Tax, *Wort*, pp. 83f.
The effect of the detail given in 6614 is quite different from that of 6594ff., for the
narrator uses the headdress to anticipate the future, he allows us to share the irony
of Marke handing over to Tristan a headdress of this symbolic force. Whereas
the dramatic irony of the headdress is visible at a first recital, that of the shield can
be appreciated only subsequently.

[2] Hellgardt, *Grundsätzliches*, p. 27, rightly criticises what he terms 'literarische
Bauhüttengeheimnisse', so often invoked as a defence of the theory of numerical
composition. The nearest I am prepared to come to the view that a medieval poet
may have built into his works effects which his contemporaries would have found
difficult to appreciate is the Whitsun chronology of the last Arthurian scene in
Wolfram's *Parzival*, as established by Weigand (see above, p. 30). Even here the
poet does not make it impossible for them to see his point, he merely reckons with
the unlikelihood.

followers after marriage to Blancheflor (2952: *Et il lor dit: 'Ne vos estuet/Pas or plorer plus longuemant:/je revandrai, se Deus m'amant;/ Que diaus a feire est nule riens'*), it is not yet clear that his journey will take years or that the conventional remark *se Deus m'amant* conceals the fact that God will help him in another sense (by taking him to the Grail castle) and that he will never return to Belrepeire.[1] The implications are more tragic when Sigune at her first meeting with the young Parzival, aware of his wish to follow in Orilus's tracks to seek vengeance for Schionatulander and fearing for his life, deliberately sends him on the wrong track (141,30ff.). Although she thereby protects him physically, she unwittingly leads him to a greater danger to his soul, since the track takes him to the encounter with Ither and the slaughter of a kinsman.[2] Neither Sigune nor the new listener can know this at the time, but the listener who can turn back narrative time by hearing the story recited a second time will bring to this scene the superior knowledge which was the monopoly of the narrator at the first recital. Those amongst Gottfried's listeners unacquainted with the *Tristan* story and hearing his version for the first time may have noticed nothing peculiar about Marke's words after he has learned that Tristan is his nephew (4307: *sit ez alsus gevaren ist,/daz doch du mir worden bist/von der vil lieben swester min,/geruochet es min trehtin,/so wil ich iemer wesen vro*). Those who know the outlines of the plot or have heard this version recited before will appreciate how shortlived the king's joy is to be.

If we move back one last stage, to the occasion when our hypothetical listener hears a story recited for the first time, we can establish that a medieval poet is not always content to leave his effects until a second recital and that he will often take steps to make his dramatic irony apparent at a first recital. He can do this either by inserting a narrator's comment to alert his audience to what is afoot or by dropping an ambiguous hint. Hartmann

---

[1] A similar example, concerning an arrival instead of a departure, occurs in Gottfried's *Tristan* when Rual welcomes Riwalin back home and expresses his relief that their country's difficulties are soon to be overcome with his help (1601ff.). Here too the audience at a first recital cannot know (although they may suspect it from 26off.) that this relief is to be shortlived and that Riwalin's death in battle is to confront his subjects with greater difficulties than ever before.

[2] Cf. Harms, *Kampf*, p. 148, although his mention of Lähelin needs to be corrected in the light of Johnson, *Ironie*, p. 137, fn. 6.

uses the latter technique in *Erec* in having Oringles claim that God was responsible for sending him to Enite in time to prevent her suicide (6251: *mich wæne in sæliger zît/ze iu got her gesendet hât*). A new listener is likely to take this at its face value at this point, especially in view of the observation made by the narrator when Oringles first came across Enite (6123: *den hâte got dar zuo erkorn/ daz er si solde bewarn*). But this apparent agreement between God's ways and Oringles's soon gives way to a tension between the two which meets one of our conditions for dramatic irony (6351: *got hete den gewalt und er den wân*). This confident belief that things are going his way and that God is harnessed to his own wishes marks Oringles down as an obvious victim of dramatic irony. Hartmann therefore reverts to him in having him brag unfeelingly to Enite that, since she has now met Oringles, her husband's death can even be counted as an advantage to her (6267: *sehet, nû wirt iu wol schîn/daz iu iuwers mannes tôt vrumt/und iu zallem heile kumt,/wan iu nû êrste wol geschiht*). His boastful tone and lack of consideration for one recently widowed stamp him as guilty of the arrogance which, in the well ordered universe of the romance, brings its own punishment and therefore alert the audience to the possibility of dramatic irony. Here it takes the form of Oringles saying something which is perfectly true, but not in the sense in which he means it. If we are to view Erec's apparent death and what follows at castle Limors as the cause of his reconciliation with Enite, it is true to say that his death (in this sense) benefits his wife (*vrumt*), brings her good fortune (*zallem heile*) for the first time (*nû êrste*), since only now is their marriage firmly based. But this reading is not what Oringles has in mind; it is so far opposed to it that the happiness which Erec soon bestows on his wife is tied to the death of this boaster.[1]

Gottfried's Marke is an obvious victim of such dramatic irony. When he promises to share both his property and his land with his favourite, Tristan (5153: *se mine triuwe in dine hant,/daz ich dir min guot und min lant/iemer geliche teile*) the listeners soon learn just how weak is his resolve to stay unmarried (5159f.) and later see the

---

[1] On the similar dramatic irony of Oringles's words to Enite in 6471ff., based on a dimension to his speech which he cannot suspect, see Green, *Alieniloquium*, pp. 125f.

unwitting irony of a future husband who regards his wife as no more than his property[1] promising to share his goods with her future lover. When Tristan is promised a cure by the Irish queen he thanks her in ecstatic terms, expressing the hope that her name will enjoy renown throughout the world (7797: *din name der müeze werden/gewerdet uf der erden!*). This hope is fulfilled, but in an unexpected sense. As the queen has the same name as her daughter Isold, it is this name (applied to the daughter) which comes to enjoy renown, not as an exemplar of healing skill, but as the name of Tristan's mistress,[2] celebrated in literature. An audience listening to a recital of *Tristan* can be presumed to have been immediately accessible to this kind of dramatic irony, even though no direct comment has been made by the narrator. This is the feature of these examples. Without any explicit pointer, the new listener is enabled to detect an ironic dimension, sometimes immediately (Tristan and the Irish queen), sometimes with a slight delay (Marke's promise to Tristan) but without necessarily having to wait until a second recital for these implications to become apparent.

Discrepancies in the present

If this is the range of possibilities open to a poet eager to exploit the potentialities of dramatic irony, there are many occasions when, especially with themes which at some stages in their transmission struck listeners as highly novel, he cannot afford to leave it to his audience to grasp the irony of a situation. He must take active steps to draw their attention to the discrepancy between what they know and a character's unawareness. The poet has to devise a number of methods to ensure that his listeners will be acquainted with some of the facts denied to a character.

The most obvious method is for the narrator to intervene with a direct commentary at the point where dramatic irony is suggested. The frequency of such drastic interventions indicates the poet's wish that his listeners should not miss the point and his

---

[1] On this see Mersmann, *Besitzwechsel*, pp. 190ff., who fails however to take his analysis of this theme (and of Marke's rôle in it) far enough.

[2] Even the renown of Isold's name as a healer will be rescued on this new level if we regard her healing powers metaphorically, as one lover's ability to cure the other's sickness (see pp. 208ff.).

realisation that a novel theme runs the risk of being deprived of many effects at a first recital. In a work dominated by the theme of deception like Chrétien's *Cligès* the narrator must see to it that we do not miss the implications of his plot. Deception in this romance commonly concerns the triangle situation of the love-plot and what leads up to it. Appositely, the narrator's commentary is expressed pointedly when it comes to the emperor's deception on his wedding-night. He makes a remark with which to introduce the scene and warns us of what is at stake (3287: *Or est l'empereres gabez*), but then, after using the conventional phrase *si com il dut* (3291) with ironic ambiguity,[1] he intervenes (3293ff.) to make sure that the irony of the victim's position (thinking to enjoy the pleasures of love out of which he has been tricked) shall not escape us. Deception is no stranger to *Flamenca*, with its similar triangle relationship. Here too it can be pointed out by the narrator's intervention, alerting us to what the victim cannot see, as when Guillem puts on a front of clerical asceticism as part of his plan of seduction, for this is explicitly compared with an equally hypocritical sermon from the *Roman de Renart* tradition (3687: *Aissi presica N'Aengris,/Mais, si-l capellas fos devis,/Ben pogra dir si con Rainartz:/GartsiBelis daus totas partz*).[2] But dramatic irony can arise from simple misunderstanding as much as from positive trickery. In Chrétien's *Lancelot* Arthur and his court are convinced that the approach of Gauvain means that he is bringing Guinevere safely back with him after rescuing her from captivity (5301ff.). But the truth is quite different and the narrator makes sure that we realise this (5311: *mes autrement est qu'il ne cuident*).

German examples follow the same pattern. In Hartmann's *Erec* the narrator allows us to see that God's control of events lies behind the hero's success in dispatching the first of the two giants (5516: *er stach in zuo der erde tôt,/als ez der hövesche got gebôt*). We are permitted an overall view of the situation which is withheld from the giants and (as a reality which he knows, rather than merely hopes for) from Erec, whilst the tension needed for dramatic irony is presented by the contrast between this outcome

---

[1] See above, pp. 232f.
[2] Cf. Lewent, *ZfrPh* 53 (1933), 54 and Topsfield, *MÆ* 36 (1967), 127.

and the boastful arrogance with which the giants entered upon this combat.[1] But the tension in this example does not merely point backwards (constituting an ironic discrepancy between arrogance and defeat), it also points forwards. If Erec cannot be aware, as we are now, that God is involved in his adventures and is assisting him, the same ignorance is shared by Enite. When Erec, exhausted by his wounds, falls to the ground apparently dead she is understandably taken in by appearances and has no grounds, like the audience, for suspecting that God would hardly have intervened to protect Erec in combat only to permit him to die shortly afterwards of the wounds received.

The dramatic irony of our knowledge of God's involvement in events as opposed to a character's ignorance is also present in Wolfram's depiction of Parzival's adventures and journeying.[2] When the narrator says of Parzival at the moment when he loses track of the Grail-knights (249,4): *alrêst nu âventiurt ez sich*, he is telling his listeners two things of which Parzival can have no knowledge, that his journeying up to this point has been under the auspices of supernatural guidance and that this guidance has now been forfeited. Elsewhere, Wolfram's examples include instances of a failure to grasp the truth of a situation. This is the case with Bene in face of the coming combat between Gawan and Gramoflanz. Here too the narrator reminds us pointedly that her confidence in the latter is only half the story and that she would not have been so cheerful if she had realised that the former was her lady's brother (686,2: *diu liez den kampf gar âne haz./sie het des künges manheit/sô vil gesehen dâ der streit,/daz si'z wolt ûzen sorgen lân./wesse ab sie daz Gâwân/ir frouwen bruoder wære,/unt daz disiu strengen mære/ûf ir hêrren wærn gezogen,/sie wære an fröuden dâ betrogen*). His technique is similar in the combat between Parzival and Feirefiz, where he conveys to us the vital information that these two lack (738,10: *ir vremde was heinlîch genuoc*).

Just as Wolfram's narrator points out what is at issue at the moment when things begin to go wrong for Parzival on his travels, so does Gottfried's come to the fore at the start of the love-potion scene. The scene is set under way by the confusion of the potion with wine. So that we shall be clear about this it is not enough to be shown the serving maid thinking she has found wine (11 670f.), we also have to be told what she has actually discovered, which can only be done by the narrator (11 672: *nein, eʒn was niht mit wine,/doch eʒ ime gelich wære;/eʒ was diu wernde swære,/diu endelose herʒenot,/von der si beide lagen tot*).[1] From this moment until their recognition of what has befallen them the audience looks down upon the lovers' ignorance of what is happening. Since the course which events take is so different from what Isold's mother had in mind concocting the potion,[2] from Isold's attitude to Tristan as the killer of her uncle and from the serving-maid's intention in going to fetch wine, we can argue that these two levels of understanding combine with a discrepancy between intention and outcome to produce a typical situation of dramatic irony. But one which we can appreciate at the vital moment only because of the narrator's intervention.

Discrepancies between present and future

This method of acquainting an audience with the necessary facts has shown us the narrator commenting on a situation as it unfolds in the narrative present. Other methods show him concerned with the future or the past, hinting at the discrepancy they provide with the present. With pointers to the future as signals to dramatic irony in the present we come to narrator's anticipations of the future which we looked at earlier as part of narrative technique.[3] In *Yvain* the narrator shows up the reliability of the hero's promise to his wife by opining that he will exceed the time-limit granted him (2667: *Je cuit, qu'il le trespassera;/Car departir nel leissera/Mes sire Gauvains d'avuec lui*). In *Cligès* he alerts us to the future treachery of Angrés of Windsor by inserting the word *ancores* into his recommendation by Arthur's advisers (423: *Par le consoil de toʒ ansanble/Fu comandee, ce me sanble,/Au conte Angrés de Guinesores,/Car il ne cuidoient ancores/Qu'il eüst baron plus de foi/An tote la terre le roi*).[4] In *Lancelot* he uses a circumlocu-

---

[1] On the further implications of these lines see Schindele, *Tristan*, p. 62.
[2] On this contrast see Green, *Alieniloquium*, pp. 156ff.
[3] See above, pp. 139ff.
[4] On this passage see Green, *Recognising*, pp. 23f.

tion to describe the hero's lack of suspicion and construct our superior knowledge (5079: *Cil qui de nul mal ne se dote*).[1] In all these cases we are given a double time perspective in place of the single view of the characters, and are shown the discrepancy between them.

German poets operate with the same discrepancy. Hartmann's description of one of the robber knights attacking Erec switches from present to future, revealing the aggressor's defeat which has not yet been narrated (3386: *ir einer hete sich ûz genomen/und was den andern vür komen,/daz er tjostierte wider in,/ûf sîn selbes ungewin*).[2] Wolfram's narrator, commenting on Herzeloyde's order to keep her son from chivalry (117,29: *Der site fuor angestlîche vart*) undermines her situation at the moment she issues her command by setting it against a future invisible to her. In the siege of Pelrapeire, the advice to take the city by storm given by one of the besiegers is juxtaposed with a glimpse of the future which includes his own death in the attack (205,9: *den rât gap Galogandres,/der herzoge von Gippones:/der brâht die burgære in nôt,/er holt' och an ir letze den tôt*).[3] The description of Marke equipping Tristan for combat contains its hint of the future, concealed from both participants but shown to us, in the headdress of the helmet (6594: *dar uffe stuont diu strale,/der minnen wisaginne,/diu sit her mit der minne/an ime vil wol bewæret wart*). The respite granted to the lovers when Tristan is allowed back at Marke's court is shown, to the listeners alone, to be of short duration (15043: *sus was in aber ein wunschleben/nach ir ungemüete geben,/swie kurz ez wernde wære*). The start of the discovery scene in the garden is chosen for an anticipation of the crisis (18122: …*biz siz ouch vollebrahten/nach allem ir leide:/si gewunnen es beide/leit unde totliche clage*). This placing of the hint at the beginning of the scene, as with the interlace mention of Marke's huntsman *before* the lovers' walk in the surroundings of the grotto, allows the audience to see the shadow of disaster

---

[1] This is followed two lines later by a descriptive comment which achieves dramatic irony this time by contrasting the narrative present with the immediate past (5081: *et siust le nain qui traï l'a*).

[2] This robber-knight's defeat is presented in the immediately following passage, but what counts is not so much the short span of time over which dramatic irony operates as rather the fact that it is present here at all.

[3] On the wider context to which this detail belongs cf. Green, *Homicide*, pp. 37ff.

cast across an otherwise idyllic scene. The dramatic irony of both episodes is essential to the poet's view of the precariousness of love in this world.

Discrepancies between present and past

The other method of emphasising the dramatic irony of a situation is to point out the discrepancy between past and present. Unlike the other methods this one can afford to be implicit and dispense with an intervention by the narrator. The reason is clear. For the dramatic irony of a situation to be visible when that situation is actually presented too much reliance may be placed on the listeners' perceptiveness if the narrator gives no commentary. The irony resting on the contrast between present and future will be visible only to those who know that future because they have heard the work recited before, so that the needs of others can only be met by a narrator's intervention. This is not necessary with a discrepancy between present and past because the poet can rely on his audience's memory of events already narrated and on their realising any deviation. If this third method is to dispense with the narrator, however, the poet must arrange that the knowledge of the past which his audience need has already been built into the work. Dramatic irony can therefore be made evident not by any express commentary of the narrator, but by the previous course of the narrative and the listeners' memory of this past.

In *Yvain* Laudine's impatience in ordering Lunete to bring Yvain to her immediately (1821ff.) must be seen as dramatic irony in view of the fact, realised by Lunete and the audience, that Yvain is already concealed in her own castle. The same is true of the last encounter between these women in the work. The mistress is tricked into a reconciliation with her husband only by being persuaded to promise her good offices in reconciling the Chevalier au Lion (whom she does not recognise as Yvain) with his wife (6602ff.). This prompts Lunete to play verbally with the situation just before revealing the facts (6742: *'Certes, dame! ja nel deïsse',/Fet Lunete, 'se ne fust voirs./Toz an est vostre li pooirs/Assez plus, que dit ne vos ai'*). Since the audience knows the facts the dramatic irony of Laudine's situation is visible to them without the need for any commentary.

Lancelot offers a string of examples concerning the misunderstandings that arise from the hero's capture. This starts with a mistake (here the narrator steps in with an explanatory comment), for some followers of Bademagu, unaware of the agreement reached between the king and Lancelot, seize the latter, hoping thereby to please their lord (4124: ...*car il cuident qu'au roi bel soit/se pris et mené li avoient/Lancelot*). This is followed by a second example when the rumour of Lancelot's supposed death is conveyed to the king (4140: *Novele qui tost vole et cort/vient au roi que ses genz ont pris/Lancelot, et si l'ont ocis*). But this false report is then carried further until it reaches Guinevere, who has no reason for not believing it (4157: *Ceste novele par tot vait,/a la reïne fu retrait,/qui au mangier estoit assise;/a po qu'ele ne s'est ocise/maintenant que de Lancelot/la mançonge et la novele ot;/mes ele la cuide veraie*). As a last stage in this series of misunderstandings the rumour that Guinevere had died (for grief) at length reaches Lancelot (4250: *A Lancelot vient la novele/que morte est sa dame et s'amie*). This comedy of errors is at length resolved, but until this point the listeners enjoy a knowledge superior to that of the lovers, because they have been privileged observers of both the narrative strands and can carry forward knowledge of what has happened on one line of action to what occurs later on the other. Although these two strands make the narrative more complex than if the action were proceeding on one course, Chrétien can dispense with comments (except at the start of this episode) because he can rely on the audience bringing their memory of what has been narrated to bear on what follows.

The same method is used repeatedly in Germany. In Hartmann's *Erec* Guivreiz's pages come to greet their lord, accompanied by Erec after their first knightly encounter, in the confident belief that Guivreiz has once more been victorious and taken his opponent captive (4595: *wan sî wâren alle/von einem wâne gemeit,/daz er nâch gewonheit/den ritter hete gevangen*). Whereas we have just witnessed the converse in the preceding narrative.

With Wolfram examples come at crucial points in the story, rich in tragic potential. This is true of Parzival's encounter with Signe after leaving the Grail-castle, for to his remark that he has just come from Munsalvæsche she replies by saying that Amfortas must indeed have come to the end of his sufferings. When she recognises that she has Parzival in front of her she launches into a eulogy so barely restrained that it once more reveals her inability to conceive that now at last things have not been put right (251,29ff.). The one slight doubt she allows herself (252,3: *ob wendec ist sîn freise*) is in a minor key and is swept aside by the flood of her words praising the Adam-like mastery of the world which, she feels confident, has been conferred on Parzival. Her enthusiasm leaves him little chance to correct her and as with every word of hers he comes to suspect the magnitude of what he has lost his sense of shame makes it more difficult for him to make his confession. It is a masterly touch that this intensely lyrical passage, revealing the full scope of what is involved in Grail-kingship, is here undercut by dramatic irony, by our knowledge of what happened (or rather did not happen) at Munsalvæsche. Signune's inability to entertain the possibility underlines the enormity of Parzival's omission. As with the narrator's comment on the withdrawal of miraculous guidance (249,4) it is the function of dramatic irony to bring home to us, suddenly and crushingly, how much has been squandered.

A little later we are brought to the brink of tragedy by dramatic irony when, after being defeated by Parzival, Orilus offers his victor in exchange for his life one of the two countries held by his brother (266,21: '*mîn leben kouf ich schône./in zwein landen krône/tregt gewaldeclîche/mîn bruoder, der ist rîche:/der nim dir swederz du wellest,/daz du mich tôt niht vellest*').[1] The irony of this offer lies in the difference in what we and Parzival know. His defeated opponent is Orilus,[2] one of the enemies of his family, and the

---

[1] On the wider significance of these lines see Johnson, *Ironie*, p. 141, and Green, *Homicide*, pp. 31f.

[2] The audience are allowed to see this by a number of pointers: by their growing realisation that the woman Parzival has come across is Jeschute (they are given clues to this earlier than Parzival himself, see above pp. 167ff.), by their suspicion that the knight accompanying her must be Orilus (about whom they had been enlightened in the earlier scene, cf. 129, 27ff.; 133, 5, whilst this information, conveyed to the listeners by the narrator, had not been shared by Parzival), and finally by the mention of Orilus's name in the second scene (260, 25; 263, 19; 264, 21; 265, 4, 25; 268, 3; 270, 9; 270, 23). The point about this repeated mention of his name is that it is made by the narrator to his listeners; nowhere is the name

brother he refers to is Lähelin, of whose enmity Parzival has learned from his mother and from whom he has sworn to exact vengeance.[1] The two lands offered for the victor to choose from with apparent magnanimity by Orilus are the lands which Lähelin has taken by force from Parzival's family, they are legally his own. The audience has been enabled to appreciate all this by what it has previously learned (together with Parzival) from Herzeloyde and Sigune, but also by their knowledge that Parzival's defeated opponent is Orilus. He is unaware of this and also that his opponent's brother is Lähelin, whose name is not mentioned in this episode. This is enough to create the disparity in understanding between Parzival and the audience. Together with the discrepancy between the victor's readiness to spare his foe and how he would have behaved if he had realised the truth, this amounts to a powerful example of dramatic irony operative at a point which would have led to further repercussions if things had taken the wrong turn.[2] If only in this negative sense of a danger narrowly avoided we can say that, as with supernatural guidance granted to Erec or withdrawn from Parzival, this use of dramatic irony opens up a view of providential control of events which we see earlier than the hero.

The same point is suggested by the words with which Trevrizent, learning of his nephew's wish to see the Grail, attempts to dissuade him from the task (468,10: *ir jeht, ir sent iuch umben grâl:/ir tumber man, daz muoz ich klagen,/jane mac den grâl nie man bejagen/wan der ze himel ist sô bekant/daz er zem grâle sî benant*). Again, we can supply facts unknown to the hermit (in this sense his accusation *ir tumber man* turns against himself). We have already

<hr/>

used in Parzival's hearing, whose understanding of this scene remains notably behind that of the audience.

[1] Cf. 128, 3ff. and 141, 6ff. Before Orilus makes his reference to his brother without naming him (266, 21ff.) the narrator reminds his listeners again that he and Lähelin are in fact brothers (261, 29f.).

[2] The irony of Parzival's encounter with Orilus is given a further twist retrospectively by the latter's words when, having been sent by his victor to Arthur's court to render his respects to Cunneware (not named by Parzival), he discovers that she is his own sister (276, 27: *och hete ichs dô genozzen / gein dem helde unverdrozzen, / wesser wie sie mich bestêt / und mir ir leit ze herzen gêt*). In assuming that he could only have profited from Parzival knowing more about his family connections, Orilus may well be correct about his sister, but is drastically wrong about his brother Lähelin.

been shown that Parzival was allowed to penetrate to Munsal-væsche, that he was *ganerbe dar* (333,30) and that he had been the beneficiary of miraculous guidance there. Trevrizent cannot know the last two facts (they have come to the audience from the omniscient narrator) and he has not yet been enlightened by Parzival on the first point (cf. 468, 19f.). In that the hermit's attempt to head the knight off from the Grail is subjected to this kind of dramatic irony this passage supplies an indirect hint that Parzival may eventually find his way back to the Grail castle.[1]

Wænen

First amongst the examples of various classes of dramatic irony I now wish to consider is the use of *wænen* or a comparable verb in the narrator's commentary on a situation to his audience. Verbs of this type can (but need not always) be used as pointers to a discrepancy between belief and reality.[2] Where this is so, the irony tends to be dramatic, for *wænen* pinpoints a character's failure to understand and indicates this to the listeners. The dramatic irony of the Greeks in *Cligès* thinking that Alexander has fallen in battle is conveyed by the narrator's express commentary,[3] but also by his choice of verb (2059: *S'an cuident lor seignor porter*), whilst the same verb recurs in the comment on the false hopes of Arthur's court in *Lancelot* (5311: *mes autremant est qu'il ne cuident*). In German it is the verb *wænen* that is generally used for this purpose, as with the young Parzival's misjudgment on first encountering knights (122,21: *der knappe wânde, swaʒ er sprach,/eʒ wære got, als im verjach/frou Herzeloyd diu künegîn*) or

---

[1] Examples from Gottfried's *Tristan* include Isold's musings on the social status of Tantris (10 020: *im solte billich unde wol / ein riche dienen oder ein lant, / des dinc also wære gewant*), for we know that she has unwittingly hit upon the truth. Or the warning to Gandin by his crew (13 331: '*herre, herre, gat her an! / und kumet min her Tristan, / die wile ir an dem lande sit, / uns begat ein übel ʒit*'), for again the audience is aware that this warning has already been made reality. Or the commentary on Marke's reaction on seeing the lovers asleep in the grotto, separated by the sword (17 511: *diu verre gelegenheit / diu was im liep unde leit: / liep meine ich von dem wane, / si wæren valsches ane*), since we have just been shown that the idea of the sword is Tristan's way of deceiving Marke yet again (17 403: *hier über vant Tristan einen sin*).

[2] See above, p. 24 and Green, *Recognising*, pp. 24ff.

[3] 2057: *Mes por neant se desconfortent.*

Riwalin's youthful heedlessness (308: *do wander, des doch niene geschach,|daz er iemer solte leben|und in der lebenden süeze sweben*).[1] Interlace points in the same direction since with the switch from one narrative strand to another the listeners, who witness both series of events, take with them knowledge of the first to their appreciation of the second and thus enjoy a knowledge superior to that of actors confined to the one action alone. In *Cligès* the various strands of a battle-scene mean that the audience is given a wider view of the whole than the participants caught up in their individual mêlée. When the narrator passes from one such mêlée to another this can be the occasion for him to use dramatic irony of the partial vision of the combatants (2036: *De tot ice rien ne savoient|Lor genz, qui estoient defors,|Mes lor escuz entre les cors|Orent trovez la matinee,|Quant la bataille fu finee;|Si feisoient un duel si fort|Por lor seignor li Greu a tort*). This switch to a new narrative strand tells us of the Greeks' misunderstanding and of the reason for their mistake, but it also gives us, in addition to the previous knowledge we bring to this scene, confirmation of the Greeks' partial view of things (*a tort*).

How closely the interlace technique ties up with dramatic irony is shown by the scene in *Lancelot* in which Meleagant (who has imprisoned Lancelot, but who knows nothing of his rival's escape from captivity, just narrated in another strand) demands the single combat with Lancelot which had been agreed upon. From Meleagant's point of view things could not be better, since he believes Lancelot to be safely out of the way so that his challenge will not be taken up, but the switch from one strand to another has shown us how ill-founded his confidence is. At this point the narrator inserts his commentary (6734: *Puis li requiert de Lancelot,|li mauvés traïtres provez|se puis fu veüz ne trovez,|ausi con s'il n'en seüst rien;|nel feisoit il, nel sot pas bien,|mes il le cuidoit bien savoir*), suggesting that although Meleagant merely pretends to know nothing about Lancelot (his captivity), in fact he does know nothing about him (his escape).

---

[1] *Dünken* can also be used with the same purpose (as with the young Parzival's encounter with the knight Karnahkarnanz, 121, 30: *den dûhter als ein got getân*) or even *dünken* in conjunction with *wænen* (as with Parzival's 'perspective impression' of the castle of Gurnemanz, 161, 25: *den tumben dûhte sêre, | wie der türne wüehse mêre: | der stuont dâ vil ûf eime hûs. | dô wânder sie sæte Artûs: | des jaher im für heilikeit, | unt daz sîn sælde wære breit*).

Failures in recognition

Another situation well known to the romance, the failure of two people to recognise each other[1] gives rise to dramatic irony. This can take the form of an encounter between two knights who would not have come to blows if they had known the truth which the narrator reveals to his listeners, and it is to this that Harms has devoted an informative book.[2] For Germany the first instructive example is given by Hartmann in the second encounter between Erec and Guivreiz: he takes care to let us know who both combatants are, that they do not recognise each other, and why they fail to do so.[3] If we add to these details the discrepancy between the combat and the fact that Guivreiz was hurrying to bring help to his friend Erec,[4] we can agree that this encounter conforms to our definition of dramatic irony. In *Iwein* the same theme is taken up in the combat between the hero and Gawein. Again the audience is left in no doubt as to the identity of each fighter, their failure to recognise each other and why this is so.[5] The discrepancy necessary to raise these facts to the level of dramatic irony is provided by the narrator's allegory on the presence of *minne* and *haz in einem vazze* (7015ff.) and by the combatants' reaction when they learn each other's identity (7491ff.).

---

[1] Dramatic irony is involved whether the misunderstanding is shared by both combatants or is confined to one only.

[2] Harms, *Kampf*. The romance is discussed at length, pp. 122ff.

[3] The listeners are shown who the two knights are and how they could not fail to meet (6862ff.), but also that neither has any clear knowledge about the other (6869: *nû enweste ir deweder niht / umbe des andern reise*) and that the setting of a moonlit, but overcast night (6894f.) makes it understandable that they do not recognise each other. The *hüetelîn* (6988) worn by Erec underneath his helmet also makes it difficult for Guivreiz to see who his defeated opponent is when he strips him of his helmet to strike him dead (6937f.). See Harms, *op. cit.*, p. 125.

[4] 6852ff.

[5] Harms, *op. cit.*, pp. 129f., has shown how the narrator mentions to his audience the names of both combatants before they arrive at the scene of their fight (6907), but that from this moment until Iwein makes a move to find out his opponent's name (7370ff.) the narrator rhetorically puts his listeners in the same position as these two knights (and *their* audience) by no longer mentioning their names. As with an ambiguous oathtaking scene, we witness events as the spectators in the narrative do, but are also given advance knowledge denied to them. Harms also explains why both knights should be unrecognisable in this scene: Iwein, because no one knows that he is identical with the Knight with the Lion, and Gawein, because he has taken deliberate steps to enter the lists anonymously (5676f., 6884ff.).

To these examples I would add two points. The first concerns the way in which the narrator goes out of his way to give realistic reasons why his characters fail to recognise each other (because of their helmets or the darkness of night, etc.).[1] These additions are not merely for the sake of verisimilitude, for by bringing it home how the misunderstanding came about between two acquaintances the narrator emphasises their misunderstanding, and thereby the presence of dramatic irony. Secondly, the misunderstanding need not arise between two friends who unwittingly fight each other, but also between two sworn foes who because of their ignorance of the situation do *not* come to blows (Chrétien's description of Gauvain's verbal encounter with Guiromelant is a leading example of this).[2] Nor need this misunderstanding arise only between two enemy knights, it can be generalised beyond this into a situation where someone shows help or affection for a sworn foe. This is expressly pointed out by Gottfried when the disguised Tristan is healed by his mortal enemy in Ireland (7911: *Du wise küniginne/diu kerte alle ir sinne/ und alle ir witze dar an,/wie si generte einen man,/umbe des lip und umbe des leben/si gerne hæte gegeben/ir lip und alle ir ere*).[3] Gottfried is careful to give us all the facts necessary: the ignorance of one party, the reason for this, and how differently the queen would have acted if she knew what we and Tristan know.[4]

Dramatic irony also arises when the listener can detect the outlines

[1] Examples of a poet taking care to motivate a failure to recognise someone are to be found in Chrétien's *Erec* 3971ff. (the heraldic device on Erec's shield has been so battered in fighting as to be no longer recognisable), *Yvain* 6110ff. (the combatants exchange no words and have no chance to recognise each other's voice), *Cligès* 1833ff. and 3485ff. (a military stratagem), Wolfram's description of the combat between Parzival and Gawan (cf. Harms, *Kampf*, pp. 155f.) and between Parzival and Gramoflanz (*ibid.*, p. 162), Arnive's failure to take account of the lapse of time when she catches sight of a heraldic device (*Parzival* 662, 10ff.). For Gottfried one could adduce the foresight with which Tristan concealed the wound inflicted on him by Morolt and the way in which this later stood him in good stead in Ireland, commented on by the narrator in 7885ff.

[2] *Perceval* 8721ff.

[3] The fact that the narrator comments expressly on the dramatic irony of this situation makes it likely that his description of the Irish queen as *diu wise küniginne* is likewise meant ironically, as a contrast between a conventional formula to describe someone skilled in magic and healing and her complete failure to understand what is at stake in this particular situation.

[4] The dramatic irony of this situation is expressly taken up again once Tristan has returned to Cornwall, 8237ff.

of hubris about to be defeated. As befits the chivalric theme of most romances, this is generally applied to a military encounter[1] and reveals to the listener that pride comes before a fall. In Chrétien's *Erec* we prick up our ears on learning of the excessive confidence displayed by Yder (783: *Mes ne cuidoit qu'el siecle eüst/ Chevalier qui tant hardiz fust/Qui contre lui s'osast conbatre*) or by the robber knights who attack Erec for booty (2935: *Tot maintenant que il les virent,/Par parole antr'aus departirent/Trestot lor hernois autressi/Con s'il an fussent ja seisi./Male chose a an coveitise;/Mes ne fu pas a lor devise,/Que bien i fu mise deffanse*).[2] In Erec's combat with the giants Hartmann's narrator achieves complex effects (5524: *Êrec erbeizete dô:/des was der rise vrô/und wânde in sâ gewunnen hân./ in trouc ob got wil sîn wân*). On the one hand he alerts the listeners to the downfall that awaits such over-confidence (by the insistent repetition of *wânde, wân* and by the glimpse of the outcome in *in trouc...sîn wân*). On the other he creates the tension of uncertainty by pretending to be in the position of the combatants and ignorant of the outcome (hence the appeal *ob got wil*).

If such remarks are placed not before, but after the boaster's discomfiture, the dramatic irony now involved is a case of the biter bit. Gottfried's *Tristan* is particularly rich in this form of irony. The narrator pours his scorn on the jealous barons at the Cornish court who, hoping to encompass Tristan's end, find themselves caught in their own trap and are shown up ironically as counsellors who can give themselves no advice (8643: *sin kunden umbe ir eigen leben/in selben keinen rat gegeben:/si rieten her, si rieten hin/und enkunden nie niht under in /geraten, daz in töhte/und daz rat heizen möhte*).[3] Other examples of the deceiver being outwitted include Gandin, tricked by Tristan's employment of the same ruse against him which he has just practised against Marke

---

[1] Although it can also be applied to the position of the lover, underlining the irony of his fond belief that he is immune to the assaults of love (as with the effect of Isold's appearance on the men at the Irish court, *Tristan* 8090ff.) or an actual scorn for love (as with Chaucer's Troilus, see above, pp. 92f., or Soredamors in Chrétien's *Cligès* 438ff., both cases placed just before each is defeated by love).

[2] Significant here is the phrase *con se*, acting as a pointer to irony by indicating the difference between expectations and reality.

[3] The way in which the barons are caught in their own snares has been brought out well by Gruenter, *Euphorion* 58 (1964), 126f. On the barons' situation see also Hahn, *Raum*, pp. 101f.

(13 413: *vriunt, ir stat an des gouches zil,|wan daz ir mit dem rottenspil|
dem künege Marke ertruget an,|daz vüere ich mit der harpfen dan:|ir
truget, nu sit ouch ir betrogen*) or the success with which Isold,
thanks to Brangæne's perspicacity, traps Marke in the snare he has
laid for her (13 860: *do verkerte sich daz:|den stric, den er ir rihtete|
und uf ir schaden tihtete,|da vie diu küniginne|den künec ir herren inne|
mit ir Brangænen lere*). There is an ironic change of fortune when
Tristan, a huntsman in the literal sense as master of the royal
hunt, but also in the metaphorical sense as the lover of Isold,[1] is
finally shown hunted down as a quarry in the grotto-scene where
Marke's huntsman comes across the tracks left by the lovers in
the dew.[2] This last example with its suggestion that fortune is
mocking Tristan opens up a wider perspective showing irony as
possibly built into the course of events. It is to this wider problem
that we must now turn.

The irony of events

To persuade us that events are directed towards an ironic end
a work must contain not just isolated instances of dramatic irony
(which is what we have been considering up to now), but a series
of such examples, especially at critical turning-points in the action.
This has been illustrated in Gottfried's *Tristan* by Haug,[3] who
proceeds from Gottfried's imagery of the 'Bärenhammer' and
the birdlime trap to show how the lesson the poet draws from
these images is applicable to the course of the narrative. It is the
ingenuity of the hero which lets him overcome a certain obstacle,
only to confront him with a greater difficulty which thus acts as
an ironic answer to the exercise of his intelligence. There would
be no point in repeating Haug's demonstration of the sustained
dramatic irony of Tristan, seeking to escape one danger, repeatedly
running into another of his own making,[4] so that I propose to consider the recurrence of dramatic irony in two other romances.

[1] See above, pp. 210f.
[2] Cf. Snow, *Euphorion* 62 (1968), 375 and fn. 23.
[3] Haug, *Aventiure*, pp. 88ff. The criticism by Schröder, *ZfdA* 104 (1975), 324ff.,
does not seem to me to touch Haug's general point.
[4] This point is made expressly by the narrator's comment on Tristan's banishment
from Cornwall (18 418: *hie merket aventiure: | Tristan vloch arbeit unde leit | und*

Of importance in *Troilus and Criseyde* is the insistent suggestion that events are under the sway of some superhuman power, be it fortune or predestination, God's providence or astrological determinism.¹ These indications, to which must be added the narrator's anticipations of the future, build up a conviction that events are moving towards a predetermined end revealed to us, but not to the actors. Something of this Chaucer may owe to Boccaccio's *Filostrato*, but references of this kind in his source are generally brief and conventional, whereas Chaucer expands them and deprives them of conventionality by adapting them to the particular situation on which he is engaged. The result is a background of determinism which constantly reminds us of the outcome and equips us with the facts necessary to understand dramatic irony.²

We know from the start (whether or not we are acquainted with Boccaccio or Benoît de Ste Maure) that Criseyde will betray Troilus (I 55: ...*Of Troilus in lovynge of Criseyde,/And how that she forsook hym or she deyde*). With this knowledge, confirmed at many subsequent points, we appreciate the irony of the lyrical depiction of the lovers' joy soon to be swept away or of Criseyde's promise of faithfulness, formulated as an unwitting curse pronounced on her future self (IV 1534: *For thilke day that I for cherisshyng/Or drede of fader, or for other wight,/Or for estat, delit, or for weddyng,/Be fals to you, my Troilus, my knyght,/Saturnes doughter, Juno, thorugh hire myght,/As wood as Athamante do me dwelle/Eternalich in Stix, the put of helle*). Knowing what is in store for Troilus we recognise the dramatic irony of his dithyrambic praise of the god of love,³ and a qualification of two words is enough to cast doubt on the highest point of his love (III 1714: *And thus Fortune a tyme ledde in joie/Criseyde and ek this kynges sone of Troie*).⁴

---

suohte leit und arbeit; / er vloch Marken unde den tot / und suohte totliche not, / diu in in dem herzen tote: / diu vremede von Isote). The ironic situation described here resembles one in *Waltharius* 779, but also the engraving by Eric Gill reproduced in Muecke, *Compass*, p. 103.

¹ On this aspect of Chaucer's work see Curry, *Chaucer*, pp. 241ff.; Patch, *Speculum* 6 (1931), 225ff.; Bloomfield, *PMLA* 72 (1957), 14ff.

² Dramatic irony in *Troilus and Criseyde* has been briefly discussed by Dempster, *Irony*, pp. 10ff.

³ III 1254ff. and 1744ff.

⁴ The insertion of *a tyme* in these lines as a pointer to dramatic irony is comparable with the use of *ancores* in *Cligès* 426 (see above, p. 266).

How closely contrived is this overall impression of events mockingly working against Troilus and his hopes can be shown by one small change effected by Chaucer. Whereas Boccaccio has Diomede's long conversation with Criseida, a crucial step in her seduction, take place on her fourth day in the Greek camp, Chaucer has altered the chronology to the tenth day, thereby synchronising this scene with the day on which Criseyde was due to return to Troy and on which we are shown Troilus confidently awaiting her return by the walls of the city.[1] Such dramatic irony can be expressly associated with fortune (with the imagery of the wheel of fortune) and govern much of the course of the narrative action, as is shown by the narrator's commentary on the young Troilus's resolve to keep himself aloof from the folly of lovers (I 215: *This Troilus is clomben on the staire,/And litel weneth that he moot descenden;/But al day faileth thing that fooles wenden*). There is an ambiguous application of this proverbial forecast,[2] since it warns us that Troilus will fall victim to love, but it also hints at the long-term future when fortune's wheel will turn in a more drastic sense and plunge him from the heights of a lover's felicity when he loses Criseyde.

Of the other romance in which dramatic irony plays a wider part than merely informing a number of scenes, Wolfram's *Parzival*, we already possess two surveys which illustrate this problem.[3] Johnson devotes an article to the specific problem of dramatic irony in this work, whilst Harms, analysing a number of encounters in *Parzival*, provides much material which, like his analysis of Hartmann's romances, suggests dramatic irony, even though he understandably nowhere makes use of what is after all not a common critical term in German. Since his concern is with combat scenes between friends or relatives who fail to recognise one another, the scenes discussed by Harms represent no more than a selection, but his choice includes a number of encounters (Parzival with Ither, with Gawan, with Gramoflanz and with Feirefiz) in which one of the combatants is ignorant of the other's identity. In each case Harms has shown us how

[1] V 841ff. See the note to 842 on p. 545 of Root's edition. This passage, mentioned earlier (p. 138) as an example of interlace technique, illustrates the potential closeness of this technique to dramatic irony.
[2] See above, pp. 27f. [3] Harms, *Kampf*, pp. 144ff. and Johnson, *Ironie*, pp. 133ff.

this situation based on misunderstanding has been elevated to dramatic irony: by informing the audience of the identity of the contestants, by making them aware of the ignorance of the contestant(s), by explaining how this misunderstanding came about and by stressing the full contrast between appearances and reality.[1] The result is to show in detail what elsewhere was only hinted at in passing,[2] namely that Parzival's offence in killing his kinsman Ither is a danger that dogs his footsteps during his knightly career and that on these subsequent occasions he narrowly avoids repeating this initial sin. Dramatic irony thus not merely plays a central role in the question of Parzival's chivalric guilt, it also links these four encounters together by demonstrating that the career of knighthood involves the danger of unwitting encounters and killings of an unrecognised opponent.

Johnson's approach is different, but it leads to a similar conclusion. He confines himself neither to knightly encounters (he includes Parzival's meeting with Trevrizent) nor to encounters with a kinsman (he therefore discusses Parzival's combat with Orilus), but shows how dramatic irony informs each of four

[1] In Parzival's encounter with Ither the listeners know in advance the identity of the combatants and of their kinship (see my review of Harroff, *MLR* 71 (1976), 955). Although Parzival knows Ither's name, he does not suspect that he is related to him, whilst Ither knows neither Parzival's name nor his kinship. The explanation for this has been given by the previous account of the hero's upbringing in Soltane, for Parzival knows nothing of the world of chivalry, whilst Ither has no grounds for seeing in this uncouth boy a knightly relative of his. The full measure of the contrast between appearances and reality is conveyed by 161, 7f. In the encounter between Parzival and Gawan we know who the latter is since we come to this scene in his company, and we are soon given narrator's hints, denied to Gawan, as to Parzival's identity (Harms, *Kampf*, pp. 155f.). The failure to recognise one another is well motivated since each has grounds for thinking that the other is Gramoflanz (Harms, *ibid.*). The gap between intention and outcome is revealed by 688, 22ff. When Parzival fights with Gramoflanz we know who each is, Parzival knows who his opponent is (since he has taken on the combat on behalf of Gawan), whilst Gramoflanz mistakenly thinks that his opponent is Gawan. Wolfram has previously accounted for the improbability of Gramoflanz being able to recognise Parzival by the externals of his armour (Harms, p. 162), and he stresses the gulf between wishes and fulfilment by having Gramoflanz insist on a combat with Gawan once he learns the truth. Finally, in the encounter between Parzival and Feirefiz we know who the former is, are soon given a hint about the latter (738, 10) which is then made much more explicit (740, 5), whilst their ignorance about each other is so complete that hostility threatens to break out again when the pagan names himself *Feirefîz Anschevîn* (745, 28; cf. Harms, p. 166). The narrator's judgment 742, 23ff. indicates the full measure of their misunderstanding of the position.

[2] By Mohr, *Schuld*, p. 206.

meetings (Parzival with Ither, with Orilus, with Trevrizent and with Feirefiz) and links them with each other to form a recognisable sequence.[1] The scenes discussed by these two scholars are not all identical, but with both the narrative span is the same, for they show us dramatic irony at various points in the hero's knightly career from beginning (Ither) to end (Feirefiz). The extent of this narrative span is suggestive, for it shows that Wolfram was ready to exploit dramatic irony in scenes with no counterpart in Chrétien's uncompleted romance. This readiness in part stems from the position in which Wolfram found himself as an adaptor of a French work, better able to spot the potentialities of dramatic irony because of his greater distance from the original.[2] To this we might add that this position of an adaptor, better placed than the original author, can be compared with that of an audience at the second recital of a novel work, better able to appreciate dramatic irony than on the first occasion because now they too have a grasp of the work in its totality.

If in these three works (*Tristan, Troilus and Criseyde, Parzival*) dramatic irony plays a large part and approaches the position of tragedy, giving rise to the impression that the whole action has been planned by an unknown power irrespective of human wishes or merits, it is not surprising that at times the victims should speak out in anger or rebellion against this power. These outbursts imply that the victims see this metaphysical power as if it were a cosmic mocker, behaving like an ironist in apparently saying one thing to them, but in reality meaning something quite different. In other words, the relationship between this superhuman power and the character (to whom some vital piece of information is not visible, as it is to the audience, so that he is led to draw a faulty conclusion) resembles that between the ironic

---

[1] Johnson, *Ironie*, p. 147. To make the network of allusions explicit: the combat with Ither is linked indirectly with the Orilus and Trevrizent encounters *via* Orilus's brother Lähelin (Parzival insultingly equates Ither with Lähelin while proving himself to be no better than a Lähelin, and Trevrizent speaks the symbolic, if not the factual truth in taking Parzival to be Lähelin). The link between Parzival's first combat and his encounter with Feirefiz is provided by the motif of Ither's sword (cf. Johnson, pp. 145f.) – the symbol of Parzival's killing of a kinsman ironically becomes, through God's intervention, the symbol of an avoidance of the same sin. Each of these encounters contains its own dramatic irony, but they are connected to form a sequence by the same feature.

[2] Cf. Johnson, *Ironie*, pp. 147f.

poet and his audience, from whom the necessary facts can also be withheld or to whom they may be presented only equivocally.[1] In *Tristan* at one point the disappointment of expectations, under the impact of grief and anger, is attributed to the devil's machinations, but in such a way that he is conceived as mockingly having had his sport with his victims. This crucial passage comes in the voyage from Ireland when Brangæne learns that Tristan and Isolde have fallen in love and blames this disastrous outcome on the devil (12127: *Brangæne sprach: 'daz riuwe got,|daz der valant sinen spot| mit uns alsus gemachet hat!'*). The emphasis on *alsus* tells us that things have gone awry, otherwise than hoped for, whilst the word *spot* suggests that the devil is ironically mocking the hopes that have been raised by Tristan's successful mission on Marke's behalf to Ireland.[2] In *Troilus and Criseyde* it is fortune who is blamed by Troilus when he learns that Criseyde is to be taken from him and handed over to the Greeks. He is conscious only that he has honoured fortune all his life (IV 267: *Have I the nought honoured al my lyve,|As thow wel woost, above the goddes alle?*), is convinced that he does not deserve such a blow (IV 260: *Then seyde he thus: Fortune, allas the while!|What have I don, what have I thus agilt?*) and can only put it down to the guile of fortune herself (IV 262: *How myghtestow for rowthe me bygile?*). By deceptively disappointing his hopes (*bygile*) fortune has mocked her servant Troilus.

This same accusation is raised in *Parzival*, only directed against God as ultimately responsible. Parzival finds it as difficult to come to terms with God as a cosmic mocker as Troilus with fortune in the same capacity. Disappointed, like Troilus, in his expectations he blames the authority he holds responsible for such mockery and the shame it brings. Like Troilus, Parzival

---

[1] Although in the text I concentrate on *Tristan, Troilus and Criseyde* and *Parzival* these are not the only works in which an ironic reversal of events is imputed to a metaphysical power. Fortune is invoked in Chrétien's *Erec* 2782ff. and *Lancelot* 6468ff. (a revealing example, even if it comes after the point where Chrétien's poetic responsibility ceases), whilst it is the authority of Love which is held responsible in *Flamenca* 902ff. and 1410ff. Apart from Brangæne's accusation of the devil, Gottfried's *Tristan* can also blame the wheel of fortune (7161ff.) or suggest God as responsible for the dramatic irony of Tristan being brought home to Cornwall whilst thinking that he is in exile (3835ff.). God is also held responsible in Hartmann's *Gregorius* 2609ff. (cf. Green, *Alieniloquium*, pp. 157f.).

[2] On the discrepancy between this outcome and the Irish queen's intentions in handing over the potion to Brangæne see Green, *Alieniloquium*, p. 157.

feels that his loyal service has not brought him the reward which he expects as a right and has given him disgrace rather than acclaim (447, 25: *ich diende einem der heizet got,/ê daz so lasterlîchen spot/sîn gunst über mich erhancte*). The *spot* and *laster* invoked here may be the attitude of others towards Parzival, but since this has been brought about by God (*erhancte*) the *spot* is ultimately, so Parzival feels, God's mockery of him and his justified hopes. To this intolerable humiliation of being an ironic God's plaything Parzival replies with his own form of defiant irony, bitterly referring to the insulting indifference of such a God as *sîn gunst*.[1] The same revealing rhyme (*got*: *spot*) occurs in the scene where Parzival, after he and Gawan have been disgraced before the Round Table, formally renounces his allegiance to God (332,1: *Der Wâleis sprach: wê waz ist got?/wær der gewaldec, sölhen spot/het er uns pêden niht gegeben,/kunde got mit kreften leben./ich was im diens under-tân,/sît ich genâden mich versan*). Again, the *spot* which Parzival has suffered (to be disgraced before such a company) is in God's gift, so that the victim sees Cundrie's message as an example of God's mockery of the hopes of one who has served Him constantly.

The parallel just hinted at between Parzival and Troilus goes further than this. With Parzival the deception lies ultimately, as Trevrizent shows him, not with God, but with himself. The discrepancy between expectation and fulfilment cannot come from a God whose essence is *triuwe*, but results instead from the false nature of Parzival's hopes, his confidence that God is adequately understood by his feudal, knightly concepts. Troilus, for his part, cannot blame fortune for being true to her acknowledged nature in taking away what she has given, but only his own blindness in not realising her nature and its relevance to his position. This parallel between the German and English heroes is important in another respect. Although Parzival blames God and Troilus fortune, this difference between the two metaphysical powers invoked is unimportant beside the fact that both heroes accuse a metaphysical authority of having ironically mocked their expectations. The relative unimportance of the precise name we attach to this cosmic mocker[2] is confirmed by the manner in

---

[1] See above, p. 186.
[2] The same conclusion has been reached by Johnson, *Ironie*, p. 149.

which Parzival, on learning the facts about his combat with Gawan, places the blame on *sælde* and *ungelücke*,[1] whilst for Brangæne responsibility lies with the devil. What counts in this kind of situation is not the name by which we know the metaphysical culprit, but the fact that an abstract power of some kind should be seen performing the rôle of mocker by guiding events to a disastrously unexpected outcome.[2]

These examples show us something of the potential scope of dramatic irony in the romance, its employment to find a metaphysical scapegoat when events unexpectedly turn against man. I have also made use of them elsewhere in finding a place for the irony of situation alongside rhetorical irony in any definition of medieval irony,[3] basing my argument on the evidence such passages provide of an abstract power seen as a cosmic mocker, behaving like the rhetorical ironist in apparently saying (or rather: in letting events apparently imply) one thing to man, but in reality meaning something quite different. In other words, this cosmic mocker is seen as a superior kind of rhetorical ironist, arranging events instead of words so as to convey one meaning to the unsuspecting victim and another meaning to an observer, like the omniscient poet, who occupies a vantage-point closer to the metaphysical realm than to the circumscribed vision of characters in his story. These abstract powers can therefore be

---

[1] Johnson, *ibid.*

[2] It is important to realise that the implications of this kind of dramatic irony are not always as metaphysically negative as they seem. We saw above (pp. 270f.) that the use of dramatic irony could open up a view of providential guidance to the audience earlier than to the actor which could assure them that events would be guided to the proper conclusion. This is particularly true of Parzival's condemnation of God, for he voices his criticism in ignorance of the full truth, unaware that he is being divinely assisted even when all guidance seems to be withdrawn from him (see above, pp. 155ff.). On the other hand, there are cases where the negative implications predominate. Amongst these I should include Gottfried's *Tristan* (cf. Haug, *Aventiure*, pp. 88ff.) and the episode in the French prose *Tristan* in which Dinadan laments the death of his friend Tristan (I quote from Vinaver, *Recherche*, pp. 175f.): '*Bien savoie gaibier sans doute a folz, a saige*, mais voici que le gabeur se voit plus gabé que nul autre, car j'ai été, moi, gabé par Celui contre qui je ne saurais me défendre. Ah! si seulement je pouvais Le gaber à mon tour! Il est vrai que pour Lui le dommage ne serait point aussi grand que le mal qu'il m'a fait.' Reproached for blaming God in this way, Dinadan replies: 'Pensez de moi ce que vous voulez ... Dieu m'a perdu, je ne veux plus être des siens, je n'ai plus cure de Lui.'

[3] Green, *Alieniloquium*, pp. 156ff.

compared with poets who make use of irony, the ones manipulating events and the others words to produce similar effects. The
similarity between these two types of irony lies behind a passage
in *Troilus and Criseyde* describing the ambiguities of the oracle
and the risk of misunderstanding in consulting the gods (IV 1405:
*He hath nat wel the goddes understonde,/For goddes speken in amphi-
bologies,/And, for a soth, they tellen twenty lyes*). It is fitting that, in
the case of an oracle, the gods should not be seen arranging
events, but rather, like poets, making use of words (*speken*), but
the force of what they say lies in the parallel not so much with
Cicero's use of *amphibolia* in speaking of an oracular saying[1] as
with the rhetorical use of the term *amphibolia* to indicate linguistic
ambiguitas,[2] the exploitation of language which underlies so much
rhetorical irony. The gods are here seen speaking like a poet,
making use of rhetoric for their own ironic purposes.

Yet the converse is also applicable to our present argument.
Bloomfield has said of Chaucer's romance something which is
equally true of the other romances we are considering. In his
capacity of knowing the outcome, of standing back sufficiently
distant from his fictional world to be able to see aspects concealed
from the actors, Chaucer sits above his creation, foresees, like
God, the doom of his own creatures, and to that extent resembles
the *Deus artifex* whose masterpiece is the created world.[3] Even
though the argument can be conducted in either direction (the
gods can be seen acting like poets, even using their rhetoric, but
the poets can also adopt an attitude towards their fictional world
comparable with God's towards His created world), there should
be no doubt as to where the historical priority belongs. To see
this we have only to recall the presence of an ironic God in the
Bible,[4] the classical view of the gods or fortune arranging human
life as if it were a play in the theatre,[5] and the Pauline and
Boethian metaphor of the theatre of life.[6] Which is another way

---

[1] Cicero, *De divinatione* II 56, 116. Suggested by Root in his editorial note to IV
1406, p. 524.
[2] Cf. Lausberg, *Handbuch*, §222.
[3] Bloomfield, *PMLA* 72 (1957), 22.
[4] Cf. Voeltzel, *Lachen* and Good, *Irony*.
[5] On this see the stimulating remarks of Salingar, *Shakespeare*, pp. 153ff.
[6] For St Paul cf. I Cor. 4, 9 and for Boethius's use of the metaphor *scaena vitae* see
De Consolatione, II, prose iii.

of saying that there might after all be, along the lines of tradition that carried this metaphor and its implications from classical antiquity down to the Middle Ages,[1] a connection between dramatic irony in Greek tragedy which was the starting-point for this chapter and the irony of mockery by a metaphysical power with which it concludes.

[1] See Curtius, *Literatur*, pp. 146ff. On survival of knowledge of the classical theatre in the Middle Ages see Norton-Smith, *Chaucer*, pp. 162ff.

9

THE IRONY OF VALUES

What I call the irony of values has connections with verbal irony (where a parody of courtly vocabulary or clichés can reflect on the courtly ideals they stand for) and with irony of the narrator (since the rôles of poet and narrator provide us with two points of view from which to question courtly conventions). Even central values of the courtly world can be subjected to a critical scrutiny, sometimes of a radical nature (Gottfried's attitude towards the chivalric ideal), but generally in a less extreme manner (the parodic clash between different views of love, where not the value of love as such is criticised, but a rival's mistaken view of it). If under four different headings we are invited to look at courtly conventions more closely, this suggests that this category of irony is far-reaching enough to merit separate treatment.

Our approach is governed by the recognition that the values most exposed to ironic questioning, chivalry and love, may be subsumed under the general ideal of courtliness,[1] so that the irony of values in the romance may be largely equated with a questioning of the courtly ideal. We shall see such questions suggested by the ambivalence and antinomies of courtly values, by the dubious nature of courtly reputation, by the concept of courtesy itself and, finally, by the way in which even the final arbiter of courtly values, the court, can be depicted on occasions.

[1] The concept of courtliness is undergoing revision at present, above all with regard to the term 'courtly love' (cf. Frappier, *Amour*, pp. 1ff.), but also concerning its justification as a general term (on this Professor P. F. Ganz is preparing a monograph, but see already Ganz, *Begriff*). None the less, until the term has been rendered critically impossible I prefer to go on using it in its accepted sense. On the rise of the courtly ideal and courtly literature in the twelfth century see above all Bezzola, *Origines* III 1 and 2, *passim*.

As with chivalry and love,[1] it is not so much the courtly ideal as some aberration from it which is the true target of the poet's irony. On those occasions when it is this ideal which he questions, he sees it as subordinate to something more embracing and doubts the justification of making an absolute value out of it.

Secular and religious

In starting with the ambivalence of some courtly values we revert to the fact that many leading terms in Middle High German literature occupy an undefined position between the two poles of secular and religious.[2] In describing its secular ideal with terms like *triuwe* and *êre* courtly literature may simply continue the secular and feudal functions of these words, but cannot ignore the fact that they have also been appropriated for religious usage. Where two dimensions can exist for the same term and even be seen in conflict, the secular function will be relativised by the religious one, which retains its force even with courtly authors. This tacit questioning of secular values by juxtaposing them alongside their religious counterparts can best be illustrated not from the courtly romance (where the dividing line between secular and religious is tactfully left blurred), but from a work like the *Rolandslied*[3] whose clerical author is more concerned to make this distinction unmistakably clear by imputing secular values to the pagans or to the traitor Genelun and condemning these by reference to the corresponding religious ones.[4]

When Genelun departs on a dangerous mission to the pagan camp he gives instructions to his followers how his son is to be brought up if he fails to come back (1694ff.),[5] but these are meant to condemn him in the author's eyes by showing him bound up, as a *miles Dei* should not be,[6] with secular commitments to wife and family. The recommendations he gives show him concerned with the education of his son not in Christian virtues,[7] but as a

---

[1] See above, pp. 89f. and 128ff.
[2] See above, p. 172.
[3] I owe the following examples to Richter, *Kommentar*.
[4] Still useful on this is Fliegner, *Rittertum*.
[5] Richter, *Kommentar*, pp. 256f.
[6] This idea goes back to II Tim. 2, 4.
[7] I take v. 1709 as a conventional phrase and not as a pious prayer.

feudal ruler trained to a life of aristocratic pomp (1698: *hêrlichen lebe*), knowing how to reward his followers (1699: *mildeclichen gebe*) and alert to military and legal obligations (1704ff.). When this educational programme is introduced with a general term (1697: *zucht schult ir in lêren*) we learn from what follows what *zucht* implies: a training in the courtly and feudal virtues of a secular ruler like that attributed by Hartmann to his courtly hero in *Der arme Heinrich* (63: *ein ganziu krône der zuht*). Within its proper place *zucht* may have an undeniable value, but in each case the poet shows us its deficiency when improperly regarded as an absolute value. In the *Rolandslied* this is because such a secular value is irrelevant to the Christian warrior's duties, a distraction from his task and a contradiction of *zucht* meaning the Christian's religious discipline and obedience (215: *habet zucht mit gûte*).[1] With Hartmann it is because no secular virtues can protect the hero from the danger which soon assails him (75ff.).[2] It is the clerical epic, however, which in its contrast between the courtly and religious functions of the same word shows up the relative force of the courtly value, as a distraction from Christian obligations.

Other values are likewise relativised whenever their secular function is placed alongside their religious connotation, as can be shown with *êre*.[3] When Olivir begins his advice to the emperor with the affirmation (940: *sô riete ich dir dîn êre*) he employs the phrase used to introduce a pagan's advice to Marsilie (430: *ich gerâte dir dîne êre*), but this parallel is not introduced (as would be possible in Wolfram's *Willehalm*) to show what is common to both armies, but rather to highlight the difference between them. The pagan's recommendation to his ruler is seen expressly in terms of secular advantages which will not have to be forgone (433: *Wilt du mir volgen/unde andere dîne holden,/sô behalte wir den lîb,/dar zû kint unde wîb/unde alle unse êre*), where we also have to read *êre* in concrete, material terms, involving social standing, but also the wealth and power on which it rests. Olivir's similar phrase is uttered in response to his ruler's wish to take advice

---

[1] Cf. Richter, *Kommentar*, p. 81, note on v. 215 (with examples for *disciplina* as a Christian virtue from Ps. 21, 11f., Hebr. 12, 7f. and Bernard of Clairvaux, *De laude novae militiae* 4).   [2] Green, *Praise*, pp. 795f.

[3] Richter, *Kommentar*, pp. 202, 229 and 237f.; Fliegner, *Rittertum*, pp. 6ff. and 42ff.

from his vassals (907: *nu râtet gotes êre*).¹ In the Christian scene invitation and response go together, the emperor's *êre* is equated with *gotes êre*. This is why Olivir's affirmation is followed by a reminder of the emperor's service of God (941: *Du hâst gode wole gedienet*) and leads to a recommendation *gote ze lobe unt ze êren* (958).² In passages like these *êre*, conceived as a secular value, is shown up in its deficiencies: not as a value to which the further enrichment of *êre* as a religious concept could theoretically be added, but as a value in conflict with the religious dimension and less than what the situation called for. As with *zucht*, this relativising use of *êre* has its parallel in Hartmann's *Armer Heinrich*. Although the summing-up of the hero's elevated position emphasises his *êre* (77: *êren unde guotes*; 81: *geprîset unde gêret*) this advantage resembles *zucht* in being powerless and irrelevant to the crisis which overcomes him.

In these examples I have confined myself to the *Rolandslied*, where the dualism between Christians and pagans makes it easy to distinguish between religious and secular usages of the same term. Konrad's target is a self-sufficient secularism which he shows up as worthless by attributing it to the pagans, but the terms we have considered (*zucht* and *êre*) are not simply secular, but more specifically values we encounter in courtly literature. What is ultimately criticised here is a courtly secularism felt to be no better than pagan idolatry.³ Although the dualistic structure of his work allowed Konrad to elaborate the contrast between courtly and religious, this contrast, although more subdued, need not be entirely absent from courtly literature, as we saw in the case of *zuht* and *êre* in *Der arme Heinrich*. Despite their secular interests courtly authors were not exclusively secular, their works still have much in common with clerical literature and the break is no absolute one.⁴ We may expect from them no wholehearted

---

¹ The following lines make it quite clear that, in contrast to the pagans' wish to lose no material advantage in the pursuit of *êre*, the emperor equates *êre* exclusively with divine favour (908: *Ja ne sûche ich nicht mêre, / wan daz wir sô gedingen, / daz wir gotes hulde gewinnen*).

² Cf. also Richter, *Kommentar*, pp. 229, note on v. 1107, and 231, note on vv. 1149–53.

³ See Fliegner, *Rittertum*, pp. 10ff.

⁴ This is suggested by the fact that Hartmann composed two legends alongside two romances and Wolfram a crusading epic as well as a romance (on his debt to clerical literature in the prologue to *Willehalm* see Ochs, *Eingang, passim*).

allegiance to secular values, but a wish to combine them with religious ones, to have their cake and eat it, implying the possibility of reservations and doubts about the absolute justification of the courtly ideal.

Social reputation

Ere is thus a courtly value which Konrad relativised by placing it in a wider religious context and Hartmann assumes its irrelevance in face of a crisis of religious proportions. It will be fitting to begin with this concept in the romance and discuss how this acknowledgement of a person's qualities by courtly society can be used to throw an ironic light either on these qualities or on society's criteria. Gottfried's *Tristan* provides some telling examples of this not least because of his extensive use of the term to designate social reputation or, in the case of the lovers, their acknowledgement by the court as the dispenser and arbiter of social reputation.[1] Whenever *êre* is shown up in a dubious light in this work this is in terms of the conflict between love and society, between the lovers and the husband who is at the same time the guardian of his court's standing, so that it is *êre* as a specifically courtly value which is here being discussed.

How little value need attach to social reputation dispensed by courtly society is displayed by Gottfried's procedure in explicitly referring to society's acknowledgement of the lovers when dramatic irony is also involved, showing us how they have just practised some deception on Marke and his court.[2] Our knowledge of what is really going on shows us the hollowness of the courtly value. We are told how Marke, regarding himself as happily married, loves and praises his wife and how this eulogy is taken up in the wider renown Isold enjoys in Cornwall (12675: *Isot diu was do starke/von ir herren Marke/geminnet unde geheret,/gepriset unde geret/von liute und von lande*). To judge by appearances, Cornwall has every reason to be satisfied with its queen, the token of the peace established with Ireland and soon, they may hope, to bless them with an heir to the throne. But we have already been

---

[1] See Maurer, *Leid*, pp. 246f.
[2] Cf. Tax, *Wort*, pp. 139 and 140; Clausen, *Erzähler*, p. 188; Green, *Recognising*, pp. 42ff.

allowed a glance behind the scenes on the wedding-night and realise the full disparity between the queen's reputation and her recent behaviour. This is forceful enough, but Gottfried goes on to overcome the slight failure of the two poles in his discrepancy to tally completely (to Isold's deception of her husband on one occasion there corresponds her present reputation, extending over a period of time). He does this by referring to further meetings between Tristan and Isold (12684ff.) and by a concluding explanation (12688: *wan nieman wande niht dar zuo;/dan dahte weder wip noch man/dekeiner slahte undinges an*) which tells us how society would have regarded the situation (*undinc*) if they had realised the truth. Behind *êre* there lurks *undinc*, so that we are left with little respect for the truth of the courtly value of *êre* on this occasion.[1]

Gottfried's *Tristan*, with its antithesis between love and courtly society, brings out the ironic implications of social reputation since we are invited to view things from the lovers' point of view. Other romances with no such gulf between the hero and society also ironise the courtly value of honour for its superficiality or irrelevance. Chrétien invites us to look critically at any glib adherence to the code of chivalric honour when, after Yvain has killed Esclados, he describes his hero's regret, on realising that his opponent is about to be buried, at losing this trophy and thus being exposed to the taunts of Keu without any tangible evidence to the contrary. Yvain sees this as bringing dishonour on himself (1346: *S'il n'an a tesmoing et garant,/Donc est il honiz an travers*), for he sees Keu not just as an individual mocker, but in his function as Arthur's seneschal who will bring him dishonour at court. If this is so, Arthur's court must employ criteria in bestowing or withholding praise which we are meant to question for Chrétien's subsequent narrative makes it clear that

---

[1] Gottfried employs the same technique, and almost identical wording, in reverting to Isold's reputation on a similar occasion (15751ff.), just after her ambiguous oath at the trial and the hoodwinking of husband and court. These passages from *Tristan* illustrate the possibility of interpreting an ironic passage on various levels: as providing a particular pointer to the presence of irony (Green, as in the last footnote), as illustrating the dramatic irony present in a scene of deception and, in the present context, as an example of the irony of the courtly value *êre*.

See also Hollandt, *Hauptgestalten*, p. 44, fn. 5, and p. 142, fn. 159, for two further comments on Gottfried's employment of *êre* as a courtly value.

he sees chivalric honour merited by deeds of service of others, not by brutally killing an opponent to avoid being laughed at. Yvain is *honiz* not because he is deprived of his trophy, but because he feels it necessary to have one at all.

The same perversion of standards, so obvious that we react against it in the direction we are meant to take, recurs in Hartmann's *Erec*, where it is easier to perceive since it is used of opponents of the hero. An instance occurs when the first group of robber knights catch sight of Erec, divide up their anticipated spoils and grant their leader his right to claim Enite for himself. When this last point is made in the terms *dô gewerten si in der êre* (3215), we realise that *êre* is employed ambiguously, suggesting the prior claim conceded to this ringleader[1] and also that this privilege is a dubious one, involving rather dishonour in such unprovoked aggression.[2] Hartmann does the same when Galoein attempts to seduce Enite with the offer of the greater social esteem she will enjoy as his wife (3792: *nû gevallet ir mir sô wol/daz ich iuch gerne machen sol/ze vrouwen disem lande:/sô habet ir âne schande/ wol gewehselt iuwer leben*).[3] As with the robber knight's prior claim (*êre*), the phrase *âne schande* is used ironically to imply its opposite, for it really would amount to disgrace if Enite were to accept this offer by betraying Erec. Nor is there any danger that she will be tempted by this, for she sees that it involves treachery (3803) and actually would amount to her lasting social disgrace (3804: *als ez diu werlt vernæme/und ez ir vür kæme,/sô wærez niuwan ir spot*). Although the poet ironises Galoein's false sense of honour by having him make such use of the phrase *âne schande*, this does not mean that his reservations extend to the concept of honour as such. It is by an appeal to a proper sense of honour, to what

---

[1] Maurer, *Leid*, p. 275, takes *êre* in this passage in the undifferentiated sense of 'Erfolg, Glück, Gewinn, Lohn'. I think it stands closer to the use of *êra* by Notker to render *primatus* (cf. Sehrt, *Glossar*, p. 43) and by Williram to translate *primus locus* (cf. Maurer, *Leid*, p. 281). On the use of *êra* in Old High German as an equivalent for *privilegium* see Green, *Lord*, p. 180.

[2] A similar irony of values is involved in Erec's encounter with the second group of robbers, cf. the use of *daz ist reht* (3331) and *billîche* (3337). See also above, p. 200.

[3] The same perverted argument is later used in the scene when Oringles claims that, in marrying him, Enite has vastly improved her position, 6471ff. (on this passage see Endres, *Studien*, pp. 68f.). That his distortion of values is like Galoein's can be seen in the way in which he too lays stress on a misconceived sense of *êre* (6472–9, 6482f., 6492–4).

society would think of the tempter's casuistry, that Enite seeks to dissuade him from his plan. Rejection of a false standard implies the presence of a true one by which it can be judged deficient, and it is the function of irony to make this distinction clear.[1]

Something similar can be shown for Wolfram's *Parzival*, concerning the related concept *prîs* instead of *êre*.[2] The episode is Gawan's combat with Lischoys, where we cannot doubt the narrator's disapproval for he interrupts his narrative to criticise their fighting merely for the sake of knightly renown (538,1: *wer solte sie drumbe prîsen,/daz die unwîsen/striten âne schulde,/niuwan durch prîses hulde?/sine heten niht ze teilen,/ân nôt ir leben ze veilen./ ietweder ûf den andern jach,/daz er die schulde nie gesach*). What is criticised is a knightly combat undertaken without necessity (*âne schulde, ân nôt*). The equation of lack of necessity with a desire to increase one's knightly reputation conveys its own criticism which, whilst it may not yet involve irony itself, tells us how we are to regard the further account of this combat. There follows

[1] A good example of a false standard rejected by an appeal to a correct one is to be found in Chrétien's *Lancelot* when Meleagant's father attempts to persuade his son to give up his unjust claim to Guinevere (3440: *Se tu la reïne li ranz, / criens an tu avoir desenor? / De ce n'aies tu ja peor, / qu'il ne t'an puet blasmes venir; / einz est pechiez del retenir / chose ou an n'a reison ne droit*). This argument reveals that Meleagant, in seeking to avoid *desenor* and *blasmes* by keeping the queen prisoner, is in fact guilty of a *pechiez* and therefore incurs *desenor* and *blasmes* on a profounder level. Elsewhere in this work the irony of courtly reputation concerns Lancelot's social disgrace in mounting the tumbril. This is how the world sees it, for they are convinced that Lancelot is guilty of some crime (410: *Tuit demandent: 'A quel martire / sera cist chevaliers randuz? / Iert il escorchiez, ou panduz, / noiez, ou ars an feu d'espines? / Di, nains, di, tu qui le traïnes, / A quel forfet fu il trovez?'*), and this is how Lancelot now judges his position vis-à-vis the queen (4347: *Dex, cist forfez, quex estre pot? / Bien cuit que espoir ele sot / que je montai sor la charrete. / Ne sai quel blasme ele me mete / se cestui non*). In fact, as the audience knows full well, Lancelot is *de cest reproche mondes* (2615) but is guilty in Guinevere's eyes of another offence. He is shamed not by mounting the tumbril, but by hesitating for a second to mount it in the service of his mistress, by pausing before acting to sacrifice everything and incur any disgrace for her sake (4484: *'Comant? Don n'eüstes vos honte / de la charrete, et si dotastes? / Molt a grant enviz i montastes / quant vos demorastes deus pas'*). When in the passage 410ff. quoted above Lancelot is held to be guilty and worthy of punishment this does not involve any social offence against the law, as his mockers take to be the case, but a private offence against the code of love. This is his *forfez*, and the *martire* (on *martire* as a term of the love lyric see Wechssler, *Kulturproblem*, pp. 277f.) that awaits him is the suffering imposed upon him by a haughty mistress. The social criterion of reputation and disgrace is here shown up as inferior to the code of love.

[2] I have discussed this elsewhere in *Homicide*, p. 30 and *Aventiure*, pp. 147f.

Gawan's demonstration of the narrator's opinion in chivalric practice. After establishing his supremacy over Lischoys, he refuses to kill a man simply because his opponent refuses him the conventional *sicherheit* (539,21ff.). He values human life higher than the formalism of a chivalric encounter and spares his opponent without any parole. But in refusing this offer and in insisting on a continuation of the combat Lischoys presents a temptation to Gawan. Gawan once more gains the upper hand and Lischoys again refuses his *sicherheit*, suggesting that his opponent will earn renown by killing him (543,7: *du maht vil prîses erben,/ob du mich kanst ersterben*).

This use of *prîs* we have to interpret as ironically as the use of *êre* by Hartmann's robber knights or of *âne schande* by Galoein. Gawan sees through this and rejects his opponent's offer, seeing in it a temptation such as Enite saw in Galoein's offer, for to kill a man needlessly (Gawan here aligns himself with the narrator by using *âne schulde*) can only harm his reputation rather than enhance it (543,10: *deiswar ine sol alsô niht tuon:/so verlür ich prîses hulde,/ erslüege ich âne schulde/disen küenen helt unverzaget*). We have here a clash between two conceptions of knightly honour: an external view which sees it as the reward for the man who defeats and kills his opponent,[1] as opposed to a moralised conception which equates honour with chivalric magnanimity. In this conflict between two conceptions of knighthood (both of which are expressly stated, like the double use of *êre* in the *Rolandslied*) Gawan demonstrates the civilising force of Arthurian chivalry by acting in accordance with the higher conception. Narrator and Arthurian knight combine to show up the inadequacy of Lischoys's view, whose conception of *prîs* is thereby ironically relativised.[2]

Courtesy

If *êre* and *prîs* are the reputation conferred by courtly society on one who superlatively conforms to its standards, any questioning of that reputation must result in a questioning of these standards,

---

[1] Cf. Kalogreant's definition of *âventiure, Iwein* 534.
[2] Schröder, *Studien*, p. 101, has similarly argued for two conceptions of *êre* in the Rüedeger episode of the *Nibelungenlied*.

of courtesy as a social ideal. Those who feel threatened by this social ideal will be more alert to its deficiencies and quicker with their criticism. This is perhaps why, like the author of the *Rolandslied* with regard to courtly attributes like *zucht* and *êre*, the clerical author of the *Kaiserchronik* can express his suspicions of the courtly ideal. He does this in his critical thumbnail sketch of the young Henry IV when he dwells on his sexual excesses (16554: *unkûsce er sich underwant:/er rait hovescen in diu lant,/er hônde di edelen frouwen,/die sîne liez er rouben*). If the poet's intention had been merely to castigate immorality he could have been content with general remarks like v. 16554 and v. 16556, but the force of the verb *hovescen* is to involve the ideal of an emergent courtliness in this picture of rampant secularism.[1]

Just as the criticism of the courtly values *zucht* and *êre* need not be confined to a clerical work, but could also find a niche in Hartmann's *Armer Heinrich* (for these values would not be regarded in the same light in a courtly legend as in a courtly romance), so too can courtliness be bluntly equated with sexual seduction in a romance, although we shall expect such forthrightness more from a victim than from a practitioner of this courtly art. This is the case in *Flamenca* when Archimbaut attempts to justify his jealousy by conjuring up the dangers to which his wife could be exposed (1196: *E que faria s'us truanz,/Que-s fenera d'amor cortes/ E non sabra d'amor ques es,/L'avia messa en follia!*). Here the modish practice of love (*amor cortes*)[2] is seen as a cloak for lack of true feeling, a technique of seduction comparable with the use of *hovescen* in the *Kaiserchronik*. Whereas in the German work the narrator himself pronounced a damning judgment by his choice of word, in the Provençal romance this is attributed to the husband who by his jealousy calls into existence the very danger he hopes to keep at bay, it cannot simply be regarded as the narrator's own opinion. Although refracted through a character,

---

[1] On another aspect of the same phenomenon see Shaw, *ZfdPh* 88 (1969), 378ff.

[2] This example needs to be added to the example from Peire d'Alvernhe quoted by Frappier, *Amour*, p. 4, in his otherwise justified attack on the concept *amour courtois* as a misleading term of modern scholarship and not of medieval poetic usage. Although it is theoretically possible to read *d'amor cortes* as 'courtly in matters of love', this is not how Lavaud and Nelli take it in their edition (p. 707: 'simulant l'amour courtois').

these words by Archimbaut testify to the persistence of a more critical view of courtliness, held seriously by the authors of the *Rolandslied* and *Kaiserchronik*, but employed for artistic purposes by the author of *Flamenca*.

Amongst the courtly authors who can voice their doubts about courtliness as a self-sufficient way of life we have to include Gottfried,[1] especially in the episode at the court of Karke where he depicts the dangers in the incipient affair between Tristan and Isold of the White Hands. Tristan, without at first feeling emotionally involved, is more preoccupied with this Isold than is safe; he performs in song and music for her as he had for her namesake, singing not for her ears alone, but to the company of the court as well. This makes it disastrously ill-judged that he sings of his own experience of love by composing *den edelen leich Tristanden* (19201), since it is this social context of his artistry that gives rise to misunderstanding of his position (19205: *oft unde dicke ergieng ouch daz:/so daz gesinde in ein gesaz,/er unde Isot und Kaedin,/der herzog und diu herzogin,/vrouwen und barune,/so tihteter schanzune,/rundate und höfschiu liedelin/und sang ie diz refloit dar in:/ 'Isot ma drue, Isot mamie,/en vus ma mort, en vus ma vie!'/und wan er daz so gerne sanc,/so was ir aller gedanc/und wanden ie genote,/er meinde ir Isote*). Because of this wider, courtly audience the theme of Tristan's art becomes a social fact which exercises its force on himself. His listeners apply his words to the Isold they know,[2] but his tacit acceptance of this compels Tristan to comply with their belief. To do otherwise would compromise his social standing at this court.

What is significant about this is not just the courtly gathering before which Tristan performs, but the emphasis that falls on his own courtliness. The term which sums up the nature of his songs is *höfschiu liedelin* (19211), his approach to this Isold is seen as an act of courtesy (19182: *doch begienger sine höfscheit*) and the same phrase is used later in their growing involvement (19334). Tristan is seen here in terms of the courtly ideal, which makes it

---

[1] This is meant without detriment to those courtly features which Gottfried views positively. On these see Stein, *DVjs* 51 (1977), 335ff.
[2] In the last four lines of the passage just quoted our attention is drawn to the presence of dramatic irony. We are told more of the situation than is visible to the court.

significant that his behaviour should be judged as a deception (19403: *und al der trügeheite,/die Tristan an si leite/so was ie daz diu volleist,/diu ir herze allermeist/an Tristandes liebe twanc,/daz er daz also gerne sanc:/'Isot ma drue, Isot mamie/en vus ma mort, en vus ma vie!'*).[1] Isold has been trapped by a pretence of emotion (which Tristan actually feels, but not for her, as she thinks). But this is a criticism often made of contemporary love-poetry (by Wolfram or by Reinmar's listeners),[2] it is implicit in Archimbaut's image of his wife's potential seducer (who only feigns affection for her and knows nothing of love itself, 1197f.) and it also informs the sketch of Henry IV (where *hovescen* is made explicit by *er hônde di edelen frouwen*). This detail of a heartless Don Juan is common to both clerical and courtly literature when criticism of sexual behaviour has to be made. With clerical authors this is because the secularism they condemn takes courtly form, in *Minnesangs Frühling* because of rival conceptions of love, and with Gottfried because an affair between Tristan and anyone other than Isold of Ireland can only invite his criticism.

It is significant that Gottfried's criticism of his hero should see him in courtly colours, for there is other evidence that the poet viewed this ideal with misgivings. If his sympathies lie with the lovers in their conflict with society, if society is represented chiefly by the court of Tintagel, and if the husband Marke presides over that court, it follows that the poet will tend to look on the values of the court critically. For the hero, as for Marke's world, *höfscheit* is an ideal social elegance in which Tristan even excels the court to which he displays his dazzling gifts,[3] but in excelling them he demonstrates that, unlike them, he is not restricted to courtly standards, but has access to other values which are closed to them and constitute a wider frame of reference within which the courtly ideal is shown up as a positive, but still relative value. The qualities which take Tristan beyond the exclusively courtly realm are summed up in such epithets as *vremede* and *der ellende gast*.[4] The former denotes his excellence in the

---

[1] Cf. also the preceding passage, 19397ff. Again, the dramatic irony of the deception is made clear to us.

[2] Cf. the dismissive comment in *Parzival* 587, 7f. (on this see Schumacher, *Auffassung*, p. 78), and the objection which Reinmar seeks to ward off in *MF* 165, 19f.

[3] Hahn, *Raum*, pp. 87f.   [4] *Ibid.*, pp. 88ff.

courtly skills, but also the fact that he is a stranger at court, literally and metaphorically,[1] whilst the latter suggests his partial allegiance to the courtly ideal,[2] the possibility that as a lover in conflict with the court he is to realise himself elsewhere. More than anyone at Tintagel Tristan incorporates courtly perfection, but as a lover he also transcends the courtly ideal. This makes it the more significant that during the period of his fall from grace as he dallies with the second Isold Gottfried plots his decline not merely in terms of a chivalry embraced as an unworthy escape from the pains of love which he is no longer willing to affirm,[3] but also in the extreme courtesy of his dealings with the substitute Isold (involving pretended rather than genuine feeling). Whatever value might attach to courtesy, it no longer suffices for one who has penetrated to the love grotto with Isold of Ireland. To see him now in an emphatically courtly context is to acknowledge the fact of his decline.

The ideal of courtesy also undergoes scrutiny in *Sir Gawain*, where two points are germane to the present argument. The first concerns the stage in the bedroom scene when the lady gains a kiss from Gawain by asking disingenuously whether he really can be Gawain since he has not yet requested a kiss himself (1297: '*So god as Gawayn gaynly is halden,/And cortaysye is closed so clene in hymseluen,/Couth not lyȝtly haf lenged so long wyth a lady,/Bot he had craued a cosse, bi his courtaysye,/Bi sum towch of summe tryfle at sum taleȝ ende*'). Gawain's reputation for courtesy is here invoked and used against him, inducing him to make a move which could have dangerous consequences, and the lady's invitation is all the more effective since it appeals to Gawain's concern for his courtly reputation. The lady is here attempting to identify courtesy with love, to fasten on Gawain the reputation for promiscuity which is his in the French romances.[4] When he says that he has no

[1] On 3379ff. see above, pp. 43f. and 186.
[2] Hahn, *op. cit.*, goes too far in suggesting an absolute difference between Tristan and Parzival in this respect. Unlike Tristan, Parzival may not be called *der ellende* with regard to Arthurian society, but he is called *der gast* (cf. 143, 24, where he is not merely a guest, but essentially a stranger at Arthur's court). His initial (and final) distance from the Round Table is important enough to be reflected in the formal patterning of the work (see below, pp. 319ff.).
[3] See above, p. 58.
[4] Cf. Brewer, *Courtesy*, pp. 75 and 80ff.

mistress (1790: '*In fayth I welde riʒt non,/Ne non wil welde þe quile*')
he is defending himself against her by showing that he is not
available for her purposes. He may give her the kiss she has asked
for, but like any kiss not spontaneously given this courteous
gesture has something impersonal about it[1] (so that sexual *cortaysye* here is as divorced from real feeling as was *amor cortes* in
Archimbaut's eyes). In thus defending himself Gawain is also
correcting the lady's understanding of his reputation: he is not
as the French literary tradition would have him be, her view of
courtesy as a cloak for promiscuity does not correspond with his.

Yet there is another aspect to the problem, regarding Gawain's
concern for his reputation for courtesy. This comes to the fore
in the third temptation scene (1770: *For þat prynces of pris depresed
him so þikke,/Nurned hym so neʒe þe þred, þat nede hym behoued/
Oþer lach þer hir luf, oþer lodly refuse./He cared for his cortaysye, lest
craþayn he were,/And more for his meschef ʒif he schulde make synne,/
And be traytor to þat tolke þat þat telde aʒt*). Here we are shown the
nature of Gawain's dilemma, but also how he hopes to resolve
it.[2] If he persists in turning down the lady's offer of love, he
must give offence to her (*lodly*), but also to his own standards of
courteous behaviour (he would sink to the level of being *craþayn*).
But to comply and accept her love would involve him in betraying his host. How Gawain judges between these possibilities is
made clear by the narrator (whose task is easier than Gawain's,
since he has no lady temptress to take into account in formulating
his words), for he says that the hero's concern for his courtesy is
not so overriding as to lead him to dismiss the danger of sin
(*He cared for his cortaysye,. . ./And more for his meschef*). In this situation even Gawain's courtesy must occupy a second place.[3]
Since his conception of courtesy is superior to the lady's exploitation of courtesy as a guise for polite adultery, this means an even
greater distancing from her equation of courtesy with love-play.

If Gawain is clear about his priorities at this point, where he
has to choose between courtesy and loyalty, it is a reflection of the
complex temptation to which he is exposed that this should no

---

[1] Brewer, *art. cit.*, p. 74.   [2] Cf. Burrow, *Reading*, p. 100.
[3] What is important here is that Gawain's courtesy is pushed into second place, but
not rejected altogether. On this see Brewer, *Courtesy*, pp. 70 and 77f.

longer be the case when, relaxing dangerously when he sees that the erotic temptation is safely past, he falls victim to the lady's offer of the girdle,[1] accepts it and makes no confession of it to his host. Gawain's loyalty is not endangered by his courtesy, but it is ultimately undermined by his love of life, his clutching at the girdle as a magical protection in the forthcoming combat. This rescues Gawain's conception of courtesy as a positive quality (his offence is not dictated by his concern for courtesy, but instead springs from his wish to save his skin), but only at the cost of shifting courtesy from the centre of the action (which it had occupied as long as the temptation was overtly sexual, involving a dilemma between courtesy and loyalty) and of giving it only a minor part. The English author, like Wolfram in *Parzival*, subordinates a knightly test of bravery to a more critical moral testing at Bertilak's castle by depicting a field of action to which knightly endeavour in combat was irrelevant.[2] To this we must add the rider that, like Gottfried in his depiction of Tristan's decline in his banishment from Cornwall,[3] he also shows up the final irrelevance of even Gawain's courtesy by pushing it from the centre of the final decisive action.[4]

The antinomies of the courtly ideal

Gawain's dilemma (how may he follow the dictates of loyalty without offending against courtesy?) serves as a bridge to the next stage of our argument which may be summed up as the antinomies of the courtly ideal, the division of this ideal into

[1] See Burrow, *Reading*, pp. 162f.   [2] See above, pp. 78f.

[3] Tristan's chivalry is presented as an unworthy distraction unbecoming a lover (see p. 58) and his courtliness, shown at Karke, as an irresponsible playing with fire (see pp. 297f.).

[4] On the irony of courtly values in *Troilus and Criseyde* two useful articles have been written by Gaylord. The one deals with the ultimate deficiencies of the ideal of *gentilesse* (*SP* 61 (1964), 19ff.), the other with the manner in which the poet invites his listeners, above all the young lovers amongst them, to scrutinise their own values more closely (*EM* 15 (1964), 25ff.). He calls this technique in the second article 'Chaucer's tender trap', an image which, applied to the audience, resembles Gottfried's technique, applied to Tristan, which Haug sees in the image of the 'Bärenhammer' used by Gottfried himself (Haug, *Aventiure, passim*). Gaylord also stresses that, with Chaucer, it is the listener who finally is responsible for catching himself in the trap (e.g. p. 34). This agrees with the point made by Weinrich, *Linguistik*, p. 63, that with irony, as opposed to lying, the victim is responsible for his own deception.

various values which can sometimes conflict with one another, making it necessary to reach a decision as to priorities and therefore to see one of these values as subordinate to another, as a relative quality rather than an absolute. The recurrence of this motif, as a theoretical generalisation or in narrative reality (both occur in *Sir Gawain*, for the narrator stands back from events to make us aware of the general issues), is enough to show that the courtly ideal is no simple wish-fulfilment pattern, but involves possible sacrifices.

Theoretical statements of the problems are not rare, but have too often been discussed only in the context of the so-called 'ritterliches Tugendsystem',[1] a wider problem which I am happy to leave untouched. If we look only at the antinomies of the courtly ideal Walther's first *Reichstonspruch* provides a classic formulation of the problem when he confesses his inability to say how three goals might be achieved without any loss (8, 11ff.). In specifying these goals the poet describes them enough to show where the potential conflict arises. Of the first two goals (both secular) he says that they are in conflict (8, 14: *diu zwei sint êre und varnde guot,/daz dicke ein ander schaden tuot*), whilst his inability to get these two, together with his third goal (a religious one, 8, 16: *gotes hulde*), into one container, the human heart, implies a further conflict between the secular values and the religious one (8, 19ff.). Whether these difficulties are caused by the political situation of the time or by the failings of the human personality,[2] only one of Walther's goals can be termed an absolute (8, 16: ...*gotes hulde,/der zweier übergulde*). Whatever secular courtly values he sees incorporated in the other two can only be relative, however desirable in themselves. What courtly literature at times presents as make-believe absolutes (Hartmann exploits this readiness in sketching the hero in *Der arme Heinrich* as a paragon of courtly virtues just before the blow strikes) is here shown up in its relativity.[3]

---

[1] The starting points for the discussion on this topic are Ehrismann, *ZfdA* 56 (1919), 137ff. and Curtius, *DVjs* 21 (1943), 343ff. respectively. See also Eifler, *Tugendsystem*.

[2] For an interpretation of Walther's poem in this light see Falk, *Nibelungenlied*, pp. 53ff.

[3] With regard to the theme of 'courtly love' Lewis, *Allegory*, p. 43, has described this state of affairs in the style of a writer of children's books.

In this Walther does not stand alone. Wernher von Elmendorf
stresses how necessary (and, by implication, how difficult) it is
to combine two components of his advice for moral conduct
(83: *dri sachin horen an den rat,|da by alle tugent nu stat:|daʒ eine daʒ
is ere, daʒ ander frome, |daʒ dritte, wi man do ʒu kome,|daʒ man
durch liebe noch leyde|ere vnd frome vmmer nicht gescheyde*). He may
question their worth when separated (89f.), but what he stresses
more is the difficulty of combining them. Ulrich von Lichtenstein
is even more categorical on the irreconcilability of four values
(*gotes hulde, êre, gemach, guot*), for he sees them all in mutual conflict
(*Frauendienst* 587, 27: *Er wær ein sælden rîcher man,|der disiu vieriu
möhte hân:|des kan ot leider nicht geschehen,|als ich di wîsen hœre jehen.|
ietwederʒ dem andern schaden tuot*) and polemicises against any easy
optimism (587, 32: *dâ von ist eʒ ein tumber muot,|ders elliu vieriu
wænet haben:|dem ist sîn hôher sin begraben*). A similar conclusion is
suggested by the use William of Conches has made of the material
of Cicero's *De officiis*, organising it under five headings in his
Moralium dogma philosophorum.[1] Two of these are entitled *De
honesto* and *De utili*, whilst two further sections point to a scale of
priorities for each (*De comparatione honestorum* and *De comparatione
utilium*) and a final section treats the possibilities of conflict
between both (*De conflictu honesti et utilis*). The fluidity of such
shifting alignments brings elasticity into what would otherwise
be rigidly systematic, but it illustrates in theoretical terms how
secular, courtly values which some may take as absolutes can be
ironically presented as only relative values when viewed in
a wider context.

Such explicitness may alert us to the implicit treatment of the
same problem in narrative action, above all in the relationship of
love with other courtly values. The difficulties to which this can
lead are latent in the *Tristan* story, but nowhere are they more
radically presented than by Thomas and Gottfried who depict
courtly refinement with greater thoroughness than in the
'version commune'. This courtliness does not prevent Thomas
from being very clear-sighted about the love he depicts, he is
alert to the hypocrisies which the adulterous affair causes[2] and
does not shrink from pointing out the moral cost that has to be

---

[1] See Bumke, *ZfdA* 88 (1957), 40.   [2] *RPh* 7 (1953/4), 121ff.

met. It has even proved possible to ask whether he may not have been utterly mistaken in trying to depict Tristan's love against a background of courtly refinement.[1] Behind this question is the disturbing possibility that the passion depicted may not be reconcilable with the social ideal of courtliness, that courtliness is powerless in the face of love of this kind. If Thomas questions the optimism of the courtly world this is what one might have expected from a radical subject like the *Tristan* story,[2] but such insight into the fragility of the courtly ideal is not confined to this theme, for we find it even in the first example of Arthurian romance.[3]

The honours lavished on Erec and Enite at Arthur's court when they marry constitute a balanced picture of the leading courtly qualities in easy harmony. Enite's beauty has been acknowledged, like Erec's chivalry in defeating Iders, both are received with courtly honours, their love for each other is assured and they bring joy to Arthur's society. Such harmony of values, one prompted by another and in turn assisting another, is a reflection of the ideal of courtly existence propagated by this first romance, but even this first exemplar hints that this ideal cannot be taken for granted and instead contains a problem. The hint is given after a eulogy of Erec, the victor of the tournament held at his wedding festivities (which has its own ironic implications),[4] and concerns his wife's initial reaction to his victory (2826: *dô daz mære ûz kam/und vrouwe Ênîte vernam/sô grôze tugent zellen/von Êrecke ir gesellen,/dô was ir sîn manheit/beide liep unde leit*). Her feelings are mixed on learning of her husband's courtly standing: his victory is *liep* to her because of the social renown he has won (2832f.), but also *leit* because she fears for his life if he further pursues *êre* (2834ff.). The poet here draws attention to the potential conflict between the enjoyment of courtly harmony and the pursuit of chivalric renown, the possibility that one might be destructive of the other. Courtly harmony is not simply presented as a fairytale achievement, ensured once and for all, but as a precarious balance. Nor is this just a passing hint, for

[1] *Ibid.*, pp. 125ff.
[2] This point has been well made by Ferrante, *Conflict*, pp. 11f.
[3] I follow here a suggestion made by Oh, *Aufbau*, pp. 22f.
[4] See Green, *Praise*, pp. 795ff.

the irony of Enite's sudden fears is that, whereas she sees the
threat to courtly harmony as coming from the dangerous pursuit
of chivalric exploits, the danger in fact comes from their love
and that it will rather be Erec's *verligen* that jeopardises his chivalric renown. Her fears point in the direction which the narrative
will take and although she is wrong in judging how the balance
might be upset she is right to see its precariousness.[1]

The antinomies of the courtly ideal also come to the fore in
Mabonagrin's account of his relationship with his mistress. Far
from this theme being voiced in passing, it is brought to our
attention again and remains a final impression. Availing herself
of a common practice in the romance (one person promises another
to do whatever he might request, where the terms of the request,
once disclosed, usually constitute an unwelcome surprise),[2]
Mabonagrin's mistress has enticed him into making such a rash
promise (9494ff.) and only later disclosed that she had in mind
for them to remain in isolation at Schoydelakurt until Mabonagrin
is defeated by a challenger (from the bondage of this promise
Erec has now released him). The usual function of the motif is
to draw attention to a weak point in the courtly edifice of values[3]
and in this case the mistress, aware like Enite of the threat to the
untroubled enjoyment of their love, has drastically eliminated this
by inveigling Mabonagrin into his promise, thus keeping him
a captive by her side.[4] Allowing for the crass exaggerations which
a caricature can claim, this episode is a final horrific illustration
of what could so easily have befallen Erec and Enite if they had
persisted in their denial of obligations to court and chivalry. To
make an absolute of one courtly value in isolation is to distort
and endanger the whole fabric, so that the romance illustrates
the shortsightedness of risking the whole for the sake of the part.

---

[1] Whether or not we see the problem in *Iwein* as a reversal of that in *Erec*, both
works are concerned with the difficulties in reconciling the values of love and
chivalry. The antinomies of these courtly values therefore inform these two
romances.
[2] This motif underlies, for example, the abduction of Guinevere in Hartmann's
Iwein and the Gandin episode in Gottfried's *Tristan*.
[3] Désilles-Busch, *Don*, pp. 19ff.
[4] With Mabonagrin's mistress the motive is jealousy of other women (9550ff.),
whereas Enite fears for her husband's life in the constant pursuit of chivalry. Both
agree in setting their love above the social obligations of courtly life.

By reverting to this theme at the concluding point of the action Hartmann rounds off his account of the marriage of Erec and Enite, but also reveals that their situation had been a representative one, that what happened to them has also befallen Mabonagrin and his mistress and could be the experience of any member of courtly society. This is another way of implying the extreme fragility of the courtly system of values. If this is a means of impressing on the listener a sense that the story is relevant to his condition, it also underlines the temporary, perhaps artificial nature of the solution reached and suggests the open-ended possibility that the problem could break out again. It is this implicit hint (for Hartmann goes no further than this in *Erec*)[1] that Wolfram has seized upon for parodic purposes in adopting the figure of Mabonagrin in *Parzival* and in suggesting that his predecessor had not gone far enough. In *Parzival* the problem of Mabonagrin, so far from having been settled by Erec's victory, has broken out again with a vengeance.[2]

Criticism of the court

There are therefore grounds to question the absolute claims made for courtly values and the criteria by which the court sets the seal of approval on characters who apparently conform to its ideal. By two quite different approaches we are led to doubt the claims of courtly society and of the court as an arbiter. We have reached the point where we have to ask whether the court as the judge of values and as the dispenser of social renown may not itself be subjected to scrutiny.

As with the irony of chivalry and love we may first consider some passages where the court is depicted not in idealising, but in very realistic terms[3] which, theoretically, may lead to the

---

[1] This faintest of hints that the conclusion of *Erec* may be no real one gives way to the more pointed suggestion in *Iwein* that the married couple's reconciliation is not really firmly based (on this see Green, *Damning*, pp. 162ff. and *Recognising*, pp. 44ff.).

[2] See above, pp. 62ff.

On the further use of the motif of the rash boon to draw attention to the possible conflict between one courtly value and another see Désilles-Busch on Chrétien's *Yvain* (pp. 50f.) and *Lancelot* (pp. 31f. and 44f.).

[3] On realistic observations about these two values see above, pp. 51ff. and 93ff.

possibility of irony. Chrétien can be very sardonic about the cowardice of the knights at Laudine's court, for his observations are made at a length which exceeds the simple need to motivate Yvain's indispensability as a guardian of Laudine's territory. Lunete can appeal to Laudine's evident knowledge of this state of affairs in arguing her case, especially in view of the approach of Arthur's knights (1628: *Que certes une chanberiere/Ne valent tuit, bien le savez,/Li chevalier, que vos avez./Ja par celui, qui miauz se prise,/N'an iert escuz ne lance prise./De jant mauveise avez vos mout,/ Mes ja n'avra si estout,/Qui sor cheval monter an ost;/Et li rois vient a si grant ost,/Qu'il seisira tot sanz deffanse*). Lunete's words are as biting here as are Keu's before the Round Table, but we are given no cause to doubt what she says. Indeed, her tart observation is borne out by their behaviour. Once she has accepted Yvain, Laudine knows her vassals well enough to realise that they will fall in readily with her wishes in order to avoid any military danger to themselves (2040ff.).[1] This is what happens when she presents Yvain to them, for they are ironically depicted eagerly recommending her to do what she has already in mind to do (2105: *A cest mot dïent tuit ansanble,/Que bien a feire lor ressanble,/ Et trestuit jusqu'au pié li vienent./De son voloir an grant la tienent;/Si se fet proiier de son buen,/Tant que aussi con maugré suen/Otroie ce, qu'ele feïst,/Se chascuns li contredeïst*). To the extent that Laudine here exercises authority (by contrast with her earlier malleability in Lunete's hands) her court is shown as consisting of pliant reeds.[2]

German literature does not stand apart in this respect. Hartmann makes the same points in *Iwein* as his predecessor, implying both the cowardice as knights and fulsomeness as courtiers of Laudine's followers.[3] Gottfried, as befits a poet who sees his lovers caught

[1] In this passage I should stress the ironic ambiguity of the word *besoing* (2043): have Laudine's courtiers advised her with regard to her need or their own? Cf. also 1855ff., where Lunete cynically banks upon these courtiers giving such advice for selfish reasons. The realism of such an observation is heightened by the pretence of an ideal state of affairs in which Laudine acts only with the certainty of her court's approval (1856f., cf. 2141f.).

[2] Chrétien can also deliver himself of generalised criticism of courtiers as time-serving flatterers (*Cligès* 2595ff., 4482f., 4485ff., 4513f.). Like his sardonic comments on the ways of women these observations arise out of a particular situation and are strictly superfluous – were it not for his wish to castigate the hypocrisies of life at court. [3] *Iwein* 2159ff. and 2393ff.

in the machinations of enemies at court, affords us glimpses behind the courtly façade. Blanscheflur's confidante is shown making shrewd calculations as to her own advantage in the advice she gives her mistress (1239f.), one innocuous line devoted to Morgan's ignorance casts a harsh light on the idealising convention of a polite courtly reception,[1] whilst Isold's musings on the human qualities of Tantris lead her to contrast his poor status, despite his personal excellence, with the shortcomings of many a ruler (10023: *diu werlt stat wunderliche,/so vil manic künicriche/ besetzet ist mit swacher art,/daz ime der einez niht enwart*). The fact that Isold is wrong in this case (she does not know that Tantris is Tristan and of royal birth) does not invalidate her observation of other instances on which her generalisation is based. Her conviction that many a ruler represents poor human material means that, in the light of medieval equation of a ruler's qualities with the status of his court (as with Erec at Karnant or with Walther's view of the mournful condition of the court of Vienna),[2] there must be many a court whose manner of life is a travesty of the courtly ideal.[3]

These are only isolated examples, but they belong to a tradition criticising the court which, whilst drawing on earlier sources (especially in classical literature), starts with any force only about the middle of the twelfth century with John of Salisbury. This tradition has been studied, from the point of view of English conditions, by Uhlig who makes the observation that the tradition is an international one and is reflected in different literary genres.[4] He establishes the continuity of general features which explain the persistence of this tradition from the twelfth century to the Renaissance: the resentment caused by the dependence of poets on the whims of court patronage, the tension between

---

[1] *Tristan* 5363ff. On the ironic function of 5364 see Clausen, *Erzähler*, p. 83.

[2] *Erec* 2966ff. and Walther 24, 33ff. (with an implicit reference to Leopold's responsibility).

[3] This is made clear in Hartmann's description of the court of Oringles in *Erec*. Their upside-down sense of values (6625ff.) is a fitting reflection of their ruler's complete lack of courtliness.

[4] Uhlig, *Hofkritik*, 27ff. Apart from the *Entheticus* and *Policraticus* of John of Salisbury Uhlig sees this tradition reflected in medieval moral philosophy, the *specula principis*, satire, letter and anecdote, and the beast epic.

what would now be called intellectuals and politicians,[1] and not least the Janus nature of the court itself, a centre of urbanity but also a hotbed of intrigue.

To these sociological factors must be added in some cases biographical details which account for an author devoting his energies to this literary tradition. With John of Salisbury, whose criticism takes the court of Henry II as its target, this impetus came from the tension between clergy and royalty in the middle of the twelfth century in Norman England, but also this writer's involvement with Thomas Becket and his banishment in 1164, events which sharpened his critical awareness of the deficiencies of life at court and of the intrigues to which he could claim to have fallen victim himself.[2] Personal reasons are not lacking in other cases. Giraldus Cambrensis uses the tradition to exact literary vengeance for his disappointment at not obtaining the see of St David's,[3] whilst the career of Peter of Blois at court, first as a stranger in Palermo and then at home in France, shows him to have been almost as much the victim of jealousy and intrigue as Tristan at Marke's court in Gottfried's version.[4]

Personal reasons combine with unchanging factors of court life to produce a literary tradition of criticism of the court. Although this tradition makes use of precedents in classical literature,[5] it begins only in the twelfth century in the person of John of Salisbury. But he is not the only author in this tradition to focus his general criticism on one court in particular, that of Henry II, for the same is true of Giraldus Cambrensis, Peter of Blois and Walter Map.[6] The implications of this are important, for it means that the first major European court to encourage literature propagating the courtly ideal[7] was also the first court

---

[1] On this see also Jaeger, *Humanism*, pp. 16ff. and 80ff.

[2] Cf. Uhlig, *op. cit.*, pp. 27ff. [3] *Ibid.*, pp. 56ff.

[4] *Ibid.*, pp. 99ff. On this aspect of Gottfried's *Tristan* see Gruenter, *Euphorion* 58 (1964), 113ff.

[5] Uhlig lists the example of classical moral philosophy (pp. 6f. and 61f.), the topos of the antithesis between town and country, where the artificialities of town life are applicable to life at court as well (pp. 11 and 48), and certain character types from Roman comedy (pp. 11 and 45ff.).

[6] Uhlig, *op. cit.*, pp. 27ff. and 51 on John of Salisbury, pp. 55ff. on Giraldus Cambrensis, p. 99 on Peter of Blois and Walter Map. See also Bezzola, *Origines* III 1, pp. 20ff., 47ff., 31ff. and 87ff. respectively.

[7] On the patronage of courtly literature by Henry II see Haskins, *Henry*, pp. 71ff.; Schirmer and Broich, *Studien*, pp. 27ff.; Bezzola, *Origines* III 1, pp. 3ff.

to attract what became an established tradition of criticism of the court. The parallels in vernacular literature are not far to seek, for the inaugurator of the Arthurian romance in Germany, Hartmann, is also the first to express reservations about the ideal of chivalry[1] and qualifications about the view of love are to be found already in the earliest romances.[2] The conclusion to which these parallels urge us is that the court encouraged a literature in which its aspirations were idealised but also occasioned a literature in which its pretensions were criticised, a state of affairs which reminds us of the two attitudes to love in two courtly genres (the romance and the fabliau) and suggests that in the present context the link between idealisation and criticism of the court may be found in irony, in a recognition of the ambivalence of courtly values.

To be sure that the occasional ironisation of the court in vernacular literature is an offshoot of the more sustained criticisms in medieval Latin we have to assume the possibility of contact between the two, not necessarily in direct borrowings, but at least suggesting that both were fed by a common experience. The contact may occasionally be a close one on a point of detail so specific as to render chance as an explanation quite unlikely. This is the case with one of Chrétien's generalisations on the fawning flattery of the courtier in *Cligès*, ingratiatingly removing a feather from his master where there was none (4485: *Qui vialt de son seignor bien estre/Et delez lui seoir a destre,/Si com il est us et costume,/Del chief li doit oster la plume,/Neïs quant il n'en i a point*). This corresponds closely to a satirical detail in the poem *De palpone et assentatore* ascribed to Walter Map (271: *Ad latus principis stat palpo blandiens,/adaptans clamidem, vestemque poliens,/et invisibiles plumas decutiens,/invisa luteo visu conspiciens*).[3] There is no need to surmise whether direct influence is to be imagined here, for Chrétien in the vernacular stands in the same tradition as Latin criticism of the court, which is enough for our purposes.[4]

---

[1] See above, pp. 66ff. and 79ff. Many of Hartmann's reservations are of course implicit in his French source.
[2] See above, pp. 91ff.
[3] The passage from Walter Map is quoted by Uhlig, *Hofkritik*, p. 92.
[4] Uhlig, *op. cit.*, pp. 124ff. has argued the same point for Chaucer's *Nun's Priest's Tale*. D. S. Brewer has kindly drawn my attention to other passages where Chaucer

This convention has however gained entry into another vernacular work and plays a vital part in it. It was not without purpose that I compared the vicissitudes to which Peter of Blois was exposed with the intrigues surrounding Gottfried's Tristan at the court of Tintagel. Our ignorance of Gottfried's life makes it otiose to wonder whether his experiences at court taught him to view it critically, as is the case with some authors about whose career we are better informed. It is enough to register that the antithesis between love and society which informs his *Tristan* was of itself liable to lead to a highly critical sketch of the society which persecutes the lovers.[1] Since Gottfried, following Thomas, wished to idealise and praise his lovers he was compelled to depict their opponents, the husband and his court, in a negative light. He does this by the manner in which the deceptions practised by Tristan as a lover differ from those which he had committed earlier in being defensive manoeuvres, meant to ward off the attacks of others.[2] Even the motives of those who seek to trap the lovers are rendered suspect, which means that Marke as centre of the court is shown up in his weakness and is demeaned by the henchmen he employs, whilst the members of his court who plot against the lovers are depicted with the conventional vices of court intriguers.[3] Although what these spies suspect is objectively the truth, the impurity of their motives (jealousy, frustrated ambition) reveals them as subjectively dishonest, hypocritically concerned, like the courtiers they are, to advance their selfish ends under the guise of public service.

It could be that, since the only court described in any detail is that of Marke the husband, this feature of the plot is sufficient explanation of the court's unattractive features. Against this we have to set the fact that the negative sketch is begun well before the love-affair starts (envy and veiled accusations are aroused by Tristan's exceptional talents and are visible as soon as he returns

---

makes the same point: *Legend of Good Women*, Prologue F, 352 and Prologue G, 328; *Romaunt of the Rose* 1050 (both quoted from Robinson's edition of Chaucer's works).
[1] Uhlig, *Hofkritik*, p. 20, fn. 56, suggests this parallel in passing, but takes it no further. But see Jaeger, *Humanism*, pp. 64ff.
[2] Cf. Hollandt, *Hauptgestalten*, pp. 110ff.
[3] *Ibid.*, pp. 136ff.

healed from the first voyage to Ireland)[1] and the significant detail
that the Irish steward, who hypocritically exploits courtly conventions to gain his own ends, is a high court official.[2] Although
Gottfried's attention is focussed on a court which, because of
Marke's double rôle of ruler and husband, happens to represent the society with which the lovers are in conflict, these
other points suggest that Gottfried's views on the nature of
any court are incorporated in his picture of this court. Just as
the Round Table represents not just Arthur's court, but the
potentialities of the medieval court at large, so does Gottfried
make use of the court of Tintagel to put across his view of
the shortcomings of any court.[3]

The Round Table

This observation needs to be qualified in so far as it implies an
absolute contrast between the function of the Round Table in
the Arthurian romance and the function of Marke's court in
Tristan, suggesting that the Round Table incorporated only the
positive potentialities of the court. That the position is more
complex, so that this model of courtly life is to be scrutinised
more closely, can be shown in the romances of Chrétien and his
German successors. Just as the court of Henry II attracted eulogistic as well as critical literature, so do the first continental romances
that ultimately derive from the literary patronage of his court
present their picture of the Round Table as an ideal focus for
love and chivalry and with some reservations. It is the merit of
Emmel's comparative survey of the structural function of the
Round Table to have shown that in the course of Chrétien's
literary career these reservations become more pronounced and
are reflected in Arthur's court being gradually edged out of the
central position which it had occupied at the beginning.[4]

---

[1] 8316ff. (coming immediately after Tristan begins his new life, 8310ff., and in
contrast with the court's previous readiness to laugh with Tristan over his
escapade, 8237ff.).
[2] See Haupt, *Truchsess*, pp. 6off., for some comments on the negative view of the
office of steward in medieval literature.
[3] Gottfried's critical view of the court has been stressed by Jackson, *Anatomy*,
pp. 144ff.
[4] In what follows I have mainly followed Emmel, *Formprobleme*.

In *Erec* and *Yvain*[1] Arthur's court symbolises an ideal of court-liness, but also provides a number of static interludes which, spaced throughout each work, interrupt the active course of the narrative made up of knightly encounters. This court is an oasis of peace and refinement from which knightly dangers are kept at bay and have to be met by the hero on his lonely wanderings. The hero starts his quest by departing from the Round Table (this is the background from which he springs) and returns to it after proving himself in his adventures (so that the Round Table also has a concluding function, to indicate the hero's final reinte-gration into courtly society). The action begins at Arthur's court and concludes with the hero's return to it. In between these extremes the hero may return to Arthur's court provisionally, so that it serves often as a formal signpost to a new stage of the action (the hero has achieved a certain degree of rehabilitation and is welcomed at this point by the Round Table, but since this still does not satisfy him he sets out once more). This alternation between the hero's isolation (on his solitary adventures) and reintegration into society (at the Round Table) is characteristic of the earliest Arthurian romance and has a bearing both on the content (chivalry is legitimised by being given a social purpose) and on the form (the scenes at Arthur's court serve as pillars spaced throughout the work).

The opening scene is set at Arthur's court in both these roman-ces. In *Erec* Arthur is shown at the opening actively in control of the situation and at the centre of events – it is he who suggests the hunt for the White Stag, rejects Gauvain's objection and himself kills the Stag. In all this Arthur shows himself as a mon-arch in control of things; it is a fitting introduction of this figure into the vernacular romance. *Yvain* likewise begins in the same setting (Calogrenant's account), but although Arthur intends to avenge his knight Yvain secretly anticipates him and sets out to face the adventure himself.[2] As regards the intermediate scenes at

---

[1] Although Emmel also includes Chrétien's *Lancelot* in her survey I have omitted this for reasons of space.

[2] Although the action of *Lancelot* begins at Arthur's court, it hardly shows it in a flattering light. The Round Table is initially in a state of helpless confusion after the stranger has appeared with his challenge, paralysed by the enormity of events with which it cannot cope.

the Round Table, we find two of these in *Erec*. The first comes when the hero has defeated Yder and marries Enide at Arthur's court whose festivities acknowledge his chivalric honour. This scene concludes the first part of the romance and can also be regarded as a concluding scene. The second intermediate scene comes at the turning-point of the second part (coming between the two series of adventures undertaken by the hero). At this point Erec, badly wounded, is enticed to rest at Arthur's court for the healing of his wound, so that his brief stay is a pointer to his external rehabilitation. With regard to these intermediate scenes *Yvain* only partly resembles *Erec*. The conclusion of the first part (after Yvain's marriage) is signalled by Arthur's arrival, Yvain's defeat of Keu, his acclaim by the Round Table and general festivities. As in *Erec*, the hero's fall from grace occurs soon after, so that here too this first intermediate scene also concludes the first part of the romance. But the second part of *Yvain* differs from the corresponding part of *Erec* in that Yvain no longer briefly returns to Arthur's court half way through, but instead encounters his wife Laudine briefly at her court. In apparent compensation for this there is another innovation, since Yvain's final adventure is his combat with Gauvain, this climax of the knightly action serving as a final proof of Yvain's chivalry and restitution to the society of the Round Table.

The concluding Arthurian scene of the whole work is quite clear in *Erec*. After the crowning exploit of defeating Mabonagrain Erec and his wife go to Arthur's court and hear there the news of the death of Erec's father. It is Arthur who crowns Erec king, thereby setting the seal on Erec's career before the Round Table itself. With *Yvain*, by contrast, we come for the first time to an Arthurian romance which is not concluded at Arthur's court, although, given the earlier connection between the Round Table and Laudine's realm when Arthur came to the magic well, Chrétien could have easily brought these two spheres together in a concluding scene. Instead, Laudine's court remains a separate authority, distinct from Arthur's and, in so far as Yvain's career is now concluded at her court, even superior to it. This detail explains in retrospect Yvain's intermediate return to Laudine, and not to Arthur, half way through the second part, and also the independent authority with which Lunete, as Laudine's messenger, could earlier accuse Yvain of infidelity before Arthur's assembled court. It implies that Laudine's court has its own criteria, and can even accuse a knight accepted into Arthur's company. Her court is a separate authority alongside Arthur's court, an innovation which dislodges Arthur from his central position and prepares the way formally for the situation in *Perceval*, where the Grail-world coexists with Arthur's realm and is superior to it.

These two romances of Chrétien plot his changing attitude towards (or growing detachment from) the ideal of Arthur's court. In *Erec* alone is Arthur an active king with real authority, so that the hero's return to his court symbolises his moral worth, since Arthur has accepted him into the Round Table. In *Yvain* Arthur has been ousted from his position of unique authority by the function of Laudine's court, and it is at this new centre that the action of the romance is now concluded. If even Chrétien, the creator of Arthur as the literary symbol of ideal chivalry in the vernacular romance, suggests the inadequacy of this figure to his artistic purpose, what reflection of this do we find in Hartmann's works? We may quickly dismiss *Iwein*, for the structure of this work (with regard to Arthur's court) corresponds closely to that of *Yvain*. This alone ensures that the distance from the Arthurian ideal attained by Chrétien is maintained by his German successor. But it is in his *Erec* that Hartmann has introduced changes which show that he has understood the implications of Chrétien's formal changes between *Erec* and *Yvain* and has accepted them for himself.

We have seen something of Hartmann's reservations about chivalry, but must consider now how these extend to its institutional embodiment, the Round Table. This can be shown by two points where he has changed the ending of *Erec* so that Arthur's court, despite its theoretical importance, no longer serves as an absolute criterion. By attaching importance to the courtly rejoicing after Erec's victory over Mabonagrin Hartmann has ensured that his return to Arthur's court is strangely muted. The story of Erec and Enite has already reached its climax at Brandigan, it is this court which now performs the climactic function which had fallen to the Round Table at the close of the first part.[1] Hartmann attempts to restore some function to Arthur's court by having Erec take the eighty widows with him to Arthur, to free them from grief by an act of symbolic courtly redemption. Even so, the function of Arthur's court is still reduced: it is no longer exercised on behalf of hero and heroine (*their* joy has been finally established at Brandigan), but for strictly minor figures. This discrepancy (the action returns to Arthur, but in a minor key) suggests that Hartmann was not fully persuaded of the structural necessity of concluding the action at Arthur's court, which in turn implies a faint doubt about the Arthurian ideal.

This is confirmed by another change. Having brought his couple back to the Round Table, Hartmann is not content with leaving them there (as was Chrétien) but takes them from the Round Table to Erec's homeland and has Erec crowned there (and not at Arthur's court, as with Chrétien). It is therefore away from Arthur's court that Erec's perfect rulership is described in almost legendary terms as a *rex pacificus* assured of divine favours in this world and the next. This transposes the work onto a new level (political and religious), transcending the *unstæte* of Erec's earlier adventures, but since Arthur's court is the embodiment of knight-errantry, this means that Arthur's court, too, is transcended in this conclusion. What with Chrétien had been the climax of his first romance (the hero's return to Arthur) has become only a preliminary climax with Hartmann.[2]

These shifts of emphasis at the conclusion agree with another change in Hartmann's version, concerning Erec's intermediate stay at Arthur's court between his two series of adventures. This scene acts as a hinge between these two series, but its central position is even more pronounced if we regard this episode at Arthur's court as the structural fulcrum of the whole romance.[3]

---

[1] Cf. Scheunemann, *Artushof*, pp. 97ff.

[2] *Ibid.*, pp. 106ff.

[3] We know since Kuhn's essay on *Erec* (now in *Dichtung*, pp. 133ff., especially p. 142) that Erec's adventures after Karnant fall into two carefully articulated series and that his brief stay at Arthur's court comes in between them. But this symmetrical arrangement goes further, for these two series are preceded by a tripartite action in the first part of the romance (arrival at Tulmein, combat, rejoicing) which agrees structurally with the tripartite Brandigan action at the end of the work (arrival at

If so, it is a strangely unimpressive fulcrum. For this is the scene in which Erec seeks to avoid Arthur's company and can only be persuaded to stay for one night, in which he regards himself as unworthy of their courtly joy and in which a vain attempt is made to heal his wound. For Erec this stay can have little importance, even though the scene is the structural turning-point of the romance. If we ask what scene, as far as Erec is concerned, is the turning-point in his career, the scene in which he begins his ascent to final success, we find it in the immediately following scene in which he frees Cadoc from the giants. This scene represents a new beginning in several respects. For the first time Erec himself perceives the presence of a challenge (5296),[1] is prompted to adventure by compassion (5335ff.), offers his knightly prowess to assist someone in distress (5343f.) and is expressly said to be the recipient of divine help in combat (5561ff.).[2] Since these are the features of an ideal adventure for Hartmann, it is in this episode that Erec first enters on the path which eventually brings him to legendary success. In other words, whilst the formal turning-point is Erec's stay at Arthur's court the thematic turning-point is found not there, but nearby, a bare mile away (5295: *kûme eine mîle*). In heightening the importance of Erec's combat with the giants Hartmann has minimised the function of Arthur's court here just as much as at the conclusion of the work.

If Hartmann plays down the function of the Round Table in *Erec* by contrast with Chrétien's version, this is what Chrétien himself does in *Yvain* (and is followed by Hartmann in *Iwein*). This makes it likely that in his changes to Chrétien's *Erec* Hartmann may have received help from *Yvain*, a romance which he also knew when he composed the first Arthurian romance in German.[3] Chrétien's development from *Erec* to *Yvain* was there-

---

Brandigan, combat, rejoicing). The scene of Erec's temporary stay at Arthur's court therefore occupies a central position in the whole work, even approximately in quantitative terms, for it occupies lines 4629[6]–5287 in a work of 10192 verses.

[1] On this detail see Ohly, *Struktur*, p. 74.

[2] Equally, this encounter between Erec and the giants is the only episode between his combat with Iders and his combat with Mabonagrin (i.e. between his first and last encounter in this romance) to be dignified by the term *âventiure* (5292). *Âventiure* is used of the Iders combat (492) and repeatedly of the last adventure in Erec's career (8384, 8398, 8414, 8481).

[3] Cf. Piquet, *Etude*, pp. 231f.

fore available to Hartmann when he wrote *Erec*, the growing distance of the French poet enabled his German successor to demonstrate a greater critical irony in his first romance. If Hartmann shows more reservations about Arthur's court in this work than Chrétien, it is because he can make good use of the later Chrétien's doubts about the earlier Chrétien. But for Hartmann to perceive and exploit such possibilities, he must have been open to the appeal of irony when applied to the Round Table.

Chrétien also retains the by now traditional structure of the Arthurian romance in his *Perceval* but, by incorporating into this the new theme of the Grail which originally had nothing to do with the Arthurian story, he changed the structure of this romance still further in the direction taken between *Erec* and *Yvain*. In the latter work Chrétien had introduced the novelty of having the action conclude somewhere else than at Arthur's court, but now in *Perceval* he extends this by having the narrative begin somewhere else than at Arthur's court, in the *gaste forest soutainne* (75) to which Perceval's mother retreats with her son. This realm of the wild forest later plays a decisive rôle in the hero's career (his adventures, his hermit uncle, Grail territory), but formally it corresponds to the non-Arthurian realm represented by Laudine's court in *Yvain*. Yet we do not remain in this wilderness for long, Perceval is quickly brought to seek Arthur to obtain chivalry. When he arrives at his court it is to find the king worried and inactive over the insult done to him by the Red Knight, a situation reminiscent of the opening of *Lancelot*. Chrétien has relativised the position of the Round Table in two ways, by edging it out of its dominant function in the opening scene and by showing up Arthur's helplessness in an uncomplimentary light.[1] After leaving the Round Table Perceval retains contact with Arthur's court by sending his defeated opponents there, but when he gains Blancheflor's hand and thereby reaches Yvain's stage when he married Laudine Chrétien does not allow Perceval and the Round Table to come together again, as with Yvain, but takes him instead into Grail territory.

---

[1] In other words, he has applied to *Perceval* two innovations for which he had been responsible in *Lancelot* and *Yvain* (using the latter innovation now of the opening of his work).

When Perceval eventually visits Arthur's court for the second time he has already passed through this other realm of the Grail from which the attack can be launched on him before Arthur's company. Like Lunete, the Grail-messenger represents a realm not subject to Arthur's authority, but whereas Laudine, as a feudal lady, belonged to the same courtly world as Arthur, the Grail-kingdom is mysteriously remote and inaccessible, the gulf between the two spheres is wider than in *Yvain*. Chrétien has built another world into the traditional pattern of the Arthurian romance and, by bringing these two worlds into collision in this scene, shows that Perceval, for all his membership of the Round Table, is not to be judged by their standards alone. Perceval only partially belongs to Arthur's world. He comes to Arthur from the wild forest of his childhood and is destined to leave the Round Table behind him for the remote wilderness of the Grail-kingdom. Similarly, when Gauvain's adventures are interrupted for Perceval's encounter with the hermit, this meeting also takes place in a wild woodland retreat. Although certainty is denied us by the fragmentary nature of Chrétien's romance, it is possible that this short intermediate stay with the hermit corresponds structurally with Erec's short stay at the Round Table for healing or, more closely, with Yvain's provisional visit at Laudine's court before his final reconciliation.[1] What is certain is that Chrétien, for all his variations, is here still working on the traditional form of the Arthurian romance, with an alternation between the hero's distance from Arthur and his occasional visits at his court. Equally certain is the fact that the Grail-world, more emphatically than Laudine's court, has ousted the Round Table from its central position and that Perceval's exploits are only partially related to Arthur's court. What we saw at work in Chrétien's development from *Erec* to *Yvain* is taken a decisive step further in *Perceval*.

In completing Chrétien's fragmentary plot Wolfram realised both these points. He perceived that the pattern was still that of the Arthurian romance.[2] In devising his own conclusion the German poet has Parzival return to the Round Table, but before the climactic scene at the Grail castle (the model for this was

[1] Emmel, *Formprobleme*, pp. 65f.   [2] *Ibid.*, pp. 66f. and 70f.

Yvain), and has him engage in unwitting combat with Gawan (again, as in *Yvain*). But he also sees that the presence of the Grail-kingdom means a diminished role for the Arthurian world, and he takes this process further than Chrétien. Like the French poet Wolfram displaces the Round Table from its initial position, yet does this not by inserting an episode before it, but instead the whole prehistory of Gahmuret and Herzeloyde. Even when Parzival leaves his mother in search of Arthur's court Wolfram has him detained on his way there by his encounter with Jeschute, and also with Signe (the latter episode an innovation of the German poet, the result of which is to push Arthur's court even more obviously away from the dominating opening position). Once at Arthur's court Parzival remains the focus of events, it is his arrival which sets things in motion. By contrast, Arthur is more passive than with Chrétien and pays little attention to Keii's behaviour.[1]

As with Chrétien, Arthur's court receives news of Parzival's exploits after he has left them from the defeated knights he sends to Cunneware. In the French work Perceval's first message was always to Arthur himself and only then to the damsel struck by Keu; with Wolfram Arthur steps into the background since Parzival sends his captives only to Cunneware (even though they also greet Arthur politely, it is not to him that they offer their *sicherheit*).[2] When Parzival next rejoins the Round Table, Arthur's company is included in Cundrie's accusation, whilst Chrétien had had the Grail-messenger first greet Arthur and his barons before accusing Perceval personally. With Wolfram Cundrie's accusation is made first against Arthur and his knights for having accepted Parzival into their midst. The poet's intentions can best be revealed by contrasting this episode with its obvious analogue, the scene where Lunete accuses Yvain before the Round Table, for never before had Arthur's court been affected by the personal guilt of an individual member; as a centre of peace and justice it had stood above the vicissitudes that befell the hero. In both the French and German versions of the *Yvain* story, as in Chrétien's *Perceval*, Arthur's court had not been affected by the accusation of one knight in their midst, but this position is no longer unas-

[1] *Ibid.*, pp. 81f.　　　　[2] *Ibid.*, pp. 84f.

sailable in Wolfram's romance. The court itself is exposed to criticism and accusation from what emerges as the higher authority of the Grail-kingdom.[1] This demotion of the Round Table is taken a step further after Parzival has left them again, for he no longer sends his defeated opponents to Cunneware (his defeat and punishment of Keii has settled that issue) or to Arthur's court itself (as Perceval still does in the corresponding scenes with Chrétien), but instead to his wife Condwiramurs.[2] His goal is now reunion with her and membership of the Grail-community,[3] no longer of Arthur's court.

This is confirmed by a structural detail in Wolfram's conclusion of Chrétien's incomplete work. Having followed *Yvain* in bringing Parzival and Gawan together in a knightly encounter, the poet is equally traditional in having Gawan accompany Parzival to Arthur's circle where his chivalry is acclaimed at what would seem to be the high-point of his career. But Wolfram takes the suggestion latent in *Yvain* one decisive step further in Parzival's unease in Arthur's company. Like Yvain, his reunion with the Round Table is followed by his dissatisfied departure from it, like Yvain he is conscious that he still lacks the love of his wife (732, 1f.), but for Parzival this love is linked with his striving after the Grail (732, 19ff.). His sadness is in conflict with the general rejoicing at Arthur's court (733, 16ff.), here he distinguishes himself profoundly from the Round Table without rejecting its values. It no longer has anything to offer him.

This inner divorce from the concerns of Arthur's court seems to be weakened by a later scene when Parzival, after his combat with Feirefiz, returns to Arthur's court with his half-brother, where we are given a last description of its festivities. This ultimate acknowledgement that Arthur's court is after all the fitting place to celebrate a climactic achievement apparently undoes the earlier suggestion that this court no longer has anything to give Parzival. In fact, Wolfram has another point to make. By

---

[1] *Ibid.*, pp. 114ff.

[2] Cf. Wynn, *Speculum* 36 (1961), 417f.

[3] On the manner in which these two goals belong together for Parzival, but with clear priority for the Grail, see Schumacher, *Auffassung*, p. 184. Less convincingly, Dewald has devoted a monograph, *Minne*, to suggesting the untroubled harmony between these goals.

devising a scene in which Parzival is finally called to the Grail and by using Cundrie as a messenger for the second time he has achieved two things. He has rounded off a long stretch of his narrative by having Parzival reconciled with the Grail-kingdom by a public announcement at the court where his earlier condemnation had been proclaimed. But by falling back again on the decisive novelty of *Yvain* (the hero is judged at Arthur's court by a representative from another court, independent of the Round Table) Wolfram has repeated the vital point that, just as Parzival's beginnings had lain outside this court, so does his final goal take him beyond their realm.[1] Once more Parzival leaves the Round Table behind him, but this time for good.

In the last few pages I have concentrated for two reasons on the structural evidence for a gradual edging of Arthur's court, the symbol of courtly values, from the centre of even the earliest romances. This kind of approach prepares us for the next chapter with its theme of structural irony, but it also confirms an important feature of much medieval irony: it achieves effects not by ignoring or rejecting a convention (in this case, the structural distribution of Arthurian scenes, as first realised in *Erec*), but by presupposing it and then introducing telling variations.

Another approach to the relativisation of Arthur's court, a thematic one, would also have been possible, but can only be briefly touched upon in conclusion here. By a thematic approach I mean one which concentrates on the narrative action (including narrator's comments on that action), rather than on the structural positioning of conventional scenes. If this thematic approach has yielded rich results in the case of Hartmann's *Iwein*[2] (suggesting that the function of Arthur's court as a guarantor of justice is not all it should be or that their concern for adventure at times smacks of self-centredness), this will not surprise us in a work where, as its structure shows, the first decisive step is taken in

---

[1] We have to take into account the possibility that Wolfram is following the example of Hartmann's *Erec*. The scene in which Parzival is called to Munsalvæsche by Cundrie is reminiscent of Hartmann's concluding scene in which messengers come to Arthur's court and accompany Erec back to his homeland where he is to take over the office of kingship.

[2] See Ohly, *Struktur*, pp. 95ff.; Schweikle, *Iwein*, pp. 10, 11f., 17f. and 21; Pütz, *GRM* 23 (1972), 193ff.; Schröder, *Darstellung*, pp. 309ff.

questioning the central importance of Arthur's court or where reservations about the justification of adventure will not leave untouched the court of Arthur as the institutional symbol of such adventures. It has even been possible, with some exaggeration, to describe Hartmann's second romance as 'eine Art Anti-Artusroman'[1] and to see in this critical distance from Arthurian values a means of toning down the otherwise harsh break between Hartmann's legends and his apparent return to the courtly ideal in *Iwein*.[2]

As the structural approach has suggested, what is true of *Iwein* is also likely to be true of *Parzival*, where doubts about Arthur's court can be insinuated by other than structural means. Wolfram can cast doubt on the Arthurian ideal by humorously confronting it with a reality not normally taken into account. When the defeated Clamide arrives at Arthur's court to give his *sicherheit*, the narrator gives a jokingly full picture of life at this court (216,23: *och wânde dô ein frouwe sân,/si solt den prîs verloren hân,/hete si dâ niht ir âmîs./ich entætes niht decheinen wîs/(eʒ was dô manec tumber lîp),/ich bræhte ungerne nu mîn wîp/in alsô grôʒ gemenge:/ ich vorht unkunt gedrenge,/estlîcher hin ʒir spræche,/daʒ in ir minne stæche/und im die freude blante:/op si die nôt erwante,/daʒ dienter vor unde nâch./mir wære ê mit ir dannen gâch*).[3] The erotic life at Arthur's court is a little too much for the narrator as a husband and he expresses his personal reservations not by actually rejecting this life at court, but by stressing its dangers and keeping his distance. Reality is also brought into the realm of fiction with similar results when the narrator attacks the widespread negative view of Keii's function as *castigator morum* (296, 16: *man saget in manegen landen wît,/daʒ Keie Artûs scheneschalt/mit siten wære ein ribbalt:/ des sagent in mîniu mære blôʒ*) by referring to the dubious company

---

[1] Schweikle, *art. cit.*, p. 21. I would accept this description only to the extent that I believe Hartmann's target to be not the Arthurian ideal as such, but the attempt to maintain its self-sufficiency.

[2] Pütz, *art. cit.*, p. 197.

[3] These lines contain another criticism of the deficiency of courtly *prîs* (216, 24) in that the narrator implies that for a woman to lose this superficial reputation would be the best way to maintain her reputation in a deeper sense. Wolfram's reference to the *gemenge* and *gedrenge* at court may be compared with the critical description of the court as *mundanis plena tumultibus* by Giraldus Cambrensis in his original preface to *De principis instructione* (*Opera* VIII, p. lvii), quoted by Uhlig, *Hofkritik*, p. 59.

attracted to Arthur's court (296,25: *Artûses hof was ein zil,/dar kom vremder liute vil,/die werden unt die smæhen,/mit siten die wæhen*). This seems to be a purely literary point (Wolfram differs from Chrétien's critical view of Keu), but in defending the necessity of Keii's function Wolfram is conceding that Arthur's court was of such mixed company that a critic of Keii's outspokenness was certainly called for, a point which he drives home, in a manner hardly flattering to Arthur, by equating the conventionally idealised court of Arthur with the contemporary and far from perfect reality of the Thuringian court (297, 16ff.).[1] A confrontation with reality is not the only way in which Wolfram relativises the Round Table in this work,[2] but it is enough to show us that in demoting this court and the courtly values it symbolises from its supreme position Wolfram is suggesting that Parzival's goal, whilst it may embrace these values, can no longer be summed up by them.[3]

This last point (Wolfram does not reject the Arthurian ideal as totally mistaken, but incorporates its values in the act of transcending them in the Grail-kingdom) is one that has been a constant feature of this chapter. The irony of values in the medieval romance is certainly not synonymous with a nihilistic dissolution of all values or even with an ascetic rejection of courtly ones, but rather a defence of central values against the threat from peripheral ones and a discussion of what is the true order of priorities. What is subjected to criticism is not the courtly ideal as such, but the belief that it can be totally self-sufficient; not this or that courtly value, but the person who fails to live up to it; not the qualities on which a courtly reputation rests, but society's naïve readiness to see its ideal attributes incorporated in one who does them little justice.[4] Seen in this light, there is no logical contradic-

---

[1] On the wider implications of this passage see Scholz, *Walther*, pp. 5ff.
[2] Cf. the terms of Kingrun's outburst on seeing his lord Clamide sent to offer *sicherheit* to Arthur's court (221, 13ff. – see Emmel, *Formprobleme*, pp. 91ff.) or the acknowledgement by Arthur of the limits set to his authority by the very existence of the Grail-kingdom (280, 28ff. and 286, 10ff. – Emmel, *op. cit.*, p. 99).
[3] On the function of the court in the *Tristan* story I can do no more than refer to Mölk's pages on the figure of Arthur in Thomas's version (*GRM* 12 (1962), 96ff.) and to the instructive parallel between the functions of Arthur and Marke drawn by Hahn, *Raum*, pp. 138f.
[4] Cf. Kellermann, *Aufbaustil*, p. 134 and the very relevant words of Heller, *Dialectics*,

tion in poets applying irony to an ideal of courtliness (or of chivalry or love) which they are in process of propagating, for they make use of irony not to undermine or destroy that ideal, but to define it more clearly and to reach agreement on the detailed choices and decisions with which it confronts society.

p. 166. See also Thurston, *Ambivalence*, pp. 228f. for a summing-up of the position with Chaucer, and Monro, *Argument*, pp. 134f. for a more theoretical observation.

Wolf, *Technik*, p. 403, fn. 34, seems to me to be correct in criticising the general argument of Tax, *Wort*, for not clearly making this kind of distinction.

10

STRUCTURAL IRONY

What precisely I have in mind by structural irony can be shown by contrast with the earlier discussion of non-verbal signals to irony,[1] where the pointer to the presence of irony consisted in the discrepancy between the ironic statement and the context in which it is made. Where the contrast is between the ironic statement and *another* context we are dealing with the specific category of structural irony. It can be detected in the romance informing the relationship between two characters or two scenes, and it is under these two headings that I wish to conduct the argument of the present chapter.

The relationship between characters (Hartmann)

With each of these types of structural irony we once more come close to the irony of values, but this is especially true of the first type, for the juxtaposition of two characters can also suggest a comparison of the values for which they stand, no matter whether we are invited to look more critically at both sets of values or only one. In other words, the range covered by the operation of structural irony is less important than the fact that here too we can entertain second thoughts about some courtly values, although we shall once more observe that this questioning does not amount to a total rejection of all courtly values, but is meant to define more closely the essentials of the courtly ideal.

This subordination of irony to a higher positive purpose can be shown in Hartmann's *Erec*. My example concerns Galoein's reaction to the way in which Enite, tricking him out of loyalty to

[1] See above, pp. 25f. and, in greater detail, Green, *Recognising*, pp. 35ff.

her husband, persuades this would-be seducer to put off the execution of his plot until the morning so that she and Erec are able to escape under cover of night. Galoein realises his mistake too late and curses himself for not having acted earlier (4096: *er sprach: 'swer sîne sache/wendet gar ʒe gemache,/als ich hînaht hân getân,/dem sol êre abe gân/unde schande sîn bereit./wer gewan ie vrumen âne arbeit?'*). There is a double irony about these words. First, in arguing in general terms[1] that a concern for *gemach* is detrimental to *êre* Galoein is voicing Hartmann's message for the whole work and in particular his judgment on Erec's own position at Karnant.[2] Secondly, Erec's past position is distorted by Galoein's didactic opinion, since there is a telling discrepancy between the poet's interpretation of this general truth and the meaning which Galoein attributes to it. He sees *gemach* as responsible for hindering his attainment of a goal so brutal (involving lust and murder) that it could never have brought him *êre*,[3] whilst the poet sees *gemach* as a danger to *êre* in the sense of chivalric renown, resulting from knightly deeds of compassion in the service of others. Galoein's words unwittingly throw light on Erec's past, but distort his position.

Hartmann also uses structural irony, where the hero's offence is illuminated by the position of another character, in connection with Erec's *verligen* on another occasion, for in the description of the wedding tournament it is applied not to his opponents, but to his competitors in Arthur's company. On the morning of the tournament Erec is so eager for knightly prowess that he rises at dawn (2487f.) before anyone else in order to practise with his spears. A *garʒûn* reports this knightly zeal to Arthur's court and upbraids the knights of the Round Table for lethargically passing their time in sleep when they could be in pursuit of chivalric

---

[1] The force of Galoein's generalisation (which he accordingly begins with *swer*) is that it applies to himself and to others, which in effect means Erec. This kind of consideration makes me dubious of the suggestion by Kramer, *Erzählerbemerkungen*, pp. 101 and 128, that a general commentary of this type has no bearing on the central problem of either of Hartmann's romances.

[2] It is ironic that this truth, however distorted, should be immediately obvious to a character like Galoein, but not to the hero of the work.

[3] In other words, Galoein's conception of *êre* is as distorted as the robbers' understanding of this value (see above, p. 293, where Galoein's use of the phrase *âne schande* shows as little perception as his use of *êre* here).

renown (2523: *die er ligende noch vant,/die begunde er strâfen/und beruofen umbe ir slâfen./er sprach: wes liget ir hie?/wer bejagete noch ie/ mit slâfe dehein êre?/hiute hât Êrec sêre/gurbort sper unde swert*). Arthur's knights are here shown in a general situation comparable with Erec's later at Karnant, even though the particular motif of love is not mentioned – they are in bed too long (*ligende, slâfen*) and thereby forgo *êre*, whilst Erec increases his renown by avoiding their fault (2536: *sus machete er im vriunde mê/und stuont ze prîse baz dan ê*). The irony of this situation is that at this stage Erec still avoids his later *verligen*, whilst this fault is imputed to the court which at Karnant is the authority that passes judgment on Erec by abandoning him. At this early point the position is reversed and Erec pays due attention to the needs of chivalry, a fact which places greater responsibility on love, the power which later distracts him from his chivalry.

Structural irony is also employed in *Iwein*, above all in the encounter between Kalogreant (and later Iwein) with the wild man, an occasion which is used to question the knights' chivalric presuppositions[1] by confronting them with a character to whom this code means nothing and to whom the concept *âventiure* must be explained in terms so simple that its primitiveness stands exposed. What concerns us now is not this definition, but the relationship between a knight and someone beyond the courtly pale. By juxtaposing two different worlds, chivalry and non-chivalry, Hartmann invites us to compare them and sets us on this path by building into his narrative an episode in which each representative, the knight and the wild man, asks his interlocutor for information on his way of life. The question prompting Kalogreant's definition of *âventiure* with its implicit questioning of this mode of life is preceded by a similar question by Kalogreant as to the wild man's function in life (489: *ambet*), introduced by a more personal inquiry about the wild man himself (486: '*mahtû mich danne wizzen lân,/waz crêatiure bistû?*') and his ethical standards (483: '*bistu übel ode guot?*'). These questions are more direct and brusque than was allowed by the etiquette of courtly converse, probably because Kalogreant condescendingly imagines that in addressing someone beyond the limits of his

[1] See above, pp. 79ff.

caste he is speaking with someone lacking in true humanity (his use of the word *crêatiure* is brutally distancing).[1] The wild man quietly answers both these questions in a manner which puts the knight in his place, for he unemphatically points out their common humanity (488: '*ein man, als dû gesihest nû*')[2] and affirms an attitude of harmless passivity (484: '*swer mir niene tuot,/der sol ouch mich ze vriunde hân*'). It is ironic that Kalogreant, holding the view that he would be thought a man if he were to kill another knight in combat (534ff.), fails to recognise the humanity of the wild man who wishes no harm to anyone else.

Such questions, and the contrasting attitudes they betray, lead us to entertain the possibility that the outwardly grotesque wild man might possess positive attributes which the knight does not and which his caste-bound attitude leaves out of account.[3] The irony of this situation (it implies a reversal of the expected situation) is taken further in the subsequent course of events. It is the knight Iwein, following the code of behaviour outlined in theoretical terms by Kalogreant, who during the period of his madness reverts to a state of wildness[4] which, disconcertingly for a courtly audience, reduces him to the level of the wild man to which Kalogreant was unthinkingly ready to assume any knight's superiority.[5]

The implications of the structural irony of this scene are apparent. It would have been theoretically possible to construct the scene symmetrically (Kalogreant's questioning of the wild man could have cast doubt on boorishness as a way of life, whilst the latter's question about adventure conversely undermined chivalric pretensions).[6] But Hartmann has not opted for this, he

---

[1] Even more so is the phrasing in Chrétien's *Yvain* 328.

[2] On the similar implications of Chrétien's version see Frappier, *Yvain*, pp. 147f.

[3] Cf. Sacker, *GR* 36 (1961), 8.

[4] *Ibid.*, p. 14.

[5] Sacker, *ibid.*, has drawn attention to one echo of the wild man's appearance in the later description of Iwein in his state of madness, for both are likened to a Moor (427 and 3348). Even more significant is the way in which Hartmann's term for the wild man (440: *walttôre*) is alluded to in the episode with Iwein (3345: *Sus twelte der unwîse / ze walde mit der spîse, / unz daz der edele tôre . . .*). See also Kern, *ZfdPh* 92 (1973), 340f.

[6] The decision for or against a symmetrical patterning of this scene was only open to Hartmann, for Chrétien has no definition of *avanture* in his version (cf. *Yvain* 361ff.).

uses each questioner to raise doubts about one way of life only, that of Kalogreant. The target of this structural irony is the chivalric ideal itself, but not in any modern nihilistic sense, for the poet allows, if not Kalogreant, at least his hero Iwein to grow in moral stature to the point where his knightly exploits are performed in the service of those in need. This ideal of active compassion therefore eventually surpasses the merely passive harmlessness in which the wild man initially outdid the knight Kalogreant.[1] From this later vantage-point we have to correct the observation just made: the target of this structural irony is not the chivalric ideal as such, but its imperfect form defined by Kalogreant and at first practised by Iwein.

In another example of the confrontation of the chivalric with the non-chivalric world Chrétien takes up the situation of his *Yvain* when he treats, at a similarly early and exposed point in his narrative, the encounter between the young Perceval and the five knights who burst in upon the forest solitude to which his widowed mother had withdrawn with him.[2] In varying this earlier motif Chrétien goes a drastic step further. No longer does a knightly hero meet a wild man, as in *Yvain*, but now a knight, the leader of the group (Wolfram's Karnahkarnanz), meets a wild man, who is in fact the hero Perceval in the uncourtly wilderness of the forest. Perceval may not be described in all the details of ugliness lavished upon the wild man in *Yvain*, for his beauty protects him from such a fate,[3] but we are left in no doubt about his wild uncouthness (e.g. 242: '*Sire, sachiez bien antreset/Que Galois sont tuit par nature/Plus fol que bestes an pasture:/Cist est aussi come une beste*').[4] In appearance and behaviour there is a wide gulf between the knightly leader and the wild boy who encounters him, but Chrétien brings the two close enough together for the possibility of a comparison when he adds the detail that this leader was made a knight by King Arthur only five days ago.[5] Since it will be only a matter of days before Perceval, in his own

[1] See above, p. 83.
[2] On the parallel situations in *Yvain* and *Perceval* see Emmel, *Formprobleme*, pp. 50f.
[3] On this motif in Wolfram's *Parzival* see Hahn, *Schönheit*, pp. 203ff. and Johnson, *Beauty*, pp. 273ff.
[4] Cf. also 975 (*vaslet sauvage*) and 1299 (*Tant est nices et bestïaus*).
[5] *Perceval* 288ff.

rough and ready manner, acquires chivalry from Arthur,[1] we may regard these two as approximately of the same age and see in the knight a courtly counterpart to Perceval, a picture of what he would have been at this moment if he had not been deprived of the social advantages of his birth.[2] This encounter between a newly dubbed knight and the wild boy is not merely a juxtaposition of two modes of life, it confronts Perceval with a counterpart of himself, a projection of his own potentialities. When Perceval, unable to comprehend the magnificence of the knight's equipment, stupidly asks him: '*Fustes vos einsi nez?*' (282), this is not simply comic,[3] it is pointedly ironic. In the sense in which Perceval means his question the knight was *not* born wearing such equipment, but in another sense it is Perceval himself who was born to this station in life and has been deprived of his birthright. In all this Chrétien's irony tells against Perceval and the ludicrous contrast he presents with the splendour of knighthood, but again the subsequent narrative turns the tables by showing us how the hero's initial distance from courtly and chivalric ideals is the means by which he is later able to surpass an exclusively Arthurian ideal and rise to the heights of Grail-kingship.[4] If ultimately the chivalry represented by the knightly leader in this scene is transcended by Perceval, it is certainly not rejected as worthless.

The relationship between characters (*Gottfried*)

For examples of structural irony of this type in Gottfried's *Tristan* I shall confine myself to the relationship between the lovers and Marke's followers, between Tristan and Gandin, and between Tristan and Isold. In these cases it is not so much what is said or done as the tacit pattern of the relationship, usually involving a reversal of what was expected, which constitutes an ironic commentary on events.

As regards the lovers and Marke's courtiers, we find this reversal of expectations in the mutual battle of wits leading to the

---

[1] Cf. Weigand, *Parzival*, pp. 21f.
[2] This point has been made by Haidu, *Distance*, p. 125, whom I follow here.
[3] As is suggested by Haidu, *ibid.*
[4] See above, pp. 318f.

lovers turning the tables on their adversaries. It is ironic in this sense that the barons of Marke's court, termed his counsellors (8635: *den rat von Curnewale*), should be depicted at their wits' end by the same word *rat* when, caught in the trap which they had laid for Tristan, they are shown derisively as knowing no way out of their dilemma (8643: *sin kunden umbe ir eigen leben|in selben keinen rat gegeben:|si rieten her, si rieten hin|und enkunden nie nicht under in|geraten, daz in töhte|und daz rat heizen möhte*). There is an obvious irony in counsellors, ready to advise the ruler, having no advice to give themselves.[1] This can only be said to arise from their relationship with Tristan when we recall that the advice which they had previously lavished on Marke was a concealed attack on his favourite whom they hoped to put out of action[2] and that their dilemma is the result of Tristan's skilled counter-move.[3] If these professional advisers are shown as intellectually bankrupt when it comes to advice for themselves, this is because of the intrigue which they have clumsily conducted against Tristan's interests as Marke's heir and beneficiary.

In another reversal of the position in which we are accustomed to see these scheming courtiers the king himself is more closely involved. This example concerns his discovery of the lovers asleep in the orchard after their love-making. Again there is an obvious irony in the husband knowing what he had long tried to find out for certain, but now struck down[4] by the enormity of his knowledge (18222: *ern wande niht, er weste:|des er da vor ie hæte gert,|des was er alles do gewert.|entriuwen ez ist aber min wan,|im hæte do vil baz getan|ein wænen danne ein wizzen*). But Gottfried takes this further by having Marke, irresolute in the face of certainty, seek out his counsellors as witnesses without telling them that he has just been a witness himself. The weakness behind such embarrassment in a ruler exacts its price from him, for when Marke, accompanied by his counsellors, returns to the orchard from which Tristan has meanwhile escaped, he now has to face the open criticism of his court for suspecting his wife without due cause (18378: '*herre*' *sprachen si* '*hier an|missetuot ir harte sere,|*

[1] See above, p. 276.
[2] Cf. their description as *Markes ratman* (8578) in the midst of their scheming.
[3] How calculated his actions are is later revealed in 8920ff.
[4] Cf. 18219: *er was aber ein verrihter man.*

iuwer wîp und iuwer ere/daz ir diu ze also maneger zit/ziehende unde zogende sit/ze lasterlicher inziht/gar ane not und umbe niht'). With this we reach a second level of irony in this episode. Through the force of circumstances these counsellors who were jealous of Tristan's position as Marke's favourite and had nothing but evil to suggest about his relationship with Marke's consort now defend the lovers against what they can only regard as an unjust calumny, and in a situation which, if they knew the facts, cryingly justified their own earlier accusations.[1]

If we stand back from detailed examples, however, and pay regard to the general course of events concerning the lovers' relationship with Marke's courtiers a similar structural irony is still evident.[2] Marke's counsellors conceive their original plan to send Tristan to certain death in Ireland out of jealousy, but this plot is thwarted by their opponent's perspicacity and skilful exploitation of circumstances to bring about the seemingly impossible. But in another sense, and certainly not as a result of the courtiers' (or even Tristan's) superior skill, events take over and lead to the result which the courtiers had wished for. Isold may not fit into their pattern for, instead of seeing in Tristan a favoured nephew and therefore her natural rival at court, she is tied irrevocably to him. But Marke, whom the barons had previously tried in vain to separate from his favourite, is now driven in this direction by their new antagonism as husband and lover. Ultimately, therefore, the king's counsellors are granted what they set their hearts upon, they live to witness the breach between uncle and nephew, but this is brought about not by any successful scheming on their part, but by events taking charge and turning full circle. Tristan's initial superiority to these counsellors is eventually converted into a position of exposed inferiority, because events more powerful than either party have driven them this far.

Tristan's encounter with Gandin is based on structural irony to the extent that the deception by which he wins back the abducted Isold is a reversal of the trick by which Gandin won her from Marke in the first place.[3] To make this parallel clear

---

[1] See Combridge, *Recht*, p. 131 and Hollandt, *Hauptgestalten*, p. 73.
[2] Cf. Gruenter, *Euphorion* 58 (1964), 128.
[3] On this episode see Hollandt, *Hauptgestalten*, pp. 103ff. and Jackson, *Anatomy*, pp. 103ff.

details are inserted whose purpose is to show how far Tristan's plan is a mirror image of what his opponent has just carried out at Marke's court. When Tristan, before approaching the abductor he is pursuing, ties up his horse, puts aside his sword and keeps only his musical instrument with him (13 282: ... *und kerte do mit listen abe/zeinem busche und bant da vaste/sin ors zuo zeinem aste./sin swert daz hancter dar an;/mit siner harpfen lief er dan*), this is an indication that he proposes to win back Isold by his artistry and not by any knightly exploit, but also that he is setting about this in the same way as his adversary, for Gandin had first arrived at Marke's court without knightly weapons and equipped only with his musical instrument (13 113: *der kam schone gecleit/mit ritterlicher schonheit/und mit herlichen siten/al eine uf Markes hof geriten/ane schilt und ane sper./über sinen rucke vuorte er/eine rotten...*).[1] On approaching Gandin Tristan says that he has heard that he is Irish (this is how Gandin had been presented to Marke, 13 107) and pretends that he too comes from Ireland (13 301: *man sagete mir an dirre zit,/daz ir von Irlande sit:/herre, dannen bin ouch ich*). This detail serves the practical purpose of allowing Tristan to linger long enough to carry out his plan and is made feasible by his command of languages, but it also strengthens the parallel between these two contestants. Without the narrator making any explicit comment we can see that the parallel extends further, for Gandin was introduced not merely as an Irishman arriving with his musical instrument, but also as a man in love with Isold who had come only with this in mind (13 125: ... *und gruozte, alse er solde,/ Marken unde Isolde;/der ritter unde der amis/was er gewesen manege wis/ und ouch ze manegem male/und kam ze Curnewale/durch ir willen von Irlant*). We know, but not Gandin, that Tristan can more fittingly be described as Isold's lover and that this is why he has followed the Irishman to the shore.

So far, the initiative in establishing this parallel has come entirely from Tristan (as a musician, as an 'Irishman', and as Isold's lover). At this point Gandin, whose ignorance of the situation has been made clear by the last two points, unwittingly puts his

---

[1] Gandin is admittedly ready to defend what he regards as his right to Isold by knightly combat (13 231ff.), but he has established this right by other means. Because of Tristan's temporary absence, there is no one to accept his challenge, neither at court (13 243ff.) nor Marke himself (13 249f.).

head into the noose by requesting Tristan to play his harp in an attempt to console the weeping Isold, offering as a reward the richest garment in his pavilion (13307: '*geselle, daz gelobe ich dir.*/ *nu sitze nider, harphe mir:/getrœstest du die vrouwen min,/dazs ir weinen lazet sin,/ich gibe dir dallerbesten wat,/die disiu pavilune hat*'). Without realising it Gandin has now set the scene for a repeat performance of the deception at Marke's court,[1] but in the converse sense, since it is now Gandin who is the patron rashly offering an indeterminate reward and Tristan who can exploit the situation for his own ends. How Tristan proposes to do this is made clear by the emphasis given to the finest garment as a fitting reward, for Gandin reverts to this explicitly a second time (13353ff.) and in general terms a third time (13406). Just as Gandin had taken Marke's general offer of reward in the very particular sense of Isold, so does Tristan understand by the finest garment promised nothing other than Isold, as he makes clear in his final jeering words to his outwitted adversary (13420ff.). The parallels between Gandin and Tristan extend right through this episode and go further than Gandin realises. Their function is to turn the tables on him by showing him caught by a trick which he has just successfully employed himself (13412ff.).

Gandin's success in cheating Marke rested on his equating the offer of a reward with Isold. It is in regarding a woman as an object to be exchanged between two men as the result of a wager that he commits his greatest offence in the poet's eyes, one which reduces an otherwise courteous and gifted knight to the level of the Irish steward.[2] But the target of Gottfried's structural irony is not Gandin alone. It takes two people to make a wager, so that, in handing his wife over as a reward, as an object, Marke proves himself guilty of the same offence.[3] The criticism latent in Tristan's final mockery of Gandin is therefore as much applicable to the weak and compliant Marke as to the person actually addressed. One last extension of this criticism is however *not* justified, for we cannot argue that Tristan, in regarding Isold as his reward

---

[1] Cf. Marke's equally imprudent words in 13192ff.

[2] On this aspect of the Irish steward, see above, pp. 116ff.

[3] That this is true of Marke from the beginning of his relationship with Isold is suggested by his offence on the wedding night in seeing no difference between Isold and Brangæne, between *golt* and *messinc* (12600ff.).

from Gandin and in equating her with a garment, is tarred with the same brush as husband and rival. For him this equation is a means to an end, a way to teach Gandin a lesson and, by freeing Isold from her abductor, to abolish her status as an object of exchange. His scornful distance from the original wager and both participants is brought out by his mockery of Gandin in hoisting him with his own petard[1] and also by the cool challenge he offers Marke on returning with Isold to his court.

His words follow the naïveté of the narrator in pretending ignorance whether the lovers sought solace together before they returned to the court (13432ff.)[2] and have to be read in this light (13441: *'herre' sprach er 'wizze crist,/so lieb als iu diu künegin ist,/ so ist ez ein michel unsin,/daz ir si gebet so lihte hin/durch harpfen oder durch rotten./ez mac diu werlt wol spotten:/wer gesach ie mere künigin/ durch rottenspil gemeine sin?/her nach so bewaret daz/und hüetet miner vrouwen baz!'*). These words are a sharp reprimand for the king's recent folly, but also an impudent concealed challenge for the future. Outwardly these lines refer to the Gandin episode they conclude, but they reveal a dimension of this episode which we, not Marke, have been allowed to glimpse. In criticising Marke for frivolously giving his wife as a prize for a musical performance Tristan refers not merely to Gandin's *rotte* but to his own harp (13445: *durch harpfen oder durch rotten*).[3] With a victor's superiority he takes the liberty of mocking at Marke's compliancy towards Gandin and also towards Tristan himself. In this light Tristan's final words jeer at Marke's weakness in face of Gandin, but also convey a hidden threat for the future, challenging him to do what he can in surveillance of his wife and expressing the lover's confidence that he will find a means to outwit him.[4]

[1] 13420ff.
[2] Cf. Gruenter, *Euphorion* 55 (1961), 386 and 388; Hahn, *Raum*, p. 28.
[3] Attention has been drawn to this by Tax, *Wort*, p. 81.
[4] What Tax sees as an 'Anspielung auf die *huote*' applies equally to Gandin *and* to Tristan, although Marke cannot realise this. Tristan's rashness in concealing a challenge behind such ambiguity has much in common with Flamenca's proposal of an oath to Archimbaut, likewise concerned with surveillance (6685ff.). In both cases the outright mocking of the outwitted husband has much in common with the fabliau.

Professor Ross also suggests an equivocation in *miner vrouwen* (13450), understood by Marke as a polite form of address ('my lady'), but possibly meant by Tristan also as the equivalent of Provençal *midons* ('my mistress').

This last example has shown us Tristan's superiority as a lover
to both Marke and Gandin, but it is part of the complexity of
Gottfried's romance that he also affords us a view of Tristan in
his relationship with Isold herself, in which his potential shortcomings become apparent. Again it is structural irony which
shows up the difference between the two. Although there are
faint hints of Tristan's failings before the period of his banishment
from Cornwall,[1] it is at this stage (as we have seen with regard to
chivalry and courtesy)[2] that his inability to measure up to the
poet's ideal and to Isold herself becomes most obvious. Tristan
plays with fire in his preoccupation with the second Isold, his
approaches by song and music (19188ff.) have a bearing on the
ideal of courtesy,[3] but they also have a structural part to play in
reminding us that Tristan, in his rôle as Tantris, had first
approached Isold of Ireland in the same way. In both instances
love (or erotic stimulation) is the result, but these two episodes
are not simply another example of the duplication of motifs to
be found in the *Tristan* story. Their function extends beyond this,
for a repetition of Tristan's experience with Isold of Ireland,
culminating in the love-grotto, with another woman (particularly when this second relationship is not fully reciprocal)[4] can
only mean a falling-off from an earlier ideal. The very presence
of this parallel implies an adverse judgment on Tristan's playing
with the second Isold's feelings.

That Tristan's stay at the court of Karke is meant to suffer by
such a comparison can be confirmed by a significant detail. In
the course of the debate with himself, in which he uses sophistry
to convince himself that the distant Isold is enjoying her married
life with Marke so that her former lover is now morally free to
seek consolation elsewhere, Tristan pulls himself up, recognises
his argument as a shabby rationalisation and realises that Isold
cannot love anyone but himself (19143ff.). At this moment of
insight into his own motives Tristan is struck by the contrast
between Isold's steadfastness and his vacillations, which is why

[1] Cf. Fromm, *DVjs* 28 (1954), 133.
[2] See above, pp. 58, 73f. and 297f.
[3] Cf. 19182: *doch begienger sine höfscheit.*
[4] Cf. 19215ff. and especially 19275ff. with the stress on the ambiguity of the name Isold.

he begins his self-criticism with a confession of disloyalty (19142: *ich ungetriuwer, waz tuon ich?*). So far, this episode stresses Tristan's decline from his former position as lover, the gap which begins to open in the unity of the couple, the difference between Tristan and his mistress.

Yet this gap is apparently closed when we recall that the words with which Tristan accuses himself of disloyalty repeat, almost literally, words with which Isold had once reproached herself.[1] Despite their separation and Tristan's vacillations, the lovers could still be seen as one in their reaction to circumstances. Isold's self-accusation comes in the episode of the magic dog Petitcreiu, sent to her as a gift by her absent lover because of its ability to charm away all grief. She realises that such freedom from care would be bought at the price of Tristan's own unhappiness and regards the mere contemplation of this possibility as a betrayal of the unity of their love (16368: *ohi ohi! und vröuwe ich mich,/wie tuon ich ungetriuwe so?*). Like Tristan, Isold catches herself here at a moment of temptation and condemns herself for even pausing to consider it. At this point we might concede a structural affinity between these situations, brought out by the verbal parallel, but still object that, because what is suggested is the unity of experience of the lovers, it would be wrong to label this an example of structural irony.

The discrepancy we need if we are to talk of irony emerges if we compare these two episodes more closely. Tristan's moment of self-awareness is only a passing one, his insight does not last long enough to prevent him from relapsing into his earlier unworthy suspicions and finding a justification for the betrayal to which his heart has already given its assent. He really does pass judgment on himself when, in a moment of lucidity, he describes himself as *ich ungetriuwer*. The position is quite different with Isold. She converts her moment of insight into a lasting condition by tearing off the dog's bell and destroying its magic power (16388ff.), sacrificing a happiness which, because of its onesidedness, she sees as no true happiness. Her self-accusation is the actual demonstration of her unshakable loyalty, an assessment which is shared by the narrator in describing her, when she

---

[1] Hahn, *Raum*, p. 124.

first receives the gift, as *diu getriuwe künigin* (16359) and at the close of the episode as *diu getriuwe stæte senedærin* (16400). In view of this difference, lurking beneath the apparent similarity between their positions, I suggest that we have here not just a structural parallel, but structural irony.

The function of Gawein

Structural irony can also underlie the possibility, from Chrétien's *Yvain* on, of plotting the hero's progress by measuring him in combat against Gauvain, the paragon of Arthurian chivalry. What I have in mind is neither the fact that the figure of Gauvain and therewith the criterion of chivalry are brought somewhat into discredit[1] nor the way in which Wolfram's Parzival even surpasses Gawan,[2] but rather what happens, as in *Sir Gawain*, when Gawain is the hero of a romance and, as it were, now has to be compared with himself if we are to judge his position. The English romance disappoints expectations by devoting itself to a hero who turns out to be all too human in his failure. There are other romances in which Gawain may fail in his quest (with Wolfram he is unsuccessful in gaining access to the Grail-castle), but this is mitigated by the fact that Gawan is not the hero of Wolfram's work, so that his failure in this respect acts as a foil to Parzival's success (just as his success elsewhere sets off the hero's fumbling.) With *Sir Gawain*, however, the position is different. Gawain is the only hero, so that his failure strikes us with a force absent from *Parzival*, pressing upon us the disturbing question whether, if even Gawain be flawed, any knight can attain to perfect chivalry. The irony of Gawain's position is that at the close of the work he returns to Arthur's court and recounts his adventures, culminating in his failure in the test. His position is reminiscent of Calogrenant's at the beginning of *Yvain*, but appearances can no longer be saved by the English poet as by his predecessors. With him Gawain's shortcoming is the central theme of the work and no mere foil to his hero's success, his work closes on a note of imperfection, whilst Calogrenant's lack of

---

[1] Cf. Frappier, *Yvain*, pp. 140ff. and *Graal*, p. 217.
[2] See Wynn, *PBB* (T) 84 (1962), 168ff. on the combat between these two.

success could be forgotten once Yvain dominated the stage. When Gawain encounters a setback as the central figure of a romance, the critical implications are far more serious than when the same happens to him in a less dominant position.

If Yvain establishes his prowess by measuring up to the standard represented by Gauvain and Parzival proves himself by going beyond his Arthurian counterpart, whilst the English hero fails in his test, this suggests that here Gawain is being measured against Gawain, but is now found wanting. There are indeed a number of well placed remarks where doubt is expressed whether he is the renowned Gawain.[1] This doubt is first voiced by the lady towards the end of the first bedroom scene (1291: *And as ho stod, ho stonyed hym wyth ful stor wordez:/'Now he þat spedez vche speche þis disport zelde yow!/Bot þat ze be Gawan, hit gotz in mynde'*) and again when she greets him on the second occasion (1481: *Sir, zif ze be Wawen, wonder me þynkkez*). The point of these remarks is obvious, for by rebuking Gawain for failing to live up to his literary reputation as a lady's man she hopes to make it more difficult for him to resist temptation. In repudiating her conception of courtesy as polite adultery Gawain rejects for himself the image attached to him in the conventional romance.[2] To this extent we can say that the hero is here measured against the conventional figure of Gawain and emerges successfully from the test.

This is still only part of the story, for the complexity of the temptation-scenes lies in the subtle stratagem by which the lady, defeated on the erotic front and apparently conceding failure, launches an attack on another front, in which she is successful, by appealing to Gawain's primitive love of life in offering him a magic girdle as protection which, because he does not admit to having received it, involves him in disloyalty towards his host. In view of this shift of emphasis it is significant that when Gawain's identity is next questioned it comes not as a doubt, but as a statement of fact made by the Green Knight at the moment of Gawain's testing (2270: '*þou art not Gawayn*', quoþ þe gome,

---

[1] These are briefly referred to, but in a different context, by Clark, *MÆ* 40 (1971), 14. See also Benson, *Art*, pp. 220ff.

[2] See Brewer, *Courtesy*, p. 75.

'*þat is so goud halden*').[1] It is bitterly ironic that Gawain should show no trust in the protective power of the girdle he has acquired and should shrink in anticipation of the blow (it is this which calls forth these words). But the Green Knight is stating the truth. The man who has betrayed his host and concealed the girdle beneath his armour is no longer the perfect Gawain presented to us at the beginning (633: *Gawan watz for gode knawen, and as golde pured*). It is now borne in upon us that Gawain has been measured against his ideal self on a second narrative level and that here he has been found wanting. A closer reading reveals an ultimate discrepancy between the hero and the conventional ideal picture of Gawain, just as Gottfried led us to acknowledge at length the force of the difference between Tristan and Isold.

The relationship between characters (Chaucer)

For a last example of structural irony operating between two characters I turn to *Troilus and Criseyde*, to the relationship between Troilus and Pandarus where each figure relativises the other so that the truth of the work is to be found in neither in isolation. These ironies have been well analysed by Muscatine.[2] What effects can be achieved by such a juxtaposition may be seen when Troilus and Pandarus express their different attitudes to the same situation. Corresponding to the conjunction of high poetry with a typical fabliau-situation in Book III we find these two adopting an elevated lyrical or down-to-earth colloquial style respectively. Troilus sees himself as the timorous lover, praying for assistance from Venus (III 705: '*Now seint Venus, thow me grace sende,*/ *Quod Troilus, 'for nevere yit no nede/Hadde ich or now, ne halvendel the drede*'), but this is immediately followed by the shrewd practicality of Pandarus (III 708: *Quod Pandarus: 'ne drede the nevere a del,*/ *For it shal be right as thow wolt desire;/so thryve I, this nyght shal I make it wel,/Or casten al the gruwel in the fire*').[3]

Even more telling is the contrast at another emotional high-point, where these two are waiting by the walls of Troy for the return of Criseyde so confidently expected by Troilus within the

---

[1] Cf. Benson, *Art*, p. 224 and Burrow, *Reading*, p. 133.
[2] Muscatine, *Chaucer*, pp. 132ff.   [3] *Ibid.*, p. 149.

time limit agreed upon. His lover's expectancy converts hope into reality and joyfully he announces that he already sees Criseyde approaching (V 1158: *Have here my trouthe, I se hire! yond she is!/ Heve up thyn eyen, man! maistow nat se?*). To this wishful thinking his companion replies with a very realistic vision (V 1160: *Pandare answerde: 'nay, so mote I the!/Al wrong, by god; what seistow, man? where arte?/That I se yond nys but a fare-carte'*).[1] The prosaic cart sums up the reality of Pandarus's world, whilst Troilus's ability to live on visions is a measure of his divorce from the facts around him. Yet from this structural relationship it would be wrong to conclude that Pandarus's realism is presented as superior to the make-believe element in Troilus's world, for even his practicality can offer Troilus no help at the end and his final words point to this bankruptcy (V1743: *'I kan no more seye'*). Nor is Chaucer ready to place Troilus's idealism, resting on an equally blinkered view of the world, above Pandarus's realism. Rather it is the case 'that each sets off and questions, enhances, and detracts from, the values represented by the other. Neither cancels the other arithmetically. This is possible because both represent positive values; their relationship produces irony not neutrality.'[2] When Muscatine later talks of 'the double view of the same situation'[3] and sees it as conducive to irony, a questioning of the simple point of view which would otherwise be taken for granted, he is in fact commenting on more than Chaucer's romance. This observation describes the structural irony, based on the relationship between two different characters, which is utilised in the romance from its beginnings with Chrétien.

The relationship between scenes (Gottfried)

This type of irony can govern the relationship between two individuals, but also between two scenes. In fact, it is often difficult to make any clearcut distinction between the two. Does Gottfried see the encounter between Tristan and Gandin as a turning of the tables in only one episode or does it represent a juxtaposition of two scenes in which first Gandin, and then Tristan is the victor? The border between these two types of

[1] *Ibid.*, pp. 146f.   [2] *Ibid.*, p. 139.   [3] *Ibid.*, p. 153.

structural irony may be uncertain whenever one scene, juxtaposed with another, follows on it immediately in the narrative, but the position is more clear-cut when the structural irony ties together two widely separated scenes. This can be shown in the case of Gottfried's Tristan and Gandin, not by comparing them in what may or may not be the one scene, but rather by comparing their joint relationship at this stage with two other episodes, one preceding it (Tristan and the Irish steward) and one following it (Tristan and Duke Gilan). Between these three scenes in which Tristan is involved structural irony can be detected.[1]

This is clear first because of the general functional similarity between Gandin and the Irish steward. Each figure, by exercising trickery, comes near to obtaining a prize which would otherwise never have come his way. In each episode what is discussed is the relationship between service and reward (the steward claims a reward for a service which he has not rendered, whilst the reward claimed by Gandin stands in no sensible proportion to his service). In each episode the prize is Isold and the initially successful, but ultimately unsuccessful deceiver is confronted with Tristan, to whom success ultimately falls. In discussing the connection between these two scenes Hollandt has observed that in Gottfried's work the justification of a deception can be inferred from its success or failure,[2] so that Tristan's intentions must be judged quite differently from those of his adversary. If these two scenes illustrate a correlation between Tristan's good intentions and his success (and, in his opponents, between unworthy aims and failure), this possesses a wider significance for Gottfried's work as a whole. Although his critical distance from chivalry means that he saw through the make-believe element in the conventional romance,[3] where the hero is infallibly successful, Gottfried is prepared to adopt the same unrealistic technique in depicting two episodes in the relationship between Tristan and Isold. He therefore realistically rejects a make-believe motif when, as with Hartmann, it is applied to chivalry, but makes use of it himself in the depiction of love.

[1] The possibility of comparing these scenes has been suggested by Hollandt, *Hauptgestalten*, pp. 106ff.   [2] *Ibid.*, p. 107.   [3] See above, pp. 54f. and 56ff.

How inessential chivalry is in these two scenes can be shown by the fact that, although Tristan disposes of the Irish steward's claims by his victory in the dragon combat, his knightly equipment is expressly laid aside for his encounter with Gandin. What counts is not Tristan as the chivalric hero of a romance, but the truth that as a lover (potential or actual) his intentions command respect – this is why he is granted success over less worthy opponents. We have seen why Tristan's intentions are worthy ones in the Gandin episode, for he sets Isold free from the status of being the object of a wager to which both Gandin and Marke reduced her. Much the same is true of the dragon episode, for here it is the steward who claims Isold as his due reward.[1] Tristan, if he receives Isold as the reward for his victory, does so not for himself, but in the name of Marke, whose relationship with Isold starts even here on an impersonal note.[2] How far Tristan stands aloof from such traffic in women is suggested by a detail. When the grateful queen of Ireland makes him an open promise (9550ff.), similar to Marke's later offer to Gandin, Tristan refuses to act like a Gandin in demanding her daughter.[3] The point of both these scenes is to establish his superiority (not as a knight) to each of his adversaries, and also to Marke, and thereby to justify the success that befalls him.

The position is similar, and yet different, in the episode in which Tristan gains the magic dog Petitcreiu from Duke Gilan, intending it as a gift to console Isold during his absence. The lover's attitude here can be compared with Gandin's at Marke's court. Just as his earlier rival had come to this court hoping to abduct Isold, so does Tristan see in the oppression of Gilan's territory by the giant Urgan a means of winning from him his most cherished possession in order to present it to his mistress.

[1] Just as in the Gandin episode blame attaches to the Irish knight and to Marke (see above, pp. 335f.), so is the Irish king also to blame in this episode for ever putting his daughter up as a reward for a man like the steward to claim.

[2] Gottfried depicts details of contemporary feudal marriage practice in his work, but suggests his attitude to it by depicting it in Marke's marriage in particular.

[3] Cf. Hollandt, *Hauptgestalten*, pp. 107f. Désilles-Busch, *Don*, pp. 54ff., has briefly discussed a similar occasion in Chrétien's *Cligès* where Alexander shows comparable sensitivity in refusing to ask for the hand of Soredamors when his victory means that he may choose what reward he will. His refusal stems from a reluctance to disregard her feelings and wishes (2193f.), to treat her as an object and not as a person.

Like Gandin, Tristan knows how to manœuvre the duke into making the rash promise on which his plan depends (15940: '*ob ich iuch des benemen kan/und iu gehilfe in kurzer zit,/daz ir des zinses ledic sit,/die wile ir iemer sult geleben:/waz welt ir mir ze lone geben?'/'entriuwen herre' sprach Gilan/'ich gibe iu gerne, swaz ich han*'). It is the nature of Tristan's plan of deception (the particular object on which he has set his heart) which makes him demand a reward from the beginning. This draws him closer to Gandin's approach to Marke (requested to play his instrument, he replies, 13190: '*herre, ine wil,/ine wizze danne umbe waz*') and shows up the difference from his earlier situation at Dublin, where it had been the queen who made the first move in offering a reward.

One might find an excuse for Tristan's self-centredness in exploiting Gilan's quandary in that his combat with the giant (unlike Gandin's musical performance) really amounts to an apposite agreement between service and reward, what he asks for is an animal and not a human being, and Tristan wishes Petitcreiu not for himself, but as a gift to Isold. Yet even when allowances are made there remains something coldly calculating in Tristan's plot to deprive someone who had shown him kindness and friendship (15775ff.) of his most cherished possession (16250ff.). Even the fact that Tristan acts in this way to obtain a gift to console Isold is no justification, for her reaction to the gift (she destroys the magic of the dog's bell rather than enjoy happiness when Tristan does not) proclaims her loyalty. In even expecting that she could welcome this gift Tristan is imputing to his mistress the less than perfect *triuwe* which he later displays at Karke.[1] We may see in his behaviour on this occasion a first indication of the lover's subsequent decline to a level lower than his mistress, and it is the function of structural irony to alert us by inviting us to compare his action in this scene with his different position in earlier scenes.

Batts has drawn attention to another example,[2] the impression we are given of Marke's court from two different points of view. What we are told of Riwalin going to Cornwall suggests that this

---

[1] Jackson, *Anatomy*, p. 119, correctly observes of Isold at this stage that she 'is wiser in the nature of true love' than Tristan.
[2] Batts, *Gottfried*, pp. 49f.

court had a reputation for courtesy, whilst from Tristan's reception we infer that life there lacked the style and polish he brought with him. This point can be taken further if, like Jackson,[1] we pay more regard to Marke's court[2] than to the difference between the two youths who come there. What is now highlighted by these two different impressions is the ambivalence of this court, a point which again takes up the irony of courtly values and of the court considered in the last chapter. When the youthful, exuberant and superficial Riwalin comes to Marke's court he has just experienced the brutalities of feudal warfare with Morgan and is therefore psychologically ready to appreciate the hedonistic and educative advantages of a renowned court. He is accordingly attracted by Marke's reputation for courtesy (420: *er hæte vil gehœret sagen,/wie höfsch und wie erbære/der junge künic wære/von Curnewale Marke,/des ere wuohs do starke*) and by the recognition that he needs to refine his own manners (455: *alda dahter beliben,/ ein jar mit ime vertriben/und von im werden tugenthaft/und lernen niuwan ritterschaft/und ebenen sine site baz*). Nor is Riwalin disappointed in his expectations (494: *diz liebet ime den hovesite./er dahte dicke wider sich:/'binamen got selbe der hat mich/ze diseme lantgesinde braht!/min sælde hat mich wol bedaht:/swaz ich von Markes tugenden ie/gehorte sagen, deist allez hie./sin leben daz ist höfsch unde guot'*). What Riwalin expects to find he does find, and he is so taken up with this that he has no eyes for anything else.

A very different picture of this same court is presented to us when Tristan goes there. What the narrator previously said of Marke's power and wealth, the material basis of courtly splendour (entrusted with overlordship over *alle künegelin* of the Saxons, 425ff., he enjoys greater renown than his neighbours, 450ff.), is shown in a very different light when Marke's political position is looked at from another point of view, with an eye to the Irish rather than to the Saxons. We are invited to do this when Tristan is at his uncle's court, for the appearance of Morolt demanding tribute informs us belatedly that there are definite limits set to Marke's regal authority and that in his youth he had been sub-

---

[1] Jackson, *Anatomy*, pp. 145f.
[2] Batts comes close to this (*op. cit.*, p. 50: 'This obviously reflects, to some degree, on the character of the King') without going any further.

jected to a humiliating tribute-agreement with Gurmun. Riwalin's impression of Marke's authority and wealth is only part of the picture, soon corrected by what we are shown from Tristan's point of view.

If it be argued that Marke's regal weakness is called for at this point to motivate the plot (to account for Morolt and thus to take Tristan to Ireland), we can weaken the force of this by pointing out that Marke's weakness is also stressed in quite a different way by the contrast between Riwalin's and Tristan's experience of his court. When he arrives there Riwalin's personal encounter is confined to two individuals, Blanscheflur and Marke. Other members of the court do not cross his horizon, the court is for him the convenient backcloth to a springtime festival and to his first experience of love. It is an ideal picture of a court, for this is how the youthful hedonist conceives the court, at least until he and we are reminded of reality when invasion threatens.[1] Again, Tristan's experience is quite different. We are shown his initial popularity with court and ruler, because this acts as a foil to the jealousy which the court soon feels for his attainments and the favours bestowed on him. From Tristan's point of view the anonymous collective of the court is dangerously particularised in the shape of jealous barons, a plotting Marjodo and a scheming Melot; it is with these creatures of the court that power ultimately rests.[2] Marke is a weakling of a ruler both externally and internally, but Riwalin sees nothing of this because he is not concerned with it, outward brilliance suffices for him. The parallel between these two arrivals at court, ultimately amounting to a discrepancy between them, shows up the difference between father and son, but also questions how far Riwalin's judgment of the court by its external brilliance corresponds to reality.

[1] As Jackson points out, *op. cit.*, p. 146, it is significantly this intrusion of the real world which leads to the conception of Tristan.
[2] This situation at Marke's court resembles Walter Map's description of the para-doxical position at the court of Henry II, where the ruler is at the mercy of his servants: *Certe domus omnis unum habet seruum et plures dominos; quod qui preest seruit omnibus; quibus seruitur domini uidentur* (quoted by Uhlig, *Hofkritik*, p. 109).

The relationship between scenes (Chrétien and Wolfram)

A juxtaposition of scenes, where one calls the other into question, has also been shown,[1] spread over a number of scenes, as the organising principle behind the start of Chrétien's *Perceval*. Each scene is presented to us as seemingly complete and meaningful in itself, but is then revealed as having a very different aspect, containing implications other than what we first expected. This is true from the opening, for if the work starts, almost like a lyric poem, with a 'Natureingang' in which the beauty of birdsong is stressed,[2] this is because of the effective contrast presented in the crashing of armour by the knights Perceval hears approaching. This contrast is not fortuitous. It sums up in acoustic terms the fact that this encounter is between two different worlds, between the wilderness and chivalry, a clash later shown to be informed by dramatic irony of a very bitter kind, since it is this encounter that Perceval's mother had sought to prevent.[3] But the speed of events as the widowed mother's defences come tumbling down does not allow us to stay content with this contrast, since it is soon followed by another, between the sound of the knights' armour, conveying the threat of demons to the inexperienced boy, and the brilliant sight of their shining equipment, arousing admiration and the equally naïve idea that these must be the angels of whom his mother has told him (138: *Ce sont ange que je voi ci*).[4] Again, this contrast is meaningful. It provides a bridge between Perceval's contentment with the wilderness up to now and his eagerness for chivalry, but his admiring equation of these knights with angels also has to be placed against the bitter disillusionment with which his mother later comments on his youthful enthusiasm (398: *Tu as veü, si con je croi,/Les anges don les ianz se plaingnent,/Qui ocient quanqu'il ataingnent*). The force of this contrast is to show the knights and what they stand for from two different points of view, as angels and as angels of death, each adequate to the experience of the person in question.

---

[1] Haidu, *Distance*, pp. 118ff., especially p. 128.
[2] Cf. 71f. and 88f.
[3] See below for the difference between Chrétien and Wolfram in the employment of irony in this scene.
[4] Cf. also 142ff.

This second contrast is replaced by a third, between the brilliance of the knight's armour and the boy's ignorance, as Perceval asks his importunate questions, prompted by the magnificence of what he sees for the first time. The discrepancy is again no fortuitous one, for it rests on Perceval's *niceté* and the stirrings of innate chivalry, the struggle between which informs so much of the narrative.[1] This last antithesis has yielded, as the latest pole, the new fact of Perceval's ignorance, particularly in regard to chivalry. This now survives as one pole in the next antithesis. When Perceval returns to his mother with the news of what he has seen, her reaction, concentrated in her bitter words about knights as angels of death, but finding longer expression in an account of the loss of her position, two other sons and her husband because of knighthood, introduces a new contrast, between the boy's ignorant enthusiasm for knighthood and her grievous awareness of its cost in human suffering. These two aspects of chivalry are brought into juxtaposition by the ambiguity of the image of the angels, but also by the different messages conveyed by these two neighbouring scenes.

If we follow, as we are invited to, the order of the narrative rather than any chronological sequence, the last point reached in this domino-like series of antitheses, the cost of knighthood in terms of death and suffering, provides the one pole in the next contrast when we learn that the mother had hoped to preserve him from the knightly fate of his brothers and father by withdrawing into the wilderness (408ff.). This contrast between the deaths caused by chivalry and a wish for innocence is charged with irony, for at the time when we learn of this decision by Perceval's mother we know already that events have caught up with her and that she has failed. Chrétien's use of irony here differs from Wolfram's (in the German romance we know of Herzeloyde's decision from the beginning,[2] so that dramatic irony is already present in Parzival's encounter with the knights). But irony is still present in the French version, in the juxtaposition of the mother's decision with what has just been narrated.[3] Finally,

[1] See Haas, *Tumpheit*, pp. 308ff.   [2] Cf. Mergell, *Parzival*, pp. 17f.
[3] Chrétien heightens the effect of irony by abandoning the *ordo naturalis* in telling us of the mother's plan (in the form of her dialogue with Perceval) after it has just

even this innocence, precarious as we know it to be, calls forth its antithesis in the insensitive harshness with which the boy ignores his mother's grief and rides off in pursuit of his own concerns even though he sees her fall to the ground as he departs. That this is no chance qualification of Perceval's innocence is suggested by his behaviour in the following scene, his meeting with the damsel in the tent, for this encounter at which we are meant to laugh is also one in which Perceval heedlessly brings pain and grief to her. With that we may break off this analysis of Chrétien's technique of stringing scenes together so that one produces the material of the next, but with an ironic relationship between each pair of scenes in that the second shows an unsuspected aspect of its predecessor, turns it round and calls earlier assumptions into question.

Despite his manifold changes,[1] Wolfram has retained enough of the general pattern of Chrétien's opening for much of what has just been said to be applicable to the German version. Rather than follow through his narrative to establish the same point it would be more illuminating to consider one detail in the German narrative where Wolfram has made independent use of structural irony, linking two scenes by contrast, where Chrétien had not. My example concerns Parzival's encounter with Karnahkarnanz and what happens subsequently, first with Jeschute and then with Ither, when he departs eager to embrace this chivalric ideal. Wolfram has altered the boy's encounter with the knights by telling us more about the intention of Karnahkarnanz in riding out and also by mentioning, as the French poet had not, his knightly adversary and telling us what he is about.[2] Of the latter (and his companion) Parzival is told that he has proved himself little better than a robber-knight by abducting a woman (122,15: 'junchêrre, sâht ir für iuch varn/zwên ritter die sich niht bewarn/kunnen an ritterlîcher zunft?/sie ringent mit der nôtnunft/und sint an werdekeit verzagt:/sie füerent roubes eine magt'). Given this information, even Parzival cannot fail to see that the task of the knight in front of him is to set right this wrong. This is why he is reminded of what

met with failure. The clash between intention and circumstances is sharper than with Wolfram.

[1] On these see Mergell, *Parzival*, pp. 13ff.
[2] *Ibid.*, pp. 23f.

his mother had taught him about God's unfailing helpfulness (119,23ff.). Even though he goes laughably wrong in taking this knight to be a god, he has chanced upon the vital fact that, as with God, the quintessence of this knight's chivalry is helpfulness (122,21: *der knappe wânde, swaz er sprach,/er wære got, als im verjach/ frou Herzeloyd diu künegîn,/do s'im underschiet den liehten schîn./dô rief er lûte sunder spot/'nu hilf mir, hilferîcher got'*). Lest his audience prove more obtuse than his hero, Wolfram's narrator makes this point clear to them at the close of this episode when he omnisciently grants them a view of the near future denied to Parzival (125,11: *ez was Meljahkanz./den ergâhte Karnahkarnanz,/mit strîte er im die frouwen nam:/diu was dâ vor an fröuden lam./sie hiez Imâne von der Beâfontâne*).

We should realise what Wolfram has achieved by such additions to Chrétien's account. He has introduced Parzival to knighthood in this scene, but has confronted him at the beginning of his wanderings with the two possibilities latent in that calling, the exercise of brutal, selfish violence and an altruistic service of others (the presence of these two possibilities means that Wolfram has already anticipated a negative view of knighthood which, with Chrétien, is voiced explicitly only when Perceval returns to his mother).[1] In face of these two possibilities we need not hesitate in deciding which exercises the greater appeal on Parzival in his eagerness to acquire knightly status. The impressionable boy has seen only Karnahkarnanz and his companions, it is the splendour of their equipment which overwhelms him (he has not even glimpsed Meljahkanz). He has been impressed, however mistaken his grounds, by the likeness between what Herzeloyde has told him of God and what he sees Karnahkarnanz doing in practice, and it is to King Arthur, the embodiment of compassionate chivalry, that this knight has directed him. There can be little doubt that Karnahkarnanz is the model which Parzival takes for himself when he sets out in search of knighthood.

Yet in two early encounters Parzival is depicted as ironically and worryingly closer to Meljahkanz than to Karnahkarnanz. If we see the former betraying chivalry by being a robber-knight, a knight (122,16: *ritter*) who robs (122,20: *roubes*), it is significant

[1] *Perceval* 427ff.

that Wolfram depicts Parzival's first step on his road to knighthood as involving robbery for, misapplying his mother's advice, he robs Jeschute of a kiss, a ring and a brooch (132,25: *Der knappe des roubes was gemeit*). Admittedly, this episode is informed by a humorous discrepancy between the boy's behaviour and the precepts he imagines he is following, and this humour can come to the fore even as Jeschute defends herself (131,22: *der knappe klagete den hunger sân./diu frouwe was ir lîbes lieht,/sie sprach 'ir sult mîn ezzen niht./wært ir ze frumen wîse,/ir næmet iu ander spîse'*). Yet humour cannot account for the whole episode, since the consequences for Jeschute are serious (punishment at the hands of Orilus, degradation and suffering over some period of time). This episode sums up on the small scale what Mohr has said of Parzival's career at large:[1] although we may at first be tempted to smile at what befalls him, this soon gives way to anxiety as we perceive more serious implications. That such anxiety is justified in this instance and that there is a tragic irony in Parzival coming close to Meljahkanz when he thinks he is becoming another Karnahkarnanz is made clear by another encounter soon afterwards. His combat with Ither is undertaken for the sake of his equipment and concludes with a worse form of robbery (475,5: *rêroup*), a detail which confirms the serious aspect of the encounter with Jeschute and establishes a disturbing continuity with the negative example of Meljahkanz. Intention and practice on Parzival's way to knighthood reveal an ironic discrepancy throughout these scenes.

The relationship between scenes (Sir Gawain)

As a last example of structural irony governing the relationship of two scenes we may return to *Sir Gawain*, to the intermeshing between the three hunting and three temptation scenes. We have looked at the transitions from one narrative strand to another as examples of the irony of interlace,[2] but what concerns us now is the more general question of the relationship between the two strands. That irony governs their overall relationship need not be doubted since this relationship prompts us to look at what is

[1] *Euphorion* 52 (1958), 3.   [2] See above, pp. 138f.

happening to Gawain in the castle in a new light. An obvious function of the hunting scenes is to provide a contrast with the temptation scenes and introduce narrative variety into the work,[1] taking the listeners from a crowded, noisy open-air setting to a stealthy encounter between two people in a bedroom. If we apparently move from the dangers of the hunt to the safety of the castle this opens up an ironic perspective when we realise that, under the metaphor of hunting standing for sexual pursuit,[2] the lady is as intent on hunting down her victim in the bedroom as her lord on tracking down his game outside. The apparent security of the indoor scenes is revealed by the parallel with the hunt outside as involving extreme danger for Gawain, but to realise this we have to see that structural irony consists in highlighting the concealed similarity between two outwardly contrasting scenes. In *Sir Gawain* two hunts are taking place simultaneously, both to the death, and the function of the more obvious hunt is to cast light on what we might not even regard as a hunt, to show the dangers in the courtly game in which Gawain is engaged.[3] To this structural irony, stripping courtly *luf-talkyng* of its polite badinage and revealing the dangers, there corresponds the dramatic irony that we, but not Gawain, know what is going on each day in the woodland (each hunting scene precedes the temptation scene of the same day) and can assess the situation as he cannot.

This is skilful enough in itself, but it is possible to go a step further[4] and see the parallel more particularly between what happens on three hunts and the course which three temptations take, in other words between the behaviour of the three different hunted animals and Gawain's reaction on three separate days. Savage bases his argument on the qualities conventionally attributed to different animals in the Middle Ages and draws a distinction between the noble game hunted by the lord on the first two

[1] Spearing, *Gawain-poet*, pp. 212f., puts this down in part to the probably heterogeneous nature of the poet's audience, his need to hold the interest of men with his hunting scenes and appeal to ladies with the bedroom scenes.

[2] See above, pp. 139 and 210f.

[3] Cf. Spearing's very pertinent observation, *Gawain-poet*, p. 217, on the subtle way in which Gawain's failure at the end of the third temptation scene is made simultaneous with the killing of the fox.

Cf. Savage, *JEGP* 27 (1928), 1ff.

days (deer and a boar) and the beast of vermin he routs out on the third day (a fox). He sees a parallel between this strand and the situation in the castle. On the first two days the lady, like her lord, finds herself pursuing noble game in Gawain and meets with failure,[1] whilst the third day sees Gawain, like the sly fox in the woodland, guilty of duplicity in accepting the girdle and not declaring it to his host. Just as the fox resorts to trickery to avoid danger by suddenly reversing direction (and thereby falls into the jaws of his foes),[2] so does Gawain have recourse to deception to save his skin and thereby fall victim to the temptation previously avoided. Insinuated by this parallel is a suggestion of the perils lurking in the ideal of courtly behaviour, but also a comparison of Gawain with a sly fox, a beast of vermin, which is hardly complimentary to one whose ideal chivalry had been initially stressed.

To interpret the narrative in this way means attributing a high degree of conscious artistry to the author of *Sir Gawain*, an exploitation of formulas to provide verbal echoes serving as connections between separate scenes. Burrow has called this 'purposive formulaic writing',[3] whilst others discount the element of purpose, seeing in the echoes in the work fortuitous products of formulaic composition.[4] The problem resolves itself into the question how far the verbal echoes linking scene with scene may be fortuitous (which they would be if merely the by-products of formulaic style) and how far the echoes are so strikingly meaningful that chance is excluded and we must assume a planning intention,[5] using standing phrases as pointers to structural contrasts of an ironic nature. In the case of *Sir Gawain* conscious intention seems to be involved, because the more obvious verbal

---

[1] If the lord is successful in his hunting on these first two days, this emphasises the parallel between his success and the lady's on the third day.

[2] 1902ff.

[3] Burrow, *Reading*, p. 72. Duggan, *Song*, especially pp. 16ff., has argued for a connection between passages with a higher density of formulas in the *Chanson de Roland* and literary excellence. In other words, the formula can be used as much as the individual word to produce intentional composition of the highest order. What is true of the epic is no less true of a romance which, like *Sir Gawain*, makes use of formulas.

[4] Cf. Spearing, *Criticism*, pp. 23f.

[5] On the need to assume conscious intention before we can talk of irony see Green, *Alieniloquium*, pp. 132ff.

echoes do not just occur anywhere, but fall at connected points in the narrative. They serve, in other words, as suggestions to the audience to look at these points together, to compare and thus to entertain the possibility of a significant contrast.

Most telling is the presence of verbal echoes between two parts of the narrative (Gawain's wager with the Green Knight and his stay at Sir Bertilak's castle) which have to be seen together by any percipient audience, regardless of whether we are convinced of the possibility of structural irony by formulaic repetition.[1] When the guide who is to conduct Gawain from the castle to his adventure tempts the knight by suggesting that he might give up his quest, he uses these words (2124: *þat I schal lelly yow layne, and lance neuer tale/þat euer ʒe fondet to fle for freke þat I wyst*). Here verbal irony is achieved by the conjunction of *lelly* with *layne*: as with the untrustworthiness of the watchman in the dawnsong,[2] for the guide to act *lelly* towards Gawain means that he shows disloyalty to others, so that his protestation of trustworthiness suggests the very opposite. The significant phrase is highlighted by its recurrence in Gawain's answer (2128) and is in any case an echo of the lady's request to him the day before when making him a gift of the girdle (1862: *And bisoʒt hym, for hir sake, disceuer hit neuer,/Bot to lelly layne fro hir lorde*). Again, verbal irony is present in her words (how little store she sets by loyalty is shown by her readiness to invoke it in order seemingly to betray her lord), but this is not enough to suggest a relationship of structural irony between these two passages. This is brought out once we realise the discrepancy between the two parallel situations. Although Gawain rejects the guide's suggestion, somewhat stuffily,[3] and puts this temptation behind him, this is undermined by the fact that he has already accepted the lady's equally dubious proposition (1864: *þe leude hym acordez/þat neuer wyʒe schulde hit wyt, iwysse, bot þay twayne for noʒte*),[4] that he has already broken

---

[1] On what follows see Clark, *MÆ* 40 (1971), 13ff.
[2] See above, pp. 127f.
[3] 2126.
[4] In this passage I wonder whether we may not assume an ironic ambiguity in the last two words, standing out by their position? On the face of it *for noʒte* gives additional emphasis to the negative *neuer* ('that nobody should ever know of it on any account'). But it would also be possible to apply the phrase to the whole sentence (not just the *þat* clause). In this second sense *for noʒte* could imply some-

faith. The function of this verbal echo, linking the guide's offer with the crucial offer of the girdle, is to show that Gawain, when rejecting the more obvious temptation, already has the ground cut from beneath him.

Equally suggestive that Gawain's real testing comes in the castle and not, as he expects, in the encounter with the Green Knight is the way in which the latter takes up words previously used by the lady. In his greeting to Gawain the Green Knight points grimly to the fitting seclusion of the place of testing (2245: *And we are in þis valay verayly oure one;/Here ar no renkes vs to rydde, rele as vus likeȝ*). This echoes the lady's more ambiguous suggestion in the bedroom (1230: *And now ȝe ar here, iwysse, and we bot oure one;/My lorde and his ledeȝ ar on lenþe faren,/Oþer burneȝ in her bedde*). For the alert listener this parallel links the two testings which Gawain has to undergo, but also reveals to him that the outcome of the beheading test has been prejudged by Gawain's failure in loyalty, a failure which arose in part from Gawain's calculation that his agreement with the lady would not be known to others (cf. 1865: *bot þay twayne*, and 1230: *we bot oure one*).

The Green Knight's doubt about Gawain's identity and its link with the lady's similar doubt we have already looked at,[1] but the former's doubts become more precise when he comments on his adversary flinching (2272: *And now þou fles for ferde er þou fele harmeȝ!/Such cowardise of þat knyȝt cowþe I neuer here*). This doubt, implying that Gawain has not lived up to himself, echoes and questions the self-satisfaction in Gawain's rejection of the guide's offer (2129: *...and I here passed,/Founded for ferde for to fle, in fourme þat þou telleȝ,/I were a knyȝt kowarde, I myȝt not be excused*). It also reminds us that, at the moment of turning the guide down, Gawain had already proved himself disloyal and cowardly in accepting the girdle to save his skin and that the use of the conditional as a remote hypothesis in *I were a knyȝt kowarde* is not justified. These links are subtle, but their appearance at decisive turns in the narrative linking two scenes in a meaningful way

thing like 'to no avail', both for the lady's part of the compact (she keeps the lord fully informed of all that goes on between her and Gawain) and for Gawain's, since the gift of the girdle avails him so little that it is actually the occasion of his failure.

[1] See above, pp. 339f.

because they assist understanding implies purpose rather than chance. In using standing or formulaic phrases far from mechanically the poet shows that he is not dependent on them like the oral poet. His use of them is alert and discriminating and demands similar qualities from his listeners, even though this does not preclude the presence among them of those who still took his formulas simply as formulas.

Parody

Structural irony may undergo one final extension when it involves an external comparison between a detail of a work and another work altogether. The other work may be one by the same author (Hausen's critique of 'Minnesang' in his crusading poem, *MF* 47, 33ff., ironises concepts which he had introduced into the German lyric in his earlier poems).[1] It may be the work of another author (Chrétien's *Cligès* as an *Anti-Tristan*[2] or Wolfram's questioning of the make-believe elements in Hartmann's chivalric universe).[3] Or a whole genre may be subjected to critical scrutiny (as when Chrétien uses *Erec* to express doubts about the concept of *fin' amors*,[4] or with the coexistence of the love-lyric and romance alongside the fabliau in the repertoire of courtly literature, where each casts doubt on the presuppositions of the other).[5] In every case the poet must be able to assume that some of his listeners are acquainted with the work or genre to which he alludes. This points to the existence of a coherent taste in courtly literature, but also means that structural irony of this external type (the allusion is to a point *outside* the work itself) is largely synonymous with parody.[6] Since this aspect of irony has already come up at several points, it need only be mentioned in passing here, as an appendix to the other two types of structural irony.

If it be thought that it is taking structural irony too far to see it governing the relationship between two works, rather than two facets of the same work, I need only mention the example of the *Canterbury Tales*. The overall unity obtained for the separate tales

---

[1] See Kienast, *Scheltliet*, above all pp. 37ff.
[2] See above, p. 114.   [3] See above, pp. 62ff.
[4] See above, pp. 107f.   [5] See above, pp. 119ff.
[6] Ménard, *Rire*, pp. 513ff., is strangely reluctant to grant any significant rôle to parody in courtly literature. How far I am from agreeing with him should be clear from the examples just quoted.

by the framework device means that any structural irony linking one tale with another can be regarded simultaneously in two different ways: as external to the tale which makes the allusion or as internal to the overall work which we know as the *Canterbury Tales* with its own narrative action of a pilgrimage from London to Canterbury. If the same links can be external or internal according to one's point of view, it would be arbitrary to exclude the external links from the structural irony we are considering, especially since this feature of the *Tales* is confirmed by the double aspect of the narrator.[1]

To equip any tale with a fictional narrator and then to place it in the wider framework of a journey on which many other narrators recount their tales opens up a double perspective: each story is presented to us not as Chaucer's (as it is still possible to regard *Troilus and Criseyde*), but as its specific narrator's tale (the Clerk, the Merchant, the Wife of Bath). This narrator's attitude to his tale will not necessarily be identical with Chaucer's and the exploitation of this discrepancy encourages us to ask questions of the tale. The most obvious case, but not the only one, is the contrast to the *Knight's Tale* presented by the immediately following *Miller's Tale*, which takes the form of a fabliau parody of the human situation depicted by the knight in terms of chivalric idealism.[2] The listener may admire the nobility of the knight's sentiments and of the code by which he conducts his life (just as the presence of Pandarus is not enough to negate the elevated sentiments attributed to Troilus), but the juxtaposition of the *Miller's Tale* with its different view of life is an external means of reinforcing the internal ironies[3] from which even the *Knight's Tale* is not immune, suggesting a distance between listener and poet on the one hand and the knight's idealised code on the other. It is the artificiality of any attempt to claim that structural irony in the *Tales* is exclusively external or only internal which justifies us in including structural irony between two works, amounting to parody, in this chapter, even if only in the form of a brief reference to its potentialities.

---

[1] On the double aspect of the narrator in the *Canterbury Tales* see Spearing's edition of the *Knight's Tale*, pp. 47f.

[2] Cf. Frost, *RES* 25 (1949), 303f.

[3] *Ibid.*, p. 304. See also Thurston, *Ambivalence, passim.*

I I

THE REASONS FOR IRONY
IN THE
MEDIEVAL ROMANCE

It is time now to draw the threads of our argument together and look at the considerations which made irony possible in the medieval romance as well as the reasons leading courtly poets to make use of it. I shall be concerned only with collective, historical reasons applicable to courtly literature or the genre of the romance at large, not with individual reasons which, in addition, may have driven any poet to make use of irony.[1]

The poet's status

We may start by giving pride of place to the fact that the courtly poet can often be regarded as something of an outsider, standing aloof from the court and its values and viewing them from a potentially critical distance. What is true of Walther (his uncertain social position forced him into this rôle,[2] which encouraged a critical, often ironic attitude towards the world of the court) is not without relevance to his colleagues in the narrative genre of the romance. This is particularly true of the French romances, most of whose authors are not knights, but clerics, perhaps active at courts in various functions, but not so thoroughly of the court as would have been the case if they had been knights.

On the uncertain status of such court clerics, neither fully-

---

[1] This concern with the genre more than with any particular example underlies my whole argument. What remains to be investigated is the use of irony by particular poets, the differences between them and also the change of emphasis between different works by the same author.

[2] The most informative discussion of this is still Burdach, *Walther*, pp. 4ff. See also Klein's interpretation of the 'Atzesprüche', *Spruchdichtung*, pp. 40ff. and Kircher, *Dichter*, pp. 49ff.

fledged ecclesiastics nor completely of the courtly world, Frappier has written,[1] stressing that it is to this class that we owe the origins of the French romance. These court poets were outsiders in two respects: from the Church to which they owed their education, but also from the aristocratic courts where they sought positions as secretaries, tutors, counsellors and poets. Their divorce from the Church may have been due to personal short-comings (as with the unfrocked priests among the *vagantes*) or to the growth of an intellectual proletariat for which the twelfth-century Church provided insufficient openings. From such clerics, equipped with a literary training meant for the Church, but thrust into the world where their intellectual talents were employed in the Civil Service of the Court, the earliest authors of the French romance were recruited.[2] The positions found for them at courts may have been influential and they continued to enjoy clerical advantages denied to laymen,[3] but this does not mean that the poets among them felt completely at home in their new sur-roundings. Worldly they may have been in taste and disposition,[4] but their literacy and education mean that their taste was quite different from that of knights nurtured on the heroic epic. They could hope to be appreciated at first only by a section of the court (the noblewomen) from whom literacy could be expected,[5] just as their clerical background could not be simply shrugged off, so that the occasional misogynous detail in courtly literature,[6] like the realistic attitude towards the idealisation of love,[7] is probably due to the incomplete assimilation of cleric to court. These *aulici clerici* may be exposed to criticism because of their worldliness and neglect of clerical obligations,[8] but it is conversely to such clerics' personal experience of the court and its intrigues that we owe the earliest examples of literature criticising the court.[9] What to some appears as an abandonment of the Church

---

[1] Frappier, *Roman*, pp. 100ff.; *Chrétien*, pp. 16f.; *Amour*, pp. 17ff.
[2] Wace refers to himself as a *clerc lisant* at the royal court, *Rou* 180.
[3] Cf. Köhler, *Trobadorlyrik*, p. 30.   [4] Cf. Frappier, *Amour*, p. 18.
[5] On this topic see Grundmann, *AfK* 26 (1936), 129ff.
[6] This has been well observed by Frappier, *Amour*, p. 18 and, in connection with the fabliau, by Tiemann, *RF* 72 (1960), 422.
[7] See Köhler, *Trobadorlyrik*, p. 30.
[8] Cf. Uhlig, *Hofkritik*, pp. 86, 104 and 114.
[9] This is illustrated by Chapters I (pp. 27ff.) and II (pp. 55ff.) in Uhlig's book.

can be regarded by others as a failure to adapt successfully to the world of the court and accept its values.[1]

What this outsider position of the clerical court-poet means for the French romance has been brought out by Bertau.[2] He stresses that the literary position in France is different from that in Germany, since none of the great French romances is written by a knight, so that the Anglo-Norman and French courts depend on the literary services of clerics of this kind, of a social class other than their own, for the literary enhancement of their way of life. These French romances do not represent, like their German equivalents, an act of self-enhancement by knightly poets, but a glorification of knighthood by outsiders, a sociological fact of French literature which Bertau sees as explaining the irony latent in the French romance from its inception. The new genre, in its homeland at least, is written to celebrate a social ideal, but by authors who do not completely identify themselves with that ideal, whose position as newcomers to the court from another cultural world gives them, for all their worldliness, enough distance from the court's values for the spark of irony to be lighted.

If the social dimension of the German romance differs from that in France in that the authors of German works are predominantly knights, this appears to deny to German literature the possibility of irony which Bertau has claimed for French and to confirm the suggestion that the German romances fail to reproduce the ironic features of their sources. My argument should have illustrated that I do not accept this evaluation of the German romance (where irony is frequently exploited, even if at different points and in different ways from the French models). Even though I would not maintain that Bertau's sociological argument is a necessary (rather than merely possible) explanation of irony in this genre, it is still possible to rescue something of his point for the position in Germany. To do this we cannot generalise the unique case of Gottfried, whose status as a cleric or, possibly,

---

[1] This uncertain position of *aulici clerici* has been discussed, with specific reference to Peter of Blois and what is termed his *sic et non* and *odi et amo* attitude, by Dronke, *MSt* 38 (1976), 190ff. A more general discussion of the position of these clerics at court is given by Jaeger, *Humanism*, pp. 16ff. and 8off.

[2] Bertau, *Literatur* I 436.

bourgeois citizen of Strassburg would explain his remoteness from chivalric values in the same way as with the non-knightly authors of the French romances.[1] However important Gottfried's case, knightly authors like Veldeke, Hartmann and Wolfram cannot be covered by this explanation. In their case I should invoke the fact of their education and literacy,[2] for these attainments were rare enough among the knights of their day to place them in a special position, drawing them, like the clerics active as poets at French courts, closer to the literate noblewomen of the German courts. Awareness of what literacy implied for his knightly status may have led Wolfram to deny his literacy (with his tongue in his cheek)[3] in order to preserve his knighthood intact, but whether or not we accept this point a knightly poet who shares the gift of literacy with noblewomen and clerics can no longer be equated with the majority of illiterate knights. His clerical training now gives him a vantage-point denied to his fellow-knights. The special position which his French colleagues enjoyed by virtue of social status as well as education is true of German poets (other than Gottfried) because of their literacy alone.

That the German poet attached some importance to this implicit distance between himself and his knightly class (even though it was less than that separating the French clerical court-poet from his audience) can be seen from the way in which he can project this situation into his narrative by depicting a comparable gulf between the hero and the courtly world, as with Parzival's upbringing in the wilderness of Soltane or Tristan's estrangement from courtly society. Both these features may be implicit in the source in question, but in each case the German poet

[1] With regard to what is now generally accepted as the initially courtly genre of the fabliau or *Schwank* it is probably the impetus of his disagreement with Bédier's bourgeois theory which led Nykrog to regard the fabliau as essentially of aristocratic origin, thereby paying too little attention to the clerical element in courtly literary production. This has been corrected by Tiemann in his important review article, RF 72 (1960), 406ff. A comparable point has been made for the German *Schwank* by Schirmer, *Versnovelle*, pp. 299ff.

[2] As indicated by their acquaintance with rhetorical theory (see above, pp. 18f., including the suggestion that even Wolfram's style is not totally divorced from rhetoric).

[3] See Green, *Oral*, pp. 163ff., especially the Excursus, pp. 265ff., dealing with Grundmann's literal reading of Wolfram's statement.

has elaborated this detail (Wolfram by the greater function and coherence he grants to the wilderness as a location other than the world of the court,[1] Gottfried by the verbal accentuation of his point by the term *vremede*).[2] The hero's distance from the court, implying his ability to transcend it, thus reflects the poet's critical aloofness from courtly values. Narrative projections of this kind, building the author's reservations into the work, are not confined to German literature. Ménard has discussed the function of Dinadan in the French prose *Tristan* as a mocking critic of the courtly and chivalric ideal and has observed that his arguments are hardly novel, for a cleric would make the same points, and that he seems to have mistaken his calling, choosing to be a knight without a genuine sense of vocation.[3] However, the independent elaboration of this technique by poets such as Wolfram and Gottfried suggests that their distance from the class for whom they wrote was not simply a sociological fact, but one on which they were prepared to build in composing their works as commentaries on the values held by that class.

The significance of this social discrepancy between poet and audience as a potential source of irony is confirmed by traces of the same phenomenon in the English romance. As regards *Troilus* we can argue that Chaucer makes good use of both the suggestions made about Gottfried's non-chivalric status, that he was a bourgeois by birth and that he was a cleric by training or calling. Despite his position as court poet, Chaucer was not of the court in the sense of being born a nobleman, for he was the son of a merchant and would accordingly, if he was to safeguard himself against accusations of being a social upstart, have to avoid giving himself airs and acting as if feudal barriers counted for nothing.[4] This potentially awkward situation, in which a poet of plebeian origins entertains and even instructs an aristocratic audience, is turned by Chaucer into an aesthetic advantage. He extends the humility formulas which both rhetoric and his social rank enjoin upon him into a sustained pose of self-deprecation which is the only position for a bourgeois poet to adopt before

---

[1] See Emmel, *Formprobleme*, pp. 70 and 73.
[2] Cf. Hahn, *Raum*, pp. 88ff.
[3] Ménard, *Rire*, pp. 459f. See also Vinaver, *Recherche*, pp. 163ff.
[4] On these implications of Chaucer's position see Birney, *PMLA* 54 (1939), 644.

an aristocratic audience,[1] but also a stance which, by his emphasis on inexperience in matters of love, keeps him out of the charmed circle of courtly values and allows him ironic or realistic comments on the topic of love. If we can regard the narrator in *Troilus* as almost a character in his own right, Chaucer resembles continental romance authors in projecting his own attitude of dubiety into the work itself, in making a virtue of his position as a social outsider by seeing in it the liberty to insinuate comments on the courtly world to which he has only conditional access as a poet.

The second outsider rôle, Chaucer as a *clerk* rather than a bourgeois, serves the same purpose. The poet emphasises his inexperience in love (thereby preserving his detachment) by suggesting that he knows of it only from bookish sources,[2] from his function as a clerk, and can at the same time use the same clerical image, as in the 'bidding prayer' at the start of the work, to imply his solidarity with his lovers and those lovers in his audience.[3] The narrator's stance is a delicate one, poised between detachment and sympathy, but the point for us is that Chaucer is again exploiting his social status, on one side of this delicate balance, to express a detachment from the courtly ideal of love which he is at pains to bring home to his aristocratic listeners.

Our knowledge of the individual poet behind *Sir Gawain and the Green Knight* is too scanty to permit any conclusion in his case. However, if we take into account the other works which he is accepted as having written a picture of his literary culture emerges which shows that he had knowledge of the two languages, Latin and French, necessary if the medieval poet was to be a *clerk*.[4] His reading in Latin betrays a knowledge of theological writings and even faint traces of contact with Virgil and Seneca, whilst on the French side his romance owes much to the courtly tradition. For reasons like these, together with the complex, literate style of *Sir Gawain*, Muscatine has suggested that its author, like Langland, might have been a cleric, perhaps a priest attached to a provincial baronial court.[5] This can only be

---

[1] Cf. Bethurum, *PMLA* 74 (1959), 514.   [2] Stevens, *Romance*, p. 221.
[3] *Ibid.*, pp. 221f.
[4] Spearing, *Gawain-poet*, pp. 12ff.
[5] Muscatine, *Poetry*, pp. 34f.

surmise, but it agrees with what we have seen with French and German romance authors, as well as with Chaucer: their reservations about the courtly ideal may in part derive from their social or cultural distance from the courtly world.

The language of courtesy

This first point has suggested a possibility of irony external to the court, arising from the poet's detachment from it, but there are other sources of irony within the courtly world itself. First amongst these is the fact of a conventional courtly etiquette and the language it developed to oil the wheels of social intercourse.[1] It is not by chance that a mode of speech like irony which avoids the pointblank (with all the danger of abruptness and aggressiveness) and which relies on a technique of indirection should be defined in Latin rhetorical handbooks by the quality of *urbanitas*.[2] The same meaning is present etymologically in the Greek ἀστεϊσμός,[3] one of the terms adopted by Latin rhetoric, together with εἰρωνεία, to denote the figures grouped under *allegoria*, figures which all convey a meaning other than what is actually said. In a more ethical context Aristotle can suggest that the ironist, by contrast with the bombastic and boastful ἀλαζών, displays a noble and refined mind by saying less, rather than more than what he means.[4] True to this rhetorical tradition, Lausberg includes under what he calls 'handlungstaktische Ironie' various linguistic forms of social politeness and mentions circumlocution, understatement and euphemism as possible examples.[5]

What classical rhetoric sees as the hallmark of the cultured town-dweller is often contrasted with the boorishness of country-dwellers, so that *urbanitas* and *eloquentia* are set up against *rusticitas* and *simplicitas*.[6] With the decline of Roman urban life the *urbs* as a centre of political authority and literary culture is replaced

---

[1] On the style of this courtly language see Bayer, *Untersuchungen*, pp. 161ff.
[2] See Haury, *Ironie*, p. 40.
[3] *Ibid.*, and Finoli, *ILRL* 92 (1958), 578.
[4] Cf. Büchner, *Hermes* 76 (1941), 341f. and Behler, *Ironie*, p. 20.
[5] Lausberg, *Elemente*, §430, 2 b.
[6] See the examples listed by Finoli, *art. cit.*, pp. 575f.

by the individual court, the *aula*,[1] so that the medieval contrast is now between those who speak the eloquent diction of the court[2] and those who are still *rustici* or *villani*, whose speech is too simple to accommodate the subtleties and circuitousness of polite social language. How allusive and manysided this language could be in poetic diction is most easily visible in the context of love, at once a private encounter and yet inseparable from society, especially when the poetry celebrating love is a public entertainment. The love-poem exists in this state of tension, proclaiming to the court that the poet is a lover, but maintaining a discreet silence on the identity of his lady, expressing the lover's hopes and wishes by means of metaphors such as *gruoz*, *gnâde*, *helfe*, which compromise neither party in public, but hint at what is involved, whilst leaving it to the lady to decide for herself how far she is to take such terms.[3]

Of the linguistic forms of social politeness mentioned by Lausberg as examples of 'handlungs-taktische Ironie' circumlocution is the most obvious case of an allusive mode of speech which avoids impolite abruptness by implying its meaning circuitously and discreetly. The social restraint and respect for others' feelings which this figure implies are obvious, especially where what is tactfully concealed is something as personal as love.[4] It is here that the periphrastic style can acquire ironic overtones. When Gottfried's Blanscheflur alludes to the impression made by Riwalin on her feelings as the harm he has done to her closest friend[5] or when the lovers in *Flamenca* draw near to mutual confession by ambiguous circumlocutions,[6] these discreetly phrased hints allow either party to retreat without loss of face, but the audience is enabled to savour the dramatic irony of seeing more than the person addressed. The same is true of the

---

[1] This is the underlying theme of the first volume of Bezzola's monumental work, *Origines*. Uhlig, *Hofkritik*, pp. 47f., also points out how the classical Latin theme of criticism of metropolitan Rome is adapted to criticism of the court in medieval literature.

[2] Finoli, *art. cit.*, p. 577, points out how a rhetorical passage in the Provençal *Leys d'Amors* refers to the *belas e cortezas paraulas* used by 'Anthismos' (for which read *asteismos*).

[3] Cf. Mohr, *Minnesang*, pp. 202 and 210.

[4] Mayer, *Topoi*, p. 245, aptly quotes *Parzival* 643, 1ff. in this connection.

[5] See above, p. 181f.   [6] See above, pp. 180f.

oath scenes in the *Tristan* story. The truth has to be implied if the oath is to be effective, but it has to be suggested indirectly (and therefore concealed from some) because of the social setting, the presence of others, in which the confession is made.[1]

Understatement resembles circumlocution in both these respects. It discreetly takes account of others' feelings by refusing to impose inflated demands upon them, by paying them the rhetorical compliment of assuming that they will grasp the true meaning, but it also opens up an ironic dimension because of the discrepancy between meaning and utterance, obvious to those whom the speaker admits into complicity. The social dimension of courtly speech is also apparent whenever the guise of hesitancy or humility is adopted, a reluctance to thrust one's own opinions upon others with excessive dogmatism. The polite use of the formula *ich wæne* to tone down remarks and make them socially acceptable is an obvious example of courtly tact,[2] but we have also come across cases where this polite formula is adapted to ironic purposes, suggesting the discrepancy between what is said with apparent naïveté and what must be meant.[3] Elsewhere Gottfried can courteously imply a readiness to agree with an opinion which he rejects (106: *der selben jehe der stüende ich bi*), but then ironise this apparent agreement and disappoint those who took it at its face value by bringing, almost as an afterthought, the true grounds for his disagreement (107: *wan ein dinc, daz mir widerstat*).[4] To discuss further the connection between irony and the speech of courtly etiquette would involve writing a stylistics of courtly diction, but at bottom this is established by the fact that irony is essentially a social mode of speech, saying and meaning different things to different groups, playing on a differentiation within the audience.

[1] See above, pp. 182f.
[2] This point has also been made by Clausen, *Erzähler*, p. 38.
[3] On the ironic use of *wænen* in this way see Green, *Recognising*, pp. 44f. and 46, but also Nellmann, *Erzähltechnik*, pp. 73f. and 139f.
[4] Cf. Clausen, *op. cit.*, p. 147.

The select audience

From this it is a short step to my next point, that irony presupposes a select group of initiated within the whole audience.[1] Fowler takes account of this feature in his definition ('Irony is a form of utterance that postulates a double audience, consisting of one party that hearing shall hear and shall not understand, and another party that, when more is meant than meets the ear, is aware both of that more and of the outsiders' incomprehension').[2] Worcester, basing himself on Horace's *pauci lectores*, makes the same point:[3] those who perceive the irony regard themselves as belonging to a small, select, secret society headed by the author, whereas the victims are countless. Once again irony achieves its effect by flattering those who perceive it and congratulating them on their superior insight. There are many examples in the medieval romance, especially where dramatic irony is involved, where two groups, the initiated and the uninitiated, can be clearly distinguished (one has only to recall the many episodes where the audience is made privy to the successful hoodwinking of Marke by Tristan and Isold). But to see the implications of this feature of irony for the romance we must take account of what is known of the medieval public for this genre.

Köhler has argued that, by contrast with the early *chanson de geste* with its essentially homogeneous public, the romance marks a stage in the progressive differentiation of the medieval literary public. It is expressly addressed only to courtly society, made up of knights and clerics, a restriction of literary appeal to a social and cultural élite which he finds programmatically expressed in the prologue to the *Roman de Thèbes* (13: *Or s'en voisent de tot mestier,/Se ne sont clerc o chevalier,/Car ausi puent escouter/Come li asnes al harper*).[4] Elsewhere French courtly literature makes it equally clear that it is addressed to knights and clerics, even if these other references lack the exclusiveness of the *Roman de Thèbes* in its refusal to address the third estate of medieval society.[5] A similar point has been made by Auerbach, who approaches the question of the medieval public from a different point of view and argues that the

---

[1] Green, *Alieniloquium*, pp. 129ff.   [2] Fowler, *Dictionary*, p. 295.
[3] Worcester, *Satire*, p. 77.   [4] Köhler, *Trobadorlyrik*, pp. 9f.
[5] Cf. Gallais, *CCM* 13 (1970), 337.

courtly audience for the romance was an emphatically élite circle, evolved at first in England and France as the first postclassical élite public with literary and cultural aspirations[1] which set them apart from the homogeneous public for the *chanson de geste*.[2] With regard to the difference between 'popular' and courtly poetry Dronke maintains that one type is meant for the whole of any given society, without distinction of class (this is the same as Köhler's point about the homogeneous public for the early *chanson de geste*), whilst the other is composed for a select, specific audience, sharing certain values or conventions with the poet which are not universally acknowledged.[3] This latter type Dronke sees exemplified in courtly literature, but we may take his distinction to apply not merely to courtly love-poetry, but also to the courtly romance.

For a number of reasons, therefore, the courtly audience is a select élite audience, set apart from the wider unified public for the heroic epic. This still does not bring us to the double audience postulated by irony, for the point of Fowler's definition is that both groups in his audience should be present on the same occasion, the one alert to and the other unaware of the ironic implication of what is said, whereas in the prologue to the *Roman de Thèbes* courtly exclusiveness meant only one élite audience for the romance. None the less, it is possible to regard the differentiation between the select courtly audience and the rest of society as the first step in a progressive differentiation, which can also be plotted *within* the courtly audience itself, giving rise to groupings within this restricted audience which serve as the basis for irony as defined by Fowler.

That courtly poets did not regard even their restricted audience as homogeneous is suggested by indications that they were concerned to appeal to and be understood by one particular grouping within this audience. Gottfried's distinction between *edelen herzen* (47) and *ir aller werlt* (50) amongst his listeners[4] not merely tells us something about his ideal of the *edelez herze*, but is also

---

[1] Auerbach, *Literatursprache*, p. 151.
[2] This is not to say that the knightly nobility could not appreciate both the *chanson de geste* and the romance, but merely that it was the latter type of narrative that gave an impetus to the differentiation of the medieval literary public.
[3] Dronke, *Love-lyric*, I 1. [4] Speckenbach, *Studien*, pp. 52f.

informative about the different levels on which he expects his romance to be understood by these two sections of his audience. He attempts to win the individual listener to his cause by flattering him into believing that, of course, he is one of the *edele herzen*, and this gives him the opportunity to play off one group against the other.

A similar differentiation amongst his listeners, based on very different criteria, is implied by Wolfram in his prologue to *Parzival*, where he is conscious that he is addressing two groups, those who will be able to make nothing of what he has to say because of their intellectual shortcomings (1,15: *diz vliegende bîspel/ist tumben liuten gar ze snel,/sine mugens niht erdenken*) and those whose wisdom consists in their ability to recognise their ignorance (2,5: *ouch erkante ich nie sô wîsen man,/ern möhte gerne künde hân,/welher stiure disiu mære gernt/und waz si guoter lêre wernt*).[1] Wolfram composes his work for the latter group (their progress from *tumpheit* to *wîsheit* parallels that of the hero),[2] but the first passage shows that he is aware that there are others amongst his listeners whose lack of perception will make them less amenable to his rhetorical purposes. When Wolfram hopes to train his listeners to a critical and attentive reception of his work[3] he has the *wîse man* in mind, but must have been aware that this was wasted labour in the case of the *tumbe liute*.[4] Elsewhere, Wolfram's narrator can appeal to particular sections of his audience[5] not because he has less hope of meeting with understanding with the others, but because the theme of his narrative at any point is

---

[1] See Haas, *Tumpheit*, pp. 31ff.

[2] *Ibid.*, pp. 36f. (with further reference to 399, 4). Nellmann, *Erzähltechnik*, p. 4, fn. 17, suggests reading 399, 4 as meaning 'young and old' on the basis of *Titurel* 170, 3. This is to assume that what is true of one work must also be applicable to another in the same sense, and it also ignores the fact that whereas *grîs* is explicitly used in *Titurel* 170, 3, the only partially synonymous *wîs* occurs in *Parzival* 399, 4. I therefore see no reason for not accepting the illuminating suggestion of Haas.

[3] This point has been well made by Harroff, *Wolfram*, although as part of a total argument about which doubts can be entertained.

[4] Although the *wîse man* is meant as a collective singular, and therefore as the logical antithesis to *tumbe liute*, Wolfram chooses to express this in terms of an antithesis between a grammatical singular and plural. Does this not imply his realisation that those who appreciate him are likely to be very much in the minority, and would this not correspond to Gottfried's emphasis on *aller* (*ir aller werlt*) in his antithesis?

[5] Nellmann, *Erzähltechnik*, pp. 5ff., especially p. 8.

likely to be of special interest to the special group he now addresses (he speaks to the *getriuwen* because his theme is *triuwe*, to ladies in particular when the subject-matter justifies it).

Nellmann's observation that Wolfram's narrator is particularly fond of directing his remarks to the ladies in his audience,[1] thus singling them out for special attention, may be applicable in a much wider sense to courtly literature if we bear in mind the rôle played by noblewomen in patronising courtly literature, the fact that their literacy made them receptive to an art which was now consciously literate[2] and capable of appreciating subtleties likely to be bypassed in any merely oral reception. Feminine taste was probably also more accessible to themes more ambitious than the simpler crudities of knightly combat with which the menfolk were satisfied. In fact, it is almost certainly the ladies whom the poet constantly had in mind when appealing to the superior insight of some of his listeners. The common feature of literacy linking poet with noblewomen places him in a closer rapport with them than with most knights in the audience, so that here too we have the makings of the double audience of irony.[3]

Written composition

From the mention of literacy it is again only a step to my next point: the greater range of ironic possibilities opened up by the transition from oral to written composition. We have already considered this in connection with the irony of the narrator, but it also belongs in any explanation of irony in courtly literature with regard to the sociological factors that determine that literature. The use of writing opens up a potentially creative gap between the poet and his work. Now he has time to stand back from it and comment on it critically, to iron out the inconsistencies by which neither the oral poet nor his audience has the time to be worried, and even to incorporate structural correlations between widely separated episodes.

To this gap between poet and work there corresponds the

---

[1] *Ibid.*, pp. 3f. [2] As is recognised by Wolfram in *Parzival* 337, 1ff.

[3] Indirectly we have reached the same point as Frappier, *Chrétien*, p. 16, when he quotes Thibaudet's observation with approval: 'le roman médiéval, c'est un clerc et une dame qui l'écoute'. Cf. also Thibaudet, *Réflexions*, p. 243.

further gap between the audience and the work, because the relationship between a manuscript text and someone capable of reading it now enables that potential reader to stand back from the work as critically as the poet who composed it under these conditions and who, acquainted with the possibility of the individual reader, would learn to take his position into account. Wolfram concedes that his *Parzival* may possibly be read by women (337,1ff.), Gottfried challenges his potential critic to consult his written source for confirmation of the veracity of his own account (2018ff.), whilst Chaucer expresses his realisation that *Troilus and Criseyde* will make its way as a work by public recital and also as a written book.[1]

Such examples suggest the awareness by the courtly author that the new conditions of written composition combine with the literacy of part of his audience to make new demands of him and to offer him novel opportunities. He can take account of critical objections in advance by revision and by removing the cause for complaint, but can also persuade the promising members of his audience to adopt this critical stance which the abandonment of the strict conditions of oral-formulaic composition has rendered possible on both sides, for the poet and for his reader.

A third gap which opens up in the romance as a product of written composition is that between poet and narrator and the novel complexity in point of view which this rendered possible. This possibility was brought about by the introduction, not of the narrator (who is essentially the reciter, a figure already known to oral tradition, now written into the literate work), but of the author or poet, composing at leisure behind the scenes, making use of, but not to be identified with, the reciter standing in front of his assembled audience.[2] This third differentiation in the written mode is as productive of irony as the others and we find it whenever (as with the pretence of humility or ignorance) what the narrator says of himself cannot also be claimed by the omniscient poet.

This threefold differentiation (paralleled by the progressive differentiation of the literary public set under way at the same time in the literate genre of the romance) means that for the poet

---

[1] See above, p. 225.   [2] Scholes and Kellogg, *Narrative*, p. 53.

there is a distinction between composition and recital and for the reading member of the audience a complementary distinction between recital and reading. Both the poet and the reader can proceed at a more leisurely and critically attentive pace than in the press of oral composition; for both of them the standing formula and traditional theme have lost the necessity they had in oral poetry. Now for the first time any discrepancy between formula and context will not be dismissed as a case of Homer nodding, but will be meant and appreciated as possibly ironic.[1] It is the novel fact of written composition of a text available to some for private reading which encourages poet and reader to stand back from the narrative, to question its implications by regarding words no longer as units of conventional formulas, but as relevant to their particular context, in short, to savour the possibilities of irony.

Patronage and rhetoric

Another condition under which courtly literature was composed has a bearing on irony. It is the social fact that the courtly poet is free to express his views openly and even to choose his subject-matter only to a limited extent, for he is much more dependent on the social resonance of his work than post-Romantic criticism always recognises. To the patronage of a feudal lord the poet owes the manuscript of his normally French source placed at his disposal for the composition of his own version, he owes him sustenance and rewards during this period and even the opportunity to recite the finished product to the court audience, whose interest he must capture and hold, not just in the impersonal contact between author and reader,[2] but in the difficult and potentially unruly encounter between poet-reciter and listeners physically present. This dependence of the courtly poet on the favours of his patron and acceptance by his listeners causes no difficulty as long as he attends to one of the conventional tasks of the medieval poet, to entertain, to praise and to flatter. His poetry in this respect will be laudatory of real individuals (as in the political

---

[1] Cf. Bäuml and Spielmann, *FMLS* 10 (1974), 248ff., especially pp. 254f.

[2] Although historically this novel type of encounter is of great importance, it remains exceptional in the Middle Ages, where it is the recital situation which is typical.

'Spruch'), of fictional characters or of the whole chivalric and courtly way of life. In each case what he has to say will compliment and please those on whom he depends, for it is their way of life which he is idealising.

Offence is more likely to be taken when the poet follows his other obligation, to compose the 'Scheltrede' alongside the 'Preisgesang'.[1] This will not be so when his criticism is directed against the enemies of his patron and of the court at which he is performing, but the risk is greater when the poet criticises or calls into doubt a fictional character with whom patron and listeners can identify, or even their contemporary mode of existence which they would rather see legitimised by undiluted praise. The argument of the earlier chapters should have made it clear that the romance-author is ready to instruct by criticising what he regards as deficiencies in the courtly way of life. If he is to minimise the danger of giving offence and frustrating his didactic intention it will be tactically advisable to disguise his criticism, to approach his goal by an indirect route,[2] in short to realise that the insinuations of irony might be more effective, and are certainly safer, than the openness of satire. How the poet resolves this dilemma we can see by considering what help rhetoric has to offer.

The medieval poet's dependence on patronage and need to flatter seem to be confirmed by the recommendations in the rhetorical handbooks.[3] The advice of Matthew of Vendôme to describe positive attributes fully and to omit negative traits (*quae tractata displicent, debent praetermitti, similiter venustas sententiae debet prolixius explicari*)[4] is often quoted in this context. Some see in this an explanation of Hartmann's idealising style by contrast with Chrétien's realism, whilst Brinkmann makes the same point of medieval literature at large,[5] that it depicts the typical and ideal

---

[1] On these two aspects of the medieval poet's task see Pörksen, *Erzähler*, pp. 156ff. and 177ff.

[2] Mohr, *Minnesang*, p. 226, refers to Walther's exploitation of his 'Narrenfreiheit' to express criticism where frankness would have been too dangerous. Tristan's disguise as a fool confers a similar liberty on him (cf. Green, *Alieniloquium*, pp. 153ff.), where his mockery of Marke is of course a form of criticism.

[3] I have discussed this problem in *Damning*, pp. 117ff.

[4] *Ars versificatoria* IV 19, in Faral, *Arts*, p. 185.

[5] On Hartmann's idealising style cf. Ehrismann, *LG* II 2, 1, p. 164; Kramer, *Erzählerbemerkungen*, pp. 152 and 180; Jackson, *Faith*, p. 58. Brinkmann makes his point in *Wesen*, p. 83.

instead of the real. Against this it can be shown that the typifying or idealising comparison (e.g. *Erec* 17: *als ein guot kneht sol*) can be used easily, if not frequently, in a critical, rather than laudatory sense, to imply conformity to a negative norm (*Erec* 5965: *ich tete als die tôren tuont*) or a failure to live up to an ideal (*Erec* 4733: *ungelîch einem guoten knehte*).[1] But if this stylistic feature can convey criticism as well as praise in courtly literature (although less often, so that this literature remains predominantly eulogistic), what are we to make of the rhetorical recommendation of Matthew of Vendôme?

We can meet the objection constituted by his suggestion that poetic descriptions should concentrate on positive features by turning to other rhetorical evidence, the traditional division into three types or *genera*, dependent on the subject treated and the rôle of the audience (*genus iudiciale*, *genus deliberativum* and *genus demonstrativum*).[2] Each of these can be used with positive or negative intent: to defend or prosecute in the first *genus*, to persuade or dissuade in the second, and to give a *laudatio* or a *vituperatio* in the third. This third *genus* may have had its origins in public ceremonies, but it was of greater importance for literary rhetoric, as is borne out by the traditional statement that this *genus* deals with descriptive details of a person which are either positive or negative. It is with Emporius, however, that we come across the most telling suggestion. He says that, since rhetoric is largely concerned with praise (criticism implies the absence of qualities which would have called forth praise, so that there are no *topoi* of criticism, only those of praise),[3] the *genus demonstrativum* is commonly, but wrongly, seen exclusively with regard to praise, even to the extent of being called the *genus laudativum*. It is this oversimplification which Emporius firmly rejects: *Demonstrativa materia, quae vulgo laudativa dicitur, non solum in praedicatione hominis alicuius aut rei, sed etiam in reprehensione consistit, unde competentius multo demonstrativa dicetur, cum eadem aliquis saepe culpabitur.*[4] From the position adopted by Emporius and his reference to a common, but mistaken, practice we could classify

---

[1] See above, pp. 231f. and also Green, *Damning*, pp. 122f.
[2] Lausberg, *Handbuch*, §61.
[3] Cf. Georgi, *Preisgedicht*, p. 30.
[4] Emporius, *Praeceptum*, p. 567.

Matthew's recommendation of praise instead of criticism as a medieval example of the same oversimplification. Here it would be Matthew who betrays his bias towards the *laudativum*, whilst Emporius, acknowledging the presence of both praise and criticism, is more objective.

The implications of this for irony are considerable, because in the medieval romance criticism tends to be voiced indirectly, as a concealed undermining of apparent praise.[1] This indirectness can be explained in two ways. Although the terms *schimpfliet* and *rüegliet* are attested for the medieval lyric,[2] the narrative poet disposes of a possibility lacking in the lyric, since he can incorporate his evaluation of persons in the narrative action. He can use a character to convey a judgment which is also his own (e.g. Erec's knights at Karnant),[3] he can shelter behind generalising, but in reality highly specific digressions (Thomas in *Tristan*),[4] he can rely on a telling discrepancy between the action and its assessment by characters (as with dramatic irony) and he can exploit the distinction between poet and narrator to hint at a critical distance from the action. The narrative poet need not pass his judgment openly, he has various ways of expressing his opinion indirectly. Secondly, these indirect possibilities open to the narrative poet mean that his criticism of a character will often be far from obvious, it may even be combined with the appearance of praise (Hartmann's eulogy of Erec at his wedding-tournament or Gottfried's description of Tristan's chivalric exploits after leaving Cornwall).[5] The narrative poet can pretend to follow the rhetorical advice given by Matthew of Vendôme (to praise, but forgo criticism), whilst in reality using this prescription for different, and more complex, ends. Indeed, it is probable that the rhetorical bias in favour of *laudatio* encouraged more sophisticated poets to express by indirect means a reservation which they were too shrewd not to feel.

In doing this, they could derive assistance from rhetoric itself, from the recommendation to control the audience's responses by indirect and concealed means (e.g. *insinuatio* or *dissimulatio*),[6] but

---

[1] Cf. Green, *Damning*, pp. 117ff.
[2] *Ibid.*, pp. 128f.
[3] *Erec* 2974ff. Cf. Green, *Damning*, p. 136.
[4] *Ibid.*, pp. 133f.
[5] *Ibid.*, pp. 151f. and 137f.
[6] Green, *Damning*, pp. 138ff.

above all from those traditional definitions of irony which illustrate it by an example of apparent praise when criticism is meant.[1] Classical authorities quote in this context the reproach addressed to Venus by Juno in the *Aeneid*, couched ironically in laudatory terms (IV 93: *egregiam vero laudem et spolia ampla refertis/tuque puerque tuus*),[2] but this kind of illustration is continued in the Middle Ages in what becomes an established ironic theory, that criticism can be effectively conveyed by the appearance of praise.[3] Theoretical definitions of this kind, giving examples from classical literature, make it clear that medieval authors acquainted with rhetoric must have known the ironic procedure of using *laudatio* to express *vituperatio*. In other words, traditional rhetoric which, as with Matthew of Vendôme, recommended the avoidance of negative, critical descriptions, also provided poets, in what it had to say about *ironia*, with the means of conveying criticism whilst appearing not to. What Matthew prescribed in rhetorical theory agreed with what tact demanded of the poet dependent on the favours of a patron, whilst rhetorical advice on the indirect mode of speech provided an answer to the poet's problem of criticising, when necessary, without giving offence. The conditions of patronage and the recommendations of rhetoric work together to make the courtly poet aware of the advantages of irony.

Secularism

Another factor encouraging irony in courtly literature concerns not the secularism of the courtly ideal, but the fact that this worldly ideal was acknowledged and espoused in literature.[4] To do this was no simple or safe matter, since it meant going against

---

[1] E.g. Quintilian, *Institutio oratoria* VIII 6, 54. The opposite ironic possibility, to insinuate praise by the appearance of blame, does not concern us. Our problem is to see how irony provided an opportunity to circumvent the general prohibition of criticism suggested by Matthew of Vendôme.

[2] E.g. Julius Rufinianus, *De schematis dianoeas*, pp. 61f.

[3] Cf. Isidore of Seville, *Etymologiae* II 21, 41 and Buoncompagno da Signa (quoted by Benton, *Clio*, p. 37). On the medieval readiness to interpret a classical text ironically see Marti, *Quadrivium* I (1956), 7ff. Kelly, *Love*, p. 73, has some very relevant words on the medieval romance authors' awareness and appreciation of the irony of Ovid's Roman comedies.

[4] On this problem in English literature of the fourteenth century see Howard, *Temptations*, pp. 282ff.

the dominant clerical current and removing prohibitions which had the force of tradition and religious authority behind them. Secularism may have been openly espoused by the *vagantes* who had rebelled against the Church and made themselves consciously outsiders, but for others the position was more delicate, especially for those clerical court-poets who had cut loose from the Church but were still hopeful of finding acceptance at court. Their secularism had to be adjusted to the responsibilities of office and avoid jeopardising the position of the court at which they served by calling down the wrath of ecclesiastical authority on too open an advocacy of worldly interests.[1]

Prudence and caution were enjoined on such poets, since, as we know all too well from the politics of the twentieth century, if it is too dangerous to speak the truth openly it will be voiced indirectly and ironically. What Heine said of Cervantes and Goethe can be applied to advocates of a courtly ideal in implicit conflict with clerical doctrine: '. . . und wie Cervantes, zur Zeit der Inquisition, zu einer humoristischen Ironie seine Zuflucht nehmen mußte, um seine Gedanken anzudeuten, ohne den Familiaren des heiligen Offiz eine faßbare Blöße zu geben, so pflegte auch Goethe im Tone einer humoristischen Ironie dasjenige zu sagen, was er, der Staatsminister und Höfling, nicht unumwunden auszusprechen wagte. Goethe hat nie die Wahrheit verschwiegen, sondern wo er sie nicht nackt zeigen durfte, hat er sie in Humor und Ironie gekleidet.'[2] There may be a difference between the Church around 1200 and the Church of the Counter-reformation, but in principle Heine's point about recourse to irony as an indirect mode when openness has its dangers is as true of the Middle Ages as of later periods. How necessary it was to show discretion and be able to fall back, if challenged, on the ambiguity of ironic speech has been stressed by Weber in the case of the most provocative example in the medieval romance, Gottfried's *Tristan*.[3] He makes the same two points to which our present argument has conducted us. Gottfried was dependent for his poetic success on his work being acceptable to his public, and this was

---

[1] On the clerical attitude towards the secular love lyric see Schmidtke, *ZfdPh* 95 (1976), 321ff.
[2] Heine, *Die romantische Schule*, pp. 85f.
[3] Weber, *Tristan*, I 290f.

only made possible by his employment of subterfuge and concealment, by a choice of words at the really sensitive points of his work which would permit an innocuous reading. Primarily for this reason, his need to shield himself from the implications of his work, modern scholarship is still so far from agreement on the ultimate meaning of his romance.

The implications of the secular nature of courtly literature can be taken a step further if we recall that this worldliness was far from being accepted as an absolute value. It had to make its way alongside Christian beliefs, and courtly literature cannot be understood in isolation from the clerical literature which preceded it in the vernacular. Christian imagery and themes persist in conjunction with secular ones of the courtly world, and one vernacular term will frequently express a religious and also a secular idea (e.g. *gnâde*, *minne*). Historically this semantic situation is the converse of Christianity appropriating Germanic heroic terminology for its own ends, but the linguistic result is the same, for in both periods the same terminology can serve very different ends. This does not constitute irony, it only creates the possibility, but this will be realised in practice when such linguistic ambiguity is consciously exploited. The absolute claims of love in the courtly world can thus be qualified by being brought up against the superior claims of the Christian idea of love,[1] or the knightly virtue of *hôher muot* is called into question by an evocation of the clerical meaning of *hôchmuot* to imply that the chivalric value is nothing but arrogance.[2] The fact that courtly literature sought to enrich and buttress its worldly ideal by adapting Christian terms and symbols to a secular purpose meant that this secular ideal could be judged by reference to external criteria and found wanting, whenever it was taken to be self-sufficient.

The critical spirit

The romance is also rendered accessible to irony by the critical, rational spirit which the poets in this genre display and which they inculcate in their listeners. Irony is an inquiring mode of

[1] See above, pp. 96f., for this position in *Troilus and Criseyde*.
[2] Cf. Hempel, *Übermuot*, pp. 163ff.

speech because it operates with an implicit discrepancy and thereby insinuates the need to inquire further into this contrast and to reach an understanding of the true situation. Similarly, the romance has been described by Vinaver as 'a questioning mode',[1] the product of trained, critical minds whose wish for a coherent, intelligible narrative pattern presupposes the hope that it would be understood by a critical and intelligent audience, even if their critical powers had largely to be wakened by authors working in the new genre. The opportunity to adopt a critical approach was provided by the transition to written composition, but it is still the poet's task to realise in practice the advantages which this new mode of composition offers. Thomas speaks for more than just himself when he states that the criterion by which he wishes his work and other versions to be judged is that of *raisun*,[2] and the same is true when Gottfried in his prologue presents the two poles in the literary dialogue as the poet's artistry and the recipient's critical perceptiveness (33: *cunst unde nahe sehender sin*).

There are indications that the poet who observes the criterion of reason is not just living up to his own standards, but is also taking into account the possible critical objections of some members of his audience.[3] A realistic question is presupposed by Gottfried's narrator when he has to say how the lovers sustained themselves in the love-grotto (16807: *Genuoge nimet hier under/ virwitze unde wunder/und habent mit vrage groze not,/wie sich Tristan unde Isot,/die zwene geverten/in dirre wüeste ernerten*).[4] Whether or not this critical question means that Gottfried's listeners were acquainted with Thomas's or Eilhart's version, their incredulity and insistence on a rationally satisfying explanation constitute a challenge to the poet. If on the other hand we regard these questioners as Gottfried's creation, without a counterpart in the real situation he faced as reciter, then the challenge would be issued by him, inviting his listeners to ask this kind of question for themselves.

At times Wolfram appears to lose patience with his listeners' reluctance to accept what he says, especially when he is describing

---

[1] *BJRL* 46 (1963/64), 488.   [2] Thomas, *Tristan* 2134ff.

[3] These have been discussed by Lofmark, *Authority*, pp. 196ff. Although Lofmark has also shown, 'Credulity', pp. 5ff., that this is not the whole story, it is what concerns us at this point.   [4] Cf. Ranke, *Allegorie*, p. 23, fn. 1.

something miraculous, as with the wonderful food provided by the Grail (238,8: *man sagte mir, diz sag ouch ich/úf iuwer ieslîches eit,/ daz vorem grâle wære bereit/(sol ich des iemen triegen,/sô müezet ir mit mir liegen)*) or Parzival's Grail-sword (435,1: *Swerz niht geloubet, der sündet*).[1] From narrator's remarks like these we can infer incredulity on the part of his audience, his concern to defend the truth of his story implies that he met criticism when his listeners were not satisfied by his simple reference to the authority of a source when the situation conflicted with common sense. Alternatively, by inventing such questions Wolfram's narrator was deliberately drawing fire upon himself, knowing that he could extricate himself by using humour, in order to wean his listeners from a naïve trust in the source and bring home to them the distinction between fictional and factual truth.

Incredulity on rational grounds can be referred to and dismissed in the legend by means of the argument that nothing is impossible for God (as in Hartmann's *Gregorius* 3132: *daz dunket manegen niht wâr:/des gelouben velsche ich./wan gote ist niht unmügelich/ ze tuonne swaz er wil:/im ist deheines wunders ze vil*). When the same argument is used in secular literature, however (as at the close of the *Schwanritter* by Konrad von Würzburg, 1630: *ich wil hie biten unde manen/alt unde junc besunder,/daz si diz fremde wunder/niht haben gar für eine lüge,/und si gelouben daz got müge/erzeigen grôz unbilde*), the impression given is that the issue is being dodged and that the critical stance of the audience is now a factor which the author has to take into account. The same is implied by the ironic use of *ich wæne*, particularly with Wolfram,[2] whose hesitant phrasing suggests that he is dealing with an attentive audience, ready to pounce if he exposes himself by an improbable exaggeration. He achieves his end more effectively by using a form of understatement, inviting them to correct it and themselves to supply the emphatic statement which would have called forth disbelief if it had come from him.[3]

---

[1] I follow the implication of Leitzmann's edition at this point, who connects 435, 1 with what precedes it by placing a colon instead of a full stop at the close of 434, 30. See also Schröder, *ZfdA* 100 (1971), 128, fn. 3.

[2] Cf. Pörksen, *Erzähler*, p. 82, and Nellmann, *Erzähltechnik*, pp. 73f. and 139f.

[3] This is the implication of Wolff's remarks on Wolfram's use of hyperbole, *Schriften*, p. 265 (cf. also pp. 272f.).

Examples like this suggest a realistic shrewdness with regard to the cruder forms of improbability, but other cases discussed by Harroff show us Wolfram training the more perceptive of his listeners to remember the most inconspicuous details, to realise their subsequent relevance to passages far removed and to learn to correlate seemingly disparate episodes.[1] The listeners capable of profiting from this training were being taught not simply how to apply the yardstick of common sense to the narrative but, much more ambitiously, how to perceive the more subtle effects of dramatic or structural irony. The growth of a critical spirit in literature and the emergence of the romance genre as a questioning mode could only encourage the use of irony and the critical questions which it is meant to provoke.

Literary polemics

Two of these points can now be combined to yield a further reason to expect irony (in the particular form of parody) in courtly literature. If the emergence of written composition for vernacular poetry opens up a literate dimension for such poetry and if the growth of a critical spirit means that the poet asks searching questions about the rational coherence of his source and his own version and also prompts his listeners to join him in such questioning, the literary atmosphere in which courtly poetry now flourishes generates critical encounters between one poet and another in terms of personal rivalry, but also concerning matters of principle, the manner in which features of the courtly ideal are to be combined and presented in literary form. A literary atmosphere in which questions and criticism are encouraged will produce literary polemics, and we have seen how such polemics can make use of the weapons of parody and irony.

This has been most readily seen in the hermetic genre of the love lyric, whose closely defined theme meant that the poet's task lay more in finding formal variations on it.[2] This has been observed by Scholz, to whom we owe a survey of the encounter between Wolfram and Walther and who maintains that the poets active in the lyric were engaged in a general competition with

---

[1] Harroff, *Wolfram, passim.*   [2] Cf. Scholz, *Walther,* p. 86.

one another, no matter whether the object was impersonal and undefined or whether it took the particular and highly personal form of polemics, literary feuds and parody.[1] Wapnewski goes much further and argues, with regard to one of Wolfram's lyrics which he now regards as a parody,[2] that medieval love-poetry was written in a permanent state of parody.[3] If this goes too far in one direction, the same can be said of the converse attempt by Wachinger to call into question almost all the polemical encounters claimed for the classical period of the German love-lyric.[4] However welcome his scepticism about some of the arguments used, the attempt itself is too radical in scope to command assent. The truth is likely to lie somewhere between Wapnewski and Wachinger, somewhere close to the suggestion by Scholz that some, but not all, of these literary encounters took a specifically polemic and parodic form. Even this is enough to substantiate my point that the highly literary atmosphere of courtly poetry was productive of irony in the shape of parody.

What is true of the lyric applies to the romance as well, although Scholz is right in qualifying this by observing that the romance is not so self-contained as the lyric, since it has the primary obligation to tell a story and construct a narrative world, so that the element of literary competition will not play so prominent a part.[5] None the less, this qualification is not enough to render parody impossible in the romance. With regard to the theme of love, Chrétien in the first Arthurian romance avails himself of the opportunity to call into question, by means of parody, the Provençal conception of love.[6] In the chapter on the irony of love we also had to devote much of our attention to the different views of love current in courtly literature, hence to the rivalries and polemics which these generated. The parody of a poetic rival's depiction of love may not occupy a central position in any of the romances with which we have been concerned, but it is for all that a feature of these works which we can ill afford to ignore.

[1] Ibid.
[2] The allusion is to an article by Wapnewski, in which he still doubted the presence of irony in the poem in question, GRM 39 (1958), 327.
[3] Wapnewski, Lyrik, p. 193.
[4] Wachinger, Sängerkrieg, pp. 95ff.
[5] Scholz, op. cit., p. 87.
[6] See above, pp. 107ff.

The same point can also be made with regard to the theme of chivalry, of Hartmann perhaps less than of his successors, because he is mainly engaged in presenting a positive view of the chivalric ideal, even though his *Iwein* begins to suggest reservations on this score. As we saw, however, it is Hartmann's optimism on this score (which his *Iwein* does not fundamentally deny) which failed to satisfy Wolfram and Gottfried and therefore prompted them to parody the chivalric ideal put forward in *Erec* and for which this first German Arthurian romance was the obvious model. Wolfram parodies this (by taking over some of Hartmann's characters briefly into his own work and showing them in a very different light)[1] not because he rejects the need for an ideal chivalry, but because Hartmann's artificial solution cannot satisfy his critical awareness of the extent of the problem. Gottfried is free to parody the same ideal more sharply because he sees it as qualifying and endangering what is for him the absolute ideal of love.[2] With regard to its two major themes the German romance makes use of parody and is impelled in this direction by the critical dialogue between poets of different views and by the markedly literary atmosphere in which courtly poetry flourished.

Normative features

We come now to two aspects of the romance which, whilst they may not actually produce irony, certainly make its use more effective and therefore encourage it indirectly. The first is the conventional and normative nature of the romance, as of medieval literature at large. The modern reader is struck by the recurrence of constant and typical features in this literature.[3] For the most part its subject-matter has been taken over from other works, its themes are the recurrent ones of love and knightly combat, its figures are largely confined to a restricted court circle, its formal features are generally dictated by traditional rhetoric and its works are commissioned by patrons and geared to the need to appeal to a courtly audience. All this implies an art-form which is conservative, traditional and collective, it suggests such a

---

[1] See above, pp. 62ff.   [2] See Jackson, *Anatomy*, pp. 142ff.
[3] Cf. Pörksen, *Erzähler*, p. 9.

degree of acceptance of what has been inherited from others that it is difficult to reconcile these conditions with what irony naturally implies, a questioning of what is taken for granted, an individual standing back from the views of the generality, a quest for new possibilities. Although these conditions cannot have brought irony about, it can be argued that, once irony had been generated in the romance for various reasons, the presence of typical, normative conditions would make the shock of that irony much more effective than if the obstacle they presented had not existed.

The force of this can be seen if we apply a criticism levelled against 'Toposforschung' as practised by Curtius to the other normative tradition of medieval literature, rhetoric. He was so concerned to establish continuity in the use of topoi from classical antiquity down through the Middle Ages that he paid too little attention to the discontinuity represented by the coming of Christianity or to deviations from the tradition on the part of individual writers of genius.[1] In this light, we have to pay equal attention to a poet's agreement with rhetorical theory *and* to his deviations from it. We have to recognise that he may adopt a traditional pattern and at the same time give it a novel slant and that his deviations from the norm may be the more effective because his listeners will be expecting this norm.[2] A normative rhetorical tradition does not make individual deviations impossible, on the contrary it gives them considerably more force whenever they occur.

The connection between this feature of medieval rhetorical practice and irony is a close one. Just as the poet who occasionally abandons the norm can shock his audience because the norm is what they expect, so can the ironist prepare a trap for his victims by allowing them to think that they understand his meaning and by leaving it to them to grasp the truth subsequently. In this sense the apparent meaning which the ironist insinuates to his victim corresponds to the traditional norm which his audience expects the rhetorical poet to observe, whilst the shock, salutary and instructive because it reveals an unexpected dimension, lies in each case in the discrepancy between what is

---

[1] Cf. Veit, *Toposforschung*, pp. 143f.   [2] Cf. Clausen, *Erzähler*, p. 11.

expected or assumed and what is actually provided. Of the many examples of this exploitation of a rhetorical expectation I shall mention here only two different types from a period well before the genesis of the romance in order to stress that, alongside the rhetorical tradition, there is also an ironic tradition in medieval literature and that the presence of the one gives added force to the other.

My examples come from Old English, where the 'rhetorical' tradition in question is the stylistic convention of formulaic expressions and standing epithets. Quirk has taught us that the conjunction of a formulaic expression with the emphasis provided by alliteration can set up an expectation, nourished by the traditional nature of these expressions in Germanic poetry, that a term will call forth one of its conventional alliterating companions (e.g. *mōd* and *mægen*).[1] He has demonstrated, however, that the author of *Beowulf* can build on this stylistic tradition, and on his audience's expectation that it will be observed, by deviating from it at carefully chosen points, overwhelming his listeners with an unexpected incongruity which shows events in a disturbingly new light (as when the first half-line of 1709, *hæleðum tō helpe*, fittingly said of Beowulf, is incongruously collocated with *Heremōd*, the symbol of evil kingship, in the second half-line).

If a traditional technique, where like is felt properly to call forth like, is here adapted to new ends, betraying a poet who knows precisely when events cannot be adequately presented by the traditional rhetoric and who is concerned to alert his audience to this incongruity, the same is true of his occasional employment of a standing epithet with a devastatingly new purpose. In heroic literature it is a traditional truth that kings are wise protectors of their peoples, but when the author of *Beowulf* describes Hrothgar as *helm Scyldinga* at a time when he can provide no defence for his subjects, or as *wīs* when he is at his wits' end, there are reasons for judging such passages as conscious irony, rather than the mechanical use of a conventional term without thought for any possible incongruity.[2] Both these classes of

---

[1] See Quirk, *Essays*, pp. 1ff.

[2] The decision in favour of conscious irony depends largely on whether we regard *Beowulf* as an example of oral composition or written literature. I opt for the latter

example in *Beowulf* reveal an author standing back sufficiently
from the act of composition to take note of an incongruity, but
in each class the effectiveness of his irony derives from his conscious break with rhetorical convention and his trapping his
audience into grasping an unsuspected truth through their
expectation of a norm which is not observed. As with judo, the
ironist uses the weight of his opponent's expectation in order to
throw him the more skilfully.

Didacticism

The other feature of the romance which encourages irony is its
element of didacticism and pedagogic intent. Of itself this feature
need not produce irony, since the wish to present a pattern of
behaviour worthy of emulation could theoretically lead, as often
in the legend, to an idealisation of that pattern from which ironic
doubts at all costs have to be kept at bay. This conviction of the
presence of a didactic ideal in Hartmann's works has led some
scholars to deny him the irony which they are prepared to acknowledge in his source, Chrétien. But quite apart from the particular
problem of Hartmann, I am not convinced that the didactic
intent of the romance must always work in this way and must
always exclude irony. Just as the legend sometimes presents an
ideal protagonist, but sometimes one who begins as a sinner[1] and
only slowly attains to sainthood, thereby standing initially closer
to the sinful Christian who is to emulate him and providing the
hope that emulation is feasible, so can the romance pay attention
to the human failings of its chivalric hero. Again, this need not
result in irony, but we are led to it whenever an author like
Wolfram draws a parallel between Parzival's fumbling quest for
the Grail and his listeners' slow realisation of what is at stake,
between God's guidance of the hero and the narrator's progressive enlightenment of his audience.[2]

---

in view of the probability that it was composed in a literate setting which allowed
the poet to escape from the restraints of formulaic language (cf. Bowra, *Poetry*,
pp. 242 and 246), but also because of the structural skill in composition shown by
Bonjour, *Digressions, passim*.

[1] See Dorn, *Heilige, passim*.

See above, pp. 284f., and Green, *Weg*, p. 21.

How close the theme of a fumbling quest lies to the indirect approach to truth which irony involves can be seen by the words used by Jankélévitch to describe the ironic procedure. It may be linguistic chance that explains his view of irony as a stylisation of the dangerous adventure,[1] but what he later has to say of the indirectness of the ironic approach and its possible gains can be closely paralleled by Parzival's experience: '...ce voyage n'est pas un détour, ni du temps perdu; ce voyage est, comme toute médiation, une épreuve; l'ironisé ne se contente pas d'annuler ou compenser purement et simplement une fausse manœuvre, ni de tenir pour zéro une fleurette de rhétorique, une fioriture ou gentillesse de langage; et, en ce sens, le déchiffrage des chiffres n'est pas le simple rétablissement du *statu quo*. La vérité à laquelle l'ironisé, enfant prodigue, retourne finalement est une vérité trempée par le péril du malentendu, par les menaces d'erreur et par le jeu du contraire avec son contraire.'[2] The similarities between this ironic victim and Parzival are striking. Both are engaged on a journey, in both cases the journey is from appearances to reality,[3] is threatened by the danger of a catastrophic misunderstanding of what is involved, and is far from being a waste of time. For Parzival the long way round is the only way open to him in his situation,[4] whilst for the victim of irony the acquisition of truth by seeking for it himself in piercing through appearances is the surest pedagogic way to ensure that he will make that truth his own. If we accept this parallel we draw close to regarding the structure of Wolfram's romance as deeply ironic and to understanding why he gives his listeners information provisionally denied to Parzival and also at times keeps them in a state of ignorance that reflects his.[5] The first technique confers upon them the privilege of dramatic irony, the realisation of Parzival's state of ignorance, whilst the second places them in his position and invites them to make his experience their own by struggling through with him to perception of the truth.

---

[1] Jankélévitch, *Ironie*, p. 60.   [2] *Ibid.*, p. 67.
[3] Jankélévitch, pp. 66f., talks of a 'voyage du sens au sens à travers les chiffres', whilst Ohly says of the knightly quest (*ZfdA* 94 (1965), 173): 'Sie schreitet durch den Schein zum Sein, das umso härter von Schein umstellt ist, je näher man zu ihm gedrungen.'
[4] Green, *Weg*, p. 18.   [5] See above, pp. 146ff.

Irony and pedagogy belong together in a sense which is true of more than just this romance by Wolfram. Irony teaches its truth not directly (therefore possibly encountering disbelief or indifference), but by suggesting something other than what is meant, to which the person addressed reacts, as intended, by making the necessary correction, flattered by the belief that the truth has been reached by his own efforts, in contradiction to what the ironist has said. To describe the workings of irony in this way is to restate the principle of Socratic irony, where the ironist, by adopting the guise of ignorance, credulity or impercipience, deliberately understates himself, not to mock his interlocutor for believing himself to be superior, but to lead him on the path of wisdom by means of a subsequent realisation of his ignorance. Defining Socratic irony in this way, as opening out from a realisation of ignorance into potential wisdom, means disagreeing with the Kierkegaardian view of Socrates' absolute negativity[1] and underlines the didactic intention behind the irony employed by Socrates. It also agrees with the suggestions made by Booth on this subject: that Plato was not so convinced of the absolute negativity of the Socratic method as to deem it futile to preserve his dialogues, that Socrates believed in something strongly enough to give his life for it and that, however tentative all approximations to the truth, some can be shown to be nearer the truth than others, whilst there is never a suggestion that truth itself is undesirable.[2]

Conclusions

These comments by Booth on Socratic irony may serve as a bridge to some concluding observations, not just on the reasons for the employment of irony in the romance, but on the argument of the whole book. Booth devotes a large part of his work to the problem of learning where to stop in one's search for irony and what he has to say needs to be taken to heart. He is aware of the dangers of an undisciplined search for irony (the loss resulting from preferring ambiguity to precision and the abandonment of intellectual responsibility this can mean).[3] He also has some

---

[1] Booth, *Irony*, p. 273.   [2] Booth, *Irony*, p. 274.
[3] Cf. Dyson, *Fabric*, p. 1 and Booth, *Irony*, p. 172.

salutary words on taking our quest too far: 'Where then do we stop in our search for ironic pleasures? Where the work "tells" us to, wherever it offers us other riches that might be destroyed by irony.'[1] If we apply this warning to the quest for irony in the romance, we have to ask ourselves how far an ironic interpretation of this genre is reconcilable with the accepted view that the purpose of the romance is to legitimise the concerns of chivalry by presenting them in an ideal light, how far we are justified in expecting works written with such an intention to accommodate an irony which might be felt to undermine the ideal presented. In other words, what are the implications for the chivalric and courtly ideal of an ironic mode informed by an essentially critical spirit?

Two problems are raised by this question. First, if irony and parody are understood as characteristic features of a 'Spätzeit', is it not improbable to expect them in a new genre such as the romance and, in the case of France and Germany, amongst the earliest examples of this genre? Secondly, is it likely that poets engaged on a novel literary expression of the secular ideal could afford to jeopardise that ideal by the use of irony?

The first objection can be met by the suggestion that the romance can be seen more in terms of a 'Spätzeit' and as less of an absolute novelty if we recall that, as a vernacular expression of secular concerns, it follows on the well-established tradition of the heroic epic, a narrative genre rendered largely out-of-date by the immediate popularity of the romance, whose irony can be directed at the deficiencies of the heroic ideal it supplants. When the brutality of a superficial view of knightly adventure is criticised by means of irony (as in *Iwein*), what is being rejected is not just the view put forward by Kalogreant but also a heroic tradition which regarded such brutality as the hallmark of heroism. There are also a number of reasons for seeing the romance, as Vinaver has called it, as a questioning mode which is particularly open to irony as a questioning mode of speech. These reasons pertain to the romance as something new, as written composition in the vernacular, since from this there follow such points as the relevance of rhetoric to the use of irony, the growth

[1] Booth, *Irony*, p. 190.

of a critical spirit among those who, whether author or reader, could read the work and stand back from it critically, the literary atmosphere of courtly poetry and the rôle of clerics as outsiders in the world of the court. These are features which characterise the conditions under which courtly literature is composed, rather than features intrinsic to the romance alone, but they mean that courtly literature, and with it the romance, shows a predisposition towards the critical, and therefore towards irony and parody, from the beginning.

This predisposition has been recorded with regard to aspects of courtly literature other than the romance. Hausen was the first to introduce the Provençal love-convention into the German lyric and also the first to break with it in the wider context of crusading obligations. Wapnewski has made a similar point about Wolfram's dawnsong, arguing that he was the first to introduce the *wahtær* into the German lyric, but also the first to dismiss him, thereby abolishing the genre itself.[1] Both the early French and German versions of Renard the Fox have been interpreted as criticising and parodying the courtly ideal, but have both been dated as contemporary with the first emergence of courtly literature in each country,[2] so that idealisation is accompanied by criticism, whilst the same point has been made about the tendency and dating of the earliest *fabliaux*.[3] Vinaver has advanced his interpretation of the negative, deflating features of Dinadan despite the early dating towards which he was driven,[4] agreeing with Utley that the formalised satire is contemporary with the formalised ideal and that, in view of the ambivalence of courtly literature, there is no objection to seeing these two acting constantly on one another.[5]

If this is true of such courtly genres, there is little reason for surprise that the romance, too, should show critical alongside idealising features, especially since in the case of Chrétien, the

---

[1] Wapnewski, *Lyrik*, p. 255. It is possibly safer to talk of questioning, rather than abolishing the genre, if one has regard for the existence of dawnsongs without the figure of the *wahtær*.

[2] This is the thesis of Jauss, *Untersuchungen*, pp. 178ff. and of Schwab, *Datierung*, *passim*.

[3] Cf. Nykrog, *Fabliaux*, pp. 72ff. with regard to the parodic tendency and Tiemann, *RF* 72 (1960), 406ff. on the question of dating.

[4] Vinaver, *Recherche*, pp. 163ff., especially pp. 170ff.   [5] Utley, *Rib*, p. 31.

founding father of the Arthurian romance, irony has been readily acknowledged as integral to the type of narrative he inaugurated. For his German successors (to some of whom a similar irony has been denied) another reason comes into operation. Their romances, dependent on French sources, are works of a second generation, they can stand back at a remove and view the work as whole in a manner impossible for Chrétien or Thomas,[1] thereby acquiring opportunities for greater irony in commentary or correlation of discrepant points.[2] The German successor has had time for reflection and comment, his rôle as an adaptor makes his position, by a 'fatalité du genre',[3] more obvious as a narrator coming between his listeners and the events he recounts, and it is from this greater distance that he acquires possibilities of irony denied to his French model. This explanation has been advanced for the greater incidence of dramatic irony in Wolfram's *Parzival* than in Chrétien's version,[4] whilst Hartmann, in his *Erec*, was able to take account not merely of Chrétien's version but also of his *Yvain*,[5] thereby profiting from his predecessor's later poetic development when rendering this early work. A similar point has been made by Wolf: by comparison with Hartmann's ability to stand back and take a wider view (and thereby to elaborate structural irony by correlating discrepant points), Chrétien gives the impression of not having completely freed himself from composing in *laisses*.[6]

The second objection, that irony weakens the ideal by exposing it to criticism, has already been implicitly met at several points in earlier chapters. With regard to the themes of chivalry and love, irony is employed to indicate more the deficiencies of one who failed to live up to the ideal than the shortcomings of that ideal.[7]

---

[1] The different stance that a second-generation author can adopt need not be restricted to those adapting from one language to another (as Huby, *Adaptation*, maintains), but is also true of a poet like Thomas who adapts and modernises an earlier theme within the same literature. None the less, crossing a linguistic frontier and entering a different literary tradition place a translated adaptation at a greater distance from the original, so that however many changes Thomas may have introduced into his version by comparison with the *Estoire*, work still remained for Gottfried in his adaptation of Thomas.

[2] Cf. Lofmark, *Authority*, pp. 139f. and *Rennewart*, pp. 108f.

[3] Fourquet, *Hartmann*, p. 29.   [4] Johnson, *Ironie*, pp. 147f.

[5] As is borne out by the parallels adduced by Piquet, *Étude*, pp. 231f.

[6] Wolf, *Sprachkunst* 2 (1971), 35, fn. 78.

[7] See above, pp. 89f. and 128ff. Cf., even in the radical case of Gottfried's *Tristan*, the words of Clausen, *Erzähler*, pp. 198f.

When a courtly ideal is apparently called into question by irony this takes the form of parodying a rival's version of that ideal, so that what comes under critical fire is a poetic colleague's imperfect understanding of the ideal, which is thus preserved and strengthened in the parodist's own positive view of its potentialities. Even when a contemporary ideal is ironised and not allowed any redeeming features at all (as with Gottfried's attitude to chivalry), this serves the constructive purpose of defending another ideal felt to be superior and more essential (in Gottfried's case it is the absolute value of love which he is not prepared to see circumscribed or subjected to conditions by being harnessed to chivalry).

In all these cases medieval irony, unlike the admittedly often nihilistic corrosiveness of modern irony, still has a positive function in strengthening the ideal, rather than necessarily weakening it, just as any irony, particularly if employed at the narrator's expense, can be a device to protect and not destroy the illusion created in the story. The same point has been made by Lewis who suggests that the romance, by allowing laughter and cynicism their place inside the poem, is able to protect itself against the laughter of the vulgar.[1] The closely allied feature of realistic details (considered like irony as modifications of an idealised presentation) has been suggested as an attempt to render this ideal world more meaningful and to communicate it more forcibly, intended to enrich the ideal and not to criticise it.[2] We are justified in regarding the irony of the medieval romance in a similar light, not as rejecting or undermining the ideal, but as more accurately defining and refining it, reducing it to what is essential by stripping away what is false or questionable or merely superficial. The same may be claimed of the study of irony in the romance, since it can lead us to discard the accretions of a degenerate Romanticism and to appreciate the romance as intellectually as well as aesthetically satisfying. Only when the point is reached in the process of interpretation where this satisfaction appears to be jeopardised, where the quest for irony begins to yield less rather than more, may we agree that this is where we should stop in our search for the pleasures of irony.

[1] Lewis, *Allegory*, p. 172.
[2] See Grosse, *WW* 22 (1972), 82ff. and Stevens, *Romance*, p. 169.

BIBLIOGRAPHY

(1) *Primary sources*

Works are listed here under the name of the author, where this is known, or under the name of the work itself, where the author is anonymous. Otherwise, entries are to be found under the name of the editor. Here, as in the text, Chrétien's works are referred to in abbreviated form, e.g. *Perceval* instead of *Contes del Graal*. Footnote references in the text give a keyword which enables the entry to be recognised.

Alexanderlied, ed. K. Kinzel, Halle, 1884.

Andreas Capellanus, *De amore libri tres*, ed. E. Trojel, Munich, [2]1964. Translated by J. J. Parry, *The art of courtly love by Andreas Capellanus*, New York, [2]1964.

Bartsch, K., *Die Schweizer Minnesänger*, Frauenfeld, 1886.

Battle of Maldon, ed. E. V. Gordon, London, 1949.

Bede, *De schematibus et tropis*, ed. K. F. Halm in *Rhetores latini minores*, Leipzig, 1863.

Beowulf, ed. F. Klaeber, New York, [3]1941.

Bernard de Ventadour, *Chansons d'amour*, ed. M. Lazar, Paris, 1966.

Bernart Marti, *Les poésies*, ed. E. Hœpffner, Paris, 1929.

Béroul, ed. A. Ewert, *The romance of Tristan by Béroul*, 2 volumes, Oxford, 1967 and 1970.

Boethius, *De consolatione philosophiae*, ed. K. Büchner, Heidelberg, 1947.

Chaucer, *Canterbury Tales*, ed. F. N. Robinson in *The works of Geoffrey Chaucer*, London, 1968.
  The General Prologue to the Canterbury Tales, ed. J. Winny, Cambridge, 1966.
  The Knight's Tale, ed. A. C. Spearing, Cambridge, 1966.
  The Merchant's Tale, ed. M. Hussey, Cambridge, 1969.
  The Wife of Bath's Tale, ed. J. Winny, Cambridge, 1965.
  Troilus and Criseyde, ed. R. K. Root, Princeton, N.J., 1954.

Chrétien de Troyes, *Cligés*, ed. A. Micha, Paris, 1957.
  Erec, ed. W. Foerster, Halle, 1934.
  Lancelot, ed. M. Roques, *Le chevalier de la Charrete*, Paris, 1963.
  Perceval, ed. A. Hilka, *Li contes del Graal*, Halle, 1932.

[394]

Yvain, ed. W. Foerster and A. Hilka, Halle, 1926.

Translated by W. W. Comfort, *Arthurian romances*, London, 1943.

Cicero, *De divinatione*, ed. W. A. Falconer, London, 1971.

De officiis, ed. W. Miller, London, 1968.

De oratore, ed. H. Rackham, London, 1968 (volume II).

Dante, *Paradiso*, ed. J. D. Sinclair, London, 1946.

Diomedes, *Ars grammatica*, ed. H. Keil in *Grammatici latini* (volume I), Leipzig, 1857.

Donatus, *Ars grammatica*, ed. H. Keil in *Grammatici latini* (volume IV), Leipzig, 1864.

Eilhart von Oberge, *Tristrant*, ed. F. Lichtenstein, Strassburg, 1877.

Emporius, *Praeceptum demonstrativae materiae*, ed. K. Halm in *Rhetores latini minores*, Leipzig, 1863.

Flamenca, ed. R. Lavaud and R. Nelli, Bruges, 1960.

Frauenlob, ed. L. Ettmüller, Quedlinburg, 1843.

Freidank, *Bescheidenheit*, ed. H. E. Bezzenberger, Halle, 1872.

Gaimar, *Lestorie des Engles*, ed. T. D. Hardy and C. T. Martin, London, 1888.

(*Sir*) *Gawain and the Green Knight*, ed. J. R. R. Tolkien and E. V. Gordon (2nd ed. by N. Davis), Oxford, ²1968. Also edited by W. R. J. Barron, Manchester, 1974.

Geoffrey of Vinsauf, *Poetria nova*, ed. E. Faral in *Les arts poétiques du XIIe et du XIIIe siècle*, Paris, 1962.

Giraldus Cambrensis, *De Principis instructione*, ed. G. F. Warner, *Giraldi Cambrensis opera* (volume VIII), London, 1891.

Gottfried von Strassburg, *Tristan und Isold*, ed. F. Ranke, Dublin and Zürich, 1967.

Hartmann von Aue, *Der arme Heinrich*, ed. H. Paul and A. Leitzmann, Halle, 1930.

Erec, ed. A. Leitzmann and L. Wolff, Tübingen, 1963.

Gregorius, ed. F. Neumann, Wiesbaden, 1958.

Iwein, ed. G. F. Benecke, K. Lachmann and L. Wolff, Berlin, 1968. Also by G. F. Benecke and K. Lachmann, Berlin, 1868. Translated by T. Cramer, Berlin, 1968.

Erec. Iwein, ed. J. Fourquet, Paris, 1944.

Heine, H., *Die romantische Schule*, ed. H. Kaufmann, *Werke und Briefe* (volume V), Berlin, 1961.

Heinrich von dem Türlin, *Diu Crône*, ed. G. H. F. Scholl, Stuttgart, 1852.

Der Mantel, ed. O. Warnatsch, Breslau, 1883.

Heinrich von Freiberg, *Tristan*, ed. R. Bechstein, Leipzig, 1877.

Heinrich von Veldeke, *Eneide*, ed. G. Schieb and T. Frings, Berlin, 1964.

Hugh of St Victor, *De grammatica*, ed. J. Leclercq in *Archives d'histoire doctrinale et littéraire du moyen âge* 18 (1943), 263ff.

Isidore of Seville, *Etymologiae*, ed. W. M. Lindsay, Oxford, 1911.

Joinville, *Histoire de Saint Louis*, ed. N. de Wailly, Paris, 1868.

Judith, ed. E. V. K. Dobbie, *Beowulf and Judith*, London, 1954.

Julian of Toledo, *De vitiis et figuris*, ed. W. M. Lindsay, Oxford, 1922.

Julius Rufinianus, *De schematis dianœas*, ed. K. Halm in *Rhetores latini minores*, Leipzig, 1863.

Kaiserchronik, ed. E. Schröder, MGH *Deutsche Chroniken*, Berlin, 1964.

Konrad von Würzburg, *Der Welt Lohn*, ed. E. Schröder, Berlin, 1959.

von Kraus, C., *Deutsche Liederdichter des 13. Jahrhunderts*, Tübingen, 1951–8.

Ludwigslied, ed. W. Braune and K. Helm, *Althochdeutsches Lesebuch*, Halle, ¹¹1949, pp. 118f.

Malory, Sir Thomas, ed. E. Vinaver, Oxford, ²1967.

Matthew of Vendôme, *Ars versificatoria*, ed. E. Faral in *Les arts poétiques du XIIe et du XIIIe siècle*, Paris, 1962.

Millstätter Exodus, ed. E. Papp, *Die altdeutsche Exodus*, Munich, 1968.

Minnesangs Frühling, ed. C. von Kraus, Leipzig, 1944.

Nibelungenlied, ed. H. de Boor, Wiesbaden, ¹⁶1961.

Niewöhner, H. and Simon, W., *Neues Gesamtabenteuer*, Dublin, 1967.

Notker der Deutsche, *Werke*, ed. E. H. Sehrt and Taylor Starck. Volume III, *Der Psalter*, Halle, 1952ff.

De arte rhetorica, ed. P. Piper in *Die Schriften Notkers und seiner Schule* (volume I), Freiburg and Tübingen, 1882.

Oswald von Wolkenstein, *Die Lieder*, ed. K. K. Klein, Tübingen, 1962.

Pfannmüller, L., *Mittelhochdeutsche Novellen*, Bonn, 1912.

Pompeius, *Commentum Artis Donati*, ed. H. Keil in *Grammatici latini* (volume V), Leipzig, 1868.

Quintilian, *Institutio oratoria*, ed. H. E. Butler (volume III), London, 1966.

Raby, F. J. E., *The Oxford book of medieval Latin verse*, Oxford, 1959.

Rolandslied, ed. F. Maurer, Leipzig, 1940.

(Des) Teufels Netz, ed. K. A. Barack, Stuttgart, 1863.

Thomas, *Roman de Tristan*, ed. J. Bédier, Paris, 1902. Also edited by B. H. Wind, Geneva, 1960.

Tristan als Mönch, ed. B. C. Bushey, Göppingen, 1974.

Ulrich von Lichtenstein, *Frauendienst*, ed. K. Lachmann, Berlin, 1841.

Wace, *Roman de Rou*, ed. H. Andresen, Heilbronn, 1877–9.

Waltharius, ed. K. Strecker, Berlin, 1947.

Walther von der Vogelweide, ed. C. von Kraus, Berlin, 1950.

Wernher von Elmendorf, ed. J. Bumke, Tübingen, 1974.

Wolfram von Eschenbach. His various works (*Parzival*, *Willehalm*, *Titurel*, lyric poems) have been quoted from the edition by K. Lachmann, Berlin, ⁶1926. Reference is sometimes made to the edition by K. Bartsch and M. Marti, Leipzig, 1929–35.

(2) *Secondary literature*

Adolf, H., 'Die Wolframsche Wendung *diu hœhste hant*', *Neophilologus* 19 (1934), 260ff.

Allemann, B., 'Ironie als literarisches Prinzip' in A. Schaefer (ed.), *Ironie und Dichtung*, Munich, 1970, pp. 11ff.

Arbusow, L., *Colores rhetorici*, Göttingen, 1963.

Auerbach, E., *Mimesis. Dargestellte Wirklichkeit in der abendländischen Literatur*, Bern, 1946.

Literatursprache und Publikum in der lateinischen Spätantike und im Mittelalter, Bern, 1958.

Baasch, K., *Die Crescentialegende in der deutschen Dichtung des Mittelalters*, Stuttgart, 1968.

Baehr, R., 'Chrétien de Troyes und der Tristan', *Sprachkunst* 2 (1971), 43ff.

Bahr, E., *Die Ironie im Spätwerk Goethes.* '... *diese sehr ernsten Scherze* ...' *Studien zum* '*West-östlichen Divan*', *zu den* '*Wanderjahren*' *und zu* '*Faust II*', Berlin, 1972.

Bäuml, F. H., 'Der Übergang mündlicher zur Artes-bestimmten Literatur des Mittelalters', in the FS for G. Eis, Stuttgart, 1970, pp. 1ff.

Bäuml, F. H. and Bruno, A. M., 'Weiteres zur mündlichen Überlieferung des Nibelungenliedes', *DVjs* 46 (1972), 479ff.

Bäuml, F. H. and Spielmann, E., 'From illiteracy to literacy: prolegomena to a study of the *Nibelungenlied*', *FMLS* 10 (1974), 248ff.

Bäuml, F. H. and Ward, D. J., 'Zur mündlichen Überlieferung des Nibelungenliedes, *DVjs* 41 (1967), 351ff.

Barron, W. R. J., 'French romance and the structure of *Sir Gawain and the Green Knight*', in W. Rothwell, W. R. J. Barron, D. Blamires, L. Thorpe (edd.), *Studies in medieval literature and languages in memory of Frederick Whitehead*, Manchester, 1973, pp. 7ff.

Batts, M. S., 'The idealised landscape in Gottfried's Tristan', *Neophilologus* 46 (1962), 226ff.

'Hartmann's humanitas: a new look at *Iwein*', in F. A. Raven, W. K. Legner, J. C. King (edd.), *Germanic studies in honor of Edward Henry Sehrt*, Coral Gables, Fla., 1968, pp. 37ff.

Gottfried von Strassburg, New York, 1971.

Bayer, H. J., *Untersuchungen zum Sprachstil weltlicher Epen des deutschen Früh- und Hochmittelalters*, Berlin, 1962.

Beck, H., *Das Ebersignum im Germanischen. Ein Beitrag zur germanischen Tier-Symbolik*, Berlin, 1965.

Bédier, J., *Les fabliaux. Etudes de littérature populaire et d'histoire littéraire du moyen âge*, Paris, ⁶1964.

Behler, E., *Klassische Ironie, romantische Ironie, tragische Ironie. Zum Ursprung dieser Begriffe*, Darmstadt, 1972.

Benecke, G. F., Müller, W. and Zarncke, F., *Mittelhochdeutsches Wörterbuch*, Leipzig, 1854–61.

Benson, L. D., *Art and tradition in 'Sir Gawain and the Green Knight'*, New Brunswick, N.J., 1965.

Benton, J., 'Clio and Venus: an historical view of medieval love', in F. X. Newman (ed.), *The meaning of courtly love*, Albany, N.Y., 1968, pp. 19ff.

Bergson, H., *Le rire*, Paris, ⁴⁵1938.

Bertau, K., *Deutsche Literatur im europäischen Mittelalter*, Munich, 1972.

Bertolucci, V., 'La retorica nel Tristano di Thomas', *SMV* 6/7 (1959), 25ff.

'Commento retorico all' *Erec* e al *Cligés*', *SMV* 8 (1960), 9ff.

Bethurum, D., 'Chaucer's point of view as narrator', *PMLA* 74 (1959), 511ff.

Beyer, J., *Schwank und Moral. Untersuchungen zum altfranzösischen Fabliau und verwandten Formen*, Heidelberg, 1969.

Beyschlag, S., 'Die Funktion der epischen Vorausdeutung im Aufbau des Nibelungenliedes', *PBB* 76 (1954), 38ff.

Bezzola, R. R., *Les origines et la formation de la littérature courtoise en occident (500–1200). Troisième partie: La société courtoise: littérature de cour et littérature courtoise*, Paris, 1963.

Bindschedler, M., *Gottfried von Strassburg und die höfische Ethik*, Halle, 1955.

'Die Dichtung um König Artus und seine Ritter', *DVjs* 31 (1957), 84ff.

Birney, E., 'The beginnings of Chaucer's irony', *PMLA* 54 (1939), 637ff.

Bizet, J.-A., *Suso et le Minnesang*, Paris, 1944.

Blamires, D., *Characterization and individuality in Wolfram's 'Parzival'*, Cambridge, 1966.

Bloch, R. H., *Medieval French literature and law*, Berkeley, Calif., 1977.

Bloomfield, M. W., 'Distance and predestination in *Troilus and Criseyde*', *PMLA* 72 (1957), 14ff.

Bogdanow, F., 'The love theme in Chrétien de Troyes's *Chevalier de la Charrette*', *MLR* 67 (1972), 50ff.

Bonjour, A., *The digressions in 'Beowulf'*, Oxford, 1950.

'Anticipations et prophéties dans le *Nibelungenlied*', *EG* 7 (1952), 241ff.

de Boor, H., *Geschichte der deutschen Literatur von den Anfängen bis zur Gegenwart*, Munich, 1949 (volume I), 1953 (volume II), 1962 (volume III).

Booth, W. C., *The rhetoric of fiction*, Chicago, 1967.

Now don't try to reason with me. Essays and ironies for a credulous age, Chicago, 1970.

A rhetoric of irony, Chicago, 1974.

Borck, K. H., *Philologische Untersuchungen zu Wolframs Liedern*, Habilitationsschrift Münster, 1959.

Borovski, C., *L'ironie et l'humour chez Gottfried de Strasbourg*, dissertation Strasbourg, 1960.

Borroff, M., *Sir Gawain and the Green Knight. A stylistic and metrical study*, New Haven, Conn., 1962.

Borst, A., 'Das Rittertum im Hochmittelalter. Idee und Wirklichkeit', *Saeculum* 10 (1959), 213ff.

Bowra, C. M., *Heroic poetry*, London, 1961.

Bracher, F., 'Understatement in Old English poetry', *PMLA* 52 (1937), 915ff.

Brackert, H., *Rudolf von Ems. Dichtung und Geschichte*, Heidelberg, 1968.

Brewer, D., 'Courtesy and the *Gawain*-poet', in the FS for C. S. Lewis, London, 1966, pp. 54ff.

'Troilus and Criseyde', in W. F. Bolton (ed.), *The Middle Ages*, London, 1970, pp. 195ff.

Brinkmann, H., *Zu Wesen und Form mittelalterlicher Dichtung*, Halle, 1928.

Studien zur Geschichte der deutschen Sprache und Literatur (volume II: *Literatur*), Düsseldorf, 1966.

Brodeur, A. G., *The art of Beowulf*, Berkeley, Calif., 1960.

Bronson, B. H., 'Chaucer's art in relation to his audience', in *Five studies in literature* (University of California Publications in English 1, 1940), pp. 1ff.

Brooks, C., 'Irony and ironic poetry', *College English* 9 (1947/48), 231ff.

Büchner, W., 'Über den Begriff der Eironeia', *Hermes* 76 (1941), 339ff.

Bullough, V. L., 'Medieval medical and scientific views of women', *Viator* 4 (1973), 485ff.

Bumke, J., 'Die Auflösung des Tugendsystems bei Wernher von Elmendorf', *ZfdA* 88 (1957), 39ff.

Wolframs 'Willehalm'. Studien zur Epenstruktur und zum Heiligkeitsbegriff der ausgehenden Blütezeit, Heidelberg, 1959.

Die romanisch-deutschen Literaturbeziehungen im Mittelalter. Ein Überblick, Heidelberg, 1967.

Die Wolfram von Eschenbach Forschung seit 1945. Bericht und Bibliographie, Munich, 1970.

Burdach, K., *Walther von der Vogelweide. Philologische und historische Forschungen*, Leipzig, 1900.

'Der gute Klausner Walthers von der Vogelweide als Typus unpolitischer christlicher Frömmigkeit', *ZfdPh* 60 (1935), 313ff.

Burger, H., 'Vorausdeutung und Erzählstruktur in mittelalterlichen Texten', in the FS for M. Wehrli, Zürich, 1969, pp. 125ff.

Burrow, J. A., *A reading of 'Sir Gawain and the Green Knight'*, London, 1965.

Ricardian poetry. Chaucer, Gower, Langland and the 'Gawain' poet, London, 1971.

Caliebe, M., *Dukus Horant. Studien zu seiner literarischen Tradition*, Berlin, 1973.

Chaytor, H. J., *From script to print. An introduction to medieval vernacular literature*, Cambridge, 1950.

Clark, C., '*Sir Gawain and the Green Knight*: its artistry and its audience', *MÆ* 40 (1971), 10ff.

Clausen, I., *Der Erzähler in Gottfrieds Tristan*, dissertation Kiel, 1970.

Cloetta, W., *Beiträge zur Literaturgeschichte des Mittelalters und der Renaissance*. Volume 1: *Komödie und Tragödie im Mittelalter*, Halle, 1890.

Coghill, N., *Geoffrey Chaucer. Troilus and Criseyde*, Harmondsworth, 1971.

Cohen, G., *La comédie latine en France au XIIe siècle*, Paris, 1931.

Combridge, R. N., *Das Recht im 'Tristan' Gottfrieds von Strassburg*, Berlin, 1964.

Cormeau, C., *Hartmanns von Aue 'Armer Heinrich' und 'Gregorius'. Studien zur Interpretation mit dem Blick auf die Theologie zur Zeit Hartmanns*, Munich, 1966.

Cramer, T., '*Sælde und êre* in Hartmanns Iwein', *Euphorion* 60 (1966), 30ff. *Hartmann von Aue. Iwein*, Berlin, 1968.

Crosby, R., 'Chaucer and the custom of oral delivery', *Speculum* 13 (1938), 413ff.

Curry, W. C., *Chaucer and the medieval sciences*, New York, 1960.

Curschmann, M., 'Oral poetry in medieval English, French and German literature: some notes on present research', *Speculum* 42 (1967), 36ff. 'Das Abenteuer des Erzählens. Über den Erzähler in Wolframs *Parzival*', *DVjs* 45 (1971), 627ff.

Curtius, E. R., 'Das "ritterliche Tugendsystem",' *DVjs* 21 (1943), 343ff. *Europäische Literatur und lateinisches Mittelalter*, Bern, 1948.

Deinert, W., *Ritter und Kosmos im Parzival. Eine Untersuchung der Sternkunde Wolframs von Eschenbach*, Munich, 1960.

Delbouille, M., 'Les chansons de geste et le livre', in *La technique littéraire des chansons de geste*, Actes du colloque de Liège (septembre, 1957), Paris, 1959, pp. 295ff.

Dembowski, P. F., 'Monologue, author's monologue and related problems in the romances of Chrétien de Troyes', *YFS* 51 (1974), 102ff.

Dempster, G., *Dramatic irony in Chaucer*, New York, 1959.

Désilles-Busch, M., '*Doner un don' – 'sicherheit nemen'. Zwei typische Elemente der Erzählstruktur des höfischen Romans*, dissertation Berlin (Freie Universität), 1970.

Dewald, H., *Minne und 'sgrâles âventiur'. Äusserungen der Subjektivität und ihre sprachliche Vergegenwärtigung in Wolframs 'Parzival'*, Göppingen, 1975.

Donaldson, E. T., *Speaking of Chaucer*, London, 1970.

Dorn, E., *Der sündige Heilige in der Legende des Mittelalters*, Munich, 1967.

Dronke, P., *Medieval Latin and the rise of European love-lyric*, Oxford, 1965. 'The rise of the medieval fabliau: Latin and vernacular evidence', *RF* 85 (1973), 275ff.

'Peter of Blois and poetry at the court of Henry II', *MSt* 38 (1976), 185ff.

Drube, H., *Hartmann und Chrétien*, Münster, 1931.

Dürrenmatt, N., *Das Nibelungenlied im Kreis der höfischen Dichtung*, Bern, 1945.

Duggan, J. J., *The Song of Roland. Formulaic style and poetic craft*, Berkeley, Calif., 1973.

Oral literature. Seven essays, Edinburgh, 1975.

Durling, R. M., *The figure of the poet in Renaissance epic*, Cambridge, Mass., 1965.

Dyson, A. E., *The crazy fabric. Essays in irony*, London, 1966.

Eggers, H., 'Non cognovi litteraturam (zu *Parzival* 115, 27)', in the FS for U. Pretzel, Berlin, 1963, pp. 162ff.

Ehrismann, G., 'Duzen und Ihrzen im Mittelalter', *ZfdW* 5 (1903/04), 127ff.

'Die Grundlagen des ritterlichen Tugendsystems', *ZfdA* 56 (1919), 137ff.

Geschichte der deutschen Literatur bis zum Ausgang des Mittelalters, Munich, 1932 (²1), 1922 (II 1), 1927 (II 2), 1935 (II 3).

Eifler, G. (ed.), *Ritterliches Tugendsystem*, Darmstadt, 1970.

Eis, G., 'Priamel-Studien', in the FS for F. R. Schröder, Heidelberg, 1959, pp. 178ff.

Emmel, H., *Formprobleme des Artusromans und der Graldichtung. Die Bedeutung des Artuskreises für das Gefüge des Romans im 12. und 13. Jahrhundert in Frankreich, Deutschland und den Niederlanden*, Bern, 1951.

Endres, R., *Studien zum Stil von Hartmanns Erec*, dissertation Munich, 1961.

Eroms, H.-W., *'Vreude' bei Hartmann von Aue*, Munich, 1970.

von Ertzdorff, X., 'Spiel der Interpretation. Der Erzähler in Hartmanns Iwein', in the FS for F. Maurer, Düsseldorf, 1968, pp. 135ff.

Everett, D., *Essays on Middle English literature*, Oxford, 1955.

Falk, W., *Das Nibelungenlied in seiner Epoche. Revision eines romantischen Mythos*, Heidelberg, 1974.

Faral, E., *Recherches sur les sources latines des contes et romans courtois du moyen âge*, Paris, 1913.

'Le fabliau latin au moyen âge', *Romania* 50 (1924), 321ff.

Les arts poétiques du XIIe et du XIIIe siècle. Recherches et documents sur la technique littéraire du moyen âge, Paris, 1962.

Fechter, W., 'Absalon als Vergleichs- und Beispielfigur im mittelhochdeutschen Schrifttum', *PBB* (T) 83 (1961/62), 302ff.

Ferrante, J. M., *The conflict of love and honor. The medieval Tristan legend in France, Germany and Italy*, The Hague, 1973.

Woman as image in medieval literature from the twelfth century to Dante, New York, 1975.

'The conflict of lyric conventions and romance form', in J. M. Ferrante and G. D. Economou (edd.), *In pursuit of perfection. Courtly love in medieval literature*, Port Washington, N.Y., 1975, pp. 135ff.

Finnegan, R., *Oral poetry. Its nature, significance and social context*, Cambridge, 1977.

Finoli, A. M., 'Χαριεντισμός festiva dictio, 'Αστεϊσμός urbana dictio', *ILRL* 92 (1958), 569ff.

Fischer, H., *Studien zur deutschen Märendichtung*, Tübingen, 1968.

Fliegner, G., *Geistliches und weltliches Rittertum im Rolandslied des Pfaffen Konrad*, dissertation Breslau, 1937.

Foulet, L., 'Sire, Messire', *Romania* 71 (1950), 1ff.

Fourquet, J., *Hartmann d'Aue: Erec, Iwein*, Paris, 1944.

Fourrier, A., *Le courant réaliste dans le roman courtois en France au moyen âge*, Paris, 1960.

Fowler, H. W., *A dictionary of modern English usage*, Oxford, 1954.

Frappier, J., *Chrétien de Troyes*, Paris, 1957.

'Le personnage de Gauvain dans la première continuation de Perceval (Conte du Graal)', *RPh* 11 (1957/58), 331ff.

'Sur la composition du *Conte du Graal*', *MA* 64 (1958), 67ff.

Le roman breton: les origines de la légende arthurienne: Chrétien de Troyes, Paris, 1959.

'Virgile source de Chrétien de Troyes?', *RPh* 13 (1959), 50ff.

'Structure et sens du *Tristan*: version commune, version courtoise', *CCM* 6 (1963), 441ff.

Etude sur 'Yvain' ou le Chevalier au Lion de Chrétien de Troyes, Paris, 1969.

Chrétien de Troyes et le mythe du Graal. Etude sur Perceval ou le Conte du Graal, Paris, 1972.

Amour courtois et Table Ronde, Geneva, 1973.

Freytag, W., *Das Oxymoron bei Wolfram, Gottfried und andern Dichtern des Mittelalters*, Munich, 1972.

Fromm, H., 'Zum gegenwärtigen Stand der Gottfried-Forschung', *DVjs* 28 (1954), 115ff.

'Komik und Humor in der Dichtung des deutschen Mittelalters', *DVjs* 36 (1962), 321ff.

'Tristans Schwertleite', *DVjs* 41 (1967), 333ff.

Frost, W., 'An interpretation of Chaucer's Knight's Tale', *RES* 25 (1949), 289ff.

Fuchs, W., *Der Tristanroman und die höfische Liebesnovelle*, dissertation Zürich, 1967.

Gaier, U., *Satire. Studien zu Neidhart, Wittenwiler, Brant und zur satirischen Schreibart*, Tübingen, 1967.

Gallais, P., 'Recherches sur la mentalité des romanciers français du moyen âge', *CCM* 7 (1964), 479ff.; II, *CCM* 13 (1970), 333ff.

Ganz, P., 'Der Begriff des "Höfischen" bei den Germanisten', in W. Schröder (ed.), *Wolfram-Studien IV*, Berlin, 1977, pp. 16ff.

Gaylord, A. T., '*Gentilesse* in Chaucer's *Troilus*', *SP* 61 (1964), 19ff.

'Chaucer's tender trap: the Troilus and the "yonge, fresshe folkes",' *EM* 15 (1964), 25ff.

le Gentil, P., 'La légende de Tristan vue par Béroul et Thomas', *RPh* 7 (1953/54), 111ff.

Georgi, A., *Das lateinische und deutsche Preisgedicht des Mittelalters in der Nachfolge des genus demonstrativum*, Berlin, 1969.

Gerz, A., *Rolle und Funktion der epischen Vorausdeutung im mittelhochdeutschen Epos*, Berlin, 1930.

Gibbs, M. E., 'Wrong ways in *Parzival*', *MLR* 63 (1968), 872ff.

Gilson, E., *La théologie mystique de saint Bernard*, Paris, 1947.

Gnaedinger, L., *Musik und Minne im 'Tristan' Gotfrids von Strassburg*, Düsseldorf, 1967.

Goebel, K. D., 'Der Gebrauch der dritten und ersten Person bei der Selbstnennung und in den Selbstaussagen mittelhochdeutscher Dichter', *ZfdPh* 94 (1975), 15ff.

Good, E. M., *Irony in the Old Testament*, London, 1965.

Goosse, A., 'Sur le Graal', *LR* 12 (1958), 302ff.

Gordon, I. L., *The double sorrow of Troilus. A study of ambiguities in 'Troilus and Criseyde'*, Oxford, 1970.

Green, D. H., *The Carolingian lord. Semantic studies in four Old High German words. Balder, frô, truhtin, hêrro*, Cambridge, 1965.

The Millstätter Exodus. A crusading epic, Cambridge, 1966.

'Der Auszug Gahmurets', in W. Schröder (ed.), *Wolfram-Studien*, Berlin, 1970, pp. 62ff.

'Irony and medieval romance', in D. D. R. Owen (ed.), *Arthurian romance. Seven essays*, Edinburgh, 1970, 49ff.

Der Weg zum Abenteuer im höfischen Roman des deutschen Mittelalters (Veröffentlichung der Joachim Jungius-Gesellschaft der Wissenschaften), Göttingen, 1974.

'Alieniloquium. Zur Begriffsbestimmung der mittelalterlichen Ironie', in the FS for F. Ohly, Munich, 1975, volume II, pp. 119ff.

'The *Alexanderlied* and the emergence of the romance', *GLL* 28 (1975), 246ff.

'On damning with faint praise in medieval literature', *Viator* 6 (1975), 117ff.

'Hartmann's ironic praise of Erec', *MLR* 70 (1975), 795ff.

'On recognising medieval irony', in A. P. Foulkes (ed.), *The uses of criticism*, Bern, 1976, pp. 11ff.

'Homicide and *Parzival*', in D. H. Green and L. P. Johnson, *Approaches to Wolfram von Eschenbach. Five Essays*, Bern, 1978, pp. 11ff.

'The concept *âventiure* in *Parzival*', *ibid.*, pp. 83ff.

'Oral poetry and written composition (An aspect of the feud between Gottfried and Wolfram)', *ibid.*, pp. 163ff.

'The pathway to adventure', *Viator* 8 (1977), 145ff.

Green, D. H. and Johnson, L. P., *Approaches to Wolfram von Eschenbach. Five Essays*, Bern, 1978.

Grisebach, C., *Zeitbegriff und Zeitgestaltung in den Romanen Chrétiens de Troyes und Hartmanns von Aue*, dissertation Freiburg, 1956.

Groos, A. B., 'Wolfram von Eschenbach's "bow metaphor" and the narrative technique of *Parzival*', *MLN* 87 (1972), 391ff.

Grosse, S., 'Vremdiu mære – Tristans Herkunftsberichte', *WW* 20 (1970), 289ff.

'Zur Frage des "Realismus" in den deutschen Dichtungen des Mittelalters', *WW* 22 (1972), 73ff.

Grosser, D., *Studies in the influence of the 'Rhetorica ad Herennium' and Cicero's 'De inventione'*, dissertation Cornell, 1953.

Gruenter, R., 'Über den Einfluss des Genus iudicale auf den höfischen Redestil', *DVjs* 26 (1952), 49ff.

'Bauformen der Waldleben-Episode in Gotfrids Tristan und Isold', in the FS for G. Müller, Bonn, 1957, pp. 21ff.

'Das *wunnecliche tal*', *Euphorion* 55 (1961), 341ff.

'Der Favorit. Das Motiv der höfischen Intrige in Gotfrids Tristan und Isold', *Euphorion* 58 (1964), 113ff.

Grundmann, H., 'Die Frauen und die Literatur im Mittelalter. Ein Beitrag zur Frage nach der Entstehung des Schrifttums in der Volkssprache', *AfK* 26 (1936), 129ff.

'Dichtete Wolfram von Eschenbach am Schreibtisch?', *AfK* 49 (1967), 391ff.

Günther, J., *Die Minneparodie bei Neidhart*, Halle, 1931.

Haas, A. M., *Parzivals tumpheit bei Wolfram von Eschenbach*, Berlin, 1964.

Hahn, I., *Raum und Landschaft in Gottfrieds Tristan*, Munich, 1963.

'Zu Gottfrieds von Strassburg Literaturschau', *ZfdA* 96 (1967), 218ff.

'Parzivals Schönheit. Zum Problem des Erkennens und Verkennens im *Parzival*', in the FS for F. Ohly, Munich, 1975, volume II, pp. 203ff.

Haidu, P., *Aesthetic distance in Chrétien de Troyes: irony and comedy in 'Cligés' and 'Perceval'*, Geneva, 1968.

van Hamel, A. G., 'Cligès et Tristan', *Romania* 33 (1904), 465ff.

Hamm, E., *Rheinische Legenden des 12. Jahrhunderts*, dissertation Cologne, 1937.

Hansen, I., *Zwischen Epos und höfischem Roman. Die Frauengestalten im Trojaroman des Benoît de Sainte-Maure*, Munich, 1971.

Harms, W., *Der Kampf mit dem Freund oder Verwandten in der deutschen Literatur bis um 1300*, Munich, 1963.

Homo viator in bivio. Studien zur Bildlichkeit des Weges, Munich, 1970.

Harrison, G. B. (ed.), *Major British Writers*, New York, 1954.

Harroff, S. C., *Wolfram and his audience. A study of the themes of quest and of recognition of kinship identity*, Göppingen, 1974.

Haskins, C. H., 'Henry II as a patron of literature', in the FS for T. F. Tout, Manchester, 1925, pp. 71ff.

Hatto, A. T., 'Poetry and the hunt in medieval Germany', *AUMLA* 25 (1966), 33ff., reprinted in *Essays on Medieval German and Other Poetry*, Cambridge, forthcoming.

'*Ine Weiz* ... Diplomatic ignorance on the part of medieval German poets', in the FS for L. A. Willoughby, Oxford, 1952, pp. 98ff.

'*Der aventiure meine* in Hartmann's *Iwein*', in the FS for F. Norman, London, 1965, pp. 94ff.

Haug, W., 'Die Symbolstruktur des höfischen Epos und ihre Auflösung bei Wolfram von Eschenbach', *DVjs* 45 (1971), 668ff.

'*Aventiure* in Gottfrieds von Strassburg Tristan', in the FS for H. Eggers, Tübingen, 1972, pp. 88ff.

Haupt, J., *Der Truchsess Keie im Artusroman. Untersuchungen zur Gesellschaftsstruktur im höfischen Roman*, Berlin, 1971.

Haury, A., *L'ironie et l'humour chez Cicéron*, Leiden, 1955.

Heinzel, R., *Kleine Schriften*, ed. M. H. Jellinek and C. von Kraus, Heidelberg, 1907.

Helff, M. M., *Studien zur Kaiserchronik*, dissertation Frankfurt, 1927.

Heller, E., *The ironic German. A study of Thomas Mann*, London, 1958.

Heller, P., *Dialectics and nihilism. Essays on Lessing, Nietzsche, Mann and Kafka*, Amherst, Mass., 1966.

Hellgardt, E., 'Grundsätzliches zum Problem symbolbestimmter und formalästhetischer Zahlenkomposition', in L. P. Johnson, H.-H. Steinhoff and R. A. Wisbey (edd.), *Studien zur frühmittelhochdeutschen Literatur. Cambridger Colloquium 1971*, Berlin, 1974, pp. 11ff.

Hempel, W., *Übermuot diu alte* ... *Der Superbia-Gedanke und seine Rolle in der deutschen Literatur des Mittelalters*, Bonn, 1970.

Hennig, J., '*Ik gihorta ðat seggen.* Das Problem der Geschichtlichkeit im Lichte des Hildebrandsliedes', *DVjs* 39 (1965), 489ff.

Herchenbach, H., *Das Präsens historicum im Mittelhochdeutschen*, Berlin, 1911.

Hermans, G., *List. Studien zur Bedeutungs- und Problemgeschichte*, dissertation Freiburg, 1953.

Hertz, W., '*Tristan und Isolde*' von Gottfried von Strassburg, Stuttgart, 1901.

Hirsch, E. D., *Validity in interpretation*, New Haven, Conn., 1974.

Hirschberg, D., *Untersuchungen zur Erzählstruktur von Wolframs* '*Parzival*'. *Die Funktion von erzählter Szene und Station für den doppelten Kursus*, Göppingen, 1976.

Höfler, O., 'Die Anonymität des Nibelungenliedes', *DVjs* 29 (1955), 167ff.

Hofer, S., *Chrétien de Troyes. Leben und Werke des altfranzösischen Epikers*, Graz, 1954.

Hoffmann, W., 'Semantische Aspekte des Mittelhochdeutschen', *Semasia* 1 (1974), 37ff.

Hollander, L. M., 'Litotes in Old Norse', *PMLA* 53 (1938), 1ff.

Hollandt, G., *Die Hauptgestalten in Gottfrieds Tristan. Wesenszüge, Handlungsfunktion, Motiv der List*, Berlin, 1966.

Homberger, D., *Gawein. Untersuchungen zur mittelhochdeutschen Artusepik*, dissertation Bochum, 1969.

Horacek, B., '*Ichne kan deheinen buochstap*', in the FS for D. Kralik, Horn, 1954, pp. 129ff.

Howard, D. A., *The relationship between poet and narrator in Gottfried's* '*Tristan*', dissertation Cambridge, 1973.

Howard, D. R., *The three temptations. Medieval man in search of the world*, Princeton, N.J., 1966.

Hrubý, A., 'Die Problemstellung in Chrétiens und Hartmanns *Erec*', *DVjs* 38 (1964), 337ff.

Huby, M., *L'adaptation des romans courtois en Allemagne au XIIe et au XIIIe siècle*, Paris, 1968.

Hübner, A., *Die* '*mhd. Ironie*' *oder die Litotes im Altdeutschen*, Leipzig, 1930.

Hunt, T., 'The rhetorical background to the Arthurian prologue', *FMLS* 6 (1970), 1ff.

'Tradition and originality in the prologues of Chrétien de Troyes', *FMLS* 8 (1972), 320ff.

'Irony and ambiguity in *Sir Gawain and the Green Knight*', *FMLS* 12 (1976), 1ff.

Iwand, K., *Die Schlüsse der mhd. Epen*, Berlin, 1922.

Jackson, W. H., 'Some observations on the status of the narrator in Hartmann von Aue's *Erec* and *Iwein*', in D. D. R. Owen (ed.), *Arthurian romance*, Edinburgh, 1970, pp. 65ff.

Jackson, W. T. H., 'The medieval pastourelle as a satirical genre', *PhQ* 31 (1952), 156ff.

'Faith unfaithful – the German reaction to courtly love', in F. X. Newman (ed.), *The meaning of courtly love*, Albany, N.Y., 1968, pp. 55ff.

The anatomy of love. The '*Tristan*' *of Gottfried von Strassburg*, New York, 1971.

'Persona and audience in two medieval love-lyrics', *Mosaic* 8, 4 (1975), 147ff.

Jaeger, C. S., *Medieval humanism in Gottfried von Strassburg's Tristan und Isolde*, Heidelberg, 1977.

Jankélévitch, V., *L'ironie*, Paris, 1964.

Jauss, H. R., *Untersuchungen zur mittelalterlichen Tierdichtung*, Tübingen, 1959.

Jeanroy, A., *La poésie lyrique des troubadours*, Paris, 1934.

Johnson, L. P., 'Lähelin and the Grail horses', *MLR* 63 (1968), 612ff.

'Characterization in Wolfram's *Parzival*', *MLR* 64 (1969), 68ff.

'Dramatische Ironie in Wolframs *Parzival*', in P. F. Ganz and W. Schröder (edd.), *Probleme mittelhochdeutscher Erzählformen. Marburger Colloquium 1969*, Berlin, 1972, pp. 133ff.

'Parzival's beauty', in D. H. Green and L. P. Johnson, *Approaches to Wolfram von Eschenbach. Five Essays*, Bern, 1978, pp. 273ff.

'*Sîne klâwen*. An interpretation', *ibid.*, pp. 295ff.

Jones, R., *The theme of love in the 'Romans d'Antiquité'*, London, 1972.

Jonin, P., *Les personnages féminins dans les romans français de Tristan au XIIe siècle. Etude des influences contemporaines*, Aix-en-Provence, 1958.

Jordan, R. M., 'Chaucerian romance?', *YFS* 51 (1974), 223ff.

Kahn Blumstein, A., *Misogyny and idealization in the courtly romance*, Bonn, 1977.

Kaiser, G., *Textauslegung als gesellschaftliche Selbstdeutung*, Frankfurt, 1973.

Kaske, R. E., 'The Aube in Chaucer's *Troilus*', in R. J. Schoeck and J. Taylor (edd.), *Chaucer criticism*, Notre Dame, Ind., 1961, volume II, pp. 167ff.

'Chaucer and medieval allegory', *ELH* 30 (1963), 175ff.

Kellermann, W., *Aufbaustil und Weltbild Chrestiens von Troyes im Percevalroman*, Halle, 1936.

Kelly, F. D., *Sens and Conjointure in the 'Chevalier de la Charrette'*, The Hague, 1966.

Kelly, H. A., *Love and marriage in the age of Chaucer*, Ithaca, N.Y., 1975.

Kern, P., 'Interpretation der Erzählung durch Erzählung. Zur Bedeutung von Wiederholung, Variation und Umkehrung in Hartmanns *Iwein*', *ZfdPh* 92 (1973), 338ff.

Kesting, P., *Maria – Frouwe. Über den Einfluss der Marienverehrung auf den Minnesang bis Walther von der Vogelweide*, Munich, 1965.

Kienast, R., *Hausens 'scheltliet' (MF 47, 33) und 'der sumer von Triere'*, Sitzungsberichte der deutschen Akademie der Wissenschaften zu Berlin, Klasse für Sprachen, Literatur und Kunst 1961, 3, Berlin, 1961.

Kircher, A., *Dichter und Konvention. Zum gesellschaftlichen Realitätsproblem der deutschen Lyrik um 1200*, Düsseldorf, 1973.

Kittredge, G. L., *Chaucer and his poetry*, Cambridge, Mass., 1915.

Klein, K. K., *Zur Spruchdichtung und Heimatfrage Walthers von der Vogelweide. Beiträge zur Waltherforschung*, Innsbruck, 1952.

Knight Bostock, J., '*Hirzwurz* und *brun*', MLR 52 (1957), 235ff.

Knoll, H. K., *Studien zur realen und ausserrealen Welt im deutschen Artusroman (Erec, Iwein, Lanzelet, Wigalois)*, dissertation Bonn, 1966.

Knox, N., *The word irony and its context, 1500–1755*, Durham, N.C., 1961.

Köhler, E., *Ideal und Wirklichkeit in der höfischen Epik. Studien zur Form der frühen Artus- und Graldichtung*, Tübingen, 1956.

Trobadorlyrik und höfischer Roman. Aufsätze zur französischen und provenzalischen Literatur des Mittelalters, Berlin, 1962.

Körner, J., *Das Nibelungenlied*, Leipzig, 1921.

Kohlschmidt, W. and Mohr, W. (edd.), *Reallexikon der deutschen Literaturgeschichte*, Berlin, ²1958.

Kolb, H., '*Der Minnen hus*. Zur Allegorie der Minnegrotte in Gottfrieds *Tristan*', *Euphorion* 56 (1962), 229 ff.

Kralik, D., *Walther gegen Reinmar*, Österreichische Akademie der Wissenschaften, Philosophisch-historische Klasse 230, 1, Vienna, 1955.

Kramer, H.-P., *Erzählerbemerkungen und Erzählerkommentare in Chrestiens und Hartmanns 'Erec' und 'Iwein'*, Göppingen, 1971.

von Kraus, C., *Die Lieder Reimars des Alten. III. Teil. Reimar und Walther. Text der Lieder*, Abhandlungen der Bayerischen Akademie der Wissenschaften, Philosophisch-philologische und historische Klasse 30, 7, Munich, 1919.

Walther von der Vogelweide. Untersuchungen, Berlin, 1935.

Krogmann, W., 'Germ. *bruna*- als Beiwort von Waffen', ZfdPh 67 (1942), 1ff.

Kuhn, Hugo, *Dichtung und Welt im Mittelalter*, Stuttgart, 1959.

Kunzer, R. G., *The 'Tristan' of Gottfried von Strassburg. An ironic perspective*, Berkeley, Calif., 1973.

Lämmert, E., *Bauformen des Erzählens*, Stuttgart, 1955.

Lausberg, H., *Handbuch der literarischen Rhetorik*, Munich, 1960.

Elemente der literarischen Rhetorik, Munich, 1963.

Lazar, M., *Amour courtois et fin' amors dans la littérature du XIIe siècle*, Paris, 1964.

van der Lee, A., *Der Stil von Hartmanns Erec verglichen mit dem der älteren Epik*, Utrecht, n.d.

Lehmann, P., *Die Parodie im Mittelalter*, Munich, 1922.

Lenaghan, R. T., 'The clerk of Venus: Chaucer and medieval romance', in the FS for B. J. Whiting, Cambridge, Mass., 1974, pp. 31ff.

Lewent, K., 'Zum Inhalt und Aufbau der *Flamenca*', ZfrPh 53 (1933), 1ff.

Lewis, C. S., *The allegory of love. A study in medieval tradition*, Oxford, 1946.

von Lieres und Wilkau, M., *Sprachformeln in der mittelhochdeutschen Lyrik bis zu Walther von der Vogelweide*, Munich, 1965.

Linke, H., *Epische Strukturen in der Dichtung Hartmanns von Aue. Untersuchungen zur Formkritik, Werkstruktur und Vortragsgliederung*, Munich, 1968.

Lofmark, C., *Rennewart in Wolfram's 'Willehalm'. A study of Wolfram von Eschenbach and his sources*, Cambridge, 1972.

'Wolfram's source references in *Parzival*', MLR 67 (1972), 820ff.

The authority of the source in Middle High German narrative poetry, dissertation London, 1973.

'On medieval credulity', in the FS for C. P. Magill, Cardiff, 1974, pp. 5ff.

Loomis, R. S., *A mirror of Chaucer's World*, Princeton, N.J., 1965.

Lord, A. B., *The singer of tales*, New York, 1965.

Lot, F., *Etude sur le Lancelot en prose*, Paris, 1918.

Luxenburger, M., *Die Zeitgestaltung in Wolframs von Eschenbach 'Parzival'*, dissertation Bonn, 1949.

MacQueen, J., *Allegory*, London, 1970.

McFarland, T., 'Ulrich von Lichtenstein and the autobiographical narrative form', in P. F. Ganz and W. Schröder (edd.), *Probleme mittelhochdeutscher Erzählformen. Marburger Colloquium 1969*, Berlin, 1972, pp. 178ff.

Madsen, R., *Die Gestaltung des Humors in den Werken Wolframs von Eschenbach*, dissertation Bochum, 1970.

Mann, J., *Chaucer and medieval estates satire. The literature of social classes and the 'General Prologue' to the 'Canterbury Tales'*, Cambridge, 1973.

Marti, B. M., 'Lucan's invocation to Nero in the light of the medieval commentaries', *Quadrivium* 1 (1956), 7ff.

Martin, J. H., *Love's fools: Aucassin, Troilus, Calisto and the parody of the courtly lover*, London, 1972.

Maurer, F., *Leid. Studien zur Bedeutungs- und Problemgeschichte, besonders in den grossen Epen der staufischen Zeit*, Bern, 1951.

'Der Topos von den "Minnesklaven",' *DVjs* 27 (1953), 182ff.

Mayer, H., *Humor im Nibelungenlied*, dissertation Tübingen, 1966.

'Topoi des Verschweigens und der Kürzung im höfischen Roman', in F. Hundsnurscher and U. Müller (edd.), *'Getempert und gemischet' für Wolfgang Mohr zum 65. Geburtstag von seinen Tübinger Schülern*, Göppingen, 1972, pp. 231ff.

Mecke, G., *Zwischenrede, Erzählerfigur und Erzählhaltung in Hartmanns von Aue 'Erec'. (Studien über die Dichter-Publikums-Beziehung in der Epik)*, dissertation Munich, 1965.

Meiners, I., *Schelm und Dümmling in Erzählungen des deutschen Mittelalters*, Munich, 1967.

Meissburger, G., *Tristan und Isold mit den weissen Händen. Die Auffassung der Minne, der Liebe und der Ehe bei Gottfried von Strassburg und Ulrich von Türheim*, Basel, 1954.

Ménard, P., *Le rire et le sourire dans le roman courtois en France au moyen âge (1150–1250)*, Geneva, 1969.

Mergell, B., *Wolfram von Eschenbach und seine französischen Quellen. II Teil: Wolframs 'Parzival'*, Münster, 1943.

Mersmann, W., *Der Besitzwechsel und seine Bedeutung in den Dichtungen Wolframs von Eschenbach und Gottfrieds von Strassburg*, Munich, 1971.

Miller, R. P., 'The wounded heart. Courtly love and the medieval antifeminist tradition', *WS* 2 (1974), 335ff.

Mills, D., 'An analysis of the temptation scenes in *Sir Gawain and the Green Knight*', *JEGP* 67 (1968), 612ff.

Milnes, H., 'The play of opposites in *Iwein*', *GLL* 14 (1960/61), 241ff.

Mölk, U., 'Die Figur des Königs Artus in Thomas' Tristanroman', *GRM* 12 (1962), 96ff.

'Das Motiv des Wiedererkennens an der Stimme im Epos und höfischen Roman des französischen Mittelalters', *RJb* 15 (1964), 107ff.

Französische Literarästhetik des 12. und 13. Jahrhunderts. Prologe – Exkurse – Epiloge, Tübingen, 1969.

Mohr, W., 'Hilfe und Rat in Wolframs *Parzival*', in the FS for J. Trier, Meisenheim, 1954, pp. 173ff.

'Obie und Meljanz. Zum 7. Buch von Wolframs *Parzival*', in the FS for G. Müller, Bonn, 1957, pp. 9ff.

'Parzival und Gawan', *Euphorion* 52 (1958), 1ff.

'Minnesang als Gesellschaftskunst', in H. Fromm (ed.), *Der deutsche Minnesang*, Darmstadt, 1961, pp. 197ff.

'Parzivals ritterliche Schuld', in *Wirkendes Wort, Sammelband II. Ältere deutsche Sprache und Literatur*, Düsseldorf, 1962, pp. 196ff.

Moleta, V., 'Style and meaning in three pastourelles', *Arcadia* 5 (1970), 225ff.

Mollard, A., 'La diffusion de l'Institution oratoire au XIIe siècle', *MA* 5 (1934), 161ff. and *MA* 6 (1935), 1ff.

'L'imitation de Quintilien dans Guibert de Nogent', *MA* 5 (1934), 81ff.

Monro, D. H., *Argument of laughter*, Notre Dame, Ind., 1963.

Moret, A., *Les débuts du lyrisme en Allemagne (des origines à 1350)*, Lille, 1951.

Mowatt, D. G., 'Irony in Hartmann's *Iwein*', in the FS for K.-W. Maurer, The Hague, 1973, pp. 34ff.

Muecke, D. C., *The compass of irony*, London, 1969.

Müller, G., *Die Bedeutung der Zeit in der Erzählkunst*, Bonn, 1947.

'Erzählzeit und erzählte Zeit', in the FS for P. Kluckhohn and H. Schneider, Tübingen, 1948, pp. 195ff.

'Über das Zeitgerüst des Erzählens', *DVjs* 24 (1950), 1ff.

Muscatine, C., *Chaucer and the French tradition. A study in style and meaning*, Berkeley, Calif., 1964.

Poetry and crisis in the age of Chaucer, Notre Dame, Ind., 1972.

Nauen, H.-G., *Die Bedeutung von Religion und Theologie im Tristan Gottfrieds von Strassburg*, dissertation Marburg, 1947.

Nayhauss-Cormons-Holub, H.-C., Graf von, *Die Bedeutung und Funktion der Kampfszenen für den Abenteuerweg der Helden im 'Erec' und 'Iwein' Hartmanns von Aue*, dissertation Freiburg, 1967.

Nellmann, E., *Wolframs Erzähltechnik. Untersuchungen zur Funktion des Erzählers*, Wiesbaden, 1973.

Neumann, F., 'Wolfram auf der Burg zu Wertheim', in the FS for H. de Boor, Munich, 1971, pp. 365ff.

Newstead, H., 'The tryst beneath the tree: an episode in the Tristan legend', *RPh* 9 (1955/56), 269ff.

'The origin and growth of the Tristan legend', in R. S. Loomis (ed.), *Arthurian literature in the Middle Ages*, Oxford, 1961, pp. 122ff.

Nickel, E., *Studien zum Liebesproblem bei Gottfried von Strassburg*, Königsberg, 1927.

Nitze, W. A., 'The character of Gauvain in the romances of Chrétien de Troyes', *MPh* 50 (1952/53), 219ff.

Nölle, M. T., *Formen der Darstellung in Hartmanns 'Iwein'*, Bern, 1974.

Norton-Smith, G., *Geoffrey Chaucer*, London, 1974.

Nottarp, H., *Gottesurteilstudien*, Munich, 1956.

de Novais Paiva, M. H., *Contribuição para uma estilística da ironia*, Lisbon, 1961.

Nykrog, P., *Les fabliaux*, Geneva, 1973.

Ochs, I., *Wolframs 'Willehalm'-Eingang im Lichte der frühmittelhochdeutschen geistlichen Dichtung*, Munich, 1968.

Ogle, M. B., 'The sloth of Erec', *RR* 9 (1918), 1ff.

Oh, E., *Aufbau und Einzelszenen in Hartmanns von Aue höfischen Epen 'Erec' und 'Iwein'*, dissertation Hamburg, 1972.

Ohly, F., 'Wolframs Gebet an den Heiligen Geist im Eingang des Willehalm', *ZfdA* 91 (1961/62), 1ff.

'Die Suche in Dichtungen des Mittelalters', *ZfdA* 94 (1965), 171ff.

'Cor amantis non angustum. Vom Wohnen im Herzen', in the FS for W. Foerste, Cologne, 1970, pp. 454ff.

Ohly, W., *Die heilsgeschichtliche Struktur der Epen Hartmanns von Aue*, dissertation Berlin (Freie Universität), 1958.

Owen, D. D. R., 'Paien de Maisières – a joke that went wrong', *FMLS* 2 (1966), 192ff.

'Burlesque tradition and *Sir Gawain and the Green Knight*', *FMLS* 4 (1968), 125ff.

(ed.), *Arthurian romance. Seven essays*, Edinburgh, 1970.

Paré, G., Brunet, A. and Tremblay, P., *La renaissance du XIIe siècle*: *les écoles et l'enseignement*, Paris, 1933.

Patch, H. R., 'Troilus on determinism', *Speculum* 6 (1929), 225ff.

Payne, R. O., 'Chaucer and the art of rhetoric', in B. Rowland (ed.), *Companion to Chaucer Studies*, Toronto, 1968, pp. 38ff.

Pearsall, D. A., 'Rhetorical "descriptio" in *Sir Gawain and the Green Knight*', MLR 50 (1955), 129ff.

Peiffer, L., *Zur Funktion der Exkurse im 'Tristan' Gottfrieds von Strassburg*, Göppingen, 1971.

Peil, D., *Die Gebärde bei Chrétien, Hartmann und Wolfram. Erec – Iwein – Parzival*, Munich, 1975.

Perry, B. E., *The ancient romances. A literary-historical account of their origins*, Berkeley, Calif., 1967.

Piquet, F., *Etude sur Hartmann d'Aue*, Paris, 1898.

L'originalité de Gottfried de Strasbourg dans son poème de 'Tristan et Isolde'. Etude de littérature comparée, Lille, 1905.

Pörksen, U., *Der Erzähler im mittelhochdeutschen Epos. Formen seines Hervortretens bei Lamprecht, Konrad, Hartmann, in Wolframs Willehalm und in den 'Spielmannsepen'*, Berlin, 1971.

Pollmann, L., *Die Liebe in der hochmittelalterlichen Literatur Frankreichs. Versuch einer historischen Phänomenologie*, Frankfurt, 1966.

Pütz, H. P., 'Artus-Kritik in Hartmanns *Iwein*', GRM 23 (1972), 193ff.

Quirk, R., *Essays on the English language, medieval and modern*, London, 1968.

Ranke, F., *Tristan und Isold*, Munich, 1925.

Die Allegorie der Minnegrotte in Gottfrieds Tristan, Berlin, 1925.

Rathofer, J., 'Der "wunderbare Hirsch" der Minnegrotte', *ZfdA* 95 (1966), 27ff.

Reble, A., *Geschichte der Pädagogik*, Stuttgart, 1964.

Reiber, T. K., *Studie zu Grundlage und Wesen mittelalterlich-höfischer Dichtung unter besonderer Berücksichtigung von Wolframs dunklem Stil*, dissertation Tübingen, 1954.

Reiffenstein, I., 'Die Erzählervorausdeutung in der frühmittelhochdeutschen Dichtung. Zur Geschichte und Funktion einer poetischen Formel', in the FS for H. Eggers, Tübingen, 1972, pp. 551ff.

Reinhold, H., *Humoristische Tendenzen in der englischen Dichtung des Mittelalters*, Tübingen, 1953.

Ribbeck, O., 'Über den Begriff des εἴρων', *RhM* N.F. 31 (1876), 381ff.

Richter, H., *Kommentar zum Rolandslied des Pfaffen Konrad – Teil I*, Bern, 1972.

de Riquer, M., 'Perceval y Gauvain en *Li Contes del Graal*', FR 4 (1957), 119ff.

Robertson, D. W., 'Historical criticism', in A. S. Downer (ed.), *English Institute Essays, 1950*, New York, 1951, pp. 3ff.

'The doctrine of charity in mediæval literary gardens; a topical approach through symbolism and allegory', *Speculum* 26 (1951), 24ff.

A preface to Chaucer. Studies in medieval perspectives, Princeton, N.J., 1963.

'The concept of courtly love as an impediment to the understanding of medieval texts', in F. X. Newman (ed.), *The meaning of courtly love*, Albany, N.Y., 1968, pp. 1ff.

Röhrig, H.-H., *Dichter und Hörer. Studien zum Formproblem des Minnesangs bis zu Walther von der Vogelweide*, dissertation Kiel, 1954.

Roetteken, H., *Die epische Kunst Heinrichs von Veldeke und Hartmanns von Aue*, Halle, 1887.

Ross, D. J. A., *Alexander and the faithless lady: a submarine adventure* (Inaugural lecture, Birkbeck College), London, 1967.

Rosskopf, R., *Der Traum Herzeloydes und der rote Ritter. Erwägungen über die Bedeutung des staufisch-welfischen Thronstreites für Wolframs 'Parzival'*, Göppingen, 1972.

Rossmann, A., *Wort und Begriff der Wahrheit in der frühmittelhochdeutschen Literatur*, dissertation Tübingen, 1952.

Rotermund, E., *Die Parodie in der modernen deutschen Lyrik*, Munich, 1963.

Gegengesänge. Lyrische Parodien vom Mittelalter bis zur Gegenwart, Munich, 1964.

Rowland, B., (ed.), *Companion to Chaucer Studies*, Toronto, 1968.

Ruberg, U., *Raum und Zeit im Prosa-Lancelot*, Munich, 1965.

'Bildkoordinationen im *Erec* Hartmanns von Aue', in the FS for W. Foerste, Cologne, 1970, pp. 477ff.

Ruggiers, P. G., *The art of the Canterbury Tales*, Madison, Wis., 1965.

Ruh, K., *Höfische Epik des deutschen Mittelalters* 1: *Von den Anfängen bis zu Hartmann von Aue*, Berlin, 1967.

Rupp, H. (ed.), *Wolfram von Eschenbach*, Darmstadt, 1966.

Rychner, J., *La chanson de geste. Essai sur l'art épique des jongleurs*, Geneva, 1955.

Sacker, H., 'An interpretation of Hartmann's Iwein', *GR* 36 (1961), 5ff.

Salingar, L., *Shakespeare and the traditions of comedy*, Cambridge, 1974.

Salmon, P. B., *The works of Hartmann von Aue in the light of medieval poetics*, dissertation London, 1957.

'Ignorance and awareness of identity in Hartmann and Wolfram: an element of dramatic irony', *PBB* (T) 82 (1960), 95ff.

'*Âne zuht*: Hartmann von Aue's criticism of Iwein', *MLR* 69 (1974), 556ff.

Savage, H. L., 'The significance of the hunting-scenes in Sir Gawain and the Green Knight', *JEGP* 27 (1928), 1ff.

Sawicki, S., *Gottfried von Strassburg und die Poetik des Mittelalters*, Berlin, 1932.

Sayce, O., 'Prolog, Epilog und das Problem des Erzählers', in P. F. Ganz and W. Schröder (edd.), *Probleme mittelhochdeutscher Erzählformen. Marburger Colloquium 1969*, Berlin, 1972, pp. 63ff.

Schaefer, A., *Ironie und Dichtung*, Munich, 1970.

Scheunemann, E., *Artushof und Abenteuer. Zeichnung höfischen Daseins in Hartmanns Erec*, Darmstadt, 1973.

Schindele, G., *Tristan. Metamorphose und Tradition*, Stuttgart, 1971.

Schirmer, K.-H., *Stil- und Motivuntersuchungen zur mittelhochdeutschen Versnovelle*, Tübingen, 1969.

Schirmer, W. F. and Broich, U., *Studien zum literarischen Patronat im England des 12. Jahrhunderts*, Cologne, 1962.

Schlösser, F., *Andreas Capellanus. Seine Minnelehre und das christliche Weltbild um 1200*, Bonn, 1960.

Schmidtke, D., 'Mittelalterliche Liebeslyrik in der Kritik mittelalterlicher Moraltheologen', *ZfdPh* 95 (1976), 321ff.

Schneider, H., *Parzival-Studien*, Sitzungsberichte der Bayerischen Akademie der Wissenschaften, Philosophisch-historische Klasse 1944/46, Heft 4, Munich, 1947.

Schnell, R., 'Vogeljagd und Liebe im 8. Buch von Wolframs *Parzival*', *PBB* (T) 96 (1974), 246ff.

Schönbach, A. E., *Über Hartmann von Aue*, Graz, 1894.

Schoepperle Loomis, G., *Tristan und Isolt. A study of the sources of the romance*, New York, 1963.

Scholes, R. and Kellogg, R., *The nature of narrative*, New York, 1966.

Scholte, J. H., 'Wolframs Lyrik', *PBB* 69 (1947), 409ff.

Scholz, M. G., *Walther von der Vogelweide und Wolfram von Eschenbach. Literarische Beziehungen und persönliches Verhältnis*, dissertation Tübingen, 1966.

Schorn, D.-H., *Die Zeit in den Tristandichtungen Eilharts und Gotfrids. Studie zur Wirklichkeitsauffassung in mittelalterlichen Dichtungen*, dissertation Cologne, 1952.

Schröder, J., *Zu Darstellung und Funktion der Schauplätze in den Artusromanen Hartmanns von Aue*, Göppingen, 1972.

Schröder, W., Review of the FS for F. Maurer, Düsseldorf, 1968, in *PBB* (T) 90 (1968), 321ff.

Nibelungenlied-Studien, Stuttgart, 1968.

'Parzivals Schwerter', *ZfdA* 100 (1971), 111ff.

'*Die von Tristande hant gelesen*. Quellenhinweise und Quellenkritik im "Tristan" Gottfrieds von Strassburg', *ZfdA* 104 (1975), 307ff.

Schröder, W. J., 'Über Ironie in der Dichtung. Der Teufel am Sakrament', *Akzente* 6 (1955), 568ff.

Schücking, L. L., *Heldenstolz und Würde im Angelsächsischen*, Abhandlungen der philologisch-historischen Klasse der sächsischen Akademie der Wissenschaften, 42, 5, Leipzig, 1933.

'Heroische Ironie im ags. *Seefahrer*', in the FS for M. Deutschbein, Leipzig, 1936, pp. 72ff.

Schulze, U., 'Literarkritische Äusserungen im Tristan Gottfrieds von Strassburg', *PBB* (T) 88 (1966/67), 285ff.

Schumacher, M., *Die Auffassung der Ehe in den Dichtungen Wolframs von Eschenbach*, Heidelberg, 1967.

Schwab, U., *Zur Datierung und Interpretation des Reinhart Fuchs*, Naples, 1967.

Schwander, A., *Das Fortleben des spätantiken Romans in der mittelalterlichen Epik (Untersuchungen zu Gottfrieds 'Tristan')*, dissertation Frankfurt, 1944.

Schweikle, G., 'Zum *Iwein* Hartmanns von Aue. Strukturale Korrespondenzen und Oppositionen', in the FS for K. Hamburger, Stuttgart, 1971, pp. 1ff.

Schwietering, J., *Die deutsche Dichtung des Mittelalters*, Potsdam, n.d. 'Die Demutsformel mittelhochdeutscher Dichter', in F. Ohly and M. Wehrli (edd.), *Julius Schwietering. Philologische Schriften*, Munich, 1969, pp. 140ff.

Philologische Schriften, ed. F. Ohly and M. Wehrli, Munich, 1969.

Sedgewick, G. G., *Of irony: especially in drama*, Toronto, 1967.

Sehrt, E. H., *Notker-Glossar. Ein Althochdeutsch-Lateinisch-Neuhochdeutsches Wörterbuch zu Notkers des Deutschen Schriften*, Tübingen, 1962.

Shaw, F., *Die Darstellung des Gefühls in der Kaiserchronik*, dissertation Bonn, 1967. 'Ovid in der Kaiserchronik', *ZfdPh* 88 (1969), 378ff.

Sidgwick, A., 'On some forms of irony', *Cornhill Magazine* 22 (1907), 497ff.

Siekhaus, H., 'Revocatio – Studie zu einer Gestaltungsform des Minnesangs', *DVjs* 45 (1971), 237ff.

Silverstein, T., '*Sir Gawain*, Dear Brutus, and Britain's fortunate founding: a study in comedy and convention', *MPh* 62 (1964/65), 189ff.

Smith, B. H., *Poetic closure. A study of how poems end*, Chicago, 1968.

Snow, A., 'Wilt, wilde, wildenære: a study in the interpretation of Gottfrieds *Tristan*', *Euphorion* 62 (1968), 365ff.

Spearing, A. C., *The Gawain-poet. A critical study*, Cambridge, 1970. *Criticism and medieval poetry*, London, 1972.

Speckenbach, K., *Studien zum Begriff 'edelez herze' im Tristan Gottfrieds von Strassburg*, Munich, 1965. 'Der Eber in der deutschen Literatur des Mittelalters', in the FS for F. Ohly, Munich, 1975, volume I, pp. 425ff.

Spitz, H. J., 'Wolframs Bogengleichnis: ein typologisches Signal', in the FS for F. Ohly, Munich, 1975, volume II, pp. 247ff.

Spitzer, L., 'Note on the poetic and the empirical "I" in medieval authors', *Traditio* 4 (1946), 414ff.

Stauffer, M., *Der Wald. Zur Darstellung und Deutung der Natur im Mittelalter*, Bern, 1959.

Stein, P. K., 'Tristans Schwertleite. Zur Einschätzung ritterlich-höfischer Dichtung durch Gottfried von Strassburg', *DVjs* 51 (1977), 300ff.

Steinmeyer, K. J., *Untersuchungen zur allegorischen Bedeutung der Träume im altfranzösischen Rolandslied*, Munich, 1963.

Stempel, W.-D., 'Mittelalterliche Obszönität als literarästhetisches Problem', in H. R. Jauss (ed.), *Die nicht mehr schönen Künste*, Munich, 1968, pp. 187ff.

Stevens, J., *Music and poetry in the early Tudor court*, London, 1961.

Medieval romance. Themes and approaches, London, 1973.

Stokoe, W. C., 'Structure and intention in the first fragment of the *Canterbury Tales*', *UTQ* 21 (1951/52), 120ff.

Strauss, D., *Redegattungen und Redearten im 'Rolandslied' sowie in der 'Chanson de Roland' und in Strickers 'Karl'. Studien zur Arbeitsweise mittelalterlicher Dichter*, Göppingen, 1972.

Strunk, G., *Kunst und Glaube in der lateinischen Heiligenlegende*, Munich, 1970.

Suchomski, J., *'Delectatio' und 'Utilitas'. Ein Beitrag zum Verständnis mittelalterlicher komischer Literatur*, Bern, 1975.

Sutherland, D. R., 'The love meditation in courtly literature', in the FS for A. Ewert, Oxford, 1961, pp. 165ff.

Tax, P. W., *Wort, Sinnbild, Zahl im Tristanroman. Studien zum Denken und Werten Gottfrieds von Strassburg*, Berlin, 1961.

'Trevrizent. Die Verhüllungstechnik des Erzählers', in the FS for H. Moser, Berlin, 1974, pp. 119ff.

Teubert, S., *Crescentia-Studien*, dissertation Halle, 1916.

Thibaudet, A., *Réflexions sur le roman*, Paris, 1938.

Thiébaut, M., *The stag of love. The chase in medieval literature*, Ithaca, N.Y., 1974.

Thirlwall, C., 'On the irony of Sophocles', *PhM* 2 (1833), 483ff.

Thompson, A. R., *The dry mock. A study of irony in the drama*, Berkeley, Calif., 1948.

Thomsen, I., *Darstellung und Funktion der Zeit im Nibelungenlied, in Gottfrieds von Strassburg 'Tristan' und in Wolframs von Eschenbach 'Willehalm'*, dissertation Kiel, 1962.

Thurston, P. T., *Artistic ambivalence in Chaucer's Knight's Tale*, Gainesville, Fla., 1968.

Tiemann, H., 'Bemerkungen zur Entstehungsgeschichte der Fabliaux', *RF* 72 (1960), 406ff.

Tilvis, P., 'Über die unmittelbaren Vorlagen von Hartmanns *Erec* und *Iwein*, Ulrichs *Lanzelet* und Wolframs *Parzival*', *NM* 60 (1959), 29ff. and 129ff.

Topsfield, L. T., 'Intention and ideas in *Flamenca*', *MÆ* 36 (1967), 119ff.

Trier, J., *Der deutsche Wortschatz im Sinnbezirk des Verstandes. Die Geschichte eines sprachlichen Feldes*, Heidelberg, 1931.

Turnell, M., *The novel in France*, London, 1951.

Tyssens, M., 'Le jongleur et l'écrit', in the FS for R. Crozet, Poitiers. 1966, volume 1, pp. 685ff.

Uhlig, C., *Hofkritik im England des Mittelalters und der Renaissance. Studien zu einem Gemeinplatz der europäischen Moralistik*, Berlin, 1973.

Utley, F. L., *The crooked rib. An analytical index to the argument about women in English and Scots literature to the end of the year 1568*, Columbus, Ohio, 1944.

Veit, W., 'Toposforschung. Ein Forschungsbericht', in M. L. Baeumer (ed.), *Toposforschung*, Darmstadt, 1973, pp. 136ff.

Vinaver, E., 'From epic to romance', *BJRL* 46 (1963/64), 476ff.

Form and meaning in the medieval romance, Presidential Address of the Modern Humanities Research Association, Cambridge, 1966.

A la recherche d'une poétique médiévale, Paris, 1970.

The rise of romance, Oxford, 1971.

Voeltzel, R., *Das Lachen des Herrn. Über die Ironie in der Bibel*, Hamburg, 1961.

Wachinger, B., *Studien zum Nibelungenlied. Vorausdeutung, Aufbau, Motivierung*, Tübingen, 1960.

Sängerkrieg. Untersuchungen zur Spruchdichtung des 13. Jahrhunderts, Munich, 1973.

Wackernagel, W., *Poetik und Stilistik*, ed. L. Sieber, Halle, 1906.

Walshe, M. O'C., 'Notes on *Parzival*, Book V', *LMS* 1 (1939), 340ff.

Wapnewski, P., 'Walthers Lied von der Traumliebe (74, 20) und die deutschsprachige Pastourelle', *Euphorion* 51 (1957), 111ff.

'Wolframs Walther-'Parodie'' und die Frage der Reihenfolge seiner Lieder', *GRM* 39 (1958), 321ff.

Hartmann von Aue, Stuttgart, 1962.

'Tristans Abschied. Ein Vergleich der Dichtung Gotfrits mit ihrer Vorlage Thomas', in the FS for J. Trier, Cologne, 1964, pp. 335ff.

'Der Sänger und die Dame. Zu Walthers Schachlied (111, 23)', *Euphorion* 60 (1966), 1ff.

'Wächterfigur und soziale Problematik in Wolframs Tageliedern', in K. H. Borck and R. Henss (edd.), *Der Berliner Germanistentag 1968. Vorträge und Berichte*, Heidelberg, 1970, pp. 77ff.

Die Lyrik Wolframs von Eschenbach. Edition, Kommentar, Interpretation, Munich, 1972.

Weber, G., *Gottfrieds von Strassburg Tristan und die Krise des hochmittelalterlichen Weltbildes um 1200*, Stuttgart, 1953.

Wechssler, E., *Das Kulturproblem des Minnesangs. Studien zur Vorgeschichte der Renaissance*, Halle, 1909.

Wehrli, M., *Allgemeine Literaturwissenschaft*, Bern, 1951.
'Wolframs Humor', in H. Rupp (ed.), *Wolfram von Eschenbach*, Darmstadt, 1966, pp. 104ff.
Formen mittelalterlicher Erzählung. Aufsätze, Zürich, 1969.
Weigand, H. J., *Wolfram's Parzival. Five essays with an introduction*, Ithaca, N.Y., 1969.
Weinrich, H., *Linguistik der Lüge*, Heidelberg, 1970.
Weise, G., *Die geistige Welt der Gotik und ihre Bedeutung für Italien*, Halle, 1939.
Wellek, R. and Warren, A., *Theory of Literature*, London, 1953.
Wells, D. A., 'Medieval literature', *YWMLS* 34 (1972), 475ff.
Wenzel, S., 'Chaucer's Troilus of Book IV', *PMLA* 79 (1964), 542ff.
Whitehead, F., 'Yvain's wooing', in the FS for E. Vinaver, Manchester, 1965, pp. 321ff.
Whiting, B. J., 'Gawain: his reputation, his courtesy and his appearance in Chaucer's Squire's Tale', *MSt* 9 (1947), 189ff.
Wiegand, H. E., *Studien zur Minne und Ehe in Wolframs Parzival und Hartmanns Artusepik*, Berlin, 1972.
Wiercinski, D., *Minne. Herkunft und Anwendungsschichten eines Wortes*, Cologne, 1964.
Willson, B., 'Literacy and Wolfram von Eschenbach', *NMS* 14 (1970), 27ff.
Winny, J., *The Wife of Bath's Prologue and Tale*, Cambridge, 1965.
Wolf, A., 'Zu Gottfrieds literarischer Technik', in the FS for H. Seidler, Salzburg, 1966, pp. 384ff.
'Erzählkunst und verborgener Schriftsinn. Zur Diskussion um Chrétiens *Yvain* und Hartmanns *Iwein*', *Sprachkunst* 2 (1971), 1ff.
Wolf, L., *Der groteske und hyperbolische Stil des mittelhochdeutschen Epos*, Berlin, 1903.
Wolff, L., *Kleinere Schriften zur altdeutschen Philologie*, Berlin, 1967.
Worcester, D., *The art of satire*, New York, 1969.
Wynn, M., 'Scenery and chivalrous journeys in Wolframs *Parzival*', *Speculum* 36 (1961), 393ff.
'Geography of fact and fiction in Wolfram von Eschenbach's *Parzivâl*', *MLR* 56 (1961), 28ff.
'Parzival and Gâwân – hero and counterpart', *PBB* (T) 84 (1962), 142ff.
Young, K., 'Chaucer's *Troilus and Criseyde* as romance', *PMLA* 53 (1938), 40ff.
Zaddy, Z. P., *Chrétien studies. Problems of form and meaning in Erec, Yvain, Cligés and the Charrete*, Glasgow, 1973.
Ziltener, W., *Chrétien und die Aeneis. Eine Untersuchung des Einflusses von Vergil auf Chrétien von Troyes*, Graz, 1957.
Zimmermann, G., *Kommentar zum VII. Buch von Wolfram von Eschenbachs 'Parzival'*, Göppingen, 1974.

INDEX OF PASSAGES DISCUSSED

The passages listed in this index are from the works mentioned in the Introduction, p. 12, but only those passages are included which are quoted and interpreted in the text. All other references to these and other poets and works are included in the general index.

GENERAL INDEX

Names of medieval authors and their works are included in this index where they are not included in the index of passages discussed. Names of fictional characters are given in the form used in the text, thus distinguishing, for example, between Gauvain (as in Chrétien's romances), Gawein (in Hartmann's), Gawan (in *Parzival*) and Gawain (in *Sir Gawain*). Although Hartmann gives no name to the character called Galoain in Chrétien's *Erec* I have referred to him for the sake of convenience in a reconstructed German form as Galoein.

Narrator (*Cont.*)
III anticipations by 139ff., 145, 162,
    164f., 167, 251f., 256, 266ff., 278
    commentary by 52, 164, 167, 228,
    234, 245f., 261, 263ff., 266ff., 272
    concealment by 145ff.
    pretence by 233ff.
    revealing and concealment by 160ff.
Neidhart von Reuental 129
nennen 148
Nibelungenlied 20, 74, 140f., 143f., 188,
    217, 255f., 295
normative features 384ff.
Notker, *De arte rhetorica* 16f.

Obie 205, 211f.
Obilot 176, 206, 211f.
Olivir 289f.
oral poetry 214ff., 223, 225ff., 373, 386
ordo artificialis 132f., 138, 148, 150, 161,
    251f.
ordo commixtus 161
ordo naturalis 132, 137, 161, 349
Orgeluse 22, 177, 179, 193f., 197f., 205,
    235
Orguelleuse 176, 191
Orilus 44f., 63, 153, 168ff., 247, 261,
    270f., 280f., 352
Oringle 107, 193
Oringles 71, 141f., 162, 164, 262, 293, 308
Ovid 58, 74, 135, 253, 377
oxymoron 171, 184ff., 207

Pandarus 33, 35, 49, 100, 138, 341f., 358
paradox 75, 101ff., 157
parallelism 26, 28, 121, 326ff., 331ff.,
    339ff., 348ff., 352ff.
parody 10f., 35, 57ff., 61ff., 66, 74f., 86,
    90, 96, 99, 103f., 106ff., 111ff.,
    115ff., 119f., 127ff., 195, 287, 357f.,
    382f., 390f., 393
Parzival 11, 30, 37f., 40, 42, 44f., 50, 53,
    59, 62, 76ff., 128, 137, 143, 146ff.,
    164ff., 174, 178, 186, 189, 193, 201,
    205ff., 231, 237, 239, 247, 261, 265,
    269ff., 272f., 279ff., 299, 319ff.,
    339f., 349ff., 362, 381, 387f.
pastourelle 104, 130
patronage 257ff., 308f., 373ff., 384
Paul, St 285
Perceval 24ff., 41, 135, 150, 160, 192,
    204, 220, 260, 330f., 348ff.
perspective, multiple 161ff., 164ff., 170,
    213, 250, 266ff., 272f., 279, 287,
    341f., 358

Peter of Blois 309, 311, 361
Petitcreiu 58, 115, 338, 344f.
Petrarch 246
Der Pfaffe und die Ehebrecherin 126
pilgrimage 220f.
Plato 389
Pompeius 4, 7
pris 294f., 323
providence 73f., 83, 144, 150ff., 154ff.,
    160, 166, 206, 271, 278, 284

quest 150, 252, 387f.
Quintilian 6f., 15, 19, 377

realism 55ff., 61f., 64, 93ff., 119f., 138,
    196, 275, 306ff., 342, 360, 374,
    382
    authenticating 56, 393
reality 72, 105, 108, 128, 186, 232, 323f.,
    347, 388
recital 215ff., 222ff., 255ff., 259ff., 268,
    281, 373
recognition, failure in 274ff.
Reinhart Fuchs 209, 391
Reinmar von Hagenau 91f., 102f., 110f.,
    123, 298
renown 54, 80, 287, 291ff., 295, 304,
    306, 327. *See also* êre *and* prîs
rhetoric 4, 14ff., 18ff., 21, 34, 49f., 97f.,
    112, 120, 148, 151, 171, 190, 196,
    212, 221, 224, 230, 235, 237, 249,
    255, 274, 284f., 362, 365ff., 373ff.,
    384ff., 390
Rhetorica ad Herennium 15
ritterschaft 57ff.
Rittertreue 125
Riwalin 57f., 109, 123, 136, 144, 175,
    181f., 202, 209, 230, 236, 253, 261,
    273, 345ff., 366
Rolandslied 84ff., 142, 195, 288ff., 295f.,
    297
Roman de Renart 184, 264, 391
Roman de Thèbes 368f.
romance genre 51, 55, 61, 73f., 80,
    83, 95, 106, 129, 140, 187, 195f.,
    213f., 218f., 222f., 252f., 256f.,
    288, 310, 319, 340, 343, 357, 359ff.
    Arthurian and *Tristan* 111ff., 119
    and fabliau 119ff., 124, 254
    and love-lyric 104ff., 107ff., 119
Round Table 41f., 49, 67f., 70ff., 80f.,
    83, 119, 204, 207f., 264, 271f., 283,
    299, 304, 307, 312ff., 327, 339
Rual 43, 60, 261